COGNITIVE NEUROSCIENCE OF ATTENTION

A Developmental Perspective

COGNITIVE NEUROSCIENCE OF ATTENTION

A Developmental Perspective

Edited by

John E. Richards
University of South Carolina

LEA LAWRENCE ERLBAUM ASSOCIATES, PUBLISHERS
1998   Mahwah, New Jersey   London

Lawrence Erlbaum Associates, Inc., Publishers
10 Industrial Avenue
Mahwah, New Jersey 07430

Cover design by Kathryn Houghtaling Lacey

Library of Congress Cataloging-in-Publication Data

Cognitive neuroscience of attention : a developmental perspective /
   edited by John E. Richards.
      p.   cm.
   Based on a conference held in May 1995 at the University of South
Carolina.
   Includes bibliographical references and index.
   ISBN 0-8058-2409-X
   1. Attention—Congresses. 2. Cognitive neuroscience—Congresses.
3. Developmental neuroscience—Congresses. I. Richards, John
Edward, 1952–
   [DNLM: 1. Attention—Congresses. 2. Neurospychology—Congresses.
3. Human development—Congresses. 4. Cognition. B F321 C676 1998].
QP405.C713   1998
612.8'2—dc21
DNLM/DLC
for Library of Congress   97-35558
                                                                   CIP

Books published by Lawrence Erlbaum Associates are printed on acid-free paper,
and their bindings are chosen for strength and durability.

Printed in the United States of America
10 9 8 7 6 5 4 3 2 1

Contents

PART II: ORIENTING TO LOCATIONS AND OBJECTS

PART III: ATTENTION, MEMORY, AND LIFE-SPAN CHANGES

Preface

The 1980s saw a new paradigm emerge in psychology—the field of cognitive neuroscience. Cognitive neuroscience has the premise that it is necessary to understand brain and neural systems in the study of cognition. Starting with animal and neuropsychological experiments, the field has emerged to using neuroimaging techniques (PET, MRI, fMRI, EEG/ERP, MEG), controlled invasive animal and human work, and experimental psychology using models of neuroscience to guide its work. One aspect of this work has been a developmental approach to cognitive neuroscience—"developmental cognitive neuroscience." The developmental approach asserts that changes in brain structure and function underlie much of cognitive development. Theories and experiments in cognitive development must rely on an understanding of neural development. Developmental research may provide a "model preparation" that aids work in cognitive neuroscience. The onset and development of specific neural–behavioral systems may tease apart the roles of separate systems in cognitive neuroscience models.

Attention has long been of interest to psychologists. William James saw it as an important field for psychological research, and it has always played a role in explanations of behavior. Cognitive psychologists, and cognitive developmental psychologists, have studied attention as a foundational area. It was only natural that in the very beginnings of cognitive neuroscience an understanding of the role of neural systems in attention was of interest. Early cognitive neuroscience studies of attention using primates and neuropsychological models have now been enhanced with neuroimaging models. The role of brain *changes* in attention *development* is a natural extension of work in this field. Techniques from neuropsychology, neuro-imaging, and neuroscience-based experimental psychology are now being applied to the study of developmental changes in attention.

Which brings us to the current book. Developmental research in young infants, in children, and in the life span provides an important complement to work with adults in the understanding of attention. Many neural systems are immature, or nonfunctional, in the young infant. The lack of these systems, corresponding behavioral characteristics, and the developmental onset of the neural and behavioral systems, provides some information about how these neural systems are expressed in intact adults. Similarly, the changes in brain systems in the elderly (e.g., correlates of Alzheimer's) and changes in attention in the elderly may be considered in a similar light. This volume provides several models of the neural bases of attention, and details how developmental research on these topics leads to a fuller understanding of the cognitive neuroscience of attention. This book pro-vides a contemporary summary of work in this area and a systematic back-ground for further study of attention development from a cognitive neu-roscience perspective.

Part I of the book deals with the neural basis of eye movements, and how attention development may be characterized based on an under-standing of development in those neural systems. Part II explores the overt and covert orienting of attention, attention directed to objects and to spatial locations, and the relation of attention development and brain development to more general issues in cognitive development. Part III contains chapters on the neural basis of attention development as related to memory, possible neural relation to individual differences in infant attention and cognition, and a life-span approach to studying attention development. Each section includes an invited "summary and commentary" chapter that highlights some of the issues raised.

The part sections are suggestions for coordinating chapters, but are not meant to be absolute boundaries. For example, many of the concepts involved in the covert shift of attention found in the second section have their basis in the neural systems controlling eye movements discussed in Part I. Thus, the chapters by Rafal, and Hood, Atkinson, and Braddick, borrow heavily on concepts introduced in the chapters by Schiller, and Maurer and Lewis; in the third section the chapter by Enns, Brodeur, and Trick on life-span changes in covert attention relies on concepts presented in Parts I and II. Similarly, the development of the object concept depends on delayed recognition memory presumed by Bell in the second section to be based on development in the frontal lobes, and thus is related to recognition memory development presented by Nelson and Dukette, and related to individual differences in infant cognition discussed by Colombo and Janowsky, the latter chapters being found in Part III. I hope that the reader benefits from the perspectives in all of the chapters when looking for information on attention development.

Preparation of the book began with a conference in May 1995. Nine of the authors, and about 50 attendees, met on a beautiful spring weekend at the University of South Carolina. The conference included formal presentations and workshops in which the neural basis of attention development was discussed. The chapters represent part of the formal presentations, which have been greatly expanded in scope. Some other chapters, and summary and commentaries, were added to expand the book over a broader range of developmental issues.

We have attempted to present an "integrated" approach across chapters within sections, as well as across sections. Rather than a series of separate chapters, many of the chapters specifically build on elements of the others. Within each section there is reference to other chapters in the section; authors refer to chapters in other sections as well. There are common experimental designs intended to address similar questions, common theoretical issues, and common sets of research data that are discussed. The summary and commentary chapters highlight some of the common issues and themes.

The Internet aided greatly in the preparation of the book. Most of the chapters were transmitted from author to editor by e-mail attachments. I was able to use word processors to read multiple formats, print and deliver copies in a similar printed format, and so forth. Many of the authors also transmitted graphics via e-mail for the figures. I developed a World-Wide-Web site that was accessible to each of the authors. As the chapters came in they were put in "html" and zipped formats. Each author could access what the others had written, develop integrated chapters based on that access, and update their own work accordingly. Most of the authors visited the Web site at least once, and many did several times. I believe that this resulted in tighter chapter integration than would have been possible by delivering 14 hard copy chapters among 25 authors. This also allowed me to transmit everything to the publisher in a common format on electronic media. The computer revolution has allowed such work. I highly recommend its usage for such an edited book.

ACKNOWLEDGMENTS

I would like to acknowledge support of this book from several sources. The College of Liberal Arts at the University of South Carolina, directed by Dean Lester Lefton, provided the funding for the conference that provided the impetus for this work. Dr. Lefton's generous allocation of money for this conference was crucial for starting this process. The Department of Psychology, chaired by Dr. Keith Davis, also provided financial support for the conference, and helped support the many details that go into preparation of a book of this kind. I was supported by a Research Scientist Development Award from the National Institute of Mental Health that gave me the extra time to do this book in a timely fashion. And finally, I received generous emotional support and patience from my family, who graciously accepted my long hours and conference trips with little complaint.

John E. Richards

Part I

ATTENTION AND
EYE MOVEMENTS

Chapter 1

The Neural Control of Visually Guided Eye Movements

Peter H. Schiller
Massachusetts Institute of Technology

Along with the eyes, Nature has created a system to move them about efficiently. The eyes of many species have become specialized in that they contain a small central region in the retina, the fovea, where the photoreceptors are tightly packed which consequently yields high acuity perception. Therefore, to be able to analyze an object in the visual scene in fine detail, the center of gaze has to be directed to it. In addition, when either the object or the person is in motion, it is desirable to maintain the center of gaze on the object. These requirements have produced two distinct systems of conjugate eye movements: the saccadic and the smooth pursuit. The function of the saccadic system is to acquire visual objects for central viewing; the function of the smooth pursuit system is to maintain objects on the fovea while either the object or the person is in motion.

Our eyes are on the move most of the time during our waking hours. We make about 3 saccadic eye movements per second, some 170,000 a day and about 5 billion in an average life time. During the intervening fixations, each of which lasts 200–500 ms, the eyes are stationary in the orbit only when neither the head nor the object viewed is in motion. If there is motion, the object remains on the fovea by virtue of the fact that the eyes engage in smooth-pursuit tracking.

The neural systems involved in the control of visually guided eye movements, the topic of this presentation, are numerous and complex yet are tremendously robust. Seldom does one hear about individuals complaining at the end of the day of having made those 170,000 saccades and endless pursuit eye movements.

That these two types of eye movements, the saccadic and the smooth pursuit, are governed at higher levels by different neural systems has been known for a long time. When the velocity of an object to be tracked is gradually increased, a sudden break in performance occurs when tracking breaks down; the eye can no longer keep up with the moving object. When this happens, the saccadic system kicks in and moves the eyes to catch up with the object. Thus there is a clear velocity discontinuum between tracking and saccadic eye movements. The two systems also have dramatically different latency responses for the initiation of smooth pursuit and saccadic eye movements. This has first been shown by Rashbass (1961) who used what is now called a step-ramp paradigm. Following fixation of a spot on a homogeneous background, it is turned off and at the same time another spot appears somewhere in the periphery, which is then ramped at various velocities. The task of the subject is to make a saccade to the target and to track it. An example of this is shown in Fig. 1.1. The data in this case were collected from a monkey (Schiller & Logothetis, 1987). Examination of the eye traces shows something quite remarkable: The eyes begin to track the peripheral spot with a latency of 75 to 100 ms in this case, and do so *before* the saccade is initiated to it with a latency of 125 to 150 ms. In fact, it has been shown, that when a large portion of the visual field is set in motion, pursuit movements can be initiated in less time than 50 ms provided the stimuli have high contrast (Miles, Kawano, & Optican, 1986). High contrast assures rapid conduction velocities through the retina.

These observations have established, therefore, at the behavioral level, that there are different neural mechanisms involved in the control of saccadic and pursuit eye movements. In what follows I first discuss the various neural systems of saccadic eye-movement generation. Both the sensory and motor aspects of eye-movement production are considered. In the last section we take a brief look at the neural systems involved in pursuit eye movement.

BRAINSTEM CONTROL OF EYE MOVEMENTS

Each eye is moved around in the orbit using six extraocular muscles. Four of these are the recti muscles, the medial, lateral, superior, and inferior. Each opponent pair may be thought of as moving the eyes along two prime axes, the horizontal and the vertical. Diagonal eye movements are brought about by the combined action of the four recti muscles. The remaining two muscles, the superior and inferior obliques, participate mostly in inducing rotatory motion, the kind of motion that comes into play when the head is tilted. One of the important functions of the oblique muscles is to counter rotate the eyes so as to keep them stable with respect to the world.

The eye and its musculature have several features that make them the delight of engineers. The eye is a nearly perfectly balanced ball that is

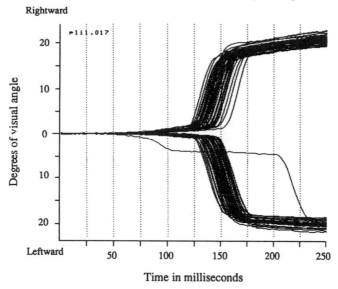

Eye-movement traces collected in step-ramp task

FIG. 1.1. Horizontal eye-movement traces obtained while a monkey performs on a step-ramp task. Following fixation of a central spot it is doused; at the same time a similar spot appears either to the right or the left of fixation at an 18° eccentricity and is moved peripherally along the horizontal axis at 20 deg/sec. Eye-movement trace collection began when the target was turned on in the periphery. The shorter latencies involved in activating the pursuit system are made evident by the fact that pursuit eye movements for the moving target actually begin before the monkey acquires it for foveal viewing with a saccade. Pursuit eye movements in this situation begin between 75 and 100 ms, whereas saccades are initiated between 125 and 150 ms. Adapted from Schiller and Logothetis (1987).

nicely viscous damped in its orbit. Unlike other muscle systems, it was not necessary to design the extraocular muscles to carry loads. The fibers of each muscle are not segmented: they run the entire length of the muscle. These facts make the analysis of eye motion readily amenable to study.

Three sets of cranial nuclei contain the neurons that innervate the six extraocular muscles of each eye through the third, fourth, and sixth cranial nerves: the oculomotor nuclei whose neurons innervate all the muscles except for the lateral rectus and the superior oblique, the trochlear nucleus whose neurons innervate the superior oblique, and the abducens nucleus whose neurons innervate the lateral rectus.

Figure 1.2 shows the response properties of a single cell in the oculo-motor nucleus whose axon innervates the inferior rectus (Schiller, 1970). Shown are the action potentials for the cell over time and the monkey's eye movements in the vertical plane. The upper set of traces were collected

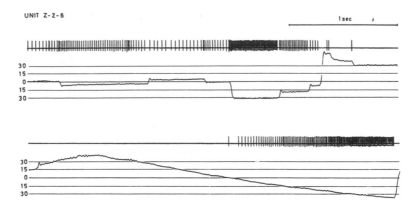

FIG. 1.2. Action potentials obtained from a single cell in the oculomotor nucleus that innervates the inferior rectus muscle. The activity of the neuron is shown along with vertical eye-movement traces. The upper set of records show neuronal activity while spontaneous eye movements are made and consist of saccadic eye movements with intervening fixations. The lower set of traces show neuronal activity during smooth-pursuit eye movement obtained by moving an object downward in front of the monkey. The rate of maintained activity of the neuron is linearly proportional to the angular displacement of the eye. Saccadic eye movements are associated with high-frequency bursts, the durations of which are proportional to saccade size. From Schiller (1970).

while the monkey looked around in the laboratory with his head restrained. Under such conditions the animal made saccadic eye movements with intervening fixations. The lower set of traces were collected while an object was moved downward in front of the monkey.

I emphasize three points about this figure. The first is that the rate of maintained activity exhibited by this neuron is proportional to the degree of downward deviation of the eye in orbit. The higher the activity the more acetylcholine is released at the terminals and consequently the more the inferior rectus contracts. It has been shown that there is a linear relationship between the degree of angular deviation of the eye and the rate of activity in neurons that form the final common path to the eye muscles. The second point is that the neuron discharges with a high frequency burst during the execution of downward saccadic eye movements; the size of the saccade is proportional to the duration of this high frequency burst. Upward saccades seen in the figure are associated with a pause of activity during which it is safe to assume that the neurons innervating the superior rectus discharge with high frequencies. The third point is that the neuron discharges in association with pursuit eye movements in a similar proportional fashion as was revealed when the monkey was fixating various objects in the stationary visual scene. This can be seen in the lower set of traces of Fig. 1.2.

I should note here one more interesting fact about the records shown in Fig. 1.2. Immediately after the execution of a saccadic eye movement brought about by a high-frequency neuronal burst, only a minimal overshoot can be seen. This is not accomplished by some sort of counteractivity in neurons innervating the antagonist muscle. If that were the case one would see in this record a brief burst immediately after the completion of an upward saccade. The remarkable ability of the eye to stop on a dime, so to speak, seems to be due simply to the excellent viscous damping achieved in tenon's capsule within which the eye resides.

Eye movements can be artificially induced by electrically stimulating many different sites in the brain. The upper portion of Fig. 1.3 shows what happens when the abducens nucleus is stimulated electrically through a microelectrode. As the duration of the high-frequency burst is increased, the size of the saccade produced gets progressively larger as might be expected on the basis of what I had just described for natural neuronal discharges.

On the basis of these observations it appears that at the level of the oculomotor complex in the brainstem, where the neurons reside whose axons innervate the extraocular muscles, the saccadic and smooth-pursuit eye movements are executed by the same set of neurons. The coding operation seen here may be termed a rate/duration code: the higher the maintained rate, the greater the angular deviation of the eye in orbit; the longer the duration of the high frequency burst seen in these neurons, the larger the saccade produced (Robinson, 1975; Schiller, 1970).

Right above the nuclei innervating the extraocular muscles there is a complement of neurons in the brain stem in which the various components of the neuronal responses associated with eye movements can be seen separately. Several classes of neurons have been identified (Fuchs, Kaneko, & Scudder, 1985). These include the following types: burst neurons that discharge in high-frequency bursts during saccadic eye movements but otherwise remain silent, omnipause neurons that fire at a constant rate but pause whenever a saccade is made, and tonic neurons whose discharge rate is proportional to angular deviation of the eye in orbit but do not have bursts or pauses associated with saccadic eye movements. It is assumed that the activity of these and several other classes of neurons drives the cells in the oculomotor, trochlear, and abducens nuclei to produce the desired saccadic and smooth pursuit eye movements.

THE SUPERIOR COLLICULUS AND SACCADIC EYE MOVEMENTS

In considering the role of the superior colliculus in eye-movement control it should first be pointed out that this structure is one that has undergone tremendous changes in the course of evolution. In more primitive animals

ABDUCENS STIMULATION

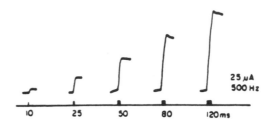

SUPERIOR COLLICULUS STIMULATION

FIG. 1.3. The effects of electrically stimulating the abducens nucleus and the superior colliculus. Stimulation frequency is held constant at 500 Hz while burst duration is systematically varied. Stimulation of the abducens nucleus shows increasing saccade size as a function of increasing burst duration. By contrast, stimulation of the superior colliculus at any given site always produces the same direction and amplitude saccade. For long duration bursts staircases of saccades are elicited in the superior colliculus; the size of each saccade remains of the same amplitude and direction. Adapted from Schiller and Stryker (1972).

8

that have little forebrain, such as toads and fish, this structure, which in these animals is called the optic tectum, is the major site of visual information processing and also participates in converting visual signals into motor outputs. Consequently, ablation of the optic tectum renders these animals virtually blind and incapable of the execution of visually triggered motor commands (Schiller, 1984).

In mammals, and particularly in primates that have a greatly expanded neocortex, visual analysis has been relegated largely to the geniculo-striate system and associated higher cortical areas. The superior colliculus, residing on the roof of the midbrain, has taken on a much more modest function which appears to involve predominantly saccadic eye-movement control (Schiller, 1984; Sparks, 1986; Wurtz & Albano, 1980). Stained coronal sections of this area reveal seven major layers. For the sake of simplicity we shall divide these into just upper and lower layers. The upper layers receive input predominantly from the retina and the occipital cortex. Single cells here respond vigorously to visual stimuli, but their receptive field properties, unlike those in the cortex, are not particularly interesting. They prefer small stimuli but are insensitive to differences in shape, orientation, and color, and most lack directional selectivity to the movement of stimuli. It is noteworthy, however, that the visual field is laid out in a neat topographic order in the colliculus, with its anterior portion representing the fovea, its posterior portion the periphery, its medial aspect the upper and its later aspect the lower visual field. In each colliculus the contralateral half of the visual field is represented.

In the deeper layers of the colliculus there is also an orderly arrangement that has to do with the coding of eye movements. To understand it, let us first consider Fig. 1.3 (Schiller & Stryker, 1972). In the lower portions of this figure eye-movement records are shown that were obtained when the colliculus was electrically stimulated. Such stimulation produces effects quite different from those obtained by abducens stimulation that is shown on the top of the figure. In the colliculus saccades of certain amplitudes and directions are elicited whose parameters are largely unaffected by the duration of the stimulation burst delivered. However, at long durations a staircase of saccades can be elicited where each ballistic eye movement has pretty much the same amplitude and direction. What determines the size and direction of each saccade is *where* in the colliculus one stimulates (Robinson, 1972; Schiller & Stryker, 1972). The lowest portion in the figure shows a staircase of tiny saccades that were obtained when the electrode was placed in the anterior portion of the structure. Thus stimulation of the anterior colliculus produces small saccades and stimulation of the posterior colliculus produces large ones. Stimulation of the medial portions of the colliculus produces upward and of the lateral portions of the colliculus downward saccades.

Systematic mapping of the receptive fields and the motor responses in the colliculus reveals a neat correspondence that can best be understood by examining Fig. 1.4. Electrodes are placed in the colliculus through which first the location of the receptive field of neurons is plotted and then the same site is electrically stimulated (Schiller & Stryker, 1972). What this kind of experiment shows is that the consequence of stimulating a small population of neurons at any given site in the colliculus triggers an eye movement that brings the fovea to that location of the visual field where the receptive fields of the neurons had been located prior to the eye movement. Thus it appears that we have a targeting system here that

Recording and stimulation in the superior colliculus

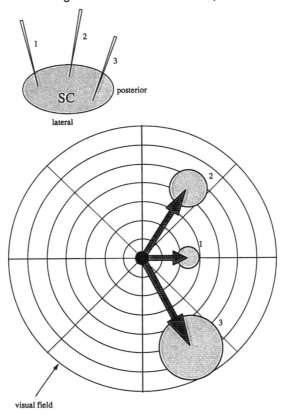

FIG. 1.4. Schematic representation of the major points derived from recording and stimulation in the superior colliculus. Electrodes are shown at three sites in the colliculus (1–3). The location of the receptive fields recorded from these three recording sites are displayed below as are the effects of electrically stimulating at these sites. The stimulation produces a saccadic eye movement that lands the center of gaze at the location where the receptive field had been prior to the movement of the eyes.

can convert a visual signal into a motor output. The calculation seems to be one that computes a retinal error signal, namely the error between the initial gaze position and the location of the target. The consequence of the stimulation is to accurately target the eye at the intended location, thereby nulling the retinal error. This process has been termed foveation mechanism.

Single cell recordings in the intermediate layers of the colliculus support this inference (Schiller & Koerner, 1971; Wurtz & Goldberg, 1972). Neuronal activity corresponds with electrical stimulation results. Neurons discharge in association with certain size and amplitude saccades as shown in Fig. 1.5 in which saccadic endpoints are plotted relative to gaze position prior to eye movement. The circles show saccadic sizes and directions not associated with neuronal activity whereas the disks show those saccades prior and during which there was a high-frequency burst of activity on

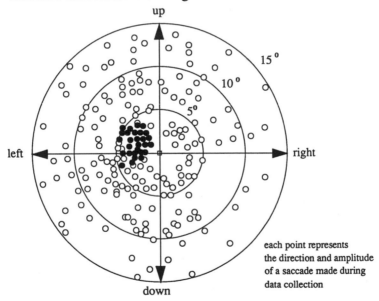

FIG. 1.5. Displayed are a polar plot of the direction and size of saccades made by a monkey while he makes spontaneous eye movements in the laboratory with his head restrained. The activity of a single cell in the superior colliculus was monitored while he did so. Saccades preceded by vigorous neuronal activity are shown as black disks. Saccades not associated with neuronal activity are shown as circles. The plot demonstrates that neurons in the superior colliculus discharge in association with a limited range of saccadic sizes and amplitudes. The area of disks denote the "motor field" or "movement field" of the cell. Adapted from Schiller and Koerner (1971).

part of the neuron for which the data shown are based. The neuron has a "motor" or "movement" field that is coded in terms of saccadic vectors. What this means of course, just to emphasize it, is that the size and direction of a saccade produced by electrical stimulation is independent of the initial position of the eye in orbit. The same is true for single-cell activity. The cell responds in association with the execution of an eye movement of a certain range of sizes and amplitudes and does so irrespective of the initial position of the eye. Many of the cells of this type also have a visual receptive field. When the sensory and motor fields are superimposed, as in Fig. 1.4, one finds that the receptive field of the cell is located in the same place relative to the fovea as is the motor field relative to the initial eye position.

On the basis of findings of this sort the idea that has emerged is that the superior colliculus carries a vector code. Different regions of the colliculus code different vectors that are in register with the visual field representation in the superficial layers of the structure (Robinson, 1972; Schiller & Sandell, 1983; Schiller & Stryker, 1972).

What we can do now is to put together what has so far been discussed to form a wiring diagram. This is depicted in Fig. 1.6. Schematized here are the eye, the brainstem, the superior colliculus, the connections among these structures, and the coding operations they perform. The final common pathway from the brainstem to the extraocular muscles carries a rate code. The input to the brainstem from the superior colliculus carries a vector code. Thus in the brainstem the vector code gets converted into a rate code. From now on we will build on this schematic diagram as we add more and more facts regarding the operation of the saccadic eye-movement system in the brain.

As an added complication I should add at this point that in the deeper layers some cells can be activated not only by visual, but also by somato-sensory and auditory stimuli (Schiller, 1984; Stein, Magalhaes-Castro, & Krueger, 1976). The somatosensory and auditory representations are arranged topographically. It has been shown, however, that unlike for the visual input, these maps do not conform to the innervation density of the somatosensory and auditory inputs from peripheral receptors. Instead, these maps are in register with the visual map suggesting that the organization in the colliculus is from the point of view of the eye (Draeger & Hubel, 1975). One might infer, therefore, that when saccadic eye move-

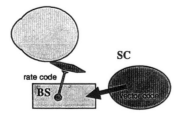

FIG. 1.6. Diagram of the basic connections and coding operations of the brainstem and the superior colliculus in the generation of saccadic eye movements.

ments are elicited by signals processed by the auditory or somatosensory systems, one pathway by which they reach the brainstem to elicit a saccadic eye movement passes through the superior colliculus.

Before moving onto other areas involved in eye-movement control, I should note that the ideas presented so far about collicular function by no means represent the final word. There is interesting ongoing research on the coding operations of this structure (Freedman, Stanford, & Sparks, in press) and I deal with some of the related issues in a later section of this review.

THE CORTICAL CONTROL OF SACCADIC EYE MOVEMENTS

Were the superior colliculus the only gateway to the brainstem for the generation of visually guided eye movements, its removal should eliminate this capacity. Yet this does not happen. Following collicular ablation a number of relatively minor deficits can be seen but unless one takes careful measurements, one would not see much (Schiller, Sandell, & Maunsell, 1987; Schiller, True, & Conway, 1980). These minor deficits include the making of fewer spontaneous saccadic eye movements, slight hypometria, and a small decrease in saccadic velocity. It stands to reason, therefore, that other neural structures play a significant role in eye-movement control. We now look at such structures in the cortex and ask what the relationship is between them and the superior colliculus.

It is a well-known fact that quite a few structures in the cortex, when electrically stimulated, elicit saccadic eye movements. These include regions of the occipital, parietal, temporal, and frontal cortices. Some of the structures in the monkey cortex are depicted in Fig. 1.7. Electrical stimulation of occipital areas elicits eye movements similar to those obtained from the colliculus but considerably higher currents are required to do so. Another area from which similar eye movements can be elicited is the frontal eye fields (Robinson & Fuchs, 1969; Schiller & Sandel, 1983). The currents required here are quite low although not quite as low as in the superior colliculus where only between 1 and 5 microamps are required. Single-cell recordings in the frontal eye fields also reveal activity related to eye movements (Bizzi, 1967; Bruce & Goldberg, 1984).

Given all these cortical areas involved in the generation of saccadic eye movements, one might well pose the question as to whether the signals from them pass through the colliculus to reach the brainstem. All of these structures are known to make extensive connections with the colliculus.

To provide an answer to this question one needs only to ablate the superior colliculus and then stimulate various cortical areas. The results

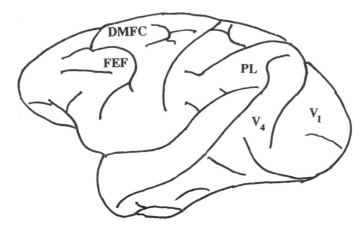

FIG. 1.7. Lateral view of the monkey brain showing some of the major cortical areas involved in the generation of visually guided saccadic eye movements. These include structures in the occipital, parietal, and frontal lobes.

of such experiments yield straightforward answers and are depicted schematically in Fig. 1.8 (Schiller, 1977). Following unilateral ablation of the superior colliculus, eye movements can no longer be elicited from posterior cortex but are still produced by frontal eye field stimulation. Also depicted is the fact that on the intact side of the brain all three areas shown, V1, the frontal eye fields (FEF) and the superior colliculus (SC), yield saccadic vectors when stimulated. Further work has shown that stimulation of parietal cortex also fails to elicit saccadic eye movements after collicular ablation (Keating, Gooley, Pratt, & Kelsey, 1983).

These findings suggest, therefore, that there are at least two parallel pathways for the generation of saccadic eye movements. One of these involves posterior cortex and the superior colliculi. The other involves the frontal cortex that presumably has direct access to the brainstem. We can therefore speak of two major parallel systems of visually guided eye movements, the anterior and the posterior.

Having discovered these two major pathways, one can ask just how important are they for the generation of saccadic eye movements? To do so, experiments can be carried out in which the frontal eye fields and the superior colliculi are ablated either singly or in pairs (Schiller et al., 1980). The results of such experiments are most dramatic. Some data for this are shown in Fig. 1.9. Monkeys were trained to pick small circular apple pieces from a slotted apple board. The slots force the animal to properly orient his hands and to therefore fixate each as he removes the apple pieces. While the monkey does this, his fixations are registered and subsequently are displayed as shown. As can be seen, frontal eye field lesions by themselves

V1 and FEF stimulation with and without collicular lesion

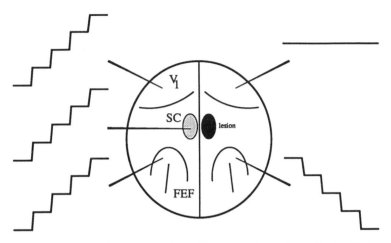

FIG. 1.8. Schematic representation of the effects of superior colliculus (SC) lesions on eye movements elicited by stimulating the striate cortex (V1) and the frontal eye fields (FEF). In intact monkeys stimulation of specific locations within each of these three sites elicits saccades of specific amplitudes and directions; prolonged stimulation elicits a staircase of saccades. Following lesion of the superior colliculus electrical stimulation no longer produces saccades from posterior cortex but continues to produce saccades from the frontal eye fields. This finding indicates that there are at least two parallel pathways involved in the generation of visually guided eye movements. From Schiller (1977).

produce virtually no lasting deficits. It should be noted, however, that immediately after such a lesion the deficits are quite notable: monkeys often fail to make saccadic eye movements to visual targets that necessitate the generation of saccadic vectors that had been represented by the removed region. Collicular lesions initially produce even more notable deficits but after a few weeks or months of recovery what remains are the kinds of minor impairments I have already noted. In contrast to lesions made to either the frontal eye fields or to the superior colliculi, paired lesions devastate eye-movement generation that show little recovery over time (panels G and H in Fig. 1.9). The quantitative data for time to completion, number of saccades per second, saccadic eye-movement velocities, and percent correct performance appear below each panel. The severity of the deficit depends on how extensive the lesions were; subsequent to complete ablation of these two areas, the monkey's eyes seem to be nailed in orbit.

It appears therefore, that the two pathways interrupted here, the one from the frontal eye fields to the brainstem and the pathways from the occipital and parietal cortices passing through the colliculus, are essential elements of the visually guided saccadic eye-movement control system. It is convenient to refer to the pathways that involve the frontal lobe in

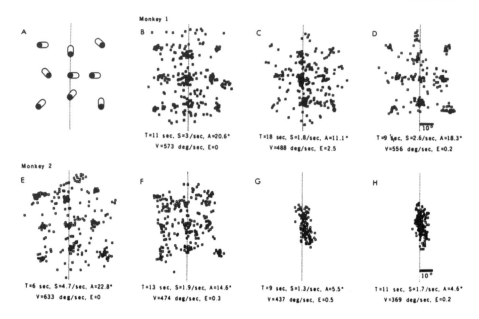

FIG. 1.9. Eye fixation patterns of two monkeys at various stages in an experiment in which the task was to pick out apple pieces in an apple board shown in A. B: fixation patterns of monkey 1 produced in the course of 10 repeated preoperative trials. C: data collected 4 days after bilateral ablation of the frontal eye fields. D: data collected 20 days later. E: shows preoperative fixation patterns for monkey 2. F: data collected four days after bilateral superior colliculus lesions. G: performance of the second monkey 57 days after having added frontal eye field lesions. H: retest of the second monkey after 134 days. Quantitative data below each display show mean number of seconds to complete a trial (T), mean number of saccades per second (S), mean saccade amplitude (A), mean saccade velocity (V), and mean number of errors (E). Frontal eye field lesions alone produce no lasting deficits. Superior colliculus lesions show mild deficits on all quantitative measures. Paired frontal eye field and superior colliculus lesions devastate performance to the extent that the animal is virtually incapable of directing his eyes to visual targets. At this stage, however, the animal can still pick the apple board clean. Adapted from Schiller, True, and Conway (1980).

eye-movement control as the anterior system and the pathways that involve the occipital and parietal cortices and the colliculus as the posterior system.

We now turn to yet another cortical system that has been identified to play a role in eye-movement control. This area, which Schlag and Schlag-Rey (1985, 1987) have termed the medial eye fields, resides in the dorsomedial portions of the frontal cortex (DMFC).

In spite of some debate (Russo & Bruce, 1996), electrical stimulation studies as well as single cell recordings strongly suggest that the operational principles of this area are quite different from those of the systems so far discussed (Chen & Wise, 1995a, 1995b; Mann, Thau, & Schiller, 1988; Schall, 1991a, 1991b; Schlag, Schlag-Rey, & Pigarev, 1992; Tanji & Kurata, 1982; Tanji & Shima, 1994; Tehovnik, 1995; Tehovnik & Lee, 1993). Electrical stimulation of the dorsomedial frontal cortex moves the eyes to certain orbital positions. Prolonged stimulation maintains the eye at a given orbital position. Just what this position is going to be depends on where in the dorsomedial frontal cortex one stimulates. These facts are shown in Fig. 1.10. Stimulation of various regions in the dorsomedial frontal cortex are made while the eye is in a variety of orbital positions by virtue of having the animal fixate a spot that appears in one of several locations on a monitor. When the dorsomedial frontal cortex is stimulated, the eye moves to a particular orbital position. If the eye is already at that location when stimulation is initiated, the eye remains at that position. Prolonged stimulation keeps the eye at that location. The figure also shows that the stimulation of different regions produces different final eye posi-

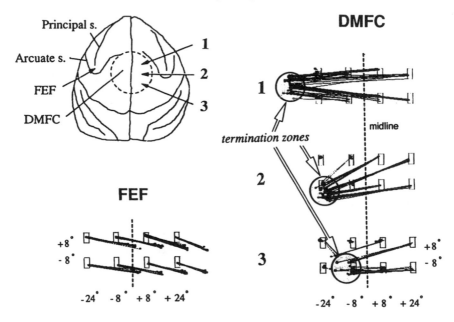

FIG. 1.10. The effects of electrically stimulating dorsomedial frontal cortex (DMFC) and the frontal eye fields (FEF). In DMFC electrical stimulation moves the eyes to a particular orbital position; different regions of this area represent different orbital positions. Prolonged stimulation maintains the eye at the orbital position represented by the stimulated site within DMFC. In contrast, stimulation of FEF produces saccades of specific amplitudes and directions as already noted in association with Fig. 8. Thus, area DMFC carries a place code, whereas the frontal eye fields, as the superior colliculus and the occipital cortex, carry a vector code. Adapted from Tehovnik and Lee (1993).

tions. In fact the orbital positions represented are laid out in an orderly fashion in this area (Tehovnik & Lee, 1993). Lastly, as a control in this animal, the effects of frontal eye field stimulation are also shown in Fig. 1.10, which demonstrates the already established vector coding operation of this area.

That the operational principles of the frontal eye fields and the dorsomedial frontal cortical area are different is supported by two other lines of evidence in addition to the stimulation work just described. The neuronal properties of single cells in these two areas are notably different: In the dorsomedial cortex it has been shown that many cells respond to both eye and limb movement, suggesting that they have multifunctional characteristics (Mann et al., 1988; Tanji & Kurata, 1982; Tanji & Shima, 1994). This is not seen in the frontal eye fields. Selective inactivation of these two areas also yields quite different effects: acute inactivation of the frontal eye fields has rather pronounced effects: animals have difficulties in making saccadic eye movements to briefly flashed visual targets that appear in the visual field contralateral to the inactivation; however, less of a deficit is evident when the targets are bright and are not extinguished prior to the initiation of a saccadic eye movement (Dias, Kiesau, & Segraves, 1995; Sommer & Tehovnik, in press). By contrast, inactivation of the dorsomedial frontal cortex produces practically no deficits to briefly presented targets. Inactivation in these kinds of experiments is accomplished by injecting various chemical agents, such as lidocaine or neurotransmitter analogues and antagonists, through a fine tube inserted into the region. Current ablation studies of area DMFC have also failed in revealing any clear-cut deficits in eye-movement control (Schiller & Chou, 1997).

How might the signals from the dorsomedial frontal cortex reach the brainstem? Unfortunately anatomical studies are not too helpful in this regard because projections have been shown to many areas including the colliculi, the frontal eye fields, and the brainstem. To gain further insight into this problem, experiments have been carried out in which dorsomedial frontal cortex was electrically stimulated after either the frontal eye fields or the superior colliculi had been ablated. Neither had a major effect on the kinds of eye movements elicited by dorsomedial frontal cortex stimulation (Tehovnik, Lee, & Schiller, 1994). This suggests that the dorsomedial frontal cortex has direct effective connections with the brainstem.

STIMULUS SELECTION AND INHIBITORY MECHANISMS

In real life the visual scene living organisms encounter is complex. Typically there is a multitude of stimuli in the scene. With each saccadic eye movement these stimuli impinge on numerous new locations on the retinal surface. One of the tasks involved in visual analysis is to make a decision, during each fixation, where to make the next saccade. Once decided, a rather accurate eye movement is made to the desired target.

To appreciate the computational problems involved in achieving such accurate acquisition of a single target that had impinged on the retina simultaneously with several other targets just prior to the initiation of the eye movement, let us first consider what happens when two locations are electrically stimulated at the same time in the superior colliculus (Robinson, 1972; Schiller, True, & Conway, 1979). Figure 1.11 provides a schematic summary of the basic facts. The top row shows what happens when the medial and lateral portions of the colliculus are stimulated with equal effectiveness. Medial stimulation produces an upward and lateral stimulation a downward saccade. Paired stimulation produces a saccade that lands the eye between these two vectors. In the lower row the effects of stimulating the anterior and posterior portions of the colliculus are shown. Individual stimulation produces a short and a long saccade. Paired stimulation produces an in-between size saccade. Thus the basic rule is that saccades

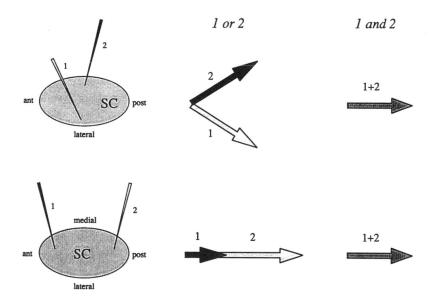

FIG. 1.11. Schematic representation of the effects of simultaneously stimulating two sites in the superior colliculus. In the first row the electrodes are located at sites that respectively elicit upward and downward eye movements. Paired stimulation with equal effectiveness produces a horizontal saccade. In the second row the anterior and posterior parts of the colliculus are stimulated that respectively elicit a small and a large horizontal saccade. Paired stimulation produces a saccade with an in-between amplitude. Thus paired stimulation produces vector averaged saccades.

produced by paired stimulation are vector averages of those obtained with individual stimulation. The same rule applies when one stimulates the frontal eye fields and even when one electrode is in the frontal eye fields and the other in the colliculus. A subtle complexity to this rule is that the actual vector average obtained also depends on the relative current levels delivered to the two sites. By manipulating these levels one can generate any saccade between those elicited by individual stimulation, the endpoints of which fall along a straight line drawn between the endpoints of the individually produced saccades.

Now clearly, when one makes saccadic eye movements to two or more simultaneously appearing targets, which is actually the most common occurrence when one looks about in the visual scene, resultant eye movements for the most part are not vector averages of these inputs. There are several reasons for this. One is that typically each object in the scene is different and is so recognized by the visual system. Hence there is little confusion as to where to look. Another is that the brain keeps track of what is out there, and therefore is able to distinguish between old and new stimuli in the scene in spite of different retinal locations being activated after each saccade. The sudden appearance of a new stimulus, such as a bird landing on a tree, will be quite different in its impact compared to the "old" objects in the scene that impinge on new retinal locations subsequent to each saccadic eye movement. The accurate acquisition of the stimuli is aided by inhibitory mechanisms that need to be disinhibited before an eye movement can be generated. I turn to such mechanisms shortly, but first I would like to elaborate a bit more as to what happens in experiments where instead of a single target, two targets are presented simultaneously. Such a situation in a way may be said to mimic electrical stimulation of two sites in the colliculus.

In one such experiment monkeys, after having fixated a central spot, either a single target or two targets were presented; the targets appeared in any of a large number of locations around the clock. When two targets appeared, the spatial separation between them was varied in blocks of trials. Figure 1.12 shows some data obtained on this task as collected recently by I-han Chou, Marc Sommer, and me (Chou, Sommer, & Schiller, 1994). The frequency with which vector averaged saccades are obtained when two identical targets are presented simultaneously varies with the spatial separation between them. With large angular separations of 90, vector averaged saccades are quite rare. In other words, the monkey looks either at one or the other of the targets and only occasionally makes saccades that land the center of gaze between the two targets. On the other hand, with an angular separation of 20, as can be seen in the lower part of the figure, the majority of saccades are vector averaged. It should be noted here that when two sites are stimulated in the colliculus that

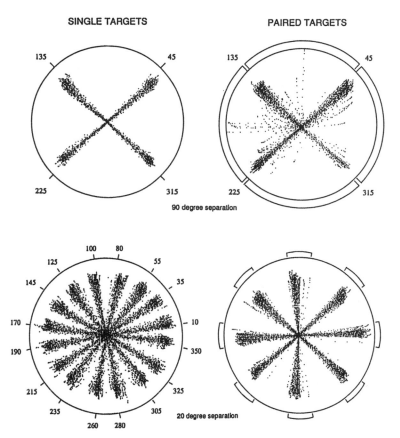

SINGLE TARGETS

PAIRED TARGETS

90 degree separation

20 degree separation

FIG. 1.12. Saccadic eye movements made to single and paired targets presented around the clock at eccentricities of 6 degrees. Eye movements on the left were obtained to singly presented targets. The paired targets, saccades to which made by the monkey are shown on the right, were presented in the experiment with angular separations of 20, 30, 60, and 90 degrees. Two of these are shown in the figure, those with 90 and those with 20 degrees of angular separation. With 90 degrees of angular separation four target locations were used, presented either singly or in pairs. The clustering obtained to single and paired targets looks similar, indicating that the monkey made few vector averaged saccades when the pairs had an angular separation of 90 degrees. With 20 degrees of angular separation (lower panels) 16 target locations were used, presented either singly or in pairs. When presented singly, 16 clusters can be seen (bottom left). When presented in pairs, only 8 clusters are evident because the majority of saccades made were vector averaged. Had the animal made accurate saccades to either one or the other of the paired targets, the clustering would look the same as for the singly presented targets. The percent of saccades made to paired targets that landed the eye within +/−4.5 degrees of the center region between the two targets yielded the following values for the 20, 30, 60, and 90 degrees of angular separation between the paired targets: 73.1%, 42.1%, 5.0%, and 2.8%. These values may therefore be said to represent the percent of vector averaged saccades made to paired targets with various angular separations. Each trial began with the appearance of the central fixation spot; after the monkey had directed its gaze to it, this spot was extinguished 100 ms prior to the appearance of the target(s). The targets were small, bright spots subtending 0.15 degrees of visual angle.

21

separately yield saccades with 90 angular separation, paired stimulation, as shown schematically in Fig. 1.11, yields vector averaged saccades. Thus the results with electrical stimulation and visual stimulation are quite different: When two identical visual stimuli are presented, the frequency with vector averaged saccades are obtained varies inversely with the angular separation between them.

What neural mechanisms then make it possible to minimize saccadic vector averaging when several targets appear simultaneously in the visual scene as it commonly happens every time an eye movement is made? An important answer to this question is provided by the elegant work of Hikosaka and Wurtz (1985) who have identified one of the possibly many inhibitory systems involved in eye-movement control. Building on the fact that the substantia nigra makes GABAergic connections with the colliculus, they showed that applying GABA blockers to the colliculus produced a plethora of involuntary saccades whose vectors were represented by the area released from inhibition by the blocker. Conversely, they showed that GABA analogues applied to the colliculus prevented the monkey from making saccades whose vectors were represented in the treated area. It appears, therefore, that the superior colliculus is clamped down by inhibition as exhibited by the rather high rate of maintained activity in substantia nigra cells that thereby constantly releases GABA in the colliculus. For the successful execution of eye movements one needs not only to send an excitatory signal to the colliculus but one needs also to release the colliculus from inhibition. This is accomplished by inputs to the substantia nigra from a great many cortical areas via the basal ganglia. Such inputs momentarily stop the activity of substantia nigra cells, thereby ceasing its inhibitory effects on the colliculus. This disinhibition, coupled with an excitatory input, is what produces a successful saccadic eye movement.

This is just one of the major inhibitory effects that has been demonstrated in the visually guided eye-movement control system. There are several other circuits that operate in a similar fashion, both at the cortical and midbrain levels. For example, we know that the two colliculi exert mutual inhibitory influences on each other (Sprague, Berlucchi, & Rizzolatti, 1973).

It is now time to add the cortical systems and the inhibitory circuits to our wiring diagram. This appears in Fig. 1.13. This figure shows the anterior and posterior systems involved in eye-movement control. The posterior system reaches the brainstem through the superior colliculus and carries a vector code. The anterior system consists of two subsystems, both of which can bypass the colliculus to reach the brainstem. The frontal eye fields carry a vector code and the dorsomedial frontal cortex carries a place code. One major inhibitory system is depicted in the diagram that clamps down the superior colliculus by virtue of the GABAergic inputs

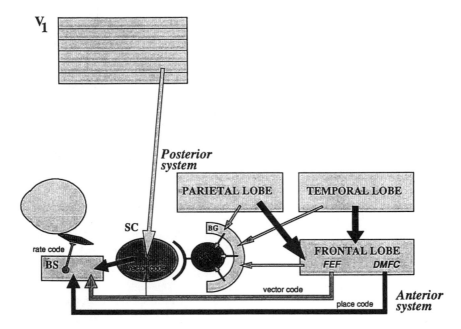

FIG. 1.13. Diagram of the basic connections and coding operations of visually guided eye-movement control with the addition of one of the major inhibitory systems that presumably plays a central role in enabling accurate targeting of individual objects in a complex visual scene.

from the substantia nigra which in turn is controlled, through the basal ganglia, by a number of cortical areas.

THE INFORMATION UTILIZED FOR SACCADE GENERATION

In the preceding section I presented evidence leading to the idea that in the superior colliculus during each fixation a retinal error signal is computed between the fovea where the fixation spot falls and the location of the target to be acquired. For example, if a target appears 10 degrees to the left of the fovea, a signal is sent down to the brainstem to move the eye 10 degrees to the left, resulting thereby in the acquisition of the target for foveal viewing.

But is this really what is happening in the system as a whole? To test this, a most interesting experiment was carried out by Hallett and Lightstone (1976), the essence of which is schematized in Fig. 1.14. The question is the following: What happens when a target stimulus is presented, in total darkness, while the eye is in midflight? Will the subsequent eye move-

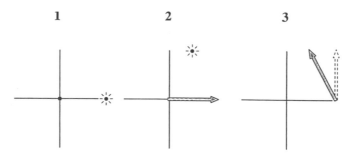

FIG. 1.14. Schematic of saccadic eye movements generated to stimuli flashed while the eye is in midflight during a saccade. Both stimuli are presented very briefly and in total darkness. When the first stimulus appears, a saccade is generated to it (1). In midflight a second target appears straight up from the fovea (2). If only a retinal error signal were computed, upon reaching the place where target one had been, a straight vertical upward saccade would be generated as indicated by the dotted arrow. Instead, the eye correctly targets the second stimulus (3). This indicates that the computational process utilizes both a retinal error and an eye-position signal.

ment to acquire the target for foveal viewing compute where it was relative to the fovea or will it take into account an eye-position signal? To answer this question two targets are presented in succession as depicted in the figure. In the first panel, following central fixation, the first target is flashed on briefly. Part way through the ballistic saccadic eye movement to this target a second spot is flashed on, so as to appear directly above the fovea as shown in the second panel. Upon completing the first saccade, the subject's task is to make a second saccade to where the second stimulus had appeared. To repeat, the question is this: Will this second saccadic eye movement be one that takes into account only the retinal error signal or will it correctly target the stimulus in space? If only the retinal error signal were taken into account, the second saccade should be one that moves the eye straight up as indicated in the third panel by the dotted arrow. But what happens instead is that the eye goes correctly to the location where the second target had actually been presented in space. This means that the computational process involves not only a retinal error signal but also a virtually instantaneous signal of the position of the eye in orbit.

A clever extension of this work has been carried out by Sparks and Mays (1983). They placed an electrode into the colliculus through which they induced saccadic eye movements with electrical stimulation. They first presented a visual target and then, before the monkey could initiate his eye movement to it, stimulated the colliculus to move the eye to some location different from where the target had appeared. This was done

while the animal was in total darkness. They asked essentially the same
question Hallett and Lightstone had asked: Will the ensuing eye movement
take into account the orbital change induced, in this case, by the electrical
stimulation? The situation is depicted in Fig. 1.15. In the left panel (A)
the basic procedure is outlined showing arrows for the two possible outcomes. After fixation a visual target is presented straight above the center
of gaze. Before the animal can shift his gaze to this target the colliculus
is stimulated, pulling the eye to position S in total darkness. The first
possible outcome, marked as T′, is that the animal makes a saccade straight
up on the basis of which one would infer that only a retinal error signal
has been coded. The second outcome is that the animal utilizes both a
retinal error and an eye position signal in generating his eye movement.
Consequently he correctly acquires the target at position T. Results by
Sparks and Mays were unequivocal and are depicted on the right panel
(B) in Fig. 1.15: the eye moves to the location where the visual target had
been presented. Also shown in this panel is an eye movement to the target
when the colliculus was not stimulated. It is clear from these data that
saccadic targeting involves taking into account both a retinal error signal
and an eye position signal.

The question that now needs to be answered is where the various components of this computation take place. Are both done in the colliculus?

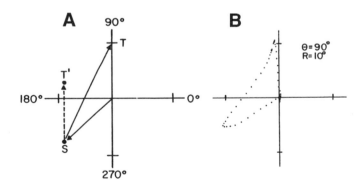

FIG. 1.15.   The effect of collicular stimulation on the acquisition of a visual
target. A: Following fixation a visual target is presented (T2); before an eye
movement is generated to it the superior colliculus is stimulated resulting
in the displacement of the eye to point S. Were only a retinal error signal
computed, the subsequent eye movement to the visual target would land at
T′. However, were both a retinal error and eye-position signal taken into
account, the eye would correctly reach the target at T. B: Actual eye-
movement traces showing (1) an eye movement directly to the target in the
absence of collicular stimulation and (2) the correct acquisition of the target
in spite of having had the eye displaced by electrical stimulation of the
superior colliculus. Adapted from Sparks and Mays (1983).

Or is some of it done in the frontal eye fields or perhaps some other structures? To provide some answers to this question several different kinds of experiments had been carried out. It has been shown, for example, that when the abducens or other oculomotor nuclei are stimulated, the system does not take into account the eye position signal (Schiller & Sandell, 1983; Sparks, 1986). This means, not surprisingly, that the computation occurs above the final common path to the eye muscles. Stimulation in other parts of the brainstem in some regions produced effects similar to those seen in the colliculus and in other regions similar to those seen with abducens stimulation. Stimulation of the frontal eye fields and the dorsomedial frontal cortex produced results similar to those found with collicular stimulation.

A set of lesion experiments suggest that the retinal error and eye position signals are most likely combined somewhere in the brainstem. In these lesion experiments either the superior colliculus or the frontal eye fields were removed and the remaining structure was eclectically stimulated using the Sparks and Mays paradigm (Schiller & Sandell, 1983). The results of this work are summarized in Fig. 1.16. It is evident that stimulation of the frontal eye fields and the superior colliculi produce similar results as indicated in the four displays on the left: The eyes correctly reach the target even after it has been pulled over by frontal eye field or superior colliculus stimulation. Lesion to either structure fails to interfere with this computational process as shown in the four displays on the right when the remaining structure is stimulated.

These studies demonstrate, therefore, that the generation of a visually guided saccade involves computations of both a retinal error signal and an eye position signal. This twofold analysis does not take place uniquely in either the frontal eye fields or in the colliculus. At this stage we do not know exactly where the eye position signal comes from. But evident from the work I have just described is that the two signals are combined somewhere in the brainstem.

THE NATURE OF THE VISUAL INPUTS TO THE
EYE-MOVEMENT CONTROL SYSTEMS

One of the remarkable facts about the visual system is that already in the retina several structurally and functionally different classes of retinal ganglion cells have been identified (Enroth-Cugell & Robson, 1966; Schiller, 1986; Schiller & Logothetis, 1990; Stone, 1983). It has been proposed that these different classes of cells extract different kinds of information from the visual scene. The two classes of retinal ganglion cells of the primate attracting the greatest attention are the so-called midget and parasol cells that in many respects appear similar to the X and Y cells first identified

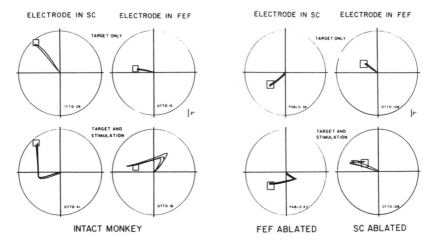

FIG. 1.16. Acquisition of visual targets when either the superior colliculus or the frontal eye fields are stimulated in the intact animal and in animals in which one of these structures has been ablated. The stimuli are correctly targeted in all cases suggesting that the computation taking into account both a retinal error signal and an eye position signal does not take place uniquely in either of these structures. It appears that this computation occurs downstream from the superior colliculus. The four displays on the left show eye-movement traces following superior colliculus and frontal eye field stimulation in the intact animal. The four displays on the right show traces obtained under similar conditions after ablation of either the superior colliculus or the frontal eye fields. The four displays on the left show stimulation of the superior colliculus and the frontal eye fields in the intact animal; the four displays on the right show stimulation of the remaining structure after the other has been ablated. Adapted from Schiller and Sandell (1983).

in the cat and subsequently in every mammalian species studied. The basic properties of these two classes of cells are delineated in Fig. 1.17. Both classes of cells have circular receptive fields that are comprised of a central excitatory region and an inhibitory surround area. The midget cells, however, have very small receptive fields; in central retina the excitatory receptive field center receives input from just one cone which renders these cells automatically color selective in primates with three cone types that are selective to long (red), medium (green) and short (blue) wavelengths. The surround mechanism of these cells, as supplied by the horizontal cells of the retina, is not purely color opponent as had until recently been thought. It now appears that the horizontal cells are promiscuous and hook up with any cone type. Thus the color opponency that arises as an interaction between the center and surround mechanisms of these cells, pits a single cone against all cone types. In addition to having small receptive fields and color opponency, it is noteworthy that the midget cells

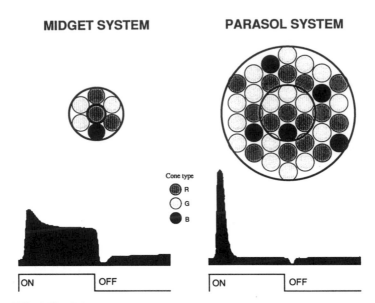

FIG. 1.17. Schematic of two major classes of retinal ganglion cells, the midget and the parasol. In central retina the receptive field center of midget cells is comprised of but a single cone that makes them automatically color selective. The surround, as created by horizontal cells, receives a mixed input from the various cone types. The receptive field diameter of the parasol cells is three times larger than the midget cells and both the center and surround of the receptive fields get a mixed input from the different cone types. The midget cells respond in a sustained fashion and the parasol cells respond transiently. R, G, and B = long (red), medium (green), and short (blue) wavelength cones. Adapted from Schiller and Logothetis (1990).

respond in a relatively sustained fashion to visual stimulation. In contrast with the midget cells, the parasol cells have much larger receptive fields; the center and surround areas receive input from many different cones suggesting that this system cannot be color selective; the responses of parasol cells to visual stimuli are transient.

Both the midget and parasol cells come in ON and OFF varieties, where the ON cells are excited by light increment and the OFF cells by light decrement (Schiller, 1995).

In addition to these two classes of retinal ganglion cells several others have also been identified (Stone, 1983). One set of these, the so-called W cells, are actually a grab-bag group that is comprised of several types of small retinal ganglion cells with a variety of receptive field properties. Some of these cells produce transient responses both to light incremental and light decremental stimuli (light and dark spots, for example). Yet another class of retinal ganglion cells is discussed later as it is involved in the generation of smooth-pursuit eye movements.

What aspects of the visual scene are analyzed by the midget and parasol systems? A number of hypotheses have been advanced on this topic (Livingstone & Hubel, 1988; Schiller, 1986, 1996; Schiller & Logothetis, 1990). One of the more popular ideas is that the midget system is devoted to the analysis of color and shape, whereas the parasol system is devoted to the analysis of luminance differences, stereopsis, and motion. Current work has come up with an alternative view based on studies in which the visual capacities of animals were examined before and after selective disruption of either the midget or parasol systems (Schiller, Logothetis, & Charles, 1990). These studies suggest that whereas for the discrimination of color differences the parasol system is essential, other visual capacities such as motion, brightness, pattern, and depth perception, can be processed by both channels. However, the midget system can perform up to much higher spatial frequencies than can the parasol system. Conversely, the parasol system can carry out these analyses up to much higher temporal frequencies. It appears therefore, that these two systems have emerged to extend the range of vision, with the midget system extending it in the spatial frequency and wavelength domains and the parasol system extending it in the temporal frequency domain.

The midget and parasol cells project to different layers of the lateral geniculate nucleus of the thalamus, which is a beautifully laminated structure in which the visual field is laid out in nice topographic order. For the representation of central retina, out to about 17 degrees of visual angle from the fovea in the old-world monkey, the lateral geniculate nucleus is comprised of six layers: the top four parvocellular layers receive input from the midget cells whereas the bottom two magnocellular layers receive input from the parasol cells. The disparity of the number of layers reflects the fact that for this central representation the number of parvocellular cells outnumbers the magnocellular cells by nearly 10 to 1. An interesting change takes place, however, with increasing eccentricity, which becomes especially apparent beyond 17 degrees where the number of layers is reduced to two parvocellular and two magnocellular ones. The proportion of parvocellular and magnocellular cells changes accordingly; in the far periphery they are just about equal in number.

These considerations highlight another important fact about these two systems. The parasol cells, perhaps by virtue of the much more extensive receptor input to them, are considerably more sensitive to contrast and motion than are the midget cells (Shapley, Kaplan, & Soodak, 1981). Thus they sacrifice the ability to discern fine detail for gaining high sensitivity. This difference should be particularly notable for the far periphery where the numerosity of the cells in the two systems is nearly the same. One might conjecture, therefore, that when a faint, rapidly moving object appears briefly in the periphery, it is predominantly the parasol system that signals its presence. One might think of a mosquito flying about silently, stalking its victim in the meadows on a hot, humid summer day. If detected at all, it is the parasol system that alerts the individual to the bloodsucker. Once foveated with a saccade, it is the midget system that provides the bulk of the information for its identification. The quick, ensuing swat might just do the bugger in. It would make good sense, therefore, for the parasol system to have a major input to the saccadic eye-movement control system. The question of the inputs from the various retinal cell types to the eye-movement control systems is addressed later.

Cells from the lateral geniculate nucleus project to area V1 where the parvocellular input terminates most densely in layer $4c\beta$ and the magnocellular input in $4c\alpha$.

Having now reached cortex I can turn to another important fact about the organization of the visual system. This fact is that there are numerous visual areas in the cortex of primates. At present more than 30 such areas have been discerned that make more than 300 interconnections (Felleman & Van Essen, 1991). Why are there so many areas? Until recently, the prevalent idea has been that each area is involved in the analysis of a different basic visual function. Thus at one time it had been proposed that area V2 is devoted to stereopsis, area V4 to color, and area MT to motion. Recent findings have questioned this attractive, if simplistic idea. It has been shown, for example, that each of these areas is not homogeneous and contains cells that respond to many different aspects of the visual scene. Furthermore, lesion studies fail to show the kind of specific basic deficit in motion, color, and stereopsis that such a theory would demand (Schiller, 1993, 1996). That the number of visual areas identified far exceeds the basic visual functions that have been denoted by psychologists and philosophers also suggests that something here does not quite fit.

In an attempt to put together the fact that there are different classes of retinal ganglion cells and that there are distinct visual areas in the cortex, an attractive unifying scheme has been proposed by Mishkin, Ungerleider, and Macko (1983) and others. According to this scheme, the midget and parasol systems remain separate beyond the striate cortex and form two information processing streams, with the midget system sending its information to the temporal lobe via areas V2 and V4, and the parasol system sending its information to the parietal lobe via area MT. The first stream has been hypothesized to be involved predominantly in color and shape analysis and the second stream in spatial analysis, motion, and depth perception.

To test these hypotheses and to determine how various retinal ganglion cells contribute to the generation of visually guided eye movements, several different kinds of experiments have been performed. I now turn to some of these.

The first approach used is to characterize the receptive field properties of those cells in the retina and in the cortex that project to the superior colliculus. This can be determined by antidromic activation. A stimulating electrode is placed into the superior colliculus while recording in either the retina or in the cortex. Electrical stimulation in the colliculus activates the axons of cells projecting there and creates action potentials traveling in the reverse direction, which when detected by the recording electrode ascertains that the neuron sampled projects to the colliculus. These kinds of experiments show that in the monkey, the prime input from the retina comes from the W-type cells that terminate in the superficial layers of the colliculus (Schiller & Malpeli, 1977). Surprisingly there is little or no direct input to the colliculus from the parasol cells in the monkey. From area V1 the input to the colliculus comes from the complex cells of layer 5 that terminate below the input from the retina.

To assess the role of the retinal and cortical inputs to the colliculus, experiments have been carried out in which area V1 was cooled to reversibly silence the cells under the cooling probe, including those that reside in layer 5 and project to the colliculus. This kind of experiment, carried out in both cat and monkey, showed dramatic results: After cooling, none of the cells in the intermediate and deeper layers of the colliculus could be driven by visual stimuli (Schiller, Stryker, Cynader, & Berman, 1974). On the other hand, the responses of the cells in the superficial layers were unaffected by cooling. An example of this appears in Fig. 1.18, showing recordings from a superficial and an intermediate layer cell. The former was unaffected and the latter was silenced upon cooling. These findings show that the cortical input is essential for visual activation of the deeper layers of the superior colliculus.

To answer the question as to what the roles are of the midget and parasol cells in driving collicular cells through the cortex, a series of experiments had been carried out using the method depicted in Fig. 1.19. The parasol or the midget systems were reversibly inactivated by injecting a variety of blocking agents into either the magnocellular or parvocellular portions of the geniculate. The effects of such inactivation were assessed by recording in the superior colliculus and also in several other cortical areas, including areas V1, V4, and MT (Ferrera, Nealy, & Maunsell, 1992; Malpeli, Schiller, & Colby, 1981; Maunsell, Nealy, & DePriest, 1990). The results of these experiments were quite interesting. It appears that the cells making their input from area V1 to the superior colliculus are driven exclusively by the parasol system. Furthermore, area MT is also driven predominantly, if not exclusively, by this system. So far so good. However, recordings in V1 showed that there are many cells that get a convergent input from the two systems. The same was found to be the case for area V4. Thus it appears that while there is some degree of specialization in

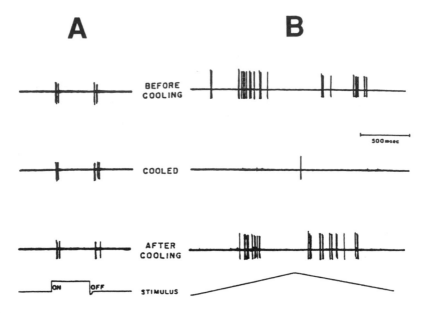

FIG. 1.18. The effect of cooling V1 on the responses of collicular cells. Cells in the top layer (A) are unaffected as they are driven directly from the retina. Cells in the rest of the colliculus, as demonstrated for one cell in B, become silent when cortex is cooled suggesting that the cortical input is crucial for the integrity of the colliculus and for eye-movement generation. From Schiller, Stryker, Cynader, and Berman (1974).

the pathways, it is not quite as neat and straightforward as had been assumed. Certainly, the temporal lobe receives, via V4, a mixed rather than a pure input from the various cell types that originate in the retina.

These considerations now bring us to the next step in our wiring diagram as shown in Fig. 1.20. Two major pathways originate in the retina in the form of the midget and parasol systems. These two systems project to different sets of layers in the lateral geniculate nucleus and terminate in different sublamina of layer 4 in area V1. The input to the superior colliculus from V1 comes from cells in layer 5 that are driven by the parasol system. On the other hand many other cells in V1 receive a convergent input from the midget and parasol systems. Therefore, one needs to postulate at least three pathways leaving V1 as far as what retinal inputs drive them: a pathway driven purely by the midget system, a pathway driven purely by the parasol system, and a pathway driven by both. In extrastriate cortex the input to MT is dominated by the parasol system, whereas the input to V4 is mixed. One infers, therefore, that the input to the temporal lobe must be mixed as well, whereas the input to the parietal lobe via MT is driven mostly by the parasol system.

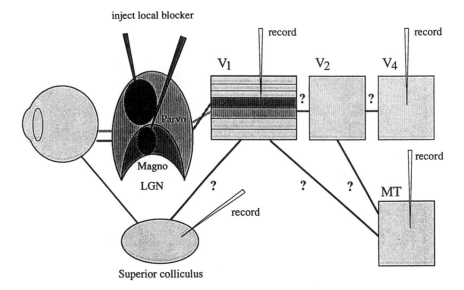

FIG. 1.19. Schematic of the method used to determine what kinds of cells originating in the retina and projecting to cortex are essential for driving cells in extrastriate cortex and in the deeper collicular layers. Recording electrodes are placed in various cortical regions and in the colliculus. Injection electrodes are placed into topographically corresponding areas in the LGN, both in its parvocellular and magnocellular divisions. The results of such experiments show the following: (1) in the striate cortex there are numerous cells that receive convergent input from the midget and parasol systems. The same is true for area V4. Area MT, however, receives its input predominantly from the parasol system. The same is true for the superior colliculus where cells are silenced only following magnocellular block.

EXPRESS SACCADES

Next I turn to a most interesting phenomenon in saccadic eye movements and consider the neural mechanisms underlying them. This phenomenon has been given the name "express saccades" by Fischer and Boch (1983). When a human or a monkey is trained to make saccades to singly appearing visual targets and one examines the latency distribution of the eye movements, surprisingly, a bimodal distribution is obtained. An example of the typical bimodal distribution of saccadic eye movements obtained in a normal monkey appears in the top panel of Fig. 1.21; eye movements falling into the first mode of the distribution are the express saccades, and those falling into the second mode are "regular" saccades. When first discovered, many criticisms were raised and it was thought that these uncommonly rapid eye movements arise only in the laboratory with singly presented stimuli on a homogeneous background and may be anticipatory in nature.

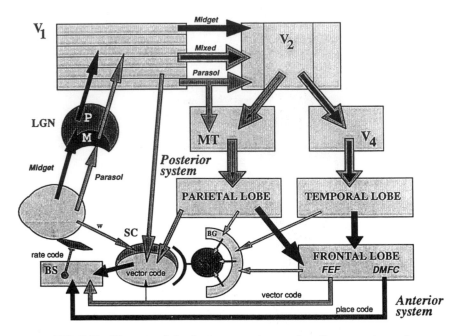

FIG. 1.20. Diagram of the basic connections and coding operations of
visually guided eye-movement control with the addition of the visual inputs
to these areas.

Although it is true that one does not see express saccades when humans
or monkeys are asked to make a discrimination between several simultaneously appearing stimuli (Schiller et al., 1987), it has been shown that
in a textured environment, while a monkey scans the visual scene, express
saccades are commonly made to suddenly appearing new visual targets
(Sommer, 1994). This suggests that express saccades are not just a laboratory curio but can occur under natural conditions.

What neural mechanisms subserve express and regular saccades? To
answer this question several lesion studies have been carried out. In doing
so a number of neat hypotheses have been advanced: Express saccades are
produced by the posterior system that involves the colliculus whereas regular saccades are the product of the anterior system and hence involves the
frontal eye fields; express saccades are driven by the parasol system, whereas
regular saccades are driven by the midget system. To test these hypotheses
lesions have been made in several structures: the superior colliculus, the
frontal eye fields, areas V4 and MT, and the parvocellular and magnocellular portions of the lateral geniculate nucleus (Schiller & Lee, 1994;
Schiller et al., 1987; Sommer, Schiller, & McPeek, 1993). The last two for
the purpose of selectively disrupting the midget and parasol systems.

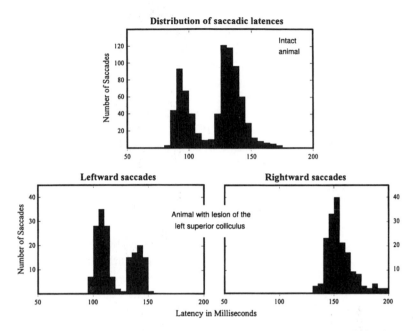

FIG. 1.21. The distribution of saccadic latencies to singly presented visual targets in an intact animal and in an animal with an ablated left superior colliculus. The distribution of saccadic latencies in the intact animal is bimodal. The first mode has been termed "express saccades" and the second "regular saccades." Following unilateral collicular ablation the monkey no longer makes express saccades to stimuli presented in the visual field that had been represented by the removed colliculus but continues to make express saccades to the intact side. This suggests that the colliculus is essential for the generation of express saccades.

The major finding of such lesion studies is shown in Fig. 1.21. Unilateral ablation of the superior colliculus eliminates express saccades made to that part of the visual field that had been represented by the colliculus prior to its removal. A normal, bimodal distribution of saccadic eye movements continues to be obtained to the intact side. In our other lesion studies we had found that the bimodal distribution of saccadic latencies is unaffected by the disruption of the midget and parasol systems, by the removal of the frontal eye fields, area V4, and area MT. Even paired area V4 and area MT lesions failed to alter the bimodal distribution of saccadic latencies. Thus the hypotheses advanced regarding the generation of express and regular saccades were only partially borne out by these lesion experiments. The superior colliculus is clearly essential for the generation of express saccades. However, it appears that the midget and parasol systems can each independently mediate express saccades. One must therefore postulate a significant input to the colliculus from the midget system.

This input cannot be uniquely from areas V4 or MT since lesions of these two areas have also failed to eliminate express or regular saccades. It should be added here that paired V4 and MT lesions leave a great number of other visual functions intact as well, such as stereopsis for example, suggesting that there are more than just two parallel streams of information emanating to higher cortical areas from V1.

It is now time to complete our wiring diagram as we know it at the present time. This final diagram of the saccadic eye-movement control system appears in Fig. 1.22. Added here are a number of new facts, including the inference, based on the lesion studies just described, that the superior colliculus receives a significant input from the midget system although its exact source remains a mystery. Other facts added are the following:

1. We know now, through the elegant work of Hendry and Yoshioka (1994) at the University of Pennsylvania, that in addition to the midget and parasol systems, the lateral geniculate nucleus, in its interlaminar regions, receives retinal input from several other classes of retinal ganglion cells which in turn drive cells that terminate in several different layers of area V1. The projection pattern of these cells to extrastriate regions is not yet known.

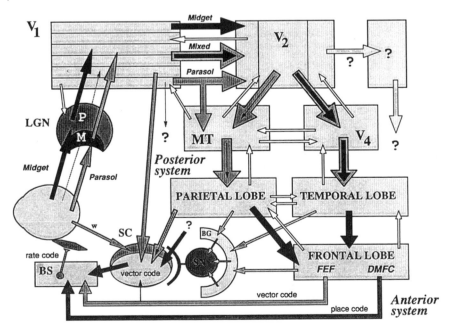

FIG. 1.22. Final diagram of the neural systems involved in visually guided saccadic eye-movement generation.

2. In addition to the two major streams emanating from area V1, there must be other, additional pathways processing visual information.

3. Feedback pathways are common throughout the system making for much more interaction among the various identified visual and oculomotor structures than had previously been thought.

FUNCTIONS OF THE ANTERIOR AND POSTERIOR SYSTEMS IN SACCADIC EYE-MOVEMENT CONTROL

At this stage in our progression through the eye-movement control system it is time to take stock and speculate about the functions of the anterior and posterior systems in saccadic eye-movement control. The weight of the evidence does suggest that these two systems play at least partially different roles in visually guided eye-movement generation. The posterior system that reaches the brainstem through the superior colliculus appears to be one that is central for the generation of rapid, reflex-like eye movements. The ability to respond rapidly to suddenly appearing targets has important survival value. This applies both to being able to acquire an object in appetitive behavior as when a bird might catch an insect, and to being able to initiate action for avoidance of a threatening object. Thus the posterior pathway appears to be important for the execution of eye movements under such conditions.

In speculating about the anterior system we need to distinguish between its two subsystems as represented by the frontal eye fields and by the dorsomedial frontal cortex. These two areas carry different codes and hence are likely to perform rather different jobs. The dorsomedial frontal cortex area, in which a place code is represented (Fig. 1.10), is likely to play a role in integrating information about the location of objects in space, both for the movement of the eyes and the limbs. Lesions of this area have so far failed to reveal a clear-cut, unique deficit in simple eye-movement control. Several studies have shown, however, that many neurons in this area respond to both eye and limb movements and that the responses are linked to the execution of motor sequences (Mann et al., 1988; Mushiake, Inase, & Tanji, 1990; Tanji & Kurata, 1982; Tanji & Shima, 1994; Tehovnik, 1995). Furthermore, it appears that the responses of neurons can undergo changes in the course of learning, suggesting that this area plays a central role in the acquisition of new hand-eye coordination skills (Aizawa, Inase, Mushiake, Shima, & Tanji, 1991; Brinkman & Porter, 1979; Chen & Wise, 1995a, 1995b; Matsuzaka, Hiroshi, & Tanji, 1992).

The frontal eye fields are also believed to play a role in execution of higher level eye movement (Bichot, Schall, & Thompson, 1996; Guitton, Buchtel, & Douglas, 1985). The area seems to be involved in object selection and the planning of sequences of eye movements that occur, for example, when the face of a person is scanned. It has also been reported that frontal eye field lesions produce deficits in predictive tracking (Keating, Gooley, & Kennedy) and in saccade generation to remembered target locations (Deng, Goldberg, Segraves, Ungerleider, & Mishkin, 1986; Dias et al., 1995; Sommer & Tehovnik, in press).

That the anterior and posterior systems have some overlap in function is suggested by the fact that after lesions of either the frontal eye fields or the colliculi there is rapid recovery of function. The likely explanation for this is that in the absence of one of these systems the other can eventually take over most of the affected functions.

SMOOTH-PURSUIT EYE MOVEMENTS

In this section I describe several aspects of pursuit eye movements. As in the case of saccades, a number of neural mechanisms contribute to the generation of pursuit eye movements. Here I deal with three of them. The first involves the generation of pursuit by the vestibular system when the organism is in motion. The second and third systems both generate pursuit by virtue of visual signals but deal most effectively with different aspect of it. When the world moves at slow velocities and the organism is not in motion, it is the accessory optic system that in many mammalian species sends essential signals for moving the eyes so as to stabilize them with respect to the visual scene. The third neural system is one that plays a central role in the tracking of individual moving objects in the visual scene and also contributes to stabilization of the eyes when the visual scene at large moves about at medium to high velocities.

When, you might ask, do we encounter the situation in which the entire visual scene or a large portion of it moves? Actually this happens all the time: when you locomote in the world, when you are driving, or when you are aboard a ship tossed about on the restless seas. Artificially the situation arises whenever you go to a panoramic, 360 degree cinema at one of the Disney parks or if you go to a Planetarium. When you go to a panoramic cinema, there are typically rails to which you are admonished to hang on. The reason is that when the world begins to move and seems to tilt by virtue of the film shown all the way around, you tend to lose your balance. That is because you are getting conflicting signals from your vestibular and visual systems. Which highlights the fact that there is a curious link between these two systems, a fact that will be better understood once we trace the circuitry involved. In real life a similar situation can also arise. It happens, for example, when you sit outside for a few hours on top of a mountain in the middle of a starry night; the stars are seen to rotate by virtue of the rotating earth. The earth's rotation is too slow and steady, of course, to be detected by the vestibular system. Now looking at stars for a prolonged time may not be something you often do, but rabbits, happily ensconced in some field at night, do it all the time, I understand. The difference under these conditions is that the rate of motion is very slow. It is so slow, in fact, that probably neither of the two systems I have noted that rely on visual input are capable of detecting it. The maximum velocity with which stars would move on the retinal surface when you or a rabbit are motionless in an open field is about 0.004 deg/sec.

To better understand the nature of tracking eye movements under conditions when either the organism or a large portion of the visual scene is in motion, experiments can be carried out in which a person is placed into an enclosure that allows one to rotate either the person or the walls of the enclosure. One can do both of these quite simply actually if you want to have the experience. You need a rotating chair and a large lamp-shade with black spots or vertical stripes painted on the inside. Then you either rotate the chair or you rotate the lampshade. If you have a willing subject you can watch the eyes to see how they move. Alternatively, of course, you can record the eye movements. In useful experiments such recording is essential. If one does that, the eye-movement signals you get look much like those depicted in Fig. 1.23. Shown here schematically is how the eyes move when the visual scene or the organism is moved at three different velocities. You can see there are two kinds of eye movements evident, which we can term the slow phase and the fast phase. During the slow phase the eye performs pursuit motion thereby stabilizing the visual scene on the retina; the visual scene in this case is the inside of the lampshade. During the fast phase the eye is reset because of the limits of ocular motility. The slow phase is more or less equivalent to smooth pursuit and the fast phase to saccades. Interestingly enough, the eye movements generated when the lampshade is rotating and when the person is rotating look pretty much the same. But they do have different names because they are initiated by different receptor organs. The eye movements generated when the lampshade is moving and the person is stable is called optokinetic nystagmus; it is initiated by visual input. The eye movement generated when the person is rotating is referred to as vestibular nystagmus, a nys-

FIG. 1.23. Schematic representation of nystagmic eye movements produced by either moving stimuli or by rotatory motion of the subject at three different velocities. The slow phase on the nystagmus occurs during tracking. The fast phase resets the eye with saccadic eye movements.

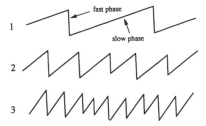

tagmus that is initiated in a reflex-like manner by the semicircular canals. This is a very rapidly conducting pathway that can start the eyes moving in less than 10 ms after the head began to rotate.

The manner in which the vestibulo-ocular reflex operates to produce vestibular nystagmus has been extensively studied. One of the interesting questions people had asked is how can this system accurately stabilize the eyes with respect to the world for one's entire lifetime? To do so, the vestibulo-ocular reflex must have a gain of 1; thus when the head moves, the eye is counterrotated so as to keep the center of gaze stationary with respect to the visual scene. It turns out, that the gain of the reflex can be changed by exposing the organism to different situations (Miles, 1983). It has been shown, for example, that if one wears lenses that magnify or minify the image, the gain of the reflex changes accordingly so that once again, the eyes become stabilized with respect to the world when the head is rotated while you are wearing the lenses. One can apparently double or half the gain within a few days by continuously wearing a set of lenses. This suggests that under normal circumstances inputs from the visual system can adjust the vestibulo-ocular reflex so as to have a gain of one.

In contrast to eye movements triggered by the vestibular system, visually triggered pursuit movements have a much longer onset latency. But remember, this latency is still a lot shorter than the latency with which saccadic eye movements are generated (see Fig. 1.1). The difference in latency between smooth-pursuit eye movements elicited by the vestibular and the visual systems can be readily experienced. Just take a lined pad and place it in front of you sideways so that the lines run vertically. First leave the pad lying in front of you and rotate your head back and forth with increasing speed. You can go to rather high velocities of head rotation and still see the lines clearly because of the rapidity with which the eyes are counterrotated in your head by virtue of the vestibular input. Next keep your head steady and move the lined pad back and forth horizontally with your hands, gradually increasing the rate of movement. You will see that the lines begin to blur even at relatively slow velocities. That is because the visual trigger takes at least 50 ms to produce eye tracking.

For the most part, the generation of smooth-pursuit movements, even as seen under conditions of nystagmus as just described, can occur effectively only when visual or vestibular information is continuously supplied. It is next to impossible to will smooth pursuit in the absence of visual or vestibular input. When pursuit is initiated to a moving target, after a very brief period the velocity of the eye movement becomes matched to the velocity of the target so that its image remains accurately within the fovea. This condition is referred to as pursuit maintenance or closed loop operation (Keller & Heinen, 1991; Koerner & Schiller, 1972). One can artificially open the loop by decoupling the eye movements from the movement of the visual scene. What happens under such conditions is quite curious. In one set of experiments what investigators have done is to immobilize one eye to which moving targets are presented while measuring the movement of the other eye, which is occluded. Ter Braak (1936) was the first person to do this clever manipulation in the rabbit. Subsequently this has also been done in the monkey by immobilizing one eye by transecting the 3rd, 4th, and 6th cranial nerves (Koerner & Schiller, 1972). Eye movements for the occluded, intact eye were then generated by presenting evenly spaced black and white vertical stripes to the immobilized eye at a slow, steady velocity. Such stripes are excellent for producing optokinetic nystagmus. When this is done, the movement of the intact eye gradually increases in velocity until it exceeds the rate of target movement several fold. The question is, why does the intact eye "run away" under such open loop conditions? Without going into technical details, one can say that the position of the target, in this case a vertical edge, is continuously monitored by the visual system relative to the position of the fovea. The disposition is to minimize the error between the two. Now this error keeps increasing, of course, since the eye is immobilized; therefore, a central processor sends a command to the motor plant to increase the rate of tracking. Continued lack of success in catching the moving target results in further signals to increase the speed of the pursuit. What is clear from this is that the pursuit system at large has several components, some of which deal with the velocity and direction of the moving visual scene, some of which generate the motor commands to move the eyes, and some that assess the accuracy of the tracking process.

The visual signals involved in the generation of optokinetic nystagmus and pursuit tracking of objects comes predominantly from direction and velocity selective neurons found in the retina and in many other parts of the visual system. To understand how such cells link up with the motor apparatus let us now turn to the second system I mentioned in the beginning of this section, the accessory optic system. This system is involved in the stabilization of the eye with respect to the visual scene at slow velocities of movement. The accessory optic system has been studied most extensively in the rabbit but has also been explored in birds and cats (Collewijn, 1975; Karten, Fite, & Brecha, 1983; Simpson, 1984). In the rabbit there are approximately 350,000 ganglion cells in each eye. A small subgroup of these, some 6 to 7 thousand cells, are the displaced cells of Dogiel. Termed *displaced* because their cell bodies instead of being in the ganglion-cell layer are closer to the cell bodies of the amacrine cells in the inner plexiform layer of the retina. Dogiel because of the name of the person who had discovered them.

Physiological studies of the cells of Dogiel of the rabbit have established that these cells respond in a directionally selective manner and do so to slow velocities ranging between 0.1 to 1.0 deg/sec. Furthermore, examination of the distribution of direction selectivities reveals that the prime axes form three lobes as shown on the top left of Fig. 1.24. What is remarkable about this layout is that these three lobes correspond to the direction of action of the semicircular canals indicated on the bottom right of the figure. The cells of Dogiel project to the three terminal nuclei in the anterior portion of the midbrain, the dorsal, medial, and the lateral. From here cells project to the dorsal cap of Kooy in the inferior olive which in turn has cells whose axons form one set of climbing fibers that project to the cerebellum. Another group of direction selective cells in the retina projects to the nucleus of the optic tract and is part of the same circuit although its cells may be selective for more rapid velocities of movement. The relevant portions of the circuit then project from the cerebellum to the vestibular nuclei that, as the name implies, receive a major input from the semicircular canals. The circuit is completed by the projections from the vestibular nucleus to the brainstem where connections are made with the brainstem oculomotor centers to generate the appropriate eye movements.

Simpson and his collaborators have conjectured that these two systems, the vestibular and the accessory optic, enable the organism to stabilize the

Major Pathways of the Accessory Optic System (AOS)

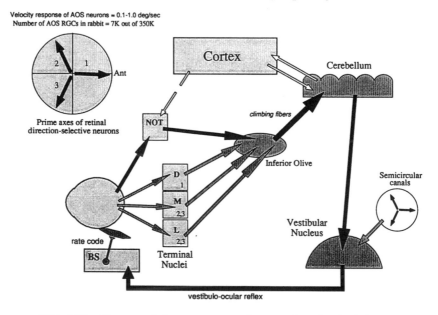

FIG. 1.24. Diagram of the structures and connections involved in eye stabilization by the accessory optic system. NOT = nucleus of the optic tract, BS = brainstem, D = dorsal, M = medial, L = lateral terminal nuclei.

eyes over the great range of velocities encountered in real life (Simpson, 1984). At very low velocities the vestibular system works poorly; hence the accessory optic system, beginning with the retinal direction selective cells, provides the crucial information for eye stabilization. At higher velocities the vestibular system kicks in and stabilizes the eyes with respect to the visual scene by virtue of the signals generated in the semicircular canals. The vestibular system, however, can stabilize the eyes only when the organism is in motion. To stabilize the visual scene or individual objects within it when they move at higher velocities, yet another system is needed. So let me turn to this third system, which also utilizes directionally selective cells. In mammals, the cells involved reside in the visual cortex and are first seen in area V1 where they are common; in fact, more than half the cells in this structure exhibit direction selectivity, and it is believed that all directions of motion are represented (Finlay, Schiller, & Volman, 1976; Schiller, Finlay, & Volman, 1976). Furthermore, most of these cells also exhibit velocity tuning. Different groups of cells respond optimally to different rates of motion; in contrast to the accessory optic system, tuning for a broad range of velocities is evident in these cortical cells, suggesting that they can contribute to the tracking of objects that move over quite a range of velocities. A high degree of specialization in direction and velocity selectivity is seen in area MT where most of the neurons have this property (Albright, 1984; Mikami, Newsome, & Wurtz, 1986). Hence this area and the regions with which it connects are believed to play a central role in motion detection and in pursuit initiation.

In the quest for further understanding of the operation of the smooth-pursuit system, another method investigators have devised is to decouple the visual signal from other extraretinal signals by briefly extinguishing the target during eye-movement tracking. As long as this period of target extinction is quite brief, the eye will continue to track. Recording from single cells under such conditions can discern whether they are involved in processing just a visual signal or if they contribute to the motor activity itself. If the cells process only visual signals, they should cease their activity when the target is extinguished. If they are tightly linked to the motor output, they should continue to discharge when the target is absent since the eye continues its tracking movement. It has been found that in area V1 and in area MT proper, cells that respond during target movement cease to do so when the target is extinguished. On the other hand, in a subdivision of area MT, referred to as MTf, in area MST, in several regions of the parietal lobe as well as in the pontine nuclei, many cells continue their discharge when pursuit is maintained during those brief periods when the target is extinguished (Komatsu & Wurtz, 1989). Such cells are therefore believed be closely linked to the execution of the motor act itself.

Two other kinds of experiments have been carried out that shed further light on the operation of the smooth-pursuit system. One of these involves electrical stimulation and the other the making of restricted lesions in the areas implicated in smooth pursuit.

Electrical stimulation experiments have shown that when areas MT and MST are stimulated during active pursuit, there is an acceleration in pursuit speed when the eye moves toward the side of the brain that is being stimulated. Conversely, when the eye pursues a target that is moving away from that side, the pursuit movement of the eye is slowed down (Komatsu & Wurtz, 1989). Both of these conditions lead to retinal slip; the retinal error so produced is often reduced by initiation of a saccadic eye movement. Stimulation of these brain sites during fixation has little effect. Similar results have also been obtained with stimulation of various pontine nuclei implicated in the generation of smooth-pursuit eye movements (May, Keller, & Crandall, 1985; Suzuki, May, Keller, & Yee, 1990).

As you might expect on the basis of what I have just said, lesions of area MT and MST produce deficits in the execution of accurate smooth-pursuit eye movements (Newsome & Wurtz, 1988). After such lesions monkeys tend to compensate by making repeated saccadic eye movements to catch up to targets that are in motion.

Interestingly enough, the deficits seen after MT and MST lesions are transitory. Even with relatively large lesions there is striking recovery after 3 months (Yamasaki & Wurtz, 1991). Similar deficits and recovery have been reported for lesions made in the pontine nuclei (May & Keller, 1988; May, Keller, & Suzuki, 1988).

The relatively rapid recovery after these lesions suggests that several pathways and neural structures must be involved in smooth-pursuit tracking of moving objects in the visual scene. Indeed, single-cell recording work has shown that cells responding during pursuit can be seen in area 7a of the parietal lobe, in the frontal eye fields and in the dorsomedial frontal cortex (Hyvarinen & Poranen, 1974; MacAvoy, Gottlieb, & Bruce, 1991; Mountcastle, Lynch, Georgopoulos, Sakata, & Acuna, 1975). Lesion work has shown pursuit deficits after frontal eye field lesions (Lynch, 1987). Anatomical work supports the possibility that the signals necessary for pursuit can bypass area MT and MST. For example, areas V2 and V3, where direction-selective cells are common, could supply the visual signals necessary and send them to the frontal eye fields or to the dorsomedial frontal cortex. From there the information could be channeled down to the pons and then of course to the brainstem. These considerations highlight the fact that the execution of most tasks involves several pathways. Such an arrangement often makes it possible to survive unscathed when various portions of the brain are damaged or at least to effectuate considerable recovery with time.

SUMMARY AND CONCLUSIONS

In this chapter the neural mechanisms underlying visually guided saccadic eye movements and smooth-pursuit movements have been delineated. Different neural networks control these two kinds of eye movements.

The networks controlling visually guided saccadic eye movements form two major systems: the anterior and the posterior. The posterior system is comprised of the visual pathways originating in the retina that pass through the lateral geniculate nucleus on the way to the visual cortex from where outputs stream to the superior colliculus and then to the brainstem oculomotor complex. This posterior system utilizes a vector code which computes predominantly a retinal error signal.

The anterior system of visually guided saccadic eye movements receives input from the occipital, parietal, and temporal cortices and is comprised of two subdivisions, one of which passes through the frontal eye fields and the other through the dorsomedial frontal cortex. The subdivision of which the frontal eye fields are a part also carries a vector code. In contrast, the subdivision that passes through the dorsomedial frontal cortex carries a place code.

The posterior system, whose prime conduit to the brainstem is through the superior colliculus, appears to play an important role in the generation of rapid, reflex-like eye movements that enable the organism to respond quickly to suddenly appearing visual stimuli. In line with this view is the fact that express saccades are eliminated by lesions of the superior colliculus. The portion of the anterior subsystem that involves the frontal eye fields is believed to contribute to higher level eye-movement generation important for object selection and for planning sequences of eye movements. The portion of the anterior subsystem that includes the dorsomedial frontal cortex is believed to integrate information about the location of objects in space and also plays a role in hand–eye coordination as well as visuomotor learning.

The neural networks controlling smooth-pursuit eye movements are also comprised of several components that perform different tasks. The accessory optic system contributes primarily to the stabilization of the eye with respect to the visual scene when the organism or the scene move at slow velocities. Higher level systems of pursuit in the cortex contribute to the tracking of selected objects when they or the organism are in motion. This system can analyze several different kinds of motion including those that necessitate interpretation of the scene in depth. Several cortical areas are involved, as a result of which lesions to any one of them produce neither unique nor long-term deficits in smooth pursuit.

It is remarkable that the movement of the eyes, which on the surface appears to be a rather simple, low-level operation, involves such extensive, complicated brain circuitry. Yet in comparison with the many complex tasks the nervous system has to perform, eye-movement control is indeed rather simple. Because of this investigators of the oculomotor system have been fortunate in making considerable progress delineating the neural mechanisms involved.

REFERENCES

Aizawa, H., Inase, M., Mushiake, H., Shima, K., & Tanji, J. (1991). Reorganization of activity in the supplementary motor area associated with motor learning and functional recovery. *Experimental Brain Research, 84,* 668–671.

Albright, T. D. (1984). Direction and orientation selectivity of neurons in visual area MT of the macaque. *Journal of Neurophysiology, 48,* 338–351.

Bichot, N. P., Schall, J. D., & Thompson, K. G. (1996). Visual feature selectivity in frontal eye fields induced by experience in mature macaques. *Nature, 381,* 697–699.

Bizzi, E. (1967). Discharge of frontal eye field neurons during eye movements in unanesthetized monkeys. *Science, 157,* 1588–1590.

Brinkman, C., & Porter, R. (1979). Supplementary motor area in the monkey: Activity of neurons during performance of a learned motor task. *Journal of Neurophysiology, 42,* 681–709.

Bruce, C. J., & Golberg, M. E. (1984). Physiology of the frontal eye fields. *Trends in Neuroscience Research, 7,* 436–441.

Chen, L. L., & Wise, S. P. (1995a). Neuronal activity in the supplementary eye field during acquisition of conditional oculomotor associations. *Journal of Neurophysiology, 73,* 1101–1121.

Chen, L. L., & Wise, S. P. (1995b). Supplementary eye field contrasted with the frontal eye field during acquisition of conditional oculomotor associations. *Journal of Neurophysiology, 73,* 1122–1134.

Chou, I., Sommer, M. A., & Schiller, P. H. (1994). Bimodal latency distribution of averaging saccades in monkey. *Society for Neuroscience Abstracts, # 573.5,* p. 1401.

Collewijn, H. (1975). Oculomotor areas in the rabbit's midbrain and pretectum. *Journal of Neurobiology, 6,* 3–22.

Deng, S.-Y., Goldberg, M. E., Segraves, M. A., Ungerleider, L. G., & Mishkin, M. (1986). The effect of unilateral ablation of the frontal eye fields on saccadic performance in the monkey. In E. Keller & D. S. Zee (Eds.), *Adaptive processes in the visual & oculomotor systems* (pp. 201–208). Oxford, England: Pergamon.

Dias, E. C., Kiesau, M., & Segraves, M. A. (1995). Acute activation and inactivation of macaque frontal eye field with GABA-related drugs. *Journal of Neurophysiology, 74,* 2744–2748.

Draeger, U. C., & Hubel, D. H. (1975). Responses to visual stimulation and relationship between visual, auditory, and somatosensory inputs in mouse superior colliculus. *Journal of Neurophysiology, 38,* 690–713.

Enroth-Cugell, C., & Robson, J. G. (1966). The contrast sensitivity of retinal ganglion cells in the cat. *Journal of Physiology (London), 187,* 517–552.

Fischer, B., & Boch, R. (1983). Saccadic eye movements after extremely short reaction times in the monkey. *Brain Research, 260,* 21–26.

Felleman, D. J., & Van Essen, D. C. (1991). Distributed hierarchical processing in the primate cerebral cortex. *Cerebral Cortex, 1,* 1–47.

Ferrera, V. P., Nealy, T. A., & Maunsell, J. H. R. (1992). Mixed parvocellular and magnocellular geniculate signals in visual area V4. *Nature, 358,* 756–758.

Finlay, B., Schiller, P. H., & Volman, S. (1976). Meridional differences in orientation sensitivity in monkey striate cortex. *Brain Research, 105,* 350–352.

Freedman, E. G., Stanford, T. R., & Sparks, D. L. (in press). Combined eye-head gaze shifts produced by electrical stimulation of the superior colliculus in rhesus monkeys. *Journal of Neurophysiology.*

Fuchs, A. F., Kaneko, C. R. S., & Scudder, C. A. (1985). Brainstem control of saccadic eye movements. *Annual Review of Neuroscience, 8,* 307–337.

Guitton, D., Buchtel, H. A., & Douglas, R. M. (1985). Frontal lobe lesions in man cause difficulties in suppressing reflexive glances and in generating goal directed saccades. *Experimental Brain Research, 58,* 455–472.

Hallett, P. E., & Lightstone, A. D. (1976). Saccadic eye movements to flashed targets. *Vision Research, 16,* 107–114.

Hendry, S. H. C., & Yoshioka, T. (1994). A neurochemically distinct third channel in the macaque dorsal lateral geniculate nucleus. *Science, 264,* 575–577.

Hikosaka, O., & Wurtz, R. H. (1985). Modification of saccadic eye movements by GABA-related substances. I. Effect of muscimol and bicuculline in monkey superior colliculus. *Journal of Neurophysiology, 53,* 266–291.

Hyvarinen, J., & Poranen, A. (1974). Function of the parietal association area 7 as revealed from cellular discharges in alert monkeys. *Brain, 97,* 673–692.

Karten, H. J., Fite, K. V., & Brecha, N. (1983). Specific projection of displaced retinal ganglion cells upon the accessory optic system in the pigeon (Columbia livia). *Proceedings of the National Academy of Sciences, 74,* 1753–1756.

Keating, E. G., Gooley, S. G., & Kenney, D. V. (1985). Impaired tracking and loss of predictive eye movements after removal of the frontal eye fields. *Society for Neuroscience Abstracts, 11,* 472.

Keating, E. G., Gooley, S. G., Pratt, S., & Kelsey, J. (1983). Removing the superior colliculus silences eye movements normally evoked from stimulation of the parietal and occipital eye fields. *Brain Research, 269,* 145–148.

Keller, E. L., & Heinen, S. J. (1991). Generation of smooth-pursuit eye movements: Neuronal mechanisms and pathways. *Neuroscience Research, 11,* 79–107.

Koerner, F., & Schiller, P. H. (1972). The optokinetic response under open and closed loop conditions in the monkey. *Experimental Brain Research, 14,* 318–330.

Komatsu, H., & Wurtz, R. H. (1989). Modulation of pursuit eye movements by stimulation of cortical areas MT and MST. *Journal of Neurophysiology, 62,* 31–47.

Livingstone, M. S., & Hubel, D. H. (1988). Segregation of form, color, movement, and depth: Anatomy, physiology, and perception. *Science, 240,* 740–749.

Lynch, J. C. (1987). Frontal eye field lesions in monkeys disrupt visual pursuit. *Experimental Brain Research, 68,* 437–441.

MacAvoy, M. G., Gottlieb, J. P., & Bruce, C. J. (1991). Smooth pursuit eye movement representation in the primate frontal eye field. *Cerebral Cortex, 1,* 217–230.

Malpeli, J., Schiller, P. H., & Colby, C. L. (1981). Response properties of single cells in monkey striate cortex during reversible inactivation of individual lateral geniculate laminae. *Journal of Neurophysiology, 46,* 1102–1119.

Mann, S. E., Thau, R., & Schiller, P. H. (1988). Conditional task-related responses in monkey dorsomedial frontal cortex. *Experimental Brain Research, 69,* 460–468.

Matsuzaka, Y., Hiroshi, A., & Tanji, J. (1992). A motor area rostral to the supplementary motor area (presupplementary motor area) in the monkey: neuronal activity during a learned motor task. *Journal of Neurophysiology, 68,* 653–662.

Maunsell, J. H. R, Nealy, T. A., & DePriest, D. D. (1990). Magnocellular and parvocellular contributions to responses in the middle temporal area (MT) of the macaque monkey. *Journal of Neuroscience, 10,* 3323–3334.

May, J. G., & Keller, E. L. (1988). Recovery from smooth pursuit impairments after successive unilateral and bilateral chemical lesion s in the dorsolateral pontine nucleus of the monkey. In H. Flohr (Ed.), *Post-lesion neural plasticity* (pp. 413–420). Berlin: Springer-Verlag.

May, J. G., Keller, E. L., & Crandall, W. F. (1985). Changes in eye velocity during smooth pursuit tracking induced by microstimulation in the dorsolateral pontine nucleus of the macaque. *Society for Neuroscience Abstracts, 11,* 79.

May, J. G., Keller, E. L., & Suzuki, D. A. (1988). Smooth-pursuit eye movement deficits with chemical lesions in the dorsolateral pontine nucleus of the monkey. *Journal of Neurophysiology, 59,* 952–977.

Mikami, A., Newsome, W. T., & Wurtz, R. H. (1986). Motion selectivity in macaque visual cortex. I. Mechanisms of direction and speed selectivity in extrastriate area MT. *Journal of Neurophysiology, 55,* 1308–1327.

Miles, F. A. (1983). Plasticity in the transfer of gaze. *Trends in Neuroscience Research, 6,* 57–60.

Miles, F. A., Kawano, K., & Optican, L. M. (1986). Short-latency ocular following response of monkey. I. Dependence on temporospatial properties of visual input. *Journal of Neurophysiology, 56,* 1321–1354.

Mishkin, M., Ungerleider, L. G., & Macko, K. A. (1983). Object vision and spatial vision: Two cortical pathways. *Trends in Neuroscience Research, 6,* 414–417.

Mountcastle, V. B., Lynch, J. C., Georgopoulos, A., Sakata, H., & Acuna, C. (1975). Posterior parietal association cortex of the monkey: command functions for operations within extrapersonal space. *Journal of Neurophysiology, 38,* 871–908.

Mushiake, H., Inase, M., & Tanji, J. (1990). Selective coding of motor sequence in the supplementary motor area of the monkey cerebral cortex. *Experimental Brain Research, 82,* 208–210.

Newsome, W. T., & Wurtz, R. H. (1988). Probing visual cortical function with discrete chemical lesions. *Trends in Neuroscience Research, 11,* 394–400.

Rashbass, C. (1961). The relationship between saccadic and smooth tracking eye movements. *Journal of Physiology (London), 159,* 326–338.

Robinson, D. A. (1972). Eye movements evoked by collicular stimulation in the alert monkey. *Vision Research, 12,* 1795–1808.

Robinson, D. A. (1975). Oculomotor control signals. In G. Lennerstrand & P. Bach-y-Rita (Eds.), *Basic mechanisms of ocular motility and their clinical implications* (pp. 337–374). Oxford, England: Pergamon.

Robinson, D. A., & Fuchs, A. F. (1969). Eye movements evoked by stimulation of frontal eye fields. *Journal of Neurophysiology, 32,* 637–648.

Russo, G. S., & Bruce, C. J. (1996). Neurons in the supplementary eye field of the rhesus monkeys code visual targets and saccadic eye movements in an oculocentric coordinate system. *Journal of Neurophysiology, 76,* 825–848.

Schall, J. D. (1991a). Neuronal activity related to visually guided saccadic eye movements in the supplementary motor area of rhesus monkeys. *Journal of Neurophysiology, 66,* 530–558.

Schall, J. D. (1991b). Neuronal activity related to visually-guided saccades in the frontal eye fields of rhesus monkeys: comparison with supplementary eye fields. *Journal of Neurophysiology, 66,* 559–579.

Schiller, P. H. (1970). The discharge characteristics of single units in the oculomotor and abducens nuclei of the unanesthetized monkey. *Experimental Brain Research, 10,* 347–362.

Schiller, P. H. (1977). The effect of superior colliculus ablation on saccades elicited by cortical stimulation. *Brain Research, 122,* 154–156.

Schiller, P. H. (1984). The superior colliculus and visual function. In I. Darian-Smith (Ed.), *Handbook of physiology, Section 1, The nervous system, Vol. 3(1), Sensory processes* (pp. 457–505). New York: Oxford University Press.

Schiller, P. H. (1986). The central visual system. *The 25th Jubilee Issue of Vision Research, 26,* 1351–1386.

Schiller, P. H. (1993). The effect of V4 and middle temporal (MT) area lesions on visual performance in the rhesus monkey. *Visual Neuroscience, 10,* 717–746.

Schiller, P. H. (1995). The ON and OFF channels of the mammalian visual system. In N. N. Osborne & G. J. Chader (Eds.), *Progress in retinal and eye research, Vol. 15* (pp. 173–195). Oxford, England: Pergamon.

Schiller, P. H. (1996). On the specificity of neurons and visual areas. *Behavior and Brain Research, 76,* 21–35.

Schiller P. H., & Chou, I. (1997). The effect of frontal eye field and dorsomedial frontal cortex lesions on visually guided eye movements. *ARVO Abstracts,* # 3070.

Schiller P. H., Finlay, B., & Volman, S. (1976). Quantitative studies of single-cell properties in monkey striate cortex. I. Spatio-temporal organization of receptive fields. *Journal of Neurophysiology, 39,* 1288–1319.

Schiller, P. H., & Koerner, F. (1971). Discharge characteristics of single units in the superior colliculus of the alert rhesus monkey. *Journal of Neurophysiology, 34,* 920–934.

Schiller, P. H., & Lee, K.-M. (1994). The effects of lateral geniculate nucleus, area V4, and middle temporal (MT) lesions on visually guided eye movements. *Visual Neuroscience, 11,* 229–241.

Schiller, P. H., & Logothetis, N. K. (1987). The effect of frontal eye field and superior colliculus lesions on saccadic and pursuit eye-movement initiation. *ARVO Abstracts,* # 303.11.

Schiller, P. H., & Logothetis, N. K. (1990). The color-opponent and broad-band channels of the primate visual system. *Trends in Neuroscience Research, 13,* 392–398.

Schiller, P. H., Logothetis, N. K., & Charles E. R., (1990). The role of the color-opponent and broad-band channels in vision. *Visual Neuroscience, 5,* 321–346.

Schiller, P. H., & Malpeli, J. (1977). The properties and tectal projections of monkey retinal ganglion cells. *Journal of Neurophysiology, 40,* 428–445.

Schiller, P. H., & Sandell, J. H. (1983). Interactions between visually and electrically elicited saccades before and after superior colliculus and frontal eye field ablations in the rhesus monkey. *Experimental Brain Research, 49,* 381–392.

Schiller, P. H., Sandell, J. H., & Maunsell, J. H. R. (1987). The effect of frontal eye field and superior colliculus lesions on saccadic latencies in the rhesus monkey. *Journal of Neurophysiology, 57,* 1033–1049.

Schiller, P. H., & Stryker, M. (1972). Single-unit recording and stimulation in superior colliculus of the alert rhesus monkey. *Journal of Neurophysiology, 42,* 1124–1133.

Schiller P. H., Stryker, M., Cynader, M., & Berman, N. (1974). Response characteristics of single cells in the monkey superior colliculus following ablation or cooling of visual cortex. *Journal of Neurophysiology, 37,* 181–184.

Schiller, P. H., True, S. D., & Conway, J. L. (1979). Paired stimulation of the frontal eye fields and the superior colliculus of the rhesus monkey. *Brain Research, 179,* 162–164.

Schiller, P. H., True, S. D., & Conway, J. L. (1980). Deficits in eye movements following frontal eye field and superior colliculus ablations. *Journal of Neurophysiology, 44,* 1175–1189.

Schlag, J., & Schlag-Rey, M. (1985). Unit activity related to spontaneous saccades in frontal dorsomedial cortex of monkey. *Experimental Brain Research, 58,* 208–211.

Schlag, J., & Schlag-Rey, M. (1987). Evidence for a supplementary eye field. *Journal of Neurophysiology, 57,* 179–200.

Schlag, J., Schlag-Rey, M., & Pigarev, I. (1992). Supplementary eye field: Influence of eye position on neural signals of fixation. *Experimental Brain Research, 90,* 302–306.

Shapley, R., Kaplan, E., & Soodak, R. (1981). Spatial summation and contrast sensitivity of X and Y cells in the lateral geniculate nucleus of the macaque. *Nature, 292,* 543–545.

Simpson, J. I. (1984). The accessory optic system. *Annual Review of Neuroscience, 7,* 13–41.

Sommer, M. A. (1994). Express saccades elicited during visual scan in the monkey. *Vision Research, 34*, 2023–2038.

Sommer, M. A., Schiller, P. H., & McPeek, R. M. (1993). What neural pathways mediate express saccades? *Commentary in Behavioral and Brain Sciences, 16*, 589–590.

Sommer, M. A., & Tehovnik, E. J. (in press). Reversible inactivation of macaque frontal eye field. *Experimental Brain Research*.

Sparks, D. L. (1986). Translation of sensory signals into commands for control of saccadic eye movements: Role of primate superior colliculus. *Physiology Review, 66*, 118–171.

Sparks, D. L., & Mays, L. E. (1983). Spatial localization of saccade targets: I. Compensation for stimulation-induced perturbations in eye position. *Journal of Neurophysiology, 49*, 45–63.

Sprague, J. M., Berlucchi, G., & Rizzolatti, G. (1973). The role of the superior colliculus and pretectum in vision and visually guided behavior. In *Handbook of sensory physiology. VII, 3, part B.*, American Physiology Society.

Stein, B. E., Magalhaes-Castro, B., & Krueger, L. (1976). Relationship between visual and tactile representations in the cat superior colliculus. *Journal of Neurophysiology, 39*, 401–419.

Stone, J. (1983). *Parallel processing in the visual system*. New York: Plenum Press.

Suzuki, D. A., May, J. G., Keller, E. L., & Yee, R. D. (1990). Visual motion response properties of neurons in the dorsolateral pontine nucleus of the alert monkey. *Journal of Neurophysiology, 63*, 37–59.

Tanji, J., & Kurata, K. (1982). Comparison of movement-related activity in two cortical motor areas of primates. *Journal of Neurophysiology, 48*, 633–653.

Tanji, J., & Shima, K. (1994). Role for supplementary motor area cells in planning several movements ahead. *Nature, 371*, 413–416.

Tehovnik, E. J. (1995). The dorsomedial frontal cortex: Eye and forelimb fields. *Behavioural Brain Research, 67*, 147–163.

Tehovnik, E. J., & Lee, K.-M. (1993). The dorsomedial frontal cortex of the rhesus monkey. Topographic representation of saccades evoked by electrical stimulation. *Experimental Brain Research, 96*, 430–442.

Tehovnik, E. J., Lee, K.-M., & Schiller, P. H. (1994). Stimulation-evoked saccades from the dorsomedial frontal cortex of the rhesus monkey following lesions of the frontal eye fields and superior colliculus. *Experimental Brain Research, 98*, 179–190.

Ter Braak, J. W. G. (1936). Untersuchungen uber optokinetischen Nystagmus. *Archives Neerlandaises de Physiologie, 21*, 308–376.

Wurtz, R. H., & Albano, J. E. (1980). Visual-motor function of the primate superior colliculus. *Annual Review of Neuroscience, 3*, 189–226.

Wurtz, R. H., & Goldberg, M. E. (1972). Activity of superior colliculus in behaving monkey. III. Cells discharging before eye movements. *Journal of Neurophysiology, 35*, 575–586.

Yamasaki, D. S., & Wurtz, R. H. (1991). Recovery of function following lesions in the superior temporal sulcus in the monkey. *Journal of Neurophysiology, 66*, 651–672.

Chapter 2

Overt Orienting Toward Peripheral Stimuli: Normal Development and Underlying Mechanisms

Daphne Maurer
McMaster University
The Hospital for Sick Children

Terri L. Lewis
McMaster University
The Hospital for Sick Children
University of Toronto

In this chapter, we discuss the development of eye movements toward targets detected in the periphery, or in the jargon typical of the literature on adults, the development of overt orienting toward exogenous stimuli (Klein, Kingstone, & Pontefract, 1992). Of prime interest are changes with age in the eccentricity from which targets can attract eye movements, or what has been called the measured visual field. Assessing the development of overt orieting toward exogenous stimuli is important for at least two reasons. First, peripheral stimuli guide shifts in visual attention. Thus, how well peripheral stimuli are detected influences how thoroughly babies search the visual world and which stimuli they bring to the fovea for more detailed examination. Second, the study of developmental patterns in overt orienting can provide insight into the development of underlying neural structures. We begin by discussing the methods that have been used to measure infants' visual fields, the basic findings, and the variables that influence the measured visual field at any age. We then address the question of why babies' performance improves with age, examining the influence of changes in peripheral sensitivity, in attention, and in other factors including motivation, optics, and the control of eye movements. Finally, we consider the neural mechanisms that may underlie the changes.

NORMAL DEVELOPMENT

Methods of Measurement and Basic Findings

As in adults, babies' overt orienting has been measured with *kinetic* perimetry and with *static* perimetry. In studies using kinetic perimetry, babies' fixation has been attracted to a 6° ball jiggled in the center of the field, then an identical ball has been moved in from the side, usually at about 3 deg/sec (Mohn & van Hof-van Duin, 1986; Schwartz, Dobson, Sandstrom, & van Hof-van Duin, 1987; van Hof-van Duin & Mohn, 1985, 1986, 1987). An observer watching the baby through a peephole in the center of the screen notes when the baby first makes an eye movement toward the periphery. The location of the stimulus at that moment constitutes the estimate of the babies' measured visual field along that meridian (assuming that the eye movement was in the correct direction). Studies using this method indicate that the measured visual field expands rapidly between 1 and 8 months of age, although even at 1 year the horizontal and lower visual fields are smaller than those of adults (Mohn & van Hof-van Duin, 1986; Schwartz et al., 1987; van Hof-van Duin & Mohn, 1987). During the first month, the measured field appears to contract (Mohn & van Hof-van Duin, 1986; Schwartz et al., 1987).

Such changes with age are difficult to interpret because three influences on the results of kinetic perimetry are likely themselves to change with age. First, the results will be affected by the latency of eye movements toward targets detected in the periphery. While a baby programs that eye movement, the target continues to move closer to center. The baby is credited with detecting it only after the observer sees that the eye movement has begun. This would not create a problem in interpreting differences between ages if the time to program an eye movement were a constant. But it is not. The latency of eye movements toward targets at a fixed location in the periphery decreases between 1 and 2 months of age (Aslin & Salapatek, 1975) and between 2 and 4 months of age (Johnson, Posner, & Rothbart, 1991; see also Goldberg, Maurer, & Lewis, 1997; Hood & Atkinson, 1993). Thus, the apparent expansion of the visual field after 1 month of age may reflect simply a decrease in the latency of eye movements.

Second, studies using this method of kinetic perimetry require babies to disengage attention from the central ball in order to look toward the peripheral ball. (Without the continuing presence of the central ball, babies would look around the field before the peripheral ball comes close enough to center for them to detect it.) Under many circumstances (but see later for exceptions), young infants have difficulty disengaging attention, especially around 1 to 2 months of age: They are less likely to make an eye movement toward a peripheral target and they take longer to do so if the central fixation stimulus remains on than if it is removed (Hood, Atkinson, & Braddick, chap. 7, this volume; Johnson et al., 1991; Richards & Hunter, chap. 4, this volume). By 4 months of age, the distracting effect of a central stimulus has diminished. Thus, developmental changes in the results of kinetic perimetry may reflect changes in the influence of a central stimulus rather than changes in peripheral vision. On this basis, one would predict a constriction of the measured visual field between birth and 1 month of age and an expansion after 2 months of age. That is the pattern that has been reported.

Third, results from kinetic perimetry will be influenced by false alarms, spontaneous eye movements that were not induced by the peripheral target. Because of developmental changes in the influence of a central stimulus and in the control of eye movements, there may well be age differences in the rate of false alarms. For example, for the reasons discussed in the previous paragraph, there may be more false alarms at birth than at 1 month of age. Indeed, in two studies there were more clearly spontaneous looks (looks in the wrong direction) at birth than at 1- to 2-months of age (Mohn & van Hof-van Duin, 1986; Schwartz et al., 1987). Investigators have attempted to control for this problem by eliminating babies with a high rate of spontaneous looks, but this approach can lead to erroneous conclusions (Maurer & Lewis, 1991). A better approach would be to measure the false alarm rate by including "dummy" trials which simulate the presentation of a peripheral target along a particular meridian.

The second method that has been used to measure babies' orienting toward peripheral targets is static perimetry. As with kinetic perimetry, the baby's attention is first attracted to the center of the field, but then a target is presented at a fixed location in the periphery. An observer notes the direction of the baby's first eye movement away from center. By presenting targets at a variety of eccentricities, it is possible to estimate the visual field for a particular type of target and meridian: the farthest target attracting significantly more eye movements than occur in that direction on control trials without a peripheral target. With static perimetry it is possible to have trials of unlimited duration, so that differences between ages in the measured extent of the field do not result from differences in the latency of eye movements. It is also possible to remove the central stimulus when the peripheral target is presented so that the results are not affected by age differences in the ease of disengaging attention from the central stimulus. It is also possible to estimate the false alarm rate from control trials without a peripheral target. However, with trials of unlimited duration and a limited number of possible responses (e.g., eye movements to the left or right), the false alarm rate is high, and as a result, experimental and control trials need to be repeated many times and/or the data will be noisy.

We have been using static perimetry to chart the development of orienting toward targets presented at 15° intervals along the horizontal meridian. In every case, a baby's fixation was first attracted to the center of the field before a target was presented at a predetermined location in the periphery or a blank control trial was presented. An observer, blind to the stimulus being presented, noted the direction of the baby's first eye movement away from center. If it was not to the left or right, the trial was repeated. For each group of babies, we compared the proportion of first eye movements toward the target at each location with the proportion in the same direction on control trials, and credited babies with detecting and orienting toward that target when there was a significant difference. All testing was monocular so that we could compare orienting toward targets in the temporal visual field (e.g., the right visual field when looking with the right eye) and in the nasal visual field (e.g., the left visual field when looking with the right eye). If the target is large, luminant, and contrasts markedly with the background, even newborns will orient toward it in the periphery (Lewis & Maurer, 1992). Figure 2.1 shows the results for newborns tested with a 6° light flashing at 3 Hz which, at its peak

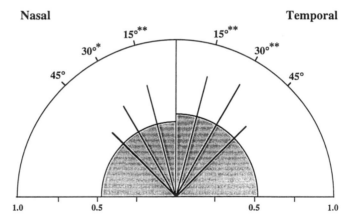

FIG. 2.1. Polar graph representing the mean proportion of trials on which newborns oriented toward a 6° light with a peak luminance of 167 cd/m². Numbers along the outer circumference indicate the locations tested in the nasal field (left half) and in the temporal field (right half). The length of line indicates the proportion of trials with orienting toward a light at a particular location, with reference proportions along the horizontal axis. The shaded area indicates the chance level of responding on blank control trials. Asterisks indicate significant orienting toward the light at that location (*$p < 0.01$; **$p < 0.001$). Adapted from *Vision Research*, Vol. 32, Lewis, T. L., & Maurer, D., The development of the temporal and nasal visual fields during infancy, p. 907, Copyright (1992) with kind permission from Elsevier Science Ltd, The Boulevard, Langford Lane, Kidlington OX5 1GB, UK.

luminance of 167 cd/m^2, had a contrast of 99%. The polargraph represents the mean proportion of trials with eye movements in the correct direction for targets at each location tested. The shaded area indicates the chance level of responding on blank control trials. As indicated by the asterisks, newborns showed significant orienting toward lights out to 30° in the temporal and nasal fields. With increasing age, babies orient toward stimuli farther and farther off to the side. For example, with the 6° light presented in the temporal field, there is a steady increase in the farthest location with significant orienting until, at 4 months of age, babies orient toward it almost as far in the periphery as do adults (see Fig. 2.2). In other studies we have found a similar expansion of the temporal field with age when babies were tested with a 3° light that had a peak luminance of 167 cd/m^2 and flashed at 3 Hz (Lewis & Maurer, 1992, Experiment 1), with a static 6° light of 165 cd/m^2 (Maurer, Nnubia, & Lewis, 1997), and with a static 6° light of only 5 cd/m^2 (Lewis, Maurer, Anvari, & Jewell, 1997). However, the age at which the field approaches adult limits depends on the characteristics of the target. In fact, with pinpoints of light, it does not do so until the school-aged years (e.g., Bowering, Maurer, Lewis, Brent, & Riedel, 1996; Liao, 1973; Wilson, Quinn, Dobson, & Bretton, 1991).

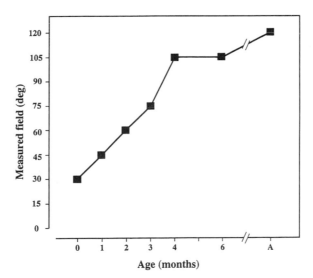

FIG. 2.2. Extent of the temporal field for infants of various ages and adults (A) tested with the 6° light. Adapted from Vision Research, Vol. 32, Lewis, T. L., & Maurer, D., The development of the temporal and nasal visual fields during infancy, p. 908, Copyright (1992) with kind permission from Elsevier Science Ltd, The Boulevard, Langford Lane, Kidlington OX5 1GB, UK.

Variables Influencing the Measured Visual Field

Estimates of the measured extent of the field in babies of a given age vary greatly between studies, probably because of variations in the parameters of the peripheral target, the method of estimating the size of the field (e.g., static or kinetic perimetry; trials of a fixed or unlimited duration), and/or the relative salience of the central fixation stimulus and the peripheral targets. For 2-month-olds, for example, estimates of the extent of the horizontal field range from 8° to 60° (Aslin & Salapatek, 1975; de Schonen, McKenzie, Maury, & Bresson, 1978; Guez, 1978; Harris & MacFarlane, 1974; Lewis & Maurer, 1992; Maurer et al., 1997; Mohn & van Hof-van Duin, 1986; Schwartz et al., 1987; Tronick, 1972; van Hof-van Duin & Mohn, 1987). De Schonen et al. (1978) obtained values ranging from 8° to 38° depending on whether the peripheral stimulus was closer or farther away from the infant than the central fixation stimulus. When the central stimulus (8° red and yellow stationary pompons) was 30 cm away and the peripheral stimuli (8° red and yellow moving pompons) were 90 cm away, 2-month-olds oriented toward the peripheral stimuli out to only 8°. However, when the central stimulus was 90 cm away and the peripheral stimuli only 30 cm away, infants oriented toward the peripheral stimuli out to 38°. Other studies have documented influences of the size of the stimulus, its luminance, its contrast, whether it was static or flickering, and the meridian on which it fell.

To study the effect of the size of the stimulus, we compared babies' orienting toward a 6° light with a peak luminance of 167 cd/m² flashing at 3 Hz with their orienting toward a light that was identical in all respects except that its diameter was only 3° (Lewis & Maurer, 1992). Figure 2.3 compares the farthest location with significant orienting for the two sizes of light. It shows that, whether the targets were in the temporal or nasal field, young infants were far more likely to orient toward them when they were 6° in diameter than when they were 3°. The one exception (in the nasal field at 6 months) is likely to be an artifact. However, despite the effect of stimulus size on the measured extent of the visual field at most ages, there is a similar developmental trend for both sizes of target: gradual expansion with age, until the adult limits are reached at about 6 months of age (presumably because both sizes of target were fairly large and both were highly luminant and of high contrast).

The luminance of the peripheral target also affects the probability that babies will orient toward it. Guez (1978) showed this indirectly when she tested 2- to 5-months-olds binocularly to determine the minimum luminance eliciting a directionally appropriate eye movement for a point source of light flashing at 3 Hz that was located at 15° or 40° in the periphery. Even 2-month-olds oriented toward the light at 40° in the periphery if its

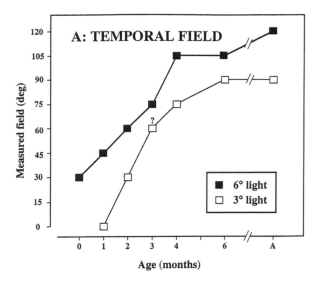

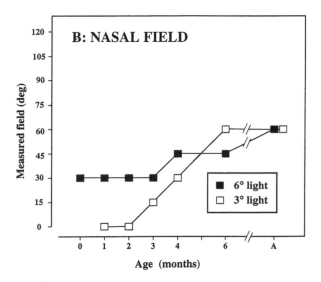

FIG. 2.3. Extent of the temporal field (Panel A) and nasal field (Panel B) for infants of various ages and adults (A). Filled symbols are for tests with the 6° light; open symbols are for tests with the 3° light. A question mark indicates that we did not find the limit of the field because infants oriented significantly toward the plotted location, which was the most peripheral position tested. Adapted from *Vision Research*, Vol. *32*, Lewis, T. L., & Maurer, D., The development of the temporal and nasal visual fields during infancy, pp. 906 & 908, Copyright (1992) with kind permission from Elsevier Science Ltd, The Boulevard, Langford Lane, Kidlington OX5 1GB, UK.

luminance was sufficiently high, although their threshold luminance for targets at 40° differed more from that of adults and older babies than did their threshold for targets at 15°. Nevertheless, like adults and older babies, they required more luminance to respond to targets farther in the periphery.

As in adults, size and luminance appear to trade off in determining whether babies will detect and orient toward a peripheral target. Thus, Schneck et al. (Schneck, Hamer, Packer, & Teller, 1984) found that 1-month-olds (tested binocularly) were as likely to orient toward a 3° target as toward a 17° target so long as the luminance of the 3° target was proportionally greater. This area-luminance trade-off held perfectly for stimuli centered at 9°, 18°, 27°, and 36° in the periphery.

The contrast between the peripheral target and its background also affect peripheral orienting during infancy. Van Hof-van Duin and Mohn (1987) tested babies with kinetic perimetry using a 6° white ball against either a black background or a grey background. At most ages, infants oriented toward the white ball when it was farther in the periphery when it was on the black background (creating 54% contrast) (Mohn & van Hof-van Duin, 1986) than when it was on the lower contrast grey background (contrast not specified). For example, 2-month-olds oriented out to 39° in the temporal field and out to 20° in the nasal field when the background was black but out to only 30° in the temporal field and 12° in the nasal field when the background was grey.

In a recent study (Lewis, Maurer, Burhanpurkar, & Anvari, 1996), we discovered that flicker also affects peripheral orienting, at least at 3 months of age and at least in the temporal field. We showed 3-month-olds a 6° light with a time-averaged luminance of 5 cd/m^2 that was either static (N = 30; luminance = 5 cd/m^2) or flickering at 6 Hz (N = 30; luminance alternating between 0 and 10 cd/m^2). (Note that these luminances are far lower than those used in the studies depicted in Figs. 2.1 to 2.3.) As shown in Fig. 2.4, flicker enhanced orienting toward lights in the temporal visual field. Infants oriented toward the flickering lights out to 60° but oriented toward the static light only at 15°. Similarly, 4-month-olds' (tested binocularly) were more likley to orient toward a stimulus presented briefly at 23° in the presence of a central stimulus when the peripheral stimulus was flickering at 5 Hz rather than static (Hicks & Richards, 1996).

The meridian on which a peripheral target is located affects not only the probability of correct orienting during early infancy but also the developmental pattern that is observed. Thus, Aslin and Salapatek (1975) found that 1- and 2-month-olds, tested binocularly with static perimetry, orient toward a 4° annulus out to 30° if it is on the horizontal or diagonal meridia, but out to only 10° if it is on the vertical meridian. Similarly, Mohn and van Hof-van Duin (1986) found that 2-month-olds, tested binocularly with kinetic perimetry, orient toward a 6° ball out to 30° if it is on the horizontal meridian, but only out to about 17° if it is on the vertical meridian. By 1 year of age, the upper field was adult-like but the horizontal and lower fields were still expanding.

When we tested babies monocularly with targets along the horizontal meridian, we found striking differences between the temporal and nasal visual fields during early infancy. When tested with the 3° light flashing at 3 Hz with a peak luminance of $167 \text{ cd}/\text{m}^2$ (see Fig. 2.3), 2-month-olds oriented toward it out to 30° in the temporal field, but failed to orient toward it even at 15° in the nasal field (Lewis & Maurer, 1992). By 3 months, they did orient toward it at 15° in the nasal field, but by then the measured temporal field had grown to at least 60°. Although less dramatic, differences are also apparent with the 6° light (see Fig. 2.3): from birth to 3 months of age, the measured nasal field does not extend beyond 30° while the temporal field grows to 75° (Lewis & Maurer, 1992). Similarly, when we tested 1-month-olds with a 26° line ($10.1 \text{ cd}/\text{m}^2$; 77% contrast) of varying width, we found that a line just 1.5° wide was adequate to attract orienting when it was located at 30° in the temporal field but that a "line" even 12.8° wide was inadequate when its nearest edge was at 20° in the nasal field (Lewis, Maurer, & Blackburn, 1985). (Adults' sensitivity is higher at 20° in the nasal field than at 30° in the temporal field—Fahle & Schmid, 1988.)

Mohn and van Hof-van Duin (1986), using kinetic perimetry, reported no difference in the rate of development of the temporal and nasal fields from the earliest age tested, 2 months of age (although inspection of the data for younger babies reported in van Hof-van Duin & Mohn [1987] does suggest slower development of the nasal field). Mayer and Fulton (1993) suggest that the relatively slow development of the nasal field is evident only with tests of static perimetry but not with tests of kinetic perimetry. That conclusion was supported by plotting the extent of the field for infants at each age as a percentage of the adult field. With our data based on static perimetry, the infants' field was a smaller percentage of the adult field for the nasal than for the temporal field until at least 4 months of age. With Mohn and van Hof-van Duin's data based on kinetic perimetry, the percentage was the same for the temporal and nasal fields from 2 months of age, the youngest age tested.

Even when targets are within both the measured temporal and nasal fields, babies' eye movements have a shorter latency toward targets in the temporal field than toward targets at the same location in the nasal field. For example, in a reanalysis of a previous study (Maurer et al., 1997), we found that 2-month-olds oriented about 400 ms more quickly toward a 6° light when it was at 30° in the temporal field than when it was at the same location in the nasal field.

Not only are there differences in babies' sensitivity and reaction time to targets in the temporal and nasal fields, but they are affected differently by flicker, at least at 3 months of age (see Fig. 2.4). Thus, flicker greatly enhanced orienting toward targets in the temporal field but had no effect on orienting toward targets in the nasal field (Lewis et al., 1996). Moreover, babies' eye movements toward targets at 15° (which were detected under all conditions) were significantly faster when the target was in the temporal field than when it was in the nasal field—but only when the targets were flickering; the latency of babies' eye movements toward static targets were equivalent for the two fields. These results suggest that during early infancy different neural mechanisms may underlie detection in the temporal and nasal fields that are differentially sensitive to flicker. Later in the chapter, we discuss the underlying neural mechanisms that are likely to be involved.

In summary, even newborns will orient toward peripheral targets if they are large, luminant, and of high contrast. With increasing age, babies orient toward targets increasingly far in the periphery, with the limit at any age determined at least in part by the characteristics of the stimulus, viz., its distance from the baby relative to any central stimulus, its size, its luminance, its contrast, the meridian on which it falls, and whether it is static or flickering. In the next section, we consider abilities that may underlie the developmental changes: increased peripheral sensitivity, improved ability to disengage attention from a competing central stimulus, and changes in other factors such as motivation, optics, control of eye movements, and the effects of sucking.

FACTORS UNDERLYING NORMAL DEVELOPMENTAL CHANGES

Improved Peripheral Sensitivity

Overt orienting improves, in part, because of increased sensitivity to peripheral targets. The strongest evidence comes from developmental studies of peripheral acuity. Babies as young as 1 month (the youngest age tested) can discriminate a striped pattern from a plain square with peripheral vision: They move their eyes first toward the striped pattern. Initially peripheral acuity appears to be quite limited. Courage and Adams (1990, 1996) reported that 1-month-olds detected stripes of 0.48 c/deg beginning at 20° in the periphery but did not detect even larger stripes beginning at 30° in the periphery. With increasing age, babies become able to detect stripes that are increasingly narrow, increasingly far in the periphery, and that have increasingly less contrast (Allen, Tyler, & Norcia, 1996; Courage & Adams, 1990, 1996; Sireteanu, Fronius, & Constantinescu, 1994; Sireteanu, Keller, & Boergen, 1984).

6-Hz FLICKER

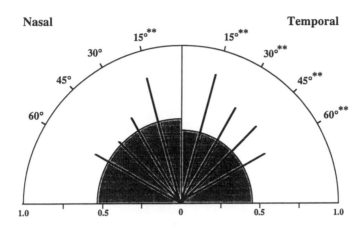

STATIC

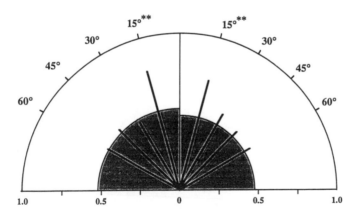

FIG. 2.4. Polar graphs representing the mean proportion of trials on which 3-month-olds oriented toward a 6° light with a time-averaged luminance of 5 cd/m^2 that was either flickering at 6 Hz (upper panel) or static (lower panel). Asterisks indicate significant orienting toward the light at that location (**$p < 0.01$). Other details as in Fig. 2.1.

Two groups of investigators have measured peripheral acuity monocularly to compare infants' sensitivity in the temporal versus nasal field (Courage & Adams, 1990, 1996; Sireteanu et al., 1994). Sireteanu et al. (1994) tested three groups of infants aged 2–5, 5–8, and 8–14 months with stripes beginning at 12.5° in the periphery and found a temporal field superiority for all three groups of infants but not for adults. Specifically, acuity was about 0.6 octaves better in the temporal field than in the nasal field for 2- to 5-month-olds, about 1 octave better for 5- to 8-month-olds, and about 1.3 octaves better for 8- to 14-month-olds (an octave is a halving or a doubling of a value). However, interesting developmental changes in temporal versus nasal acuity might have been missed because infants younger than 2 months were not tested and each group of infants included a broad span of ages. Moreover, because of a strong bias to look toward the temporal field, the results for the oldest group may be artifactual. In a similar study, Courage and Adams (1990, 1996) tested 1-, 2-, and 3-month-olds and adults with stripes beginning at 10°, 20°, or 30° in the periphery. The 1-month-olds "were extremely difficult to test. . . . and their performance was highly variable" when tested monocularly (Courage & Adams, 1990, p. 126). For older infants and adults, acuity at 30° was about 1 octave better in the temporal field than in the nasal field.

However, the studies of temporal–nasal differences in acuity should be interpreted with caution. First, because investigators have used large stimuli (9° wide in the studies by Courage and Adams; 15° wide in the study by Sireteanu et al.), the stimulus may have been effectively smaller in the nasal field since the farther edge of the pattern would be more likely to fall outside the nasal field than outside the temporal field. Second, temporal-nasal differences at 10°–20° in the periphery might have been underestimated because part of the stimulus in the temporal field would have included the blind spot. Third, the data are likely to be noisy because very few stripe sizes were tested and they covered a wide range of spatial frequencies. Perhaps for these reasons, the studies include a number of surprising results given previous evidence of adults' greater acuity in the temporal field than at comparable locations in the nasal field (e.g., Fahle & Schmid, 1988) and of our findings of greater temporal–nasal differences in light sensitivity in infants than in adults. These surprising results include: *no* temporal–nasal differences in adults (Sireteau et al., 1994); *larger* differences in adults than infants at 10° and 20° (Courage & Adams, 1990, 1996); and *worse* acuity at 20° in the temporal field than at 20° in the nasal field for 1-months olds (Courage & Adams, 1990).

Previous behavioral studies of peripheral acuity for striped patterns (Courage & Adams, 1990, 1996; Siretaneau et al., 1984, 1994) and for single lines (Lewis et al., 1985) have all estimated acuity from group data. In a recent study, we collected enough data from each baby to estimate individual thresholds. We measured the peripheral acuity of 2-, 5-, and 12-month-olds tested binocularly with horizontal stripes in portholes beginning at 10° or at 30° in the periphery. At the beginning of each trial, the baby's fixation was attracted straight ahead. Then a pair of stimuli was presented: in one porthole, a striped pattern; in the other porthole, a grating that matched the mean luminance of the stripes of 57.5 cd/m² and which was of such high spatial frequency that it looked grey. The observer, who did not know the location or size of the stripes, noted the direction of the baby's first eye movement.

To obtain optimal performance and sensible psychometric functions from individual babies, we first "trained" the infants to move their eyes toward the stripes. Using stripes twice the width of the largest to be tested, we reinforced correct responses with puppets, keys, or other objects presented directly below the stripes and continued training trials until the baby had made four correct responses in a row. Reinforcement was continued during the subsequent testing. Each baby was tested with four spatial frequencies roughly one octave apart and spanning the range where the baby was likely to be "correct" 75% of the time. (A fifth spatial frequency was added halfway through the procedure, if necessary.) To determine threshold acuity, we used the method of constant stimuli and presented each spatial frequency 20 times. Most babies required more than one session to complete the procedure. Thresholds were estimated by fitting logistic functions to the psychometric functions for each baby and taking the threshold as the spatial frequency corresponding to 75% correct.

Figures 2.5 and 2.6 show the thresholds obtained at each age and eccentricity when we tested different babies at 10° and 30° (Experiment 1; Fig. 2.5) and when we tested a different group of babies with the two eccentricities interleaved (Experiment 2; Fig. 2.6). Each dot represents the threshold for an individual baby at one eccentricity and the arrows point to the geometric mean. At both 10° and 30°, acuity improved between 2 and 5 months of age, an improvement that could not be explained by changes in the slope or fit of the psychometric functions. There was no further improvement by 12 months of age, even though acuity at both eccentricities was still below adult values, but more so at 10° than at 30°. Siretaneau et al. (1994) reported a similar developmental pattern for stripes beginning at 12.5° in the periphery: rapid improvement in peripheral acuity over the first 6 months followed by much smaller change until 10–14 months, at which point acuity was still not adult-like. Allen et al. (1996) also report rapid improvement in peripheral acuity between 2 and 5 months, but perhaps because they recorded visually evoked responses rather than orienting responses or because the peripheral stripes started closer to center (at 8°), they obtained adult-like acuities by 6 months of age. Just as we found that acuity at 30° is more mature at 5- to 12-months

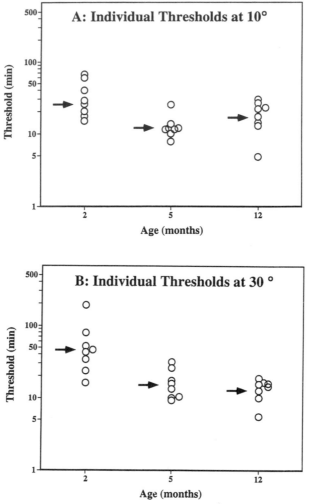

FIG. 2.5. Peripheral acuity at three different ages for horizontal stripes located at 10° (Panel A) or at 30° (Panel B) in the periphery. Each dot represents the acuity for one baby. Each baby was tested at only one age and location. Arrows point to the geometric mean.

than is acuity at 10°, they found that peripheral acuity at 8° matured more rapidly than central acuity.

In adults, acuity falls off sharply with eccentricity, largely because of a decrease in the density of ganglion cells (Fahle & Schmid, 1988; Grigsby & Tsou, 1994). Adults' acuity at 30° is typically 1.5–2 octaves poorer than their acuity at 10° (Fahle & Schmid, 1988; Grigsby & Tsou, 1994). In Experiment 2, 2-month-olds showed the expected fall-off in acuity between

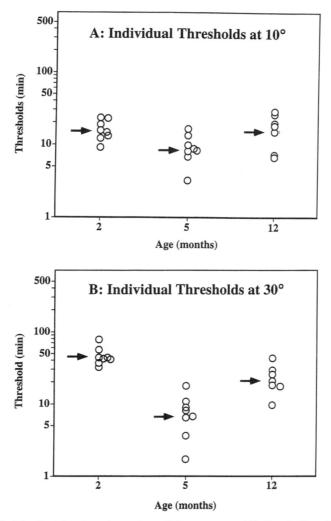

FIG. 2.6. Peripheral acuity at three different ages at 10° (Panel A) and at 30° (Panel B) in the periphery. Each baby was tested at one age at both locations. Other details as in Fig. 2.5.

10° and 30° (see Fig. 2.6). Similarly, Courage and Adams (1990, 1996) reported poorer acuity in 1- to 3-month-olds tested with stripes beginning at 20° or 30° than for stripes beginning at 10°. However, unlike adults and younger infants, the acuity of the 5- and 12-month-olds we tested was similar at 10° and 30° in both Experiments 1 and 2. One possibility is that the peripheral acuity of young infants drops off only when the striped stimulus falls near the edge of the field—as would be true for a 1- to 3-month-old shown a 15° pattern beginning at 30° (our study) or a 9°

pattern beginning at 20°–30° (Courage & Adams, 1990, 1996). In that case, the farther edge of the pattern may be outside of the effective visual field or at least not clearly visible. By 5 months of age, the visual field likely extends well beyond the farthest edge of such patterns because of the rapid expansion in the extent of the field that occurs over the the first half year of life (see Figs. 2.2 and 2.3A). This analysis suggests that during the first year, infants' peripheral acuity falls off with eccentricity only to the extent that it is limited by the edges of the visual field. Together with Allen et al. (1996), the results suggest that different parts of the retina mature at different rates with faster maturation of the midperiphery (30°) than of the near periphery (10°) and faster maturation of the near periphery (8°) than of the central retina.

Despite the unequal development of acuity in different parts of the periphery, it is clear that acuity improves over the first 6 months at every eccentricity that has been tested. Thus, some of the improved orienting toward exogenous peripheral stimuli probably results from improved ability to see the targets.

Improved Ability to Disengage Attention

Overt orienting may also improve with age because babies get better at not being distracted by a competing central stimulus. A number of studies have reported that 1- to 2-month-olds are slower and/or less likely to move their eyes toward a peripheral target if the central fixation stimulus remains on than if it is turned off as the peripheral target appears, and that the distracting effect of the central stimulus decreases by 3- to 4-months of age (Hood et al., chap. 7, this volume; but see Goldberg et al., 1977). Fast directionally appropriate eye movements are most likely to occur when the heart rate indicates that the baby has just ceased attending to the central stimulus (Richards & Hunter, chap. 4, this volume) or when there is a short gap between the offset of the central fixation stimulus and the presentation of the peripheral target (Hood et al., chap. 7, this volume). The studies described earlier in the section on normal development all used a central fixation stimulus that either remained on when the peripheral target was presented (studies using kinetic perimetry) or was turned off just after the baby started fixating it and just as the peripheral target came on, without a gap (studies using static perimetry). It is tempting to speculate that babies' responses to peripheral targets may have been diminished by having to disengage attention from a central stimulus that was still present or that had just disappeared and that these adverse effects were greater at the younger ages.

The presence of a central stimulus can also influence babies' ability to discriminate between peripheral stimuli. This was apparent when we showed 3-month-olds (tested binocularly) pairs of stimuli chosen because babies of that age look longer at one member of the pair: a checkerboard that they prefer to a smaller pattern of rectangles; and a pattern of solid circles forming figure eights that they prefer to the same pattern of rectangles (see Fig. 2.7) (Maurer & Lewis, 1979, 1981). The first pair required a gross discrimination that could be based on size, shape, color, contour, and so on; the other pair required a finer discrimination that could be based only on the shape of the internal elements. For one group of babies,

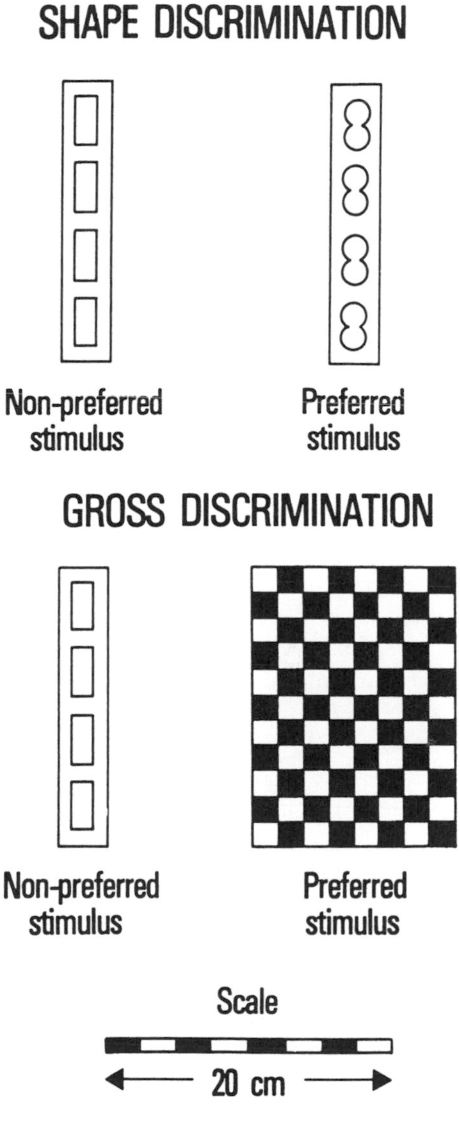

SHAPE DISCRIMINATION

Non-preferred stimulus   **Preferred stimulus**

GROSS DISCRIMINATION

FIG. 2.7. The stimuli used to test peripheral discrimination in 3-month-olds. The checkerboard was black-and-white. The other stimuli contained white elements on a red background. The top pair differ only in the shape of their internal elements. The bottom pair differ in many respects and hence require a gross discrimination. Reprinted from Figure 1 in Maurer, D., & Lewis, T. L. (1981). The influence of peripheral stimuli on infants' eye movements. In D. F. Fisher, R. A. Monty, & J. W. Senders (Eds.), *Eye movements: Cognition and visual perception.* Hillsdale, NJ: Lawrence Erlbaum Associates, p. 22. Reprinted with permission from Lawrence Erlbaum Associates.

Non-preferred stimulus   **Preferred stimulus**

Scale

← **20 cm** →

there was no competing central stimulus; for the other group, the peripheral stimuli were presented while the baby fixated a a vertical white line, 4.5° wide by 29° long. Whether or not the central line was present, babies made the gross discrimination when the targets began 10°, 20°, and 30° in the periphery (the only locations tested): at each eccentricity, their first eye movements were toward the checkerboard significantly more than 50% of the time. However, the presence of the central line had a detrimental effect on babies' ability to make the fine discrimination: they looked first toward the preferred cirular shapes out to 10° in the absence of the central line but showed no evidence of discriminating the shapes with peripheral vision when the central stimulus was present. Thus, fixation of a central stimulus interferes with the processing of subtle peripheral information like the shape of a stimulus, even in infants as old as 3 months.

However in a recent study, we found that even younger infants do not always have difficulty disengaging attention from a central stimulus (Goldberg et al., 1997). We tested newborns, 1-month-olds, and 4-month-olds ($N = 252$) monocularly along the horizontal meridian with a 6° light flashing at 3 Hz while an identical central light either remained on or was turned off. Except for a difference in eye movement bias for newborns, the central stimulus had no effect on the latency or direction of eye movements at any age, and hence no effect on the measured nasal or temporal fields. Assuming that any difficulty in disengaging attention would affect performance more when the central stimulus remains on during the entire presentation of the peripheral target than when it is turned off as the peripheral target comes on, these data indicate that, under some circumstances, young infants are perfectly well able to disengage attention from a central stimulus to make an eye movement toward a peripheral target. Note that the conditions for the group tested with the central stimulus going off in this study were identical to those in our study of the expansion of the temporal and nasal field (illustrated in Figs. 2.1–2.3). Thus, the developmental changes that we observed (an expansion of the visual field between birth and 4 months of age with more rapid development of the temporal field than of the nasal field) are unlikely to have resulted from changes in the ability to disengage attention.

The conditions under which young infants have especial difficulty disengaging attention (i.e., show "sticky fixation") are not obvious from the literature because of differences across studies in the characteristics of the peripheral stimulus and whether it was identical to the central stimulus. The studies most easily compared are Aslin and Salapatek's study of 1- and 2-month-olds (1975) and our study of newborns, 1-month-olds, and 4-month olds (Goldberg et al., in press). In both studies, babies were tested with peripheral targets at a number of eccentricities, the peripheral and central stimuli were identical, and the analyses were based on a comparison of experimental trials with peripheral targets and control trials without. Both studies found no effect of the central stimulus on the measured extent of the visual field (which is based on differences between experimental and control trials). However, the results of the studies differ in one important respect: in Aslin and Salapatek's study, the babies showed sticky fixation—the central stimulus reduced eye movements on *both* experimental and control trials; in our study (Goldberg et al., 1997), the babies did not show sticky fixation—the presence of the central stimulus affected 1-month-olds' tendency to make eye movements on *neither* experimental nor control trials. Aslin and Salapatek's stimuli were smaller and dimmer than ours and static rather than flickering. Thus, babies may be more likely to show sticky fixation when the stimuli are less salient and/or static. This is unlikely to be the only explanation because many of the studies reporting sticky fixation used peripheral targets that were even larger than our lights and, like our lights, were nonstatic stimuli presented against a highly contrasting background (Atkinson, Hood, Wattam-Bell, & Braddick, 1992, Experiment 4; Hood & Atkinson, 1990, 1993). Another possibility is that sticky fixation is more likely to be observed when babies are tested binocularly, as in all previous studies, rather than monocularly, as in our study (see later section on underlying neural mechanisms for a discussion of why this might be the case).

Other Factors

Increased Motivation. As they get older, babies might become more motivated to move their eyes toward stimuli they can see in the periphery. Since most investigators use direction of eye movements as the measure of peripheral detection, an increased tendency to orient toward detected peripheral stimuli would be interpreted as an increase in the effective visual field. Certainly, babies do not always move their eyes toward stimuli they detect in the periphery (Richards & Hunter, chap. 4, this volume). However, increased motivation is an unlikely explanation for especially poor orienting toward stimuli in the nasal field since there is no reason to assume that any increased motivation would favor eye movements along one meridian but not along another. Thus, although motivational factors might contribute to the measured expansion of the visual field during infancy, it seems unlikely that they contribute to differences in temporal and nasal detection.

Better Optics. Optical factors cause peripheral stimuli to appear blurred and this blur increases with increasing distance from the optic axis (Davson, 1963; Duke-Elder & Abrams, 1970). Changes with age in the shape of the eyeball (Mann, 1964; Sorsby, Benjamin, Sheridan, Stone, & Leary, 1961) and in the cornea and lens (Brown, 1961; Mann, 1964; Parks, 1966) might reduce optical blur and contribute to the observed expansion of the visual field. However, optical blur has little influence on adults' ability to detect peripheral stimuli and has virtually no effect outside the central 30° (Atchison, 1987; Benedetto & Cyrlin, 1975; Frankhauser & Enoch, 1962; Frisén & Glansholm, 1975). In fact, Elizabeth Bowering confirmed the minor contribution of optical defocus to peripheral detection in two patients with very large refractive errors because the natural lens had been removed as treatment for congenital cataract (Bowering, 1992; Bowering, Maurer, Lewis, & Brent, in press; Bowering et al., 1996). She used the Goldmann perimeter to measure the extent of the visual field along eight meridia, both while the patients were wearing an appropriate optical correction (+14.50 D for patient JW and +17.25 D for patient KS) and while they were wearing no optical correction whatsoever. The differences in the extent of the visual field under the two conditions were minimal. For example, when tested with target III2e (a 24' stimulus of 31.8 cd/m^2), the field was only about 2° smaller for KS and only about 0.5° smaller for JW when tested with *no* optical correction compared to tests with the appropriate high powered plus lenses. Thus it is unlikely that differences in optical defocus would account for changes with age in the measured extent of the visual field of normal infants.

A related issue is whether changes in the optics of the eye can account for reductions with age in differences between temporal and nasal detection. Developmental changes in the shape of the eyeball, cornea, and lens all appear to be symmetrical around the optic axis (Brown, 1961; Mann, 1964; Parks, 1966; Sorsby et al., 1961) and therefore are an unlikely explanation. However, peripheral blur increases with increasing distance from the optic axis rather than from the visual axis (Davson, 1963; Duke-Elder & Abrams, 1970). In adults, the line of sight is displaced about 5° temporally on the retina from the optic axis (Alpern, 1962). Thus, a stimulus at 20° in the nasal field would be further from the optic axis than a stimulus at 20° in the temporal field, causing the nasal stimulus to be slightly more blurred than the temporal stimulus. This effect is probably exaggerated slightly in newborns because their line of sight may be displaced about 8° temporally from the optic axis (Slater & Findlay, 1972, 1975). Thus, as the fovea shifts nasally on the retina with development, optical blur for stimuli in the nasal field would be diminished. Nonetheless, the differences between adults and newborns in the location of the fovea are far too small to account for the especially slow growth of the nasal field during early infancy or for the especially poor sensitivity within it.

Improved Control of Eye Movements. Important changes in eye movements occur during infancy, including changes in the length, form, latency, and accuracy of saccades (see chapters by Hood et al.; Johnson & Gilmore;

and Richards & Hunter). Of prime interest here is whether such changes can account for the observed improvements with age in overt orienting toward peripheral targets. They likely make at least some contribution. For example, as eye-movement control improves, variability should decrease, making it more likely that a difference will occur between experimental and control trials, especially in the parts of the field where the target has a weak effect (i.e., at the edge of the field). Thus, improvements in the control of eye movements might contribute to the observed expansion of the visual field with age. However, in many respects, improvements in the control of eye movements would be irrelevant. In our studies, to be credited with peripheral detection, babies had only to move their eyes in the appropriate direction more often than they looked in the same direction on blank control trials—the latency of eye movements, the number of saccades to reach the target and, in fact, whether they ever did reach the target, were all irrelevant. We propose that the change in eye movements themselves play a minor role in the observed expansion of the visual field during normal development. Rather, the development of the cortical mechanisms that leads to improved eye movements during early infancy (see chapters by Hood et al. and Johnson & Gilmore; see also later section on underlying neural mechanisms) also leads to increased peripheral sensitivity. These cortical mechanisms are more sensitive to peripheral stimuli than are subcortical mechanisms, at least in monkeys (Cowey, 1967; Cowey & Weiskrantz, 1963; Mohler & Wurtz, 1977).

Similarly, it is likely not the eye movements themselves that are primarily responsible for especially poor orienting toward stimuli in the nasal visual field during early infancy. In all of our studies, babies made nasal eye movements but did so as frequently on experimental trials as they did on control trials with no target. Moreover, if the nasal target was sufficiently large or sufficiently close to center, babies oriented toward it more often than they oriented in the nasal direction on control trials: They did so from birth when tested with the 6° light (Lewis & Maurer, 1992) and even 1-month-olds tested with lines of varying width located 20° in the nasal field did so if the line was increased to a square 25.6° wide (Lewis et al., 1985). Thus, the differences in orienting toward the temporal and nasal fields do not reflect merely a difficulty in making nasal eye movements (or an observer's difficulty in detecting nasal eye movements). As discussed in the section on underlying neural mechanisms, they likely reflect immaturities in cortical pathways.

Sucking. Competition from an ongoing activity, such as sucking on a pacifier, may interfere with young infants' orienting toward exogenous peripheral stimuli (MacFarlane, Harris, & Barnes, 1976). Most published studies on developmental changes in the measured extent of the visual field allowed babies to suck on a pacifier "when needed." Because more of the younger subjects likely "needed" a pacifier, these studies may have underestimated the measured extent of the field in young babies, and may have exaggerated the amount of developmental change.

In a recent study (Maurer et al., 1997), Nneka Nnubia investigated the effect of sucking on babies' overt orienting toward exogenous stimuli using a design that differed from the one previous study (MacFarlane et al., 1976) in that babies were given an unlimited time to respond on each trial and blank control trials were used to evaluate whether sucking affected babies' bias to move the eyes in a particular direction. We used static perimetry with a 6° static light of 165 cd/m² against a black background of 0.5 cd/m² to test the monocular visual fields of 32 1-month-olds and 32 2-month-olds. Each baby was given a pacifier during one of the two testing sessions. Sucking increased the latency of eye movements but did not influence their direction nor constrict the measured extent of the field. Thus, sucking is unlikely to account for the expansion of the visual field with age that has been observed in studies that gave babies unlimited time to respond.

In summary, the expansion of the measured visual field with age probably reflects increased peripheral sensitivity and improved control of eye movements but not increased motivation, improved optics, or increased ability to avoid interference from fixation on a central stimulus or another activity like sucking. In the next section, we examine the role of visual experience in the development of peripheral orienting.

THE ROLE OF VISUAL EXPERIENCE

Studies of children treated for dense, central cataracts allow one to examine the influence of visual experience on the development of peripheral vision. In our studies we have included only patients whose cataracts were so dense that they prevented fixation and following and/or they prevented an ophthalmologist from seeing clearly into the eye (no red reflex through an undilated pupil and/or no visualization of the fundus). Such cataracts prevent patterned input from reaching the retina, and may do so from birth (congenital cataracts) or following a period of putatively normal visual input (traumatic or developmental cataracts). The cataractous lenses are removed surgically and the then aphakic eyes fitted with contact lenses to focus visual input on the retina. The eyes are given years to recover, and then tested while wearing a contact lens of the appropriate power to focus the peripheral targets on the retina. In unilateral cases, the fellow normal eye is patched following treatment to promote usage of the previously deprived eye. Although patching 50% of the waking time throughout early childhood was recommended for this cohort, compliance varied and hence we can examine the effect of various amounts of patching.

We have used three methods to examine peripheral vision following an earlier period of visual deprivation: kinetic perimetry with the Goldmann perimeter to plot the edges of the visual field; static perimetry with the Octopus perimeter to measure sensitivity at 20° in the nasal field and 30° in the temporal field—the locations that revealed poorer sensitivity nasally than temporally during early infancy; and contrast sensitivity along the horizontal meridian. In each case, patients were required to maintain central fixation while detecting targets in the periphery; unlike babies, they were not required to make eye movements toward the detected targets. The results indicate that visual deprivation causes large deficits in peripheral vision, even when the deprivation begins after infancy. (Patients unable to maintain central fixation could not be tested and hence the results may underestimate the deficits.)

One effect of visual deprivation is a constriction of the visual field. This was apparent when Elizabeth Bowering used the Goldmann perimeter to measure the visual fields of normal subjects aged 5 years to adult ($N = 88$) and those of 44 children treated for dense and central cataracts in one ($N = 25$ tested eyes) or both eyes ($N = 31$ tested eyes), all of whom were at least 5 years old at the time of the test (Bowering, 1992; Bowering et al., 1996, in press). Compared to age-matched controls, children who had been visually deprived by cataracts had severely restricted fields, even when the deprivation had begun as late as 6 years of age. The losses were largest in the temporal field, the part of the field that is slowest to reach an adult extent for a pinpoint of light. Figure 2.8 shows the losses for various parts of the visual field and also illustrates the larger losses in eyes that were deprived for more than 6 months than in eyes that were deprived for a shorter time. The difference was significant in all parts of the field except the superior field, the part of the field that is first to reach an adult size. For the dimmer light, the losses in the deprived eye were greater after monocular deprivation than after binocular deprivation of comparable duration. Thus, visual deprivation interferes with the normal development of the edges of the field, with the largest effect on the part of the field that is slowest to develop.

The large restrictions after binocular deprivation indicate that visual deprivation interferes with the normal development of peripheral vision. The fact that the restrictions were even greater after monocular deprivation indicates that unfair competition between the eyes can have an additional adverse effect. That conclusion is bolstered by the finding that the restrictions were smaller when there had been extensive patching of the fellow eye, but only in the temporal field, the part of the field that is slowest to develop (Bowering, 1992; Bowering et al., 1996, in press). (Mean field

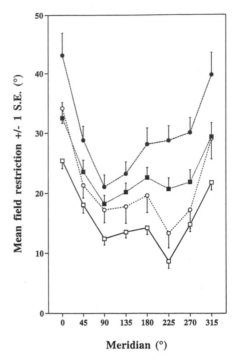

Meridian (°)

FIG. 2.8. Mean field restrictions and standard errors along eight meridia in children treated for dense and central cataracts. The temporal field includes 0° and 315°; the superior field 45°, 90°, and 135°; the nasal field 180°; and the inferior field 225° and 270°. Data are for children with less than 6 months deprivation tested with a pinpoint of light 6.4′ wide with a luminance of 318 cd/m^2 (open squares) and of 31.8 cd/m^2 (filled squares) and for children with more than 6 months deprivation tested with the more luminant target (open circles) and the less luminant target (filled circles). Adapted from *Journal of Pediatric Ophthalmology & Strabismus*, in press, Bowering, E. R., Maurer, D., Lewis, T. L., & Brent, H. P., Constriction of the visual field of children after early deprivation, Figure 2, Copyright (1997) with kind permission from SLACK Incorporated, 6900 Grove Road, Thorofare, NJ 08086.

restrictions at 0° temporally were 24°, 37°, and 35° for good, fair, and poor patchers, respectively.) Together, the results suggest that different aspects of peripheral vision develop at different rates and that the more slowly developing aspects are most dependent on normal visual input.

Studies of sensitivity along the horizontal meridian indicate that visual deprivation also interferes with sensitivity to targets throughout the periphery. Thus, when we measured the contrast sensitivity of 11 children treated between 5 and 16 months of age for congenital cataracts in one ($N = 6$) or both eyes ($N = 5$), we found that sensitivity was depressed both when the sine waves were located in the center of the field and when they were located at 10°, 20°, or 30° in the periphery along the horizontal meridian (Maurer & Lewis, 1993; Tytla, Lewis, Maurer, & Brent, 1991). In every case, the contrast had to be higher for the patient to detect the grating than for an age-matched normal control, with a larger difference at higher spatial frequencies. Thus, deprivation also interferes with sensitivity to targets anywhere along the horizontal meridian. For the five children treated for bilateral cataracts, the loss of sensitivity was constant across the visual field: at each eccentricity, every patient required 1–1.5 log units more contrast than normal to see the highest spatial frequency the eye could resolve. In contrast, all six of the children treated for unilateral cataracts showed larger losses when the gratings were in the nasal field than when they were in the temporal field. Similarly, the light sensitivity of children treated for unilateral congenital cataract is reduced significantly more when the target is in the nasal field (at 20°) than when it is in the temporal field (at 30°) (Bowering, Maurer, Lewis, & Brent, 1993). In other groups, light sensitivity is reduced equally at both locations (see Fig. 2.9).

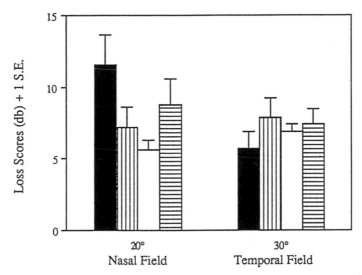

FIG. 2.9. Mean losses and standard errors in peripheral light sensitivity for patients relative to age-matched normals at 20° in the nasal field and 30° in the temporal field. Data are for children treated for unilateral congenital (filled bars), unilateral noncongenital (vertically striped bars), bilateral congenital (open bars), and bilateral noncongenital (horizontally striped bars) cataracts. Although all groups showed reduced light sensitivity, only the children treated for unilateral congenital cataract showed significantly greater losses at 20° nasally than at 30° temporally. Reprinted with permission from Figure 2 in Bowering, E. R., Maurer, D., Lewis, T. L., & Brent, H. P. (1993). Sensitivity in the nasal and temporal hemifields in children treated for cataract. *Investigative Ophthalmology & Visual Science, 34,* 3506, © the Association for Research in Vision & Ophthalmology (ARVO).

Interestingly, there are large reductions even when the deprivation began in the early teenage years, so late that acuity and contrast sensitivity were unaffected by the deprivation and are normal.

These results parallel our findings that during infancy there is slower growth of the nasal field than the temporal field, and initially lower sensitivity for targets at 20° in the nasal field than for targets at 30° in the temporal field (Lewis et al., 1985; Lewis & Maurer, 1992). Like the results for the far edges of the temporal field, they suggest that slowly developing parts of peripheral vision are most affected by visual deprivation or unfair competition between the eyes. Moreover, the development of peripheral vision depends on visual experience until at least the teenage years.

Control experiments indicated that only a small part of the loss in the measured extent of the visual field (4–5°) could be attributed to optical factors such as aphakia (the absence of a natural lens in the eye) or peripheral defocus (Bowering et al., 1996, in press). Thus, the bulk of the deficit in peripheral vision after deprivation is likely to be neural. In the next section, we consider the neural structures that are likely to underlie the improvements in overt orienting during normal development and the deficits after visual deprivation.

UNDERLYING NEURAL MECHANISMS

Development of Neural Systems

Schiller (chap. 1, this volume) has provided a detailed analysis of many of the pathways and structures controlling visually guided eye movements. He proposed four eye-movement systems that project from the retina, through the lateral geniculate nucleus and primary visual cortex. The first neural system, which Schiller calls the posterior system, controls reflexive saccades and reaches the superior colliculus directly from the primary visual cortex or via the parietal cortex. The second neural system, the anterior system, is concerned with locating objects in space and planning sequences of saccades to selected objects. The anterior system bypasses the superior colliculus and involves projections from the frontal eye fields and the dorsomedial frontal cortex to the brainstem. The third neural system controls smooth pursuit and involves the middle temporal (MT), middle superior temporal (MST), and parietal areas of the cortex. The fourth system provides an inhibitory pathway to the superior colliculus from a variety of cortical areas via the substantia nigra and basal ganglia. Although not emphasized by Schiller (this volume), other pathways and structures likely contribute to visually guided eye movements, such as direct projections from the retina to the superior colliculus and/or the pulvinar (see later section on temporal–nasal differences). There appears to be considerable redundancy among structures in the mediation of orienting toward peripheral targets. Lesions of any one of them alter but do not obliterate peripheral orienting, whereas multiple lesions (e.g., frontal eye fields and superior colliculus) typically eliminate it (Schiller, this volume). So poor orienting toward peripheral stimuli in the baby is likely to reflect poor functioning of several of these structures, or of the connections between them. Of course, a structure could play a more important role during infancy than it does after the system is completely developed.

Studies of these structures in humans and monkeys indicate that most are very immature at birth. All retinal neurons and synapses are generated prenatally, even those in the far periphery (LaVail & Rakic, 1983; Mann, 1964; Nishimura & Rakic, 1983; Provis, van Driel, Billson, & Russell, 1985). Although the peripheral retina beyond about 5° is more mature than the central retina, even in the peripheral retina, the outer segments of cones are much shorter than in the adult retina, ganglion cells have not yet reached their adult size, and the uptake of most neurotransmitters is much lower than in the adult (Abramov, Gordon, Hendrickson, Hainline, Dobson, & LaBossier, 1982; Brown, Dobson, & Maier, 1987; Drucker & Hendrickson, 1989; Hendrickson & Kupfer, 1976; Hollyfield, Frederick, & Rayborn, 1983; Horsten & Winkelman, 1962; Mann, 1964; Provis et al., 1985; Weidman, 1975). However, one neurotransmitter, 3H-glycine, is taken up by cells in the peripheral retina at about twice the adult rate (Hollyfield et al., 1983).

Higher levels of the visual system appear much more immature at birth. During the first 10 weeks of life, cells in the lateral geniculate nucleus (LGN) of the monkey have a low rate of spontaneous activity, respond sluggishly to visual stimulation after a long latency and fatigue easily (Blakemore & Vital-Durand, 1986). Nonetheless in the newborn monkey, LGN cells are morphologically mature (except for an excessive number of spines) and in their proper layers, the retinotopic map is established, all cells respond to visual stimulation, and glucose is utilized at the adult rate when the monkey is awake (Blakemore & Vital-Durand, 1986; Garey & de Courten, 1983; Gottlieb, Pasik, & Pasik, 1985; Kennedy, Sakurada, Shinohara, & Miyaoka, 1982). In the 8-day-old monkey (the youngest age studied), cells in the parvocellular layers of the LGN are fully grown and those in the magnocellular layers are 90% of their adult size (Headon, Sloper, Hiorns, & Powel, 1985). In humans, adult-like lamination of the LGN is present prenatally (Dekaban, 1954; Hitchcock & Hickey, 1980), but in other ways the LGN matures more slowly than in the monkey. At birth, cells are only 60% of their adult size, and they are not fully grown until 12 months of age in the parvocellular layers and until 24 months of age in the magnocellular layers (Hickey, 1977). Moreover, the proliferation and subsequent thinning of spines on cell bodies and on dendrites takes much longer than in the monkey (Garey & de Courten, 1983).

In most respects, development of the striate cortex lags behind that of the LGN (Rakic, 1974). In the monkey, all neurons are generated prenatally (Rakic, 1974, 1991). By birth, dendritic branching is complete (Boothe, Greenbough, Lund, & Wrege, 1979) and orientation selectivity and ocular dominance columns are evident (Kennedy et al., 1982; LeVay, Wiesel, & Hubel, 1980; Wiesel & Hubel, 1974). Postnatal changes include a 25%–75% increase in cortical volume during the first 4 months (Gottlieb et al., 1985; O'Kusky & Colonnier, 1982); an increase in cortical thickness during the first few months followed by a gradual decrease (Bourgeois & Rakic, 1993; Zielinski & Hendrickson, 1992) and perhaps a subsequent increase (Bourgeois & Rakic, 1993); a substantial increase in myelination (Gottlieb et al., 1985) and in glucose utilization (Kennedy et al., 1982); a doubling of the number of synapses during the first 3–6 months followed by a gradual decrease to adult values (Bourgeois & Rakic, 1993; Mates & Lund, 1983; O'Kusky & Colonnier, 1982; Rakic, 1991; Zielinski & Hendrickson, 1992); the final maturation of the ocular dominance columns during the first 6 weeks (LeVay et al., 1980); and changes in the laminar distribution of feedback projections from higher cortical areas (Barone, Dehay, Berland, Bullier, & Kennedy, 1995). The monkey's frontal, parietal, and temporal cortices are also very immature at birth (Kennedy et al., 1982), even more immature than the striate cortex (Bachevalier, Ungerleider, O'Neill, & Friedman, 1986).

The pattern of development for the human's striate cortex is similar to that described for the monkey, except that some changes are more pronounced and/or occur at a slower rate. Thus, cortical volume increases six-fold during the first four months instead of by 25%–75% (Huttenlocher & de Courten, 1987); neuronal density decreases by twice as much as in the monkey (Leuba & Garey, 1984; O'Kusky & Colonnier, 1982); unlike the case with the monkey's striate cortex, there is substantial growth of dendrites after birth and continued migration of cells to different layers (Becker, Armstrong, Chan, & Wood, 1984; Conel, 1939, 1941, 1947; Takashima, Chan, Becker, & Armstrong, 1980); and synaptic density reaches its maximum level at 8 months instead of at 6 months (Huttenlocher, de Courten, Garey, & van der Loos, 1982; Huttenlocher & de Courten, 1987). Additional evidence of cortical immaturity is that most enzymes occur at much lower levels than in the adult (Diebler, Farkas-Bargeton, & Wehrlé, 1979), and glucose utilization occurs at a much lower rate (Chugani, 1994; Chugani & Phelps, 1986). In humans, as in monkeys (Bachevalier et al., 1986), development of the striate cortex appears to precede development of other visual areas of the cortex. For example, in the infant's prestriate cortex, there are fewer large cells, axons are smaller, and they have less myelin (Conel, 1941, 1947, 1951).

In the infant's parietal cortex, fibers are less dense than in the striate cortex; dendritic branching, neurofibrils, and extra-large pyramidal cells are less well developed; and the thickness of the cortex reaches adult values at a later age (Conel, 1941, 1947, 1955, 1967). In the frontal lobe (which contains the frontal eye fields and the dorsal medial frontal cortex), synaptogenesis and subsequent thinning to adult values occurs much later than in the striate cortex (Huttenlocher, 1979, 1994; Huttenlocher & de Courten, 1987; Rabinowicz, 1986), and glucose utilization increases more slowly (Chugani, 1994; Chugani & Phelps, 1986).

The little information available on the development of other areas involved in peripheral vision indicates many immaturities and some differential rates of maturation. In the monkey, glucose utilization is adult-like at birth in the superior colliculus, but significantly below adult levels in the pulvinar (Kennedy et al., 1982). Nonetheless, the pulvinar does show an adult pattern of distribution and density of opiate receptor sites (Bachevalier et al., 1986). Within the human newborn's superior colliculus, all cells in the superficial layers are fully differentiated, but only some synapses are present and there is the exuberance of spines typical during early development (Robertson, 1982).

Studies of visually deprived monkeys indicate that, unless the deprivation extended from birth past 2 years of age, retinal ganglion cells have a normal morphology (reviewed in Boothe, Dobson, & Teller, 1985). Cells in the lateral geniculate nucleus also respond normally to visual stimulation (reviewed in Blakemore, 1988), even after 5 years of monocular deprivation from birth (Levitt, Movshon, Sherman, & Spear, 1989), but cells in the primary visual cortex do not. After relatively short periods of monocular deprivation, the deprived eye can drive very few cells in the primary visual cortex (reviewed in Blakemore, 1988; Boothe et al., 1985; Crawford, 1988; Movshon & Van Sluyters, 1981), and those few respond abnormally (Blakemore, 1988; but see Crawford, 1988). After comparable periods of binocular deprivation, the effects are not as severe: some cortical cells respond normally (cf. Crawford, Blake, Cool, & von Noorden, 1975; Crawford, Pesch, von Noorden, Harwerth, & Smith, 1991) but, as with monocular deprivation, very few can be stimulated by both eyes (e.g., Crawford, et al., 1991). Therefore, after either monocular or binocular deprivation, abnormal input from the primary visual cortex to either the anterior or posterior eye movement systems described by Schiller could underlie the behavioral deficits observed in the peripheral vision of visually deprived children. Greater deficits after monocular than after binocular deprivation can be explained by the more severe effects of monocular deprivation on the visual cortex.

In summary, studies of the young monkey and human indicate that the immaturities observed in human infants' peripheral vision could be caused by immaturities in any of the structures involved in adults' peripheral vision. Similarly, studies of visually deprived monkeys indicate that the deficits observed in the peripheral vision of visually deprived humans could be caused by abnormalities in the visual cortex or in its projections to any of the structures involved in adults' peripheral vision. We attempt to narrow the possibilities by considering whether there are neural parallels to the developmental patterns evident in the data of normal babies: the initially greater sensitivity to stimuli in the temporal field than to those in the nasal field, the gradual expansion of the field from the center out, and the disengagement of attention. We also consider neural parallels to the deficits after deprivation.

Temporal–Nasal Differences

In the section on normal development, we reviewed evidence that young infants orient toward a light farther in the periphery if it is in the temporal field than if it is the nasal field, especially if the baby is young, the target is small and/or the target is flickering. Even for targets closer to center, babies orient more quickly toward temporal targets and the size of the smallest effective target is smaller. Thus, there appears to be slower post-natal development of sensitivity in the nasal field. That interpretation is supported by our findings on the effects of visual deprivation: Visual dep-rivation in one eye shortly after birth has a more deleterious effect on sensitivity in the nasal field than in the temporal field (see earlier section on the role of experience).

The asymmetry during early infancy is much larger than that seen in normal adults. In adults, much of the difference in the size of the two fields can be explained by the nose physically blocking stimuli in the far periphery of the nasal field. Adults' slightly greater sensitivity in the tem-poral than the nasal field (e.g., Fahle & Schmid, 1988) can be explained by a greater density of receptors and ganglion cells in the nasal retina (Curcio & Allen, 1990; Curcio, Sloan, Kalina, & Hendrickson, 1990; Øster-berg, 1935), especially more eccentrically (Perry & Cowey, 1985) and a corresponding difference in the geniculostriate pathway (Gottlieb et al., 1985; Blakemore & Vital-Durand, 1986; LeVay, Connolloy, Honde, & van Essen, 1985). Perhaps young infants show larger temporal–nasal differences than adults because infants have more blockage by the nose or greater differences between fields in the density of receptors, ganglion cells, LGN cells, or cells in striate cortex. None of these possibilities seems likely. Young infants' noses are flatter than those of adults and hence block less of the nasal field (Lewis & Maurer, 1992). In monkeys, there is little or no change in the density of photoreceptors for the nasal versus temporal hemi-retinae between birth and adulthood (Packer, Hendrickson, & Curcio, 1990). In humans, vascularization of the nasal retina (which receives input from the temporal field) does occur more rapidly than vascularization of the temporal retina (which recieves input from the nasal field), but both are nearly complete before term age (Quinn, 1992). Receptors in the two hemi-retinae grow at equal rates until 37 weeks of gestation, then those in the nasal retina may grow more rapidly than those in the temporal retina so that at 40 weeks their diameters average 50% more (Provis et al., 1985). Unfortunately, there were problems in the preservation of the only two specimens studied between 37 weeks and term age: in the 37-week specimen, a small tear near the macula caused additional shrinkage locally, and in the 40-week specimen, the peripheral retina shrank "excessively." Thus the evidence on differential rates of growth for receptors in the temporal and nasal retinae in humans is inconclusive.

In the monkey, LGN cells in layers receiving input from the nasal field grow at the same rate as LGN cells in layers receiving input from the temporal field (Gottlieb et al., 1985). There are temporal–nasal differences in the spatial resolution of LGN cells, but they are no larger in newborn monkeys than in adult monkeys (Blakemore & Vital-Durand, 1986). Indirectly these data confirm that there are no temporal–nasal differences in the input to the LGN (i.e., from the retina) that are larger in newborn monkeys than adult monkeys. Within the geniculostriate pathway, crossed pathways (which mediate detection in the temporal visual field) appear to develop at the same rate as uncrossed pathways (which mediate detection in the nasal visual field; LeVay et al., 1980; Rakic, 1976). Thus, studies of infant monkeys suggest that larger temporal–nasal differences in babies than in adults arise from (a) immaturities beyond the lateral geniculate nucleus or (b) in extrageniculate pathways.

A plausible explanation is that the slow development of geniculostriate pathways limits cortical input to the superior colliculus and other subcortical areas such as the pulvinar. Absent or scarce input from cortex to these areas would have more effect on orienting toward nasal targets than toward temporal targets. This is because direct retinal input to structures outside the geniculostriate pathway such as the superior colliculus is predominately from crossed axons of retinal ganglion cells in the nasal retina, which receive input from the temporal visual field, at least in the cat. For example, in the cat, the temporal retina has little direct input to the superior colliculus, but rather influences collicular cells mainly via an uncrossed projection through the lateral geniculate nucleus and layers 4 and 5 of the visual cortex (Kanaseki & Sprague, 1974; Rosenquist & Palmer, 1971; Sterling, 1973; Wässle & Illing, 1980). Bilateral lesions of the occipito-temporal cortex leave the cat unresponsive to stimuli in the nasal visual field but orienting normally to stimuli in the temporal visual field (Sherman, 1974, 1977). After visual deprivation from shortly after birth, cats also have especially poor sensitivity in the nasal visual field, presumably because the deprivation has deleterious effects on cortical projections to the superior colliculus (reviewed in Bowering et al., 1993). In kittens, the indirect projection to superior colliculus through the cortex is relatively late to mature (reviewed in Stein, McHaffie, & Stein, 1985) and, as would be expected, so is orienting toward stimuli in the nasal visual field (Sireteanu & Maurer, 1982).

As with kittens, temporal–nasal asymmetries in babies have been attributed to the early control of orienting by retinotectal pathways that cannot readily support nasal orienting (Braddick, Atkinson, & Hood, 1996; Braddick et al., 1992; Lewis & Maurer, 1992; Maurer & Lewis, 1991; see also Hood et al., chap. 7, this volume; Rafal, chap. 6, this volume). The diminution of the asymmetry during infancy has been explained by the development of cortical control over the superior colliculus and other subcortical structures that is equally effective for both fields. The argument has been based on evidence that in monkeys, as in cats, the projection from the retina to the superficial layers of the superior colliculus contains more fibers from the nasal retina (temporal field) than from the temporal retina (nasal field), although the asymmetry is smaller in monkeys than in cats (Hendrickson, Wilson, & Toyne, 1970; Hubel, LeVay, & Wiesel, 1975; Pollack & Hickey, 1979; Wilson & Toyne, 1970). This anatomical asymmetry could cause a behavioral asymmetry through connections from cells in the superficial layers of the superior colliculus to cells in deeper layers that control eye movements and/or to other subcortical structures (Moschovakis, Karabelas, & Highstein, 1988). The asymmetry would be most likely to be apparent when there is less cortical influence over the superior colliculus because the subject is young, because the characteristics of the stimulus match the properties of collicular cells, or because the cortex was damaged by visual deprivation. It might also be more apparent when the stimulus elicits little response from developing cortical structures because it is small or dim. As predicted, binocular deprivation from shortly after birth degrades monkeys' peripheral vision, especially in the nasal visual field (Wilson et al., 1989).

Studies of humans with cortical damage support the hypothesis that nasal–temporal asymmetries can arise from an absence of cortical input to the superior colliculus and other subcortical structures. Thus, adults who had suffered bullet wounds or other forms of damage to the cortex often have especially poor detection in the nasal visual field (Engler, Zihl, & Pöppel, 1993; Koerner & Teuber, 1973). More convincing is a study of a baby (LAH) who had had the left cortical hemisphere removed at 8 months of age to relieve seizures (Braddick et al., 1992). The superior colliculus and rest of the subcortex were apparently intact. When tested 8 to 10 months later with a stripe at 23° in the affected field, LAH oriented 100% of the time if it was in the temporal periphery but only 12% of the time if it was in the nasal periphery. These results imply some subcortical parthway, such as the retinotectal pathway from the nasal retina, is sufficient to mediate orienting toward targets in the temporal visual field but not toward targets in the nasal visual field. For nasal orienting, some cortical input is necessary.

The same conclusion arises from Rafal's study of five adults following small unilateral lesions to the primary visual cortex that rendered them blind to stimuli in the opposite field (Rafal, Smith, Krantz, Cohen, & Brennan, 1990; Rafal, chap. 6, this volume): their eye movements toward targets in the good field were delayed by the brightening of a box in the blind temporal field. There was no effect of distracters in the blind nasal field and no effect when the patients were asked to press a key when the target appeared rather than to make an eye movement. Rafal et al. (1990) concluded that the human retinotectal pathway appears to be sufficient to influence the oculomotor system when it is transmitting information from the nasal retina (temporal field) but not when it is transmitting information from the temporal retina (nasal field).

Remnants of a temporal bias on the oculomotor system can also be detected in normal adults. When they are presented with targets in both the temporal and nasal visual fields, normal adults move their eyes toward the temporal target 80% of the time (Posner & Cohen, 1980), even when the temporal target was presented slightly later than the nasal target. Similarly, eye movements toward a validly cued target 10° in the periphery are faster if the cue appeared in the temporal field than if it occurred in the nasal field (Rafal, Henik, & Smith, 1991; Rafal, this volume). The cost of invalid cuing is also larger in the temporal field: The subsequent eye movement away from the temporal field is slower than the subsequent eye movement away from the nasal field. The temporal bias seems to especially influence reflexive saccades toward peripheral targets because it is less likely to occur if there is no peripheral target or if the oculomotor system is not involved (e.g., temporal order judgments) (Posner & Cohen, 1980; Rafal, this volume). Together with the data from patients following cortical damage, the data from normal adults support the hypothesis that some subcortical pathway, such as the retinotectal pathway, can mediate orienting toward temporal targets in humans but that it is not sufficient to mediate orienting toward nasal targets. As Rafal concludes: in humans the "phylogenetically older retinotectal pathway retains an important role in controlling visually guided behavior." These data provide "further support for using temporal–nasal hemifield asymmetries as a marker for investigating the function of the retinotectal pathway in humans" (Rafal et al., 1991, p. 326; see also Rafal, this volume).

That hypothesis is also supported by studies of inhibition of return in normal adults, patients, and newborns. Rafal (this volume; see also Hood et al., this volume) reviews evidence that inhibition of return arises in the oculomotor system, that it is mediated by extrageniculate subcortical structures such as the retinotectal pathway, and that, as would be expected, it is stronger when the cue falls in adults' temporal field than when it falls in their nasal field. If inhibition of return is mediated subcortically, it should be present in newborns, at least under conditions that do not require covert orienting, and the effect should be stronger for temporal than for nasal cues. Simion, Valenza, Umiltà, and Dalla Barba (1995) confirmed that prediction. After a newborn fixated a central red bulb, a checkerboard was presented beginning at 15° in the temporal or nasal field. Once the baby made an eye movement toward the checkerboard, it was turned off, fixation was attracted back to center, and two identical checkerboards were presented to the left and right for 5 seconds. Newborns looked significantly more often toward the checkerboard on the novel side, but the effect was much stronger if the initial checkerboard had been in the temporal field than if it had been in the nasal field. Together with the results from patients and normal adults, these results suggest that newborns' eye movements are influenced by extrageniculate subcortical pathways such as the retinotectal pathway that favor the temporal field.

This framework can be used to interpret our finding of a differential effect of flicker in the temporal and nasal fields (see Fig. 2.4). Three-month-olds oriented toward a dim 6° light (time averaged luminance = 5 cd/m^2) much farther in the temporal field when it was flickering at 6 Hz than when it was static. There was no beneficial effect of flicker in the nasal field. In fact, babies oriented toward this target only out to 15° when it was static in the temporal field, static in the nasal field, or flickering in the nasal field (in contrast to orienting to it out to 60° in the temporal field when it was flickering). One explanation is that the dim light evoked little response from either retinotectal or developing cortical pathways, especially when it was farther in the periphery—unless it was flickering. Cells in the superficial layers of the monkey's superior colliculus (where direct retinal input terminates) respond better to flashing than to static stimuli (Schiller & Koerner, 1971). Thus the flickering stimulus may have been sufficient to evoke responses via the retinotectal pathway, but could do so only for the temporal field. If this interpretation is correct, then as the cortical pathways mature and exert more influence over the control of eye movements, we would expect the temporal–nasal asymmetry to diminish since adults are almost equally sensitive to flicker in both visual fields (Grigsby & Tsou, 1994).

That human subcortical systems mediating reflexive orienting are more responsive to dynamic than to static stimuli is supported by a study of adults who, following right cerebral infarcts, both neglected to attend to objects to the left and failed to detect their presence (Butter, Kirsch, &

Reeves, 1990). As is usual in such patients, they bisected lines, not at their true center, but farther to the right. However, small squares to the left—that the subjects failed to perceive—decreased the error, and had a significantly larger effect if two squares jumped back and forth between two locations than if four squares remained statically on the screen. Butter et al. conclude that the squares activated a subcortical system (like the deeper layers of the superior colliculus and the mesencephalic reticular formation) that is more sensitive to transient than to static stimuli.

That the localization of static and dynamic stimuli is mediated by different neural pathways is also suggested by the study of a subject with severely impaired visual localization (McCloskey & Palmer, 1996; McCloskey et al., 1995). Whether reaching for objects or indicating their location on a computer screen, she confuses right with left significantly more than half the time, although she accurately identifies the axis on which the object is located and its distance in the periphery. No such errors occur for auditory or tactile localization. Interestingly, localization is severely impaired for targets that are static, of higher contrast, or of longer duration but is nearly normal for targets that are flickering, moving, very brief, or of lower contrast. McCloskey and his colleagues concluded that the visual system uses two pathways for computing visual location: a transient system specialized for processing rapidly changing visual stimuli such as those that are moving, flickering, or very brief and a static system for processing steady, stationary stimuli of long duration. Our data suggest that, during early infancy, peripheral localization is mediated primarily by a subcortical transient system that is more effective for the temporal field than for the nasal field. Later peripheral localization may be mediated by cortical systems that are (almost) equally effective for both fields. As the cortical systems exert increased control over peripheral orienting, temporal–nasal asymmetries should decline and the speed and accuracy of eye movements toward either field should increase. However, the subcortical transient system may continue to operate under some circumstances (Posner & Cohen, 1980; Rafal et al., 1991).

At least at some ages, the scanning of static and flickering stimuli may also be mediated by different neural pathways. Bronson (1990) reported that infants as old as 14 weeks of age (the oldest age tested) revert to a more immature pattern of scanning when the display is flickering rather than static: Scanning between features declines and the accuracy of saccades decreases. Bronson proposed that, shortly after birth, saccades are mediated primarily by the retinotectal pathway, which responds best to transient events such as a flickering stimulus. Later, saccades begin to be mediated by cortical pathways, which respond to both transient and sustained events. As those pathways are developing, scanning of a static stimulus is mediated by the emerging cortical pathways but scanning of a flickering stimulus is mediated by the earlier retinocollicular pathways. Hence saccadic control reverts to more immature forms for flickering stimuli.

So far, we have emphasized temporal–nasal asymmetries in the retinotectal pathway as an explanation of the more rapid development of eye movements toward targets in the temporal field than in the nasal field and of smaller deficits in sensitivity to targets in the temporal field after monocular deprivation from birth. The same emphasis on the retinotectal pathway has occurred in explanations of temporal-nasal asymmetries in normal adults' automatic eye movements (Posner & Cohen, 1980; Rafal et al., 1991), in their inhibition of return (Rafal, this volume), in the effect of distractors in the blind field of adults with unilateral cortical lesions (Rafal et al., 1990), in the orienting of a baby missing one cortical hemisphere (Braddick et al., 1992), and in newborns' inhibition of return (Simion et al., 1995; see also Hood et al., this volume; Rafal, this volume). A recent study has challenged these explanations. Williams, Azzopardi, and Cowey (1995) reinvestigated the temporal–nasal asymmetry in retinal projections to the primate superior colliculus using a more rigorous quantitative technique than in previous studies. They injected horseradish peroxidase into the superior colliculus and pretectum of four adult monkeys, and counted the retinal ganglion cells that were retrogradely labeled. Overall, they found 1.57 more labeled cells in the nasal retina (temporal field) than in the temporal retina (nasal field). This does show a small bias favoring the temporal field, but a bias that was no greater than that in the axons in the optic nerve following ablation of the superior colliculus (1.54). Hence, the temporal–nasal bias in the retinotectal projection appears to be no greater than that in the geniculostriate projection and is so small that it is not likely to account for large temporal–nasal differences in behavior. Williams et al. (1995, p. 577) conclude that their finding "invalidates the proposal that prominent differences in the properties of 'blindsight' in monocular nasal and temporal visual fields arise from differences in the projection from the nasal and temporal retina to the midbrain" (i.e., superior colliculus). They might have drawn the same conclusion about development.

If the study by Williams et al. is definitive, then the use of temporal–nasal differences as a marker that a behavior is controlled by the retinotectal pathway may apply to cats but not primates. There are three reasons why it might not be definitive. First, all four monkeys had had lesions to the rostral superior temporal sulcus 1 to 5 years before the study of retinotectal projections. Thus, it is possible that there had been reorganization of the nervous system following the initial lesion and that the monkeys differed from normal monkeys. However, any such reorganization is not likely to have affected a pathway as peripheral as the retinotectal pathway and the same pattern has been observed in normal adult monkeys (Cowey, personal communication, November 28, 1996). Second, there was great variability among the four monkeys in the ratio of temporal:nasal projections to the superior colliculus and pretectum. In fact, the results for all four differed significantly from the 1.53 ratio found in the optic nerve, but two showed significantly greater asymmetries and two significantly smaller asymmetries, so that overall there was no significant difference. The authors indicate that such variability is typical of tracing studies (Cowey, personal communication, November 18, 1996) and that it may arise from variability among animals in temporal:nasal ratios or might reflect "differences in placement of the tracer" and hence the extent of labeling (Williams et al., 1995). Third, HRP was injected into the superior colliculus and pretectum, and hence the retrograde labeling will have been influenced by the temporal:nasal ratios for both structures, which may not be the same. This fact combined with the likely variation in the placement of HRP leaves uncertainty about the ratio of temporal:nasal input to the superior colliculus versus the pretectum in normal adult monkeys. It also leaves open the possibility than any asymmetry is greater in infants than in adults and the possibility that even a small asymmetry will have more impact when a behavior is mediated by the retinotectal pathway than by the geniculostriate pathway because the former contains far fewer fibers. Nevertheless, it signals that one should be cautious about ascribing temporal–nasal differences in overt orienting to mediation by the retinotectal pathway.

Williams et al. (1995) offer the alternative possibility that temporal–nasal asymmetries after cortical lesions are caused by asymmetrical retinal input to subcortical nuclei other than the superior colliculus such as the inferior pulvinar and accessory optic nuclei of the pretectum. They note that these structures receive a mostly crossed input directly from the nasal retina, which could mediate orienting toward stimuli in the temporal visual field, but receive very little input from the temporal retina.

The pulvinar might well play a role in newborns' orienting toward peripheral targets. Both the medial and inferior pulvinar receive direct retinal input (Itaya & van Hosen, 1983). The projections are predominantly contralateral (i.e., from the nasal retina or temporal visual field), and those in the medial pulvinar terminate mostly on its dorsolateral surface. Both regions contain cells which, like cells in the superior colliculus, fire before visually guided eye movements: Their responses are enhanced if a stimulus in their visual field is a target for a subsequent eye movement but not before a spontaneous eye movement (reviewed in Robinson, 1993). These responses occur at latencies so short that they may be based on direct retinal input rather than the input from the parietal cortex that the pulvinar also receives (Benevento & Port, 1995). Cells in the dorsolateral and adjacent medial pulvinar also have color and form preferences that are manifested at latencies shorter than responses in inferotemporal cortex and hence may be based on input from the retina either directly or via other subcortical structures (Benevento & Port, 1995). Many pulvinar cells respond well to flashing stimuli (e.g., Bender, 1982; Robinson, Petersen, & Keys, 1986). Studies of humans after lesions or during PET imaging and of monkeys after chemical modulation of the pulvinar suggest that the pulvinar also plays some role in shifting and focussing attention (reviewed in Robinson, 1993). Collectively, these data suggest that the properties of some regions of the pulvinar match the abilities of the young infant: better localization in the temporal than the nasal field (as is favored by crossed input from the retina), better localization of flickering targets than of static targets within the temporal field, sensitivity to primitive facedness (Johnson & Morton, 1991), and rudimentary ability to discriminate color (Adams, Maurer, & Cashin, 1990). Studies of metabolic activity in the newborn monkey indicate that the pulvinar might be functional at birth, although its level of activity is less mature than that in the LGN or superior colliculus (Kennedy et al., 1982). A limitation on this argument is that it is not clear how activity in the pulvinar would affect newborns' behavior, except through its reciprocal connections with cortical visual areas (Robinson & McClurkin, 1989).

The accessory optic system, on the other hand, likely does not mediate the temporal–nasal asymmetry observed in newborns and in children treated for unilateral cataract. Although the direct retinal projection is primarily crossed in cats, monkeys, and humans (Baleydier, Magnin, & Cooper, 1990; Fredricks, Giolli, Blanks, & Sadun, 1988; Grasse & Cynader, 1982, 1984; Hoffmann, Distler, & Ilg, 1992) and, at least in cats, is functional shortly after birth (Distler & Hoffmann, 1993) and unaffected by early monocular deprivation (Grasse & Cynader, 1987), measurements of receptive field properties suggest that it is not involved in detecting a peripheral stimulus. In cats, the mammals that have been studied most extensively, all three nuclei of the accessory optic system (the dorsal, medial, and lateral terminal nuclei) have exceptionally large receptive fields, typically 40°–60° in diameter (Grasse & Cynader, 1982, 1984). They respond best to large textured patterns, moving in a specific direction, and give little or no response to a small target such as a 1° × 5° bar of light (Grasse & Cynader, 1982, 1984). Rather than playing a role in peripheral vision, the accessory optic system of the cat, monkey, and human is most likely involved in the mediation of optokinetic nystagmus, smooth pursuit, and oculomotor–vestibular interactions (Grasse & Cynader, 1982, 1984; Hoffmann, Distler, & Erickson, 1991; Hoffmann et al., 1992; Schiff, Cohen, Buttner-Ennever, & Matsuo, 1990).

Whatever the particular role of the superior colliculus, the pulvinar and the accessory optic system, the collective evidence indicates that temporal-nasal asymmetries occur when the cortex is not functioning well because it is immature, because it was removed, or because it was damaged. Thus, the developmental diminution of temporal–nasal asymmetries reflect increasing cortical influence on the control of eye movements, whereas increased temporal–nasal asymmetries after monocular deprivation in humans reflect abnormal cortical influence on the control of eye movements.

Other Neural Mechanisms

Evidence From Data on the Expansion of the Field. It is difficult to pinpoint the mechanisms underlying the gradual expansion of the field. Some of the expansion may arise from the growth of the infant's eye. As the eye grows, a stimulus of a given size will fall on an increasingly larger area of the retina (see Hamer & Schneck, 1984, for calculations). Mayer and Fulton (1993), citing data in part from Larsen (1971), stated that the sagittal length of the eye of 6-month-olds relative to adults agrees well with the horizontal extent of the visual field of 7- to 8-month-olds as measured by kinetic perimetry. Based on this, they concluded that "the growth of the infant eye may be sufficient to explain an increase in kinetic field extent with age" (Mayer & Fulton, 1993, p. 126). However, the sagittal length of the eye is about 73% of that of adults at birth and about 81% of that of adults at 6 months of age (Larsen, 1971, Tables 2 and 3). This modest increase over the first 6 months of life is not sufficient to explain the expansion of the visual field during that time as measured by either kinetic or static perimetry. For example, with kinetic perimetry, the extent of the temporal and nasal fields grows from about 32% of that of adults at 2 months of age (youngest age tested) to about 67% of that of adults at 7 months of age (data from Mohn and van Hof-van Duin, 1986, as replotted by Mayer and Fulton, 1993). With static perimetry and a 3° light, the temporal visual field grows from 0% of that of adults at 1 month (no detection) to 100% of that of adults at 6 months (data from Lewis and Maurer, 1992, as replotted by Mayer and Fulton, 1993). Even the nasal visual field measured by static perimetry and a 6° light (data from Lewis and Maurer, 1992, as replotted by Mayer and Fulton, 1993), grows from 25% of adult extent at birth to 50% of adult extent at 6 months. These increases are far greater than the increase in the sagittal length of the eye during the first 6 months. Thus the growth of the eye could account for no more than a small portion of the growth of the measured field with age and the expansion likely reflects neural changes.

Most of the structures involved in peripheral vision (see above) are organized topographically, that is, adjacent cells have receptive fields in adjacent parts of the visual field. Thus, later maturation of one part of a structure would affect only certain parts of the visual field, for example, the more peripheral parts. Moreover, there appears to be less redundancy among the structures for the control of orienting toward the far periphery than of orienting toward the near periphery. For example, silencing the monkey's superior colliculus or frontal eye fields by ablation or anesthesia decreases the frequency and accuracy of eye movements toward peripheral targets and increases their latency, but does not obliterate them (Albano & Wurtz, 1982; Butter, Weinstein, Bender, & Gross, 1978; Keating, Kenney, Gooley, Pratt, & McGillis, 1986; Kurtz & Butter, 1980; Mohler & Wurtz, 1977; Schiller, this volume; Schiller, Sandell, & Maunsell, 1987; Schiller, True, & Conway, 1980; van der Steen, Russell, & James, 1986). However, the eye movements tend to be too small, so that the eye is less likely to reach targets in the far periphery than in the near periphery. This is true whether the eye movements are made spontaneously toward peripheral targets or elicited electrically (Hikosaka & Wurtz, 1986; Mohler & Wurtz, 1977; Schiller et al., 1980; van der Steen et al., 1986). Similarly, the accuracy of detecting peripheral stimuli decreases, but much more for stimuli in the far periphery than for those in the near periphery (Albano, Mishkin, Westbrook, & Wurtz, 1982; Butter et al., 1978; Latto & Cowey, 1971).

From the literature it is impossible to speculate about which structure(s) might be so immature at birth as to limit infants' orienting toward the far periphery. For the kitten there are two obvious candidates: the retina and the superior colliculus. The more central regions of the kitten's retina may mature before the peripheral regions (Donovan, 1966; Johns, Russoff, & Dubin, 1979; but see Stone, Rapaport, Williams, & Chalupa, 1982), and electrical stimulation of the superior colliculus initially elicits only short saccades toward the near periphery (Stein, Clamann, & Goldberg, 1980). However, there have been no developmental studies of the superior colliculus in monkey or man, and in both species most evidence indicates a centrifugal pattern of retinal development only during fetal development (Provis et al., 1985; Rakic, 1977; but see Hollyfield et al., 1983). Within the primate lateral geniculate nucleus, cells with input from all parts of the visual field are immature, and there are no anatomical or electrophysiological differences for those with input from the near versus the far periphery, except that the spatial resolution of cells with receptive fields within 10° of center improves dramatically after birth, with little change for cells with receptive fields anywhere beyond 10° (Blakemore & Vital-Durand, 1986; Hickey, 1977). Such a difference cannot explain the gradual expansion of the visual field that we found for stimuli beginning 15° in the periphery. Nor are there obvious differences in the growth of the volume, surface area, or thickness of the areas of the monkey's visual cortex receiving input from the central versus peripheral visual fields (Gottlieb et al., 1985). Although during some periods the area receiving input from the central visual field grows more rapidly, at other times it grows more slowly. Of course, detailed comparison of areas receiving input from different parts of the periphery might reveal differences, as might comparisons of the electrophysiological properties of cells. Thus, there is little basis on which to explain the general expansion of the visual field with age. Similarly, there is little basis on which to explain the shrinkage of the field after deprivation in humans, except that the deficits are likely to be of cortical origin.

Evidence From Studies on the Disengagement of Attention. As discussed earlier in this chapter, babies sometimes have difficulty disengaging attention from one target in order to move their eyes toward another target in the periphery. Such sticky fixation is especially strong between 1 month and 3–4 months of age, although it does not occur under all circumstances even at 1 month of age. The onset and waning of sticky fixation have been attributed to changing influences on the superior colliculus. The onset has been attributed to the development of an inhibitory pathway from the deeper layers of the primary visual cortex through the substantia nigra and basal ganglia to the superior colliculus, which is not yet regulated by input from the parietal and/or frontal cortex (Johnson, 1990, 1994a, 1995; Rothbart, Posner, & Rosicky, 1994). Babies' improved ability to disengage attention after 3–4 months is assumed to reflect the maturation of cortical influence over the superior colliculus, particularly from the parietal and frontal cortices (Atkinson et al., 1992; Braddick et al., 1996; Hood, 1995; Hood et al., this volume; Johnson, 1990, 1994b; Rafal, this volume; Rothbart et al., 1994).

Results from a baby (PP) with apparently intact superior colliculi who had had the right cortex removed for treatment of seizures provide a test of the neural explanation of sticky fixation (Braddick et al., 1992; see also Hood et al., this volume). The baby was tested in the good field (i.e., the right field which had cortical representation) and the "blind" field (i.e., the left field which had no cortical representation) at 7 to 12 months of age, ages at which normal infants have no trouble disengaging attention from a central stimulus to orient toward a peripheral target (although the diminution is not so apparent for the conditions the authors tested in this study—Hood & Atkinson, 1993). The peripheral target was a vertical black-and-white stripe 23° off to the side, phase reversing at 6 Hz, either presented alone or accompanied by a schematized face that was altered at the same rate. When the target was presented alone in the affected field, PP moved his eyes toward the it nearly 100% of the time. Thus, human subcortical pathways are sufficient to mediate binocular overt orienting toward exogenous peripheral stimuli, at least during infancy. The most likely basis is via direct retinal input to the superior colliculus. In contrast to the good performance when the central stimulus was removed, when it remained on, PP was much less likely to move his eyes toward the peripheral target. When he did orient appropriately, it was often after blinking or nodding his head seemingly to "unlock" central fixation. Thus, some cortical structures do seem to play a role in facilitating disengagement from a central stimulus in order to allow eye movements toward a peripheral target, and their maturation may be responsible for the diminution of sticky fixation in normal infants between 1 and 3–4 months of age.

The sticky fixation observed in PP also indicates that sticky fixation can occur in the absence of cortical input to subcortical structures. Hence, the maturation of input from the deeper layers of the primary visual cortex to the substantia nigra and basal ganglia is not *necessary* for its onset at about 1 month of age. However, binocular input through that pathway may contribute to sticky fixation in the normal 1-month-old. That hypothesis is suggested by the fact that sticky fixation has been observed in previous studies when babies were tested binocularly but not in our studies when they were tested monocularly (see earlier section on improved ability to disengage attention). The cells in the deeper layers that project to the substantia nigra and basal ganglia are mainly binocular (Hubel & Wiesel, 1977; Sparks & Pollack, 1977). Thus, although the results from the baby missing one cortical hemisphere indicate that binocular input from this pathway is not necessary for sticky fixation (Braddick et al., 1992), such input may make it more difficult for the young infant to disengage attention from an attractive central stimulus, especially if the baby is so young that there is little processing of the peripheral target by the parietal or frontal cortices. (Presumably the cells in the deeper layers of primary visual cortex, although binocular, do not mediate stereopsis, which does not develop until 3–5 months of age—Birch, 1993.) It may also be the case that cells receiving input from near the fovea are not as responsive when they receive monocular as opposed to binocular input and hence babies' attention may not be as thoroughly engaged by the central stimulus when they view it monocularly. As a result, they readily look away from center whether or not the central stimulus remains on. An interesting test of this hypothesis would be to compare the effects of a central stimulus on 1-month-olds' orienting toward peripheral targets when tested monocularly versus binocularly.

Collectively the evidence suggests that binocular fixation may inhibit the superior colliculus from initiating eye movements toward peripheral targets, at least in part via binocular input from the deeper layers of the primary visual cortex through the substantia nigra and basal ganglia. Such sticky fixation becomes stronger as the primary visual cortex matures but then wanes as the superior colliculus begins to be influenced by higher cortical areas such as the parietal and temporal cortices.

SUMMARY AND CONCLUSIONS

Even newborns can orient toward exogenous peripheral targets if the targets are large, luminant, and of high contrast. The effective field for overt orienting increases with age, and at any age depends on the size and luminance of the stimulus. The improvement arises in part from increased sensitivity to peripheral targets that likely results from maturation of many parts of the nervous system beginning in the retina. It arises also from improved control of eye movements. Orienting toward targets in the temporal field develops more quickly than orienting toward targets in the nasal field, presumably because it is facilitated by extrageniculate subcortical structures. The slower development of orienting toward nasal targets reflects increasing cortical influence, mainly from the primary visual cortex. That influence initially causes the baby to have difficulty disengaging attention from a central stimulus, at least when tested binocularly. Only when the frontal and parietal cortices also begin to influence eye movements are babies able to readily disengage attention from one stimulus in order to make a saccade toward a peripheral target. Although cortical influences over overt orienting develop considerably during the first 6 months of life, their development stretches over many years: It takes many years for peripheral sensitivity to become completely adult-like and it does not develop normally in the absence of visual input at any time up to the teenage years.

ACKNOWLEDGMENTS

We thank John Richards, Bob Rafal, David Robinson, Louis Benevanto, Luisa Mayer, Robin Walker, Janet Atkinson, Mark Johnson, Alan Cowey, and Bruce Hood for comments on an earlier draft of this chapter. Some of the data reported in the chapter formed the undergraduate honors thesis at McMaster University of Kelly Blackburn, Andrea Clarke, Christina Soleas, Shelley Jobson, Ross Breithaupt, Anita Burhanpurkar, Lisa McKee, and Sima Anvari; the first year graduate project at McMaster University of Melissa Goldberg; the master's thesis at McMaster University of Nneka Nnubia; and the Ph.D. thesis at McMaster University of Elizabeth Bowering. We thank Dr. Henry Brent, former Director of the Contact Lens Clinic at The Hospital for Sick Children in Toronto, for his valuable advice and for providing the patients treated for cataracts. We also thank McMaster University Hospital in Hamilton, The Hospital for Sick Children in Toronto, and St. Joseph's Hospital in Hamilton for providing space for the studies, The Hospital for Sick Children and St. Joseph's Hospital for the use of the Goldmann perimeter, Bob Barclay for providing contact lenses, and Rolfe Morrision for statistical advice. This research was supported in part by the National Science and Engineering Council of Canada grant OGP0009797, by the Medical Research Council of Canada grants 9975A, MA8894 and MT-11710, and by the National Institutes of Health (Bethesda, Maryland) grant EY03475. Correspondence should be directed to Dr. Daphne Maurer, Department of

Psychology, McMaster University, Hamilton, Ontario, Canada, L8S 4K1 (e-mail: Maurer@McMaster.ca).

REFERENCES

Abramov, I., Gordon, J., Hendrickson, A., Hainline, L., Dobson, V., & LaBossier, E. (1982). The retina of the newborn human infant. *Science, 217*, 265–267.

Adams, R., Maurer, D., & Cashin, H. (1990). The influence of stimulus size on newborns' discrimination of chromatic from achromatic stimuli. *Vision Research, 30*, 2023–2030.

Albano, J. E., Mishkin, M., Westbrook, L. E., & Wurtz, R. H. (1982). Visuomotor deficits following ablation of monkey superior colliculus. *Journal of Neurophysiology, 48*, 338–351.

Albano, J. E., & Wurtz, R. H. (1982). Deficits in eye position following ablation of monkey superior colliculus, pretectum and posterior-medial thalamus. *Journal of Neurophysiology, 48*, 318–337.

Allen, D., Tyler, C., & Norcia, A. (1996). Development of grating acuity and contrast sensitivity in the central and peripheral visual field of the human infant. *Vision Research, 36*, 1945–1953.

Alpern, M. (1962). Introduction to movements of the eyes. In H. Davson (Ed.), *The eye, Vol. 3* (pp. 3–5). New York: Academic Press.

Aslin, R. N., & Salapatek, P. (1975). Saccadic localization of visual targets by the very young human infant. *Perception and Psychophysics, 17*, 293–302.

Atchison, D. A. (1987). Effects of defocus on visual field measurement. *Ophthalmologica, 173*, 364–374.

Atkinson, J., Hood, B., Wattam-Bell, J., & Braddick, O. (1992). Changes in infants' ability to switch visual attention in the first three months of life. *Perception, 21*, 643–653.

Bachevalier, J., Ungerleider, L. G., O'Neill, J. B., & Friedman, D. P. (1986). Regional distribution of 3H naloxone binding in the brain of a newborn rhesus monkey. *Developmental Brain Research, 24*, 302–308.

Baleydier, C., Magnin, M., & Cooper, H. M. (1990). Macaque accessory optic system: II. Connections with the pretectum. *Journal of Comparative Neurology, 302*, 405–416.

Barone, P., Dehay, C., Berland, M., Bullier, J., & Kennedy, H. (1995). Developmental remodelling of primate visual cortical pathways. *Cerebral Cortex, 5*, 22–38.

Becker, L. E., Armstrong, D. L., Chan, F., & Wood, M. M. (1984). Dendritic development in human occipital cortical neurons. *Brain Research, 315*, 117–124.

Bender, D. (1982). Receptive-field properties of neurons in the macaque inferior pulvinar. *Journal of Neurophysiology, 48*, 1–17.

Benedetto, M. D., & Cyrlin, M. N. (1975). The effect of blur on static perimetric thresholds. In A. Heijl & E. L. Greve (Eds.), *Proceedings of the Sixth International Visual Field Symposium* (pp. 563–567). Dordrecht, The Netherlands: Dr. W. Junk Publishers.

Benevento, L., & Port, J. (1995). Single neurons with both form/color differential responses and saccade-related responses in the nonretinotopic pulvinar of the behaving macaque monkey. *Visual Neuroscience, 12*, 523–544.

Birch, E. E. (1993). Stereopsis in infants and its developmental relation to visual acuity. In K. Simons (Ed.), *Early visual development, normal and abnormal* (pp. 224–236). Committee on Vision, Commission on Behavioural and Social Sciences and Education, National Research Council. New York: Oxford University Press.

Blakemore, C. (1988). The sensitive periods of the monkey visual cortex. In G. Lennerstrand, G. K. von Noorden, & C. C. Campos (Eds.), *Strabismus and amblyopia: Experimental basis for advances in clinical management* (pp. 219–234). New York: Plenum.

Blakemore, C., & Vital-Durand, F. (1986). Organization and post-natal development of the monkey's lateral geniculate nucleus. *Journal of Physiology, 380,* 453–491.

Boothe, R. G., Dobson, V., & Teller, D. Y. (1985). Postnatal development of vision in human and nonhuman primates. *Annual Review of Neurology, 8,* 495–545.

Boothe, R. G., Greenbough, W. T., Lund, J. S., & Wrege, K. (1979). A quantitative investigation of spine and dendrite development of neurons in visual cortex (area 17) of Macaca Nemestrina monkeys. *Journal of Comparative Neurology, 186,* 473–490.

Bourgeois, J.-P., & Rakic, P. (1993). Changes of synaptic density in the primary visual cortex of the macaque monkey from fetal to adult stage. *Journal of Neuroscience, 12,* 2801–2820.

Bowering, E. R., Maurer, D., Lewis, T. L., & Brent, H. P. (1993). Sensitivity in the nasal and temporal hemifields in children treated for cataract. *Investigative Ophthalmology & Visual Science, 34,* 3501–3509.

Bowering, E. R., Maurer, D., Lewis, T. L., Brent, H. P., & Riedel, P. (1996). The visual field in childhood: Normal development and the influence of deprivation. *Developmental Cognitive Neuroscience Technical Report,* No. 96.1.

Bowering, E. R., Maurer, D., Lewis, T. L., & Brent, H. P. (in press). Constriction of the visual field of children after early deprivation. *Journal of Pediatric Ophthalmology & Strabismus.*

Bowering, M. E. R. (1992). *The peripheral vision of normal children and of children treated for cataracts.* (Doctoral dissertation, McMaster University). Dissertation Abstracts International.

Braddick, O., Atkinson, J., & Hood, B. (1996). Striate cortex, extrastriate cortex, and colliculus: Some new approaches. In F. Vital-Durand, O. Braddick, & J. Atkinson (Eds.), *Infant vision* (pp. 203–220). Oxford: Oxford University Press.

Braddick, O., Atkinson, J., Hood, B., Harkness, W., Jackson, G., & Vargha-Khadem, F. (1992). Possible blindsight in infants lacking one cerebral hemisphere. *Nature, 360,* 461–463.

Bronson, G. W. (1990). Changes in infants' visual scanning across the 2- to 14-week age period. *Journal of Experimental Child Psychology, 49,* 101–125.

Brown, A. M., Dobson, V., & Maier, J. (1987). Visual acuity of human infants at scotopic, mesopic and photopic luminances. *Vision Research, 27,* 1845–1858.

Brown, C. A. (1961). The development of visual capacity in the infant and young child. *Cerebral Palsy Bulletin, 3,* 364–372.

Bruner, J. (1973). Pacifier-produced visual buffering in human infants. *Developmental Psychobiology, 6,* 45–51.

Butter, C. M., Kirsch, N. L., & Reeves, G. (1990). The effect of lateralized dynamic stimuli on unilateral spatial neglect following right hemisphere lesions. *Restorative Neurology and Neuroscience, 2,* 39–46.

Butter, C. M., Weistein, C., Bender, D. B., & Gross, C. G. (1978). Localization and detection of visual stimuli following superior colliculus lesions in rhesus monkeys. *Brain Research, 156,* 33–49.

Chugani, H. (1994). Development of regional brain glucose metabolism in relation to behavior and plasticity. In G. Dawson & K. Fischer (Eds.), *Human behavior and the developing brain* (pp. 153–175). New York: Guilford.

Chugani, H. T., & Phelps, M. E. (1986). Maturational changes in cerebral function in infants determined by [18]FDG positron emission tomography. *Science, 231,* 840–843.

Conel, J. L. (1939). *The postnatal development of the human cerebral cortex: Vol. I. The cortex of the newborn.* Cambridge, MA: Harvard University Press.

Conel, J. L. (1941). *The postnatal development of the human cerebral cortex: Vol. II. The cortex of the one-month infant.* Cambridge, MA: Harvard University Press.

Conel, J. L. (1947). *The postnatal development of the human cerebral cortex: Vol. III. The cortex of the three-month infant.* Cambridge, MA: Harvard University Press.

Conel, J. L. (1951). *The postnatal development of the human cerebral cortex: Vol. IV. The cortex of the six-month infant.* Cambridge, MA: Harvard University Press.

Conel, J. L. (1955). *The postnatal development of the human cerebral cortex: Vol. V. The cortex of the fifteen-month infant.* Cambridge, MA: Harvard University Press.

Conel, J. L. (1967). *The postnatal development of the human cerebral cortex: Vol. VIII. The cortex of the six-year child.* Cambridge, MA: Harvard University Press.

Courage, M. L., & Adams, R. J. (1990). The early development of visual acuity in the binocular and monocular peripheral fields. *Infant Behavior and Development, 13,* 123–128.

Courage, M. L., & Adams, R. J. (1996). Infant peripheral vision: The development of monocular visual acuity in the first 3 months of postnatal life. *Vision Research, 36,* 1207–1215.

Cowey, A. (1967). Perimetric study of field defect in monkeys after cortical and retinal ablations. *Quarterly Journal of Experimental Psychology, 19,* 232–245.

Cowey, A., & Weiskrantz, L. (1963). A perimetric study of visual field defects in monkeys. *Quarterly Journal of Experimental Psychology, 15,* 91–115.

Crawford, M. L. J. (1988). Electrophysiology of cortical neurons under different conditions of visual deprivation. In G. Lennerstrand, G. K. von Noorden, & C. C. Campos (Eds.), *Strabismus and amblyopia: Experimental basis for advances in clinical management* (pp. 207–218). New York: Plenum.

Crawford, M. L. J., Blake, R., Cool, S. J., & von Noorden, G. K. (1975). Physiological consequences of unilateral and bilateral eye closure in macaque monkeys: Some further observations. *Brain Research, 84,* 150–154.

Crawford, M. L. J., Pesch, T. W., von Noorden, G. K., Harwerth, R. S., & Smith, E. I., III. (1991). Bilateral form deprivation in monkeys: Electrophysiologic and anatomic consequences. *Investigative Ophthalmology & Visual Science, 32,* 2328–2336.

Curcio, C. A., & Allen, K. A. (1990). Topography of ganglion cells in human retina. *Journal of Comparative Neurology, 300,* 5–25.

Curcio, C. A., Sloan, K. R., Kalina, R. E., & Hendrickson, A. E. (1990). Human photoreceptor topography. *Journal of Comparative Neurology, 292,* 497–523.

Davson, H. (1963). *The physiology of the eye.* Boston: Little, Brown.

de Schonen, S., McKenzie, B., Maury, L., & Bresson, F. (1978). Central and peripheral object distances as determinants of the effective visual field in early infancy. *Perception, 7,* 499–506.

Dekaban, A. (1954). Human thalamus. *Journal of Comparative Neurology, 100,* 63–94.

Diebler, M. F., Farkas-Bargeton, E., & Wehrlé, R. (1979). Developmental changes of enzymes associated with energy metabolism and the synthesis of some neurotransmitters in discrete areas of human neocortex. *Journal of Neurochemistry, 32,* 429–435.

Distler, C., & Hoffmann, K.-P. (1993). Visual receptive field properties in kitten pretectal nucleus of the optic tract and dorsal terminal nucleus of the accessory optic tract. *Journal of Neurophysiology, 70,* 814–827.

Donovan, A. (1966). The postnatal developmental of the cat retina. *Experimental Eye Research, 5,* 249–254.

Drucker, D. N., & Hendrickson, A. E. (1989). The morphological development of extrafoveal human retina. *Investigative Ophthalmology & Visual Science, 30,* 226. (Abstract)

Duke-Elder, S., & Abrams, D. (1970). *System of ophthalmology. Vol. V: Ophthalmic optics and refraction.* London: Henry Kimpton.

Engler, U., Zihl, J., & Pöppel, E. (1993). Incongruity of homonymous visual field defects. *Clinical Vision Sciences, 8,* 355–363.

Fahle, M., & Schmid, M. (1988). Naso-temporal asymmetry of visual perception and of the visual cortex. *Vision Research, 28,* 293–300.

Frankhauser, F., & Enoch, J. M. (1962). The effect of blur upon static perimetric thresholds. *Archives of Ophthalmology, 68,* 120–131.

Fredericks, C. A., Giolli, R. A., Blanks, R. H., & Sadun, A. A. (1988). The human accessory optic system. *Brain Research, 454,* 116–122.

Frisén, L., & Glansholm, A. (1975). Optical and neural resolution in peripheral vision. *Investigative Ophthalmology, 14,* 528–536.

Garey, L. J., & de Courten, C. (1983). Structural development of the lateral geniculate nucleus and visual cortex in monkey and man. *Behavioral Brain Research, 10*, 3–13.

Goldberg, M. C., Maurer, D., & Lewis, T. L. (1997). Influence of a central stimulus on infants' visual fields. *Infant Behavior and Development, 20*, 359–370.

Gottlieb, M. D., Pasik, P., & Pasik, T. (1985). Early postnatal development of the monkey visual system. I. Growth of the lateral geniculate nucleus and striate cortex. *Developmental Brain Research, 17*, 53–62.

Grasse, K. L., & Cynader, M. S. (1982). Electrophysiology of medial terminal nucleus of accessory optic system in the cat. *Journal of Neurophysiology, 48*, 490–504.

Grasse, K. L., & Cynader, M. S. (1984). Electrophysiology of lateral and dorsal terminal nuclei of the cat accessory optic system. *Journal of Neurophysiology, 51*, 276–293.

Grasse, K. L., & Cynader, M. S. (1987). The accessory optic system of the monocularly deprived cat. *Developmental Brain Research, 31*, 229–241.

Grigsby, S. S., & Tsou, B. H. (1994). Grating and flicker sensitivity in the near and far periphery: Naso-temporal asymmetries and binocular summation. *Vision Research, 34*, 2841–2848.

Guez, J. R. (1978, March). *The development of peripheral vision in infants.* Paper presented at the meeting of the Southwestern Society for Research in Human Development, Dallas, TX.

Hamer, R. D., & Schneck, M. E. (1984). Spatial summation in dark-adapted human infants. *Vision Research, 24*, 77–85.

Harris, P., & MacFarlane, A. (1974). The growth of the effective visual field from birth to seven weeks. *Journal of Experimental Child Psychology, 18*, 340–348.

Headon, M. P., Sloper, J. J., Hiorns, R. W., & Powel, T. P. S. (1985). Size of neurons in the primate lateral geniculate nucleus during normal development. *Developmental Brain Research, 18*, 51–56.

Hendrickson, A., & Kupfer, C. (1976). The histogenesis of the fovea in the macaque monkey. *Investigative Ophthalmology, 15*, 746–756.

Hendrickson, A., Wilson, M. E., & Toyne, M. J. (1970). The distribution of optic nerve fibres in Macaca mulatta. *Brain Research, 23*, 425–427.

Hickey, T. L. (1977). Postnatal development of the human lateral geniculate nucleus: Relationship to a critical period for the visual system. *Science, 198*, 836–838.

Hicks, J., & Richards, J. E. (1996). Stimulus movement and peripheral stimulus localization by 20- and 26-week old infants. *Infant Behavior and Development, 19*, 505. (Abstract)

Hikosaka, O., & Wurtz, R. H. (1986). Saccadic eye movements following injection of lidocaine into the superior colliculus. *Experimental Brain Research, 61*, 531–539.

Hitchcock, P. F., & Hickey, T. L. (1980). Prenatal development of the human lateral geniculate nucleus. *Journal of Comparative Neurology, 194*, 395–411.

Hoffmann, K.-P., Distler, C., & Erickson, R. (1991). Functional projections from striate cortex and superior temporal sulcus to the nucleus of the optic tract (NOT) and dorsal terminal nucleus of the accessory optic tract (DTN) of macaque monkeys. *Journal of Comparative Neurology, 313*, 707–724.

Hoffmann, K.-P., Distler, C., & Ilg, U. (1992). Callosal and superior temporal sulcus contributions to receptive field properties in the macaque monkey's nucleus of the optic tract and dorsal terminal nucleus of the accessory optic tract. *Journal of Comparative Neurology, 321*, 150–162.

Hollyfield, J. G., Frederick, J., & Rayborn, M. (1983). Neurotransmitter properties of the newborn human retina. *Investigative Ophthalmology & Visual Science, 24*, 893–897.

Hood, B. (1995). Visual selective attention in infants: A neuroscientific approach. In L. Lipsitt & C. Rovee-Collier (Eds.), *Advances in infancy research, Vol. 9* (pp. 163–216). Norwood, NJ: Ablex.

Hood, B., & Atkinson, J. (1990). Sensory visual loss and cognitive deficits in the selective attentional system of normal infants and neurologically impaired children. *Developmental Medicine and Child Neurology, 32,* 1067–1077.

Hood, B., & Atkinson, J. (1993). Disengaging visual attention in the infant and adult. *Infant Behavior and Development, 16,* 405–422.

Hornsten, G. P. M., & Winkelman, J. E. (1962). Electrical activity of the retina in relation to histological differentiation in infants born prematurely and at full-term. *Vision Research, 2,* 269–276.

Hubel, D. H., LeVay, S., & Wiesel, T. N. (1975). Mode of termination of retinotectal fibres in macaque monkey: An autoradiographic study. *Brain Research, 96,* 25–40.

Hubel, D. H., & Wiesel, T. N. (1977). Functional architecture of macaque monkey visual cortex. *Proceedings of the Royal Society of London B, 198,* 1–59.

Huttenlocher, P. R. (1979). Synaptic density in human frontal cortex—developmental changes and effects of aging. *Brain Research, 163,* 195–205.

Huttenlocher, P. R. (1994). Synaptogenesis in human cerebral cortex. In G. Dawson & K. Fisher (Eds.), *Human behavior and the developing brain* (pp. 137–152). New York: Guilford Press.

Huttenlocher, P. R., & de Courten, C. (1987). The development of synapses in striate cortex of man. *Human Neurobiology, 6,* 1–9.

Huttenlocher, P. R., de Courten, C., Garey, L. J., & van der Loos, H. (1982). Synaptogenesis in human visual cortex—evidence for synapse elimination during normal development. *Neuroscience Letters, 33,* 247–252.

Itaya, S., & van Hosen, G. (1983). Retinal projections to the inferior and medial pulvinar nuclei in the old-world monkey. *Brain Research, 269,* 223–230.

Johns, P. R., Rusoff, A. C., & Dubin, M. W. (1979). Postnatal neurogenesis in the kitten retina. *Journal of Comparative Neurology, 187,* 545–556.

Johnson, M. (1990). Cortical maturation and the development of visual attention in early infancy. *Journal of Cognitive Neuroscience, 2,* 81–95.

Johnson, M. (1994a). Dissociating components of visual attention: A neurodevelopmental approach. In M. Farah & G. Radcliffe (Eds.), *The neural basis of high-level vision* (pp. 241–268). Hillsdale, NJ: Lawrence Erlbaum Associates.

Johnson, M. (1994b). Visual attention and the control of eye movements in early infancy. In C. Umiltà & M. Moscovitch (Eds.), *Attention and performance XV: Conscious and nonconscious information processing* (pp. 291–310). Cambridge, MA: MIT Press.

Johnson, M. (1995). The development of visual attention: A cognitive neuroscience perspective. In M. S. Gazzaniga (Ed.), *The cognitive neurosciences* (pp. 735–747). Cambridge, MA: MIT Press.

Johnson, M., & Morton, J. (1991). *Biology and cognitive development: The case of face recognition.* Oxford, England: Blackwell.

Johnson, M., Posner, M., & Rothbart, M. (1991). Components of visual orienting in early infancy: Contingency learning, anticipatory looking, and disengaging. *Journal of Cognitive Neuroscience, 3,* 335–344.

Kanaseki, T., & Sprague, J. M. (1974). Anatomical organization of pretectal nuclei and tectal laminae in the cat. *Journal of Comparative Neurology, 158,* 319–338.

Keating, E. G., Kenney, D. V., Gooley, S. G., Pratt, S. E., & McGillis, S. L. B. (1986). Targeting errors and reduced oculomotor range following ablations of the superior colliculus or pretectum/thalamus. *Behavioral Brain Research, 22,* 191–210.

Kennedy, C., Sakurada, O., Shinohara, M., & Miyaoka, M. (1982). Local cerebral glucose utilization in the newborn macaque monkey. *Annals of Neurology, 12,* 333–340.

Klein, R., Kingstone, A., & Pontefract, A. (1992). On orienting of visual attention. In K. Raynor (Ed.), *Eye movements and visual cognition: Scene perception and reading* (pp. 46–63). New York: Springer-Verlag.

Koerner, F., & Teuber, H. (1973). Visual field defects after missile injuries to the geniculo-striate pathway in man. *Experimental Brain Research, 18*, 88–113.

Kurtz, D., & Butter, C. (1980). Impairments in visual discrimination performance and gaze shifts in monkeys with superior colliculus lesions. *Brain Research, 196*, 109–124.

Larsen, J. S. (1971). The sagittal growth of the eye. *Acta Ophthalmologica, 49*, 873–886.

Latto, R., & Cowey, A. (1971). Visual field defects after frontal eye-field lesions in monkeys. *Brain Research, 30*, 1–24.

LaVail, M. M., & Rakic, P. (1983). Cell genesis in the rhesus monkey retina. *Investigative Ophthalmology & Visual Science, 24*, 7. (Abstract)

Leuba, G., & Garey, L. J. (1984). Development of dendritic patterns in the lateral geniculate nucleus of monkey: A quantitative Golgi study. *Developmental Brain Research, 16*, 285–299.

LeVay, S., Connolly, M., Honde, J., & van Essen, D. C. (1985). The complete pattern of ocular dominance stripes in the striate cortex and visual field of the macaque monkey. *Journal of Neuroscience, 5*, 486–490.

LeVay, S., Wiesel, T. N., & Hubel, D. H. (1980). The development of ocular dominance columns in normal and visually deprived monkeys. *Journal of Comparative Neurology, 191*, 1–51.

Levitt, J. B., Movshon, J. A., Sherman, S. M., & Spear, P. D. (1989). Effects of monocular deprivation on macaque LGN. *Investigative Ophthalmology & Visual Science, 30*, 296. (Abstract)

Lewis, T. L., & Maurer, D. (1992). The development of the temporal and nasal visual fields during infancy. *Vision Research, 32*, 903–911.

Lewis, T. L., Maurer, D., Anvari, S. H., & Jewell, D. (1997). The influence of flicker on infants' orienting toward peripheral targets. *Investigative Ophthalmology & Visual Science, 38*, S64. (Abstract)

Lewis, T. L., Maurer, D., & Blackburn, K. (1985). The development of young infants' ability to detect stimuli in the nasal visual field. *Vision Research, 25*, 943–950.

Lewis, T. L., Maurer, D., Burhanpurkar, A., & Anvari, S. H. (1996). The influence of flicker on 3-month-olds' peripheral vision. *Investigative Ophthalmology & Visual Science, 37*, S1067. (Abstract)

Liao, F. (1973). Perimetry in young children. *Japanese Journal of Ophthalmology, 17*, 277–289.

MacFarlane, A., Harris, P., & Barnes, I. (1976). Central and peripheral vision in early infancy. *Journal of Experimental Child Psychology, 21*, 532–538.

Mann, I. (1964). *The development of the human eye*. London: British Medical Association.

Mates, S. L., & Lund, J. S. (1983). Neuronal comparison and development in lamina 4C of monkey striate cortex. *Journal of Comparative Neurology, 221*, 60–90.

Maurer, D., & Lewis, T. L. (1979). Peripheral discrimination by three-month-old infants. *Child Development, 50*, 276–279.

Maurer, D., & Lewis, T. L. (1981). The influence of peripheral stimuli on infants' eye movements. In D. F. Fisher, R. A. Monty, & J. W. Senders (Eds.), *Eye movements: Cognition and visual perception* (pp. 21–29). Hillsdale, NJ: Lawrence Erlbaum Associates.

Maurer, D., & Lewis, T. L. (1991). The development of peripheral vision and its physiological underpinnings. In M. J. Weiss & P. R. Zelazo (Eds.), *Newborn attention: Biological constraints and the influence of experience* (pp. 218–255). Norwood, NJ: Ablex.

Maurer, D., & Lewis, T. L. (1993). Visual outcomes after infantile cataract. In K. Simons (Ed.), *Early visual development: Normal and abnormal* (pp. 454–484). Committee on Vision, Commission on Behavioral and Social Sciences and Education, National Research Council. New York: Oxford University Press.

Maurer, D., Nnubia, N., & Lewis, T. L. (1997). The effect of sucking on babies' orienting toward peripheral visual stimuli. *Infant Behavior and Development, 20*, 397–404.

Mayer, D. L., & Fulton, A. B. (1993). Development of the human visual field. In K. Simons (Ed.), *Early visual development: Normal and abnormal* (pp. 117–129). Committee on Vision,

Commission on Behavioural and Social Sciences and Education, National Research Council. New York: Oxford University Press.

McCloskey, M., Rapp, B., Yantis, S., Rubin, G., Bacon, W., Dagnelie, G., Gordon, B., Aliminosa, D., Boatman, D., Badecker, W., Johnson, D., Tusa, R., & Palmer, E. (1995). A developmental deficit in localizing objects from vision. *Psychological Science, 6,* 112–117.

McCloskey, M., & Palmer, E. (1996). Visual representation of object location: Insights from localization impairments. *Current Directions in Psychological Science, 5,* 25–28.

Mohler, C. W., & Wurtz, R. H. (1977). Role of striate cortex and superior colliculus in visual guidance of saccadic eye movements in monkeys. *Journal of Neurophysiology, 40,* 74–94.

Mohn, G., & van Hof-van Duin, J. (1986). Development of the binocular and monocular visual fields of human infants during the first year of life. *Clinical Vision Sciences, 1,* 51–64.

Moschovakis, A., Karabelas, A., & Highstein, S. (1988). Structure-function relationships in the primate superior colliculus. I. Morphological classification of efferent neurons. *Journal of Neurophysiology, 60,* 232–262.

Movshon, J. A., & Van Sluyters, R. (1981). Visual neural development. *Annual Review of Psychology, 32,* 477–522.

Nishimura, Y., & Rakic, P. (1983). Synaptogenesis in the inner plexiform layer of the fetal monkey retina. *Investigative Ophthalmology & Visual Science, 24,* 7. (Abstract)

O'Kusky, J., & Colonnier, M. (1982). Postnatal changes in number of neurons and synapses in visual cortex (area 17) of macaque monkey: A sterological analysis in normal and monocularly deprived animals. *Journal of Comparative Neurology, 210,* 291–306.

Østerberg, G. (1935). Topography of the layer of rods and cones in the human retina. *Acta Ophthalmologica* (Kobenhaven), Supplement 6.

Packer, O., Hendrickson, A. E., & Curcio, C. A. (1990). Developmental redistribution of photoreceptors across the *Macaca nemestina* (Pigtail Macaque) retina. *Journal of Comparative Neurology, 298,* 472–493.

Parks, M. M. (1966). Growth of the eye and development in vision. In S. Liebman & S. Gellis (Eds.), *The pediatrician's ophthalmology* (pp. 15–26). Saint Louis: C. V. Mosby.

Perry, V. H., & Cowey, A. (1985). The ganglion cell and cone distributions in the monkey's retina: Implications for central magnification factors. *Vision Research, 25,* 1795–1810.

Pollack, J. G., & Hickey, T. L. (1979). The distribution of retino-collicular axon terminals in rhesus monkey. *Journal of Comparative Neurology, 185,* 587–602.

Posner, M., & Cohen, Y. (1980). Attention and the control of movements. In G. E. Stelmach & J. Requin (Eds.), *Tutorials in motor behavior* (pp. 243–258). Amsterdam: North-Holland.

Provis, J. M., van Driel, D., Billson, F. A., & Russell, P. (1985). Development of the human retina: Patterns of cell distribution and redistribution in the ganglion cell layer. *Journal of Comparative Neurology, 233,* 429–451.

Quinn, G. (1992). Retinopathy of prematurity: Natural history and classification. In J. Flynn & W. Tasman (Eds.), *Retinopathy of prematurity* (pp. 7–22). New York: Springer-Verlag.

Rabinowicz, T. (1986). The differentiated maturation of the cerebral cortex. In F. Faulkner & J. M. Tanner (Eds.), *Human growth: A comprehensive treatise, 2nd Edition, Vol. 2: Postnatal growth neurobiology* (pp. 385–410). New York: Plenum.

Rafal, R., Henik, A., & Smith, J. (1991). Extrageniculate contributions to reflex visual orienting in normal humans: A temporal hemifield advantage. *Journal of Cognitive Neuroscience, 3,* 322–328.

Rafal, R., Smith, J., Krantz, J., Cohen, A., & Brennan, C. (1990). Extrageniculate vision in hemianopic humans: Saccade inhibition by signals in the blind field. *Science, 250,* 118–121.

Rakic, P. (1974). Neurons in rhesus monkey visual cortex: Systematic relation between time of origin and eventual disposition. *Science, 181,* 425–427.

Rakic, P. (1976). Prenatal genesis of connections subserving ocular dominance in the rhesus monkey. *Nature, 261,* 467–471.

Rakic, P. (1977). Prenatal development of the visual system in the rhesus monkey. *Philosophical Transactions of the Royal Society of London, 278,* 245–260.

Rakic, P. (1991). Development of the primate cerebral cortex. In M. Lewis (Ed.), *Child and adolescent psychiatry* (pp. 11–28). Baltimore: Williams & Wilkins.

Robertson, T. W. (1982). Prenatal development of the human superior colliculus. *Society for Neuroscience, 8,* 450. (Abstract)

Robinson, D. (1993). Functional contributions of the primate pulvinar. *Progress in Brain Research, 95,* 371–380.

Robinson, D., & McClurkin, J. (1989). The visual superior colliculus and pulvinar. In R. Wurtz & M. Goldberg (Eds.), *The neurobiology of saccadic eye movements* (pp. 337–360). Amsterdam: Elsevier.

Robinson, D., Petersen, S., & Keys, W. (1986). Saccade-related and visual activities in the pulvinar nuclei of the behaving rhesus monkey. *Experimental Brain Research, 62,* 625–634.

Rosenquist, A. C., & Palmer, L. A. (1971). Visual receptive field properties of cells of the superior colliculus after cortical lesions in the cat. *Experimental Neurology, 33,* 629–652.

Rothbart, M. K., Posner, M. I., & Rosicky, J. (1994). Orienting in normal and pathological development. *Development and Psychopathology, 6,* 635–652.

Schiff, D., Cohen, B., Buttner-Ennever, J., & Matsuo, V. (1990). Effects of lesions on the nucleus of the optic tract on optokinetic nystagmus and after nystagmus in the monkey. *Experimental Brain Research, 79,* 225–239.

Schiller, P., & Koerner, F. (1971). Discharge characteristics of single units in superior colliculus of the alert rhesus monkey. *Journal of Neurophysiology, 34,* 920–936.

Schiller, P. H., Sandell, J. H., & Maunsell, J. H. (1987). The effect of frontal eye field and superior colliculus lesions on saccadic latencies in the rhesus monkey. *Journal of Neurophysiology, 57,* 1033–1049.

Schiller, P. H., True, S. D., & Conway, J. L. (1980). Deficits in eye movements following frontal eye-field and superior colliculus ablations. *Journal of Neurophysiology, 44,* 1175–1189.

Schneck, M. E., Hamer, R. D., Packer, O. S., & Teller, D. X. (1984). Area-threshold relations at controlled retinal locations in 1-month-old infants. *Vision Research, 24,* 1753–1763.

Schwartz, T. L., Dobson, V., Sandstrom, D. J., & van Hof-Van Duin, J. (1987). Kinetic perimetry assessment of binocular visual field shape and size in young infants. *Vision Research, 27,* 2163–2175.

Sherman, S. M. (1974). Visual field of cats with cortical and tectal lesions. *Science, 185,* 355–357.

Sherman, S. M. (1977). The effect of superior colliculus lesions upon the visual fields of cats with cortical ablations. *Journal of Comparative Neurology, 172,* 211–230.

Simion, F., Valenza, E., Umiltà, C., & Dalla Barba, B. (1995). Inhibition of return in newborns is temporo-nasal asymmetrical. *Infant Behavior and Development, 18,* 189–194.

Sireteanu, R., Fronius, M., & Constantinescu, D. H. (1994). The development of visual acuity in the peripheral visual field of human infants: Binocular and monocular measurements. *Vision Research, 34,* 1659–1671.

Sireteanu, R., Kellerer, R., & Boergen, K.-P. (1984). The development of peripheral visual acuity in human infants: A preliminary study. *Human Neurobiology, 3,* 81–85.

Sireteanu, R., & Maurer, D. (1982). The development of the kitten's visual field. *Vision Research, 22,* 1105–1111.

Slater, A. M., & Findlay, J. M. (1972). The measurement of fixation position in the newborn baby. *Journal of Experimental Child Psychology, 14,* 349–364.

Slater, A. M., & Findlay, J. M. (1975). Binocular fixation in the newborn baby. *Journal of Experimental Child Psychology, 20,* 248–273.

Sorsby, A., Benjamin, B., Sheridan, M., Stone, J., & Leary, G. A. (1961). Refraction and its components during growth of the eye from the age of three. *Medical Research Council Special Report Series* (Serial No. 301). London: Her Majesty's Stationery Office.

Sparks, D. L., & Pollack, J. G. (1977). The neural control of saccadic eye movements: The role of the superior colliculus. In B. A. Brooks & F. J. Bajandas (Eds.), *Eye movements* (pp. 179–219). New York: Plenum Press.

Stein, B. E., Clamann, H. P., & Goldberg, S. J. (1980). Superior colliculus: Control of eye movements in neonatal kittens. *Science, 210*, 78–80.

Stein, B. E., McHaffie, J. G., & Stein, N. L. (1985). Ontogenetic changes in the cat superior colliculus. In R. N. Aslin (Ed.), *Advances in neural and behavioral development, Vol. 1* (pp. 79–106). Norwood, NJ: Ablex.

Sterling, P. (1973). Quantitative mapping with the electron microscope: Retinal terminals in the superior colliculus. *Brain Research, 54*, 347–354.

Stone, J., Rapaport, D. H., Williams, R. W., & Chalupa, L. (1982). Uniformity of cell distribution in the ganglion cell layers of prenatal cat retina: Implications for mechanisms of retinal development. *Developmental Brain Research, 2*, 231–242.

Takashima, S., Chan, F., Becker, L. E., & Armstrong, D. L. (1980). Morphology of the developing visual cortex of the human infant: A quantitative and qualitative Golgi study. *Journal of Neuropathology and Experimental Neurology, 39*, 487–501.

Tronick, E. (1972). Stimulus control and the growth of the infant's effective visual field. *Perception and Psychophysics, 11*, 373–376.

Tytla, M. E., Lewis, T. L., Maurer, D., & Brent, H. P. (1991). Peripheral contrast sensitivity in children treated for congenital cataract. *Investigative Ophthalmology & Visual Science, 32*, 961. (Abstract)

van der Steen, J., Russell, J. S., & James, G. O. (1986). Effects of unilateral frontal eye field lesions in eye-head coordination in monkeys. *Journal of Neurophysiology, 55*, 696–714.

van Hof-van Duin, J., & Mohn, G. (1985). The development of visual function in preterm infants. *Ergebnisse der experimentellen Medizin, 46*, 350–361.

van Hof-van Duin, J., & Mohn, G. (1986). Visual field measurements, optokinetic nystagmus and the visual threatening response: Normal and abnormal development. In J. Barrie (Ed.), *Detection and measurement of visual impairment in pre-verbal children* (pp. 305–316). Documenta Ophthalmological Proceedings Series 45.

van Hof-van Duin, J., & Mohn, G. (1987). Early detection of visual impairments. In H. Galjaard, H. F. R. Prechtl, & M. Velickovic (Eds.), *Early detection and management of cerebral palsy* (pp. 79–100). Dordrecht, The Netherlands: Martinus Nijhoff.

Wässle, H., & Illing, R. B. (1980). The retinal projection to the superior colliculus in the cat: A quantitative study with HRP. *Journal of Comparative Neurology, 190*, 333–356.

Weidman, T. A. (1975). Fine structure of the developing retina. In K. M. Zinn (Ed.), *The developing visual system, Vol. 15* (pp. 65–84). Boston: Little, Brown.

Wiesel, T. N., & Hubel, D. H. (1974). Ordered arrangement of orientation columns in monkeys lacking visual experience. *Journal of Comparative Neurology, 158*, 307–318.

Williams, C., Azzopardi, P., & Cowey, A. (1995). Nasal and temporal retinal ganglion cells projecting to the midbrain: Implications for "blindsight." *Neuroscience, 65*, 577–586.

Wilson, J. R., Lavallee, K. A., Joosse, M. V., Hendrickson, A. E., Boothe, R. G., & Harwerth, R. S. (1989). Visual fields of monocularly deprived macaque monkeys. *Behavioural Brain Research, 33*, 13–22.

Wilson, M., Quinn, G., Dobson, V., & Breton, M. (1991). Normative values for visual fields in 4- to 12-year-old children using kinetic perimetry. *Journal of Pediatric Ophthalmology and Strabismus, 28*, 151–153.

Wilson, M. E., & Toyne, M. G. (1970). Retino-tectal and cortico-tectal projections in Macaca mulatta. *Brain Research, 24*, 395–406.

Zielinski, B. S., & Hendrickson, A. E. (1992). Development of synapses in macaque monkey striate cortex. *Visual Neuroscience, 8*, 491–504.

Chapter 3

Toward a Computational Model of the Development of Saccade Planning

Mark H. Johnson
MRC Cognitive Development Unit, London

Rick O. Gilmore
Pennsylvania State University

Gergely Csibra
MRC Cognitive Development Unit, London

Eye movements are among the first actions available to the infant to explore and learn about the world. To make accurate eye movements in most natural circumstances, however, requires the integration of information not only about the retinal location of a target, but also about the position of the eyes, head, and torso relative to each other and the location of the target in space. This is especially true in situations where the observer is moving through the environment or shifting gaze with combined eye and head movements. The problem of integrating visual information with signals specifying the configuration and motions of the body is common to most forms of visually guided action, and thus eye-movement control can serve as a model system for investigating the development of action planning in general.

In this chapter we explore three central questions related to the computational processes that underlie the development of saccadic eye movement planning: (a) what are the representations that drive saccades early in life, (b) how do they change in development, and (c) why do they change? These questions are motivated on several grounds. Studies with adults and nonhuman primates have shown that while visual information processing in the brain can be broadly distributed, there is a considerable functional specificity within localized regions that is remarkably consistent across individuals and species. Evidence from the postnatal development of the brain suggest that to a large extent this functional specificity is the *outcome* of normal development, and not its predecessor. However, different parts of the brain appear to develop at different rates and reach functional maturity at different times. Consequently, the representations that guide behavior, and the manner in which infants process visual information for action planning, may change as the substrates that carry out these sensorimotor computations develop. Our exploration of these questions will rest upon an examination of evidence from behavioral experiments, neurophysiological and neuroanatomical studies, and computational considerations. In the first section, we review evidence about the patterns of development in the brain's multiple visual orienting and attention pathways. Then, we discuss evidence concerning the representations that appear to be instantiated in these pathways. This leads us to discussion about how information processing for saccades might change in accord with the development of individual pathways and the interactions between them. Finally, we present some recent evidence from neuroimaging studies of saccade planning and discuss some of the issues that need to be addressed by future integrated models of the development of these processes.

THE PATTERNS OF POSTNATAL BRAIN DEVELOPMENT

Bronson (1974, 1982) proposed that many aspects of the development of visual orienting in infants can be accounted for by increasing cortical involvement in perception and the control of eye movements. His claim that the primary visual pathway is not fully functioning until around 2 or 3 months postnatal age was supported by a variety of electrophysiological, neuroanatomical, and behavioral studies. Atkinson (1984) and Johnson (1990) updated and extended Bronson's original account in the light of more recent information about the neural basis of visual orienting and infant perceptual capabilities. In particular, Johnson (1990) discussed neuroanatomical and behavioral evidence that retinal input to the cortical pathways underlying oculomotor control increased over the first 6 months of life.

The hypothesis put forward by Johnson (1990) accounted for changes in the development of visual orienting over the first few months of life in terms of the maturation of several, relatively independent, functional visuomotor pathways. These pathways were derived from proposals initially put forward to account for adult primate electrophysiological and lesion data by Schiller (1985) and which have been recently updated (Schiller, chap. 1, this volume) to account for new data. The pathways are as follows: (a) a pathway from the retina to the superior colliculus (possibly via the deeper layers of V1) involved in rapid input-driven (exogenous) eye movements toward simple, easily discriminable stimuli, and fed mainly by the peripheral visual field; (b) a *posterior* cortical pathway in which largely broad-band or magnocellular inputs from primary visual cortex, the middle temporal area (MT/V5), and parietal cortex converge on the intermediate and deep layers of the superior colliculus; (iii) an *anterior* cortical pathway in which both broad-band and color-opponent streams of processing converge in the frontal cortex and subsequently project directly to brainstem oculomotor nuclei. This pathway appears to be involved in the detailed and complex analysis of visual stimuli such as the temporal sequencing of eye movements within complex arrays, and anticipatory saccades; (iv) a final pathway for the control of eye movements involves tonic inhibition of the colliculus via the substantia nigra and basal ganglia. Schiller (1985; chap. 1, this volume) has proposed that this pathway ensures that the activity of the colliculus can be regulated. More recent findings suggest that this oculomotor pathway forms an integrated system with the frontal eye fields and parietal lobes (e.g., Alexander, DeLong, & Strick, 1986) and that it plays some role in the regulation of subcortical processing by these cortical structures.

Johnson (1990) asserted that, first, the characteristics of visually guided behavior of the infant at particular ages is determined by which of these pathways is functional, and second, which of these pathways is functional is influenced by the developmental state of the primary visual cortex (V1). The basis of this claim at the neuroanatomical level lies in three sets of observations: (a) that the primary visual cortex is the major (though not exclusive) "gateway" for input to the three cortical pathways (ii, iii, iv) (Schiller, 1985; this volume), (b) the primary visual cortex shows a postnatal continuation of the prenatal "inside-out" pattern of growth of the cortex, with the deeper layers (5 and 6) showing greater dendritic branching, greater dendritic length, and greater extent of myelinisation than more superficial layers at birth (e.g., Becker, Armstrong, Chan, & Wood, 1984; Huttenlocher, 1990; Purpura, 1975; Rabinowicz, 1979), and (c) there is a restricted pattern of inputs and outputs from the primary visual cortex (e.g., the efferents to V2 depart from the upper layers (see, e.g., Burkhalter & Bernardo, 1989; Rockland & Pandya, 1979). These three observations, and some associated caveats, are discussed in more detail in Johnson (1994, 1995a) and recent findings related to these ideas are discussed elsewhere (Richards & Hunter, chap. 4, this volume; Maurer & Lewis, chap. 2, this volume; Hood, Atkinson, & Braddick, this volume).

Johnson (1990) proposed that the inside-out pattern of dendritic growth allows prediction of the *sequence* of development of layers in the cortex. This differential developmental sequence is useful in combination with another of the observations mentioned earlier: that particular layers show particular patterns of inputs and outputs. Thus, if we know sequences of development of particular layers within the cortex, Johnson argued, we can then predict the sequence of development of the particular patterns of inputs and outputs that they possess. One of these predictions is that as development proceeds upward through the layers, more output pathways will come online. In fact, in primary visual cortex this effect may be exacerbated because the afferents from the Lateral Geniculate Nucleus (LGN) grow up through the deeper layers (possibly forming temporary synapses on the way) until they reach their adult termination sites in layer 4 (at about 2 months of age in the human infant). Therefore, as the innervation passes up through the layers, different output pathways may start to feedforward information to other cortical areas.

The hypothesized relative restriction on projection patterns yielded the prediction that output from V1 to pathway (ii) should be stronger than the projection to pathway (iii) at early stages of development. This prediction from cellular development has implications for information processing: The functions subserved by pathway involving structure MT (pathway ii) should appear earlier in development than those of the pathway involving the frontal eye fields (pathway iii). Employing this logic, Johnson (1990) attempted to account for characteristics of the visually guided behavior of the infant in terms of the sequential development of pathways underlying visual orienting.

Although Johnson (1990) was able to account for a number of phenomenon associated with development of visual orienting, such as the externality effect and saccadic pursuit tracking in newborns, "obligatory attention" in 1 month olds (see also Hood, Atkinson, & Braddick, this volume), the development of smooth-pursuit tracking by 2 months, and the onset of anticipatory saccades by 4 months, the framework he presented proved limited in the following respects. First, the framework was couched in terms of neural systems that regulate output in a competitive way. No attempt was made to elucidate the internal mechanisms of these systems. Second, while the framework attempted to move beyond the simple subcortical to cortical shift originally posited by Bronson (1974) by providing a specific account of partial cortical functioning, it still involved the sequential development of a number of discrete neurocognitive systems with no clear implications of graded development within a system, other than it being initially "weaker" in its influence on output. Third, the framework presupposed that the pathway from the retina to the colliculus can mediate functional oculomotor behavior very early in life. In mature animals, eyemovement related responses from the superior colliculus depend on cortical input (Schiller, chap. 1, this volume), so it is not known to what extent functional cortical projections are necessary for orienting behavior mediated by the retinocollicular pathway early in life (see also Richards & Hunter, chap. 4, this volume). Finally, and most importantly from an information-processing perspective, the Johnson (1990) framework failed to specifically address the nature of the representations associated with the neurocognitive pathways.

NEURAL REPRESENTATIONS OF VISUAL SPACE
FOR SACCADES

Saccade processing in its simplest form involves converting a signal specifying a target's location into eye muscle commands which move the orbits into a position that centers the target on both foveas. The question of how the visual system codes the spatial location for a saccade can be asked in a precise way: In what coordinate frame or frame of reference are saccade targets represented? There are at least three possibilities. Saccade targets could be represented by their positions relative to the fovea in an eye-based or *retinocentric* frame; they could be defined relative to the center of the head in a *craniocentric* frame; or target locations could be represented relative to the center of the trunk or egocenter in an *egocentric* frame. These frames follow a logical hierarchy. Craniocentric coordinates combine retinocentric location and eye position relative to the head; egocentric coordinates combine retinocentric location, eye position relative to the head, and head position relative to the trunk. Specifying a target location in coordinates relative to any body part other than the retina requires the systematic integration of visual information, its position or velocity relative to the retina, and somatosensory information specifying eye, head, or body positions and velocities.

Retinocentric Representations

The retinocentric representation is the simplest computational scheme that has been proposed to account for saccade control (Young & Stark, 1963). In this framework, a target's distance and direction from the fovea is directly transformed into motor commands that center the target upon it. The retinocentric model is supported by evidence that the pathway from the retina to the superior colliculus appears to instantiate a retinocentric representation of space. Retinal input to the subcortical pathway terminates densely in the upper layers of the superior colliculus in a retinotopic pattern (Schiller, Malpeli, & Schein, 1979). Upper cells in the colliculus have retinotopic receptive fields, and when stimulated electrically, many cells elicit saccades that bring the eyes to fixate on the center location of the cell's receptive field, suggesting that these neurons code the retinotopic goal of an eye movement (Robinson, 1973; Schlag-Rey, Schlag, & Shook, 1989). Many cells in the intermediate and deep layers of the colliculus, which project directly to the brainstem oculomotor nuclei, also fire when subjects make saccades of a certain direction and amplitude (Schiller & Stryker, 1972; Sparks, Holland, & Guthrie, 1975), and the saccade responses are topographically organized (Robinson, 1972; Sparks et al., 1975; Wurtz & Goldberg, 1972), so that cells near one another respond to movements of a similar direction and amplitude. Electrostimulation of the deep layers of the structure results in saccades of fixed amplitude and direction independent of eye position. This supports the proposal that this nucleus transforms retinocentric position into eye-movement commands directly (see also Schiller, this volume).

Craniocentric Representations

Despite the appealing simplicity and physiological evidence for retincentric representations, behavioral and neural evidence from studies with adult primates have suggested that in some circumstances saccades are planned in craniocentric or egocentric, not retinocentric coordinates. Moreover, these higher order representations appear to derive from processing outside the colliculus.

Behavioral studies have shown that in adults information about the eyes' position and movement influences both the perception of the relative directions of visual targets flashed during saccades and the production of saccades (Matin & Pearce, 1965). The influence of eye position on saccade planning and other visual perceptual abilities suggests that a craniocentric or egocentric frame underlies mature saccade processing. The double-step saccade paradigm (Aslin & Shea, 1987; Becker & Jürgens, 1979; Feustel, Shea, & Aslin, 1982; Findlay & Harris, 1984; Lisberger, Fuchs, King, & Evinger, 1975; Westheimer, 1954) has been used to determine whether and how viewers plan saccades to multiple targets simultaneously and what spatial information is used in controlling saccades (Hallett & Lightstone, 1976a, 1976b). In this task (see Fig. 3.1), participants are instructed or trained to make saccades to sequences of two targets flashed briefly in different positions in a dark visual field. Typically, the second target appears and disappears shortly before or during the first saccade. Retinal information alone does not permit subjects to localize the second target accurately since the saccade to the first stimulus shifts the center of gaze and with it the second target's position relative to the retina. Accordingly, to make accurate saccades to the location of both stimuli, subjects must plan the direction and magnitude of the saccade to the second stimulus based on either the stimulus position defined relative to the head (craniocentric coordinates) or body (egocentric coordinates). Adult subjects make saccades directly toward the second target without delay or significant error in most circumstances suggesting that retinal position alone does not control mature saccade planning, but that eye or head position information plays a central role in determining the location of visual targets for even the most briefly presented of saccade targets (Hallett & Lightstone, 1976a, 1976b). Further, by manipulating the timing of the targets, Dassonville and colleagues (Dassonville, Schlag, & Schlag-Rey, 1992, 1993) found that the eye position signal used

Double Step Saccade Paradigm

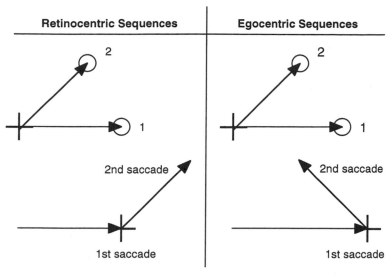

FIG. 3.1. Schematic depiction of the double-step saccade paradigm. While a subject maintains fixation at the location of the crosshairs, two visual targets flash one after the other. Subjects are instructed to make saccades to the targets. The figure indicates where subjects would look if they had coded the target locations using retinal positions alone (retinocentric sequence) or had represented the targets in a head- or body-centered representation (egocentric sequence).

for localizing and planning the second saccade is not instantaneously available, but requires several hundred milliseconds to update; therefore, in some conditions even adults make saccadic errors either to the retinocentric locations of the targets (Dassonville et al., 1992; Honda, 1989) or the vector average of these retinal positions (Aslin & Shea, 1987; Becker & Jürgens, 1979; Findlay, 1982; Honda, 1989). These results suggest that in adults the accurate localization of saccade targets is typically carried out in craniocentric or egocentric coordinates, but information about retinocentric position is maintained separately and may influence saccade planning in circumstances where the internal perception of eye position is inaccurate.

Craniocentric coordinates could underlie a unified saccade planning system that controls responses to both visual and auditory targets because the ears are also fixed with respect to the head. Further, neural and computational evidence supports the contention that craniocentric representations may be used by the brain. Extensive neurophysiological, neuropsychological, and neuroanatomical findings point to the parietal cortex as a crucial region in the brain for computations related to spatial processing and action planning (Goodale & Milner, 1992; Ungerleider & Mishkin,

1982). The parietal cortex receives information from and projects to visual, somaesthetic, proprioceptive, auditory, vestibular, oculomotor, limb control, and limbic centers (see Stein, 1992; also Andersen, Snyder, Li, & Stricanne, 1993, for reviews). Damage to parietal cortex causes a variety of spatial orienting and cognitive deficits in humans that appear to reflect the influence of multiple, body-centered and even object-based frames of reference (Behrmann & Tipper, 1994; Farah, Brunn, Wong, Wallace, & Carpenter, 1990; Moscovitch & Behrmann, 1994). Furthermore, there are two critical saccade planning areas in the parietal cortex, 7a and LIP, in which the neurons fire both in response to visual targets and fire in association with saccades. These cells have large retinocentric receptive fields. Some 30% have response properties that vary systematically with changes in the position of the eyes in the orbit (Andersen, Essick, & Siegel, 1985). Although the distribution of these cells is not systematic in the sense that the parietal cortex contains a topographic map of visual space in craniocentric coordinates, the cells with retinal and eye position sensitivity are sufficiently numerous and broadly tuned to constitute a distributed representation of craniocentric space (Andersen et al., 1993). These findings are also consistent with those that have found that the output of the SC incorporates information about eye position in planning saccades (Mays & Sparks, 1980a). These signals, however, appear to originate from cortical sources which project to the deep layers of the SC such as the parietal and frontal cortex (Schlag, Schlag-Rey, & Dassonville, 1991) or oculomotor regions of the brainstem or cerebellum (Schiller, this volume).

Additionally, computational simulations of visual spatial processing have shown that by systematically combining retinal and eye position signals in a neural network, units whose receptive fields approximate those of parietal neurons emerge (Goodman & Andersen, 1989; Pouget, Fisher, & Sejnowski, 1993; Zipser & Andersen, 1988). Zipser and Andersen (1988; Andersen & Zipser, 1988) presented a connectionist model in which the hidden layer units developed response properties closely resembling those observed within areas 7a and LIP. The basic architecture of their model is shown in Fig. 3.2. The model was a three-layered net with the input layer divided into two components, a "retina" in which a single visual target was represented by a Gaussian pattern of activity, and eye position units which coded the position of the eye in the head monotonically. Training consisted of presenting several hundred patterns of random eye position and retinal input to the network, and adjusting the weights between nodes in the layers according to the backpropagation algorithm (Rumelhart & McClelland, 1986). The trained output was the eye position independent, head-centered location of the target stimulus. Zipser and Andersen (1988) reported that after several hundred trials the network became very accurate in representing visual targets in craniocentric coordinates and the response

Architecture of Zipser & Andersen (1988) Network

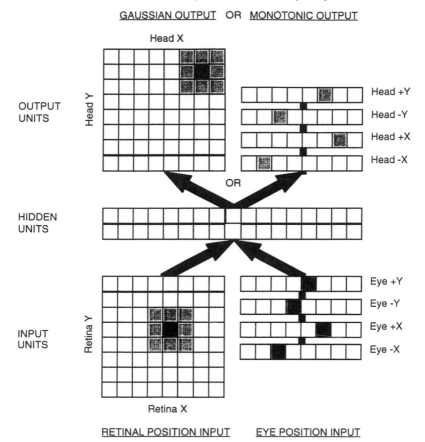

FIG. 3.2. Architecture of the Zipser and Andersen (1988) neural network model. Inputs are both the retinal position of a stimulus and the position of eyes relative to the head. One of two output representations was tested: a 2D Gaussian format similar to the retinal input and a monotonic representation of the XY coordinates of the target in head-centered coordinates. When trained using the backpropagation algorithm, the network's hidden units resembled those found in eye movement-related regions of the posterior parietal cortex.

patterns of nodes in the hidden layer strikingly resembled those of cells found in regions of the parietal cortex, area 7a and LIP. That is, the cells were sensitive to both retinal and eye positions. Goodman and Andersen (1989) extended this result by showing that a network similarly trained could generate signals corresponding to saccades which would align the center of the retina with a specified target, in a manner similar to that observed by stimulating posterior parietal regions.

Egocentric Representation

The craniocentric model is probably the dominant view of saccade planning, but it cannot easily account for the fact that most skilled shifts of gaze involve the coordinated movement of both the head and eyes (Bizzi, 1974). Because a shift in the position of the head relative to the trunk also shifts the origin of the craniocentric frame of reference, the direction of visual targets and the motor commands that move the head and eyes might be coded in an egocentric spatial frame of reference centered at the trunk. Andersen and colleagues have provided physiological evidence in support of the notion that posterior parietal cortex may instantiate multiple representations of space (Andersen et al., 1993). These authors have found visually responsive cells that modulate their firing based on changes in retinal, eye in head, and head on trunk coordinates (Brotchie, Andersen, Snyder, & Goodman, 1995). Whereas a body-centered or egocentric frame of reference poses potentially difficult problems for saccade planning, it might serve as common point of reference for spatial sensory systems not isolated to the head, such as the sense of touch (see Moscovitch & Behrmann, 1994) and might prove useful in generating other more complex other forms of action such as visually guided reaching or locomotion. For example, Guenther and colleagues (Guenther, Bullock, Greve, & Grossberg, 1994) demonstrated how a neural network system that combined retinotopic position, eye and head position signals could be trained to determine the 3D spatial position of a target in the visual environment. This simulation used random head, but not eye, movements to points in space and a simulated vestibular ocular reflex that kept a given spatial target in fixation in order to calibrate the set of retina, eye, and head positions that corresponded to 3D target positions. Still, the fact that young infants have poor eye and head control suggests that accurate egocentric representations of space are not present from birth.

Summary

A retinocentric representation of saccade targets has an attractive computational simplicity and is apparently instantiated in the subcortical visual pathway from the retina to the upper layers of the superior colliculus. Nevertheless, behavioral studies with adults suggest that saccades are normally planned in craniocentric or egocentric coordinates, whereas neural and computational evidence suggests that the parietal cortex plays a central role in the representation and processing of spatial information in multiple body-centered frames of reference. In the next section we discuss how patterns of brain development imply specific changes in visual spatial representations early in life.

HOW DO REPRESENTATIONS FOR ACTION CHANGE
DURING DEVELOPMENT?

The gradual development of visuomotor areas strongly suggests that information processing, and by extension representations of visual space, change as babies' neurocomputational circuitry develops through interaction with experience. For example, a number of authors have recently suggested that some of the changes in visual orienting and saccade planning behavior that take place after birth may be attributable to the emergence of functioning in the parietal cortex (Hood, Atkinson, & Braddick, chap. 7, this volume; Johnson 1994, 1995b). These claims are based on a number of sources of evidence including (a) developmental neuroanatomy, (b) resting PET scans, and (c) the functional role of the parietal cortex in saccade planning and covert shifts of visual attention (see also Hood et al., this volume; Maurer & Lewis, chap. 2, this volume). In this section we review some recent empirical studies from our laboratory that explore the dynamics of representational change for saccades in early infancy.

If subcortical systems dominate the orienting responses of younger infants, then the representations associated with subcortical processing should most strongly influence saccade planning early in life and there should be a gradual shift in the representation controlling action as cortical systems become functional and begin to influence shifts of gaze. Consequently, we predicted that retinocentric information should dominate younger infants' saccade planning and that there should be a shift toward craniocentric or egocentric saccade planning in accord with the gradual development of parietal visual attention areas. We tested this hypothesis with three separate experiments based on the double-step saccade paradigm described previously.

In two experiments (Gilmore & Johnson, 1997), 4- to 6-month-old infants viewed a display that attracted their attention to one of three computer monitors and was followed by sequences of two brief visual targets that flashed on the other monitors, one after the other, in a randomly selected pattern (see Fig. 3.3A). The targets elicited sequences of eye movements that were recorded on videotape and subsequently coded for direction and latency. Sequences were classified as *retinocentric* if the babies' saccades corresponded to the pattern that would occur if the infant had merely assigned to each saccade a distance and direction equal to the target's position on the retina at the time it appeared (see Fig. 3.3A, col. 2). Sequences were classified as *egocentric* (because the head was fixed, not free) if they visited both target locations in order (see Fig. 3.3, col. 3). Single target control trials (Fig. 3.3B) were presented as a control for the possibility that 4- and 6-month-olds could differ in their capacity to make long eye movements independent of the specific form of spatial representation.

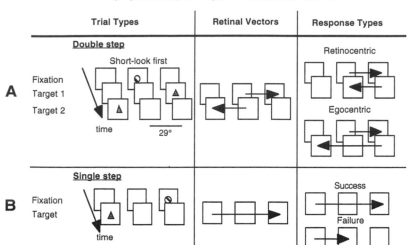

FIG. 3.3.   Design of the one-dimensional infant versions of the double-step task. Column 1 shows the sequence of stimuli for double- and single-step trials. Column 2 shows the retinal position vectors. Column 3 depicts the scheme for coding responses.

Figure 3.4 summarizes the results from the two studies. It shows that the relative proportion of egocentric to retinocentric sequences was significantly smaller in the group of 4- to 5-month-olds than in the 6-month-old groups. A marginally significant difference in the proportion of long looks relative to short ones was found in the first study but not the second. The smaller proportion of egocentric saccades to the target location in the younger group suggested that younger infants less reliably integrated retinal and somatosensory sources of spatial information and therefore relied on a retinocentric coding of visual target position in planning saccade sequences. The fact that the mean proportion of successful long saccades in the control trials did not differ significantly argues against an alternative explanation in terms of differences in the ability to make long saccades. We interpret the results as meaning that a retinocentric representation of space dominates saccade planning in the youngest of infants in most circumstances, but gradual development of cortical, probably parietal, circuitry permits functional egocentric representations to subsequently emerge.

Another experiment sought direct evidence for the presumed diminishing collicular role in saccade planning. In this study we attempted to elicit saccades to the location equivalent to the vector sum or average of two simultaneously presented targets. Stimulation of many cells in the superior colliculus elicits saccades equivalent to the retinal error between the current fixation point and the center of the cell's receptive field (Mays

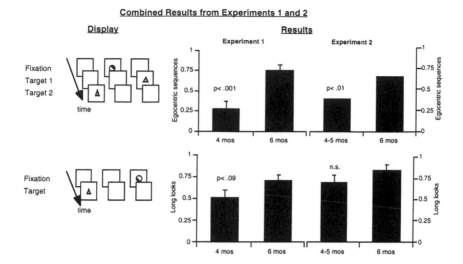

FIG. 3.4. Results from one-dimensional infant double-step tasks. In both studies, younger (4–5-month-old) infants made significantly more retino-centric and fewer egocentric sequences than did 6-month-olds.

& Sparks, 1980a; Robinson, 1972; Schlag-Rey et al., 1989). The stimulation of two or more such cells results in a saccade that is the average of each stimulated cell's retinal error or movement vector (Robinson, 1972), sug-gesting that normal saccade commands involve vector averaging (Mays & Sparks, 1980b; Van Gisbergen, Van Opstal, & Tax, 1987) or weighted averaging (Ottes, Van Gisbergen, & Eggermont, 1984) of responses asso-ciated with the active population of cells. Adult observers make retinocen-tric vector average saccades in circumstances when the distances between targets are small or the responses are speeded (Aslin & Shea, 1987; Becker & Jürgens, 1979; Findlay, 1982; Honda, 1989). We reasoned that because the averaging of retinal position vectors is a hallmark of processing in the superior colliculus, the prevalence of vector averaging in infants' saccades may serve as a marker for the extent of influence of the subcortical reti-nocollicular pathway.

Accordingly, we recorded the saccades of 12 infants in each of three age groups (2, 4, and 6 months) who viewed pairs of brief (200 ms) visual targets presented simultaneously in a two dimensional array (Johnson et al., 1996; see Fig. 3.5). We predicted that the extent of spontaneous saccade errors to the retinal vector average location would decline in older groups of infants. Figure 3.6 shows the proportion of vector average responses declined significantly between 2 and 6 months as predicted. A follow-up analysis confirmed that saccade planning toward one target was affected by the presence of the second target, as the vector average hypothesis predicts. But

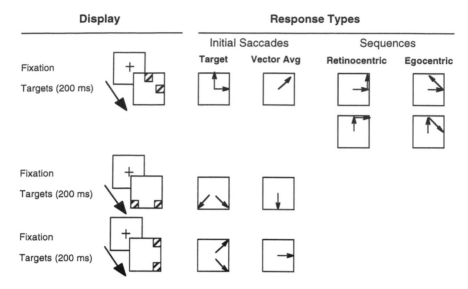

FIG. 3.5. Design of two-dimensional infant double-step task with simultaneous targets.

because data were not collected about the accuracy of saccades to single targets or the baseline rates of responding in the absence of any target, we cannot rule out the possibility that some age-related improvements in saccade accuracy account for a portion of the observed decline in vector average reponses.

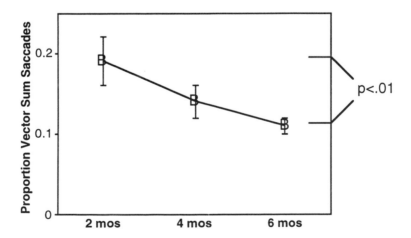

FIG. 3.6. Results from two-dimensional infant double-step task with simultaneous targets. The proportion of saccades to the vector average/sum location declined significantly from 2 to 6 months.

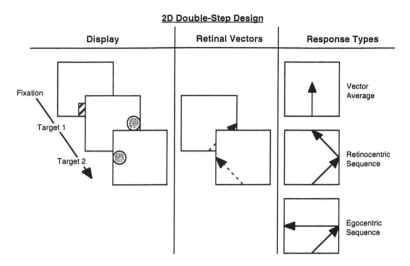

FIG. 3.7. Design of the two-dimensional infant double-step task with sequential targets.

Finally, we recently examined the patterns of saccade sequences made by 3- and 7-month-olds infants performing a two-dimensional version of the double-step task (Gilmore & Johnson, in press; see Fig. 3.7). In this experiment younger babies made more initial saccades to the retinal vector average location (3 months: .15 of first looks; 7 months: .06), more retinocentric saccade sequences ending at a location where no stimulus flashed (3 months: .50 of sequences; 7 months: .25), and fewer egocentric sequences to the actual target locations (3 months: .08 of sequences; 7 months: .40). Thus, in three separate experiments we observed an increase with age in egocentric saccade sequences to sequential saccade targets, and in two studies we observed a decline in initial saccades to the sum or average of the two targets' retinal positions. The combined results support the hypothesis that the representations for saccades between 2 and 7 months of age shift from retinocentric to cranio- or egocentric in accord with the graded experience-dependent development of cortical, especially parietal, centers where these higher order representations are instantiated.

TOWARD AN INTEGRATED FRAMEWORK

At the outset we set forward three questions that served to guide our explorations of the computational issues in saccade development: What are the representations that drive saccades early in life; how do they change in development; and why do they change? An assessment of information processing in the primate visual attention pathways showed the subcortical and cortical (parietal) pathways represent visuomotor space in different ways. Combined with evidence concerning patterns in the postnatal development of the human brain, we predicted that retinocentric representations, which are mediated by the subcortical pathway, would dominate saccade planning in young infants, and that craniocentric and egocentric representations, which are mediated by the cortical, parietal pathway, would emerge gradually during the first year of life. It is in the period around 6 months that spatial processing circuitry in the parietal cortex is presumed to develop rapidly. Behavioral evidence from two studies using the double-step saccade paradigm supported these predictions. Egocentric saccade sequences increased between 3 and 7 months, while retinocentric and vector sum saccades declined over this period. In short, the subcortical to cortical shift in saccade control is paralleled by a shift from retinocentric to cranio- or egocentric spatial processing.

This account is far from complete, however. For example, it fails to explain fully what benefits, in computational or behavioral terms, the infant derives from changes in visual representation, and what drives their emergence. It is easy to demonstrate that representations of visual space in head or body-centered coordinates are more useful in planning a variety of visually guided actions—looking, reaching, kicking, locomotion—than those defined solely in retinal coordinates. This flexibility comes at a price, however; more complex representations for action require additional degrees of freedom, and this raises a critical question about how such a system could emerge without extensive periods of calibration.

Higher order frames of reference involve increasing numbers of inputs—eye position relative to the head and head position relative to the body—whose spatial and temporal resolution must be precise in order to guide behavior accurately. Because signals specifying retinal position, eye position, and head are independent, any errors associated with each of these variables would sum. Consequently, the further removed a frame used for saccade control lies from direct retinal input, the greater the potential error between perceived and actual position in that frame. As a result, in order to minimize each individual error component and the total error, calibration of the separate signals that contribute to each spatial representation may be essential. Even for the simplest retinocentric model, the saccade system must calibrate the relationship between retinal position and saccade commands, given the general lack of patterned visual input for saccades prior to birth. Aslin (1993) explored this possibility in a simple model which made essentially random saccades and modified its parameters by comparing the resulting retinal stimulation after the saccade with the initial retinal input. Aslin concluded both that the retinal to motor mapping must have some sort of primitive structure, perhaps similar to the topography and processing characteristics of the subcortical pathway, and that learning the retinal to motor mapping would take a large number of random saccade learning trials. For representations in craniocentric space, the need for calibration and the period of learning is even greater, of course. Motor commands must be calibrated with actual (proprioceptive) or predicted (efference copy) movements of the eyes in order to determine an accurate internal signal of eye position. Similarly, saccade processing in an egocentric frame would require the calibration of both eye position and head position signals, which include skin and muscle proprioceptive information, vestibular, and visual information from optic flow patterns.

Consequently, it may be impractical for the infants' visuomotor system to depend on error prone higher order representations until the calibration process has made sufficient progress. Therefore, we believe that the use of a retinocentric representation early in life corresponds to a form of bootstrapping procedure, which provides the infant with sufficient information to move the eyes toward visual targets and to sample the range of retinal, eye, and even head positions that result from the active visual exploration of a patterned visual environment. The retinocentric representation is not as powerful, accurate, or flexible as the head-, trunk-, and other body-centered representations that emerge later on in development to control visually guided behavior, but it is sufficient to provide a framework for learning to proceed and it is embodied in a visuomotor pathway that is functioning from very early in postnatal life. Obviously, this account predicts that active visual exploration plays a vital role in the normal development of visual spatial processing systems in the cortex, a claim consistent with a broad range of experiments on the development of other forms of visually guided behavior (Walk, 1978).

This discussion raises an intriguing alternative to the way in which we have characterized spatial representations and their development. In this view, which we call the *dynamic retinal update model*, information processing involved in saccade planning retinotopic representations of visual space that shift dynamically in accord with changes in eye position *that are about to be made* (Duhamel, Colby, & Goldberg, 1993; Duhamel, Goldberg, Fitzgibbon, Sirigu, & Grafman, 1992). There is both behavioral and physiological evidence to support this claim. Duhamel and colleagues (Duhamel et al., 1992) studied an adult patient with lesions to the left parietal and frontal cortex who showed failures on the double-step paradigm. The patient failed to make a second saccade toward the ipsilesional side when the first saccade was in the contralesional direction, despite showing no deficits on ipsilesional saccades when single targets were presented alone. The absence of ipsilesional deficits suggested that there was no selective damage to representations of that side of craniocentric or egocentric space. Instead, the authors interpreted these results as supporting a failure to update internal retinotopic representations in accord with planned or recently performed saccades. In addition, behavioral data on double-step saccade tasks which varied the intervals between targets and saccade onset suggested that accuracy in orienting to the target's positions in craniocentric space improved as the interval between targets increased or as actual eye position grew closer to the first saccade goal (Dassonville et al., 1993). Physiological studies have shown that some cells in saccade-related areas of the parietal cortex shift their normally retinotopic receptive fields in advance of a saccade that is about to bring a target into the appropriate position on the fovea.

Taken together, these results imply that spatial representation in the brain is dynamic, dependent on current and planned actions, and in the mature animal relies on circuitry in the parietal lobe (Duhamel, Colby, & Goldberg, 1993). This suggests that young infants may fail to demonstrate higher order, egocentric, representations for saccades not because they lack these representations per se, but because they do not have accurate internal representations of eye position or have representations that do not update sufficiently rapidly to influence saccade planning. Although our current behavioral data do not speak to this question directly, a number of avenues for future work including additional behavioral studies, computational modeling, and neuroimaging offer promise for a clearer understanding of the neurodevelopment of visually guided action. We now discuss these approaches.

Behavioral Markers for Neurocognitive Systems

One way to unravel the emerging interaction between the different pathways outlined by Schiller and others is to develop "marker tasks" for studying their function. Marker tasks are versions of tasks associated with particular neural pathways through cognitive neuroscience studies involving brain imaging, brain damaged patients, or animal studies, which are suitable for testing human infants. We have illustrated the use of marker tasks for computations in the parietal cortex and in the superior colliculus. To understand the function of each of the visual attention pathways and the interactions among them we must develop additional tasks that indicate the emergence of functional processing in a given region or pathway (see Maurer & Lewis, this volume; Hood, Atkinson, & Braddick, this volume; Richards & Hunter, this volume; Rafal, this volume).

For example, an indicator of frontal cortex damage in humans is an inability to suppress involuntary automatic saccades toward targets, and an apparent inability to control volitional saccades (Fischer & Breitmeyer, 1987; Guitton, Buchtel, & Douglas, 1985). Guitton et al. (1985) studied normal subjects and patients with frontal or temporal lobe lesions in a so-called "anti-saccade" task. In this task subjects are instructed to *not* look at a briefly flashed cue, but to make a saccade in the opposite direction (Hallett, 1978). Guitton et al. (1985) reported that although normal subjects and patients with temporal lobe damage could do this task with relative ease, patients with frontal damage, and especially those with damage around the FEF, were severely impaired. In particular, the frontal patients had difficulty suppressing unwanted saccades toward the cue stimulus.

Clearly, one cannot give verbal instructions to a young infant to look to the side opposite from where the cue stimulus appears. Instead, infants must be motivated to look at the second of two opposite peripheral stimuli more than at the first (Johnson, 1995b). This can be done by making the second stimulus reliably more dynamic and colorful than the first. After a number of such trials infants may learn to inhibit their tendency to make a saccade to the first stimulus (the cue) when it appears, in order to respond as rapidly as possible to the more attractive second stimulus (the target). Four-month-olds showed a significant decrease in frequency of looking to the first (cue) stimulus over a number of such trials (Johnson, 1995b). A second experiment demonstrated that this decrement was not due to differential habituation to the simpler stimulus. Since 4-month-olds are able to inhibit saccades to a peripheral stimulus, it seems reasonable to infer that their FEF circuit is functioning by this age.

Other tasks recently administered to infants are consistent with increasing endogenous control exerted by prefrontal regions over shifts of attention and saccades around 6 months of age. For example, Goldman-Rakic and colleagues (Funahashi, Bruce, & Goldman-Rakic, 1989, 1990) used an oculomotor delayed-response paradigm to study the properties of neurons in the dorsolateral prefrontal cortex of macaque monkeys. In this task the monkey plans a saccade toward a particular spatial location, but must wait for a period (usually between 2 and 5 sec) before executing the saccade. Single unit recording in the macaque indicates that cells in the dorsolateral prefrontal cortex code for the direction of the saccade during the delay. Further, reversible microlesions to the area result in selective amnesia for saccades to a localized part of the visual field. A recent PET study on human subjects has confirmed the involvement of prefrontal cortex (and parietal cortex) in this task (Jonides, Smith, Koeppe, Awh, Minoshima, & Mintun, 1993). Gilmore and Johnson (1995) devised an infant version of the oculomotor delayed-response task. The results indicate that six month olds can delay saccades successfully for at least 5 seconds, suggesting some influence of this region of the prefrontal cortex on eye movement control by this age.

Additional behavioral tasks might examine other spatially oriented behaviors that emerge between 4 and 6 months of age, but whose computational aspects have been largely unexplored—e.g., saccades guided by sound or visually guided reaching. Auditory localization relies on timing, intensity, and frequency differences between the two ears, whose position with respect to the head is fixed. Consequently, auditory localization must use craniocentric representations of target locations, while reaching presumably depends on trunk or even arm-centered representations. Although the relationship between brain development and behavioral development in these domains is less well known, both may provide information about spatial processing in the cortex. For example, the initial representation of auditory information in the nervous system is frequency, not location based, so accurate auditory localization may require cortical processing mechanisms (Muir, Clifton, & Clarkson, 1989), and neural representations of space in arm-centered coordinates have recently been reported in the premotor cortex (Graziano, Yap, & Gross, 1994) of monkeys trained to reach for visual targets.

Computational Studies of Sensorimotor Transformations

Previous computational studies of visuomotor processing have provided powerful tools for exploring theories about the function of these systems in mature animals, but only recently have they provided insights into the problems faced by the developing organism. A critical issue for future simulations is the incorporation of more realistic assumptions about the sources of information for learning. The Zipser and Andersen (1988) model trained a network to predict craniocentric target position, but in the actual biological system there is probably no teaching signal that specifies these coordinates veridically. Nor is there a simple relationship between craniocentric position, eye, and retinal position because a given position in space corresponds to an infinite combination of eye and retinal positions. A potentially useful tool exploring how complex sensorimotor transformations might be learned in the absence of veridical error signals is the forward model approach (Jordan & Rumelhart, 1992). In this scheme, the network learns to change its output by predicting what it will sense next, given the current input and a proposed output. In the context of saccade planning, this would correspond to the brain learning to predict what the pattern of retinal stimulation will appear like and what eye position will be given a visual scene and a planned saccade as input. It is intriguing to note that the parietal cells that apparently remap retinotopic space in accord with future eye movements (Duhamel et al., 1993) are broadly consistent with the predictions of the forward model. The development of biologically plausible models of sensorimotor behavior that incorporate realistic learning and processing constraints should be the ultimate goal of future modeling efforts.

Functional Brain Imaging of Action Planning

Finally, in order to understand the unique contributions of the multiple visual attention pathways and their complex interactions, it is essential that we gather direct information about the activity of the brain in the course of visual orienting behavior. A general hypothesis advanced in this chapter is that cortical (egocentric) representations for saccade planning gradually emerge through the infant's interaction with the environment mediated by subcortical retinocentric representations. We have begun to gather evidence pertaining to this hypothesis through the use of high-density event-related potential recordings of the brain electric activity from the scalp surface of infants.

In adults, there are a number of characteristic saccade-related potentials (SRPs) preceding the onset of a saccade (for a review, see Kurtzberg & Vaughan, 1982). In case of visually triggered, target-directed saccades one can normally record two of them: the presaccadic positivity which is a gradually increasing centro-parietal activity, culminating in the second, which is the sharp parietal spike potential just prior to target onset (see Fig. 3.8). Both probably originate from the eye-movement related areas of the parietal cortex, but the activity of the supplementary eye field (SEF) may also contribute to the presaccadic positivity. Although the amplitude of these components vary with certain experimental manipulations (Csibra,

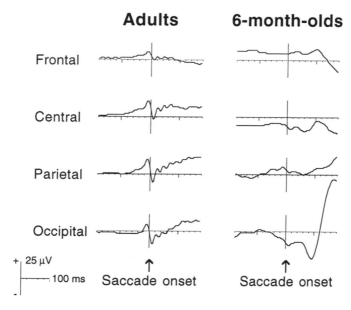

FIG. 3.8. Characteristic examples of saccade-related potentials in adults (left column) and 6-month-old infants (right column).

Johnson, & Tucker, 1997), they seem to be obligatory constituents of the adult SRPs and may reflect important aspects of cortical saccade planning such as constructing predictive retinotopic maps of the visual field.

Evidence from infants, however, has revealed that these SRP components are weak, less synchronized to the saccade execution, or even completely absent in 6-month-olds (Csibra, Tucker, & Johnson, 1996; see also Vaughan & Kurtzberg, 1989). At least in the procedures we have studied, their waveforms do not appear to show the characteristic presaccadic spike (see Fig. 3.8). Nevertheless, at the parietal lead the average SRP amplitude just preceding the saccade onset tends to be more positive than in the earlier periods. This tendency, however, is an aggregate of entirely different waveforms obtained from individual infants. Approximately half of the infants we have studied display positive–negative patterns resembling the adult spike, but these components are more elongated in time and less clearly aligned to the saccade execution than the adults' spike. Others show only a positive-going deflection that later transforms into the postsaccadic visual potentials and still others do not manifest anything comparable with the adults' presaccadic potentials. In summary, at 6 months of age the eye-movement related areas in the parietal cortex appear to be functioning in some infants but their activity is unlikely to be reliable enough to directly control saccade execution.

This conclusion is consistent with the idea that saccade planning at this age is still largely under subcortical control and the parietal circuits are still in the learning (calibration) phase that is needed to take over the control over the subcortical pathways. This conclusion is strengthened by the fact that the SRP components associated with the processing of the retinal input during and after the saccade are not reduced—in fact, they seem to be enhanced in 6-month-olds as compared to adults (Csibra et al., 1996). These postsaccadic components, which are already present in newborns (Vaughan & Kurtzberg, 1989), reflect the visual processing of the refixated retinal input. In addition to the occipital region they extend to the parietal and posterior temporal areas. The integration of the pre- and postsaccadic retinotopic maps together with the information about the direction of the executed saccade and the position of the eyes is essential for building higher order representations for action control. The electrophysiological data suggest that this integration is not yet complete by 6 months of age.

The absence or weakness of sophisticated spatial representations for guiding saccades does not mean, however, that the cerebral cortex plays no role in visually guided behavior. Various pathways enable the cortex to modulate (inhibit or disinhibit) the functioning of subcortical centers thereby influencing the eye movements. As mentioned earlier, 4-month-olds can inhibit automatic saccades toward peripheral stimuli (Johnson, 1995b), which indicates that the FEF is functioning by that age. Event-related potential results from our laboratory also suggest that structures in the frontal cortex play an active role in regulating reflexive eye movements in 6-month-old infants (Csibra et al., 1996). Specifically, if a central fixation stimulus goes off 200 ms prior to the onset of a peripheral target, a left frontal positivity is observed just after the target onset (see Fig. 3.9). In these trials the saccadic reaction times are also considerably smaller than in the trials where the fixation stimulus stays on (by over 50 ms). In addition to releasing of suppression of reflexive eye movements within the SC (Dorris & Munoz, 1995), the fixation offset can also exert its effect via the FEF by facilitating target-directed saccades initiated by the SC. Although this

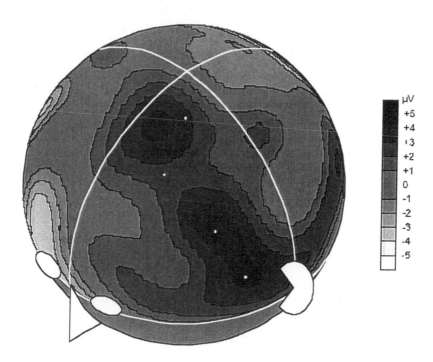

FIG. 3.9. Scalp voltage surface map of a difference potential recorded from 12 6-month-old infants by a high-density electrode array incorporating 62 sensors. The potential is the average amplitude difference in the postarget 100–200 ms interval between trials when the fixation stimulus went off 200 ms prior to target onset and trials when it stayed on. White spots mark the electrode locations where the difference is statistically significant ($p < .005$).

cortical regulation of subcortical activity does not require complex spatial mapping, it may indirectly contribute to the construction of more sophisticated spatial representations by regulating action in a way that trains cortical circuits appropriately.

One general implication of the foregoing results is that even if at the behavioral level infants seem functioning similarly to adults, their performance might be based on the working of somewhat different neural structures. Functional neuroimaging techniques, such as recording event-related brain potentials, can help us to uncover such subtle differences.

CONCLUSION

An adequate computational model of the development of saccadic control must integrate information from infant visual orienting behavior, theoretical and modeling studies of mechanisms for sensorimotor transformations, and an examination of the patterns of postnatal brain development. We have sketched out some of the considerations for such a model. The finding that infants' representation of space for saccades changes in the first several months of life points out the rich, and as yet largely untapped, potential for explorations of the neural mechanisms of spatial cognition early in life. Surely the time is now ripe for a thorough examination of the development one of the most fundamental forms of adaptive behavior: perception and action in space.

ACKNOWLEDGMENTS

We thank Leslie Tucker, Sarah Minister, Sarah Hesketh, and Margaret Brockbank for assistance with the experiments reported and with the preparation of this manuscript. We acknowledge financial support from the Medical Research Council of the United Kingdom. Additional financial support was provided by the National Academy of Sciences, The Scientific Research Society, and the American Psychological Association to ROG, and by a grant from the Human Frontiers Scientific Foundation to MHJ and GC.

REFERENCES

Alexander, G. E., DeLong, M. R., & Strick, P. L. (1986). Parallel organization of functionally segregated circuits linking basal ganglia and cortex. *Annual Review of Neuroscience, 9,* 357–382.

Andersen, R. A., Essick, G. K., & Siegel, R. M. (1985). Encoding of spatial location by posterior parietal neurons. *Science, 230*, 456–458.

Andersen, R. A., Snyder, L. H., Li, C. S., & Stricanne, B. (1993). Coordinate transformations in the representation of spatial information. *Current Opinion in Neurobiology, 3*, 171–176.

Andersen, R. A., & Zipser, D. (1988). The role of the posterior parietal cortex in coordinate transformations for visual-motor integration. *Canadian Journal of Physiology & Pharmacology, 66*, 488–501.

Aslin, R. N. (1993). Perception of visual direction in human infants. In C. E. Granrud (Ed.), *Visual perception and cognition in infancy*. Hillsdale, NJ: Lawrence Erlbaum Associates.

Aslin, R. N., & Shea, S. L. (1987). The amplitude and angle of saccades to double-step target displacements. *Vision Research, 27*(11), 1925–1942.

Atkinson, J. (1984). Human visual development over the first six months of life: A review and a hypothesis. *Human Neurobiology, 3*, 61–74.

Becker, L. E., Armstrong, D. L., Chan, F., & Wood, M. M. (1984). Dendritic development on human occipital cortex neurones. *Brain Research, 315*, 117–124.

Becker, W., & Jürgens, R. (1979). An analysis of the saccadic system by means of double step stimuli. *Vision Research, 19*, 967–983.

Behrmann, M., & Tipper, S. P. (1994). Object-based attentional mechanisms: Evidence from patients with unilateral neglect. In C. Umiltà & M. Moscovitch (Eds.), *Attention and performance XV: Conscious and nonconscious information processing* (pp. 351–375). Cambridge, MA: MIT Press.

Bizzi, E. (1974). The coordination of eye-head movement. *Scientific American, 231*, 100–106.

Bronson, G. W. (1974). The postnatal growth of visual capacity. *Child Development, 45*, 873–890.

Bronson, G. W. (1982). Structure, status and characteristics of the nervous system at birth. In P. Stratton (Ed.), *Psychobiology of the human newborn* (pp. 99–118). Chichester, England: Wiley.

Brotchie, P. R., Andersen, R. A., Snyder, L. H., & Goodman, S. J. (1995). Head position signals used by parietal neurons to encode locations of visual stimuli. *Nature, 375*, 232–235.

Burkhalter, A., & Bernardo, K. L. (1989). Organization of corticocortical connections in human visual cortex. *Proceedings of the National Academy of Sciences, 86*, 1071–1075.

Csibra, G., Johnson, M. H., & Tucker, L. (1997). Attention and oculomotor control: A high-density ERP study of the gap effect. *Neuropsychologia, 35*, 855–865.

Csibra, G., Tucker, A. L., & Johnson, M. H. (1996). Neural correlates of saccade planning in infants: A high density ERP study. *Developmental Cognitive Neuroscience Technical Reports, No. 96.3*, MRC Cognitive Development Unit, London.

Dassonville, P., Schlag, J., & Schlag-Rey, M. (1992). Oculomotor localization relies on damped representation of saccadic eye displacement in human and nonhuman primates. *Visual Neuroscience, 9*, 261–269.

Dassonville, P., Schlag, J., & Schlag-Rey, M. (1993). Direction constancy in the oculomotor system. *Current Directions in Psychological Science, 2*(5), 143–147.

Dorris, M. C., & Munoz, D. P. (1995). A neural correlate for the gap effect on saccadic reaction times in monkey. *Journal of Neurophysiology, 73*, 2558–2562.

Duhamel, J. R., Colby, C. L., & Goldberg, M. E. (1993). The updating of the representation of visual space in parietal cortex by intended eye movements. *Science, 255*, 90–92.

Duhamel, J. R., Goldberg, M. E., Fitzgibbon, E. J., Sirigu, A., & Grafman, J. (1992). Saccadic dysmetria in a patient with a right frontoparietal lesion: The importance of corollary discharge for accurate spatial behaviour. *Brain, 115*, 1387–1402.

Farah, M. J., Brunn, J. L., Wong, A. B., Wallace, M. A., & Carpenter, P. A. (1990). Frames of reference for allocating attention to space: Evidence from the neglect syndrome. *Neuropsychologia, 28*(4), 335–347.

Feustel, T. C., Shea, S. L., & Aslin, R. N. (1982). Saccadic eye movements to successive target steps. *Investigative Opthalmalogy and Visual Science, Supplement, 22*(105), 14.

Findlay, J. M. (1982). Global visual processing for saccadic eye movements. *Vision Research, 22,* 1033–1045.

Findlay, J. M., & Harris, L. R. (1984). Small saccades to double-stepped targets moving in two dimensions. In A. Gale & B. Johnson (Eds.), *Theoretical and applied aspects of eye movement research* (pp. 71–78). Amsterdam: Elsevier.

Fischer, B., & Breitmeyer, B. (1987). Mechanisms of visual attention revealed by saccadic eye movements. *Neuropsychologia, 25,* 73–83.

Funahashi, S., Bruce, C. J., & Goldman-Rakic, P. S. (1989). Mnemonic coding of visual space in the monkey's dorsolateral prefrontal cortex. *Journal of Neurophysiology, 61*(2), 331–349.

Funahashi, S., Bruce, C. J., & Goldman-Rakic, P. S. (1990). Visuospatial coding in primate prefrontal neurons revealed by oculomotor paradigms. *Journal of Neurophysiology, 63*(4), 814–831.

Gilmore, R. O., & Johnson, M. H. (1995). Working memory in infancy: Six-month-olds' performance on two versions of the oculomotor delayed response task. *Journal of Experimental Child Psychology, 59,* 397–418.

Gilmore, R. O., & Johnson, M. H. (in press). Body-centered representations for visually-guided action emerge during early infancy. *Cognition*

Gilmore, R. O., & Johnson, M. H. (1997). Egocentric action in early infancy: Spatial frames of reference for saccades. *Psychological Science, 8,* 224–230.

Goodale, M. A., & Milner, A. D. (1992). Separate pathways for perception and action. *Trends in Neuroscience, 15*(1), 20–25.

Goodman, S. J., & Andersen, R. A. (1989). Microstimulation of a neural network model for visually guided saccades. *Journal of Cognitive Neuroscience, 1,* 317–326.

Graziano, M. S. A., Yap, G. S., & Gross, C. G. (1994). Coding of visual space by premotor neurons. *Science, 266,* 1054–1057.

Guenther, F. H., Bullock, D., Greve, D., & Grossberg, S. (1994). Neural representations for sensorimotor control. III. Learning a body-centered representation of a three-dimensional target position. *Journal of Cognitive Neuroscience, 6*(4), 341–358.

Guitton, H. A., Buchtel, H. A., & Douglas, R. M. (1985). Frontal lobe lesions in man cause difficulties in suppressing refexive glances and in generating goal-directed saccades. *Experimental Brain Research, 58,* 455–472.

Hallett, P. E. (1978). Primary and secondary saccades to goals defined by instructions. *Vision Research, 18,* 1270–1296.

Hallett, P. E., & Lightstone, A. D. (1976a). Saccadic eye movements to flashed targets. *Vision Research, 114,* 107–114.

Hallett, P. E., & Lightstone, A. D. (1976b). Saccadic eye movements towards stimuli triggered by prior saccades. *Vision Research, 16,* 99–106.

Honda, H. (1989). Perceptual localization of visual stimuli flashed during saccades. *Perception and Psychophysics, 45,* 162–174.

Huttenlocher, P. R. (1990). Morphometric study of human cerebral cortex development. *Neuropsychologia, 28,* 517–527.

Johnson, M. H. (1990). Cortical maturation and the development of visual attention. *Journal of Cognitive Neuroscience, 21,* 81–95.

Johnson, M. H. (1994). Dissociating components of visual attention: A neurodevelopmental approach. In M. J. Farah & G. Radcliffe (Eds.), *The neural basis of high-level vision* (pp. 241–268). Hillsdale, NJ: Lawrence Erlbaum Associates.

Johnson, M. H. (1995a). The development of visual attention: A cognitive neuroscience Perspective. In M. S. Gazzaniga (Ed)., *The cognitive neurosciences* (pp. 735–750). Cambridge, MA: MIT Press.

Johnson, M. H. (1995b). The inhibition of automatic saccades in early infancy. *Developmental Psychobiology, 28*(5), 281–291.

Johnson, M. H., Gilmore, R. O., Tucker, L. A., & Minister, S. L. (1996). Vector summation in young infants. *Brain and Cognition, 32,* 237–243.

Jonides, J., Smith, E. E., Koeppe, R. A., Awh, E., Minoshima, S., & Mintun, M. A. (1993). Spatial working memory in humans as revealed by PET. *Nature, 363,* 623–625.

Jordan, M. I., & Rumelhart, D. E. (1992). Forward models: Supervised learning with a distal teacher. *Cognitive Science, 16,* 307–354.

Kurtzberg, D., & Vaughan, H. G., Jr. (1982). Topographic analysis of human cortical potentials preceding self-initiated and visually triggered saccades. *Brain Research, 243,* 1–9.

Lisberger, S. G., Fuchs, A. F., King, W. M., & Evinger, L. C. (1975). Effect of mean reaction time on saccadic responses to two-step stimuli with horizontal and vertical components. *Vision Research, 15,* 1021–1025.

Matin, L., & Pearce, D. G. (1965). Visual perception of direction for stimuli flashed during voluntary saccadic eye movements. *Science, 148,* 1485–1488.

Mays, L. E., & Sparks, D. L. (1980a). Dissociation of visual and saccade related responses in superior colliculus neurons. *Journal of Neurophysiology, 43,* 207–232.

Mays, L. E., & Sparks, D. L. (1980b). Saccades are spatially, not retinocentrically coded. *Science, 208,* 1163–1165.

Moscovitch, M., & Behrmann, M. (1994). Coding of spatial information in the somatosensory system: Evidence from patients with neglect following parietal lobe damage. *Journal of Cognitive Neuroscience, 6*(2), 151–155.

Muir, D. W., Clifton, R. K., & Clarkson, M. G. (1989). The development of a human auditory localization response: A U-shaped function. *Canadian Journal of Psychology, 43,* 199–216.

Ottes, F. P., Van Gisbergen, J. A., & Eggermont, J. J. (1984). Metrics of saccade responses to visual double stimuli: Two different modes. *Vision Research, 21*(10), 1169–1179.

Pouget, A., Fisher, S. A., & Sejnowski, T. J. (1993). Egocentric spatial representation in early vision. *Journal of Cognitive Neuroscience, 5*(2), 150–161.

Purpura, D. P. (1975). Normal and aberrant neuronal development in the cerebral cortex of human fetus and young infant. In N. A. Buchwald & M. A. B. Brazier (Eds.), *Brain mechanisms of mental retardation.* New York: Academic Press.

Rabinowicz, T. (1979). The differential maturation of the human cerebral cortex. In F. Falkner & J. M. Tanner (Eds.), *Human growth: Vol. 3. Neurobiology and nutrition.* New York: Plenum Press.

Robinson, D. A. (1972). Eye movements evoked by collicular stimulation in the alert monkey. *Vision Research, 12,* 1795–1808.

Robinson, D. A. (1973). Models of the saccadic eye movement control system. *Kybernetik, 14,* 71–83.

Rockland, K. S., & Pandya, D. N. (1979). Laminar origins and terminations of cortical connections of the occipital lobe in the rhesus monkey. *Brain Research, 179,* 3–20.

Rumelhart, D. E., & McClelland, J. L. (Eds.). (1986). *Parallel distributed processing: Explorations in the microstructure of cognition. Vol. 1: Foundations.* Cambridge, MA: MIT Press.

Schiller, P. H. (1985). A model for the generation of visually guided saccadic eye movements. In D. Rose & V. G. Dobson (Eds.), *Models of the visual cortex* (pp. 62–70). Chichester, England: Wiley.

Schiller, P. H., Malpeli, J. G., & Schein, S. J. (1979). Composition of geniculo-striate input to superior colliculus of the rhesus monkey. *Journal of Neurophysiology, 42,* 1124–1133.

Schiller, P. H., & Stryker, M. (1972). Single-unit recording and stimulation in superior colliculus of the alert rhesus monkey. *Journal of Neurophysiology, 35,* 915–924.

Schlag, J., Schlag-Rey, M., & Dassonville, P. (1991). Spatial programming of eye movements. In J. Paillard (Ed.), *Brain and space* (pp. 69–78). Oxford, England: Oxford University Press.

Schlag-Rey, M., Schlag, J., & Shook, B. (1989). Interactions between natural and electrically evoked saccades. I. Differences between sites carrying retinal error and motor command signals in monkey superior colliculus. *Experimental Brain Research, 76,* 537–547.

Sparks, D. L., Holland, R., & Guthrie, B. L. (1975). Size and distribution of movement fields in the monkey superior colliculus. *Brain Research, 113*, 21–34.

Stein, J. F. (1992). The representation of egocentric space in the posterior parietal cortex. *Behavioral and Brain Sciences, 15*, 691–700.

Ungerleider, L. G., & Mishkin, M. (1982). Two cortical visual systems: Separation of appearance and location of objects. In D. L. Ingle, M. A. Goodale, & R. J. W. Mansfield (Eds.), *Analysis of visual behavior* (pp. 549–586). Cambridge, MA: MIT Press.

Van Gisbergen, J. A., Van Opstal, A. J., & Tax, A. A. (1987). Collicular ensemble coding of saccades based on vector summation. *Neuroscience, 21*(2), 541–555.

Vaughan, H. G., Jr., & Kurtzberg, D. (1989). Electrophysiologic indices of normal and aberrant cortical maturation. In P. Kellaway & J. L. Noebels (Eds.), *Problems and concepts in developmental neurophysiology* (pp. 263–287). Baltimore, MD: John Hopkins University Press.

Walk, R. D. (1978). Depth perception and experience. In R. D. Walk & H. L. Pick (Eds.), *Perception and experience.* New York: Plenum Press.

Westheimer, G. (1954). Eye movement responses to a horizontally moving visual stimulus. *Archives of Opthalmology, 52*, 932–941.

Wurtz, R. H., & Goldberg, M. E. (1972). Activity of superior colliculus in behaving monkey. 3. Cells discharging before eye movements. *Journal of Neurophysiology, 35*(4), 575–586.

Young, L. R., & Stark, L. (1963). Variable feedback experiments testing a sampled data model for tracking eye movements. *IEEE Transactions, Human Factors, 4*, 38–51.

Zipser, D., & Andersen, R. A. (1988). A back-propagation programmed network that simulates response properties of a subset of posterior parietal neurons. *Nature, 331*, 679–684.

Chapter 4

Attention and Eye Movement in Young Infants: Neural Control and Development

John E. Richards
Sharon K. Hunter
University of South Carolina

Attention has two characteristics: selectivity and intensity (Berg & Richards, in press; Berlyne, 1970; Ruff & Rothbart, 1996). Selectivity refers to the focusing of activity on the object to which attention is directed, whereas, intensity refers to the depth of processing that occurs concomitant with attention. For visual attention, selectivity often refers more specifically to the control of the direction of visual regard. This involves the general direction of gaze, as well as the control of eye movements during attentive tasks. Spatial selectivity is implemented in the visual domain as the active control of fixation in the direction to which attention is directed and the inhibition of eye movements in directions that would interfere with the current task. Thus, an important part of the study of visual attention's selectivity is an understanding of eye-movement control during attention.

There are many changes in the eye movements of infants across the first few months. These include changes in the characteristics of the eye movements themselves, as well as changes in how psychological variables affect eye movement. The thesis of this chapter is that many of these changes occur because of changes in the underlying neural systems controlling eye movement. Even further, there is an interaction of the eye-movement systems and changes in central nervous systems controlling attention. Development of eye movements is, therefore, considered to be a joint product of neural system development and developmental changes in attention. Thus, attention's "selectivity" characteristic in infant development may be physically implemented in eye-movement control systems that show development during the early part of infancy.

This chapter discusses three eye-movement systems that are involved in the development of infant fixation and attention. These are a short-latency reflexive eye-movement system, a longer-latency attentive saccadic system, and smooth-pursuit eye movements. Developmental changes in the neural areas controlling these eye movements, and the relation of these eye movements to early infant behavior, are presented.

THREE NEURAL SYSTEMS CONTROLLING EYE MOVEMENTS

In the earlier chapter concerning the neural control of visually guided eye movements, Schiller (this volume) discussed neural pathways and structures involved in the generation of eye movements. He presented two systems, posterior and anterior, consisting of several pathways responsible for various eye movements. There are three eye-movement systems that may be abstracted from this model. These three systems control reflexive saccades, target-directed saccades, and smooth-pursuit eye movements.

The system controlling reflexive saccades is the simplest of the systems. This system involves the "posterior" eye-movement control pathways (Schiller, this volume). The parasol cells in the retina are the primary input cell for this pathway. These cells have large visual fields, transient on- or off-responses, are predominantly located in the peripheral retina, and respond to broadband stimuli. Thus, they are optimized for responding to transient or moving stimuli in the peripheral visual field. They project to magnocellular layers in the lateral geniculate nucleus, and then to specific layers of the primary visual cortex. These layers of the primary visual cortex connect to the superior colliculus directly, or via the parietal cortex (Schiller, this volume), or via other areas of the cortex (e.g., suprasylvian cortex, Stein, 1988). Layers 5 and 6 of the visual cortex send, via corticotectal pathway, information to both the superficial and deep layers of superior colliculus, thus ensuring the functional integrity of the retinal image analysis (superficial superior colliculus layers) and the motor–visual properties of the deep layers of the superior colliculus, and reflexive saccade movements.

There are several characteristics of the "reflexive" saccadic system that are important for this chapter. First, it is the deeper (middle and deep) layers of the superior colliculus that are involved in this pathway (Schiller, this volume). The retinal input directly to the superior colliculus (primarily "W-cells"), however, is primarily restricted to the superficial layers. Second, there is little evidence for connectivity from the superficial to the deeper layers of the superior colliculus, so retinal-driven motor activity in the superior colliculus must be mediated by cortical pathways. Also, the superficial layers, unlike the deeper layers, do not show the receptive field enhancement that is contingent on eye movement (Mohler & Wurtz, 1976, 1977; Wurtz & Mohler, 1976). Cortical visual systems, therefore, must mediate the retinal driving of the deeper layers of the superior colliculus. Third, cortex ablations, or microstimulation, show that the visual cortex, including areas 17, 18, 19, and lateral suprasylvian areas, mediate the parasol cells driving for at least 75% of the colliculus deeper layer activity (Berson, 1988). Additionally, in light of the scarcity of corticotectal pathways from V1 to deeper superior colliculus layer (Carpenter, 1976; Cusick, 1988; Sparks, 1986; Sparks & Groh, 1995; Stein, 1988), the cortical influence might involve other cortical areas (e.g., suprasylvian cortex, Stein, 1988). Finally, cortical ablation eliminates both intentional and reflexive saccades, whereas spontaneous saccades and quick phases remain (Tusa, Zee, & Herdman, 1986). Ablation of the primary visual cortex does not affect the visual responsiveness of the cells in the superficial superior colliculus. Visual cortex ablation does, however, remove the visual responsiveness of the deep layers (Schiller, this volume).

The second neural system controls target-directed saccades, and attention-influenced saccades. This system involves both the "anterior" and "posterior" eye-movement control pathways (Schiller, this volume). The midget cells are the primary input cell for this pathway. These cells have small visual fields, sustained on- or off-responses, are predominantly located in the focal retina, and have color-opponent properties. Thus they are optimized for detailed pattern and color analysis. They project to the parvocellular layers in the LGN and then to specific layers of the primary visual cortex. Their major projections are then to parts of the cortical system involved in object identification (e.g., V4, inferotemporal cortex, "IT"; Schiller, this volume). At the same time, aspects of both the midget and parasol systems are integrated at the level of V1, MT, and the parietal lobe. The former pathway (V4 and IT), involving the "what" processing stream, is necessary for identifying a specific target. The latter pathway (MT, parietal), involving the "where" system, may identify spatial location. These two systems must then be integrated to identify both the location and the type of object for target-directed saccades. Finally, the anterior system bypasses the superior colliculus in its connection to the brainstem and primarily uses the frontal eye fields or dorsal-motor frontal cortex to control eye movements.

There are several characteristics of this *target-directed* eye-movement system that are important for this chapter. First, this is a longer latency system. It involves processing of stimulus information and location, and thus must take longer than the reflexive system. Second, this system involves several areas of the cortex that are known to be affected by attention. For example, the posterior parietal cortex and V4 have cells that are selectively enhanced in attention-demanding tasks, and nontargets are selective attenuated. This system ultimately controlling the target-directed eye-movement systems has been labeled the "posterior attention system" by Posner (Posner, 1995; Posner & Petersen, 1990). Third, this target-detection system is intimately involved in "selectivity" aspects of attention. Stimuli that are identified as targets are selectively enhanced in this system, particularly in the posterior parietal cortex and in V4. At the same time, in these cortical areas nontarget stimuli are attenuated. This system then has inhibitory influence over the superior colliculus (via frontal eye fields, and perhaps temporal lobe) to inhibit reflexive saccades to nontarget stimuli. Attention's selectivity is implemented as the active control of fixation toward targeted stimuli and the inhibition of eye movements that would interfere with the target task.

The third neural system of interest here is the one controlling smooth-pursuit eye movement. As part of a longer latency system, this pathway controls smooth-pursuit eye movements and is involved in motion detection and pursuit. This pathway involves the parasol cells in the retina, magnocellular layers of the LGN, and several higher cortical areas, such as V1, middle temporal, middle superior temporal, and parietal lobe areas. Cells in V1 respond to "retinal slip" when moving stimuli cross the visual field. Cells in the superficial layer of the superior colliculus may be primarily involved in the analysis of retinal image slip, particularly for computing retinal movement (e.g., vestibuloocular reflex and smooth pursuit). Motion-sensitive cells in V1 become active as a result of this retinal slip, and affect cells in the middle temporal (MT) and medial superior temporal (MST) cortex. MT and MST respond to such motion by initiating eye movements. It appears that MT responds primarily to the retinal slip information, and provides information to the smooth-pursuit system about the motion of potential pursuit targets. MST initiates motor commands necessary for the execution (maintenance) of smooth-pursuit eye movements, such as target velocity. Cells in MT and MST have direct connections to pontine or brainstem areas that control eye muscles. Once smooth-pursuit eye movements begin, the systems controlling the vestibuloocular reflex and optokinetic nystagmus (see Schiller, this volume, Fig. 1.24) participate in the control of eye movements during targeted smooth pursuit.

Smooth pursuit is the phylogenetically youngest of the eye movements. It is unique to frontal-eyed, foveate animals. The cortical aspects of this system have developed relatively late in evolution, but uses several systems known to be established in several species (e.g., vestibuloocular reflex, optokinetic nystagmus). The smooth-pursuit system therefore has a phylogenetically recent system that originates eye movements (middle temporal and medial superior temporal areas), and uses the phylogenetically primitive system to preserve accurate targeting.

DEVELOPMENT OF NEURAL SYSTEMS
CONTROLLING EYE MOVEMENTS

The three neural systems controlling eye movements show different developmental changes over the course of early infancy. These developmental changes are hypothesized to underlie behavioral development in the young infant. These developmental changes, and models describing the relation between the neural and behavioral changes, are presented.

Theories of Development

"Neurodevelopmental" models of infant vision posit different developmental courses for these eye-movement systems (Bronson, 1974; Johnson, 1990, 1995; Johnson, Posner, & Rothbart, 1991; Maurer & Lewis, 1979; Richards, 1990; Richards & Casey, 1992). The most well-known of these is the "two visual systems" model of Bronson (1974). Bronson's model consists of a primary and secondary visual system. The primary visual system has excellent visual acuity, overrepresents the fovea, and is devoted to fine pattern visual analysis. The secondary system, on the other hand, has poor visual acuity, represents the fovea and periphery, responds to stimulus location and movement much more than pattern, and is devoted to the detection and localization of targets in the peripheral field and saccades to those targets. Bronson proposed that the secondary system is phylogenetically older, mature at birth, and, therefore, responsible for the newborn infant's visual behavior. The primary system, however, does not begin to play a role until 1 or 2 months of age. Other theories of developmental changes in eye-movement control are similar to that of Bronson's (1974; Karmel & Maisel, 1975; Maurer & Lewis, 1979; cf. Salapatek, 1975) in that they postulate two parallel systems that show different developmental rates.

More recent models by Johnson (1990, 1995; Johnson et al., 1991) and by Richards (1990) and Richards and Casey (1992) are based on recent neurophysiological models of eye-movement control and, therefore, have a much more complicated picture. Although some details about the neural systems underlying eye-movement behavior differ in these models, they are very similar.

Johnson (1990, 1995; Johnson et al., 1991), based on Schiller's model (Schiller, 1985; this volume), uses four pathways to explain eye-movement development. Three correspond to those discussed earlier, that is, a short-latency system involving the retina and superior colliculus, a smooth-pursuit pathway based on the middle temporal cortex, and a frontal eye field-directed pathway. A fourth pathway included in Johnson's model is an inhibitory pathway from the substantia nigra to the superior colliculus. In his model, Johnson traces the developmental changes in eye movements and the parallel developmental changes in the underlying neural pathways. The differential development of the neural systems is then used to explain how the behavioral development may occur.

The models by Johnson (1990, 1995; Johnson et al., 1991) and others (Richards, Bronson) make concrete predictions and explanations of developmental changes. The reflexive saccade system, probably controlled by visual field information via the retina and superior colliculus and motor information via the short-latency pathway discussed earlier, is the first to develop and is functioning at a high level of maturity at birth or shortly thereafter. The second system to develop is the inhibitory pathway from the basal ganglia to the superior colliculus and probably systems in the cortex that control this inhibitory pathway. This pathway inhibits peripheral stimulus orienting in the presence of focal stimuli and may result in some types of "unusual" fixation-holding in 1- to 2-month-old infants, that is, "sticky fixation" (see chapters by Hood, Atkinson, & Braddick and Maurer & Lewis, this volume). The target-directed saccadic system involving the midget and parasol pathways from the retina, through the lateral geniculate nucleus, layers 4, 5, and 6 of V1, and the middle temporal area, is the third system to develop. This system is undeveloped at birth because the cortical systems do not have the functional maturity needed to operate. Based on the changes in the functioning and structure of the cortical systems, it has been speculated that this system shows rapid development from 2 to 6 months (Johnson, 1990, 1995; Johnson et al., 1991). The fourth system is involved in smooth-pursuit control and has the longest development course. The maturation of layers 2 and 3 of V1 allows for functioning of the frontal eye fields, and as with the predictive saccadic system, its functional onset seems to be in the 1 to 2 month period for the human infant. Many of the structures involved show some rapid development in the first few months following birth; however, the magnocellular pathways themselves have an extended developmental course. Thus, one would expect that this system is far from mature at 6 months and may even show development through the first 2 years.

Figure 4.1 shows a hypothesized developmental course for the reflexive saccades, targeted-saccades, and smooth-pursuit movements in the first year. Presumably, the short-latency saccadic system involved in tracking should not be affected by attention and should show little developmental change from 2 to 6 months. The longer-latency target-saccadic system should show the effects of attention and have a rapid developmental increase from 2 to 6 months. Finally, the longer-latency smooth-pursuit system should show the effects of attention but should have a more gradual development over this age range and not be at its full strength at 6 months.

Development of Eye Movement Systems

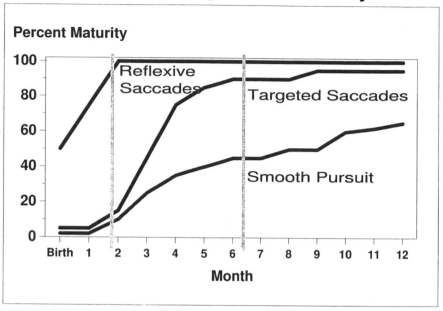

FIG. 4.1. Development of three visual systems involved in visual tracking. The "percent maturity" shown as a function of months, from birth through 12 months. There are three lines, corresponding to the reflexive saccades, targeted saccades, and smooth-pursuit systems.

Development of Neural Structures Involved in Eye Movements

The major development of the mammalian visual system, particularly that of primates, primarily occurs prenatally. This includes initial generation of neurons, synapse connection, and so forth. Postnatal development in primates consists primarily of maturation of the laminar nature of the visual cortex, completion of immature myelinization, and developmental changes in connectivity. Other species that have been widely studied (e.g., rodent or cat) have a more extensive postnatal development that corresponds to the prenatal primate visual development (see Maurer & Lewis, chap. 2, this volume, for a more detailed discussion).

Many postnatal changes in the primate visual system, in perspective to the total development of the primate visual system, seem more like fine tuning or modification of a nearly complete system. This corresponds as well to developmental changes in eye movements. Many of the systems exist at birth but, with development, become more extensive, fine tuned, able to respond to a wide array of conditions, and subject to voluntary control. For example, the differential development of the early-developing parvocellular and late-developing magnocellular pathways parallels development of behaviors based on these systems.

Developmental changes relying on the magnocellular pathways are seen in smooth pursuit. The incorporation of the middle temporal area into the visual system is relatively late, being based on the higher cortical use of the broadband system. Visual cortex changes in layers 4 and 5 of V1 become mature near 2 to 3 months of age, and these pathways are sufficient for visual pathways to the middle temporal area. Thus, smooth-pursuit eye movements show extensive developmental changes beginning near 6 to 8 weeks, changes across the period from 3 to 6 months, and continues adjustments beyond that period (past 1 year).

An example of a system with strong input from the parvocellular, narrowband discrimination pathways is target saccades controlled by the frontal eye fields. The parvocellular layers in the lateral geniculate nucleus show very rapid development between 3 and 6 months of age, and reach adult size and functional characteristics early (6 months). Narrowband pathways through the visual cortex are well developed by 6 months. Thus, frontal eye fields-driven saccades, which depend on fine visual discrimination pathways, should show rapid change from 3 to 6 months, but finish developmental changes by around 6 months of age.

Postnatal changes also occur in the layered nature of the visual cortex. The layered aspect of the visual cortex exists at birth; however, while layers 5 and 6 are more developed at birth, layers 1–4 show more development after birth. Layers 5 and 6 of V1 project to the superior colliculus (and lateral geniculate nucleus) and are responsible for retinal image analysis and are perhaps involved in reflexive saccades. The other layers (2, 3, and particularly level 4) participate in more sophisticated visual analysis (movement, stereopsis, form, pattern, color). These areas show rapid increases in size, complexity, and interconnections from birth through 8 to 9 months of age in the human.

Because layers 2, 3, and 4 are less developed at 1 to 2 months than layers 5 and 6, it might be expected that components of visual behavior that rely on their use (e.g., V4, inferior temporal cortex, middle temporal cortex, frontal eye fields) are relatively unused at this age. By 3 months of age layer 4 is capable of supporting activity. Between 3 and 6 months the highest layers (2 and 3) are becoming capable of supporting neural activity, although they continue to show development for several months (Banks & Salapatek, 1983; Conel, 1939–1963).

Many of the more complex eye movements are governed by higher cortical centers. This is particularly true of voluntary, intentional eye movements, such as targeted saccades (i.e., frontal eye fields and parietal cortex area PG). However, the actual developmental progression of these areas is much less well-known than that of the visual cortex or subcortical visual systems.

It is likely that these systems show two types of developmental changes. First, they undoubtedly have intrinsic changes in structure, function, synaptic connections, size, and so forth. These changes are very likely to occur later than those in the primary and secondary visual areas. For example, development in frontal areas occurs over several years of postnatal life, and development is not restricted to the first 6 months, or even through the first year. Second, their connectivity to other cortical or subcortical systems changes. For example, the layers of the visual cortex have pathways differentially distributed to the higher cortical centers. The functionality of these higher centers would, therefore, have to wait for the development of the primitive systems. The middle temporal lobes' control of smooth eye movements, for example, must wait for the development of broadband connections in layers 4 and 5 of the visual cortex, and in the columns of V2. Given the need for stimulus input for development, several of these higher centers' development may not begin until they receive input from the lower centers.

DEVELOPMENTAL CHANGES IN EYE MOVEMENTS

There are several reviews of eye movements in young infants (e.g., Hainline, 1988; Hainline & Abramov, 1985, 1992). Some include a discussion of the issues involved in measuring eye movements in infants (Aslin, 1985; Shupert & Fuchs, 1988); others, concerning infant visual perception, or visual capacity, also include sections about eye movements (e.g., Banks & Salapatek, 1983). The following sections summarize the developmental changes in eye movements.

Reflexive Saccades

By all theoretical and empirical accounts, the most mature eye-movement system at birth involves short-latency, reflexive superior colliculus saccades. Some theorists assume (e.g., Bronson, 1974; Johnson, 1990, 1995; Johnson et al., 1991) that the retinotectal pathway (retina to superior colliculus) is responsible for these short-latency, reflexive saccades in the newborn and very young infant. However, it is unlikely that retinal input to the superior colliculus directly affects superior colliculus-driven eye movements for two reasons. First, the cells likely involved in this reflexive saccadic eye movement are the parasol cells. These cells do not form a major input from the retina to the superior colliculus directly, but involve cortical pathways. Second, direct retinal-superior colliculus connections are primarily in the superficial layers of the superior colliculus. This layer is involved in retinal image slip and other receptive functions, but does not have the motor cells as do the deeper layers of the superior colliculus. Again, these deeper layers, involving both receptive and motor fields, receive input from the retina indirectly via the cortex (see Schiller, this volume).

There are two implications of the early existence of these reflexive saccades. First, and perhaps most obvious, the first eye movements that infants make postnatally are reflexive and saccadic in nature. Both Bronson (1974) and Johnson (1990, 1995; Johnson et al., 1991) affirm this. The second implication of the existence of these early eye movements is that the neural pathways serving them must exist at birth. This system involves the magnocellular, broadband pathways and connections between V1 (layers 5 and 6), secondary visual areas, and corticotectal connections. Thus, a minimal broadband pathway must exist between these structures in order for this reflexive pathway to function at birth.

Saccades made by infants have some distinct characteristics. These saccades usually are of fixed length, and, in some cases, the infant may approach a target with several small, equal-sized saccades. For example, Aslin and Salapatek (1975) reported that 1- and 2-month-olds localized 10° targets with single or double saccades while targets at 20, 30, or 40° were localized with a series of equally spaced, small saccades (hypometric). The magnitudes of saccades across these target distances were not equal; infants' saccades increased in magnitude as target distance increased. Salapatek, Aslin, Simonson, and Pulos (1980) suggested that the series of hypometric saccades may be due to an initial computation of target position, which is accurate, but which uses several small saccades. With increasing age the ability of the infant to localize a target depends on the increasing use of higher cortical areas implicated in spatial attention for accurate single saccade localization (e.g., parietal cortex area PG/frontal eye fields system). Other studies have demonstrated a developmental progression in the ability to localize targets with single saccades. For example Roucoux, Culee, and Roucoux (1982, 1983) found that at 8 weeks, infants could localize targets at 15° with a single saccade; 30° at 12 weeks; and 45° at 16 weeks.

Hypometric saccades have not been reported in all studies of infant eye movements, such as those found when infants scan an interesting visual stimulus (Hainline & Abramov, 1985; Hainline, Turkel, Abramov, Lemerise, & Harris, 1984). In this case, infants were scanning an interesting visual stimulus in the focal visual field. These hypometric and step-like saccades have not been reported in studies of adult saccades to peripheral targets. A typical sequence for multiple eye movements in adults involves a large saccade that traverses the majority of the eccentricity, and then one or two small "corrective" saccades for final localization of the target (Becker, 1976; Prablanc & Jennerod, 1975; Prablanc, Masse, & Echallier, 1978).

So, why the apparently conflicting data? One difference between these studies may be the type of stimulus used. The stimuli used by Hainline et al. were complicated textured patterns or simple patterns that filled the viewing area. The stimuli of the former studies were small targets, filling only a small portion of the visual field. They also were in the peripheral visual field. Studies using small targets require that the infant execute a saccade to a specific spatial location. In the full stimulus presentation the infant may choose a large variety of locations at different eccentricities. Thus, moving (Roucoux et al., 1982, 1983) or peripheral stimuli may result in hypometric saccades, whereas the static stimulus filling the visual field do not.

There are only a few studies in which other saccade characteristics have been systematically investigated. One study conducted by Ashmead (1984) showed that each of the small saccades was a well-formed main sequence saccade. Main sequence refers to the relation between the saccade's velocity and amplitude (or duration and amplitude). That the main sequence was intact suggests that part of the infant's immaturity is in the use of spatial location to foveate objects, implicating the immaturity of the systems involved in spatial attention. Thus, early saccades may be more "reflexive," subcortical, in nature.

Attention may play a role in saccadic eye movement in infants. A report by Hainline et al. (1984) suggests that attention enhances the main sequence relation for infants, but that during inattention it is irregular. Saccades by 14 to 151 day-old infants (1–4.5 months) to complex (interesting) targets showed the same main sequence relation (Bahill, Clark, & Stark, 1975) as with adults. That is, the velocity–amplitude relation was the same across different degrees of targets. However, with relatively simple (uninteresting) stimuli, the slope of the velocity–amplitude function was much lower for infants. The main sequence for adults is unaffected by attention manipulations.

Head movements may occur with saccadic eye movements in order to localize targets, and these head movements may also be hypometric (Regal, Ashmead, & Salapatek, 1983; Regal & Salapatek, 1982). In adults, saccades to target eccentricities less than about 20° occur without head movements, whereas target localizations to larger eccentricities usually involve head movements (Tomlinson & Bahra, 1986a, 1986b). It is unknown whether target eccentricity has a similar effect in infants.

Smooth Pursuit

Perhaps the second major postnatal developmental change in human eye movement is in smooth-pursuit motor movements. Smooth pursuit involves retinal image slip, processing of broadband information through the visual cortex, origination of smooth pursuit by the middle temporal and medial superior temporal areas, and cerebellar adjustment of eye movements.

The systems for retinal image slip exist at birth. By 2 months of age, the layers of primary visual cortex sending efferents to the higher CNS levels mature. These include projections to both the secondary visual area and the middle temporal area. Smooth-pursuit origination, therefore, is possible by this age, and as demonstrated in behavioral studies, begins.

In behavioral studies, smooth pursuit shows developmental changes at least through 12 months of age, and probably beyond. This may be due to at least three developmental reasons. First, the slowly maturing broadband magnocellular pathways probably change for 1 to 2 years, suggesting continuing changes in smooth-pursuit functioning. The areas of smooth pursuit origination (middle temporal and medial superior temporal areas) may also show developmental changes over an extended period. These developmental changes may be internal or involve connections with other brain areas. A second reason is that attention-based smooth-pursuit movements involve the parietal cortex area PG. This higher cortical level may also show developmental changes.

Smooth pursuit, therefore, is immature in human infants at birth and develops slowly over the next 2 to 3 months. Behaviorally, newborn infants show little sustained smooth-pursuit tracking, although some periods of smooth pursuit exist to slow velocity objects (e.g., 15% of approximate 370 ms duration to velocities of less than 19° per sec; Kremenitzer, Vaughan, Kurtzberg, & Dowling, 1979). Most newborn tracking is based on saccadic eye movements. Five-week-olds use head and eye movements to track objects moving at 11° per sec, but saccades and poorer smooth pursuit occurred at 23° per sec. Eight-week-old infants track 13° per sec stimuli primarily with smooth pursuit, but 39° per sec or 45° per sec with a combination of smooth pursuit and saccades (Roucoux et al., 1982, 1983). By 12 months of age, infants track stimuli at 45° per sec well, although still not as well as adults (Roucoux et al., 1982, 1983).

Figure 4.2 shows data from Aslin (1981), which displays tracking behavior of 6- and 10-week-old infants, and adults. As you can see, infants younger than 6 weeks of age show little smooth pursuit. Instead, they track the object with a series of saccades. Between ages 6 and 8 weeks, segments of smooth pursuit are interspersed with saccadic interruptions. Infants continue to use saccades to track the object, and, in the 6-week-old, often seem to be corrective of inaccurate smooth-pursuit direction. By 10 to 12 weeks of age, the smooth pursuit becomes nearly as accurate as that of adults. At this age, saccadic interruptions rarely occur (Aslin, 1981, 1985; see Shea & Aslin, 1984). Like adults (e.g., Barnes, 1979), infants often do smooth-pursuit target tracking with a combination of smooth-pursuit eye movements and localizing head movements (Roucoux et al., 1982, 1983).

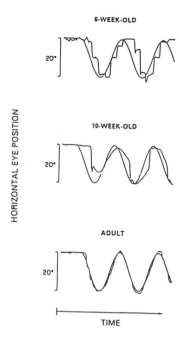

FIG. 4.2. Smooth-pursuit eye-movement development.

Some research has indicated that smooth-pursuit functioning might occur earlier with velocity and stimulus manipulations. Adults track objects with smooth-pursuit eye movements up to 72° per sec. Newborn infants track targets with velocities as slow as 9° per sec with few (<15%) smooth-pursuit eye movements, although they do exist (Kremenitzer et al., 1979). Therefore, newborn infants may be able to track very low target velocities (10° per sec or less), with very large targets (12°), although with poor pursuit latencies and gain (Hainline, 1988; Hainline & Abramov, 1985, 1992). These results suggest that parts of the system for smooth pursuit may be in place very early, but functions poorly or under severely restricted conditions.

It may be, for example, that the slow tracking velocities are required because of the retinal image slip information, or the connections through the visual system, are slow due to inadequate or immature myelinization. Also, part of the smooth-pursuit system controlling gain (accuracy), such as the cerebellum connections, may not exist at all. With increasing age, the maximum velocity for which smooth pursuit is predominant and accurate increases.

Localizing saccades that result in head movements may indirectly cause the slow eye-movement systems (e.g., smooth pursuit, vestibuloocular reflex) to participate in target localization. As discussed earlier, head movements following saccades are accompanied by "compensatory ocular responses" that move the eye in the direction opposite to the initial saccade and head movement in order to preserve target localization. In adults and older children, compensatory ocular responses are primarily vestibuloocular responses (Barnes, 1979; Funk & Anderson, 1977; Pelisson, Prablanc, & Urquizar, 1988; Uemura, Arai, & Shimazaki, 1980; Zangemeister & Stark, 1982). This is probably true for infants as well (Finocchio, Preston, & Fuchs, 1987; Regal et al., 1983). The vestibuloocular reflex exists in function similar to adult function at least by 1 to 2 months (Regal et al., 1983; Reisman & Anderson, 1989). The neural components of the human vestibular system are well-established and functional at birth. However, parameters of the vestibuloocular response change to some degree with age, such as a decrease in the gain of the response (Ornitz, Kaplan, & Westlake, 1985; Reisman & Anderson, 1989).

Frontal Eye Fields Saccades

Third in the developmental progression of eye movements are those movements controlled by the frontal eye fields pathways. Beginning at age 2 to 3 months, there is rapid development in the primary visual cortex in layers 2, 3, and 4 and a corresponding rapid development in the narrowband, color-opponent form discrimination pathways of the visual system. These probably include connections to V2, V3, and inferior temporal cortex. These lower level systems are antecedent to the mature functioning of the frontal eye fields–parietal cortex area PG control of attentional eye movements.

These areas seem to mature rather quickly, reaching adult levels by 6 to 9 months of age. So, although they start their rapid development later than the smooth-pursuit systems, their development is rapid. However, similar to smooth-pursuit eye-movement control, not much is known about development of the higher CNS structures that control attention-directed eye movements (e.g., frontal eye fields, parietal area PG).

DEVELOPMENTAL CHANGES IN INFANT ATTENTION—SUSTAINED ATTENTION DEVELOPMENT

The three eye-movement systems that have been presented show behavioral developmental patterns that parallel the development of the underlying neural systems. This suggests that development of these neural systems is responsible for developmental patterns seen in behavioral changes. However, another important development is occurring in infant behavior in a similar age range. This is the development of "sustained attention." Developmental changes in attention also may play a role in the behavioral development seen in these eye-movement systems. Specifically, the tar-geted-saccadic system and the smooth-pursuit system likely are strongly influenced by attention, whereas the reflexive saccadic system is not directly enhanced by attention. We now take a diversion to show some changes in attention that occur over the early period of infancy that may be related to these eye-movement systems.

Many studies by the first author have shown that heart rate (HR) in young adults is an index of different attention types. In the young infant HR has been shown to index at least four visual information-processing phases (Graham, 1979; Graham, Anthony, & Zeigler, 1983; Porges, 1980; Richards, 1988; Richards & Casey, 1992). These phases include the automatic interrupt, the orienting response, sustained attention, and attention termination.

Heart rate and cognitive activity differ during these attention phases. The automatic interrupt is characterized by a brief biphasic deceleration–acceleration, or small deceleration in HR, and behaviorally reflects the initial detection of stimulus change. Stimulus orienting is characterized by a marked deceleration in HR and involves the evaluation of stimulus novelty. Heart rate remains below prestimulus levels during sustained attention. This phase involves subject-controlled processing of stimulus information. During the final phase, attention termination, HR returns to prestimulus levels and the infant continues to fixate on the stimulus. Since the infant may be easily distracted during this time (Casey & Richards, 1988; Richards, 1987) or looks away voluntarily from the stimulus, it is assumed that the infant is no longer processing information in the stimulus.

Infant looking behavior differs dramatically during these phases. For example, looking back and forth between two interesting visual stimuli depends on the phase of attention and the type of stimulus. For two novel stimuli, the duration of individual looks to one of two stimuli is much longer during sustained attention than during attention termination. However, if one of the stimuli is novel and the other is familiar, infants will look at the novel stimuli longer than the familiar stimuli during sustained attention, but will look at both stimuli with equal duration during attention termination. Thus HR, indexing the level of arousal in attentional systems, covaries with infant fixation patterns (Richards & Casey, 1990).

Heart rate changes during sustained attention are also paralleled by behavioral indices of sustained attention. These include focusing on a central stimulus (e.g., Richards, 1987), exhibiting recognition memory (Richards & Casey, 1990), maintaining fixation on a central stimulus in the presence of a peripheral distracting stimulus (Hicks & Richards, submitted; Hunter & Richards, 1997; Lansink & Richards, 1997; Richards, 1987, 1997), and acquiring stimulus information (Richards, in press). The "selective" aspect of attention has been demonstrated in several studies to be particularly true of sustained attention. Infants will not be distracted from viewing a central stimulus during sustained attention, and are poorer in localizing a peripheral stimulus if sustained attention to a central stimulus is in progress. Alternatively, the presence of a focal stimulus alone during "inattention" (attention termination phase) does not inhibit localization of peripheral stimuli. Thus, it is during sustained attention that the selective aspect of attention is manifested (Berg & Richards, in press).

There are important developmental changes occurring in infant attention, as defined by these heart rate defined attention phases. Specifically, a consistent pattern of developmental changes in sustained attention has emerged from several studies (Casey & Richards, 1988; Richards, 1987, 1989a, 1989b). The level of HR change during sustained attention, which is a reflection of cognitive processing intensity, increases from 14 to 26 weeks of age. This age change parallels the finding of an increasingly sustained HR response for the older age infants during the sustained period of attention (Richards, 1985). This change in HR during sustained attention parallels some of the behavioral manifestations of attention. This includes, for example, an increasing ability of infants to acquire familiarity with stimulus characteristics in a fixed length of time (Richards, in press). This occurs primarily during sustained attention, rather than the other attention phases. For younger ages (e.g., 8 weeks), behavioral and HR indices of attention are not as well-synchronized as they are at older ages (Hicks & Richards, submitted; Richards, 1989b).

Why are HR changes in infants during fixation indexing infant attention phases? The answer to this lies in an understanding of the neural systems affecting HR, and "arousal" attention systems. The neural control of this HR change likely originates from a "cardioinhibitory" center in the frontal cortex. This area has reciprocal connections with several areas, all of which are part of the limbic system, and thus involved in the mesencephalic reticular formation arousal system (Heilman, Watson, Valenstein, & Goldberg, 1987; Mesulam, 1983). The mesencephalic reticular formation and the limbic system (Heilman et al., 1987; Mesulam, 1983), as well as dopaminergic and cholinergic neurotransmitter systems (Robbins & Everitt, 1995) control this arousal form of attention. This arousal-sustained alertness system sustains attention and maintains an alert, vigilant state. This system subserves several component systems, including audition, visual–spatial attention, and form–color object discrimination (Posner, 1995; Posner & Petersen, 1990). Attention, then, may operate in a nonselective manner on visual areas, including enhancing form and color discrimination, motion detection and visual tracking, and eye movements.

Heart rate changes during attention in infants are an index of the arousal system. Therefore, they may indirectly index the sensitivity of the visual system to external stimuli. Heart rate may reflect the arousal effects occurring in the nondifferentiated areas of V1 and V2. Heart rate changes during attention should be closely associated with the eye-movement changes found in higher cortical areas also, because these areas are closely associated with the cingulate's input to the parietal cortex area PG–superior colliculus–frontal eye fields attention network, and contribute to the arousal found in the selective attention networks. Arousal also contributes to the form discrimination network, represented by V4 and inferior temporal cortex. Arousal contributes to the selective attention properties of those areas by heightening the selective responsiveness of the visual fields in V4 and inferior temporal cortex. Thus HR changes should also occur when the processing of pattern or configuration information is the primary activity, and significant eye movements do not occur.

The changes in sustained attention that occur from 3 to 6 months of age may partially form the basis for changes in eye movements across this age range. As presented earlier, the targeted-saccadic system is controlled by several cortical areas that are influenced by attention. These areas show both selective enhancement of targets for attention, and attenuation of neural and behavioral responses to nontargeted stimuli during attention. The hypothesized developmental changes in the eye-movement systems (Johnson, 1990, 1995; Johnson et al., 1991; Richards, 1990; Richards & Casey, 1992) that control these systems is paralleled by HR and behavioral changes in sustained attention.

These changes in attention parallel the eye-movement systems. The early looking system of the infant is predominated by the reflexive saccade system that is relatively unaffected by attention. This is consistent with the finding that HR changes during fixation are relatively unsynchronized with peripheral stimulus localization in the 8-week-old infant (Hicks & Richards, submitted; Richards, 1989b). As sustained attention develops, and at the same time as the cortical areas controlling targeted saccades develop, the infant begins to focus fixation on attention-eliciting stimuli and withstand distraction by peripheral or nontargeted stimuli. Thus, changes in eye-movement behavior in the period from 14 to 26 weeks may be caused by parallel developmental changes in the neural systems underlying eye movements and developmental changes in sustained attention. The similar developmental changes in eye-movement systems and sustained attention suggest that they may be complementary perspectives of the same underlying phenomenon.

How does this fit together? What are the behavioral results of the interaction between developing neural structures, developing eye movements, and developing attention? The following are two examples of the interaction of attention and eye movements in infants.

EXAMPLE: EYE AND HEAD MOVEMENTS
DURING ATTENTION

In the opening section of this chapter we briefly discussed the neural pathways indicated by Schiller (this volume) to be involved in eye-movement generation. Two of those pathways were said to control the generation of saccadic eye movements, while a third controls smooth-pursuit eye movements. One of the saccadic pathways is the short-latency system from the retina to the superior colliculus via primary visual cortex. The second pathway is a longer latency pathway involving the retina, primary visual cortex, V2, posterior parietal cortex, and frontal eye fields. It is this second, longer-latency saccadic pathway that is thought to be affected by attention.

Localizing head movements that accompany saccadic eye movements center the eye with respect to the head so that eye control muscles do not have to actively hold the orbit at large eccentricities. The relation between head movements and target eccentricity in infants has been informally reported in some studies (Regal & Salapatek, 1982; Regal et al., 1983; Roucoux et al., 1982, 1983), and the findings suggest an increase in the number of head movements accompanying peripheral stimulus localization with increases in eccentricity. In general, it has been found that eye movements usually precede head movements (Regal & Salapatek, 1982; Regal et al., 1983; Roucoux et al., 1982, 1983; Tronick & Clanton, 1971). However, head movement initiation probably occurs at the same time as that of eye movements, but the delay is a result of biomechanical lag (Zangemeister & Stark, 1982).

Peripheral stimulus localization is one method that has been used to study developing eye and head movements in infants. The study of eye movements in this paradigm has often been based on visual judgments of eye movements (e.g., Atkinson, Hood, Braddick, & Wattam-Bell, 1988; Atkinson, Hood, Wattam-Bell, & Braddick, 1992; de Schonen, McKenzie, Maury, & Bresson, 1978; Harris & MacFarlane, 1974; Hood & Atkinson, 1993; Richards, 1987, 1997). A few studies have investigated the characteristics of saccadic eye movements used for stimulus localization, but none have studied the velocity–amplitude relation for peripheral stimulus localization in infants.

As has been reported in many studies, the presence of a competing stimulus in the central or focal visual field results in a lower localization percentage of a peripheral stimulus. It is not, however, the presence of competing stimuli that inhibits peripheral stimulus localization. Rather, the lower localization percentage is due to the engagement of attention to the visual stimulus. Using the HR changes known to be associated with infant attention or inattention, it has been shown that the latency of looking toward a peripheral stimulus is longer in 3- to 6-month-olds when attention is engaged with the central stimulus than when the infant is fixating the central stimulus but attention is unengaged (Richards, 1987, in press).

Similarly, the probability of detecting a peripheral target of limited duration is lower if the infant is attending to a central visual stimulus than when inattentive fixation is occurring (Finlay & Ivinskis, 1984; Richards, 1997). When a central stimulus is present but attention is unengaged, peripheral stimulus localization occurs at latencies and with probabilities similar to the noncompeting situation when the central stimulus is absent (Finlay & Ivinskis, 1984; Richards, 1987, 1997). Recent work has suggested that the presence of a central stimulus and attention to that stimulus changes the infant's response bias such that a response is less likely during attention to the central stimulus than during inattention, or without a central stimulus (Hicks & Richards, submitted; Richards, 1997).

Richards and Hunter (1997) examined attentional effects on head and eye movements in infants. Specifically, the study looked at the probability of head movements accompanying localization and the affect attention to a focal stimulus had on them, and the study examined the characteristics of saccadic eye movements during attention and in relation to head movements.

Infants were tested at 14, 20, and 26 weeks of age (3, 4.5, and 6 months) in an interrupted stimulus paradigm (see Fig. 4.3). In this paradigm, a trial

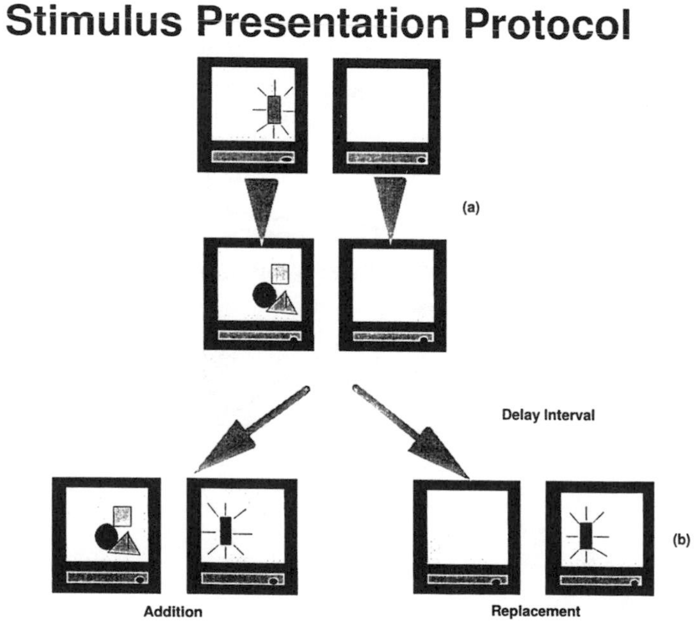

Stimulus Presentation Protocol

FIG. 4.3. Interrupted stimulus paradigm. (a) Infant's fixation is engaged on a stimulus in the central visual field. (b) Interrupting stimulus is presented in the periphery.

begins once the infant's fixation is engaged on a stimulus in the central visual field. Another stimulus is then presented at some distance in the periphery. The presentation of this peripheral stimulus either occurs immediately (concurrent with the central visual stimulus) or after some delay.

For this particular study, stimuli were placed at eccentricities of either 25, 35, or 45° in the periphery. The delay for presentation of the peripheral stimulus was manipulated to result in differing attention level; specifically: the peripheral stimulus was presented after focal localization of a simple blinking dot; the focal and peripheral stimulus were presented simultaneously; the peripheral stimulus was presented after a 2 sec delay; the peripheral stimulus was presented after a significant HR deceleration; or the peripheral stimulus was presented after HR returned to its prestimulus level after a significant deceleration. Also, on some trials the focal stimulus remained on, while in other trials it was removed upon presentation of the peripheral stimulus.

The results of this study showed a developing inhibition of saccadic localization of peripheral stimuli in 3- to 6-month-old infants. As you can see in Fig. 4.4, peripheral stimulus localization occurred less frequently near the beginning of fixation and when a significant HR deceleration had occurred (sustained attention) than when no focal stimulus was present or after HR had returned to prestimulus level (attention termination).

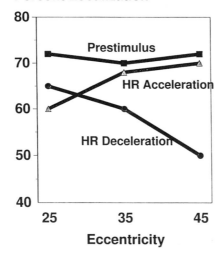

FIG. 4.4. Percentage of peripheral stimulus localizations as a function of peripheral stimulus eccentricity and attention conditions. Note the eccentricity effect occurred primarily during sustained attention (HR deceleration condition).

Localization of the peripheral stimulus was accompanied by head movements on more than two thirds of the trials, and the likelihood of head movements was positively associated with stimulus eccentricity (see Table 4.1). However, there were unusual localizing head movements in the attention conditions in the absence of localizing saccades or changes in fixation for the two older age groups. During attention conditions the 6-month-olds often made "localizing head movements" toward the peripheral stimulus while fixation remained on the focal stimulus. Because infant attention modulates eye movement, characteristics of infants' eye–head relations during infant attention may be different than during inattention.

There was a strong relation between peak velocity and amplitude of the localizing saccades during the prestimulus period with a simple nonpatterned stimulus array (Fig. 4.5A). There were no age changes in this main sequence relation, and it is assumed that adult-like relations characterize these velocity–amplitude relations. In contrast, in the two conditions under which focal stimulus attention is maximally engaged (2 sec and HR deceleration) unusual velocity–amplitude relations were found. This consisted of a faster peak velocity relative to saccade amplitude than during prestimulus periods. This effect occurred primarily in 20- and 26-week-old infants (Fig. 4.5B). These age differences were not found in any other condition, nor in the prestimulus period or the saccades to the blinking dot.

These findings suggest that there was an increasing inhibition of the reflexive peripheral saccades during sustained attention over the age range from 3 to 6 months. The distinction between sustained attention and attention termination became sharper with increasing age (14 to 26 weeks), both in distraction times and in the characteristics of reflexive peripheral localization. The emergence of attention-directed targeted saccades and fixation to the focal stimuli, controlled by the posterior attention system and the frontal eye fields, was accompanied by the suppression of reflexive peripheral saccades over this age range.

The interpretation of the effect of attention on the main sequence, and on peripheral stimulus localization generally, involves an understanding of the brain systems controlling eye movement during attention. Earlier

TABLE 4.1
Localizations With and Without Accompanying Head Movements on
Peripheral Stimulus Present Trials as a Function of Delay Conditions

	Prestim	Immediate	2-Sec	HR Dec	HR Acc	All Types
Number of PS Trials	144	200	184	165	141	824
PS Localization	78.3%	66.3%	83.3%	76.4%	80.9%	75.9%
Saccade Only	25.7%	38.5%	20.6%	48.5%	29.0%	32.7%
Saccade & Head Movement	74.3%	61.5%	79.4%	51.5%	71.1%	67.3%

Main Sequence

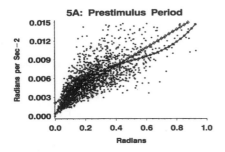
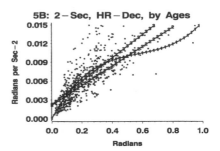

FIG. 4.5. Main sequence relation between maximum saccade velocity and total amplitude of saccade. 5A: Prestimulus saccades, with linear equation and best-fitting polynomial equation; 5B: Saccades to peripheral stimulus in 2-s and HR deceleration conditions, with separate regression lines for 14-, 20-, and 26-week-old infants. 5B: 1–14 week-olds, 2–20 week-olds, 3–26 week-olds.

in the chapter, we referred to the pathway from the lateral geniculate nucleus to the frontal eye fields for the control of targeted saccades during attention (Schiller, this volume). The HR changes during attention probably index a general arousal–alertness system (Heilman et al., 1987; Mesulam, 1983; Posner, 1995; Robbins & Everritt, 1995) that "invigorates" the posterior attention network (Richards & Casey, 1992). The saccades that manage to avoid this inhibition may be unusual. Perhaps saccade amplitude is programmed and then attention-based inhibitory systems affect saccade parameters.

The changes in the main sequence relation for the attention conditions in the two older age groups, and the unusual head movements toward the peripheral stimulus in the absence of localizing saccades, reflect the inhibition of the reflexive system by the attention system. These results are consistent with the *neurodevelopmental* model with which we began this chapter, hypothesizing a focal attention system that over this age range increasingly inhibits reflexive saccadic eye movements used to localize peripheral stimuli (Johnson, 1990, 1995; Richards, 1990; Richards & Casey, 1992).

There are two unanswered questions posed by this study. First, some characteristics of saccades (e.g., main sequence relations, "corrective" rather than "hypometric" saccades) were found to develop over the entire age range of the study. This suggests that the onset of these phenomena should occur at earlier ages, perhaps in the 8- to 11-week-old range. Second, differences affecting peripheral stimulus localization between sustained attention and attention termination were found in relatively "intact" levels at the earliest age (14 weeks). Studies with 8-week-olds (Richards, 1989a, 1989b; Hicks & Richards, submitted) have suggested that the sustained attention–attention termination differential effect is much less pronounced.

EXAMPLE: DEVELOPMENT OF SMOOTH PURSUIT UNDER ATTENTION AND INATTENTION

The eye-movement systems presented by Schiller (1985; this volume) were shown in previous sections to show developmental changes in early infancy, both in the neural systems controlling the eye movement, and in behavioral studies of eye-movement characteristics. There were three systems that have been discussed in this chapter that were recently examined in two studies (Richards & Holley, submitted). These systems are: (a) a short-latency reflexive system involving the retina, LGN, primary visual cortex, and superior colliculus, (b) a longer-latency system involving the parvocellular retina and LGN cells, that involves several higher cortical areas (V1, V2, posterior parietal cortex, FEF, and SC), and (c) a longer-latency system involving the magnocellular retina and LGN cells, and several higher cortical areas (V1, V2, V4, MT, MST). These systems differ in the type of eye movements that are controlled, the involvement of attention in the eye movements, and developmental course. The first two systems control saccadic eye movements, with the short-latency pathway being involved in reflexive peripheral saccades and the second system involved in the control of attention-directed saccades. This system controls smooth-pursuit eye movements, and is heavily involved in motion detection and pursuit. Like the second system, it is strongly affected by attentive behavior.

The changes in these behaviors were recently studied (Richards & Holley, submitted). In this study infants at 8, 14, 20, and 26 weeks of age were presented with a small sinusoidal moving stimulus that ranged in speed from 4 to 24° per sec while EOG was used to record eye movements. We used EOG on the outer canthi of the eyes, which measures electrical activity in the eye relative to the head. The composite EOG was separated into saccadic and smooth-pursuit components. Attention phases were once again determined by the changes in HR previously noted. Sustained attention was defined as occurring following a significant HR deceleration; stimulus orienting any period prior to sustained attention; attention termination as the return of HR to its prestimulus level following sustained attention. The distinction between attention and inattention, and smooth pursuit and saccades, allowed us to examine the three eye-movement systems (reflexive-saccades; attentive-saccades; attentive-smooth pursuit).

Now to some results from the eye-movement data. Figure 4.6 shows the coherence between the composite EOG signal and the moving stimulus.

Stimulus Tracking Across Testing Age

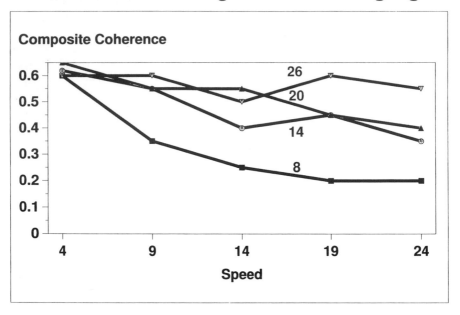

FIG. 4.6. The coherence between composite EOG and tracking stimulus, as a function of tracking speed, for the four age groups. An increase in coherence at the higher speeds occurs over this age range.

This represents how well the infant tracks the signal regardless of the nature of the eye movements. This is separated for the four age groups, plotted for the horizontal stimulus, and at the different tracking speeds. There is a large drop-off in the tracking of the 8-week-olds at very slow speeds, and a gradual increase over the next three ages in the level of tracking. This is shown by the increased sustaining of the coherence between the signal and the eye movements for the four ages over the increases in tracking speed. This generally shows an increase in visual stimulus tracking over this age range.

Figure 4.7 shows the number of saccades made during the tracking at the different ages. The graph on the left is when HR has significantly decelerated below prestimulus level. This represents sustained attention to the visual tracking stimulus. The graph on the right is when HR has returned to its prestimulus level, though the infant continues to fixate toward the TV stimulus. During the attention–HR change, there is an increase over age in the number of saccades toward the tracking stimulus as speed increases. This seems to peak for the 3-month-olds at about 14 degrees per sec, and then decline at the fastest speed. The 20- to 26-week-olds show increases in saccade

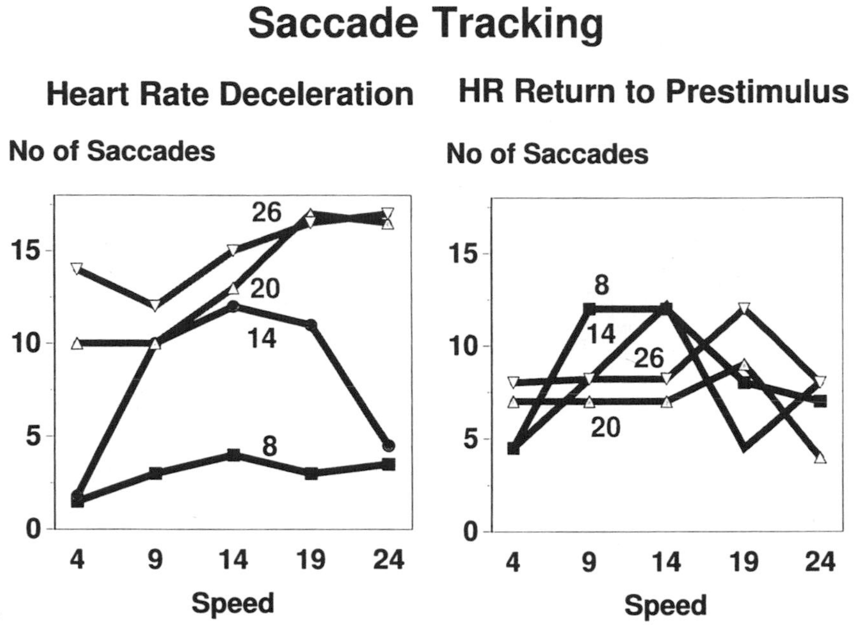

Saccade Tracking

Heart Rate Deceleration   HR Return to Prestimulus

No of Saccades   **No of Saccades**

FIG. 4.7. Number of saccades, as a function of stimulus speed, for the four age groups. Left graph is HR deceleration, and right graph is return of HR to prestimulus level.

number over the faster speeds all the way until the fastest speed. Thus, although smooth-pursuit tracking is becoming poor, and saccadic system needs to be used, the visual pursuit continues. Saccadic tracking during attention represents a longer-latency system involving the parvocellular retina and LGN cells that involves several higher cortical areas (V1, V2, posterior parietal cortex, FEF, and SC). This shows a dramatic increase from 2 to 4.5 months, and not much change to 6 months.

The right side of Fig. 4.7 is the number of saccades during the inattentive period when HR has returned to prestimulus levels. Note that tracking still occurs, though coherence between the visual stimulus and the EOG movements is lower. However, there is no age difference in this condition, and the tracking does not increase dramatically with visual stimulus speed. Saccadic tracking during inattentive periods was found to be the poorest, and did not change over the age ranges studied. Remember, saccades during "inattention" represent a short-latency system involving the retina, LGN, primary visual cortex, and superior colliculus. This system is thought to exist at or near birth (or at least by 1–2 months) and control saccadic eye movements to peripheral targets.

Changes in smooth-pursuit tracking are shown in Fig. 4.8. This shows the coherence between the smooth-pursuit eye movements, and the track-

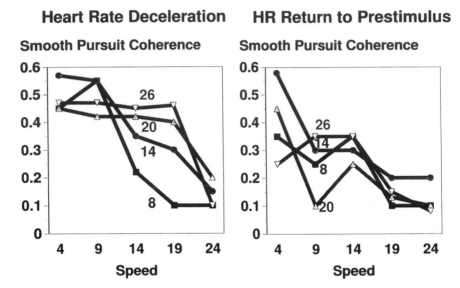

FIG. 4.8. Coherence between smooth-pursuit eye movements and visual stimulus, as a function of stimulus speed, separate for the four ages. Left graph shows HR deceleration, and right graph shows return of HR to prestimulus level.

ing stimulus, as a function of the stimulus speed, separately for the four age groups. Again, on the left is the data for the HR deceleration period, and the right shows the data for when HR has returned to its prestimulus level. The coherence decreases with the tracking speed for the four ages. However, in the graph at left, representing attention, there is a steady increase over the four ages in the coherence–speed function. Again, as with the saccadic tracking number, the smooth-pursuit coherence following the return of HR to its prestimulus level is not as good, and does not show the dramatic age differences as the attention-based tracking does.

There was a gradual increase in the level of smooth-pursuit tracking across these ages, particularly during attention. Smooth-pursuit tracking represents a longer-latency system involving the magnocellular retina and LGN cells, and several higher cortical areas (V1, V2, V4, MT, MST). This system shows development starting after 2 months, and has a very long developmental course (up through 18–24 months). Like the attentive-saccadic system, it is strongly affected by attentive behavior.

It is worth comparing the results in Fig. 4.7 and Fig. 4.8 with the hypothetical graph in Fig. 4.1. This hypothetical graph shows a rapid increase in saccadic tracking in the short-latency system. This is represented by saccadic tracking that occurs in the infant during "inattentive" periods. Though not shown in the graphs, there is also some evidence that this type of age function (no age change in this age) is typical of the saccadic eye movements during stimulus orienting. Second, the "attention-directed" saccadic tracking system shows a rapid development over this age range. By 6 months, it is at peak maturity level, and doesn't change much after that. Third, the smooth-pursuit system shows gradual development over this age range, and is closely related to attention as with the attention-directed saccadic system, but shows development in much later periods of infancy and perhaps into early childhood.

The "attentive-saccadic" system and the "attentive smooth-pursuit" system are involved in focal stimulus attention. These systems show changes over the entire period from 2 to 6 months. The "reflexive-saccadic" system, that exists at birth, is the system that controls peripheral stimulus localization and is inhibited during focal stimulus attention. The developmental changes in these systems needs to be studied in the time period before 14 weeks of age, with a systematic study of the effect of the newly emerging focal sustained attention systems on the reflexive-saccadic system.

Similarly, the changes in the eye-movement systems affected by attention occur over this entire age range and would likely be involved in the development of response inhibition and covert attention that would be studied in Experiment months of age. This tracking ability continues to change over the first year, and well into the second year, perhaps peaking by the end of that year.

SUMMARY AND CONCLUSIONS

The selectivity of attention is a vacuous notion that needs to be filled in with specific details. In the case of visual attention, selectivity often involves the *competition* between eye-movement systems. The systems controlling fixation enhance focal field processing, and those systems involving peripheral stimulus localization are inhibited. Alternatively, some saccadic eye-movement control may be enhanced during attention. The increasing development of the predictive system in the smooth-pursuit study is an example that not just fixation is enhanced, but eye-movement systems that aid in the task requirements are enhanced (either saccades or smooth pursuit).

This chapter has presented two main theses. First, we asserted that developmental changes in the neural systems controlling eye movement form the basis for changes in overt eye-movement behavior. The changes in these neural systems arise as individual systems begin to function, as individual systems reach maturity, and as the interaction between these systems occurs. The "cognitive developmental neuroscience" models of eye-movement control predict specific patterns of development in overt behavioral systems.

Second, it has been asserted that developmental changes in sustained attention also occur over the same time period as these overt and neural changes. These changes in sustained attention may form the basis for much of the development of two eye-movement systems, targeted saccades and smooth-pursuit eye movements. The changes in sustained attention and in the neural systems act as complementary changes that show up in infants' overt eye-movement responses in psychological tasks. In the case of eye movements, overlapping developmental trajectories between the various eye-movement control systems, and development in sustained attention, results in unique patterns of developmental changes in the effect of attention on eye movements in young infants. These overt behavioral changes may be best understood as a confluence of the developmental changes in the underlying systems and the increasing coordination of those changes in the first few months of infancy.

ACKNOWLEDGMENTS

The writing of this chapter was supported by grants from the National Institute of Child Health and Human Development, #R01-HD18942 and a Research Scientist Development Award from the National Institute of Mental Health, #K02-MH00958.

REFERENCES

Ashmead, D. (1984). Parameters of infant saccadic eye movements. *Infant Behavior and Development, 7,* 16.

Aslin, R. N. (1981). Development of smooth pursuit in human infants. In D. F. Fisher, R. A. Monty, & J. W. Senders (Eds.), *Eye movements: Cognition and visual perception.* Hillsdale, NJ: Lawrence Erlbaum Associates.

Aslin, R. N. (1985). Oculomotor measures of visual development. In G. Gottlieb & N. A. Krasnegor (Eds.), *Measurement of audition and vision in the first year of postnatal life: A methodological overview* (pp. 391–417). Bethesda, MD: NIH.

Aslin, R. N., & Salapatek, P. (1975). Saccadic localization of visual targets by the very young human infant. *Perception and Psychophysics, 17,* 293–302.

Atkinson, J., Hood, B., Braddick, O. J., & Wattam-Bell, J. (1988). Infants' control of fixation shifts with single and competing targets: Mechanisms for shifting attention. *Perception, 17,* 367–368.

Atkinson, J., Hood, B., Wattam-Bell, J., & Braddick, O. J. (1992). Changes in infants' ability to switch visual attention in the first three months of life. *Perception, 21,* 643–653.

Bahill, A. T., Clark, M. R., & Stark, L. (1975). The main sequence: A tool for studying human eye movements. *Mathematical Bioscience, 24,* 191–204.

Banks, M. S., & Salapatek, P. (1983). Infant visual perception. In M. M. Haith & J. J. Campos (Eds.), *Handbook of child psychology: Infancy and psychobiology* (Vol. 2, pp. 435–572). New York: Wiley.

Barnes, G. R. (1979). Vestibuloocular function during coordinated head and eye movements to acquire visual targets. *Journal of Physiology, 287,* 127–147.

Becker, W. (1976). Do correction saccades depend exclusively on retinal feedback? A note on the possible role of non-retinal feedback. *Vision Research, 16,* 425–427.

Berg, W. K., & Richards, J. E. (1997). Attention across time in infant development. In P. J. Lang, R. F. Simons, & M. T. Balaban (Eds.), *Attention and orienting: Sensory and motivational processes* (pp. 347–368). Mahwah, NJ: Lawrence Erlbaum Associates.

Berlyne, D. E. (1970). Attention as a problem in behavior theory. In D. I. Motofsky (Ed.), *Attention: Contemporary theory and analysis* (pp. 25–49). New York: Appleton-Century-Crofts.

Berson, D. M. (1988). Retinal and cortical inputs to cat superior colliculus: Composition, convergence, and laminar specificity. In T. P. Hicks & G. Benedek (Eds.), *Vision within extrageniculo-striate systems* (pp. 17–26). New York: Elsevier.

Bronson, G. W. (1974). The postnatal growth of visual capacity. *Child Development, 45,* 873–890.

Carpenter, M. B. (1976). *Human neuroanatomy.* Baltimore, MD: Waverly Press.

Casey, B. J., & Richards, J. E. (1988). Sustained visual attention in young infants measured with an adapted version of the visual preference paradigm. *Child Development, 59,* 1515–1521.

Conel, J. L. (1939–1963). *The postnatal development of the human cerebral cortex* (Vols. 1–7). Cambridge, MA: Harvard University Press.

Cusick, G. G. (1988). Anatomical organization of the superior colliculus in monkeys: Corticotectal pathways for visual and visuomotor functions. In T. P. Hicks & G. Benedek (Eds.), *Vision within extrageniculo-striate systems* (pp. 1–16). New York: Elsevier.

de Schonen, S., McKenzie, B., Maury, L., & Bresson, F. (1978). Central and peripheral object distances as determinants of the effective visual field in early infancy. *Perception, 7,* 499–506.

Finlay, D., & Ivinskis, A. (1984). Cardiac and visual responses to moving stimuli presented either successively or simultaneously to the central and peripheral visual fields in 4-month-old infants. *Developmental Psychology, 20,* 29–36.

Finocchio, D. V., Preston, K. L., & Fuchs, A. F. (1987). A quantitative analysis of the vestibuloocular reflex in 3-month-old infants. *Investigative Ophthalmology and Visual Science Supplement 28,* 313.

Funk, C. J., & Anderson, M. F. (1977). Saccadic eye movements and eye-head coordination in children. *Perceptual and Motor Skills, 44,* 599–610.

Graham, F. K. (1979). Distinguishing among orienting, defense, and startle reflexes. In H. D. Kimmel, E. H. van Olst, & J. F. Orlebeke (Eds.), *The orienting reflex in humans* (pp. 137–167). Hillsdale, NJ: Lawrence Erlbaum Associates.

Graham, F. K., Anthony, B. J., & Zeigler, B. L. (1983). The orienting response and developmental processes. In D. Siddle (Ed.), *Orienting and habituation: Perspectives in human research* (pp. 371–430). Sussex, England: Wiley.

Hainline, L. (1988). Normal lifespan developmental changes in saccadic and pursuit eye movements. In C. W. Johnston & F. J. Pirozzolo (Eds.), *Neuropsychology of eye movements. Neuropsychology and neurolinguistics* (pp. 31–64). Hillsdale, NJ: Lawrence Erlbaum Associates.

Hainline, L., & Abramov, I. (1985). Saccades and small-field optokinetic nystagmus in infants. *Journal of the American Optometric Association, 56,* 620–626.

Hainline, L., & Abramov, I. (1992). Assessing visual development: Is infant vision good enough. *Advances in Infancy Research, 7,* 39–102.

Hainline, L., Turkel, J., Abramov, I., Lemerise, E., & Harris, C. (1984). Characteristics of saccades in human infants. *Vision Research, 24,* 1771–1780.

Harris, P., & MacFarlane, A. (1974). The growth of the effective visual field from birth to seven weeks. *Journal of Experimental Child Psychology, 18,* 340–348.

Heilman, K. M., Watson, R. T., Valenstein, E., & Goldberg, M. E. (1987). Attention: Behavior and neural mechanisms. In V. B. Mountcastle, F. Plum, & S. R. Geiger (Eds.), *Handbook of physiology* (pp. 461–481). Bethesda, MD: American Physiological Society.

Hicks, J. M., & Richards, J. E. (1997). *The effects of stimulus movement and attention on peripheral stimulus localization by 8-, 14-, 20- and 26-week-old infants.* Paper submitted for publication.

Hood, B. M., & Atkinson, J. (1993). Disengaging visual attention in the infant and adult. *Infant Behavior and Development, 16,* 405–422.

Johnson, M. H. (1990). Cortical maturation and the development of visual attention in early infancy. *Journal of Cognitive Neuroscience, 2,* 81–95.

Johnson, M. H. (1995). The development of visual attention: A cognitive neuroscience perspective. In M. S. Gazzaniga (Ed.), *The cognitive neurosciences* (pp. 735–747). Cambridge, MA: MIT Press.

Johnson, M. H., Posner, M. I., & Rothbart, M. K. (1991). Components of visual orienting in early infancy: Contingency learning, anticipatory looking and disengaging. *Journal of Cognitive Neuroscience, 3,* 335–344.

Karmel, B. Z., & Maisel, E. G. (1975). A neuronal activity model for infant visual attention. In L. B. Cohen & P. Salapatek (Eds.), *Infant perception: From sensation to cognition* (Vol. 1, pp. 77–131). New York: Academic Press.

Kremenitzer, J. P., Vaughan, H. G., Kurtzberg, D., & Dowling, K. (1979). Smooth-pursuit eye movements in the newborn infant. *Child Development, 50,* 442–448.

Lansink, J. M., & Richards, J. E. (1997). Heart rate and behavioral measures of attention in six-, nine-, and twelve-month-old infants during object exploration. *Child Development, 68,* 610–620.

Maurer, D., & Lewis, T. L. (1979). A physiological explanation of infants' early visual development. *Canadian Journal of Psychology, 33,* 232–252.

Mesulam, M. M. (1983). The functional anatomy and hemispheric specialization for directed attention. *Trends in Neuroscience, 6,* 384–387.

Mohler, C. W., & Wurtz, R. H. (1976). Organization of monkey superior colliculus: Intermediate layer cells discharging before eye movements. *Journal of Neurophysiology, 39,* 722–744.

Mohler, C. W., & Wurtz, R. H. (1977). Role of striate cortex and superior colliculus in visual guidance of saccadic eye movements in monkeys. *Journal of Neurophysiology, 40,* 74–94.

Ornitz, E. M., Kaplan, A. R., & Westlake, J. R. (1985). Development of the vestibuloocular reflex from infancy to adulthood. *Acta Oto Laryngological, 100,* 180–193.

Pelisson, D., Prablanc, C., & Urquizar, C. (1988). Vestibuloocular reflex inhibition and gaze saccade control characteristics during eye-head orientation in humans. *Journal of Neurophysiology, 59,* 997–1013.

Porges, S. W. (1980). Individual differences in attention: A possible physiological substrate. In B. Keogh (Ed.), *Advances in special education* (Vol. 2, pp. 111–134). Greenwich, CT: JAI.

Posner, M. I. (1995). Attention in cognitive neuroscience: An overview. In M. S. Gazzaniga (Ed.), *Cognitive neurosciences* (pp. 615–624). Cambridge, MA: MIT Press.

Posner, M. I., & Petersen, S. E. (1990). The attention system of the human brain. *Annual Review of Neuroscience, 13,* 25–42.

Prablanc, C., & Jennerod, M. (1975). Corrective saccades: Dependence on retinal reafferent signals. *Vision Research, 15,* 465–469.

Prablanc, C., Masse, D., & Echallier, J. F. (1978). Error-correcting mechanisms in large saccades. *Vision Research, 18,* 557–560.

Regal, D. M., Ashmead, D. H., & Salapatek, P. (1983). The coordination of eye and head movements during early infancy: A selective review. *Behavioural Brain Research, 10,* 125–132.

Regal, D. M., & Salapatek, P. (1982). Eye and head coordination in human infants. *Investigative Opthalmology and Visual Science, 22,* 85.

Reisman, J. E., & Anderson, J. H. (1989). Compensatory eye movements during head and body rotation in infants. *Brain Research, 484,* 119–129.

Richards, J. E. (1985). The development of sustained attention in infants from 14 to 26 weeks of age. *Psychophysiology, 22,* 409–416.

Richards, J. E. (1987). Infant visual sustained attention and respiratory sinus arrhythmia. *Child Development, 58,* 488–496.

Richards, J. E. (1988). Heart rate changes and heart rate rhythms, and infant visual sustained attention. In P. K. Ackles, J. R. Jennings, & M. G. H. Coles (Eds.), *Advances in psychophysiology* (Vol. 3, pp. 189–221). Greenwich, CT: JAI.

Richards, J. E. (1989a). Development and stability of HR-defined, visual sustained attention in 14-, 20-, and 26-week-old infants. *Psychophysiology, 26,* 422–430.

Richards, J. E. (1989b). Sustained visual attention in 8-week-old infants. *Infant Behavior and Development, 12,* 425–436.

Richards, J. E. (1990). *Neurophysiological basis of eye movements, and the effect of attention on eye movements in the development of infant saccades, smooth pursuit, and visual tracking.* Unpublished manuscript.

Richards, J. E. (1997). Peripheral stimulus localization by infants: Attention, age and individual differences in heart rate variability. *Journal of Experimental Psychology: Human Perception and Performance,* 667–680.

Richards, J. E., & Casey, B. J. (1990). Infant visual recognition memory performance as a function of heart rate defined phases of attention. *Infant Behavior and Development, 13,* 585.

Richards, J. E., & Casey, B. J. (1992). Development of sustained visual attention in the human infant. In B. A. Campbell, H. Hayne, & R. Richardson (Eds.), *Attention and information processing in infants and adults* (pp. 30–60). Hillsdale, NJ: Lawrence Erlbaum Associates.

Richards, J. E., & Holley, F. A. (1997). *The effect of attention on the development of eye movements in 2 to 6 month old infants.* Manuscript submitted for publication.

Richards, J. E., & Hunter, S. K. (1997). Peripheral stimulus localization by infants with eye and head movements during visual attention. *Vision Research.*

Robbins, T. W., & Everitt, B. J. (1995). Arousal systems and attention. In M. S. Gazzaniga (Ed.), *Cognitive neurosciences* (pp. 703–720). Cambridge, MA: MIT Press.

Roucoux, A., Culee, C., & Roucoux, M. (1982). Gaze fixation and pursuit in head free human infants. In A. Roucoux & M. Crommelinck (Eds.), *Physiological and pathological aspects of eye movements* (pp. 23–31). The Hague: Dr. W. Junk Publishers.

Roucoux, A., Culee, C., & Roucoux, M. (1983). Development of fixation and pursuit eye movements in human infants. *Behavioural Brain Research, 10,* 133–139.

Ruff, H. A., & Rothbart, M. K. (1996). *Attention in early development.* New York: Oxford University Press.

Salapatek, P. (1975). Pattern perception in early infancy. In L. Cohen & P. Salapatek (Eds.), *Infant perception.* New York: Academic Press.

Salapatek, P., Aslin, R. N., Simonson, J., & Pulos, E. (1980). Infant saccadic eye movements to visible and previously visible targets. *Child Development, 51,* 1090–1094.

Schiller, P. H. (1985). A model for the generation of visually guided saccadic eye movements. In D. Rose & V. G. Dobson (Eds.), *Models of the visual cortex* (pp. 62–70). New York: Wiley.

Shea, S. L., & Aslin, R. N. (1984). Development of horizontal and vertical smooth pursuit in human infants. *Investigative Opthalmology & Visual Science, Supplement 25,* 263.

Shea, S. L., & Aslin, R. N. (1990). Oculomotor responses to step-ramp targets by young human infants. *Vision Research, 30,* 1077–1092.

Shupert, C., & Fuchs, A. F. (1988). Development of conjugate human eye movements. *Vision Research, 28,* 585–596.

Sparks, D. L. (1986). Translation of sensory signals into commands for control of saccadic eye movements: Role of primate superior colliculus. *Physiological Reviews, 66,* 118–171.

Sparks, D. L., & Groh, J. M. (1995). The superior colliculus: A window for viewing issues in integrative neuroscience. In M. S. Gazzaniga (Ed.), *Cognitive neurosciences* (pp. 565–584). Cambridge, MA: MIT Press.

Stein, B. E. (1988). Superior colliculus-mediated visual behaviors in cat and the concept of two corticotectal systems. In T. P. Hicks & G. Benedek (Eds.), *Vision within extrageniculo-striate systems* (pp. 37–54). New York: Elsevier.

Tomlinson, R. D., & Bahra, P. S. (1986a). Combined eye-head gaze shifts in the primate: I. Metrics. *Journal of Neurophysiology, 56,* 1542–1557.

Tomlinson, R. D., & Bahra, P. S. (1986b). Combined eye-head gaze shifts in the primate: II. Interactions between saccades and the vestibuloocular reflex. *Journal of Neurophysiology, 56,* 1558–1570.

Tronick, E., & Clanton, C. (1971). Infant looking patterns. *Vision Research, 11,* 1479–1486.

Tusa, R. J., Zee, D. S., & Herdman, S. J. (1986). Effect of unilateral cerebral cortical lesions on ocular motor behavior in monkeys: Saccades and quick phases. *Journal of Neurophysiology, 56,* 1590–1625.

Uemura, T., Arai, Y., & Shimazaki, C. (1980). Eye-head coordination during lateral gaze in normal subjects. *Acta Oto Laryngologica, 90,* 191–198.

Wurtz, R. H., & Mohler, C. W. (1976). Organization of monkey superior colliculus: Enhanced visual response of superficial layer cells. *Journal of Neurophysiology, 39,* 745–765.

Zangemeister, W. H., & Stark, L. (1982). Gaze latency: Variable interactions of head and eye latency. *Experimental Neurology, 75,* 389–406.

Chapter 5

Summary and Commentary: Eye Movements, Attention and Development

Louise Hainline
Brooklyn College of CUNY

Many of the most important concepts in psychology have proved elusive to define and frustrating to study. The prime example is probably intelligence. Another is attention. The difficulties of finding comprehensive definitions of such constructs that map cleanly onto an agreed-upon, comprehensive sets of methods and measures are well illustrated by the decades of work on both topics. Yet in both cases, the obvious evidence of such psychological processes in everyday life is sufficient to maintain healthy research efforts and continuing attempts to harness the concepts theoretically. In 1890, William James said of attention that "everyone knows what [it] is"; for James, it implied withdrawing from something in order to deal effectively with others (James 1890/1950, p. 403). Since that time, researchers have used attention to mean, *inter alia*, selection, search, mental effort, concentration, and arousal, risking the possibility, as Eysenck and Keane (1990) remarked, that a concept "used to explain everything" might "turn out to explain nothing." Still the interest in attention perseveres.

This volume reflects an ambitious attempt to approach the attention construct developmentally, focusing on visual attention from the perspective of neural development. The chapters in this section illustrate the multiple ways in which attention has been characterized in recent work. The authors appear to be in general agreement that attention involves the selective deployment of information-processing resources. They also manifest general agreement that visual attention can be both overt (i.e., manifested in external behaviors such as orienting eye movements) and covert (implicitly

163

a kind of mental orienting, inferred from changes in response probabilities as a function of specific environmental events). This distinction is somewhat fluid, as it appears to depend on the information available to the observer; if there were no obvious orienting eye movements but under some form of brain imaging, for example, one could "see" the brain change response, the question is whether this is best described as covert or overt orienting. The most relevant example of the problem of the observer's perspective is demonstrated in Richards' technically demanding research measuring eye movements and visual orienting simultaneously with heart rate; Richards and colleagues (e.g., Richards & Hunter, this volume; Richards & Casey, 1992) and Finlay and Ivinkis (1984) have shown that infants sometimes show heart rate changes associated with attention to visual events occurring in both the visual periphery and in the central field, without accompanying eye movements. An empirical question is whether the lack of overt eye movements uniquely characterizes a different type of attention, and if so, what its characteristics are developmentally.

NEURAL CONTROL OF OCULOMOTOR BEHAVIOR IN THE MATURE PRIMATE

As the clearest sign of overt attention is an orienting eye movement, many of these chapters take as inspiration the excellent lead chapter by Peter Schiller on the current knowledge of the neural substrate for oculomotor systems. Previously, one of the best chapters for nonphysiologists on how the brain controls movements of the eyes was Schiller's (1985) work. Chapter 1 in this volume brings that work up to date in terms of current research. Its clear descriptions and diagrams illustrate the complex neural connections that function in support of oculomotor behaviors in the mature primate. It is hard to know what metric to use to evaluate scientific progress; by a simple "arrow" index, in just over a decade, Schiller's model for saccadic control shows significant signs of progress. In 1985, Schiller required 35 arrows (some 21 ascending and 14 descending; see Fig. 1 in the 1985 chapter). In the equivalent figure (Fig. 1.22) in this volume, there are more than 50 (about evenly distributed between ascending and descending connections and including those going to as yet undiscovered regions). Thus, by this simple measure, we have experienced a more than 67% increase in our understanding of this complex sensorimotor system in 12 years. And given the number of question marks in the current figure, one has the strong suspicion that the next few years will bring even more connections to light. Schiller's new chapter will be heavily used by those attempting to understand how the brain controls eye movements in different circumstances, both because of its expository clarity and its well-designed figures.

Schiller describes the mature endpoint of oculomotor development in fine detail. However, the chapter is a challenge for developmentalists because from a physiological perspective, comparatively little is known about the development of these pathways, except in the most general sense: In most cases, the specific elements are both less elaborated and less well functioning at younger ages. As reviewed by Maurer and Lewis (chap. 2, this volume), we have a bit of data on the structural development of different components (superior colliculus (SC), area V1, etc.) in species such as cat and nonhuman primate, but at present, we lack much information about functional properties of the developing system from studies with any species using the recording methods responsible for the modeling described by Schiller. As a result, the student of attentional development, interested in using various eye movements as an index, is left in an uncomfortable position of having to infer neural organization from noninvasive measures.

MEASURES OF INFANT ATTENTION

The measures of behavior we have to work with in research with the human infants are relatively nonspecific, in the sense that they are all influenced by more than one psychological process. Researchers have made good use of behavioral measures such as total looking time, widely used in studies of novelty preference and habituation (see, e.g., chap. 12, this volume, by Colombo & Janowsky) and indices such as direction or latency of first look (as in studies of perimetry, described in Maurer & Lewis, chap. 2, this volume). Other researchers (e.g., Johnson, Gilmore, & Csibra, and Hood, Atkinson, & Braddick, chaps. 3 and 7, this volume) have used observation of ocular orientation to achieve an intermediate level of resolution by having observers rate where within relatively broad areas infants are directing glances. And still other research uses more fine grain measures of specific eye-movement parameters (with measures of saccade length, as in studies with EOG by Richards and colleagues (see Richards & Hunter, chap. 4, this volume) and other methods for recording eye movements like corneal reflection techniques, employed by researchers such as Bronson (1990, 1991) and my research group (e.g., Hainline, 1993). There are also attempts to understand underlying mechanisms of attention by indexing gross physiological responses such as heart rate changes, as in the studies of Richards and colleagues (cf. Richards & Hunter, chap. 4, this volume), combining gross attentional measures with refined heart rate analysis to great benefit, and gross brain responses such as visual evoked responses and event-related potentials (cf. chap. 9 by Bell and chap. 11 by Nelson & Dukette, this volume).

Still, we should be frank about the fact that no one of these measures can be inextricably linked to a particular neural control system, and therefore differences in them across age may be, indeed almost certainly is, multiply determined. It is interesting that in a book on CNS development and attention, for example, that little mention is made of a factor well known to modulate attentional measures in infants, namely, changes in gross arousal and behavioral state (e.g., Berg & Berg, 1987). Evidence is abundant that in early infancy, voluntary infant attention is positioned on a pedestal of cyclic, largely endogenously controlled periods of arousal which have a strong influence on the responsivity of an infant at any given time. The extent to which external versus such internal events influence infant behaviors changes markedly in the first few months, presumptively because of changing relationships between brainstem and higher centers in the control of gross arousal. The practical effect of this is that for most experiments, the dropout rate is typically higher for subjects up to 1–2 months than for older infants and the behavior of younger subjects is generally more variable. It is harder to get younger infants in the optimal waking states to allow behaviors such as attention to be measured in equivalent situations, as such states are both briefer and less stable than they are in older infants. These factors have statistical implications when one compares across age. More importantly, after some years when arousal was rather understudied, recent physiological research (e.g., Castro-Alamancos & Connors, 1996; Kinomura, Larsson, Gulyás, & Roland, 1996; Munk, Roelfsema, König, Engel, & Singer, 1996; Steriade, 1996) reminds us of the influence of the brainstem reticular formation on attention and visual responsiveness, even in mature organisms.

A related problem is that attention to stimuli must be preceded by detection of those stimuli; sensory thresholds are also changing during infancy, and markedly so over the first 6 months. This means that research intending to study the existence or functioning of a particular neural pathway by direct comparison of the response probabilities of infants of different ages to a single combination of stimulus parameters risks confusing changes in sensory thresholds with attention, typically attributed to more central neural processes. The extensive work by Maurer and Lewis (see chap. 2, this volume), for example, shows clear evidence that there is no single perimetric function at a given age in infancy; rather the response probability for a given peripheral location depends crucially on stimulus parameters such as size, intensity, and temporal rate. For example, 1-month-old infants who show no response to target A, a $3°$, 30 cd/m^2 light, flashing at 3 Hz may demonstrate reliable detection of target B, a $5°$, 40 cd/m^2 light, flashing at 6 Hz, presented in the same eccentric location. Two-month-olds might immediately orient to both targets. Is the lack of overt orienting to Target B in the 1-month-old due to differences in the neural bases of attention, or simply an improvement in sensory detection thresholds? If only Target A had been employed, one would have no way to decide. It was only after testing numerous combinations of these factors, that Maurer and Lewis had sufficient evidence to posit a consistent nasal–temporal asymmetry reflecting something pervasive about the neural representation of visual space.

Although tedious, it is important to establish a parametric set of stimuli that allows demonstration of equipotentiality of basic sensory detection for different ages of infants. Such data are a prerequisite for interpreting attentional differences across age as due to the contribution of a particular neural system at a higher functional level in the nervous system. This is particularly a problem when orientational eye movements are the primary dependent measure, as in most cases, the infant is required to make a response to a visual stimulus situated away from the central visual field. Acuity is not uniform across the visual field. We now have both behavioral and electrophysiological measures of infant acuity and contrast sensitivity at different eccentricities in human infants (e.g., Allen, Tyler, & Norcia, 1996; Courage & Adams, 1996) and infant monkeys (Kiorpes & Kiper, 1996); interestingly the results of these studies imply different developmental histories for the relative spatial sensitivities of the central and peripheral retinae in young humans and monkeys, which could complicate an uncritical use of the infant monkey as a human model. An example of the appropriate use of such a control in reported by Hood, Atkinson, and Braddick (chap. 7, this volume) in the stimulus pretesting done in their studies of inhibition of return (IOR); in that work, peripheral targets (patterns of stripes) were equated for peripheral detection before IOR was measured. Unfortunately, such experimental controls are relatively still rare in studies of infant attention.

Similar concerns relate to the distance at which a target is presented, particularly if a target is relatively far from the infant; changes in both spatial sensitivity and the accommodative response of the lens with age mean that less information is available about a target at a given viewing distance for younger than older infants; indeed, sensory factors are probably responsible for the commonly observed fact that young infants have a kind of zone of attention to objects before them, with attention falling off dramatically when objects are more than a meter or so away (e.g., Hainline, Riddell, Grose-Fifer, & Abramov, 1992). Appropriate controls equating for target detectability require that infants of different ages be shown psychophysically equivalent stimuli, rather than physically equal stimuli, especially important when presence or absence of a response is a key variable. Merely picking stimuli that are above threshold for the youngest ages may not be sufficient, as even above threshold stimuli can differ in their potency across age in eliciting a response. More work is clearly needed on this issue, but the possibility of developmental changes in simple detection thresholds for a given sensory target cannot be ruled out without further evaluation when differences in measured attention are found across infant ages.

REVERSE ENGINEERING THE INFANT NERVOUS SYSTEM

Younger and older infants are clearly neurologically different; the issue is how well we can use simple behavioral and gross electrophysiological measures to map where those neurological differences lie. The logic of much of the work described in the early chapters in this volume could be termed *physiologizing* (as opposed to physiology), an attempt to infer specific underlying physiological mechanisms from nonphysiological, or in the case of measures like multiple-electrode EEG, VEP, and ERP, gross-physiological measures. Even using direct physiological recording, it has proved difficult to study the interaction among complex neural systems, as Schiller's chapter demonstrates. The problem of inferring the underlying control circuits from behavior and gross physiology alone is substantially more challenging, even assuming that the neural control circuits in a young infant are less complex. It is as if we are in a position of having to deduce the circuit diagram of a television from observing the picture we see and the way the external controls affect the picture. It's a difficult bit of reverse engineering, and given the complexity, must be tentative and subject to revision by conflicting data. Several of these chapters discuss Bronson's (1974) proposal that the behavior of young infants could be explained by positing that their behavior is under the control only of subcortical structures, with cortically mediated behaviors emerging only later in infancy. The Bronson model was among the first to attempt to explain infant behavior in direct physiological terms. The original proposal was quickly criticized as behaviors that Bronson claimed were not possible for young infants such as shape and orientation discrimination and evidence of habituation in newborns (e.g., Slater, Morison, & Rose, 1982; Slater, Morison, & Somers, 1988) began to be demonstrated.

Regardless of such disconfirming evidence, the subcortical–cortical developmental hypothesis has been attractive to others building physiological explanations for the differences in behaviors between younger and older infants (see, e.g., Atkinson, 1984; Johnson, 1990). Although the later models acknowledge the likelihood of gradual transitions in the control of behavior by various cortical structures, the logic in support of them shows a heavy emphasis on binary (present–absent) data on infant abilities at different ages. The most common form of evidence relies on the absence of behaviors at a young age, followed by the appearance of a behavior (e.g., habituation, smooth pursuit, inhibition of return, etc.) at a later age. Statistically, of course, this unfortunately usually implies acceptance of the null hypothesis and logically devolves to discussions of certain neural centers "coming online" at a given age, when the first occurrence of a target behavior is reported. There has been a tendency in the literature for these null predictions to be reversed by subsequent work done with slight experimental modifications; in addition to the work by Slater, cited earlier, other examples can be seen in the data on inhibition of return in newborns (e.g., Simion, Valenza, Umiltà, & Barba, 1995; Valenza, Simion, & Umiltà, 1994) or the increasing evidence for the rudiments of smooth pursuit, discussed later. Less commonly, the logic is based on data apparently showing a particular behavior in young infants (e.g., asymmetry of monocular optokinetic nystagmus, vector-averaged saccades) in younger subjects that "disappear" in older subjects.

What is at issue, of course, is the old developmental question of whether a specific set of developments is most profitably considered as neurally stagelike (in our engineering metaphor, like a two-pole switch, with higher neural centers first "off" and then "on"), or whether it is better characterized as a continuous process, with earlier stages being in some way simpler, weaker, less complex, and so on, but not qualitatively different than later stages (more like a gain control mechanism or a rheostat, in which higher centers simply exert more influence over time, as they get "turned up"). Our current measures do not lend themselves readily to interpretation as degrees of cortical functioning, and the models we have now probably too stage-like, focused on asking *whether* a given cortical structure is influencing early infant behavior, rather than *how much* a behavior obviously under cortical control is being influenced by higher control circuits at different ages (and we might add, in a given experimental setting). With more careful attention to measures and comparisons of results across ages, perhaps we will develop more nuanced understandings than present models provide. The work on multiple electrode cortical recordings reported in Johnson et al. (chap. 3, this volume) may be a significant step in that direction.

VECTOR AVERAGE SACCADES AS A MARKER TASK OF COLLICULAR INVOLVEMENT

Let us take a specific neural structure proposed to control infant attentional behavior to illustrate some of the difficulties of this type of neural modeling. Many of the existing models of infant oculomotor development (Atkinson, 1984; Bronson, 1974; Johnson, 1990, 1995), reviewed in several chapters in this volume, posit a functioning, completely subcortical (retino-tectal or retino-collicular) circuit for saccadic control in early infancy. Yet Schiller's chapter confirms that at least in the adult monkey, there are no direct connections between the SC's superficial, sensory layers (receiving direct input from the retina and topographically mapped to retinal position) and deeper layers (coding for eye movements of particular sizes and to particular locations in the visual field). The deep layers receive only cortical inputs, so a complete sensorimotor loop necessarily involves the cortex. There is relatively little physiology on the development of the SC, most notably for our case, in infant monkey. Although there might be functional neural connections in the immature organism that are deleted or rerouted over the course of development, at the moment, there is no strong direct physiological evidence of the existence of such pathways directly connecting the superficial and deep layers without cortical input in young primates or humans. With firm data only about the mature endpoint, and little hard evidence of the functional physiology of young primates, attempts to explain infant development in terms of as yet undiscovered neural structures must be regarded with circumspection; from a scientific perspective, "physiologizing" is much more equivocal than physiology.

Inevitably, testing simple models of complex systems has its difficulties. Johnson et al. (chap. 3, this volume) suggest that research organized around the helpful concept of marker tasks can serve to direct research toward data relevant to the models. Among the many situations that can elicit behaviors, it is reasonable to ask what makes for a good marker task, particularly when a neural subsystem in the mature organism has more than one defining characteristic. Johnson et al. propose that a relevant marker task for the direct control system mediated by the superior colliculus is evidence of vector summation in responses stimulated by two brief spatially separated targets presented simultaneously in a demand saccade paradigm. The superior colliculus has a retinotopic spatial organization or map, such that stimulation in different sections produces predictable directional eye movements. Further, simultaneous stimulation of two different SC locations reliably produces a saccade that represents the vector average of those that would be seen to stimulation of each locus individually (Schiller, chap. 1, this volume, Fig. 1.11).

Gilmore, Johnson, Tucker, and Minister (1996) reasoned that if vector summation is a valid marker task of SC-controlled eye movements, the prevalence with which vector summation occurs may indicate the degree to which infant eye movements are under the control of what they term the retino-collicular pathway. Target locations tested in infants at 2, 4, and 6 months are illustrated in Fig. 3.5 in the Johnson et al. chapter. The study found an overall effect of age (Fig. 3.6, Johnson et al., chap. 3, this volume), with 2-month-olds showing significantly more vector averages than 6-month-olds, taken as support for the prediction. As Fig. 3.5 in Johnson et al. (chap. 3, this volume) illustrates, the Gilmore et al. study actually included three trial types (i.e., at 90° midpoints, vs. either horizontal or vertical corners). The results for the different trials show a more complex pattern of results than implied by the average performance. The percentage of vector sum responses showed a clear decline with age only for the midpoint type trials; on the other two types of trials, the reduction in averaged saccades was much weaker or nonsignificant. Apparently, the age differences from the midpoint trials were sufficient to carry the main effect of age, but the percentage of vector-averaged saccades even for 2-month-olds averages less than 25% of all saccades (see Johnson et al., chap. 3, Fig. 3.6). If the saccadic orienting of younger and older infants were under the control of subcortical structures whose hallmark is vector averaging in such a situation, and cortical structures were relatively undeveloped, one would expect a stronger pattern of response across all conditions. Instead, the results suggest that some more gradual process is occurring, which could be attentional, sensory, or spatial, or some combination of all of them.

Gilmore (personal communication, 1997) reports that there was an effect of eccentricity in the vector averaging frequencies observed with infants. On trials that show a decline in saccadic vector averaging across age, targets were closer to the central fixation point (12°) than those on which infants continued to show vector averaging at 4 and 6 months (17°). Only at 7 months is there a decline in vector averaging for targets at 17°. Gilmore proposed that the age differences might occur because there is more extensive projection from the peripheral retina to the SC, so that localization to more peripheral targets will be controlled by the SC for a longer period of time. At this time however, there are no physiological data from young primates to either support or refute this explanation for older infants' behavior. The Maurer and Lewis work on developmental changes in peripheral visual fields would not to lead one to suspect, *a priori*, different processes for localizing 12° vs. 17° targets by 6–7 months of age. As the viewing was binocular, the results cannot be due to a nasal–temporal asymmetry. The pattern of results obtained in the vector averaging study complicates acceptance of the simple hypothesis that led to the study, namely, that behavioral transitions in infants between 2 and 4 months of age are due to the introduction of cortically controlled processes between those ages.

A further problem with this marker test is that according to Schiller, vector averaged saccades can also be elicited by two-point stimulation in the frontal eye fields (FEF), a cortical region thought to be responsible for more conscious, planned saccades; in his hierarchical model, Johnson (1995) suggests that the FEF does not influence infant orienting behavior until after 4–5 months of age. Vector averaging is also produced by electrical stimulation of one point in the SC and one in the FEF. Thus vector averaging alone does not appear to be a definitive test for SC-driven eye movements, particularly if head position, and thus retinal mapping, is kept constant across stimulus presentations. There are also a number of adult studies that show adults' saccades to multiple targets in some circumstances demonstrate a kind of vector-averaging or "center of gravity" spatial distribution, despite the fact that there is no reason to doubt cortical processes being active in the normal adult brain (e.g., Findlay, 1982; Coeffe & O'Regan, 1987; Shepard, Findlay, & Hockey, 1986). More recent research supports the conclusion that these effects are probably not saccadic errors due to low-level processes, but occur because these saccades were programmed when covert spatial attention was distributed across a wide region of the visual field, rather than at one specific small target (He & Kowler, 1989; Kowler, Anderson, Dosher, & Blaser, 1995). Rather than reflecting saccades controlled by the SC, the imprecise saccades observed by Johnson and colleagues could also reflect the coarseness of the infant's spatial maps, present at many neural levels in the brain (see, e.g., Banks & Crowell, 1993; Rizzolatti, Riggio, & Sheliga, 1994). The effect of attention on saccadic target selection is not well understood even in adults (e.g., Deubel & Schneider, 1996), but it likely to be more complex in infants than current models imply.

THE CASE OF SMOOTH PURSUIT AS A MARKER TASK

Another marker task that has been proposed in support of the hypothesis that cortical processes are relatively little involved in the oculomotor behavior of young infants is the purported absence of smooth pursuit in early infancy; smooth pursuit requires a response to retinal slip and is generally regarded as requiring contributions from cortical motion processing centers such as temporal cortical area MT. Most individuals taking this perspective on pursuit development use as their reference data presented by Aslin (1981), in which he reported that infants under the age of 6–8 weeks failed to show any pursuit to bar targets moving in a sinusoidal velocity profile back and forth across a display. In this study, smooth pursuit emerged only after 2 months of age. However, this not the entire story, and it is surprising to see how extensively the models rely on the Aslin (1981) conclusions. There have also been a number of studies in the literature for some time (e.g., Kremenitzer, Vaughn, Kurtzberg, & Dowling, 1979; Roucoux, Culee, & Roucoux, 1983) that contradict the conclusion of absent smooth pursuit in the youngest infants; these studies indicate that infants are capable of episodes of smooth pursuit, even if they do not sustain it for lengthy periods or at high speeds. The most recent studies in this area have been consistent in supporting the view that the basic smooth-pursuit mechanisms are intact and functional even early in infancy, supporting adult-like pursuit, but over a more limited parameter space than in adults (e.g., Buquet, Charlier, Desmidt, & Querleu, 1993; Carchon & Bloch, 1996; Krinsky, Scanlon, & Hainline, 1990; Phillips, Finocchio, Ong, & Fuchs, 1994, 1995, 1997; Shea & Aslin, 1990).

The bulk of these data provides little support for a position that an essential difference between younger and older infants is the absence of smooth pursuit. Rather, these studies report obvious smooth eye movements in response to stimulus movement, although the prevalence depends on the characteristics of the stimulus such as the target speed (best in the range of 7–15 degrees per sec) and the velocity profile (better in response to constant velocity ramp than to motion such as a sinusoidal velocity profile, as used by Aslin, 1981; such a velocity profile requires continuous calculation of the relative error of eye and target position which may unduly tax the computational capacities of the infant system). We have here another example of why parametric examination of the stimulus conditions at different ages is essential. The smooth pursuit of early infancy is demonstrated mostly for constant, midrange velocities. It seems that pursuit targets do not, as has been claimed, have to be large, as long as they are sufficiently above threshold; the targets in Krinsky et al. (1990) and in Phillips et al. (1997) were small lighted targets around 1.5° across. In contrast to the claim that young infants show no smooth pursuit, the preponderance of the data shows that the systems responsible for smooth pursuit exist and function in early infancy. At the same time, there is no question that pursuit improves with age over infancy, again implying a gradual recruitment of higher levels of performance. In adults, smooth pursuit at higher speeds requires considerable concentration and is a motivated, voluntary response.

It is unlikely that early pursuit is really subcortical optokinetic nystagmus (OKN), as has sometimes been claimed. OKN is generally not stimulated by targets on the order of a few degrees, and is typically defined as a biphasic alternation of reversing slow and fast phases, not a unidirectional mixture of pursuit and forward saccades. OKN has often figured into discussions of subcortical–cortical models, particularly in the case of monocular OKN which is notably asymmetric in young infants. Under many conditions of stimulation, infants younger than a few months show obvious, high-amplitude, low-frequency nystagmic responses to monocularly presented patterns moving in a temporal-to-nasal direction, with less obvious low-amplitude, high-frequency or no obvious nystagmic responses to monocular patterns moving in a nasal-to-temporal direction (see, e.g., Preston & Finocchio, 1993). There are numerous studies reporting a developmental change in this response, which by analogy to the cat has been attributed to increasingly cortically mediated mechanisms. The exact neural pathways responsible for the development of symmetry at lower velocities are still not well understood, despite decades of study. The simplicity of the explanation that early asymmetric OKN is subcortical has been compromised by the failure to find clear correlations with other cortical functions as symmetry emerges. Also, at high velocities of stimulus movement even adults show the same monocular asymmetry, suggesting that the developmental difference is not in the presence or absence of the OKN asymmetry, but the range of stimulus speeds where it is observed. Also, Phillips et al. (1995) reported that the monocular optokinetic nystagmus seen in young infants begins with a fast phase, indicative of the mechanism responsible for smooth pursuit, rather than a slow period of build-up more typically associated with subcortical mechanisms. These data, at least, are more consistent with the perspective that what changes developmentally is the range of conditions that will elicit appropriate eye movements to moving targets, not the presence or absence of the basic oculomotor behaviors themselves.

SOME RECOMMENDATIONS

Attention is clearly not an all-or-nothing phenomenon. Richards and his colleagues (Richards & Hunter, chap. 4, this volume; Richards & Casey, 1992) have delineated a cycle of at least four phases for simple visual attention to an environmental event that are not directly observable from simple observation but reflect qualitatively different stages of attention and information processing. The use of multiple measures such as adding heart rate recording to observations of gross attentional deployment can be quite powerful in giving us perspective on the underlying attentional processes. Yet relatively few researchers regularly record heart rate as a measure of infant attention. If the goal is to characterize stages in an attentional cycle, one might not need an extremely high level of precision in recording heart rate to make it a useful adjunct to measures of looking time. It might be profitable then to encourage attention researchers experienced in heart rate recording to evaluate a form of recording heart rate good enough to allow the use of heart rate as a measure in a broader range of developmental laboratories.

It remains to be seen whether any method that allowed plug-and-play heart rate recording would be robust enough to differentiate different phases of attention, but new sensor technologies might make this feasible. Ideally, such methods could involve other than chest electrodes, and would employ telemetry to avoid the "wired baby" situation. Such recording techniques would obviously need to be validated against more rigorous recording methods, just as simple observations of eye movements have sometimes been validated by more complex recording of eye movements to establish baseline levels of recording sensitivity. Such methods could be an important adjunct to future studies of infant attention.

Another recommendation is for infant researchers to exercise care in borrowing descriptive terms from the adult literature. Such terms may need refinement when used with developing organisms. For example, in the various chapters in the book, eye movements are sometimes termed endogenous if they are controlled by purposive, cognitive mechanisms, and exogenous if they are controlled reflexively by the characteristics of external stimuli. The implication is that endogenous movements are more mature than exogenous movements. Yet in the infancy period, eye movements during REM sleep and spontaneous eye movements in the dark are sometimes also referred to as under endogenous control, in this case by lower neural centers; thus they are closer to reflexive than voluntary processes. In that sense, direct control of eye movements by stimuli may be more, not less mature. Also, even during adulthood, the majority of the thousands of saccades that we make during our waking hours are rather more reactive than specifically planned; sometimes such saccades are also called spontaneous. Planned saccades to specific targets or produced as the result of a plan to search for specific targets are relatively less frequent. It is not clear that it is particularly appropriate to refer to the former as immature and the latter as mature. They clearly do, however, involve different attentional mechanisms. *Active* versus *passive* orienting (cf. e.g., Rizzolatti et al., 1994) might be useful terms to explore.

In all this work, it is a good idea to occasionally pull back from selective attention on attention, per se, and take a systems perspective. In this case, it means looking at the developmental tasks of the whole infant, not just the oculomotor system, as exhibited in natural circumstances, not just the austere circumstances of the laboratory. As I have pointed out in other work (Hainline & Abramov, 1991), focusing on how the infant is deficient from the adult case is not incorrect, but can be overdone if it leaves the impression of an organism cut off from or at the mercy of outside forces. We need to ask whether the conclusions being drawn from a set of studies make sense in terms of other things we know about the infant. We also need to keep in mind, as pointed out earlier, that the infant has many systems developing simultaneously, and that they are interacting in complex ways.

SUMMARY AND CONCLUSIONS

The intent of this discussion is not to imply that attempts at "physiologizing" the infant are not worthwhile, only that we must be careful to do it in a way that leads to new insights rather than limiting our understanding of development. The study of neural development in the human is a demanding kind of science to do, and one needs a good deal of data to do it well. The most successful examples of this kind of work are those in which human infants and young monkeys have been given equivalent behavioral tasks, and the results related to known developmental phenomena derived from standard physiological measures in the monkey case. The work on visual sensory development by Kiorpes and her colleagues is one example of such a program. Another is found in Diamond and colleagues' efforts to explain the development of Piagetian A error in terms of maturation in prefrontal cortical structures; that research program draws on both considerable behavioral data on a related task (delayed response) and ablation data from monkey, as well as the human behavioral data from infants on the Piagetian task (see Bell, chap. 9, this volume for a discussion of this and related research). By mapping the types of errors and their time courses in the two research domains, one gets the satisfactory feeling, if not assurance, that the changes in infant behavior are likely to be directly related to the development of specific structures in the prefrontal cortex.

In the present case, we lack this kind of evidence for most of the attentional tasks described here, and even worse, in some cases, the predictions from adult monkey physiology contradict what has been proposed for the human infant. Finding the data to decide between discontinuous ("switch") and continuous ("gain") models is difficult. Changes in neural conduction speed with myelinization alone (with existing circuits intact) can have major impact on how motor behaviors will be displayed in a given experimental situation (e.g., for a given exposure time or stimulus speed), even with all neural centers functional. Different levels of responsivity at different ages may also reflect changes in stimulus detectability due to sensory development at all neural levels. Add to this endogenously controlled modulations in overall arousal caused by cyclical state microcycles during waking, as well as exogenously controlled changes in the attention cycle defined by heart rate, as measured by Richards and colleagues, and it becomes very difficult to read physiological development from simple differences in the behaviors of infants of different ages. Collaborations between infant researchers who can suggest interesting human questions and researchers who have more direct techniques for studying underlying mechanisms are rare and very beneficial to our progress. Maybe if we could only talk Peter Schiller into working with infant monkeys . . .

REFERENCES

Allen, D., Tyler, C. W., & Norcia, A. M. (1996). Development of grating acuity and contrast sensitivity in the central and peripheral visual field of the human infants. *Vision Research, 36*, 1945–1953.

Aslin, R. N. (1981). Development of smooth pursuit in human infants. In D. F. Fisher, R. A. Monty, & J. Senders (Eds.), *Eye movements: Cognition and visual perception* (pp. 31–52). Hillsdale, NJ: Lawrence Erlbaum Associates.

Atkinson, J. (1984). Human visual development over the first six months of life: A review and a hypothesis. *Human Neurobiology, 3,* 61–74.

Banks, M. S., & Crowell, J. A. (1993). Front-end limitations to infant spatial vision: Examination of two analyses. In K. Simons (Ed.), *Early visual development, normal and abnormal* (pp. 91–116). New York: Oxford University Press.

Berg, W. K., & Berg, K. M. (1987). Psychophysiological development in infancy: State, startle and attention. In J. D. Osofsky (Ed.), *Handbook of infant development, 2nd Ed.* (pp. 238–317). New York: Wiley.

Buquet, C., Charlier, J. R., Desmidt, A., & Querleu, D. (1993). Evaluation of spatial discrimination of infants with visual pursuit of pattern stimuli. *Investigative Ophthalmology and Visual Science, Supplement, 34,* 1357.

Bronson, G. W. (1974). The postnatal growth of visual capacity. *Child Development, 45,* 873–890.

Bronson, G. W. (1990). Changes in infants' scanning over the 2- to 14-week age period. *Journal of Experimental Child Psychology, 49,* 101–125.

Bronson, G. W. (1991). Infant differences in rate of visual encoding. *Child Development, 62,* 44–54.

Carchon, I., & Bloch, H. (1996). Eye-head relations in neonates and young infants. In F. Vital-Durand, J. Atkinson, & O. Braddick (Eds.), *Infant vision* (pp. 249–264). Oxford, England: Oxford University Press.

Castro-Alamancos, M. A., & Connors, B. W. (1996). Short-term plasticity of a thalamocortical pathway dynamically modulated by behavioral state. *Science, 272,* 274–277.

Coeffe, C., & O'Regan, J. K. (1987). Reducing the influence of non-target stimuli on saccadic accuracy: Predictability and latency effects. *Vision Research, 27,* 227–240.

Courage, M. L., & Adams, R. J. (1996). Infant peripheral vision: The development of monocular visual acuity in the first 3 months of postnatal life. *Vision Research, 36,* 1207–1215.

Deubel, H., & Schneider, W. X. (1996). Saccade target selection and object recognition: Evidence for a common attentional mechanism. *Vision Research, 36,* 1827–1837.

Eysenck, M., & Keane, M. (1990). *Cognitive psychology: A student's handbook.* London: Lawrence Erlbaum Associates.

Findlay, J. M. (1982). Global visual processing for saccadic eye movements. *Vision Research, 22,* 1033–1046.

Finlay, D., & Ivinkis, A. (1984). Cardiac and visual responses to moving stimuli presented either successively or simultaneously to the central and peripheral visual fields in 4-month-old infants. *Developmental Psychology, 20,* 29–36.

Gilmore, R. O., Johnson, M. H., Tucker, L. A., & Minister, S. L. (1996). Vector summation in young infants' saccades. *Infant Behavior and Development, 19,* 475.

Hainline, L. (1993). Conjugate eye movements of infants. In K. Simons (Ed.), *Early visual development, normal and abnormal* (pp. 47–79). New York: Oxford University Press.

Hainline, L., & Abramov, I. (1991). Assessing infant development: Is infant vision good enough? In C. Rovee-Collier & L. P. Lipsitt (Eds.), *Advances in infancy research, Vol. 7* (pp. 39–102). Norwood, NJ: Ablex.

Hainline, L., Riddell, P. M., Grose-Fifer, J., & Abramov, I. (1992). Development of accommodation and convergence in infancy. *Behavioural Brain Research, 49,* 33–50.

He, P., & Kowler, E. (1989). The role of location probability in the programming of saccades: Implications for "center-of-gravity" tendencies. *Vision Research, 29,* 1165–1181.

James, W. (1890/1950). *The principles of psychology.* New York: Dover.

Johnson, M. (1990). Cortical maturation and the development of visual attention in early infancy. *Journal of Cognitive Neuroscience, 2,* 81–95.

Johnson, M. (1995). The development of visual attention: A cognitive neuroscience perspective. In M. S. Gazzaniga (Ed.), *The cognitive neurosciences* (pp. 735–747). Cambridge, MA: MIT Press.

Kiorpes, L., & Kiper, D. C. (1996). Development of contrast sensitivity across the visual field in macaque monkeys (*Macaca nemestrina*). *Vision Research, 36,* 239–247.

Kowler, E., Anderson, E., Dosher, B., & Blaser, E. (1995). The role of attention in the programming of saccades. *Vision Research, 35,* 1897–1916.

Kinomura, S., Larsson, J., Gulyás, B., & Roland, P. E. (1996). Activation by attention of the human reticular formation and thalamic intralaminar nuclei. *Science, 272,* 512–515.

Kremenitzer, J. P., Vaughan, H. G., Kurtzberg, D., & Dowling, K. (1979). Smooth-pursuit eye movements in the newborn infant. *Child Development, 50,* 442–448.

Krinsky, S., Scanlon, M., & Hainline, L. (1990). In pursuit of smooth pursuit: A repeated excursion approach. *Infant Behavior and Development, 13,* 462.

Munk, M. H. J., Roelfsema, P. R., König, P., Engel, A. K., & Singer, W. (1996). Role of reticular activation in the modulation of intracortical synchronization. *Science, 272,* 271–274.

Phillips, J. O., Finocchio, D. V., Ong, L., & Fuchs, A. F. (1994). Development of tracking strategies in human infants during smooth target motion. *Investigative Ophthalmology and Visual Science, Supplement, 35,* 2031.

Phillips, J. O., Finocchio, D. V., Ong, L., & Fuchs, A. F. (1995). Development of binocular and monocular OKN in human infants. *Investigative Ophthalmology and Visual Science, Supplement, 36,* 1649.

Phillips, J. O., Finocchio, D. V., Ong, L., & Fuchs, A. F. (1997). Smooth pursuit in 1- to 4-month-old infants. *Vision Research.*

Preston, K. L., & Finocchio, D. V. (1993). Development of vestibuloocular and optokinetic reflexes. In K. Simons (Ed.), *Early visual development, normal and abnormal* (pp. 80–90). New York: Oxford University Press.

Richards, J. E., & Casey, B. J. (1992). Development of sustained visual attention in the human infant. In B. A. Campbell, H. Hayne, & R. Richardson (Eds.), *Attention and information processing in infants and adults* (pp. 30–60). Hillsdale, NJ: Lawrence Erlbaum Associates.

Rizzolatti, G., Riggio, L., & Sheliga, B. M. (1994). Space and selective attention, In C. Umiltà & M. Moscovitch (Eds.), *Attention and performance XV: Conscious and nonconscious information processing* (pp. 231–265). Cambridge, MA: MIT Press.

Roucoux, A., Culee, C., & Roucoux, M. (1983). Development of fixation and pursuit eye movements in human infants. *Behavioural Brain Research, 10,* 133–139.

Schiller, P. (1985). A model for the general of visually guided saccadic eye movements. In D. Rose & V. G. Dobson (Eds.), *Models of the visual cortex* (pp. 62–70). Chichester, England: Wiley.

Shea, S. L., & Aslin, R. N. (1990). Oculomotor responses to step-ramp targets by young human infants. *Vision Research, 30,* 1077–1092.

Shepard, M., Findlay, J. M., & Hockey, R. J. (1986). The relationship between eye movements and spatial attention. *The Quarterly Journal of Experimental Psychology, 38,* 475–491.

Simion, F., Valenza, E., Umiltà, C., & Dalla Barba, B. (1995). Inhibition of return in newborns is temporal-nasal asymmetrical. *Infant Behavior and Development, 18,* 189–194.

Slater, A. M., Morison, V., & Rose, D. (1982). Perception of shape by the new-born baby. *British Journal of Developmental Psychology, 1,* 135–142.

Slater, A. M., Morison, V., & Somers, M. (1988). Orientation discrimination and cortical function in the human newborn. *Perception, 17,* 597–602.

Steriade, M. (1996). Arousal: Revisiting the reticular activating system. *Science, 272,* 225–226.

Valenza, E., Simion, F., & Umiltà, C. (1994). Inhibition of return in newborns. *Infant Behavior and Development, 17,* 293–302.

Part II

ORIENTING TO LOCATIONS AND OBJECTS

Chapter **6**

The Neurology of Visual Orienting: A Pathological Disintegration of Development

Robert Rafal
University of California, Davis
and Northern California Veteran's Administration Health Care System

Our neural machinery for visual orienting, like the rest of us, is the product of a long evolutionary history (Ingle, 1973). All vertebrates have primitive midbrain circuits for reflexively orienting the eyes toward salient events occurring in the visual periphery. In foveate mammals, including humans, these archetypal pathways function to align high acuity regions of the retina with objects of potential interest; but they must also be integrated with cortical mechanisms involved in strategic search under endogenous control. As mammals, humans have a phylogenetically new visual cortex that receives its dominant input from the retina through the thalamus (its lateral geniculate nucleus). This new system is superimposed on the ancient pathways from the retina to the midbrain, and these two systems must be coordinated to provide coherent experience and behavior.

The evolutionary challenges of integrating subcortical and cortical systems to meet the adaptive demands facing each species have determined individual solutions in different mammals depending on their specializations. Study of the comparative neurology of these differences in mammals can provide us with clues on this intriguing problem in psychobiology (Stein & Meredith, 1993). Yet, to gain insights on our own unique evolutionary history, perhaps the most direct approach is to study the development of contemporary humans through ontogeny, maturation, aging, and disease (see Enns, Brodeur, & Trick, chap. 13, this volume).

Insofar as the study of development can give us glimpses of our evolutionary history, then there is also a sense in which pathology can disar-

181

ticulate postnatal development and reveal the principles that drive it. It is a cardinal principle of neurology that disease processes affecting higher centers—especially cerebral cortex—are revealed by the re-appearance of primitive reflexes. In the fetus, stimulation of the foot produces a "flexion reflex" with flexion of the trunk, the hip, knee, ankle and dorsiflexion of the great toe. In the newborn infant, the Babinski sign (dorsiflexion of the great toe with fanning of the others when the sole of the foot is stimulated) remains as a remnant of this reflex response; and with the beginning maturation of the cortico-spinal tract, this sign, too, disappears by the age of 6 months. If there is subsequent damage to the cortico-spinal tract, due to a lesion of the motor cortex, spinal cord, or pathways connecting them, the Babinski sign reappears as this primitive reflex becomes disinhibited—a useful localizing sign for the clinical neurologist. Similarly, the sucking and rooting reflexes disappear after the nursing years; but can reappear in a patient with Alzheimer's disease. Presumably these primitive reflexes remain hard wired in the nervous system but are inhibited after infancy—until a cortical insult causes them to be disinhibited.

Implicit here is the notion that the nervous system routinely goes about its business through an orchestration of reflexes by endogenous processes which can activate or inhibit them. The development of midbrain visuo-motor reflexes in babies and children is a story of increasing cortical regulation throughout maturation. Subsequent lesions in adults can, in some ways, reverse this developmental process and produce regressions in visuomotor flexibility.

With the encephalization of visual function in mammals during evolution, the phylogenetically ancient visuomotor reflex pathways of the midbrain have been integrated into a complex, distributed network of brain systems for coordinating visually guided and goal-directed behavior. Other chapters in this volume describe the maturation of this network during development, allowing for more complex and flexible visual behavior (Enns et al., chap. 13; Hood et al., chap. 7; Johnson et al., chap. 3; Mauer & Lewis, chap. 2; Schiller, chap. 1). This chapter considers some of the effects of pathology on visual orienting in the adult. These neurologic disorders, by disarticulating development, can help us understand the neural basis of attention in humans. The purpose is not to detail a catalogue of all of the distressing and intriguing neurologic syndromes that disrupt attention. [For more extensive treatments of some of classic cortical syndromes such as hemispatial neglect or Balint's syndrome that result from unilateral or bilateral lesions of the parietal lobes, respectively, see Rafal (1996a, 1996b).] The emphasis here is on pathologic explorations of a few selected midbrain visuomotor reflexes whose development is considered in other chapters of this volume. Studies that I review shed light on the functions of some of these reflex pathways in the adult brain, and on the higher brain mechanisms that regulate them in health and disease. Three mid-brain reflexes are considered: the visual grasp reflex; inhibition of return; and the fixation reflex (as manifest by the fixation offset effect).

THE VISUAL GRASP REFLEX

I first was attracted to the study of visually guided behavior when, at the start of my neurology training I cared for patients who, like the gentleman shown in Fig. 6.1, had a degenerative neurologic disease called progressive supranuclear palsy or PSP. Note in the figure that he doesn't look at me and establish eye contact while we are discussing his medication (Fig. 6.1, top left). Even when I lean toward his face, this potent looming and socially imperative stimulus fails to trigger an orienting response (top right). He isn't blind and he does see me: When I call him by name and ask him to

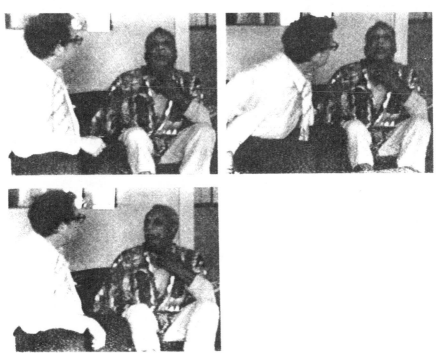

FIG. 6.1. Loss of spontaneous social orienting in a patient with progressive supranuclear palsy. The patient doesn't establish eye contact while discussing his medication with me (top left). Even when I loom toward him with my face, he doesn't orient (top right). When I ask him to look at me, though, he is able to (bottom). (Reprinted from Rafal & Grimm, 1981.)

look at me, he can (bottom left). This figure illustrates the striking loss of spontaneous social orienting that is due to the midbrain pathology in this disease.

Human infants, even newborns, are attracted to orient to the human face (Johnson & Morton, 1991). The reader with any military training will know from harsh experience that this social orienting is a very powerful reflex. Troops being inspected on parade are required to stand to attention with the eyes fixed straight ahead. They are not permitted to turn toward the inspector when approached; and even when directly confronted and interrogated, they are expected to "look through" the drill instructor. It is very hard not to orient to someone who approaches you, looks you in the eye, and yells at you. To inhibit this social orienting reflex takes great discipline (which is, for military purposes after all, the point of the exercise). After being punished with enough pushups, the recruit can learn to inhibit the powerful impulse to orient. Having had to do my share, I was intrigued by the lack of visual regard in these patients, and by their loss of a spontaneous visual grasp reflex.

Orienting and Visually Guided Behavior in Progressive Supranuclear Palsy

In submammalian vertebrates, the visual grasp reflex is mediated by a reflex pathway from retina to the optic tectum of the midbrain. In mammals, this part of the brain is called the superior colliculus, but its role in vision and visually guided behavior has been something of a puzzle. Mammals have evolved a completely new cortical visual system based on visual input from the retina to the lateral geniculate nucleus and thence to the primary visual, or striate, cortex in the occipital lobe.

My interest in the possible functions of the phylogenetically ancient retino-tectal pathway to the midbrain in humans was sparked because the distinguishing pathological feature of PSP is a severe degeneration of the dorsal midbrain including the superior colliculus and peri-tectal region. This is a heterogeneous degenerative disorder which, like Parkinson's disease with which it shares many clinical features, also affects the basal ganglia as well as other subcortical nuclei. However, the collicular pathology is unique to PSP and accounts for its distinguishing clinical feature—a paralysis of eye movements, especially in the vertical plane.

The midbrain pathology of this disease produces not only a compromise of eye movements, but also results in a striking and pervasive derangement of visually guided behavior (Rafal, 1992; Rafal & Grimm, 1981). Although visual acuity is not affected, patients with PSP *behave as if they were blind,* even at a stage in the disease when their eyes are not totally paralyzed. They do not orient to establish eye contact with persons who approach them or engage them in conversation; nor do they look down at their plate while eating, but rather grope for their food without looking (Fig. 6.1, bottom right). The plight of these patients tells us that midbrain visuomotor reflexes retain an important role in human visually guided behavior in daily life.

In several experiments done with Michael Posner in the early 1980s, we showed that PSP patients are not only slow in moving their eyes, but in moving their attention as well (Posner, Cohen, & Rafal, 1982; Posner, Rafal, Choate, & Vaughn, 1985; Rafal, Posner, Friedman, Inhoff, & Bernstein, 1988). We also found that these patients were deficient in generating another visual reflex, inhibition of return, which I return to later (Posner et al., 1985). First, though, I review some converging evidence, from another group of patients, that implicates the midbrain pathways in generating a visual grasp reflex in humans. These are patients with blindness in one visual field, or hemianopia, due to destruction of primary visual cortex. Having examined, in PSP patients, what visual reflexes are lost in patients with midbrain degeneration due to PSP, we can also ask whether these reflexes are preserved in patients who lack visual input to cortex or conscious awareness of the visual signals that elicit them.

Blindsight: Saccade Inhibition by Signals in the Hemianopic Field

What visuomotor function is preserved when only the retinotectal pathway is competent to process visual input? Humans who become hemianopic due to destruction of the primary visual (striate) cortex are rendered clinically blind in the entire hemifield contralateral to the lesion, and cannot see even salient signals, such as a waving hand, within the scotoma (the blind area). They are unable to report such events and deny any awareness of them. In no other animal, including monkeys, do striate cortex lesions produce such profound and lasting blindness. It is thus clear that the geniculo-striate pathway in humans is dominant over the phylogenetically older retinotectal pathways. It is perhaps not surprising that the neuroscience community came to view the older pathway as being vestigial in humans, providing little service to normal vision.

Yet its remarkable how well these patients compensate for their visual loss. With time they get about beautifully and their function in everyday life gives only an occasional hint that they have lost half their visual field. Recent studies in hemianopic human patients have provided some evidence that this remarkable compensation may be mediated, in part, by preserved retinotectal visual pathways. These pathways process information that, although not accessible to conscious awareness, can nevertheless trigger orienting responses toward the hemianopic field. This "blindsight" has been demonstrated by requiring hemianopic subjects to move their eyes or reach toward signals that they cannot "see" and by employing forced-choice discrimination tasks (Weiskrantz, 1986). The physiologic mechanisms mediating blindsight remain uncertain, and the role of the retinotectal pathway is controversial. In some patients there is "residual vision" that could be mediated by spared geniculostriate fibers, and that could reflect degraded cortical vision near the perceptual threshold (Fendrich, Wessinger, & Gazzaniga, 1992). Other investigators propose that blindsight reflects processing of visual input from retinotectal afferents to the superior colliculus.

Figure 6.2 (top) shows an experiment used to demonstrate that blindsight can be mediated by extrageniculate visual pathways (Rafal, Smith, Krantz, Cohen, & Brennan, 1990). This experiment showed that a peripheral visual signal reflexively activates the midbrain oculomotor system. This study examined patients who had suffered an occipital stroke destroying the geniculostriate pathway; they were blind in visual field opposite the lesion, and could not report the presence or absence of stimuli presented there. Subjects maintained fixation on the middle of a video display, and on each trial made a saccadic eye movement to a target that appeared in the *intact* hemifield. Blindsight was inferred from the effect that resulted from the presentation of an unseen distractor in the blind hemifield (which had the same eccentricity and luminance as the saccade target), simultaneous with or immediately preceding the target.

This study exploited a lateralized neuroanatomic arrangement of retino-tectal pathways, distinguishing them from those of the geniculostriate system; namely, more direct projections to midbrain, extrageniculate pathways from the temporal hemifield. The use of temporal–nasal asymmetries as a marker for collicular mediation is discussed in more detail elsewhere in this volume (see Mauer & Lewis, chap. 2). The geniculostriate pathway, which is the dominant pathway to visual cortex in the occipital lobe, carries both crossed and uncrossed fibers, so that the visual cortex of each hemisphere receives binocular projections representing the contralateral visual field from both eyes. In contrast, the more primitive midbrain pathways have more crossed fibers from the contralateral eye. Moreover, these projections are asymmetrically represented with a greater representation of the temporal hemifield (temporal meaning toward the temple, in contrast to nasal—toward the nose). Thus, a functional asymmetry between temporal and nasal hemifield activation can serve as a marker for extrageniculate mediation, and perhaps midbrain involvement.

The results (Fig. 6.2, bottom) showed that unseen distractor signals presented to the blind, temporal (but not nasal) hemifield of hemianopic patients increased the latency of saccades directed to targets presented in the intact visual field. These results provide direct evidence that there is a reflexive activation of retinotectal pathways to prime the oculomotor

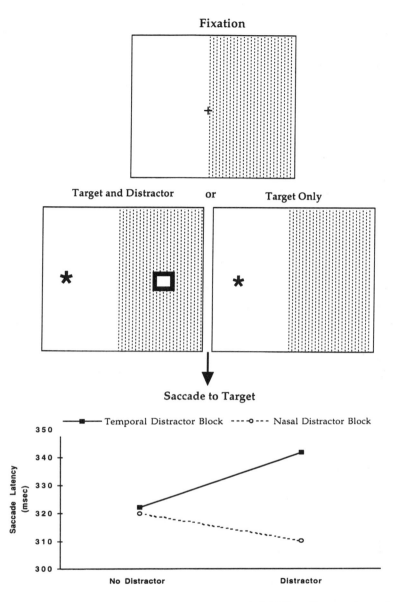

FIG. 6.2. Saccade inhibition by signals in the hemianopic field. Top: The experimental display and task for a patient with right hemianopia. The hemianopic field is depicted by stippling. The task was to make a saccadic eye movement to a target appearing on the left (in the intact field). On some trials the box on the right brightened—the distractor. The patient did not see the distractor. On blocks in which the right eye was patched the distractor was in the nasal hemifield; on blocks in which the left eye was patched the distractor was in the temporal hemifield. In this experiment the effect of the unseen distractor on saccade latency was measured compared to the no distractor condition. Bottom: Results of the experiment for five hemianopic patients. Mean of the median saccade latency (in ms) in the distractor and no distractor conditions are shown for blocks in which the distractor in the blind field was temporal and nasal.

system, and that this activation, possibly by inhibition of the contralateral superior colliculus, slows saccades to the opposite field. An advantage for orienting toward the temporal field has also been demonstrated in hemianopic infants after hemispherectomy (Braddick, Atkinson, Hood, Harkness, Jackson, & Vargha, 1992).

The clinical observations in patients with PSP and hemianopia converge with a large body of experimental research in animals on the role of midbrain visuomotor pathways for reflexive orienting. The clinical findings confirm that these pathways make an important contribution to regulating visually guided behavior in human adults. During early stages of postnatal development, these reflexes dominate visually guided behavior. With maturation, they come under increasing control of cortical systems which integrate the primitive reflexes into a more complex and flexible repertoire of voluntary and goal directed behaviors, presumably through mechanisms that can activate or inhibit the more primitive midbrain pathways. The following sections review some effects of cortical pathology on the regulation of the visual grasp reflex.

Parietal Lobe Lesions Disinhibit the Visual Grasp Reflex:
Visual Neglect and the Sprague Effect

Figure 6.3 shows a patient with left hemispatial neglect caused by a recent large stroke in the right frontal and parietal lobes. The figure on the left shows that he has his head and eyes directed to his right and he ignores me as I approach him from his left. He is not blind in his left visual field because, when his attention is not directed to the right and he is told to expect something on his left, he did usually detect objects presented in his left visual field. However, as shown in the figure on the right, whenever two objects were presented simultaneously in both fields, he oriented to the one on his right and did not detect the one in the left field. This clinical sign is called visual extinction, and is part of the syndrome of hemispatial neglect.

In this syndrome there is an impairment of orienting attention to the field contralateral to the lesion, and this results in a loss of conscious awareness of information from that field. In addition, as seen in Fig. 6.3, there is also a pathologically disinhibited orienting toward the *ipsilesional* field (on the side of the lesion). This reciprocal disorder in which a parietal lesion causes both impaired orienting to the contralesional field and disinhibited "hyper-orienting" to the ipsilesional field has promulgated what Kinsbourne dubbed the "hemispheric rivalry" account of visual orienting (Kinsbourne, 1977, 1993). Each hemisphere generates a bias to orient to its contralesional field, and the two hemispheres mutually inhibit one another. A lesion in one hemisphere produces an ipsilesional orienting

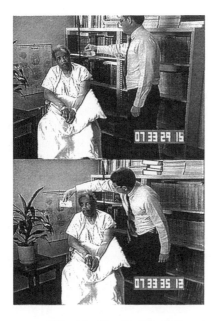
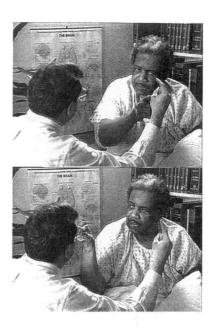

FIG. 6.3. Hemispatial neglect in a patient with a recent large right fronto-parietal stroke. Left: Although he is not blind in his left visual field, the patient doesn't notice me as I approach from his left side (top) but orients promptly when approached from the right (bottom). Right: Visual extinction on double simultaneous stimulation. Although he almost always reported detecting a finger wiggling in his left visual field when wiggled by itself (top), he did not see the wiggling finger in the left field when a finger was wiggled simultaneously in the right field.

bias that is the result of both impaired orienting to the contralesional field *and* a disinhibited visual grasp reflex toward the ipsilesional field.

Reciprocal hemispheric inhibition could be mediated through cortical, or subcortical connections—or through both. One account of the neural basis for mutual hemispheric inhibition emphasizes mutually inhibitory callosal connections between homologous regions of cerebral cortex of the two hemispheres. According to this account, when one hemisphere is lesioned, homologous regions of cerebral cortex in the opposite hemisphere, that normally receive inhibitory projections from the damaged region through the corpus callosum, become disinhibited; and the disinhibited regions produce hyper-orienting of attention to the ipsilesional side. We have recently (Seyal, Ro, & Rafal, 1995) obtained some support for this hypothesis by examining the effects of transcranial magnetic stimulation (TMS) on sensory thresholds for tactile detection in normal subjects. TMS uses a transient magnetic field on the scalp to induce a very brief electrical stimulation that inactivates the underlying cortex for a few hundred ms—in essence an ultra temporary lesion. A suprathreshold (i.e., sufficiently strong to activate a twitch in the contralateral thumb when applied over motor cortex) TMS stimulus transiently inactivates subjacent cortex. This study examined whether the hemisphere opposite the TMS stimulus would show signs of disinhibition, manifested as a reduced threshold to detect a tactile stimulus in the thumb *ipsilateral* to the TMS lesion. Results supported the attentional disinhibition account by showing a reduced ipsilateral tactile threshold after parietal (3 or 5 cm posterior to motor cortex) TMS, but not when TMS was applied at control locations over the motor cortex or 5 cm anterior to it.

Another mechanism contributing to ipsilesional hyper-orienting, more pertinent to the theme of this chapter, postulates an interaction between cerebral cortex and subcortical visuomotor reflexes of the midbrain. According to this account, the unlesioned parietal lobe becomes disinhibited and tonically increases activity in the superior colliculus ipsilateral to it; while the colliculus on the side of the lesion loses the tonic activation from the damaged parietal lobe. As a result, parietal lesions also produce an imbalance in the activity of subcortical structures involved in orienting such as the superior colliculus. The ipsilesional superior colliculus becomes dysfunctional while the contralesional superior colliculus becomes disinhibited, and this results in exaggerated reflexive orienting to signals in the ipsilesional field.

Sprague's experiments in the cat confirmed that this kind of cortical–subcortical interaction is important in regulating visually guided orienting behavior (Sprague, 1966). Neglect was produced in cats by removing occipital and parietal cortex. It was then shown that vision in the contralesional field improved if the *opposite* superior colliculus was removed. A similar result is obtained if the inhibitory connections are severed between the contralesional substantia nigra *pars reticulata* and the ipsilesional colliculus (Wallace, Rosenquist, & Sprague, 1989, 1990). Converging evidence for midbrain mediation of the Sprague effect was also demonstrated by Sherman who sectioned the interhemispheric commisure in cats, and showed that the Sprague effect was restricted to the temporal hemifield (Sherman, 1974).

The Sprague effect is thought to work in the following way (see Fig. 6.4). Parieto-occipital projections to the ipsilateral superior colliculus normally exert a tonic facilitation on it. After parietal lesions the colliculus looses this tonic activation (Hovda & Villablanca, 1990). At the same time the opposite (contralesional) colliculus becomes hyperactive due to increased activation from its parietal lobe that, as we saw earlier, is disinhibited. This imbalance is sustained and aggravated by the mutually inhibitory connections between the two colliculi themselves. The more active contralesional superior colliculus is released from inhibition and produces disinhibited reflexive orient-

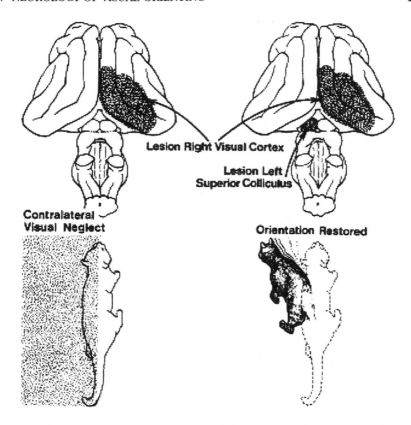

FIG. 6.4. The Sprague effect. After a lesion of cat visual cortex (top left) there is neglect of contralesional space (the cat doesn't orient toward food). A secondary lesion of the opposite superior colliculus (top right), or of the commissural fibers transmitting inhibitory input to the colliculus on the side of the cortical lesion, restores orienting to the field contralateral to the cortical lesion (bottom right). From Stein and Meredith (1993).

ing to signals in the field ipsilateral to the cortical lesion. If the contralesional superior colliculus is then removed (or the fibers of passage from the substantia nigra *pars reticulata* to the opposite colliculus), the hyper-orienting, and hence neglect, is ameliorated.

The Sprague effect demonstrates (at least in cats) that disinhibition of subcortical visual pathways on the side opposite the cortical lesions aggravates neglect caused by cortical lesions, and that prevention of visual input to the disinhibited contralesional midbrain can alleviate neglect. Are there any clinical applications of this phenomenon in rehabilitation? Now it is obviously not an option to surgically remove the contralesional superior colliculus in humans who have suffered parietal lobe strokes. It is possible, however, to decrease contralesional collicular activation, and reflexive orienting, by occluding the ipsilesional eye with a patch (Posner & Rafal, 1987); and, indeed, patching the eye on the side of the lesion has been shown to help reduce symptoms of neglect (Butter, Kirsch, & Reeves, 1990).

It seems likely that both cortical and subcortical imbalances contribute to the rightward bias of attention in patients with left hemispatial neglect. The subcortical imbalance is presumably more pronounced during the period of extensive diaschesis in the acute stage following the injury. Diaschesis refers to the occurrence, after large acute cortical injuries, of dysfunction of remote but closely connected brain regions until there is time for reorganization of the system. Diaschesis in remote brain regions can be measured with imaging studies as a decrease in brain blood flow or metabolism, and characteristically persists for 6 months or more. After acute parietal injury, there is a decrease in function in the ipsilesional colliculus (Deuel, 1987; Deuel & Collins, 1984)—and an increase in orienting driven by the contralesional colliculus.

This subcortical imbalance between the colliculi is thought to produce not just a turning bias, but also a shift in the spatial frame of reference such that the contralesional space is more weakly represented (Karnath, 1994; Kinsbourne, 1994). Neglect resulting from degradation of the left side of the spatial representation caused by the rightward orienting bias can be reduced transiently by production of a countervailing orienting bias through vestibular activation. One way of activating the vestibular apparatus is with caloric stimulation. The ear canal is irrigated with cold (or warm) water to deactivate the inner ear or to induce conduction currents of the endolymph in the inner ear. This produces vertigo—a spinning sensation similar to what one feels after getting off a spinning bar stool or rolling down a hill. The world is perceived to spin in the opposite direction—a displacement of the spatial frame of reference. Caloric stimulation has been shown to transiently alleviate not only visual (Cappa, Sterzi, Vallar, & Bisiach, 1987; Rubens, 1985) and somatosensory (Vallar, Bottini, Rusconi, & Sterzi, 1993) neglect, but also the lack of awareness of the deficit (anosognosia; see Bisiach, Rusconi, & Vallar, 1991). A shift in spatial representation by vibration of neck muscles (Karnath, Christ, & Hartje, 1993) or by optokinetic stimulation (a stripped drum rotated in front of the eyes) (Pizzamiglio, Frasca, Guariglia, Inaccia, & Antonucci, 1990) can also decrease neglect.

Preserved Reflexive Orienting to Neglected Signals

In a recent experiment, Shai Danziger, Alan Kingstone, and I showed that *covert* attention was oriented toward signals in the neglected, contralesional field of patients with hemispatial neglect, even when these signals were not consciously seen because of extinction. Two patients with hemispatial neglect were tested in a precueing experiment in which ipsilesional, contralesional, or bilateral cues were presented prior to the presentation of the detection target for RT measurement. Orienting to the cues was inferred from the effect of peripheral precues on subsequent RT to detect targets at the cued location. Exposure duration of the precues was titrated to that which produced consistent *extinction*; durations at which, by explicit report, the patients consistently and convincingly insisted that only ipsilesional signals were present. The critical comparison was between the condition in which, for contralesional targets, only invalid *ipsilesional* cues had occurred and that in which there was a bilateral cue. The patients experienced the ipsilesional and bilateral cue displays as identical, because the contralesional cue was extinguished. The critical question was whether the bilateral cue would differ in its effects, in comparison to only ipsilesional, invalid cues, on contralesional target detection; that is, would the extinguished, contralesional cue summon attention to facilitate subsequent detection of targets at that location relative to the condition in which only an invalid ipsilesional cue had occurred. Both patients were faster to detect a contralesional target on double (extinction) cue trials than on single, invalid ipsilesional cue that preceded contralesional targets. Thus, the extinguished cue did summon attention toward its location, even thought the patient had not been consciously aware of it. This observation provides evidence that subcortical mechanisms may continue to orient attention to automatically facilitate subsequent processing, even when the signals summoning attention are not consciously perceived.

Effects of Frontal Eye Field Lesions on Visually Guided and Voluntary Saccades: A Reverse Sprague Effect

Acute lesions in the superior part of the dorsolateral prefrontal cortex—including the frontal eye field (FEF) can also produce the syndrome of hemispatial neglect. However, the neglect is typically transient. There are extensive direct and indirect projections from this part of cortex, especially from the FEF, to the midbrain including the superior colliculus and the substantia nigra *pars reticulata*. An acute lesion to the FEF causes a kind of shock to connected regions, the phenomenon of diaschesis discussed earlier, that can be measured experimentally as hypometabolism in remote structures including the superior colliculus (Deuel & Collins, 1984). So the acute neglect seen after FEF lesions may result, in part, because the ipsilesional superior colliculus is transiently dysfunctional.

However, the neglect seen after small acute lesions in the region of the FEF is typically short lasting. In the chronic, compensated state, lesions restricted to the FEF do not result in persistent neglect or any evident impairments in daily life—or on clinical examination of eye movements at the bedside. The chronically reorganized state of fronto-collicular circuitry after FEF lesions is a complex one. One of the net effects of chronic FEF lesions may be a disinhibited visual grasp reflex toward *contralesional* signals—the opposite of what is seen in patients with neglect. One way in which this has been revealed in humans is by the observation that patients with lesions of the FEF have difficulty in making so-called antisaccades *away* from visual signals because they are unable to "inhibit reflexive glances" toward them, especially toward signals in the contralesional field (Guitton, Buchtel, & Douglas, 1985).

More recently we investigated the effects of chronic unilateral lesions of the human frontal eye fields on the latencies of eye movements in experiments that compared visually guided saccades and voluntary saccades (Henik, Rafal, & Rhodes, 1994). The patients in this study are part of a pool of individuals who have suffered brain injuries, mostly from strokes, and who have been gracious in helping us to investigate the consequences of these injuries. Each was selected for having a single, unilateral lesion restricted to the dorsolateral prefrontal cortex. All had recovered from the acute phase of the illness during which diaschesis can have a major affect on remote structures; most were studied several years after the ictus. All were competent and independent individuals, and have been active participants in our laboratories at the Martinez VA Hospital over a number of years.

Now, of course, it is unusual for a brain injury to respect functional boundaries, except by chance. So only 2 of the 16 patients in this group had lesions restricted chiefly to the frontal eye fields (FEF). In order for us to make inferences about FEF function, we used the following approach. We compared the 9 patients in this frontal lesion group in whom the lesion included the FEF (including the two patients whose lesion was largely restricted to this region) with 7 neurological control patients who had frontal lesions that spared the FEF. The region involved in these patients includes that area believed to be the human homologue of the FEF based on PET studies (Paus, 1996). (This includes the most posterior part of the middle frontal gyrus where it joins the precentral sulcus. Brodman's area 8, classically also considered part of the FEF, lies somewhat anterior to the center in the averaged lesion in this group. Area 8 is at the watershed of the middle and anterior cerebral artery territories and so is not as often involved by middle cerebral artery stroke.) Figure 6.4 shows the composite neuroimage reconstructions for the patients in each of the groups. For each patient the CT or MRI brain scan was reviewed and the lesions seen on each section were drawn onto templates from a standard brain atlas. The lesion on each section was then traced, using a graphic tablet, into a computer program that was used to superimpose the lesions of the patients. The scale on the figure refers to the percentage of patients in the group who had a lesion in the region indicated (Fig. 6.5). The patients were tested in two

FRONTAL EYE FIELD LESION

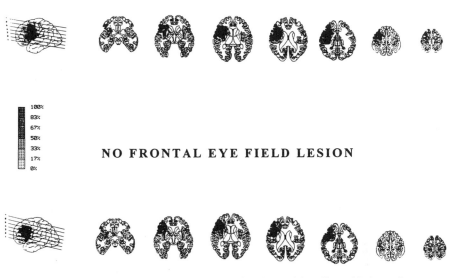

NO FRONTAL EYE FIELD LESION

FIG. 6.5. Neuroimage reconstructions of patients with unilateral lesions of the dorsolateral prefrontal cortex that involve the region of the FEF, and of the group of neurological control patients with frontal lesions sparing the FEF. The scale indicates the percentage of patients in the group have a lesion in the area indicated. All lesions are reflected on the left side. The lines on the lateral reconstructions correspond to the axial sections shown.

saccade tasks: visually guided saccades to targets that appeared 10° to the left or right; and voluntary saccades from a symbolic arrow cue at the center of the display that pointed to a marker target, 10° to the left or right.

For the neurological control patients whose frontal lesions spared the FEF, the latencies of voluntary saccades were, as for normal controls, longer than for visually guided saccades. However, the frontal lesion did not produce an asymmetry of eye movements. Saccade latencies were not different for contralesional and ipsilesional fields for either kind of eye movement. The results are shown for the FEF lesion patients in Fig. 6.6.

Voluntary saccades were slower to the contralesional field. In contrast, visually guided saccades were slower to the ipsilesional field. In the ipsilesional field the patients' visually guided saccade latencies were, quite abnormally, no faster than their latencies for voluntary saccades to that field. These results indicate that frontal eye field lesion have two separate effects on eye movements: The frontal eye fields are involved in generating endogenous saccades and lesions in this region therefore increase their latency; frontal eye field lesions produce a profound influence on the *opposite*

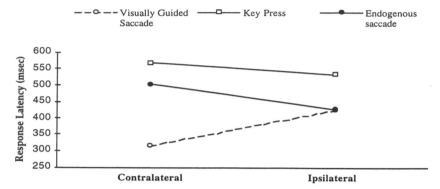

FIG. 6.6. Mean of the median latencies for visually guided and voluntary saccades, and key press RTs for nine patients with frontal eye field lesions.

superior colliculus. It seems not to generate a visual grasp reflex, and saccades made toward signals in the field ipsilesional to it must be made voluntarily without the usual advantage of this midbrain reflex. Note in Fig. 6.6 that this asymmetry for responding to targets in the field ipsilesional or contralesional to FEF lesions is specific to the oculomotor system. A control experiment was conducted using the same display as that used to make visually guided saccades, but with choice RT key press responses while the eyes remained fixed. These key press RTs to contralesional targets were actually *slower* than for ipsilesional targets—the opposite pattern of that found for saccade latencies.

Thus unilateral lesions of the FEF, in the chronic state, can produce a kind of reverse Sprague effect. One explanation of this apparent reversed Sprague effect is that FEF lesions disinhibit the ipsilesional substantia nigra *pars reticulata*, resulting in inhibition of the superior colliculus *opposite* to the FEF lesion. Yet in experimental animals the Sprague effect doesn't emerge as a simple disinhibition effect immediate upon placement of the lesion—it evolves often a week or so after collicular resection (Wallace et al., 1989). It may also be that the dysfunctional contralesional colliculus, resulting from chronic, unilateral FEF lesions, reflects a recovery process that involves a considerable amount of plasticity and reorganization.

A recent study using transcranial magnetic stimulation (TMS) in normal subjects investigated whether this reverse Sprague effect reflects a plastic reorganization following recovery from brain injury, or the immediate effect of FEF inactivation. The effects of TMS are very transient. They presumably do not cause much in the way of remote diaschesis effect, and certainly don't allow time for plastic reorganization. When TMS was applied over the FEF, there was an increase in latency for voluntary saccades to the contralateral field—the same pattern as seen in patients with chronic focal lesions. However, unlike the patients study, the TMS had no affect on ipsilateral visually guided saccades (Ro, Henik, Machado, & Rafal, 1997). As discussed earlier, TMS over the parietal lobe can be shown to have an immediate effect of disinhibiting the opposite cerebral hemisphere (Seyal et al., 1995). Since TMS of the FEF did not have the effect on ipsilesional visually guided saccades that occurs with chronic lesions of the FEF, we concluded that the reverse Sprague effect after chronic FEF lesions is the result of plastic reorganization as part of the compensation for brain injury.

Taken together, these kinds of observations emphasize the importance of appreciating brain and behavior relationships in the context of a dynamic biological system. Behavior after acute lesions reflects not just dysfunction in the lesioned area, but also the remote effects of diaschesis. On the other hand, behavior in the chronic phase after can reflect plastic reorganization of brain function and compensatory changes. These considerations emphasize the importance of converging approaches to studying cognitive neuroscience; the study of both acute and chronic lesions can be revealing when the findings of both kinds of investigations are integrated with one another and with other methods for studying brain function in humans.

Effects of Aging and Alzheimer's Disease on the Visual Grasp Reflex

We have seen that visual signals reflexively activate the oculomotor system through midbrain pathways. Thus far we have been considering eye movements, that is, overt movements of the eyes. Our studies in PSP patients show, however, that the midbrain is also involved in activating reflexive *covert* shifts of visual attention that are summoned by signals in the visual periphery even if the eyes do not move (Posner et al., 1982; Posner et al., 1985; Rafal et al., 1988). We obtained converging evidence for a midbrain role in covert reflexive orienting in a study of normal subjects that showed that covert attention shifts were generated more effectively by signals in the temporal than in the nasal hemifield (Rafal, Henik, & Smith, 1991).

Can reflexive covert orienting of attention also be inhibited? That is, if subjects are instructed to actively inhibit these signals—not just to ignore them, but to move their attention away from them, are they able to do so? One way of looking at this question is with experiments in which a peripheral cue predicts that a target will appear in the *opposite visual* field. In one such experiment (Posner et al., 1982) a peripheral cue was valid on 20% of trials: The cue instructed the subject to expect the target in the visual field *opposite to the cue.* The subjects were neurologically normal young adults. Results showed that for short cue-target intervals of 50–200 ms, detection RT was faster at the location of the cue, even though the task conditions gave the subjects a strong incentive to inhibit orienting to the cue signal, and to shift their attention toward the contralateral hemifield instead. Warner et al. used a modification of this paradigm to show that, with practice, subjects were able to inhibit this reflexive orienting of attention to the cue (Warner, Juola, & Koshino, 1990).

I examined the effects of normal aging on the ability to *inhibit* reflexive orienting to peripheral signals (Rafal & Henik, 1994). There were 10 young adults (mean age = 27) and 10 older subjects (mean age = 69). The results for the young subjects are shown on the top of Fig. 6.6 and the data for the older subjects are shown on the bottom. In this experiment a faster detection RT for targets at the cued location (solid lines) indicates that the subject had oriented to that location at the time the target appeared—a covert attentional visual grasp reflex. Faster detection RT for targets appearing in the field contralateral to the cue (dashed lines) indicates that the subject had been successful in inhibiting the reflexive orienting to the cue, and in reorienting toward the opposite hemifield where the target is expected.

Figure 6.7 (top) shows that the younger subjects had a small reflex orienting grasp effect which was present only at the shortest (50 ms) interval. By the 300 ms interval detection RT is quicker for targets in the expected field contralateral to the cue. The older subjects (bottom) have a much more robust and prolonged covert visual grasp reflex. Detection RT is faster for targets appearing at the location of the cue through the 300 ms cue–target interval; only at the longest (500 ms) interval do these older subjects show evidence for having reoriented way from the cue.

This result confirms that there is an automatic orienting, a so-called visual grasp reflex, toward a peripheral signal. Attention is summoned, at least briefly, to the stimulated location even when the individual has an incentive to try to ignore it. These findings also demonstrate how it is possible to study endogenous mechanisms that inhibit and regulate this reflex, what neural structures mediate this control, and how they are affected by age and disease processes. A recent study has used this same experimental paradigm to demonstrate that patients with Alzheimer's disease have a stronger visual grasp reflex which they are less able to inhibit than do normal elderly individuals (Maruff & Currie, 1995).

The Visual Grasp Reflex in Attention Deficit Disorder

We have also recently used this experimental paradigm to investigate whether children with attention deficit disorder (ADD) have difficulties in inhibiting the visual grasp reflex as a factor contributing to their difficulties. Mark Chaterjian and Penny Garrison tested nine children from the ADD clinic at UC Davis Medical Center in Sacramento on this paradigm and compared them with 10 matched normal control children. The results

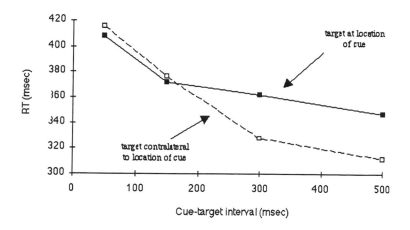

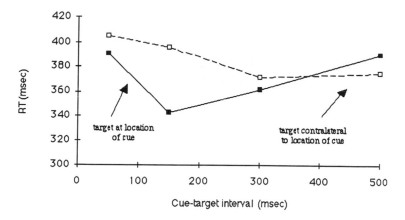

FIG. 6.7. Reflexive orienting toward, and endogenous orienting away from, a peripheral cue in younger and older adults. Mean detection RT is shown for each group as a function of interval between the to-be-ignored precue, and the detection target. An initial visual grasp reflex in normal young adults is indicated by a small RT advantage for target appearing at the location of the cue at the shortest cue–target intervals (top). By 300 ms, however, detection RT is faster for targets appearing at the expected location in the field opposite the cue. The subjects have inhibited the visual grasp reflex by this time, and have voluntarily reoriented their attention to the expected location. Older adults (bottom) show a more pronounced and prolonged visual grasp reflex, and do not begin to show an advantage in RT for targets at the expected location until after 300 ms following the cue onset.

are shown in Fig. 6.8. It is interesting to note that normal children are very quick to inhibit the visual grasp reflex, and show evidence at having voluntarily shifted attention to the expected location within 50 ms of the cue. The children with ADD, compared to the normal children, are slower to inhibit the visual grasp reflex and do not show evidence of having voluntarily reoriented attention to the expected location until after 150 following the cue. (The temporal dynamic of the visual grasp reflex in this study can't, unfortunately, be compared directly to the data in adults shown in Fig. 6.6. The testing was done on different equipment, and the cues in the aging study were larger and brighter than those used in the ADD study and may have activated a more vigorous visual grasp reflex. For a systematic study of the effects of maturation and aging on the ability to inhibit the visual grasp reflex, see Enns et al. (chap. 13, this volume).)

INHIBITION OF RETURN

Posner and Cohen (1984) showed that a luminance change in the visual periphery not only summons attention, but also activates a subsequent inhibitory effect that slows detection of signals at the stimulated location. They called this inhibitory effect "inhibition of return," and suggested that it functions to favor novelty in optimizing the efficiency of visual search. Consistent with such a function was their observation that the effect lasts long enough for several saccades to take place, up to 3–5 seconds (Tassinari, Biscaldi, Marzi, & Berlucchi, 1989). Moreover, if an eye movement is made after the cue signal, the inhibition does not move with the retina but seems to tag the location in the environment (Posner & Cohen, 1984).

A number of lines of converging evidence suggest that generation of inhibition of return is closely related to oculomotor behavior rather than to shifts of covert attention. First, although inhibition of return does not occur after endogenously deployed shifts of covert attention (produced in response to an arrow in the center of a visual display, rather than a peripheral visual cue), it does occur after an endogenously generated saccade (Posner et al., 1985; Rafal, Calabresi, Brennan, & Sciolto, 1989). If a saccade is made to a peripheral location and the eyes are then moved back to the center, keypress responses were delayed to signals presented at the location to which the saccade had just been made. Moreover, simply preparing an endogenous saccade is sufficient to generate inhibition of return, even when no saccade is actually made, and even when no peripheral signal occurs prior to the target (Rafal et al., 1989; Schmidt, 1996). The next section reviews evidence that midbrain oculomotor pathways mediate the generation of IOR.

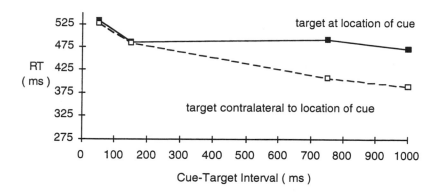

ADD Children (N=9)

target at location of cue

target contralateral to location of cue

RT
(ms)

Cue-Target Interval (ms)

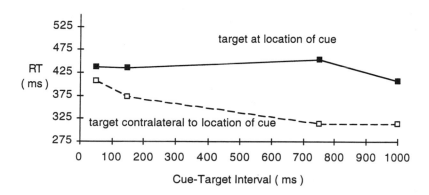

Normal Children (N=10)

target at location of cue

target contralateral to location of cue

RT
(ms)

Cue-Target Interval (ms)

FIG. 6.8. The visual grasp reflex in attention deficit disorder. Top: Results in ADD children. Bottom: Results in normal control children. Mean detection RT is shown for each group as a function of interval between the to-be-ignored precue and the detection target. Normal children show evidence of attempting to inhibit the visual grasp reflex; an advantage is present for targets at the expected location contralateral to the cue even at the 50-ms interval, indicating that even this early, the subjects were inhibiting the visual grasp reflex and were voluntarily allocating their attention at the expected location. The ADD children don't begin to show an advantage for the expected target location until some time more than 15 ms after the distracting cue.

Evidence for Midbrain Mediation of Inhibition of Return

The presence of IOR in earliest infancy (Simion, Valenza, Umiltà, & Dalla Barba, 1995) suggests that midbrain mechanisms may be competent to generate it. To determine the importance of the retinotectal pathway in generating inhibition of return in adults, we sought evidence from three converging sources: First we showed that IOR was affected in PSP patients (Posner et al., 1985). We then demonstrated that IOR is activated more robustly in normal adults by signals in the temporal hemifield than by those in the nasal hemifield (Rafal et al., 1989). Finally, in a recent study we showed that IOR could be activated by signals in the blind field of hemianopic patients (Danziger, Fendrich, & Rafal, 1997).

In the studies in normal subjects and PSP patients, brightening of a peripheral box was used to summon attention. The first cue was then followed, on some trials, by brightening of a center box which summoned attention back to the center. The target then appeared, with equal probability, either at the first cued location, or in the uncued contralateral visual field. Inhibition of return was measured as a slower detection RT for targets at the location of the first cue. In the PSP patients inhibition of return was compared in the vertical and horizontal planes, since vertical eye movements are characteristically more impaired in this disease than are horizontal eye movements. In the normal subjects we compared the activation of inhibition of return by cues in the temporal and nasal hemifields under monocular viewing conditions.

The PSP patients showed no inhibition of return in the vertical plane (Posner et al., 1985). In normal subjects (Rafal et al., 1989), signals presented to the temporal hemifield generated a larger inhibition of return (Fig. 6.9). Both observations provide converging evidence for a midbrain role in generating IOR.

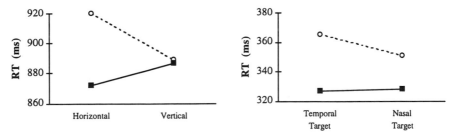

FIG. 6.9. Converging evidence for an extrageniculate contribution to inhibition of return in humans. Mean detection RT is shown for targets appearing at the cued location (dashed lines) in comparison to RT for targets appearing at uncued locations. Left: IOR is not activated due to impaired vertical orienting in PSP patients ($N = 6$), but is preserved in the horizontal plain; Right: IOR is more effectively activated by signals in the temporal hemifield of normal subjects ($N = 20$).

An experiment was also done in hemianopic patients to determine whether midbrain visuomotor centers are sufficient to generate IOR in the absence of visual input through the geniculostriate cortical pathway. Figure 6.10 shows an experiment done (Danziger, Fendrich, & Rafal, 1997) in two patients with left hemianopia to measure whether signals presented in the blind field (the scotoma) would activate IOR. Both patients had had right occipital strokes from posterior cerebral artery infarction destroying primary visual cortex. They could not detect any visual signals to the left of the midline. While the patients faced the display for the experiment shown in Fig. 6.10 (top), we first confirmed that they were not aware of signals in the left visual field, and that they were unable to make any explicit inference about the location of visual signals in that field: One of the two boxes in the left field was briefly brightened and the patients were asked to guess whether it had been the top or bottom. The performance

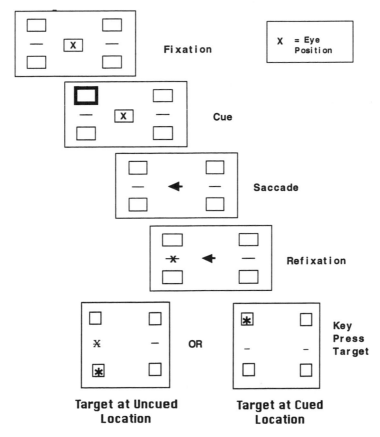

FIG. 6.10. Display used to test whether IOR is activated by unseen signals presented within the scotoma of hemianopic patients.

of both patients was at chance at this task. Thus, neither of these two patients demonstrated "blindsight" at the locations tested as conventionally measured using two alternative force choice responses. Both patients did have small "islands" of above chance detection (without conscious experience of awareness of the signals) at other locations in their visual fields using the methods of Fendrich et al. (1992). These islands have been argued to represent areas of residual cortical processing below the subjective threshold. Because our purpose was to test for midbrain generation of IOR, we wanted to avoid testing these regions that might have some residual cortical representation. Having confirmed the absence of any awareness of the location of visual signals at the locations to be probed for IOR, the experimental task then used the brightening of the same boxes as stimuli to determine if they would activate IOR.

The sequence of events in each trial is depicted in Fig. 6.10. One of the two boxes in one field (the seeing field on half the trials and the blind field on the other half) was briefly flashed. Then an arrowhead appeared at the center of the display instructing the patient to move the eyes to a marker in the field indicating the midpoint between the two boxes. Once the eyes had moved to this position, both boxes were of course visible to him, one above and one below. A detection target then appeared, with equal probability, either in the box that had been cued in that field or in the other box. Inhibition of return was measured as a slower detection RT for targets appearing at the previously cued box. In one patient the results demonstrated a reliable IOR in both fields, and that the IOR in the blind field was as large as that produced by signals in the seeing field.

These results in this patient provide converging evidence for midbrain generation of IOR. They also confirm neurophysiological findings that the colliculus is mapped in oculocentric, not retinotopic, coordinates (Glimcher & Sparks, 1992; Mays & Sparks, 1980). However, oculocentric collicular mapping may be dependent on inputs from visual cortex, since oculocentric programming of eye movements in the double saccade paradigm appears to depend on the maturation of cortico-collicular afferents (see Johnson et al., chap. 3, this volume). Furthermore, the second hemianopic patient we tested using the same methods and did not show any hint of IOR from signals in the hemianopic field. The lack of consistency in finding "blindsight" effects in hemianopics remains a vexing puzzle, and the implications of our finding of IOR in a single hemianopic patient remain uncertain.

Looking Forward to Looking, I: Voluntary Saccade Preparation Activates Inhibition of Return

It was argued earlier that IOR is activated by midbrain oculomotor centers. Midbrain pathways can be activated to generate IOR either by a peripheral visual signal (perhaps directly through the retino-tectal pathway), or by the programming of a voluntary saccade (perhaps via pathways from the frontal eye fields to the midbrain). An acid test of this account requires demonstrating that IOR can be generated by the preparation of a voluntary saccade to the location at which an observer is actively attending.

Table 6.1 shows the results of an experiment (Rafal, Ro, & Ingle, 1995) in normal individuals designed to show that IOR is activated by the preparation of a saccade toward a location even while that location is actively attended, and a saccade is eventually executed toward it. In this experiment, subjects viewed a display consisting of two unfilled boxes, 8° to left and right of a central fixation dot. The subjects' task was to make a saccade to a target signal (a 1° asterisk) that appeared in one of the two peripheral boxes, and saccade latency was the dependent variable. Each trial began with the presentation, for 100 ms, of a precue plotted at fixation which could be, with equal probability, uninformative about the location of the forthcoming target (a diamond shape), or an arrowhead pointing left or right which predicted the subsequent target's location with 100% probability. Thus, on half the trials subjects had prepared a saccade before the target appeared, and on half they did not. In a control task, the subjects viewed the same display, but their task was to make a choice RT key press response. In this control task, on arrowhead trials, subjects developed a valid expectation of the location of the forthcoming target and presumably oriented covertly, but they had not been required to prepare an eye movement. Except on catch trials (15%) the target appeared either 200 ms or 700 ms after onset of the cue. The results of this experiment for saccade and key press tasks are shown in the table.

In the key press task there was a benefit, in RT, for an informative precue of about 30 ms. This benefit was present at the early (200 ms) cue-target interval and persisted until the later (700 ms) cue-target interval. In the saccade task a benefit in saccade latency from an informative precue was present at the 200 ms cue-target interval, suggesting that subjects had prepared a saccade in response to the precue. However, at the later (700 ms) cue-target interval the benefit was no longer present and was replaced by inhibition. The significant Cue × Interval interaction in the saccade

TABLE 6.1
Effects of Saccade Preparation on Latencies
for Manual and Saccadic Responses

Precue	Key Press RT (ms) Cue–Target Interval		Saccade Latency (ms) Cue–Target Interval	
	200 ms	700 ms	200 ms	700 ms
Uninformative	344	316	292	289
Informative	314	288	255	303

task ($F[1, 9] = 6.0$, $p < .05$) is attributable to the increase in saccade latency in the valid precue condition between the 200 ms and the 700 ms interval ($t[df\, 9] = -4.6$, $p < .025$).

In the key press task, in which informative precues enabled subjects to covertly orient attention to the location of the expected target, but did not instruct the preparation of a saccade, there was a benefit of the informative precue that remained stable for 700 ms. The key press findings confirm that endogenous covert orienting does not generate inhibition of return. In the saccade task, subjects had an incentive both to covertly orient to the location of the expected target, and also to prepare a saccade toward it. The benefit for an informative precue at the 200 ms cue–target interval in the saccade task indicates that subjects did use the advance information to orient to the cued location. Because subjects continued to expect the target at the cued location, just as they did in the key press task, they can be assumed to have remained covertly oriented to it. The loss of benefit from the informative precue at the later cue-target interval demonstrates that IOR was generated by preparing the saccade and its effects accumulated over time at the location to which the saccade was prepared, even while subject continued to actively attend to the same location.

These results demonstrate that saccade preparation activates IOR even when attention is not actively withdrawn from the attended location, and even when the prepared saccade is not canceled. They are also consistent with other evidence that IOR is generated by oculomotor systems independent from those for covert visual orienting, and that IOR and covert orienting can have simultaneous and independent effects on detection of signals at the same location. Our efforts now are focusing on the anatomic circuits between cortex and midbrain that mediate the voluntary generation of IOR. We are studying patients with unilateral cortical lesions to identify the neural substrates for the cortical regulation of this primitive reflex.

Location and Object-Based Inhibition of Return: Cortical Involvement in the Inhibitory Tagging of Objects

Thus far, we have been considering the orienting of attention to locations in space. The experimental approach has mainly adapted Posner's methods that first demonstrated that humans can allocate attention to locations in the visual field (Posner, 1980; Posner & Cohen, 1984). This ability serves the obvious function of ensuring detection of objects of interest and of bringing to bear foveal vision and a cognitive commitment to the locations they occupy. The purpose of attention mechanisms for orienting to locations is to expedite further processing of objects at those locations and responses to them. Once attention is oriented to a location containing a selected object, the reference frame in which attention operates then must also be that of the object (and its spatial relations with the observer and with other objects).

There is growing evidence from a number of converging sources, including neuropsychology, that early vision parses the visual field into candidate objects preattentively, and that attention operates on this parsed representation. Moreover, this parsed representation may exist in several more modular action-specific spatial representations. For example, the study of hemispatial neglect has shown that perceptual processing can proceed to the level of semantic classification in the absence of attention or conscious awareness; and that preattentive vision parses the scene to extract figure from ground, group objects and define their primary axis (see Rafal, 1996b, for a review). Patients neglect not only the contralesional side of the visual field, but can also neglect the contralesional side of objects—even if the object moves from the contralesional to the ipsilesional field (Behrman & Tipper, 1994; Behrmann & Moscovitch, 1994; Tipper & Behrmann, 1996).

So although the phylogenetically primitive midbrain pathways for reflexive orienting play an important role in getting attention to objects of potential interest, it is obvious that these mechanisms must be integrated with higher cortical systems involved in object-based attention. Consider the problem of searching a crowd for the face of a friend. Inhibition of return might serve a useful function by facilitating a systematic search if it prevents attention from returning to individuals who we've already looked at and didn't recognize. However, because people in crowds, as in many real-world situations, can and do move, it is not sufficient for inhibition of return to prevent return of attention to the *location* we've just sampled; it must keep track of the person.

Tipper and colleagues (Tipper et al., 1997; Tipper, Driver, & Weaver, 1991; Tipper, Weaver, Jerreat, & Burak, 1994) have shown that inhibition of return can in fact tag and track objects that move using the following experimental paradigm (see Fig. 6.11a.) At the start of each trial, three black squares appeared on a light gray background, one in the middle, and one in each field equidistant from the middle. The two peripheral squares were located in opposing corners of an imaginary square. Simple key press RT was measured for detecting a target probe which appeared, with equal probability, in one of the two peripheral squares. Trials began with the cuing of one of the two peripheral squares by "flickering" it. Two hundred ms after the onset of the cue in the outer square, the central square was cued in the same manner. At the same time, the peripheral squares began to move smoothly around the central square in either a clockwise or counterclockwise direction. This rotation could cause the squares either to move within the same hemifield or to cross the midline into the opposite hemifield. After a rotation of 90°, the squares stopped and (except on catch trials) a target appeared 500 ms after the onset of

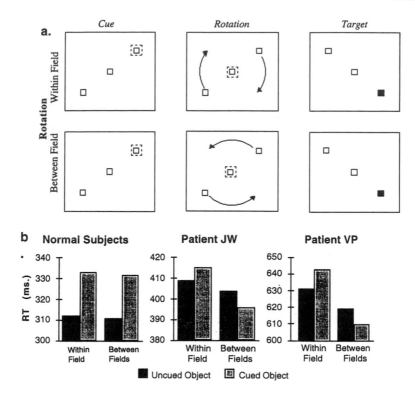

FIG. 6.11. (a) The experiment for measuring object-based IOR. Top: A within field rotation of the cued object, with the target appearing in the cued object. Bottom: A between field rotation of the cued object, with the target appearing in the uncued object. (b) Experimental results in normal subjects and two split brain patients. RT is shown in ms for detection of targets within cued and uncued objects that have moved either within a visual hemifield, or across the midline into the opposite visual hemifield. For normal control subjects (left), detection is slowed for cued objects—an object-based inhibition of return (IOR)—whether they move within or between hemifields. Callosotomy patients J. W. (middle) and V. P. (right) both show object-based IOR for within field object movements; but a facilitation of detection for the cued object when it moves across the midline.

the cue, either in the box which had been cued or, with equal probability, in the uncued box.

As shown in Fig. 6.11b (left), normal subjects showed an inhibition in detecting signals in the cued object whether it moved within or between fields. Thus, inhibition of return can effect detection in an object based reference frame. In other experiments, Tipper and his colleagues have used a modification of this paradigm to show that cueing an object actually activates two inhibitory tags: one that remains at the cued *location* and another that moves with the tagged object if it moves.

It is not known if both inhibitory tags originate in the midbrain, and this tag transmitted to two independent cortical reference frames, location, and object, or whether the two effects are generated by entirely independent mechanisms. One possibility is that they are each totally independent effects: one, location-based, generated through the retino-tectal pathway; and the other, object-based, generated from visual input through the geniculostriate system. Another possibility, more phylogenetically parsimonious, is that the inhibitory tag generated by the midbrain as a primitive reflex for guiding eye movements is also transmitted to cortical processors where they are adapted to be maintained in an object-based representation of space. In either case, the object-based IOR tag capable of tracking moving objects and aiding strategic search should presumably require registration in some cortical representation capable of such complex computations.

We used Tipper's experimental paradigm to determine whether object-based IOR requires cortical mediation by testing whether object-based IOR would transfer between the left and right visual fields in patients whose corpus callosum had been sectioned. If object-based IOR is maintained by a cortical representation requiring an intact corpus callosum for inter-hemispheric transfer, then it should be manifest only for objects moving within a visual field, and it should be lost if the object crosses the midline into the opposite visual field. Figure 6.11b also shows the results of this experiment in two split-brain patients, JW and VP. Both of these individuals had undergone complete transection of the corpus callosum for treatment of severe epilepsy. As shown in Fig. 6.11b, both split-brain patients showed IOR when the cued object moved within the same visual field. However, when the boxes moved such that they crossed the midline into the opposite visual field, there was no inhibition and, instead, a facilitory effect was observed with detection being faster in the cued box. These results indicate that a peripheral luminance change simultaneously activates both a facilitory and an inhibitory effect on attention. Both the inhibitory and facilitory effects are object-based and both may last for several hundred ms. However, the inhibitory effect requires an intact corpus callosum for interhemispheric transfer, while the facilitory effect is transferred subcortically.

THE FIXATION OFFSET EFFECT

Saslow (1967) first observed that the offset of a fixation point decreased the latency of saccades to visual targets in an experiment in which there was a temporal gap between fixation offset and target onset. This facilitation has been called the "gap effect." A gap of approximately 200 ms is optimal for reducing saccade latencies, and under some circumstances a robust gap effect may generate a bimodal distribution of saccade latencies, with a separate peak of very fast "express saccades" with latencies of less than 100 ms. Kingstone and Klein (1993a, 1993b) showed that simultaneous fixation offset with target onset results in reduced saccade latencies—a fixation offset effect (FOE). They argued that the gap effect may consist of at least two components: the FOE, and an alerting effect that accrues during the gap foreperiod. While the FOE, the gap effect, and "express saccades" may be related phenomena, the existence of express saccades as a distinct class of eye movements in humans has been controversial (Wenban & Findlay, 1991).

The gap effect has attracted the interest of both physiologists and psychologists for two reasons: First, animal experiments implicated the superior colliculus as the neural substrate for the effect (Schiller, 1977; Schiller, Sandell, & Maunsell, 1994) and second, the phenomenon was a rich one for relating attention to eye movements (Fischer & Breitmeyer, 1987). Munoz and Wurtz (1992, 1993a, 1993b) have identified "fixation neurons" in the deeper part of the intermediate layer of the rostral pole of the superior colliculus whose activity is correlated with sustained fixation, and whose inactivation is associated with disinhibition of reflexive saccades. They (Munoz & Wurtz, 1992) proposed that the decrease in activity of the fixation neurons with fixation offset represented a neural correlate of express saccades.

Within the colliculus there is neural machinery for two opponent processes, the visual grasp reflex and the fixation reflex. Oculomotor behavior is determined by the coordination integration of these two reflexes. We are now beginning to study the voluntary processes that control these opponent midbrain reflexes, and are trying to identify the neural mechanisms for cortico–subcortical interaction that are involved.

Looking Forward to Looking, II: Saccade Preparation Modulates the FOE for Visually Guided Saccades

The fixation offset effect decreases as babies mature (see chaps. 3 and 7 by Johnson et al. and by Hood et al., this volume). The effect may perhaps serve as a marker for a midbrain fixation reflex, and its decrement with maturation reflects the development of cortical inhibition of this reflex. However, normal subjects can learn to increase the size of the fixation offset effect with practice and even to make express saccade while the fixation point remains visible (Fischer & Breitmeyer, 1987). The implication here is that normal subjects may be able to voluntarily inhibit collicular pole fixation neurons even while the are being activated by a visual fixation stimulus.

We have recently been investigating whether normal adults can modulate the FOE when they voluntarily prepare an eye movement. In one experiment the conditions were identical to the last one described to measure IOR induced by saccade preparation. The only modification in this experiment was that there was an additional manipulation of fixation offset or overlap with the target. In one condition (overlap) the precue remained visible until the target appeared and the subject responded; in the other (fixation offset) condition, the precue disappeared simultaneously with the onset of the target. In any case the subjects' task was simply to make a saccade to the target as soon as it appeared. The variables in this experiment included, in addition to precue type (prepare saccade or no orienting prior to target) and precue to target interval, the additional variable of fixation overlap versus fixation offset.

The results of this experiment replicated the previous finding that IOR was generated at long precue to target intervals as found in the earlier experiment. Figure 6.12 shows the size of the fixation offset effect at the two intervals. There was a strong reduction of the FOE in the saccade preparation condition—and this suppression of the FOE was present even at the 75 ms precue to target interval, well before IOR had become fully manifest.

It seems clear then, that this midbrain fixation reflex is under some voluntary control. It appears that it can be voluntarily inhibited when a saccade is prepared, even when a fixation point is visible to activate fixation neurons in the rostral pole of the superior colliculus. Perhaps even when the fixation point is on, saccade preparation permits activation of projec-

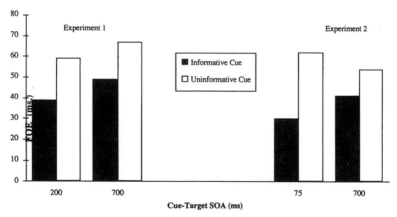

FIG. 6.12. The FOE (mean saccade latency in the overlap condition minus mean saccade latency with fixation offset simultaneous with the target) as a function of whether or not the target was preceded by an informative cue that enabled preparation of a voluntary saccade. In one experiment the cue–target intervals used SOAs of 200 and 700 ms; the second used SOAs of 75 and 700 ms. Saccade preparation reduces the FOE even at the short cue–target intervals—well before saccade preparation generates IOR (see Table 6.1).

tions from the FEF that inhibit the rostral pole fixation neurons in the ipsilateral colliculus, and thereby prime (or disinhibit) prelude burster neurons to expedite saccade latencies. Or perhaps these projections don't directly influence the activity of the pole fixation neurons per se but, instead, inhibit their effects on prelude bursters presynaptically. In either case, this is a fascinating example of voluntary control over a visuomotor reflex, and we hope to learn much about these circuits with further investigations of the effects of saccade preparation on the FOE in normal individuals and neurological patients.

Looking Forward to Looking, III: Saccade Preparation Modulates the FOE for Antisaccades

The FOE had, until recently, been described only with visually guided saccades to exogenous visual signals. For example, Reuter-Lorenz, Hughes, and Fendrich (1991) found no FOE for choice RT key press responses, or in an antisaccade task. The lack of FOE for antisaccades seemed to indicate that the FOE did not affect endogenous saccades. A recent study by Forbes and Klein (1996), however, demonstrated a FOE for endogenous saccades (made in response to spoken words). They found a FOE for endogenous saccades which was as large as that for visually guided saccades; the FOE for both was larger than for antisaccades.

Forbes and Klein argued that collicular disinhibition conferred by the FOE does benefit endogenous saccades. They offered an explanation for the reduced FOE in the antisaccade task, an account that serves as the basis for the next series of experiments described here. They argued that antisaccades are a special type of endogenous saccade task in that the subject must also actively inhibit a reflexive saccade on each trial. They proposed that, because the subject is endogenously inhibiting the colliculus, the fixation offset does not disinhibit it, and hence there is a reduced FOE for antisaccades. The usual FOE experiment, including that of Forbes and Klein, is a choice saccade task in which the subject does not know in which field the target is to appear, and cannot prepare a saccade before the fixation offset and target. In the antisaccade task, for example, the subject does not know where the visual target signal will appear and must, therefore, inhibit *both* colliculi until the target appears, in order to prevent reflexive saccades to the wrong location. If, however, the subject performing an antisaccade task knew in advance where the target signal was to appear and to prepare a saccade in the opposite direction, would he or she be able to maintain inhibition of the colliculus contralateral to the location of the expected target, while disinhibiting the other colliculus involved in programming the saccade to the opposite field?

We recently tested this prediction in an experiment that compared the effects of saccade preparation on the FOE for both prosaccades (toward the target) and for antisaccades (away from the target). We reasoned that when an individual prepares an endogenous saccade, FEF projections to midbrain may be activated to phasically disinhibit fixation neurons in the colliculus (or to prevent their effects on collicular oculomotor output). In the prosaccade task, saccade preparation may disinhibit the colliculus before the fixation offset, so that the colliculus is already disinhibited and therefore the benefit of fixation offset will confer a smaller FOE advantage. In an antisaccade task, however, subjects will not benefit from fixation offset in the uninformative precue condition—they can't predict on which side the target will appear and must keep pole neurons active bilaterally, perhaps even after the fixation point is turned off, in order to prevent a visual grasp reflex toward the target when it appears. When there is an informative precue, on the other hand, that tells subjects to inhibit orienting to one side while preparing to move the eyes in the opposite direction, subjects may selectively disinhibit the colliculus on the side ipsilateral to the expected target signal, enabling it to benefit more from fixation offset then it could if the subject had to maintain tonic inhibition of both colliculi until the target appeared. The display was the same as for the last experiment described except that subject made an antisaccade away from the target. In separate blocks, a control condition was run in each subject (the order being counterbalanced) that replicated the previous results of prosaccade preparation effects on FOE.

The results of this experiment are shown for 20 normal subjects in Fig. 6.13. As expected, prosaccades had shorter latencies than antisaccades ($F[1, 23] = 11.0, p < .005$), an informative precue that enabled saccade preparation decreased saccade latency ($F[1, 23] = 89.9, p < .0001$), and saccade latency was less in the fixation offset than in the fixation overlap condition ($F[1, 23] = 52.0, p < .0001$). Saccade preparation, however, had opposite effects on the FOE for prosaccades and antisaccades ($F[1, 23] = 15.4, p < .001$). A significant FOE was found in every condition ($p < .0025$ by t test for all). However, in the prosaccade task the FOE was less when a saccade was

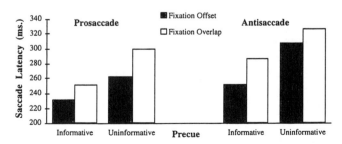

FIG. 6.13. Fixation offset effect on saccade latency (in ms) for prosaccades and antisaccades showing a differential effect of saccade preparation from informative precues on the FOE in the two tasks.

prepared ($F[1, 23] = 28.5$, $p < .0001$); while for the antisaccade task the FOE was augmented by saccade preparation ($F[1, 23] = 30.5$, $p < .0001$).

These results, then, confirm previous findings that, in a choice saccade task (uninformative precue condition), the FOE is less for antisaccades than for prosaccades (Forbes & Klein, in press; Reuter-Lorenz, Hughes, & Fendrich, 1991). A new finding of this experiment is that saccade preparation augments the FOE in the antisaccade task, and is consistent with our hypothesis that individuals are able to selectively disinhibit the colliculus contralateral to the field toward which an endogenous saccade has been prepared We also find the opposite pattern for prosaccades: The FOE is greater in the uninformative precue condition. We interpret this observation to indicate that saccade preparation disinhibits the same collicular mechanism as does fixation offset; therefore, there is less further benefit from fixation offset when a saccade is prepared in a prosaccade task. We are now testing patients with FEF lesions in these pro- and antisaccade tasks to determine the role of the FEF in modulating midbrain circuits involved in the FOE.

CONCLUSIONS

This chapter has revisited some selected midbrain visuomotor reflexes whose maturation in early infancy and childhood are detailed in other chapters of this volume: the visual grasp reflex, inhibition of return, and the fixation reflex (as measured by the fixation offset effect). Evidence for midbrain mediation of these reflexes in humans was reviewed in light of the effects of focal lesions. A theme was developed in which the dissolution of cortical regulation of these reflexes by disease reveals the opposite side of the developmental coin. The visual grasp reflex and the fixation reflex may be opponent states within the colliculus. Voluntary effort can bias one state or the other during saccade preparation; and the ability to do so must depend on cortical centers. Currently my lab is investigating the effects of chronic lesions of the frontal eye fields and the parietal lobe on the ability to voluntarily regulate these reflexes.

Inhibition of return is generated through midbrain visuomotor pathways, and can be activated either by a peripheral luminance change, or by the voluntary preparation of an endogenous saccade. IOR may not be a unitary phenomenon. Separate spatial and object-based effects may be activated through entirely separate subcortical and cortical systems. On the other hand, they might share a common midbrain origin; the midbrain tag made available to separate cortical representations evolved for specific purposes.

The selected midbrain reflexes considered here provide an attractive model for the complimentary study of development and pathology. Hopefully, the principles we glean from this kind of convergence will help provide a framework for understanding the psychobiology of cognitive development. The interpretation of neuropsychological observations and data requires a biological perspective that appreciates the evolutionary history of our species, the dynamic interactions between cortical and subcortical components of a distributed network, and the plastic reorganization of functional anatomy after brain injury.

ACKNOWLEDGMENT

This work was supported by U.S. PHS Grant RO1 MH 41544.

REFERENCES

Behrmann, M., & Moscovitch, M. (1994). Object-centered neglect in patients with unilateral neglect: Effects of left-right coordinates of objects. *Journal of Cognitive Neuroscience, 6*, 1–16.

Behrman, M., & Tipper, S. P. (1994). Object-based visual attention: Evidence from unilateral neglect. In C. Umiltà & M. Moscovitch (Eds.), *Attention and performance XIV: Conscious and nonconscious processing and cognitive functioning* (pp. 351–376). Hillsdale, NJ: Lawrence Erlbaum Associates.

Bisiach, E., Rusconi, M. L., & Vallar, G. (1991). Remission of somatoparaphrenic delusion through vestibular stimulation. *Neuropsychologia, 29*, 1029–1031.

Braddick, O., Atkinson, J., Hood, B., Harkness, W., Jackson, G., & Vargha, K. F. (1992). Possible blindsight in infants lacking one cerebral hemisphere. *Nature, 360*, 461–463.

Butter, C. M., Kirsch, N. L., & Reeves, G. (1990). The effect of lateralized dynamic stimuli on unilateral spatial neglect following right hemisphere lesions. *Restorative Neurology and Neuroscience, 2*, 39–46.

Cappa, S. F., Sterzi, R., Vallar, G., & Bisiach, E. (1987). Remission of hemineglect and anosognosia after vestibular stimulation. *Neuropsychologia, 25*, 775–782.

Danziger, S., Fendrich, R., & Rafal, R. D. (1997). Inhibitory tagging of locations in the blind field of hemianopic patients. *Consciousness and Cognition, 6*, 291–307.

Deuel, R. K. (1987). Neural dysfunction during hemispatial neglect after cortical damage in two monkey models. In M. Jeannerod (Ed.), *Neurophysiological and neuropsychological aspects of spatial neglect*. Amsterdam: North-Holland.

Deuel, R. K., & Collins, R. C. (1984). The functional anatomy of frontal lobe neglect in monkeys: Behavioral and 2-deoxyglucose studies. *Annals of Neurology, 15*, 521–529.

Fendrich, R., Wessinger, C. M., & Gazzaniga, M. S. (1992). Residual vision in a scotoma: Implications for blindsight. *Science, 258*, 1489–1491.

Fischer, B., & Breitmeyer, B. (1987). Mechanisms of visual attention revealed by saccadic eye movements. *Neuropsychologia, 25*, 73–84.

Forbes, K., & Klein, R. M. (1996). The magnitude of the fixation offset effect with endogenously and exogenously controlled saccades. *Journal of Cognitive Neuroscience, 8*, 344–352.

Glimcher, P. W., & Sparks, D. L. (1992). Movement selection in advance of action in the superior colliculus. *Nature, 355*, 542–545.

Guitton, D., Buchtel, H. A., & Douglas, R. M. (1985). Frontal lobe lesions in man cause difficulties in suppressing reflexive glances and in generating goal directed saccades. *Experimental Brain Research, 58,* 455–472.

Henik, A., Rafal, R., & Rhodes, D. (1994). Endogenously generated and visually guided saccades after lesions of the human frontal eye fields. *Journal of Cognitive Neuroscience, 6,* 400–411.

Hovda, D. A., & Villablanca, J. R. (1990). Sparing of visual field perception in neonatal but not adult cerebral hemispherectomized cats. Relationship with oxidative metabolism in the superior colliculus. *Behavioral Brain Research, 37,* 119–132.

Ingle, D. (1973). Evolutionary perspectives on the function of the optic tectum. *Brain Behavior and Evolution, 8,* 211–237.

Johnson, M. H., & Morton, J. (1991). *Biology and cognitive development: The case of face recognition.* Oxford, England: Basil Blackwell.

Karnath, H. O. (1994). Disturbed coordinate transformation in the neural representation of space as the crucial mechanism leading to neglect. *Neuropsychological Rehabilitation, 4,* 147–150.

Karnath, H. O., Christ, K., & Hartje, W. (1993). Decrease of contralateral neglect by neck muscle vibration and spatial orientation of trunk midline. *Brain, 116,* 383–396.

Kingstone, A. F., & Klein, R. M. (1993a). Visual offsets facilitate saccadic latency: Does pre-disengagement of visuo-spatial attention mediate this gap effect? *Journal of Experimental Psychology: Human Perception and Performance, 19,* 1251–1256.

Kingstone, A. F., & Klein, R. M. (1993b). What are express saccades? *Perception and Psychophysics, 54,* 260–273.

Kinsbourne, M. (1977). Hemi-neglect and hemisphere rivalry. In E. A. Weinstein & R. P. Friedland (Eds.), *Advances in neurology* (pp. 41–49). New York: Raven Press.

Kinsbourne, M. (1993). Orientational bias model of unilateral neglect: Evidence from attentional gradients within hemispace. In I. H. Robertson & J. C. Marshall (Eds.), *Unilateral neglect: Clinical and experimental studies* (pp. 63–86). Hillsdale, NJ: Lawrence Erlbaum Associates.

Kinsbourne, M. (1994). Mechanisms of neglect: Implications for rehabilitation. *Neuropsychological Rehabilitation, 4,* 151–153.

Maruff, P., & Currie, J. (1995). An attentional grasp reflex in patients with Alzheimer's disease. *Neuropsychologia, 33,* 689–702.

Mays, L. E., & Sparks, D. L. (1980). Saccades are spatially, not retinocentrically, coded. *Science, 208,* 1163–1165.

Munoz, D. P., & Wurtz, R. H. (1992). Role of the rostral superior colliculus in active visual fixation and execution of express saccades. *Visual Neuroscience, 9,* 409–414.

Munoz, D. P., & Wurtz, R. H. (1993a). Fixation cells in monkey superior colliculus. I. Characteristics of cell discharge. *Journal of Neurophysiology, 70,* 559–575.

Munoz, D. P., & Wurtz, R. H. (1993b). Fixation cells in monkey superior colliculus. II. Reversible activation and deactivation. *Journal of Neurophysiology, 70,* 559–575.

Paus, T. (1996). Location and function of the human frontal eye-field: A selective review. *Neuropsychologia, 34,* 475–484.

Pizzamiglio, L., Frasca, R., Guariglia, C., Inaccia, R., & Antonucci, G. (1990). Effect of optokinetic stimulation in patients with visual neglect. *Cortex, 26,* 535–540.

Posner, M. I. (1980). Orienting of attention. *Quarterly Journal of Experimental Psychology, 32,* 3–25.

Posner, M. I., & Cohen, Y. (1984). Components of visual orienting. In H. Bouma & D. Bouwhuis (Eds.), *Attention and Performance X* (pp. 531–556). London: Lawrence Erlbaum Associates.

Posner, M. I., Cohen, Y., & Rafal, R. D. (1982). Neural systems control of spatial orienting. *Philosophical Transactions of the Royal Society of London, B298,* 187–198.

Posner, M. I., & Rafal, R. D. (1987). Cognitive theories of attention and the rehabilitation of attentional deficits. In R. J. Meir, L. Diller, & A. L. Benton (Eds.), *Neuropsychological rehabilitation* (pp. 182–201). London: Churchill & Livingston.

Posner, M. I., Rafal, R. D., Choate, L., & Vaughn, J. (1985). Inhibition of return: Neural basis and function. *Cognitive Neuropsychology, 2,* 211–228.

Rafal, R. (1992). Visually guided behavior in progressive supranuclear palsy. In I. Litvan & Y. Agid (Eds.), *Progressive supranuclear palsy: Clinical and research approaches* (pp. 204–222). Oxford, England: Oxford University Press.

Rafal, R. D. (1996a). Balint's syndrome. In T. E. Feinberg & M. J. Farah (Eds.), *Behavioral neurology and neuropsychology* (pp. 337–356). New York: McGraw-Hill.

Rafal, R. D. (1996b). Hemispatial neglect: Neuropsychological approaches and issues. In T. E. Feinberg & M. J. Farah (Eds.), *Behavioral neurology and neuropsychology* (pp. 319–336). New York: McGraw-Hill.

Rafal, R., Calabresi, P., Brennan, C., & Sciolto, T. (1989). Saccade preparation inhibits reorienting to recently attended locations. *Journal of Experimental Psychology: Human Perception and Performance, 15,* 673–685.

Rafal, R. D., & Grimm, R. J. (1981). Progressive supranuclear palsy: Functional analysis of the response to methysergide and antiparkinsonian agents. *Neurology, 31,* 1507–1518.

Rafal, R. D., & Henik, A. (1994). The neurology of inhibition: Integrating controlled and automatic processes. In D. Dagenbach & T. Carr (Eds.), *Inhibitory processes in attention, memory and language* (pp. 1–51). San Diego: Academic Press.

Rafal, R., Henik, A., & Smith, J. (1991). Extrageniculate contributions to reflexive visual orienting in normal humans: A temporal hemifield advantage. *Journal of Cognitive Neuroscience, 3,* 323–329.

Rafal, R. D., Posner, M. I., Friedman, J. H., Inhoff, A. W., & Bernstein, E. (1988). Orienting of visual attention in progressive supranuclear palsy. *Brain, 111,* 267–280.

Rafal, R. D., Ro, T., & Ingle, H. (1995, October). Saccade preparation inhibits detection at actively attended locations. *Proceedings of the 36th Annual Conference of the Psychonomics Society,* Los Angeles.

Rafal, R., Smith, J., Krantz, J., Cohen, A., & Brennan, C. (1990). Extrageniculate vision in hemianopic humans: Saccade inhibition by signals in the blind field. *Science, 250,* 118–121.

Reuter, L. P., Hughes, H. C., & Fendrich, R. (1991). The reduction of saccadic latency by prior offset of the fixation point: An analysis of the gap effect. *Perception and Psychophysics, 49,* 167–175.

Reuter-Lorenz, P. A., Hughes, H. C., & Fendrich, R. (1991). The reduction of saccadic latency by prior offset of the fixation point: An analysis of the gap effect. *Perception and Psychophysics, 50,* 383–387.

Ro, T., Henik, A., Machado, L., & Rafal, R. D. (1997). Transcranial magnetic stimulation of the prefrontal cortex delays contralateral endogenous saccades. *Journal of Cognitive Neuroscience, 9,* 433–440.

Rubens, A. B. (1985). Caloric stimulation and unilateral visual neglect. *Neurology, 35,* 1019–1024.

Saslow, M. G. (1967). Effects of components of displacement-step stimuli upon latency for saccadic eye movements. *Journal of the Optical Society of America, 57,* 1024–1029.

Schiller, P. H. (1977). The effect of superior colliculi ablations on saccades elicited by cortical stimulation. *Brain Research, 122,* 154–156.

Schiller, P. H., Sandell, J. H., & Maunsell, J. H. (1994). The effect of frontal eye field and superior colliculus lesions on saccadic latencies in the rhesus monkey. *Experimental Brain Research, 98,* 179–190.

Schmidt, W. C. (1996). "Inhibition of return" without visual input. *Neuropsychologia, 34,* 943–952.

Seyal, M., Ro, T., & Rafal, R. (1995). Increased sensitivity to ipsilateral cutaneous stimuli following transcranial magnetic stimulation of the parietal lobe. *Annals of Neurology, 38,* 264–267.

Sherman, S. M. (1974). Visual fields of cats with cortical and tectal lesions. *Science, 185,* 355–357.

Simion, F., Valenza, E., Umiltà, C., & Dalla Barba, B. (1995). Inhibition of return in newborns is temporo-nasal asymmetrical. *Infant Behavior & Development, 18*(2), 189–194.

Sprague, J. M. (1966). Interaction of cortex and superior colliculus in mediation of peripherally summoned behavior in the cat. *Science, 153,* 1544–1547.

Stein, B. E., & Meredith, M. A. (1993). *The merging of the senses.* Cambridge, MA: MIT Press.

Tassinari, G., Biscaldi, M., Marzi, C. A., & Berlucchi, G. (1989). Ipsilateral inhibition and contralateral facilitation of simple reaction time to non-foveal visual targets from non-informative visual cues. *Acta Psychologia, 70,* 267–291.

Tipper, S. P., & Behrmann, M. (1996). Object-centered not scene-based visual neglect. *Journal of Experimental Psychology: Human Perception and Performance, 22,* 1261–1278.

Tipper, S. P., Driver, J., & Weaver, B. (1991). Object-centered inhibition of return of visual attention. *Quarterly Journal of Experimental Psychology, 43*(2), 289–298.

Tipper, S., Rafal, R., Reuter-Lorenz, P. A., Starreveld, Y., Ro, T., Egly, R., Weaver, B., & Danziger, S. (1997). Object based facilitation and inhibition from visual orienting in the human split brain. *Journal of Experimental Psychology: Human Perception and Performance, 23,* 1522–1532.

Tipper, S. P., Weaver, B., Jerreat, L. M., & Burak, A. L. (1994). Object- and environment-based inhibition of return of visual attention. *Journal of Experimental Psychology: Human Perception and Performance, 20,* 478–499.

Vallar, G., Bottini, G., Rusconi, M. L., & Sterzi, R. (1993). Exploring somatosensory hemineglect by vestibular stimulation. *Brain, 116,* 71–86.

Wallace, S. F., Rosenquist, A. C., & Sprague, J. M. (1989). Recovery from cortical blindness mediated by destruction of nontectotectal fibers in the commissure of the superior colliculus in the cat. *Journal of Comparative Neurology, 284,* 429–450.

Wallace, S. F., Rosenquist, A. C., & Sprague, J. M. (1990). Ibotenic acid lesions of the lateral substantia nigra restore visual orientation behavior in the hemianopic cat. *Journal of Comparative Neurology, 296,* 222–252.

Warner, C. B., Juola, J. F., & Koshino, H. (1990). Voluntary allocation versus automatic capture of visual attention. *Perception and Psychophysics, 48,* 243–251.

Weiskrantz, L. (1986). *Blindsight: A case study and implications.* Oxford, England: Oxford University Press.

Wenban, S. M., & Findlay, J. M. (1991). Express saccades: Is there a separate population in humans? *Experimental Brain Research, 7,* 505–510.

Chapter 7

Selection-for-Action and the Development of Orienting and Visual Attention

Bruce M. Hood
Harvard University

Janette Atkinson
Oliver J. Braddick
University College London

ATTENTION AS A SELECTION-FOR-ACTION MECHANISM

Attention is a term that is widely used in cognitive science but very rarely defined adequately. It can be used interchangeably with the term *selection* but both of these terms are of little use unless some effort is made to explain the purpose and the mechanism whereby selection is taking place. Broadbent (1971), who was an early proponent of the information-processing approach to understanding behavior, proposed that selective attention reflected the underlying capacity limitations of the human brain:

> If there were really sufficient machinery available to the brain to perform such an analysis for every stimulus, and then use the results to decide which should be selected, it is difficult to see why any selection at all should occur. The obvious utility of a selection system is to produce an economy in mechanism. (p. 147)

For Broadbent (1971), the reason for selection was to protect the brain from information overload. He stated: "selection takes place in order to protect a mechanism of limited capacity" (p. 178). However, this argument is clearly circular in that the evidence for limited capacity is the occurrence of selection and yet selection exists *in order* to protect the limited capacity which in turn, is evoked to explain selection.

219

Furthermore, the argument for the limited capacity of a central processor is less persuasive when the computational resources at later stages of information processing are considered. For example, the visual system is not a converging but rather, a highly diverging system that may not have the obvious capacity limitations as suggested (van der Heijden, 1995). While each eye sends approximately 10^6 afferents from retinal ganglion cells, the cortical visual system has approximately 10^{11} cortical cells involved in further processing of the visual signal. This means that for every retinal ganglion cell input, there is subsequent processing by approximately 100,000 cortical visual neurons.

If the central processor is not the limiting factor, why does selective attention take place? In recent years, *selection-for-action* (Allport, 1987) has provided a pragmatic approach to understanding bottlenecks of attention. The survival of an individual is determined by the efficiency of actions which are under a number of constraints. These constraints include an unpredictable environment in which the organism must respond rapidly. Actions must also be organized in some form of priority system, otherwise chaos would ensue. Furthermore, as many actions share common subcomponents, mechanisms must operate to coordinate the selection and timing of actions in order to avoid interference between them. Selection-for-action is a set of principles that supports behavioral coherence. This coherence or maintenance is necessary because of the potential conflicts that may arise, disrupting the planning and execution of actions. On the other hand, complementary mechanisms must also exist to interrupt maintenance when changes in either internal and external circumstances call for a change in priority assignment. For Allport (1987), attention has evolved as a selection-for-action mechanism that enables the organism to execute, or at least prepare to execute, a coherent pattern of motor activity, selected from a range of potential actions that may compete for the same underlying resources.

A good example of selection-for-action in operation is the organization of the primate saccadic eye movement system. Saccades have to be coordinated because they are actions directed in space that can not occur simultaneously. For example, looking left can not occur at the same time as looking right. Likewise, it not possible to maintain fixation on an object of interest at the same time as generating a saccade toward a peripheral target. Selection-for-action principles must coordinate between the need to inspect the world and the need to orient toward peripheral visual events that may signal a potential threat or opportunity.

For example, as Fig. 7.1 illustrates, controlled inspection of the visual scene is achieved by voluntary or endogenous saccades. However, the endogenous system is effortful, takes up processing resources, and may place the organism at a disadvantage in situations where a rapid response is

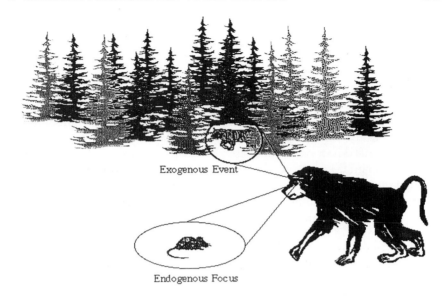

Exogenous Event

Endogenous Focus

Dissociation Between Endogenous and Exogenous Attention

FIG. 7.1. The focus of visual attention can be determined by internal, endogenous goals but may be interrupted by exogenous events that represent a threat. On the other hand, it is equally important to be able to ignore exogenous events if the endogenous goals have a higher priority.

required; namely to avoid a potential threat. Therefore, a second exogenous system exists to rapidly orient the eyes to certain types of events. This second system is not under voluntary control and requires fewer resources as it is specialized for detecting when and where events occur rather than determining what the event is. However, there must also be some means of inhibiting exogenous orienting, otherwise gaze would always be determined by external events. Bob Rafal (this volume) refers to this form of exogenous orienting as the "visual grasp reflex" and has suggested that it is very similar to other infantile reflexes that re-emerge as a result of disinhibition following cortical injury later in life.

Not only are endogenous and exogenous mechanisms functionally separate, but neuroanatomical and neurophysiological evidence indicates that they may be subserved by relatively independent neural structures that relay control commands to the eye movement generators (Schiller, this volume). Furthermore, studies of patients with localized lesions concur with animal models of the orienting system (Rafal, this volume). In particular, the endogenous system is predominantly mediated by anterior cortical visual areas whereas the exogenous system is predominantly subcortical with less cortical involvement. Although these mechansims are quite distinct, there is a high degree of connectivity between them. As noted earlier this is necessary, given that both systems must compete for the same motor output.

Evidence from anatomical studies (Conel, 1939) and recent positron emission tomography studies (Chugani & Phelps, 1986) support a vast amount of behavioral data indicating that subcortical structures are relatively mature in comparison to cortical structures in the young infant. This is likely to have implications for the emergence of endogenous control. Indeed, most models of visual development are based on the idea that early visual behavior in the human infant predominantly reflects the activity of subcortical systems and that changes in visual behavior over the first months of life reflect the onset of cortical mechanisms (Atkinson, 1984; Bronson, 1974; Johnson, 1990). This chapter summarizes the current state of knowledge concerning the development of orienting over the first year of life and proposes that the data are best interpreted as not only the maturation of endogenous mechanisms, but also the emergence of the necessary coordination with the exogenous system as required for effective selection-for-action. However, we acknowledge that not all aspects of attention can be fully accounted for in terms of motor planning as selection can take place at levels where the motor limitations are not clear. In particular, attention to objects, independent of their spatial coordinates, is difficult to reconcile with selection-for-action (Baylis, this volume; Rafal, this volume).

VISUAL PATHWAYS FOR ORIENTING

Orienting occurs whenever the organism has to align receptors with a sensory source. Although this is achieved by coordinating a number of different motor systems including the eye, head, and posture, only eye movements are considered here. For primates, the visual system is the primary modality, which is designed to sample external information in a series of coordinated eye movements that shift and fixate approximately 3 to 4 times per second under normal viewing conditions. One main reason for this is that the receptor layout is not homogeneous across each retina. The high cone density in the fovea optimizes the processing of spatial detail, while in the periphery, color sensitivity and spatial resolution are greatly reduced, but flicker sensitivity and the ability to register high velocities (Baker & Braddick, 1985) are relatively enhanced. A full review of all of the neural structures involved in generating eye movements is beyond the scope of this chapter and much of the following summary is based on the initial classification of four independent pathways proposed by Schiller (1985). Readers are referred to Schiller (this volume) for an updated and fuller account of the visual pathways for orienting.

Retinotectal Pathway

The superior colliculus (SC) is a subcortical structure that plays a major role in orienting by integrating multimodal information from both cortical and subcortical structures prior to issuing commands to generate orienting behavior. There are both direct inputs from the retina and indirect afferents via visual cortical areas. Approximately 10% of retinal ganglion cells project to the SC (Perry & Cowey, 1984b). The colliculus on each side receives a direct input from the ipsilateral nasal retina (temporal visual field) and a crossed input from the contralateral temporal retina (nasal visual field). There is some anatomical evidence to indicate that there is proportionally larger projection from the temporal visual field (Hendrickson, Wilson, & Toyne, 1970; Hubel, LeVay, & Weisel, 1975) which may account for behavioral asymmetries in responding to targets appearing in the two hemifields (see what follows for alternative findings).

Each colliculus has a retinotopic representation of the visual field and in primates, the central visual field is greatly magnified reflecting the importance of the foveal field in primate visual behavior. There have been many studies of the receptive field properties of visual neurons in the SC in an effort to determine how they differ from processing in the cortical visual system. In spite of varying studies using different techniques, there is good general agreement about the main properties of SC visual neurons. They are primarily designed to detect novel, moving stimuli by coding for position and direction of movement. However, even coordinating these orienting properties is believed to involve cortical influence as SC activity needs to be modified to avoid automatic or reflexive responding (Schiller, 1985). This is supported by the finding that temporary inactivation of the visual cortex by reverse cooling eliminates responses of many SC neurons (Schiller, Stryker, Cynader, & Berman, 1974). The role of cortical visual areas in SC activity is further substantiated by the sparse connections between the superficial layers and the deep layers from which efferents project to the eye movement generators in the brainstem. Therefore, much of the retinal input to the superficial layers reaches the eye movement generators in deeper layers via an indirect route through the primary visual cortex. The issue of direct retinal input to the deeper layers is still controversial and has not been resolved (for review, see Sparks & Hartwich-Young, 1989). Although there appears to be sufficient evidence for an entirely subcortical direct projection from the retina to the layers of the SC involved in eye movement control, their function is unknown (Moschovakis, Karabelis, & Highstein, 1988). This issue is very important for models which attribute aspects of visual behavior wholly to the subcortical pathway, independent of cortical influence (see Maurer & Lewis, this volume).

The SC is a complicated structure involved in many behaviors (for review, see Stein & Meredith, 1993). It appears to be particularly suited

for detecting the location of visual events and triggering coordinated orienting responses. It may be capable of these responses via the retinotectal
pathway, independently of cortical influence. However, as part of the corticotectal and corticocortical pathways, the SC is likely to play a role in
responding to visual stimuli that are processed by cortical mechanisms. In
terms of the distinction made earlier in the chapter, the retinotectal and
corticotectal pathways may be thought of as the neural substrates that
mediate exogenous orienting as it is the occurrence of external events that
trigger orienting in this relatively direct route to the eye movement generators in the brainstem.

Corticotectal and Corticocortical Pathway

The remaining 90% of retinal ganglion cells project to visual cortex
through the dorsal lateral geniculate nucleus (Perry & Cowey, 1984a) which
can be regarded as a relay station to the primary visual area (V1). The
cortex is heavily involved in orienting as V1 is a major component of at
least two other pathways. One is the corticotectal projection back down to
the SC involving V1 and the middle temporal visual area (MT). The other
major pathway is predominantly cortical as it projects to extrastriate visual
areas through to association areas involved with higher order visual processing such as object recognition (temporal cortex) and location analysis
(parietal cortex). The output of this pathway feeds through to the Frontal
Eye Fields (FEF) in the prefrontal cortex which are eye movement command centers that project to both the SC and eye movement generators
in the brain stem.

    The striate visual processing area or V1 has been regarded as the cortical
gateway to visual awareness in view of the phenomenological blindness
that is experienced following its destruction (Cowey & Stoerig, 1991). From
V1 there are corticocortical projections to the extrastriate visual processing
areas as well as cortical areas involved with higher order visual analysis.
Visual pathways can be segregated into two main channels on the basis of
the type of visual signal they convey. This arises from the visual input at
the retinal level from two classes of ganglion cells which differ in terms
of their anatomical and functional significance (for review, see Schiller,
this volume). These channels remain relatively segregated throughout the
visual system and have been called the parvocellular (P) and magnocellular
(M) pathways; though Schiller (Schiller & Logothetis, 1990) uses the pic-
torially more accurate terms "midget" and "parasol" systems to convey what
the cell bodies look like under the microscope.

    There are a number of other differences that may have significance for
models of orienting as direct pathways involving the SC are exclusively

magnocellular (parasol) whereas the cortical visual pathways contains both streams (midget & parasol). There is also some evidence to indicate that the pathways may mature at different rates during the first year (Hickey & Peduzzi, 1987) and there are a number of models proposing that this differential maturation may account for some of the changes in visual behavior in the infant (Colombo, 1995; Johnson, 1990; Lewis, Maurer, & Brent, 1989; Richards & Hunter, this volume). However, such distinctions should be not be viewed as a discrete division of function rather than a means of extending the range of visual processing in the spatial, wavelength, and temporal domains (Schiller, 1996).

As noted earlier, the visual stream that eventually feeds through to prefrontal cortical mechanisms for controlling saccades, contains both parvocellular (midget) and magnocellular (parasol) information and is involved in a much richer analysis of the visual scene. It is likely to be the pathway responsible for endogenous orienting where the direction of the eye movement is based on heuristic principles derived from higher level processing. This is a much slower, voluntary system that enables the observer to direct their gaze to wherever they wish and plan or make anticipatory eye movements. However, the corticotectal pathway that projects back down to the SC is exclusively magnocellular and may be related to exogenous orienting. This pathway has been strongly implicated in the generation of eye movements in collaboration with the SC as destruction or temporary inactivation obliterates responses in the deep layers of the SC (Schiller et al., 1974).

Nigrocollicular Pathway

In addition to excitatory corticotectal and corticocortical pathways, there is also an inhibitory pathway that acts on the SC via the substantia nigra. A number of cortical areas, including frontal and parietal mechanisms, are believed to exert an inhibitory influence on the SC via this nigrocollicular pathway (Hikosaka & Wurtz, 1983). The inhibitory pathway curtails the orienting activity of the SC and can be regarded as a pivotal mechanism in selection-for-action as it may be critical for coordinating the exogenous and endogenous systems. Cells in the substantia nigra are normally very active but become less so when potential visual targets are presented or prior to saccades. Therefore, the nigrocollicular pathway which exerts tonic inhibition upon the colliculus, must itself be disinhibited. The process may originate in the endogenous eye movement control system of the cortical visual pathways. The nigrocollicular pathway projects to the deeper layers of the SC where there are visual neurons that are active during fixation and other cells which are temporally related to saccades.

The Reciprocity of Fixation and Saccades in the SC

Recently, Munoz and colleagues (Munoz & Guitton, 1989; Munoz & Wurtz, 1993a, 1993b, 1993c) reported a coordination of fixation and saccadic mechanisms within the SC that is consistent with selection-for-action principles. In addition to the large body of research to indicate that the SC is involved in saccade generation, studies have demonstrated that the SC controls the periods of fixation as active states involved in a reciprocal relationship with orienting (Wurtz & Munoz, 1995). Within the deeper layers of the SC, there are both fixation and saccade cells that are mutually inhibitory. For example, increasing the activity of fixation cells by direct stimulation leads to reduced activity of saccade cells which is manifest as increased saccadic latencies and behavioral locking of gaze. Reducing the activity of fixation cells by a GABA agonist leads to fixation instability and rapid orienting or express saccades. Therefore, within the SC there is selection-for-action coordination between the exogenous and endogenous system. The endogenous system, mediated by cortical structures, may inhibit orienting by modulating the activity of fixation cells in the deep SC layers via the nigrocollicular pathway (Wurtz & Munoz, 1995).

POSTNATAL MATURATION OF CORTICAL VISUAL SYSTEM

Early models of the developing visual system made a distinction between subcortical and cortical mechanisms and proposed that newborn visual behavior was subserved initially by subcortical structures that were relatively mature at birth (Bronson, 1974). In particular, the retinocollicular pathway was believed to be mediating visual behavior in the first months. At around 3 months of age, the cortical visual system was believed to come online, adding more function and efficiency to the existing system. Later models of visual development (Atkinson, 1984; Bronson, 1982; Johnson, 1990) are essentially extensions and refinements of this dichotomous model.

Johnson (1990, this volume) proposed the most recent version of the maturational model of the development of visual attention. In his account, the four visual pathways based on the Schiller (1985) model not only project to separate brain sites but are conveyed within different cortical layers. The progressive maturation of the primary visual cortex from the deeper to more superficial layers enables different pathways to become functional during relatively defined postnatal months. To begin, the newborn is believed to have mature subcortical structures with partial functioning in cortical area V1. Thus the retinocollicular and corticotectal pathways are functional within the first month. Next to come on line between 1 and 2 months is the cortical inhibitory pathway that operates with the nigrocollicular pathway. The effect of this onset is to damp down the activity of the excitatory visual pathways. The behavioral consequence is a reduction in orienting around 1 to 2 months of age. However, within a month the corticocortical pathway becomes enabled as connections in the upper layers of the visual cortex become operational. This pathway proceeds from V1 to other extrastriate visual areas as well as parietal and frontal areas. In particular, the output from this pathway can exert a direct influence on both the SC and eye movement generators via projections from the FEF. The emergence of greater cortical influence in both excitatory and inhibitory mechanisms is believed to underpin the shift from predominantly exogenously controlled overt orienting in the young infants to increasing endogenous control over the first 3 to 4 months.

OVERT AND COVERT ORIENTING IN INFANTS

Orienting is usually overt in that we make an eye movement to the selected target, but it can also be covert in the *absence* or *anticipation* of executing a movement. The best demonstrations of covert orienting have used cuing paradigms, in which subjects are faster to respond to a target if the previous cue indicates that it is likely to appear at that location (Posner, 1978). Likewise, subjects are much slower to respond to the target if the cue incorrectly directs their attention to a different location. To account for this, Posner proposed that there was an attentional spotlight that could move independently of the motor response. In covert orienting, this spotlight moves in advance of the motor response and facilitates performance when the cue and target occur at the same spatial location but disrupts performance when the cue invalidly directs attention to the wrong location. There is considerable debate about whether covert visual attention is simply premotor activity prior to an unexecuted motor response (e.g., Rizzolatti, Riggio, Dascola, & Umiltà, 1987) or rather a mechanism, independent of motor preparation (Klein, 1980; Klein, Kingstone, & Pontefract, 1992; Posner & Cohen, 1984). In this chapter we adopt the position that many of the experimental results from studies of covert orienting in infants can be understood as reflecting premotor activity, as required by the selection-for-action hypothesis.

As noted earlier, in addition to the overt–covert distinction, orienting can also be exogenously or endogenously determined (Klein et al., 1992). Infant visual orienting studies have been concerned with measuring eye movements, which are either spontaneous (endogenous) or elicited by stimulus presentation (exogenous). Note that the terms *endogenous* and *exogenous* are not mutually exclusive as endogenous movements are usually directed toward exogenous visual information and likewise, exogenous orienting will be dependent on the internal or endogenous state of the observer. Rather, the terms reflect the relative contribution of internal versus external factors in triggering an eye movement.

Exogenous Overt Orienting

Most early studies of infant eye movements were measures of exogenous orienting. Part of this focus was an interest in mapping the extent of visual field or how far out in space infants would move their eyes to locate a target. This could be easily measured in the vertical and horizontal planes by presenting stimuli at increasing eccentricities and determining whether the infant made an orienting eye movement toward the target. Measuring the extent of the visual field in depth is achieved by optical refraction techniques (Braddick, Atkinson, French, & Howland, 1979). In general, the finding is that the visual field is initially limited in all dimensions (see later for exceptions) but undergoes rapid expansion over the early months. Maurer and Lewis (this volume) have conducted a systematic analysis of the various spatial and temporal factors that determine orienting in young infants and how these factors change over time. However, an intriguing finding in the early studies was that the visual field measures depended strongly upon whether or not there were competing visual targets and this effect appears to be age dependent. For example, Tronick (1972) using a simple orienting task reported that the visual field increased from 15° to 40° for a particular target in the horizontal plane between 2 and 10 weeks of age. This led to the conclusion that there is improvement in the sensory processing of more distant targets. However, subsequent studies (Aslin & Salapatek, 1975; Harris & MacFarlane, 1974) revealed these age effects were highly dependent on whether there was more than one visible target in the field. In particular, a second target in the center of the visual field was likely to compete for eye movements to the periphery. Furthermore, the competition effect is greatly increased if the central target moves indicating that increases in the visual field may be partly due to allocating visual attention among targets and not simply visibility. A similar finding emerged in a series of studies by Finlay and colleagues (Finlay & Ivinski, 1982, 1984) who measured orienting in 3- to 4-month-olds with competing foveal and peripheral targets which could rotate at different speeds. Although heart rate measures indicated that infants detected a change in the peripheral stimulus, making an eye movement toward it was dependent on the relative salience of the two targets as determined by rate of rotation. If the two targets rotated at the same speed, eye movements to the peripheral target occurred 40% of the time. If the central target rotated slower in comparison to the peripheral target, eye movements to the peripheral target occurred 75%.

Competition effects can also explain another infant visual attention phenomenon known as the externality effect. In general, the scanning patterns of infants younger than 4 months of age are less extensive than those of older infants (Salapatek, 1975). In particular, infants tend to concentrate their fixations on the outer most contours of visual stimuli. For example, Milewski (1976, 1978) demonstrated that young infants failed to scan the internal features of figures made up of a geometric shape surrounded by a high contrast boundary of a different shape (e.g., a circle surrounded by a square). Although 5-week-olds could discriminate the stimuli on the basis of the shape of the outer boundary, they did not discriminate the internal shape and hence the term externality effect. Four-month-olds were capable of discriminating the compound figures on the basis of a change in either the internal or external contours. The explanation for the externality effect was that younger infants engaged in more limited scanning and tended to be visually captured by the outer boundary. This has been confirmed by recent eye movement studies which are capable of determining where an infant is fixating during a stimulus presentation (Bronson, 1990; Haith, 1980).

Processing external contours may be the basis for early face perception as newborns use the hairline and outer contour to discriminate their mother's face from that of a stranger (Pascalis, de Schonen, Morton, Deruelle, & Fabre-Grenet, 1995). The most likely explanation is that the hair, especially if dark, is the most salient feature of the face as it contains the most contrast within the visual resolution of the newborn. However, externality effects can be overcome if internal features move (Bushnell, 1979; Girton, 1979) and so face processing may be less prone to externality effects during natural movement of the mouth and eyes.

Sensory Factors

Competition effects decrease with age significantly over the first 3 months of age as indicated by an increase in the visual field (Harris & MacFarlane, 1974) and more extensive scanning between visual targets (Bronson, 1990; in press). Although attention factors have been implicated, sensory mechanisms may also contribute to the reduction of the competition effect. For example, there are relative differences in visual resolution between central and peripheral targets and these are known to change with age (for review, see Maurer & Lewis, this volume). In other words, older infants may be more likely to orient to peripheral targets because they can see them that much more clearly. There may also be lateral masking effects where the visibility of a peripheral target is compromised by a more salient target in the central field. With these issues in mind, Atkinson and her colleagues (Atkinson, Hood, Braddick, & Wattam-Bell, 1988; Atkinson, Hood, Wattam-Bell, &

Braddick, 1992) set out to examine the competition effects in 1- and 3-month-old infants using targets that had been equated for detectability by setting them to threshold for each age group. To do this, initial studies estimated the just detectable contrast level for peripheral target for the two age groups. In line with other measures of visual development, there was an improvement in the ability of 3-month-olds to detect a contrast target, in that their threshold was significantly lower than that of 1-month-olds. Two conditions were tested which are illustrated in Fig. 7.2.

The first was a noncompetition condition where the infant fixates a central target that disappears and is replaced with an identical peripheral target set to the same contrast threshold. Note that noncompetiton condition is the same as the fixation offset effect (FOE) discussed by Rafal (this volume). In order to test the competition effect, trials were introduced where the central stimulus remains on following the onset of the peripheral target. The main effects observed were on the latency to make an eye movement to the peripheral target. Overall, 3-month-olds were much faster to orient to peripheral targets than 1-month-olds in both conditions. Both age groups were slower to orient to the peripheral target in the competition condition compared to noncompetition condition but this effect was significantly more pronounced in the younger infants even though all targets have been adjusted for visual detectability in each age group. This suggests

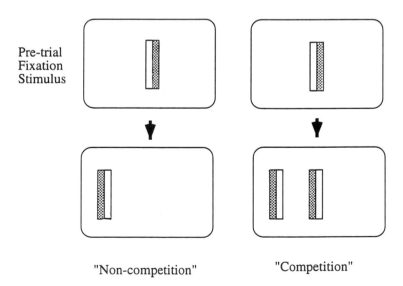

Pre-trial
Fixation
Stimulus

"Non-competition"   "Competition"

FIG. 7.2. Example of competition and noncompetition stimulus display. All infants are significantly slower to orient to the peripheral target on the competition condition in comparison to the noncompetition condition but the effect is significantly more pronounced in the infants younger than 3 months compared to older subjects.

that sensory factors alone can not account for the competition effect. A number of studies have confirmed that the competition effect reduces significantly over the first months of life (Hood & Atkinson, 1990b, 1993; Johnson, Posner, & Rothbart, 1991).

Sticky Fixation

In addition to increased response latencies during competition conditions, there is an orienting phenomenon observable around about 1 to 2 months of age that may be significant in relation to selection-for-action. A number of researchers have noted that infants at this age often exhibit prolonged periods of fixation with some apparent difficulty in looking away from salient visual stimuli. In some situations, the infants can become distressed if they are unable to unlock their gaze. The observation was first reported by Stechler and Latz (1966) who coined the term "obligatory attention" and it was subsequently verified by others (de Schonen, McKenzie, Maury, & Bresson, 1978; Johnson et al., 1991). In an effort to emphasize the oculomotor aspects of the phenomenon, Hood (1991, 1995) used the term "sticky fixation" and speculated that it is likely to reflect deficiencies in the mechanisms that allow the capture of fixation control to be overridden by a new stimulus. Although it is often reported anecdotally for 1-month-olds in the normal environment it can be reliably produced in laboratory experiments where there is a single high-contrast, dynamic target in an otherwise blank visual field. However, this is a highly unusual visual environment and so the effect may be less obvious in the real world where there are many potentials targets that may attenuate such capture effects (Hood, 1995). This hypothesis is supported by the finding that the effect is reduced when there is more than one visual target that may compete for attention (Hood, Murray, King, Hooper, Atkinson, & Braddick, 1996).

This finding emerged in a longitudinal study of 36 infants who were tested on a visual habituation experiment as newborns and then followed up at 2, 4, and 6 months of age using the same paradigm. As shown in Fig. 7.3, infants exhibited significantly longer periods of visual fixation at 2 months in comparison to other ages, producing an inverted "U" shape for visual fixation over the first 4 months. This is consistent with sticky fixation at 2 months and has been found in another longitudinal habituation study that reported that fixation durations increase specifically between 1 and 2 months and then drop again by the third month (Slater, Brown, Mattock, & Bornstein, 1996). On the other hand 2-month-olds made more refixations than newborns if two visual targets were presented, suggesting that a single salient target engages attention more effectively than multiple targets. One possibility is that multiple targets trigger orienting whereas single targets have no competition. Another important

Longitudinal Habituation Measures

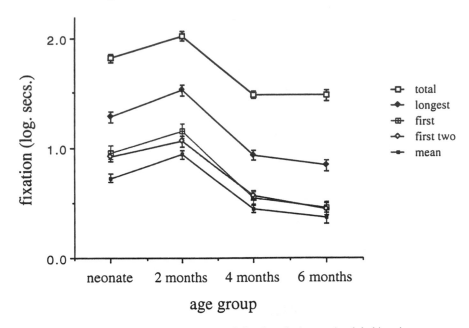

FIG. 7.3. Longitudinal measures of fixation during a visual habituation experiment. The total measure corresponds to the total accumulated looking time during the habituation. Longest is the absolute value of the longest single period of fixation. First is the absolute value of the first fixation in the experiment. First two is the mean of the first two looks and mean is the average of all fixations during habituation. All measures have been converted to the natural logarithm of the value in seconds. Repeated measures of analysis reveal that the elevation in measures at 2 months in relation to the neonate and older ages is significant.

aspect of this phenomenon to be explored is the finding that sticky fixation is less likely under monocular viewing conditions (Goldberg, Maurer, & Lewis, 1993; Maurer & Lewis, this volume). The absence of binocularity in the early months and sudden onset around 2 to 3 months may be associated with the apppearance of sticky fixation about the same time. In addition to positing neuronal mechanisms (Maurer & Lewis, this volume), it is tempting to speculate the potential function of sticky fixation as a behavior that could help to calibrate a rapidly developing stereoptic system.

Sticky fixation may be similar to the gaze apraxia resulting from bilateral parietal damage or Balint's syndrome in adult patients (Balint, 1909). Although spontaneous eye movements are relatively normal, if the patient's attention is captured by a salient target, they may be unable to readily release fixation. Under these circumstances, they may be able to do so only by blinking and jerking their head away (Cogan & Adams, 1953). Blinking may form part of the mechanism for shifting visual attention as it often accompanies saccadic responses (Hall, 1945). Interestingly, there is an inverse relationship between the frequency of saccade-associated blinks and the complexity of the visual array (Watanabe, Fujita, & Gyoba, 1980). This is consistent with the single-target salience effect noted before (Hood et al., 1996). Although developmental studies of saccade-related blinking have not yet been conducted, exogenous blinking in response to an approaching target is relatively rare in infants below 3 months of age (Petersen, Yonas, & Fisch, 1980; van Hof-van Duin & Mohn, 1986) and is a cortical function mediated by visual area 7a in the parietal lobes. It is also a response that is impaired following parietal damage in the adult (Anderson & Gnadt, 1989). Furthermore, there are reports that blinking was used to overcome sticky fixation in at least one neurologically impaired child (Braddick et al., 1992). At the moment, the function and basis for this behavior remain speculative.

Gap Effect

Sticky fixation may be an extreme example of competition where fixation mechanisms are not coordinated with saccade mechanisms. The noncompetition condition avoids this conflict. In adults, Saslow (1967) demonstrated that the introduction of a temporal gap between the offset of a central fixation stimulus and the onset of peripheral target greatly facilitated saccadic response times in comparison to trials where there was an overlap between the offset fixation stimulus and peripheral target (competition). More recently, Fischer and colleagues (Fischer, 1993; Fischer & Boch, 1983; Fischer & Ramsperger, 1984) reported that saccadic responses can be divided into two populations of regular fast saccades and a second population of much shorter "express" saccades. Not all researchers have been able to demonstrate a bimodal distribution of fast and express saccades and there is some question about whether they are a real distinct category of orienting eye movements or a consequence of training and particular experimental conditions (for review, see Fischer, 1993). However, facilitated saccadic latencies are reliably found with a temporal gap.

To test whether infants benefit from temporal gaps, Hood and Atkinson (1993) tested infants from 6 weeks to 6 months of age with the competition–noncompetition paradigm (Atkinson et al., 1988; 1992). In addition, two gap conditions were included in which there was a temporal gap (either 240 ms or 720 ms) between the offset of the central stimulus and the onset of the peripheral target. In line with the adult studies, all age groups showed a significant difference between the noncompetition condition and gap conditions supporting the idea that disengagement is an active process that takes time to complete.

As in previous studies, the competition condition produced the longest latencies for all ages, including a group of adults that have been explicitly instructed to make an eye movement as quick as possible. Interestingly, the effect was significantly more pronounced in the 6-week-olds while there was no significant difference between 3- and 6-month-olds. The overlap duration of the competing central stimulus was 2 seconds. Only the 3- and 6-month-olds were capable of orienting to the peripheral before the offset of the central stimulus while 6-week-olds waited until the central stimulus offset before orienting to the peripheral target. This suggests that the mechanisms that enable infants to disengage fixation become functional between 1 and 3 months and show little change over the 3 to 6 month period studied in these experiments.

As fixation and saccades can not occur simultaneously in the orienting paradigm, selection-for-action can explain the gap effect. Disengaging the fixation mechanism in the overlap situation is a process that takes time to complete and so introducing a gap between the offset of the fixation stimulus and onset of the peripheral target bypasses the disengagement component and shortens the response time. The selection-for-action explanation is supported by the finding that gap effects are found in other situations where responses are spatially oriented and mutually exclusive. For example, when a manual response has to be made to the left versus right, gap effects are found but not when the manual response is not spatially directed (Bekkering, Pratt, & Abrams, 1996). As the manual response does not have to be directed in space, then the source of conflict arising from executing the action in one part of the space as opposed to another part, is avoided.

Endogenous Overt Orienting

Endogenous overt orienting refers to voluntary eye movements that are determined by internal states. As noted earlier, such eye movements are not exclusively endogenous in that saccades are usually made to external visual stimuli. Rather, it is the choice of when and which visual event to orient to that is determined by endogenous factors. In general, studies of endogenous orienting in infants have looked at the pattern of spontaneous scanning of complex visual stimuli. Like studies of exogenous orienting, these usually report that initially scanning is limited and slow with the range and rate of refixation increasing over the early months (for review, see Banks & Salapatek, 1983). However, the account of such developmental trends is invariably in terms of the changing influence of exogenous visual factors such as contrast, luminance, or flicker of the targets.

Nevertheless, endogenous mechanisms, which may reflect a number of factors such as cognition, arousal, or motivation, which also change with age, are critical internal states that affect eye movements. As Hainline (1993) has correctly pointed out, many studies of infant orienting fail to acknowledge the various factors that contribute to the endogenous state of the infant. For example, only recently has the role of arousal been systematically investigated in relation to orienting (for review see Richards, this volume). Furthermore, Hainline is very critical of studies that compare infant visual performance to other groups such as adults, patients, or animals, as there are likely to be many differences between the endogenous states of the various groups. This criticism applies also to the significance of marker tasks in which performance on a task is believed to reflect specific neurological activity (Johnson, 1996). However, while null results and differences in performance may not be very informative as there may be alternative explanations—when similarities do emerge between groups using similar paradigms, this suggests that these tasks may be illustrating fundamental principles of how the system is organized independently of age (Hood & Atkinson, 1993). The job of the experimenter is to investigate what are the sources of similarity as well as differences.

COVERT ORIENTING

Under some circumstances we can dissociate the direction of attention from the locus of fixation (James, 1890). In this stituation, there is an endogenous shift of covert attention as the observer is voluntarily attending to a location in the absence of any overt orienting. However, as the monkey and tiger illustration in Fig. 7.1 shows, attention can be shifted exogenously by a visual event in the periphery. This has been demonstrated experimentally using either covert endogenous or exogenous cues, prior to a target onset, that influence the performance of the observer responding to the target (Posner, 1978). Endogenous cues are events that have to be interpreted, such as a symbol that informs the observer of the impending location of a target. For example, if a letter such as "R" or an arrow pointing to the right appears prior to a peripheral target presentation, subjects will be faster to respond to a target appearing in the right field if the cue is valid on most trials. A typical validity ratio of 80:20 means that the cue will be valid on 80% of trials. On invalid trials the cue directs attention to the opposite location leading to inhibited responses. Posner (1980) suggested that attention is similar to a spotlight that can be shifted covertly prior to a target location thereby, enhancing responses to that location. On invalid trials, as the spotlight is pointing to the wrong location, responding is inhibited as the observer now has to reorient the spotlight to the correct location. Unlike endogenous cues, exogenous cues are brief visual events that can appear at the target location. Exogenous cues automatically trigger a shift of visual attention and are difficult to ignore. Also, unlike endogenous cues, exogenous cues have a biphasic effect on performance with the benefits from valid cuing turning into costs as the stimulus onset asynchrony increases (see the following discussion of inhibition of return). Developmental studies of these two types of covert orienting reveal that exogenous cuing undergoes comparatively little change from 6 years of age onwards whereas endogenous cuing is much more variable (see Enns, Brodeur, & Trick, this volume). This supports the idea that exogenous cues operate much more automatically in comparison to endogenous cues that may be based on higher level cognitive processes.

Exogenous Covert Orienting and Inhibition of Return

According to Posner's analogy (1980) the onset of the cue causes a spotlight of attention to automatically shift to the location independently and prior to any response. Following an initial period of facilitation when responses are enhanced to targets appearing at the cued location, a period of inhibition ensues whereby responses to the cued location become poorer relative to uncued locations. This phenomenon is known as "inhibition of return" (IOR) and reflects the finding that subjects are inhibited on returning their attention to the previously cued location. It affects both the saccadic response time to make an eye movement towards the target as well as manual response to press a key with the target onset (Maylor, 1985; Posner & Cohen, 1984). According to Posner, this an evolutionary adaptive mechanism that ensures that once a location is attended to either overtly or covertly, it becomes inhibited, thereby biasing responses towards novel locations (Posner, Rafal, Choate, & Vaughan, 1985). However, as Tipper, Driver, and Weaver (1991) point out, observers usually move through the environment and so object-based IOR would be more useful than absolute spatial location. Furthermore, there is increasing evidence for mechanisms of attention that operate on objects rather than space (Duncan, 1984; Kahneman & Treisman, 1984). This interpretation found some support from studies demonstrating that the inhibition is also defined in object-based coordinates and can move in accordance with an object's movements (Gibson & Egeth, 1994; Tipper et al., 1991). Recently, a more thorough analysis has indicated that both object-based and environment-based IOR occur in the cued orienting paradigm (Tipper, Weaver, Jerreat, & Burak, 1994). However, the object-based inhibition effects are smaller than environment-based IOR and are heavily dependent on the object being continually visible during the duration of the stimulus onset asynchrony. This suggests that covert attention directed to the object-based representation is more due to continuous tracking than object representation alone. Furthermore, most studies of IOR have shown that the effect is only found for detection tasks and not perceptual discriminations suggesting that is more related to event onsets rather than determining the exact nature of the event (Schmidt, 1996a; Terry, Valdes, & Neill, 1994).

In our opinion, the most satisfactory account of IOR evokes the selection-for-action argument. Rafal, Calabresi, Brennan, and Sciolto (1989) demonstrated that the effect is attributable to the planning or execution of eye movements, even though other responses such as the manual response time is the dependent measure. However, when subjects are asked to prepare a manual response to the cue in preparation of the target, IOR is not observed. In other words, the phenomenon is not a general consequence of any motor activity but rather appears to attributed to the automatic activation of the oculomotor system by visual events (Tassinari, Aglioti, Chelazzi, Marzi, & Berlucchi, 1987). Note that this is still a feature of many manual response tasks. Exogenous events such as peripheral cues automatically trigger eye movements but if the subject is instructed to maintain fixation, this motor program is canceled. Therefore, reapplying the same directional motor program when the target appears at the same location is ineffectual in comparison to targets appearing at other spatial locations that require a different set of directional parameters. This is supported by the finding that IOR is mapped in terms of relative motor direction and not absolute spatial location (Berlucchi, Tassinari, Marzi, & Di Stefano, 1989). Relative motor direction is mutually exclusive whereas relative amplitude is a simple adjustment of the gain and the last parameter to be entered into the motor command for speeded responses (Keele, 1981). IOR is also found with overt orienting responses. If endogenous cues such as an arrow pointing left or right are used, IOR only occurs if the subject is instructed to prepare an eye movement even though no saccade is actually executed (Rafal et al., 1989). More recently, it has been demonstrated that IOR can occur in the auditory domain in the absence of visual input so long as the observer has prepared an eye movement (Schmidt, 1996b).

Tipper and colleagues (1994) argued that object-based and environment-based IOR exist simultaneously and may be mediated by relatively independent neural substrates. In particular, they suggested that environment-based IOR is associated with eye movements (Rafal et al., 1989) and may be subserved by the SC. The SC does not encode object features and so the object-based IOR is likely to be mediated by cortical structures that feed into the orienting system. Developmental studies of contingency learning are consistent with this account in that 3-month-olds learn contingency on the basis of location but not object identity whereas 6-month-olds learn contingency on the basis of location and object identity (Colombo, Mitchell, Coldren, & Atwater, 1990). There is also one recent infant study that reports that overt orienting is initially determined by environment-based IOR before object-based IOR (Harman, Posner, Rothbart, & Thomas-Thrapp, 1994).

Inhibition of return has been reported in infants using both overt orienting (Clohessy, Posner, Rothbart, & Vecera, 1991) and covert orienting tasks (Hood, 1993; Hood & Atkinson, 1990a, 1991; Johnson & Tucker, 1993, 1996). These two types of orienting paradigms are illustrated in Fig. 7.4. In the overt tasks, infants are cued to one side by a single cue. After

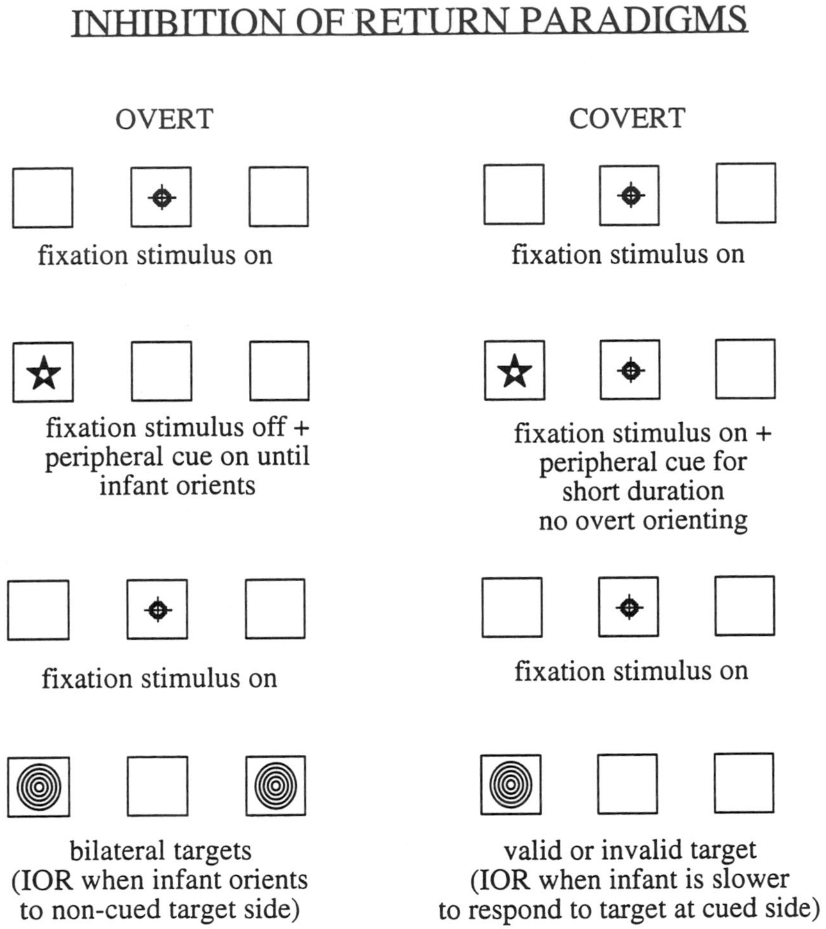

INHIBITION OF RETURN PARADIGMS

FIG. 7.4. Paradigms for overt (Clohessy et al., 1991) and covert (Hood & Atkinson, 1990a) inhibition of return in infants. In the overt paradigm, the infant orients to the peripheral cue and then orients back to the central point of fixation. In the covert paradigm, the central stimulus at the point of fixation remains visible during the cue presentation and competes for the infant's attention. No overt movement to the cue is observed and hence the shift is deemed to be covert. If a gap greater than 200 ms is introduced, infants tend to orient to the opposite location to the cued side in the overt paradigm or are significantly slower to orient to a single target at the cued side compared to the uncued location in the covert paradigm.

orienting to one side and then returning to the center, IOR can be demonstrated in that infants are significantly more likely to orient to the opposite location with a bilateral target presentation. This is also reflected in a faster response time. In the covert orienting tasks, infants are presented with a salient central fixation target which inhibits orienting to the peripheral cue. When the central stimulus is extinguished, infants are much slower to make a saccade to a peripheral target appearing at the same side as the cue compared to trials where the target and cue are on opposite sides (Hood & Atkinson, 1990a). When a bilateral target presentation is used, there is also a bias to orient to the location not previously cued (Johnson & Tucker, 1993, 1996).

At first, there appeared to be a good correspondence between the age of onset for both overt (Clohessy et al., 1991) and covert (Hood & Atkinson, 1990a; Johnson & Tucker, 1996) IOR between 3 to 6 months of age. However, a number of recent studies have demonstrated earlier overt IOR. If the target eccentricities are reduced to 10° rather than the usual 20°–30°, 3-month-olds are more likely to orient to the opposite location with a bilateral presentation, though the latency data does not reach significance (Harman et al., 1994). This eccentricity effect was interpreted as a constraint on IOR when targets are further than a single saccadic eye movement away from the point of central fixation. However, this interpretation seems unlikely as later studies demonstrated IOR for both the latency and direction of saccade in the newborns with targets at 30° (Valenza, Simion, & Umiltà, 1994).

As yet, there are no reports of covert IOR in newborns, but those studies that have found IOR following overt shifts during the pretest report that it only occurred on trials in which the infant had made an eye movement to the cue during the pretest. This suggests that covert IOR will not be found until infants are old enough to plan and then cancel the motor program during covert orienting. As Rafal's (Rafal et al., 1989) study has shown, selection-for-action can account for both phenomena if covert orienting is considered to be activating the same motor program as overt orienting.

Visual Field Asymmetry: Marker for SC Pathway?

Interestingly, the effects of IOR are not evenly distributed across the visual field. Under monocular viewing conditions, adults experience a temporal hemifield dominance of IOR; namely that cues presented in the temporal field exert a greater influence on subsequent targets at that location compared to nasal cues and targets (Rafal et al., 1989). This finding is consistent with other behavioral asymmetries of the nasal–temporal visual hemifields which are believed to reflect an asymmetry of retinocollicular projections (for review see Maurer & Lewis, this volume). In very young infants who have a functional retinocollicular projection but possibly immature cortical pathways, there is a significant tendency to orient to targets presented in the temporal visual field in comparison to the nasal field. In line with the visual field data, there is also greater IOR for cues and targets presented in the temporal field of the newborn under monocular viewing conditions (Simion, Valenza, Umiltà, & Barba, 1995). These findings are consistent with Posner's hypothesis that IOR is closely associated with the functioning of the SC as patients with localized damage to this structure do not show normal IOR (Posner et al., 1985).

However, a recent anatomical study (Williams, Azzopardi, & Cowey, 1995) casts doubt on the theory that nasal–temporal asymmetries are due to relatively more crossed (temporal visual field) compared to uncrossed (nasal visual field) retinocollicular projections. Rather, other subcortical nuclei such as the inferior pulvinar which receives little ipsilateral retinal input has been suggested as alternative subcortical sites for the asymmetry (Williams et al., 1995; for discussion, see Maurer & Lewis, this volume).

Endogenous Covert Orienting

As already noted, exogenous cues automatically engage the orienting system in the covert tasks and so it is difficult to dissociate the cue effects as acting on an attention system as distinct from those acting on the motor system. To address this issue, Johnson and colleagues (Johnson, Posner, & Rothbart, 1994) trained 4-month-old infants to orient to the opposite side from a lateralized visual cue in anticipation of a target 400 ms later. Following training, the infants were presented with trials in which the target appeared at the same side only 100 ms later. As infants were faster to respond to these targets, Johnson et al. (1994) concluded that the cue caused a shift in attention and not a facilitation of the eye movement as the infants should be planning a saccade in the opposite location. However, the use of different SOAs between the training and test trials as well as the possible IOR effects due to invalid cuing from peripheral cues make the results difficult to interpret.

One way to avoid IOR effects is to use central cues, but infants must be trained to learn the contingency between a central cue and the location. Once again, Johnson et al. (1991) demonstrated that 4-month-olds could learn the contingency between two central visual stimuli and either the left or right peripheral location following training with 18 trials. Other studies have also shown that visual contingency learning and anticipatory eye movements can be demonstrated between 3 and 4 months of age (for review, see Haith, 1993).

In a recent line of research, Hood and colleagues (Hood, Willen, & Driver, 1997) have adapted the joint attention paradigm to induce covert endogenous shifts of visual attention without training. This was achieved by adapting the standard infant joint attention task (Scaife & Bruner, 1975) into a Posner central cuing paradigm. In the joint attention procedure an adult faces the infant and directs their gaze towards the child. When the infant looks at the adult, he or she then turns their head and eyes to look to one side. By 10 to 12 months of age, most infants will turn to the corresponding direction as the adult, indicating that they have determined the cues for a shift in mutual or joint attention. During the second year, infants will begin to turn on the basis of a shift of the direction of eyes alone, independently of the movement of the adult's head.

However, one recent theory has postulated the existence of an Eye Direction Detector (EDD) which is sensitive to deviation of the eyes alone as an indicator of the direction of attention (Baron-Cohen, 1996). This is believed to be operating within the first year as it forms one of the fundamental building blocks of social communication. Furthermore, several lines of neuropsychological and neurophysiological evidence suggest that gaze detection may be a specialized visual module with its own dedicated neural basis. For example, 64% of neurons in the monkey superior temporal sulcus that respond to face stimuli have been found to be selectively tuned to the direction of the gaze of the face (Perrett, Smith, Potter, Mistlin, Head, Milner, & Jeeves, 1985). Furthermore, adult prosopagnosics who lose the ability to recognize the human face may have a selective deficit in the ability to detect the direction of gaze (Campbell, Heywood, Cowey, Regard, & Landis, 1990).

Although studies of gaze detection in young infants have determined that they can discriminate aligned gaze from deviated gaze on a schematic face following habituation (Vecera & Johnson, 1995) as early as 4 months, this does not determine whether this discrimination serves to shift the infant's own attention. To test whether eye direction produces a shift in infant attention, we adapted the Posner cuing paradigm where responses to a target are facilitated if the location of the target is validly prespecified by a preceding cue in comparison to trials where the cue incorrectly shifts the respondent's attention away from the location of the ensuing target (Posner, 1978).

The display is shown in Fig. 7.5. A full-size color image of a real female face was presented to the infants. The image opened and closed her eyes twice a second in order to attract the infants' attention to the salient features. When the infant looked at the eyes, a trial was initiated where the eyes on the faces looked briefly to one side. After a short delay, the face disappeared and a peripheral target then appeared at the same (valid) or opposite side (invalid) and the direction and latency to initiate an orienting saccade was measured. An analysis of latencies revealed that 4-month-old infants were significantly faster to orient to the target if gaze

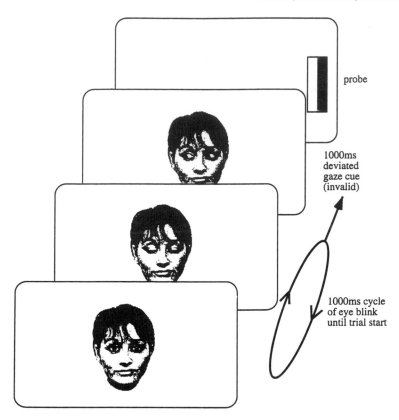

probe

1000ms
deviated
gaze cue
(invalid)

1000ms cycle
of eye blink
until trial start

FIG. 7.5. Example of stimulus sequence on an invalid trial. The gaze shifted
for 1000 ms before the face disappeared and a peripheral probe was
presented. The latency and direction of the first saccade were determined
from video recordings. Infants were significantly faster to orient to the validly
cued probe and made proportionally more errors (20% vs. 12%) on invalid
trials compared to valid trials. A significantly greater proportion of infants
(93%) looked away from the probe on invalid trials compared to valid trials
(63%).

had validly cued the target. More strikingly, infants were twice as likely to
make an error of orienting away from the target when the gaze cue was
invalid compared to valid trials and this occurred in most infant in which
a reasonable number of trials had been obtained.

These findings were observed in the youngest infants tested at 10 weeks
through 28 weeks of age. This is considerably younger than most reports of
joint attention (Corkum & Moore, 1995). One possible explanation for the
lack of orienting in very young infants is that they are less likely to orient to
a peripheral target when there is an interesting adult in the central visual
field. In other words, there is a competition effect operating in the traditional

joint attention paradigm. Nevertheless, the presence of significant attentional effects produced by the direction of gaze supports Baron-Cohen's (1996) hypothesis that there is an eye direction detector operating very early in development. It remains to be seen whether future studies will push this capacity to an earlier age, although it seems unlikely given the low levels of visual acuity with younger infants and their limited scanning of the internal features of a face. On the other hand, attentional effects from gaze detection appear to become more reliable with age and may be a function of the infant's familiarity of the face. Not only is a more familiar face one that is likely to have had a good contingency history of social interaction but studies of facial expression indicate a greater allocation of attention to the mother as indicated by the amplitude of negative components of the event-related potential (Nelson & Dukette, this volume).

EXOGENOUS AND ENDOGENOUS CUING: ATTENTIONAL SHIFTS OR SELECTION-FOR-ACTION?

We initially began by proposing that attentional effects of orienting are really consequences of selection-for-action or motor preparation. Recently, a similar proposal has been made by Rizzolatti and his colleagues (Rizzolatti et al., 1987; Rizzolatti, Riggio, & Sheliga, 1994) who have put forward a premotor theory of spatial attention. In their account, shifts of attention activate the same neural mechanisms in advance of those that would be innervated by executing the actual motor response, hence premotor. Spatial attention is therefore preparation to perform goal-directed, spatially coded movements. Furthermore, as foveal vision and saccades play such an important role in acting on the world for primates, many spatial attention effects reflect oculomotor preparation. Although there are opponents of this account (Klein et al., 1992) there is mounting evidence that shifts of attention act directly on the oculomotor system. For example, Rizzolatti et al. (1994) found that vertical saccades to the same target in space would be deviated toward a covertly attended location that was to either side of the vertical meridian. Using similar logic, Kustov and Robinson (1996) found that fixed vector saccades, which are evoked by direct collicular stimulation in the monkey, were deviated by both exogenous and endogenous cues in an attention paradigm. In line with the premotor account, they found that a totally naive animal who was trained on a manual version of the exogenous and endogenous cuing paradigm, also exhibited deviated evoked saccades by direct stimulation. The authors conclude that, "shifts of attention, however evoked, are tightly coupled with the preparation to make oculomotor responses to the attended area" (p. 77). On the other hand, it seems likely that the factors influencing endogenous control are more complicated than the simple sensory cuing from exogenous events and this is supported by the different developmental course when the two mechanisms are compared (Enns et al., this volume).

SUMMARY AND CONCLUSIONS

In terms of the four dimensions of orienting, exogenous and endogenous mechanisms can shift visual attention either overtly or covertly in the 3- to 4-month-old infant, as indicated by saccadic response times. Prior to 3 months, orienting is more heavily influenced by exogenous events than perhaps the endogenous control system. The exogenous and endogenous mechanisms may be subserved by relatively separate neural pathways that are different stages of development in the young infant. In particular, the exogenous system may be predominantly mediated by the midbrain and striate cortical visual areas. Endogenous orienting is much less automatic and may use a number of higher level processes in deciding where to direct the eyes next. However, selection-for-action predicts that when there is conflict between exogenous and endogenous mechanisms, which are both competing for the same resources, behavior is impaired and response times are increased. When there is a single target in an otherwise homogeneous visual field there is no competition and orienting is achieved by simple mechanisms. These may be predominantly exogenous in the youngest infants. However, when there is more than one target, and especially if there is a salient target in the foveal region stimulating those mechanisms that maintain fixation, orienting requires active disengagement of the fixation system before an orienting saccade can occur. If exogenous events do not automatically cause disengagement, then endogenous mechanisms which may be mediated by cortical structures are required to inhibit fixation maintenance. This ability to voluntarily disengage improves with age as indicated by the reduction of the competition effect, especially between 1 and 3 months of age. Sticky fixation reflects the relatively inefficiency of the oculomotor disengagement mechanisms with solitary, salient targets which is especially pronounced at around 2 months of age. As the gap paradigm bypasses the need for disengagement, facilitated response times are observed at all ages tested. Overt inhibition of return reflects the relatively inefficiency of executing the same motor during a refractory period. Covert inhibition of return is essentially unexecuted overt orienting which produces the same pattern. It is caused by the triggering of the exogenous orienting system that can be voluntarily countermanded by the endogenous system to maintain fixation. These premotor accounts of attentional shifts are supported by recent neurophysiological studies revealing that both exogenous and endogenous cues that shift attention prior to either eye movements or manual responses operate by activating oculomotor preparation.

ACKNOWLEDGMENTS

Preparation of this chapter was supported by an Alfred P. Sloan Fellowship in neuroscience to the first author and a Medical Research Council of Great Britain grant to the second and third authors.

REFERENCES

Allport, A. (1987). Selection for action: Some behavioral and neurophysiological considerations of attention and action. In H. Heuer & A. F. Sanders (Eds.), *Perspectives on perception and action* (pp. 395–479). Hillsdale, NJ: Lawrence Erlbaum Associates.

Anderson, R. A., & Gnadt, J. W. (1989). Posterior parietal cortex. In R. H. Wurtz & M. E. Goldberg (Eds.), *The neurobiology of saccadic eye movements* (pp. 315–335). Amsterdam: Elsevier.

Aslin, R. N., & Salapatek, P. (1975). Saccadic localization of visual targets by the very young human infant. *Perception and Psychophysics, 17,* 293–302.

Atkinson, J. (1984). Human visual development over the first six months of life. A review and a hypothesis. *Human Neurobiology, 3,* 61–74.

Atkinson, J., Hood, B., Braddick, O. J., & Wattam-Bell, J. (1988). Infants' control of fixation shifts with single and competing targets: Mechanisms of shifting attention. *Perception, 17,* 367–368.

Atkinson, J., Hood, B., Wattam-Bell, J., & Braddick, O. J. (1992). Changes in infants' ability to switch attention in the first three months of life. *Perception, 21,* 643–653.

Baker, C. L., & Braddick, O. J. (1985). Eccentricity-dependent scaling of the limits for short-range motion perception. *Vision Research, 25,* 803–812.

Balint, R. (1909). Seelenlähmung des 'Schauens', optische Ataxie, räumliche Störung der Aufmerksamkeit. *Monatschrift für Psychiatrie und Neurologie, 25,* 51–81.

Balint, R. (1909). Psychic paralysis of gaze, optic ataxia and disturbances of spatial attention. *Monographs for Psychiatry and Neurology, 25,* 51–81.

Banks, M., & Salapatek, P. (1983). Infant visual perception. In P. H. Mussen (Ed.), *Handbook of child psychology. Vol. II: Infancy and developmental psychobiology* (pp. 435–571). New York: John Wiley.

Baron-Cohen, S. (1996). *Mindblindness. An essay on autism and theory of mind.* Cambridge, MA: MIT Press.

Bekkering, H., Pratt, J., & Abrams, R. A. (1996). The gap effect for eye and hand movements. *Perception & Psychophysics, 58,* 628–635.

Berlucchi, G., Tassinari, G., Marzi, C. A., & Di Stefano, M. (1989). Spatial distribution of the inhibitory effect of peripheral non-informative cues on simple time to non-fixated visual targets. *Neuropsychologica, 27,* 201–221.

Braddick, O. J., Atkinson, J., French, J., & Howland, H. C. (1979). A photorefractive study of infant accommodation. *Vision Research, 19,* 1319–1330.

Braddick, O. J., Atkinson, J., Hood, B., Harkness, W., Jackson, G., & Vargha-Khadem, F. (1992). Possible blindsight in infants lacking one cerebral hemisphere. *Nature, 360,* 461–463.

Broadbent, D. E. (1971). *Decision and stress.* London: Academic Press.

Bronson, G. W. (1974). The postnatal growth of visual capacity. *Child Development, 45,* 873–890.

Bronson, G. W. (1982). Structure, status and characteristics of the nervous system at birth. In P. Stratton (Ed.), *Psychobiology of the human newborn* (pp. 99–118). Chichester, England: Wiley.

Bronson, G. W. (1990). Changes in infants' visual scanning across the two- to fourteen week period. *Journal of Experimental Child Psychology, 49,* 101–125.

Bronson, G. W. (in press). The growth of visual capacity: Evidence from infant scanning patterns. In C. Rovee-Collier & L. Lipsett (Eds.), *Advances in infancy research* (Vol. 11). Norwood, NJ: Ablex.

Bushnell, I. W. R. (1979). Modification of the externality effect in young infants. *Journal of Experimental Child Psychology, 28,* 211–229.

Campbell, R., Heywood, C., Cowey, A., Regard, M., & Landis, T. (1990). Sensitivity to eye gaze in prospagnosic patients and monkeys with superior temporal sulcus ablation. *Neuropsychologica, 28,* 1123–1142.

Chugani, H. T., & Phelps, M. E. (1986). Maturational changes in cerebral function determined by 18FDG positron emission topography. *Science, 231,* 840–843.

Clohessy, A. B., Posner, M. I., Rothbart, M. K., & Vecera, S. P. (1991). The development of inhibition of return. *Journal of Cognitive Neuroscience, 3,* 345–356.

Colombo, J. (1995). On the neural mechanisms underlying developmental and individual differences in visual fixation in infancy: Two hypotheses. *Developmental Review, 15,* 97–135.

Colombo, J., Mitchell, D. W., Coldren, J. T., & Atwater, J. D. (1990). Discrimination learning during the first year: Stimulus and positional cues. *Journal of Experimental Psychology: Learning, Memory, & Cognition, 16,* 98–109.

Cogan, D. G., & Adams, R. D. (1953). A type of paralysis of conjugate gaze (ocular motor apraxia). *Archives of Ophthalomology, 50,* 434–442.

Conel, J. L. (1939). *The postnatal development of the human cerebral cortex* (Vols. 1–3). Cambridge, MA: Harvard University Press.

Corkum, V., & Moore, C. (1995). Development of joint visual attention in infants. In C. Moore & P. J. Dunham (Eds.), *Joint attention: Its origins and role in development* (pp. 61–83). Mahwah, NJ: Lawrence Erlbaum Associates.

Cowey, A., & Stoerig, P. (1991). Reflections on blindsight. In D. Milner & M. Rugg (Eds.), *The neuropsychology of consciousness* (pp. 11–37). New York: Academic Press.

de Schonen, S., McKenzie, B., Maury, L., & Bresson, F. (1978). Central and peripheral object distances as determinants of the effective visual field in early infancy. *Perception, 7,* 499–506.

Duncan, J. (1984). Selective attention and the organization of visual information. *Journal of Experimental Psychology: General, 113,* 501–517.

Finlay, D. C., & Ivinski, A. (1982). Cardiac and visual responses to stimuli presented foveally and peripherally as a function of speed of moving stimuli. *Developmental Psychology, 18,* 692–698.

Finlay, D. C., & Ivinski, A. (1984). Cardiac and visual responses to moving stimuli presented either successively or simultaneously to the central and peripheral visual fields in four-month-old infants. *Developmental Psychology, 20,* 29–36.

Fischer, B. (1993). Express saccades and visual attention. *Behavioral Brain Research, 16,* 553–610.

Fischer, B., & Boch, R. (1983). Saccadic eye movements after extremely short reaction times in the monkey. *Brain Research, 260,* 21–26.

Fischer, B., & Ramsperger, E. (1984). Human express saccades: Extremely short reaction times of goal directed eye movements. *Experimental Brain Research, 57,* 191–195.

Gibson, B. S., & Egeth, H. (1994). Inhibtion of return to object-based and environment-based locations. *Perception & Psychophysics, 55,* 323–339.

Girton, M. R. (1979). Infants' attention to intrastimulus motion. *Journal of Experimental Child Psychology, 28,* 416–423.

Goldberg, M. C., Maurer, D., & Lewis, T. L. (1993). The influence of a central stimulus on infants' visual fields. *Investigative Ophthalmology & Visual Science, 34,* 1354.

Hainline, L. (1993). Conjugate eye movements of infants. In K. Simons (Ed.), *Early visual development: Normal and abnormal* (pp. 47–79). Oxford, England: Oxford University Press.

Haith, M. M. (1980). *Rules that babies look by.* Hillsdale, NJ: Lawrence Erlbaum Associates.

Haith, M. M. (1993). Future-oriented processes in infancy: The case of visual expectations. In C. E. Granrud (Ed.), *Visual perception and cognition in infancy* (pp. 235–264). Hillsdale, NJ: Lawrence Erlbaum Associates.

Hall, A. (1945). The origin and purpose of blinking. *The British Journal of Ophthalmology, 29,* 445–467.

Harman, C., Posner, M. I., Rothbart, M. K., & Thomas-Thrapp, L. (1994). Development of orienting to locations and objects in human infants. *Canadian Journal of Experimental Psychology, 48,* 301–318.

Harris, P. L., & MacFarlane, A. (1974). The growth of the effective visual field from birth to seven weeks. *Journal of Experimental Child Psychology, 18,* 340–384.

Hendrickson, A., Wilson, M. E., & Toyne, M. J. (1970). The distribution of optic nerve fibres in Macca mulatta. *Brain Research, 23,* 425–427.

Hickey, T. L., & Peduzzi, J. D. (1987). Structure and development of the visual system. In L. Cohen & P. Salapatek (Eds.), *Handbook of infant perception* (pp. 1–42). New York: Academic Press.

Hikosata, O., & Wurtz, R. H. (1983). Visual and oculomotor functions of monkey substantia nigra pars reticulata I–IV. *Journal of Neurophysiology, 49,* 1230–1301.

Hood, B. M. (1991). *Development of visual selective attention in infants.* Unpublished doctoral dissertation. University of Cambridge.

Hood, B. M. (1993). Inhibition of return produced by covert shifts of visual attention in 6-month-old infants. *Infant Behavior and Development, 16,* 255–264.

Hood, B. M. (1995). Shifts of visual attention in the infant: A neuroscientific approach. In C. Rovee-Collier & L. Lipsett (Eds.), *Advances in infancy research* (Vol. 9, pp. 163–216). Norwood, NJ: Ablex.

Hood, B., & Atkinson, J. (1990a). Inhibition of return in infants. *Perception, 19,* 369.

Hood, B., & Atkinson, J. (1990b). Sensory visual loss and cognitive deficits in the selective attentional system of normal infants and neurologically impaired children. *Developmental Medicine and Child Neurology, 32,* 1067–1077.

Hood, B., & Atkinson, J. (1991). Shifting covert attention in infancy. *Investigative Ophthamology and Visual Science, 31,* 965.

Hood, B. M., & Atkinson, J. (1993). Disengaging visual attention in the infant and adult. *Infant Behavior and Development, 16,* 405–422.

Hood, B. M., Murray, L., King, F., Hooper, R., Atkinson, J., & Braddick, O. (1996). Habituation changes in early infancy: Longitudinal measures from birth to 6 months. *Journal of Reproductive and Infant Psychology, 14,* 177–185.

Hood, B. M., Willen, J. D., & Driver, J. (1997, April). *An eye direction detector triggers shifts of visual attention in human infants.* Paper presented at the Society for Research in Child Development, Washington, DC.

Hubel, D. H., LeVay, S., & Weisel, T. N. (1975). Mode of termination of retinotectal fibres in macaque monkey: An autoradiographic study. *Brain Research, 96,* 25–40.

Johnson, M. H. (1990). Cortical maturation and the development of visual attention in infancy. *Journal of Cognitive Neuroscience, 2,* 81–95.

Johnson, M. H. (1996). *Developmental cognitive neuroscience.* Cambridge, MA: Blackwell.

Johnson, M. H., Posner, M. I., & Rothbart, M. K. (1991). Components of visual orienting in early infancy: Contingency learning, anticipatory looking, and disengaging. *Journal of Cognitive Neuroscience, 3,* 335–344.

Johnson, M. H., Posner, M. I., & Rothbart, M. K. (1994). Facilitation of saccades toward a covertly attended location in early infancy. *Psychological Science, 5*, 90–93.

Johnson, M. H., & Tucker, L. A. (1993). The ontogeny of covert visual attention: Facilitatory and inhibitory effects. *Abstracts of the Society for Research in Child Development, 9*, 424.

Johnson, M. H., & Tucker, L. A. (1996). The development and temporal dynamics of spatial orienting in infants. *Journal of Experimental Child Psychology, 63*, 171–188.

Kahneman, D., & Treisman, A. (1984). Changing views of attention. In R. Parasuraman & D. Davies (Eds.), *Varieties of attention* (pp. 29–61). San Diego, CA: Academic Press.

Keele, S. W. (1981). Behavioural analysis of movement. In M. Brookhart & V. Mouncastle (Eds.), *Handbook of physiology, Section 1: The nervous system* (pp. 1391–1414). Bethesda, MD: American Physiology Society.

Klein, R. (1980). Does oculomotor readiness mediate cognitive control of visual attention? In R. S. Nickerson (Ed.), *Attention and performance VIII* (pp. 259–276). Hillsdale, NJ: Lawrence Erlbaum Associates.

Klein, R., Kingstone, A., & Pontefract, A. (1992). Orienting of visual attention. In K. Raynor (Ed.), *Eye movements and visual cognition: Scene perception and reading* (pp. 46–65). New York: Springer-Verlag.

Kustov, A. A., & Robinson, D. L. (1996). Shared neural control of attentional shifts and eye movements. *Nature, 384*, 74–77.

Lewis, T. L., Maurer, D., & Brent, H. P. (1989). Optokinetic nystagmus in normal and visually deprived children: Implications for cortical development. *Canadian Journal of Psychology, 43*, 121–140.

Maylor, E. A. (1985). Facilitatory and inhibitory components of orienting in visual space. In M. I. Posner & B. B. Marin (Eds.), *Attention and performance XI* (pp. 189–204). Hillsdale, NJ: Lawrence Erlbaum Associates.

Maurer, D., & Lewis, T. L. (1991). The development of peripheral vision and its physiological underpinnings. In M. J. Weiss & P. R. Zelazo (Eds.), *Newborn attention: Biological constraints and the influence of experience* (pp. 218–255). Norwood, NJ: Ablex.

Milewski, A. E. (1976). Infants' discrimination of internal and external pattern elements. *Journal of Experimental Child Psychology, 22*, 229–246.

Milewski, A. E. (1978). Young infants' visual processing of internal and adjacent shapes. *Infant Behavior and Development, 1*, 359–371.

Moschovakis, A. K., Karabelas, A. B., & Highstein, S. M. (1988). Structure-function relationships in the primate superior colliculus. I. Morphological classification of effect neurons. *Journal of Neurophysiology, 60*, 232–262.

Munoz, D. P., & Guitton, D. (1989). Fixation and orientation control by the tecto-reticulo-spinal system in the cat whose head is unrestrained. *Review of Neurology, 145*, 567–579.

Munoz, D. P., & Wurtz, R. H. (1993a). Fixation cells in the monkey superior colliculus: I. Characteristics of cell discharge. *Journal of Neurophysiology, 70*, 559–575.

Munoz, D. P., & Wurtz, R. H. (1993b). Fixation cells in the monkey superior colliculus: II. Reversible activation and deactivation. *Journal of Neurophysiology, 70*, 576–589.

Munoz, D. P., & Wurtz, R. H. (1993c). Superior colliculus and visual fixation. *Biomedical Research, 14*, 75–79.

Pascalis, O., de Schonen, S., Morton, J., Deruelle, C., & Fabre-Grenet, M. (1995). Mother's face recognition by neonates: A replication and extension. *Infant Behavior and Development, 18*, 79–86.

Perrett, D., Smith, P., Potter, D., Mistlin, A., Head, A., Milner, A., & Jeeves, M. (1985). Visual cells in the temporal cortex sensitive to face view and gaze direction. *Proceedings of the Royal Society of London, B223*, 293–317.

Perry, V. H., & Cowey, A. (1984a). Retinal ganglion cells that project to the dorsal lateral geniculate nucleus in the macaque monkey. *Neuroscience, 12*, 1101–1123.

Perry, V. H., & Cowey, A. (1984b). Retinal ganglion cells that project to the superior colliculus and pretectum in the macaque monkey. *Neuroscience, 12*, 1125–1137.

Pettersen, L., Yonas, A., & Fisch, R. O. (1980). The development of blinking in response to impending collision in preterm, full-term, and postterm infants. *Infant Behavior and Development, 3*, 155–165.

Posner, M. I. (1978). *Chronometric explorations of the mind.* Hillsdale, NJ: Lawrence Erlbaum Associates.

Posner, M. I. (1980). Orienting of attention. *Quarterly Journal of Experimental Psychology, 32*, 3–25.

Posner, M. I., & Cohen, Y. (1984). Components of visual orienting. In H. Bouma & D. G. Bouwhuis (Eds.), *Attention and performance X* (pp. 531–556). Hillsdale, NJ: Lawrence Erlbaum Associates.

Posner, M. I., Rafal, R. D., Choate, L. S., & Vaughan, J. (1985). Inhibition of return: Neural basis and function. *Cognitive Neuropsychology, 2*, 211–228.

Rafal, R. D., Calabresi, P. A., Brennan, C. W., & Sciolto, T. K. (1989). Saccade preparation inhibits reorienting to recently attended locations. *Journal of Experimental Psychology: Human Perception and Performance, 15*, 673–685.

Rizzolatti, G., Riggio, L., Dascola, I., & Umilta, C. (1987). Reorienting attention across the horizontal and vertical meridians: Evidence in favour of a premotor theory of attention. *Neuropsychologica, 25*, 31–40.

Rizzolatti, G., Riggio, L., & Sheliga, B. M. (1994). Space and selective attention. In C. Umiltà & M. Moscovitch (Eds.), *Attention and performance, 15: Conscious and nonconscious information processing* (pp. 231–265). Hillsdale, NJ: Lawrence Erlbaum Associates.

Salapatek, P. (1975). Pattern perception in early infancy. In L. Cohen & P. Salapatek (Eds.), *Infant perception: From sensation to cognition. Basic visual processes* (Vol. 1, pp. 133–248). New York: Academic Press.

Saslow, M. G. (1967). Effects of components of displacement-step stimuli upon latency of saccadic eye movements. *Journal of the Optical Society of America, 57*, 1024–1029.

Scaife, M., & Bruner, J. S. (1975). The capacity for joint attention. *Nature, 253*, 265–266.

Schiller, P. H. (1985). A model for the generation of visually guided saccadic eye movements. In D. Rose & V. G. Dobson (Eds.), *Models of the visual cortex* (pp. 62–70). Chichester, England: Wiley.

Schiller, P. H. (1996). On the specificity of neurons and visual areas. *Behavioral Brain Research, 76*, 21–35.

Schiller, P. H., & Logothetis, N. K. (1990). The color-opponent and broad-band channels of the primate visual system. *Trends in Neuroscience, 13*, 392–398.

Schiller, P. H., Stryker, M., Cynader, M., & Berman, N. (1974). The response characteristics of single cells in the monkey superior colliculus following ablation or cooling of the visual cortex. *Journal of Neurophysiology, 35*, 181–194.

Schmidt, W. C. (1996a). Inhibition of return is not detected using illusory line motion. *Perception and Psychophysics, 58*, 883–898.

Schmidt, W. C. (1996b). Inhibition of return without visual input. *Neuropsychologica, 34*, 943–952.

Simion, F., Valenza, E., Umiltà, C., & Barba, B. D. (1995). Inhibition of return in newborns is temporo-nasal asymmetrical. *Infant Behavior and Development, 18*, 189–194.

Slater, A. M., Brown, E., Mattock, A., & Bornstein, M. (1996). Continuity and change in habituation in the first 4 months from birth. *Journal of Reproductive and Infant Psychology, 14*, 187–194.

Sparks, D. L., & Hartwich-Young, R. (1989). The deep layers of the superior colliculus. In R. H. Wurtz & M. E. Goldberg (Eds.), *The neurobiology of saccadic eye movements* (pp. 213–256). Amsterdam: Elsevier.

Stechler, G., & Latz, E. (1966). Some observations on attention and arousal in the human infant. *Journal of the American Academy of Child Psychiatry, 5*, 517–525.

Stein, B. E., & Meredith, M. A. (1993). *The merging of the senses.* Cambridge, MA: MIT Press.

Tassinari, G., Aglioti, S., Chelazzi, L., Marzi, C. A., & Berlucchi, G. (1987). Distribution in the visual field of the costs of voluntarily allocated attention and the inhibitory after-effects of covert attention. *Neuropsychologica, 25*, 55–72.

Terry, K. M., Valdes, L. A., & Neill, W. T. (1994). Does "inhibition of return" occur in discrimination tasks? *Perception & Psychophysics, 55*, 279–286.

Tipper, S. P., Driver, J., & Weaver, B. (1991). Short report: Object-centered inhibiton of return. *Quarterly Journal of Experimental Psychology, 43A*, 289–298.

Tipper, S. P., Weaver, B., Jerreat, L. M., & Burak, A. L. (1994). Object-based and environment-based inhibition of return of visual attention. *Journal of Experimental Psychology: Human Perception and Performance, 20*, 478–499.

Tronick, E. (1972). Stimulus control and the growth of the infant's effective visual field. *Perception & Psychophysics, 11*, 373–376.

Valenza, E., Simion, F., & Umiltà, C. (1994). Inhibition of return in newborns. *Infant Behavior and Development, 17*, 293–302.

van der Heijden, A. H. C. (1995). Modularity and attention. *Visual Cognition, 2*, 269–302.

van Hof-van Duin, J., & Mohn, G. (1986). Visual field measurements, optokinetic nystagmus, and the threatening response: Normal and abnormal development. *Documenta Ophthalmologica Proceedings Series, 45*, 305–315.

Vecera, S. P., & Johnson, M. H. (1995). Gaze detection and the cortical processing faces: Evidence from infants and adults. *Visual Cognition, 2*, 59–87.

Watanabe, Y., Fujita, T., & Gyoba, J. (1980). Investigation of blinking contingent upon saccadic eye movement. *Tohoka Psychologica Folia, 39*, 121–129.

Williams, C., Azzopardi, P., & Cowey, A. (1995). Nasal and temporal retinal ganglion cells projecting to the midbrain: Implications for "blindsight." *Neuroscience, 65*, 577–586.

Wurtz, R. H., & Munoz, D. P. (1995). Role of monkey superior colliculus in control and fixation. In M. S. Gazzaniga (Ed.), *The cognitive neurosciences* (pp. 533–548). Cambridge, MA: MIT Press.

Chapter 8

Visual Parsing and Object-Based Attention: A Developmental Perspective

Gordon C. Baylis
University of South Carolina

In common usage, the term *attention* is used in two main ways reflecting a distinction that has been noted since the time of William James. One sense is that we optimize the level of processing—a theme addressed by Richards and Hunter in this volume. A second distinct meaning of attention is the selection of some information for processing—a theme that is the subject of several other chapters in this volume. The present chapter addresses an issue that is central to selection: If attention is directed, what is it directed *to*? The information used to direct attention must result from processes that occur prior to the allocation of attention (termed preattentive processes). It is certainly clear that the systems used to shift attention develop over the first few years of life (e.g., Maurer & Lewis, chap. 2, this volume). However, we also need to consider how the preattentive systems develop, in order to understand the overall performance of infants at different stages of development.

Inherent in the notion of selective attention is a paradox: If attention selects those parts of the visual scene to which processing should be directed, how is attention controlled? Put another way: How we do we know what to process without first processing it? A polarization of explanations of this issue led to many years of controversy between those who believed that selection occurred prior to the analysis of the visual scene (Early Selection; see Broadbent, 1958) versus those who believed that the entire visual scene was analyzed, and that selection occurred subsequent to this (Late Selection; see Deutsch & Deutsch, 1963).

This controversy has never been resolved, perhaps for the reason that each view has a certain elegance. Early Selection is computationally efficient because only a small (hopefully relevant) subset of the visual scene is analyzed, but has the drawback that the control of attention is unclear. By contrast, Late Selection means that computational economy is sacrificed for precision in the control of attention. Recent developments in the field of attention may define a minimum level processing that occurs throughout the visual field, and show how this processing enables attention to be controlled in an adaptive fashion.

ATTENTION IN THE SPOTLIGHT

A popular metaphor for early selection has been a spotlight (e.g., Posner, 1980) that "illuminates" some part of the visual array, enhancing processing within its beam. Initially most spotlight theories suggested simply that the beam was directed to some region or other within an unanalyzed visual array. Certainly there is abundant evidence that attention can be directed both overtly and covertly to regions defined by spatial coordinates. Much of this work (e.g., Rafal, chap. 6, this volume) supports the notion that processing can be enhanced within some region (or regions), and considers how attention is directed to regions, and how it may be moved between them. Such work begs one important issue: why those regions? On what information is the decision to attend based?

Without intelligent control, surely an attentional "spotlight" cannot be advantageous. It would be like a spotlight randomly moved across a stage: Some of the actors can be seen, some cannot; but no distinction is made between the relevant and the irrelevant. Some information is needed order to direct attention adaptively; controversy has been how much preattentive processing takes place in order to provide this information.

Some spotlight theorists have suggested that a simple "salience map" (e.g., Folk, Remington, & Wright, 1994) would suffice to guide the spotlight of attention. According to such a view, minimal analysis of the visual array might result in a space-based representation of the power in the intensity domain (or else power in the time-derivative of intensity domain). This computation would generate a weighting factor biasing the probability that attention will be directed to different parts of the visual array. This very simple analysis would explain many data, such as the tendency to shift attention toward bright regions, or regions of sudden onset (Posner, 1980; Yantis, 1993; Yantis & Jonides, 1984).

A somewhat different view follows from the introspection that we attend to things or objects in our visual world. Object-based views of attention suggest that the visual array is first decomposed into visual objects, and that attention is directed to these. Thus the targets of attention are not arbitrary regions of an unprocessed visual array, but regions likely to correspond to objects in the visual scene. The term "object-based attention" has been used in different ways by different authors, yet what the various object-based views have in common is the assertion that allocation of attention is in part determined by preattentive parsing. We now examine the evidence that such preattentive decomposition of the visual scene takes place, and how its implications on subsequent attention mean that attention is object based in a number of ways.

PERCEPTUAL GROUPING

Wertheimer (1915, 1923) noted that our visual world does not appear as a homogeneous array of visual information but as a scene organized into visual forms. This organization occurs without effort and so spontaneously that these processes of visual parsing may be easy to overlook. Wertheimer and the Gestaltists went on to describe a series of laws or principles of organization. These include textbook examples such as grouping by proximity, by similarity, by common motion, or by good continuation (see Fig. 8.1a–d), but also include principles such as convexity–concavity that have been described more recently (see Kanizsa & Gerbino, 1976).

Grouping principles share two important properties. First, to a first approximation these are properties of objects in the visual scene. For example, in the case of common motion, regions of the visual array that share motion path and velocity are likely to represent movement of parts of a single object. Regions with differential motion are unlikely to represent parts of a single object, but instead are likely to correspond to different objects. Similarly, in the case of proximity, because objects are typically spatially contiguous, adjacent points in the visual array are more likely to represent points on one object rather than different objects. The second interesting point about grouping principles is that they are computationally simple to implement. Thus the computation of grouping may represent considerable informational gain (i.e., it may estimate which regions of the visual scene are likely to be related to objects) but at very low cost of computation. Therefore grouping can be applied the entire visual array (due to its economy) and is of great utility in the control of visual attention (as it provides estimated objects to which attention may be directed).

A number of studies suggest, however, that the grouping of items within the visual scene, according to Gestalt principles may occur when it is not advantageous to do so, and even when it is truly disadvantageous. The groups produced may define the possible limits of attentional focus. That is, when attention is directed to some item in the visual array, attention may automatically spread to those items phenomenally grouped with the target.

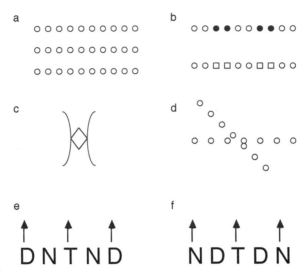

FIG. 8.1. Perceptual grouping principles first described by the Gestaltists. (a) grouping by proximity—the items group into three rows. (b) two examples of grouping by similarity—the items group into pairs of similar items; (c) uniform connectedness leads us to see this a single form, rather than the initials of the person who first described it; (d) good continuation: Note that items in the center group with those in the same line, and not with closer items than are not in that line; (e) when a target (T) is presented, flanked by nearby neutral letters (N) and far distractor items (D), interference from the distractors is seen when they move with the target; (f) when distractors are close to the target but do not move with it, the interference is absent.

A classic measure of selective attention concerns the extent to which distractors disrupt performance of a target task. Eriksen and Eriksen (1974) had participants classify target letters presented at central fixation. Distractor letters flanked each target at various separations, and could be neutral letters or letters associated with the same or opposite response to that required by the target. Slower responses in the presence of incongruent distractors were taken as evidence that these distractors were identified. The decline in such interference for more distant distractors was taken as evidence that less processing takes place outside an attentional spotlight focused on the target.

Driver and Baylis (1989) suggested that the reduced interference from more distant distractors might simply reflect a reduction in grouping between target and distractors when more distant. This study used displays that set grouping by common motion against grouping by proximity, and found that distant distractors that moved with the target could interfere more than closer distractors in a separate motion group (see Fig. 8.1e–f).

Thus interference from distractors was high in displays of the form of Fig. 8.1e, but not for displays of the form shown in Fig. 8.1f. Driver and Baylis concluded that attention is directed to Gestalt groups rather than to raw locations. This precedence of common motion over proximity can disappear with minor changes in stimuli and procedure (see Kramer, Tham, & Yeh, 1991) presumably because when two powerful factors conflict, the one that predominates depends on the exact circumstances. The precedence of motion remains a robust finding with the original displays, and subsequent studies have made a similar point for other grouping factors. Kramer and Jacobson (1991) found more interference for distractors grouped with the target by connectedness or common color. Harms and Bundesen (1983) and Baylis and Driver (1992) showed that distractors sharing the target's color caused more interference than those of a different color. Finally, Baylis and Driver (1992) found that grouping of a grid of characters into rows could similarly affect the extent of distractor interference.

These results support the notion that an initial analysis of the items in the visual scene leads to grouping according to simple Gestaltic principles. When attention is directed to part of one of these groups, it may spread to include the entire group, so that the visual grouping determines the units of attention. Relatively little processing is required to derive these groups, which are of course not associated directly with any particular object in the visual world. However, these forms (often termed "candidate objects") represent estimates of what regions of the visual array are most likely to have resulted from objects in the real world. The fact that attention tends to spread among all items that are grouped into a candidate object, is one sense in which attention may be object-based.

OBJECT-LIMITED ATTENTION

If attention tends to spread throughout a candidate object, can it spread *between* objects? That is, is attention distributed to include all of one object, but no more? To address this issue, Duncan (1984) had subjects make perceptual judgments of two superimposed objects—a box and a line (see Fig. 8.2a). He found that subjects could make two judgments about the same object (the orientation and texture of the line, for example) as easily as they could make a single judgment. On the other hand, when subjects had to make two judgments about both objects (e.g., the texture of the line and the position of a gap in the box) they were very much slower and less accurate than when making single judgments. Duncan interpreted these data to suggest that subjects show a cost when attention has to be distributed across more than one object.

Such an interpretation has been questioned by Watt (1988) and by Baylis and Driver (1993), on the grounds that the within-object judgments were

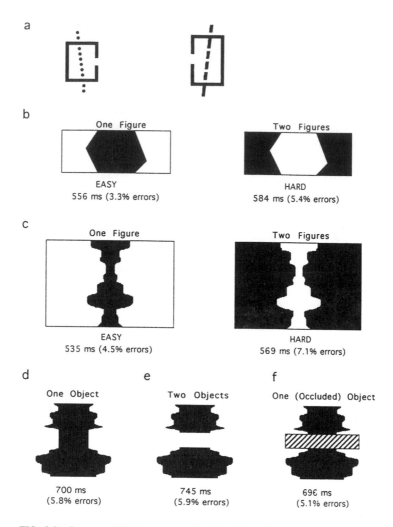

FIG. 8.2. Perceptual judgments are harder when they involve more than one object. (a) multi-attribute displays used by Duncan (1984). (b–c) whether ambiguous displays are seen as either one or two figural objects affects the reaction time and error rate to judge apex height (b) or symmetry (c). (d–f) Attention may cover an entire object even when parts of that object are occluded, leading it to appear as two regions in 2-D. Thus (f) is seen as a single (occluded) object with the result that RTs to judge symmetry are not elevated compared to single object conditions (d). On the other hand, when the scene must be parsed as two objects, a RT cost is seen due to the need to allocate attention to more than one object.

more similar in terms of spatial frequency than the between-object judgments. In other words, the apparent two-object cost may have been a cost of making judgments in more than one spatial frequency band. To investigate the possibility of a two-object cost while avoiding such pitfalls, Baylis and Driver (1993) had subjects make judgments of the relative height of two apices on a video monitor. In this study subjects were slower and made more errors if the apices belonged to two different objects, compared to when they were on the same object. In one experiment, displays that could be interpreted either as one- or two-object displays (see Fig. 8.2) and manipulated which interpretation subjects had by their task instructions.

Judgments involving two objects were slower and less accurate than equivalent judgments that involved only a single object. This was true even when the one-object and the two-object displays were physically the same, with the number of objects being manipulated by task set. Thus no objections based on the stimulus properties can be advanced to explain this two-object cost. A similar two-object cost has also been seen when subjects are making judgments of symmetry (see Baylis & Driver, 1995a, Experiment 3).

These and other experiments (e.g., Baylis, 1994; Duncan, 1993) suggest that the optimal extent of attention is a single candidate object that is produced in the preattentive phase of visual parsing. It may be hard to confine attention to less than one object, and it may be hard to extend attention beyond a single object. These are two important aspects to object-based attention.

OBJECT-BASED ORIENTING OF ATTENTION

We have seen that visual objects may define the extent of attention, but these experiments do not show that attention is directed to the objects. An alternative explanation might be that attention is directed to the region of space that contains a visual object. We now consider whether attention is applied to an object, or to a location in space. Posner (1980) interpreted his results to mean that attention is directed to a region of the visual display where a target might appear. However, the spatial locations in many of these cuing studies contained an object—the outline box in which the target could appear. It is possible that attention was being directed to the box as an object, rather than the location signaled by the box.

Egly, Driver, and Rafal (1994) used displays like those shown in Fig. 8.3a to examine the possible contribution of visual parsing to spatial cuing. Attention was directed to one end of one of the rectangles, by brightening, similar to Posner's (1980) study. This cue was predictive of the location of the target, so would be expected to attract both endogenous and exogenous attention to that region. Thus, on most trials the target occurred at the location validly predicted by the cue (V). On a minority of invalid trials the

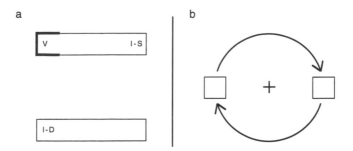

FIG. 8.3. (a) The studies of Egly et al. (1994) suggest that covert orienting is applied to an object rather than a spatial location. When one end of a box brightens, it predicts that a target will appear in that location. These valid (V) trials are the majority, but on a minority of trials, the target can occur at a location not signaled by the cue. These invalid trials can either be on the same object (I–S) or on the other object (I–D). There was a much greater invalidity effect in the latter case. (b) Tipper et al. (1991) examined IOR to a cued box, when the entire display slowly rotated so that the cued box now occupied the location previously occupied by the uncued box. These authors found that IOR followed the object, and did not remain at a fixed spatial location.

target could appear in a location other than that cued, again following Posner (1980). These invalid target trials could be of two types: The target could appear either at the opposite end of the cued rectangle (I–S), or at the end of the other rectangle (I–D). Both the invalid target positions were an equal distance from the location of the cue, so no spatial account of cuing would predict any difference between these two conditions.

When targets appeared at an uncued location that was nonetheless located on the same object as the cue (I–S), a modest increase in reaction time to detect the target was seen compared to validly cued trials. However, when targets appeared at the uncued location on a different object (I–D trials) a much larger reaction time cost was seen. These results are consistent with the notion that attention tends to spread to include the entire object, or that it is hard to move or spread attention across more than one object. In either case, the interpretation is that attention must be directed *to* an object, not simply to the region of space occupied by an object.

A different approach to disconfounding objects and location was used by Tipper, Driver, and Weaver (1991). This study investigated the phenomenon of inhibition of return (IOR) first described by Posner and Cohen (1984). With exogenous cues, target detection is initially faster, but as the time between the cue offset and the target onset increases, this reduction in reaction time eventually reverses, so that cued locations are now slower than uncued. This attentional cost has been termed IOR, and may be long lasting. Tipper et al. investigated whether this IOR applied to the cued object or to the location by making the location of the objects move (see Fig. 8.4b). The crucial finding was that IOR moved with the boxes, and did not remain at the initial location of the box when it was cued. This suggests that the IOR reflected a process applied to the object, and not to the location of that object. Similar results have been found by Gibson and Egeth (1994) who used drawings of cubes that appeared to rotate in depth. Cuing one face of the cube led to IOR that moved with that face, even though it was subsequently projected to a different location in 2-D. A discussion of the neural substrate of IOR is given in Rafal (chap. 6, this volume).

Posner and Cohen (1984) speculated that IOR may reflect inhibitory processing applied to cued locations after they have been examined. They further suggested that this may be used to ensure efficient visual search through a large set of targets—inhibition of previously searched targets will prevent back-tracking and perseveration on targets (see also Klein, 1988). Regardless of the exact mechanism of IOR, it represents another sense in which attention is object-based—processing is applied to a region defined by an object, and the location of that region is updated as the object moves. It may be noted, in passing, that many studies suggest that people are indeed able to track the locations of a number of moving objects for extended periods (Kahneman, Treisman, & Gibbs, 1992; Pyly-shyn & Storm, 1988; Yantis, 1992).

FIGURE–GROUND SEGMENTATION

Rubin (1915) pointed out that visual parsing introduced a special type of heterogeneity into the visual scene—the organization into visual forms (termed "figure") against a formless background ("ground"). Figures typically appear closer, more saturated and higher in contrast than comparable ground (see also Koffka, 1935). Introspective observations such as these have since been supported and extended by psychophysical studies (e.g., Coren & Porac, 1983). Abundant evidence has also been collected on the stimulus factors which lead one region to become figure. For example, regions that contrast highly with the general illumination tend to become phenomenal figures, as do relatively small shapes, surrounded shapes (Koff-ka, 1935), symmetrical shapes (Bahnsen, 1928; Driver & Baylis, 1996), convex shapes (Kanisza & Gerbino, 1976), and regions that are rich in high spatial frequencies (Klymenko & Weisstein, 1986). However, until recently, there has been less progress in giving a computational explanation of the subsequent figure–ground difference that results.

Rubin used displays such as his 2-D faces–vase engraving (Fig. 8.4a) to demonstrate an important result of figure–ground segmentation on shape

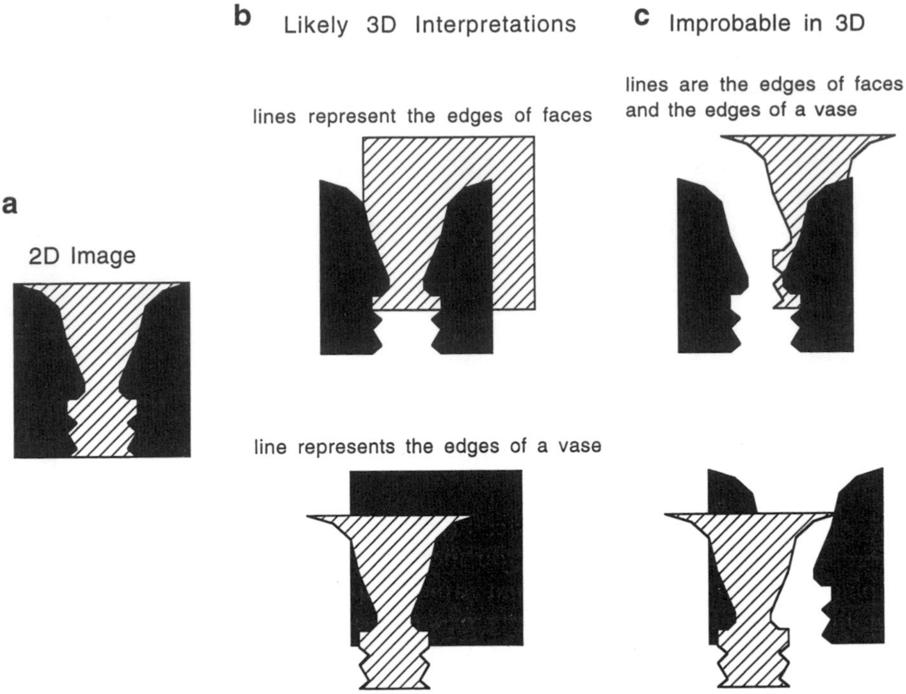

b Likely 3D Interpretations   **c** Improbable in 3D

lines are the edges of faces
lines represent the edges of faces   and the edges of a vase

a

2D Image

line represents the edges of a vase

FIG. 8.4. The classic faces–vase engraving of Rubin. (a) represents a 2-D scene that must be interpreted in 3-D; (b) shows likely scenes that would project such an image; (c) shows scenes that would project the 2-D scene, but could only occur as a result of an extremely unlikely set of coincidences.

perception. What is striking about this display is that we can experience it as a pair of faces, or as a vase (Fig. 8.4b or 8.4c), but not as both at the same time. These phenomenal experiences of this 2-D image are really theories about the three-dimensional (3-D) real world that can be projected onto two dimensions as this faces–vase scene. These theories make crucially different proposals about the nature of the curved lines. In both cases the lines are determined to represent an occlusion contour—the limiting line where one object partially occludes an object or background behind it. These two interpretations differ concerning which region is seen as the occluder object (in front) and which as the background (in back).

A computational approach to the process of vision describes an initial visual process that converges with figure–ground phenomenology. Early computational approaches to vision included attempts to describe visual scenes in a "blocks world" (see, e.g., Waltz, 1975). The input visual scenes were line drawings of arrangements of children's blocks, and the task of the machine vision system was to create a 3-D description of the blocks and their interrelations. A necessary first step in this process was to decide which lines represented occlusion contours, and which object these edges belonged to. That is, each line segment in the scene either represented a junction of two faces of one object, or represented where one object lay closer to the viewer than another object, and thus partially occluded that object. These occlusion contours correspond to the edge of the occluding object, and not to the occluded object, so should be assigned to the region that is part of the occluder. This assignment of a line to one of the two regions it adjoins represents an estimate about the 3-D arrangement of the visual scene that is projected as the 2-D image.

This computational description of edge-assignment is in essence the same as the process of figure–ground segmentation—assigning an edge to one region determines that region to be closer to the viewer (i.e., figural). The two lines in Rubin's faces–vase display can either be assigned to the central vase, or to the faces on the sides. These lines cannot belong to two objects, hence we can only have one of the two interpretations at a given time. Moreover, since the occlusion contour is unrelated to the occluded object, this (or any background) has a shape unrelated to this occlusion contour. Only the occluder (figure) has the shape of the occlusion contour.

The phenomenal demonstrations of figure–ground segmentation (or edge assignment) suggest lines tend to be assigned to regions that they adjoin, and that the viewer usually does not have access to unassigned lines. However, these studies do not show that this edge-assignment is obligatory, merely that it can occur. A recent study by Driver and Baylis (1996) suggests that the assignment of an edge to one of the regions it adjoins is an obligatory process.

In this study, Driver and Baylis (1996) studied the ability of subjects to perceive the shapes of figure and ground in an online task that was not subject to the many possible criticisms of the studies of Rubin. Subjects were presented with a display in which a random "stepped" contour divided a rectangle into a smaller and brighter green region, and a larger, dimmer red region (see Fig. 8.5a). This display was presented briefly (for 180 ms) and was followed 500 ms later by a test display comprising a pair of test shapes that either looked like the figure (Fig. 8.5b) or like the ground region (Fig. 8.5c). These test shapes were intermediate in brightness and size between the figure and ground, and were presented in gray. As such the test shapes were equally similar to the regions determined to be figure and ground in the initial displays.

Subjects' task in this study was to judge which of the two shapes in the test display was the same as the shape in the initial figure–ground display. Subjects were never alerted to the possibility of figural assignment, and task instructions explicitly required subjects to concentrate only on the jagged line itself. Nonetheless, subjects were faster and more accurate at judging displays that were shaded like the figure parts of the initial display than when the test display was shaded like the ground (see data in Fig. 8.5b and c). At

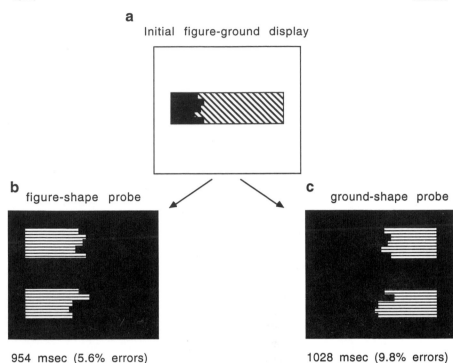

a

Initial figure-ground display

b figure-shape probe

c ground-shape probe

954 msec (5.6% errors)   1028 msec (9.8% errors)

FIG. 8.5. Subjects are instructed to remember the shape of the jagged line in displays like (a). The smaller bright green region is seen as figural, and the line is assigned to that side. As a result, when asked to recognize this edge from a pair of shapes, subjects perform better when shapes like the previous figure (b), than when presented with shapes that resemble the non-figural regions of the initial display.

the end of testing subjects were debriefed and asked about their phenomenal experience of the figure–ground displays. An overwhelming majority of them reported that the initial display did appear to be automatically segregated into figure and ground in the manner that we would expect.

These results show that subjects cannot confine their attention to the jagged lines alone. The lines are automatically assigned to just one of the two regions they adjoin—the figure. The shape of the figural part of the initial display appears to be represented better in some way than that of the ground, causing subsequent recognition of the shape of the figure to be better than recognition of the ground shape. This is both a replication of the seminal work of Rubin, and an extension of his work in an online task. They extend Rubin's findings by showing that the figure–ground difference does not occur as a result of differential memory (as may have been the case with Rubin's long testing intervals). Furthermore, our subjects were explicitly instructed not to see one side or the other as figure (in contrast to Rubin's subjects who were instructed to see just one side as the figure). Our results therefore suggest that the assignment of an edge to its figural side is an obligatory process. The failure of subjects to confine attention to just the edge can be seen as another sense in which attention may be object-based: Whenever attention is directed to an edge, the entire (figural) object to which the edge has been assigned will be attended.

A further result of these studies is the suggestion that the figure and ground are different shapes. Phenomenally this may seem to be an obvious and trivial finding—compare the pairs of test items in Fig. 8.5b and c; these are clearly "different" from each other. On the other hand, we need a computational explanation of how a single edge could generate two distinct "shapes" depending on how it is assigned. This issue is discussed in a later section.

THE RELATION OF FIGURE–GROUND ASSIGNMENT TO ATTENTION

Investigations into the difference between figural and ground regions suggest that figures are brighter, appear closer, have more distinct shape and are recognized better than regions that have been parsed as ground (see Koffka, 1935; Weisstein & Wong, 1987; Wong & Weisstein, 1982). These attributes are very similar to the characteristics of attended regions. One might wonder whether figure–ground segmentation can be logically distinguished from the allocation of attention, if figural assignment and attention are the same. In fact, figural assignment and attention do influence each other, but in an important and nontrivial manner, as shown by Baylis and Driver (1995b; Driver & Baylis, 1996).

Before discussing the relation of covert attention shifts to figural assignment, it is important to distinguish two forms of covert attention shifts (i.e., shifts not involving movements of the eyes). Cognitive research (e.g., Jonides, 1981; Posner, 1980) has distinguished at least two such covert shifts, which may be related to different eye-movement control systems (see also Schiller, chap. 1, this volume). The first is a relatively automatic shift of attention that appears to be driven by stimulus attributes, and is largely outside the control of the observer. These *exogenous* attention shifts occur even when the cues do not predict the location of a target (in other words if the target is just as likely to be at a cued or at an uncued location). Exogenous cues occur at, or close to, the location of the target, and so attention is directed toward the cue. The second type of covert orienting (*endogenous* orienting) requires that the cues have predictive value concerning the target location, that is, the target is more likely to be located at the cued location than at an uncued location. The signaled location may or may not be spatially close to the cue. Thus a centrally placed arrow, that points left or right according to the likely position of a subsequent target can act as an endogenous cue.

Driver and Baylis (1996) used a modification of the figure–ground task outlined in the previous section to study attention and figural assignment. Subjects were presented with an initial display, divided by a jagged edge, where the two sides were equivalent in terms of brightness, size, surround-edness, and so forth (see Fig. 8.6b). Thus the assignment of the edge to one side or the other (or figural assignment) was not possible. However, a precue (Fig. 8.6a) was used to bias the interpretation of this display, in an attempt to influence attention and figural assignment to one side or the other. This

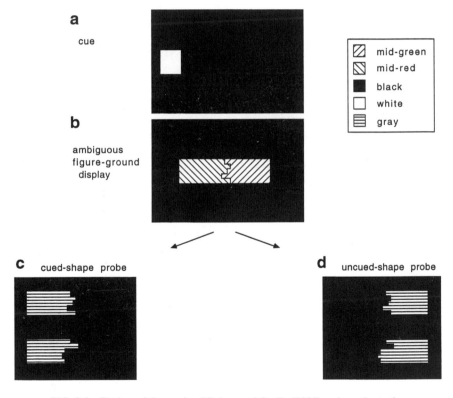

FIG. 8.6. Design of the study of Driver and Baylis (1996) to investigate the relation between covert orienting and figural assignment. A precue was presented that was either uninformative as to which side would later be tested (exogenous cuing only), or predicted 75% of the test displays (endogenous cuing). If this cue induced figurality this would bias the otherwise ambiguous figure–ground display (b), with the result that the cued-shape test (c) displays would lead to superior performance than the uncued-shape tests displays (d).

precue was a small bright rectangle presented adjacent to the lateral edge of one side of the display, presented for 80 ms immediately prior to the display. The ability of subjects to recognize the jagged edge was tested by means of a pair of shapes that were shaded to correspond to the cued side or the uncued side. The cues were shown to reliably attract attention to the cued side, inducing a sense of "filling in" from the cued side.

For one group of subjects, the precue was not informative. That is, the test displays were just as likely to correspond to the shape on the cued side or the uncued side of the display. For the other group of subjects, the test shapes occurred three times as often on the side where the precue was presented. The results in terms of speed and accuracy of recognition were clear (see data in Fig. 8.6b and c). When the cues carried no predictive value, there was no difference in recognition on the cued and uncued side. Exogenous orienting appears to be unable to bias figure–ground segmentation, and thus induce a figural advantage on the cued side. On the other hand the very same cues, when they predicted the side that was to be tested, led to a recognition advantage on that side. Summoning an endogenous shift of attention appears to affect figure–ground assignment, in that the region to which attention is directed becomes figural.

These results, together with previous work such as that of Rubin and others, lead us to propose the following relation between covert orienting and figural assignment. When figural assignment due to image factors (such as brightness and size) can proceed unambiguously, attention is exogenously drawn to the figural regions. In this case, figural assignment determines an (exogenous) attention shift. In contrast, where figural assignment cannot proceed on the basis of image factors alone, endogenous allocation of attention can lead one part or other to acquire figural status. A good example of an ambiguous display would be Rubin's faces–vase engraving. In such cases, attention shifts can determine figural assignment. In a real world setting, these ambiguous scenes are probably rare, so that typically it is figural assignment that exogenously determines the allocation of attention.

IMPLICATIONS OF FIGURE–GROUND SEGMENTATION ON SHAPE DESCRIPTION

As edges are located within the visual scene, their shape needs to be described in order to provide some basis for later perception and recognition. Baylis and Driver (1995a), following Rubin (1915) and Attneave (1974) suggested that the figural assignment of a particular edge is a crucial factor in determining the shape that edge acquires. Informally it is easy to see why the shape of an edge changes as the assignment of that edge changes. We tend to describe curved line segments in terms of their convexity–concavity, so one might ask: "Is a **C** convex or concave?". Of course the answer is that it is either—it is convex with respect to the right side, concave with respect to the left. To describe a curved line, we first have to "assign" it to one side or the other.

The precedence of edge-assignment over shape-description has been challenged by Peterson and colleagues (Peterson, 1994; Peterson & Gibson, 1993, 1994; Peterson, Harvey, & Weidenbacher, 1991). The position taken by Peterson et al. is that it is possible to describe the shape of lines prior to their assignment to a region, and indeed that this shape information may be used in the determination of figure and ground. Although these results show that recognition of shape information *can*, in ambiguous cases, influence edge-assignment, they do not account for the many cases where unambiguous edge-assignment takes place in an obligatory fashion prior to the generation of shape-descriptions.

The differences in curvature become more extreme with more complex line shapes. Consider how we might describe the shape of the curved line in Fig. 8.7a. We can either see this line as the edge of the black region (in which case we see this as three broad domes pointing to the right), or as the edge of the gray region (in which case we see four sharp peaks pointing to the left). Not only is the description of the shape different, but the decomposition of the curve into component parts is different, with the result that we can see this as comprising either three or four parts. A computational algorithm for the decomposition into components of any curve has been suggested by Hoffman and Richards (1984). When any two objects intersect, the points at which they join corresponds to a line of high concavity, or in 2-D, points of sharp concavity (see Fig. 8.7b). Thus, by induction, points of sharp concavity may correspond to the junctions between component parts that make up a whole shape. Considerable evidence suggests that our descriptions of everyday objects often entail decomposition according to this rule of part-decomposition at points of negative minima of curvature (i.e., concavities). Note that this method is computationally very straightforward, simply requiring computation of second derivatives of distance. However, because concavities are determined to be part-boundaries the curve must be assigned to one side or the other, in order to determine which is concavity, which convexity (as we saw in the case of a C). This means that reversing the assignment of a line will radically alter its decomposition into parts, inasmuch as concavities (part-boundaries) and convexities (part-centers) interchange.

Baylis and Driver (1995a) suggested that this part-decomposition rule may explain a paradox first explicated by Mach (1885/1959). Symmetry is much more salient and easy to detect than literal repetition (compare the two objects in Fig. 8.7c). This salience of symmetry is seen at a very young age (as young as 4 months old, see what follows). This is paradoxical because

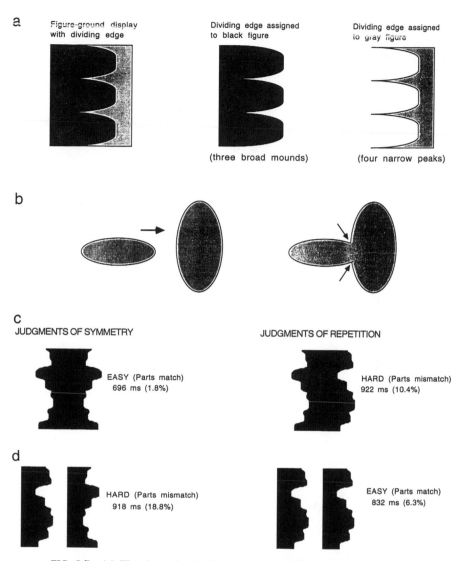

Figure-ground display
with dividing edge

Dividing edge assigned
to black figure

Dividing edge assigned
to gray figure

(three broad mounds)

(four narrow peaks)

b

c

JUDGMENTS OF SYMMETRY

JUDGMENTS OF REPETITION

EASY (Parts match)
696 ms (1.8%)

HARD (Parts mismatch)
922 ms (10.4%)

d

HARD (Parts mismatch)
918 ms (18.8%)

EASY (Parts match)
832 ms (6.3%)

FIG. 8.7. (a) The shape-description of the curved line in that divides the gray from the black depends on whether this line is seen as belonging to the gray or the black region. We typically see concavities as the junctions between parts, and describe accordingly. (b) The value of using concavities to signal part-boundaries. Since the intersection of any two objects leads to concavities at their point of intersection, induction suggests that concavities may signal junctions between objects or parts. (c) Baylis and Driver (1995a) suggested that symmetry was so salient and easy to judge because the part-descriptions of the two sides correspond. In contrast, literal repetition causes mismatching part-descriptions on the two sides of the object. (d) However, figure–ground assignment can be manipulated so that symmetrical objects do not have corresponding part-descriptions, whereas repeated objects do. This manipulation renders judgments of symmetry harder, and judgments of repetition easier.

267

detection of symmetry in a pair of lines requires a reflection and a translation, whereas detection of literal repetition requires only a translation.

Baylis and Driver (1995a) proposed that the ease of symmetry detection was due to the fact that shape is not described for unassigned lines, but for edges that are already assigned to one (figural) region that they bound. Furthermore, if shapes are decomposed according to a rule such as the concavity rule of Hoffman and Richards (1984) then the two sides of symmetrical objects will receive identical part-descriptions. Of course this will not be the case for objects with repeated contours, where a convexity on one side opposes a concavity on the other. No clear correspondence of the part-descriptions exists for the two sides of a repeated object. Thus judgments of repetition require a more time-consuming point-by-point comparison of the two contours (Baylis & Driver, 1994). As a result, RTs to judge symmetry are much shorter than RTs to judge repetition in a single object. The figural assignment of the lines could be altered so that the part-descriptions of the two sides of a symmetrical object no longer correspond, whereas the two sides of a repeated object do (see Fig. 8.7d). Baylis and Driver predicted that now, judgments of symmetry should be much harder, whereas judgments of repetition should be easier. This pattern of data was seen (see Fig. 8.7c and d) suggesting that the ease of detecting symmetry compared to repetition was at least in part due to the correspondence of part descriptions of the two sides of a symmetrical object.

The results of Baylis and Driver (1995a) underscore the importance of the assignment of edges in the scene, and how a reversal of this assignment can lead to a radical change in the shape description of the objects. These results show again that the assignment of edges may be an obligatory process, because otherwise subjects would be insensitive to this manipulation of figural assignment, and so would not show the large decrement in performance judging symmetry in Fig. 8.7d.

VISUAL PARSING AND DISORDERS OF ATTENTION

One approach to understanding the relation of attention to the preattentive processes of visual parsing is to examine whether visual parsing is affected when attention is dysfunctional, as in neuropsychological disorders of attention. Presumably any processes that are unaffected by disorders of attention cannot require attention, and thus may occur preattentively. Furthermore, the way in which attention breaks down may shed light on the manner in which attention is directed to the results of preattentive visual parsing.

Visual hemineglect (neglect) is a relatively common result of unilateral brain damage, due to strokes or other injury (see Bisiach & Vallar, 1988).

Most typically, neglect may be associated with damage to the right parietal lobe, although damage to many regions of the brain may be associated with this disorder (see Rafal, chap. 6, this volume). Traditionally, neglect has been characterized as a disorder of the attention system, which had until recently been thought to be primarily spatial in nature. As a result, neglect is typically thought of as a spatial disorder, such that damage to the right parietal lobe results in failure to attend to the visual field contralateral to the lesion (contralesional), in this case the left visual field. Recent work, however, suggests that visual parsing is intact in the contralesional field, and that the distribution of intact and absent attention depends on this visual parsing.

For many years it has been known that neglect patients may copy only the ipsilesional half of a drawing, so that a patient with a right-hemisphere lesion may copy only the right-hand side of a drawing (e.g., a cat; Driver & Halligan, 1991). What is less clear is why the left side is neglected. Is it neglected because it lies to the left of the patient (scene-based neglect) or because it is the left side of the drawing (object-based neglect). This distinction could not be made in many early studies of drawing by neglect patients because the two reference frames (scene or object) were confounded—the drawings were placed in the patient's midline, so the left part of the object was also within the left side of the visual scene. However, if patients are given a visual scene containing many objects, they may copy the ipsilesional side of each object, even those lying on the contralesional side of the page (e.g., Gainotti, Messerli, & Tissot, 1972).

One possibility is that figure–ground segmentation is intact in neglect patients and that this allows the patient to determine the locations of the figures (objects to be copied) within the scene. The logic behind this notion is that because visual parsing precedes normal attention, it should equally be expected to precede the dysfunctional attention seen in neglect (e.g., Driver & Baylis, 1995). The contralesional neglect may occur at a subsequent stage of allocation of attention to figural objects. On the other hand, these studies were carried out with unrestricted viewing, so this apparent figure-based neglect may arise because the patient is fixating each figure in turn, and perhaps recentering each figure at their own midline, and then neglecting the contralesional side of the visual scene.

Driver, Baylis, and Rafal (1992) used a computerized task to examine the existence of figure-based neglect in CC who had suffered a large right-hemisphere stroke. We used a short-term edge-matching task similar to that described earlier for normal subjects. An initial figure–ground display like those shown in Fig. 8.8a was presented, and the task was to remember the jagged dividing edge for comparison with a subsequent probe display. The probe displays comprised a single jagged line presented centrally (see examples in Fig. 8.8a). This line was equally likely to match or mismatch

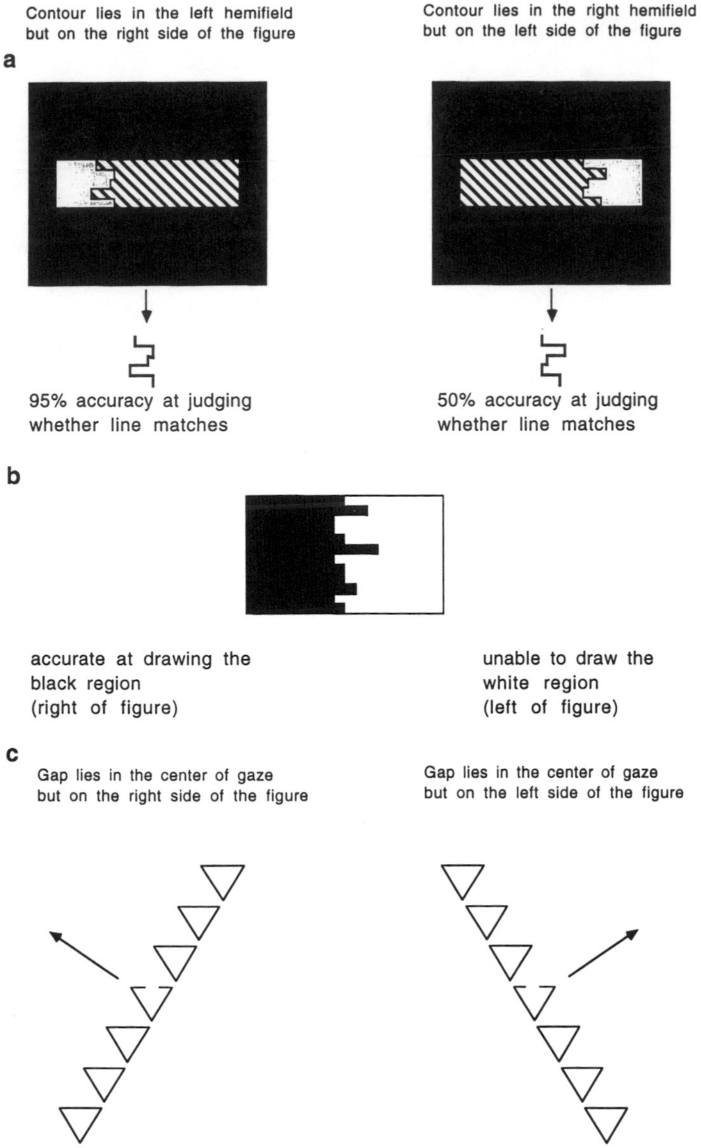

FIG. 8.8. Neglect may be figure-based in that patients are unable to match or draw a contour that lies on the contralesional side of the figure, even when this is in ipsilesional side of the patient. Conversely, the are able to match and draw shapes that are in the contralesional hemifield, when these are on the ipsilesional side of the figure. Data in (a) come from a matching task, where figural assignment is due to image-based factors (Driver et al., 1992). Data in (b) are from a drawing task, where figural assignment is due to intentional allocation of attention (Marshall & Halligan, 1994). (c) shows the two types of displays used by Driver et al. (1994) to show axis-based neglect. The different contexts of the central target triangle make this triangle point such that the gap is on the right (left diagram), or left (right diagram) with respect to the target's own principal axis.

the preceding jagged dividing edge, and the patient had to say "Yes" or "No" respectively. Line probes were used to ensure that the entire probe could be perceived, so any neglect would arise only in the initial figure–ground display.

The jagged edge in the initial figure–ground stimulus could be on the left or right (Fig. 8.8a). If neglect applies to the entire contralesional field one would expect CC to perform worse in the former case as the critical jagged edge falls to his left. However, the opposite pattern was observed (see accuracy data in Fig. 8.8a); the patient showed reasonable accuracy when the initial figure was in his left visual field, but was at chance when the figure was on his right. Thus, the patient's left neglect applied to the left of the figures segmented from the initial display, rather than to the left visual field. This result suggests that figure–ground segmentation was intact throughout both visual fields of this patient despite his severe impairment in attention. If visual parsing can proceed despite such an attentional impairment, this provides further evidence that visual parsing does not require attention, and occurs prior to the allocation of attention.

A similar figure-based neglect has been documented by Marshall and Halligan (1994). They presented a left-neglect patient with ambiguous figure ground displays, where a single jagged edge divided a rectangle into equally sized black and white regions (see Fig. 8.8b). The patient was asked to draw a copy of the jagged edge from the black shape, or from the white shape. Even though the jagged edge was equivalent for adjoining black and white shapes, the left-neglect patient could accurately copy it only when it was described as belonging to the shape on his left (i.e., when it belonged to the right of the perceived figure).

These studies on figure-based neglect suggest that an attentional reference frame may be centered on the figures within a visual scene as well as being centered in the entire visual scene. However, this reference frame is not distorted compared to an egocentric frame—"left" and "right" still correspond in the object-based and the observer- or scene-based reference frames. If object- or figure-based reference frames are truly distinct from a "recentered" scene-based reference frame, they should be able to have left and right defined with respect to the object, rather than the observer of the scene.

Driver, Baylis, Goodrich, and Rafal (1994) studied three patients with visual neglect in a task where the left and right sides of a visual object were defined independent of the overall left and right of the scene, to understand which reference frame would determine neglect. In this task, patients were asked to detect the presence or absence of a small gap in one side of an equilateral triangle presented in the center of a video monitor. This target triangle lies in the center of the example displays shown in Fig. 8.8c. With respect to the patients, their visual scene, and the monitor, the gap was always in the center, and so would be expected to be attended, because it did not lie to the contralesional side of these reference frames. (For a more complete discussion of potential reference frames of attention other than object-based frames, the reader is directed to Farah, Brun, Wong, Wallace, & Carpenter, 1990.)

However, the context of the target triangle was manipulated by means of flanking "context" triangles, so that the target triangle was seen to point in one direction or another. From the direction of pointing of any object, its left and right are defined directly, so as the triangle pointed to the top left (left side of Fig. 8.8c) the side with the gap would lie on its right. Conversely, when the target triangle pointed to the top right, the gap would be on its left (right side of Fig. 8.8c). This provides a method of disconfounding the left and right of the observer versus the left and right of the object in a manner that was not done in the study of CC (Driver et al., 1992).

When object-based coordinates were disentangled in this way, an interesting effect was seen. When the direction of pointing was such that the gap lay on the left of the triangle, the patients were much more likely to miss the gap than when it was on the right. Thus the attentional reference frame of the patients was defined by the inherent direction (and hence left and right) of the triangles. The participants neglected the contralesional side of the triangle, where side was defined by the triangle itself. This suggests that the attentional reference frame (which appears to be intact in neglect patients; see Grabowecky, Robertson, & Treisman, 1993; Baylis & Baylis, in press-a) will have its principal axes defined by the object itself.

Balint's Syndrome (Balint, 1909) provides further insights into the relation of visual objects to the distribution of attention. Balint's syndrome is a rare disorder of attention that occurs with bilateral lesions, typically bilateral lesions of the parietal lobes. Classic descriptions (see Holmes, 1918; Holmes & Horax, 1919) of this syndrome include the symptom simultanagnosia—the inability to perceive more than one object at once. When this symptom is examined, clearly the attentional limit of a Balint's patient truly is one object, and is not limited to a particular spatial extent. Thus two objects can be held such that they overlap in the field of view of a Balint's patient, and still they attend to only one of the two.

Interestingly, quite high-level factors can determine the perceptual span of a Balint's patient. In one study we examined the ability of a Balint's patient to report letters that were presented visually (Baylis, Driver, Baylis, & Rafal, 1994). This patient had sustained lesions that almost completely destroyed both of his parietal lobes, with minimal damage beyond this lobe. In line with his clinical simultanagnosia, RM was able to report only one, or at best two, letters out of an array of four presented to him.

However, when the four letters made up a word, he was able to report the entire word, and indeed was able to spell out the letters that made up that word. This result supports the notion that the organization of the visual input determines the extent of a single object. When the objects are letters, then a letter was the attentional extent, and hence one letter is the perceptual limit of this patient. On the other hand, when the object was a (single) word, he was able to attend to, and perceive the entire word. Persons without brain damage may be able to attend and perceive beyond one object by virtue of their ability to rapidly switch attention between the objects that are generated in the initial visual parsing. Patients like RM may enable us to assay the attentional limit of a system that has lost the ability of attention switching that the parietal lobes provide (see further discussion by Rafal, chap. 6, this volume).

SUMMARY OF OBJECT-BASED ATTENTION IN ADULTS

Studies examining the relation of visual parsing and figure–ground segmentation to attention suggest that the entire visual scene is subjected to an obligatory parsing. This parsing includes the grouping of items that are likely to be related together, the assignment of edges to the region to which they are most likely to belong, and shape-description of the figural objects. This process is distinct from attention, and appears to operate prior to the allocation of attention (see also Baylis & Baylis, in press-a; Grabowecky et al., 1993). The results of the initial preattentive parsing provide stubborn constraints on subsequent perceptual processes, but also has a profound effect on the manner of allocation of attention.

Many of the processes of attention shifting appear to have access to the information derived from this process. As noted by Schiller (chap. 1, this volume), there may be at least three systems whereby overt shifts of attention take place. With the exception of reflexive saccades, these systems have access to highly processed visual information, including a description of the visual scene in terms of figure and ground. Indeed, evidence outlined earlier suggests that the initial preattentive parsing provides powerful constraints on the subsequent allocation of attention. Although attention may ostensibly be directed to a particular spatial location, the distribution of attention may more closely conform to the object at a particular location.

Because the preattentive processes of visual parsing are distinct from the allocation of attention, the course of development of these two systems is unlikely to coincide. Therefore in considering the development of systems to allocate attention appropriately, it is crucial to consider the development of the parsing processes that constrain the direction and distribution of attention.

VISUAL PARSING IN INFANTS

Numerous studies have suggested that infants even as young as 4 months old may show a looking preference for symmetrical objects (e.g., Bornstein & Krinsky, 1985). Many teleological explanations have been advanced as to why infants should prefer symmetrical objects, such as the likelihood that biologically meaningful stimuli may often display symmetry about a vertical midline. However, no *computational* explanation has been advanced to explain why this particular regularity of form is detected so readily and at such a young age.

Baylis and Driver (1995a) suggested for adults that the computational ease of detecting symmetry and its salience is because the edges in a visual scene are automatically assigned to one of the regions that they bound, as shape-descriptions are produced. Given the extensive research on shape preferences in infants (from Fantz, 1965, on) it is reasonable to assume that such a low-level algorithm may be present very early in visual development, even at birth. Given that infants do show a preference for objects that are symmetrical about a vertical midline, it is likely that this preference is similar to the preference seen in adults. Thus the preference for symmetry by infants may depend on the presence of matching part-descriptions. To test this, we studied symmetry detection by infants aged 6 to 7 months old (Baylis & Branson, in press).

In our study, 6-month-old infants sat on their parent's lap, facing a video monitor, while their gaze was monitored along with a computer-driven clock. To ensure that infants fixated the center of the monitor we presented a flickering, color-alternating pattern of dots. As soon as this occurred, the flickering dots were replaced by a pair of visual objects, each approximately 4° tall, and centered 6° to either side of fixation. The stimuli were based on those used by Baylis and Driver (1995a), in that the assignment of the curved edges was manipulated by altering the shading. Each pair of stimuli had the same type of shading, but one was regular (i.e., showing symmetry or literal repetition), and one was irregular (see example displays in Fig. 8.9). These conditions were randomly intermixed, and the side on which the regular stimulus appeared was counterbalanced.

In which conditions would we expect infants to show a looking preference? Certainly the single-object symmetry would be expected to produce such a preference, based on the results of prior studies in which infants have shown such a preference. If the symmetry detected by these infants is based on the lines only, then one would also expect a preference for the symmetrical stimulus in the noncorresponding displays (Fig. 8.9b). On the other hand, if shape-description is based on *assigned* edges, then no such preference would be seen because the part-descriptions of the two sides of the objects would not correspond.

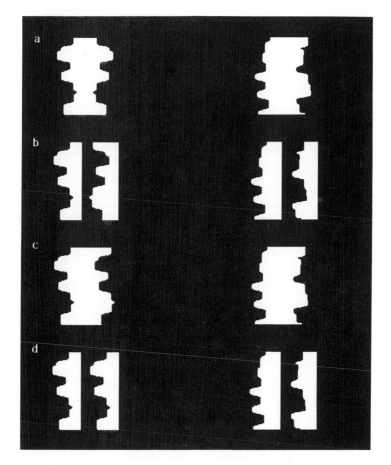

FIG. 8.9. Examples of the four types of trial, where two stimuli are presented to either side of the video monitor. The shapes on each trial were always different and produced anew according to a random algorithm.

Would we predict that infants will show a looking preference for any object displaying literal repetition? According to theories that stress either visual experience or utility, we would not expect any such preference because, like adults, infants are unlikely to encounter objects showing this regularity. On the other hand, if infants are sensitive to matching part-descriptions, we might expect them to show a looking preference to repeated objects where the part-descriptions of the two sides correspond (Fig. 8.9d).

Looking preferences were assessed in two ways, and are shown in Fig. 8.10. The proportion of trials in which infants first looked toward the regular stimulus is given (first looks), as is the total time spent looking at the regular stimulus (total time). In this experiment, the pattern of data is the same whichever method of assessing looking preference is used. It can be seen

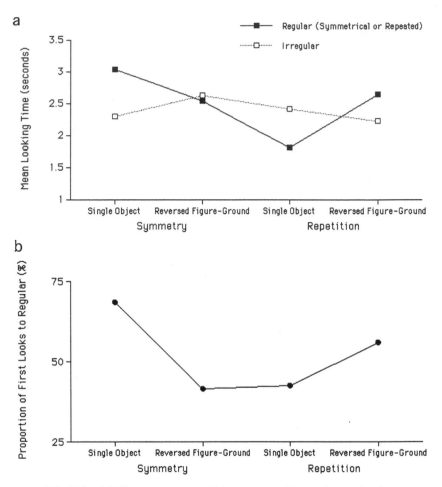

FIG. 8.10.   (a) The mean amount of time spent looking at the regular (i.e., symmetrical or repeated) stimulus (filled symbols) or irregular stimulus (open symbols) when presented in pairs. The only significant difference is the preference for the single symmetrical object over the single asymmetric object. (b) The mean proportion of trials on which the subject first fixated the regular or irregular stimulus.

from this figure that infants showed a clear preference for single symmetrical objects over the single asymmetric objects that are paired with them. Such a looking preference has been seen in 12-month-old infants (Bornstein, Fernandsen, & Gross, 1981), and some evidence of a preference for looking at symmetrical forms has been noted as early as 4 months. This result might be predicted from many theories of symmetry detection in the infant, so does not afford support for a theory based on part-descriptions.

On the other hand, when infants are presented with a choice between a symmetric object, and an asymmetric object as in Fig. 8.9b, no clear looking preference is seen (Fig. 8.10). In this kind of display, the shading is such that the lines will not be assigned equivalently, and so will not receive matching part-descriptions in the case of the symmetrical object. The lack of a looking preference with this type of display suggests that 6-month-old infants are insensitive to symmetry of lines per se, but are sensitive to the matching part-descriptions of the two sides of symmetric shapes, as has been suggested for adults (Baylis & Driver, 1995a).

Another point of convergence between the infant data and the data from young adults concerns sensitivity to literal repetition. With single visual shapes, our infants did not show any preference to look at the repeated object over the object with unrelated sides (see Fig. 8.11), suggesting that they are insensitive to this form of visual regularity. This parallels the observation that adults find literal repetition very much less salient than symmetry (Mach, 1885/1959), and that judgments of repetition take considerably longer than judgments of symmetry (Baylis & Driver, 1995a). Baylis and Driver suggested that the difficulty that adults have in detecting literal repetition is because this judgment cannot be performed on the basis of the extant part-descriptions. Indeed, judgments of repetition require another method of computation, such as point-by-point comparison (Baylis & Driver, 1994).

If young infants are insensitive to literal repetition because the part-descriptions do not match, one should be able to restore sensitivity to this by rendering the part-descriptions so that they do match, as in Fig. 8.10d. When Baylis and Driver (1995a) altered edge-assignments in this way for adult subjects, they greatly facilitated judgments of repetition. If the infants in this study are sensitive to the match in part-descriptions, a preference

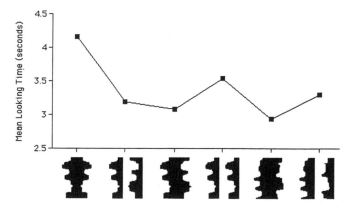

FIG. 8.11. The mean amount of time that 6- to 7-month-old infants will continue to fixate a single, centrally located stimulus.

for this type of repeated display should be observed. However, as can be seen from Fig. 8.11, no such preference is observed, although there is a small, nonsignificant trend in this direction.

Why are infants insensitive to the matching part-descriptions on the repeated side of Fig. 8.9d? One possibility is that these displays are so complex that infants identify four objects but may not identify which should be related to each other. Another possibility is that they are sensitive to the matching part-descriptions on, for example, the left side of Fig. 8.9d, yet are also attracted by the mismatching figure–ground assignment of the object on the right. In order to investigate these possibilities, we repeated carried out a study in which only one object was presented at a time. In this study, we used 10 new subjects, aged 6- to 7-months-old, and attracted their attention to the center of the monitor as before. In this experiment, one of six types of objects could appear at the center of the monitor. Examples of these stimuli would be the left sides of Fig. 8.9a–d, plus two further types like the right sides of Fig. 8.9a and b. We timed how long infants would maintain fixation on the stimulus at the center of the monitor before looking off to one side or the other.

The mean amount of time infants would look at the different stimuli are shown in Fig. 8.11. It can be seen that only one of the stimuli is preferred to any of the others, and this is a symmetrical object where the part-descriptions of the two sides match. This result is consistent with those of the previous study, and suggest that infants do not base their looking preferences on the correspondence of part-descriptions alone. If this was the case, then the corresponding repetition displays might be expected to show elevated looking times compared to the equivalent unrelated displays.

It is clear that an alteration of figure–ground assignment has different effects in these 6-month-olds compared to young adult subjects. One point of agreement is that the salience of symmetry is disrupted by altering figure–ground assignment such that the part-descriptions of the two sides no longer correspond. Such a disruption leads to markedly elevated RTs to judge symmetry in adults, and eliminates any looking preferences in 6-month-old infants. The main difference between these two subject groups in the converse alteration of figure–ground assignment with literal repetition. In young adults, changing the shading so that the part-descriptions correspond in a repeated object leads to a reduction in RTs and error rates in judging repetition. In contrast, this does not introduce a looking preference for these stimuli in the young infants. One possible reason for this is that the infants may not be able to perceive these as a single figure, and may not be able to spread their attention over the two separate objects.

We are currently running experiments to understand the source of this difference in visual parsing between infants and adults, but whatever the final explanation, these results show that an understanding of figure–

ground segmentation is important in studying the attention and perception of young infants. We have also carried out experiments to determine the age at which young children may begin to show the adult pattern (Baylis & Baylis, in press-b). In this study, participants faced a computer monitor on which pairs of stimuli like those in Fig. 8.9 were presented. The 7-year-old children who took part in this study were instructed to press a key on the side of the keyboard that the symmetrical or repeated object was shown. Two separate experiments were conducted, one where the task was finding the symmetrical object, one where the task was detection of repetition. The results are shown in Fig. 8.12b, along with data for young adults performing the same task (Fig. 8.12a). These data suggest that at this age, children are showing essentially the same pattern of data as the adults.

When this task was modified slightly, and carried out by 3-year-olds, a slightly different pattern emerged. (The main modification was that the experimenter pressed the keys, and the child was instructed to pick the "prettiest" pattern out of the two—because it was found that subjects at this age could not be reliably instructed as to the nature of symmetry and repetition.) These results are given in Fig. 8.12c. These preference data suggest that 3-year-olds may prefer symmetrical objects with corresponding part-descriptions over similar asymmetric objects, but do not show a reliable

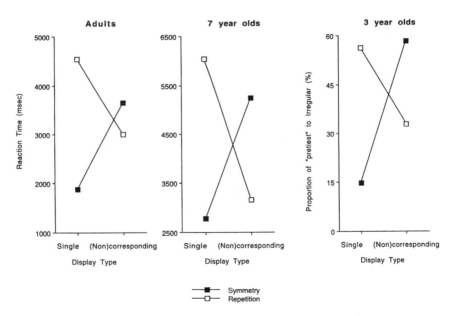

FIG. 8.12. (a–b) The mean RT to correctly judge which side of a display the regular (i.e., symmetrical or repeated) stimulus lay, in young adults (a) and 7-year-old children (b). (c) shows the proportion of times that 3-year-old children failed to consider the regular object as the "prettier" of the two.

preference when the part-descriptions do not correspond. These children show a modest preference for repeated objects where the part-descriptions correspond, but none where they do not. These preliminary data suggest that the adult pattern of data, where correspondence of part-descriptions plays a leading role, may not emerge until after 3 years of age.

THE BRAIN SUBSTRATE OF FIGURE–GROUND SEGMENTATION

Recent research suggests that attention is object-based due to the preattentive visual parsing that demarcates the visual scene into figural objects and their background. Attention may be directed to the objects that are produced in this parsing, and may spread to the extent of a single object, but not beyond. Thus visual parsing crucially constrains the distribution of attention. Increasingly, it is becoming clear that the system for parsing the visual scene takes some time to achieve its adult level of sophistication. In studying the cognitive neuroscience of attention, it is important to consider the developing nature of visual parsing and its underlying neural substrate.

Despite the clear dependence of attentional systems on visual parsing, it is clear that visual parsing is a modular system, in that it can be dissociated from both perception and the allocation of attention. Kartsounis and Warrington (1991) and Baylis and Baylis (1997) have described patients who have deficits in shape recognition that are due to a failure of figure–ground segmentation in the absence of other deficits. For example, the patient CB (Baylis & Baylis, 1997) was unable to spontaneously parse Fig. 8.13 into (symmetrical) red objects against a green background, despite her ability to make explicit judgments of symmetry. In neither CB, nor the case reported by Kartsounis and Warrington (1991) is it possible to localize the site of brain

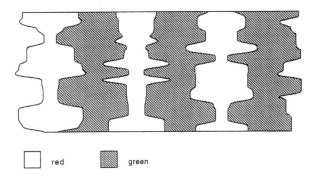

□ red   ▨ green

FIG. 8.13. When a bicolored display of this type is shown to normal subjects they will spontaneously see red symmetrical objects against a green background, due to the powerful effect that symmetry has on figure–ground organization (see Bahnsen, 1928). However, CB did not exhibit this effect due to her deficient ability to assign edges to figural regions.

damage that led to the figure–ground segmentation deficits. However, suggestive evidence in the case of CB points to damage within the occipital lobe.

Investigations into the neural substrate of figure–ground segmentation suggest that edge-assignment must take place relatively early in the visual system. For example, recordings of the activity of single cells in the cortex of the awake, behaving monkey show that cells in inferior temporal cortex may respond to the figural shape, rather than on the basis of any local edge information (Baylis & Driver, 1995a, unpublished data). Furthermore, investigations into the neural basis of the Bregman (1981) effect suggest that even complex edge-assignment has occurred before the inferior temporal cortex. The effect first noted by Bregman (1981) was that perception of objects could take place with ease in the presence of occlusion only if the occluders themselves could be seen (see Fig. 8.14). This effect has typically been explained in terms of high-level factors—that perception of occluded objects can only proceed if there are occluders present that can "explain" the loss of parts of the occluded object. On the other hand, it has been suggested recently (e.g., Baylis, in press), that the difficulties arise from the obligatory nature of edge-assignment. The edge-segments that should be assigned to the occluder cannot, if there is no (visible) occluder present. As a result of the fact that they must be assignment to some region, they are assigned, incorrectly to the occluded object.

In our study (Baylis, in press) we were interested in the effects of partial image occlusion on the responses of face-selective cells in the inferior temporal lobe of the macaque. We found that the presence of occluders had effects on the responses of cells in the inferior temporal cortex that were analogous to the effects of occlusion on perception by the whole organism. An example of the responses of such a cell are shown in Fig. 8.15. This cell

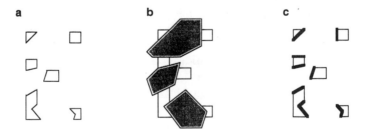

FIG. 8.14. The occluded large E within display (a) is difficult to see due to the fact that partial occlusion has occurred, yet the occluders are not visible. It has been suggested (e.g., Baylis, in press) that this is due to an inability to assign those edge-segments (shown in bold in (b)) which should be assigned to occluders. Because edge segments must be assigned, they are inappropriately assigned to the E, rather than to the occluders. With visible occluders (c), there is no difficulty making the appropriate edge-assignments, and thus recognition of the large E is possible.

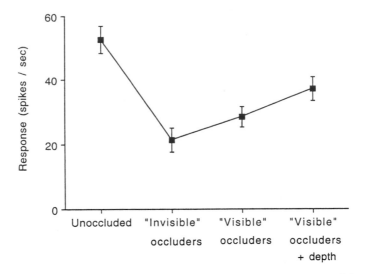

FIG. 8.15. The results of recording face cells in the temporal lobe of the awake monkey while the monkey is looking at occluded and unoccluded images of faces. With "invisible" occluders, a large reduction in the evoked activity is seen. This is less with "visible" occluders (analogous to Fig. 8.14c) this reduction in evoked response is ameliorated. When a difference in depth is introduced between the occluder and the face, this response returns close to that for the unoccluded face.

responded vigorously to the sight of a face (in this case the face of a human). When parts of the image were removed, but no occluders were visible, the responses of this cell were markedly reduced. However, when the occluders were rendered visible, the response was greater. When the occluders were placed at depth between the monkey and the face, the responses approached those to the unoccluded face. (In people, this manipulation can almost completely mitigate the effects of occlusion.) In this case, the rather complex assignment of edges in an image that includes occluders must presumably take place prior to the inferior temporal cortex.

These studies suggest that figure–ground segmentation may take place within the visual cortex of the occipital lobe. Indeed the opponent-surround cells of area V4 are at least consistent with the possibility that this region is involved in the detection of areas that contrast with the background. Such as substrate in the early stages of the visual system, which mature relatively early, would explain why many of the automatic aspects of edge-assignment seem at least partially functional very early. Effortful reversal of "incorrect" edge-assignment may be harder in young children because the connections to and from later parts of the visual system take longer to mature. However, at this time much of our discussion of the neural systems subserving edge-assignment and figure–ground segmentation must remain largely speculative.

CONCLUSIONS

The assignment of edges to a figural region that they adjoin is a largely obligatory process that provides important constraints on the allocation of attention. We know that this process of figure–ground assignment occurs in very young children but may not reach its adult level of sophistication until relatively late in childhood. Further work is needed to more fully specify the neural substrate of this crucial process, and to trace the maturation of these neural systems in development.

ACKNOWLEDGMENTS

The author gratefully acknowledges the intellectual contribution of Dr. Jon Driver of the University of London. Many of the themes and ideas in this chapter developed in the course of our collaborative research. I also gratefully acknowledge the research collaborations of Dr. Leslie Baylis, Steve Tuholski, Steve Branson, Ellison Cale, Aaron Williamon, Wendi Jones, and Karen McCord. Much of this work was supported by the generous intramural funding provided by the Department of Psychology, the College of Liberal Arts, and the Research and Productive Scholarship Fund of the University of South Carolina.

The author was supported by a grant from the National Science Foundation (SBR 96-16555) and by PHS Grant R29 NS27296.

REFERENCES

Attneave, F. (1974). Multistability in perception. *Scientific American, 225,* 63–71.

Bahnsen, P. (1928). Eine Untersuchung uber Symmetrie und Asymmetrie bei visuellen Wahrnehmungen [A study of symmetry and asymmetry in visual parsing]. *Zeitschrift fur Psychologie, 108,* 355–361.

Balint, R. (1909). Seelenhamung des "Schauens," optisches ataxie, raumlische stoung des afmersamkeit. *Monatschr Psychiatrie und Neurologie, 25,* 51–81.

Baylis, G. C. (1994). Visual attention and objects: Two-object costs without convexity differences. *Journal of Experimental Psychology: Human Perception and Performance, 20,* 208–212.

Baylis, G. C. (in press). Effects of partial image occlusion on the face-selective responses of cells in macaque temporal lobe. *Experimental Brain Research.*

Baylis, G. C., & Baylis, L. L. (1997). Deficit in figure-ground segregation following closed head injury. *Neuropsychologia, 35,* 1133–1138.

Baylis, G. C., & Baylis, L. L. (in press-a). Effects of brain damage on selective reaching. In S. Jackson & S. P. Tipper (Eds.), *Selection for action.* Mahwah, NJ: Lawrence Erlbaum Associates.

Baylis, G. C., & Baylis, L. L. (in press-b). *Detection of symmetry and repetition by children and adults.*

Baylis, G. C., & Branson, S. (in press). *Looking preferences for symmetry in infants: The importance of shape-descriptions.*

Baylis, G. C., & Driver, J. (1992). Visual parsing and response competition: The effect of grouping factors. *Perception and Psychophysics, 51,* 145–162.

Baylis, G. C., & Driver, J. (1993). Visual attention and objects: Evidence for hierarchical coding of location. *Journal of Experimental Psychology: Human Perception and Performance, 19,* 451–470.

Baylis, G. C., & Driver, J. (1994). Parallel computation of symmetry but not repetition within single visual shapes. *Visual Cognition, 1,* 377–400.

Baylis, G. C., & Driver, J. (1995a). Beyond edges in vision: Symmetry detection, part decomposition, and attention to objects. *Journal of Experimental Psychology: Human Perception and Performance, 21,* 1323–1342.

Baylis, G. C., & Driver, J. (1995b). One-sided edge-assignment in vision: 1. Figure-ground segmentation and attention to objects. *Current Directions in Psychological Science, 4,* 140–146.

Baylis, G. C., Driver, J., Baylis, L. L., & Rafal, R. (1994). Perception of letters and words in Balint's syndrome. *Neuropsychologia, 32,* 1273–1286.

Bisiach, E., & Vallar, G. (1988). Hemineglect in humans. In F. Boller & J. Grafman (Eds.), *Handbook of neuropsychology: Vol. 1* (pp. 195–222). Amsterdam: Elsevier.

Bornstein, M. H., Fernandsen, K., & Gross, C. G. (1981). Perception of symmetry in infancy. *Developmental Psychology, 17,* 82–86.

Bornstein, M. H., & Krinsky, S. J. (1985). Perception of symmetry in infancy: The salience of vertical symmetry and the perception of pattern wholes. *Journal of Experimental Child Psychology, 39,* 1–19.

Bregman, A. L. (1981). Asking the "What for?" question in auditory perception. In M. Kubovy & J. R. Pomerantz (Eds.), *Perceptual organization* (pp. 99–119). Hillsdale: NJ: Lawrence Erlbaum Associates.

Coren, S., & Porac, C. (1983). Subjective contours and apparent depth: A direct test. *Perception & Psychophysics, 33,* 197–200.

Deutsch, J. A., & Deutsch, D. (1963). Attention: Some theoretical considerations. *Psychological Review, 70,* 80–90.

Driver, J., & Baylis, G. C. (1989). Movement and visual attention: The spotlight metaphor breaks down. *Journal of Experimental Psychology: Human Perception and Performance, 15,* 448–456.

Driver, J., & Baylis, G. C. (1995). One-sided edge-assignment in vision: 2. Part decomposition, shape description, and attention to objects. *Current Directions in Psychological Science, 4,* 201–206.

Driver, J., & Baylis, G. C. (1996). Edge-assignment and figure-ground segmentation in visual matching. *Cognitive Psychology, 31,* 248–306.

Driver, J., Baylis G. C., Goodrich, S. J., & Rafal, R. D. (1994). Axis-based neglect of visual shapes. *Neuropsychologia, 32,* 1353–1365.

Driver, J., Baylis, G. C., & Rafal, R. D. (1992). Preserved figure-ground segmentation and symmetry perception in visual neglect. *Nature, 360,* 73–75.

Driver, J., & Halligan, P. W. (1991). Can visual neglect operate in object-centred coordinates? An affirmative single-case study. *Cognitive Neuropsychology, 8,* 475–496.

Duncan, J. (1984). Selective attention and the organization of visual information. *Journal of Experimental Psychology: General, 113,* 501–517.

Duncan, J. (1993). Similarity between concurrent visual discriminations: Dimensions and objects. *Perception & Psychophysics, 54,* 425–430.

Egly, R., Driver, J., & Rafal, R. (1994). Shifting visual attention between objects and locations: Normality and pathology. *Journal of Experimental Psychology: General, 123,* 161–177.

Eriksen, B. A., & Eriksen, C. W. (1974). Effects of noise-letters on identification of a target letter in a nonsearch task. *Perception & Psychophysics, 16,* 143–149.

Fantz, R. L. (1965). Visual perception from birth as shown by pattern selectivity. *Annals of the New York Academy of Science, 118*, 793–814.

Farah, M. J., Brunn, J. L., Wong, A. B., Wallace, M., & Carpenter, P. A. (1990). Frames of reference for allocation of spatial attention. *Neuropsychologia, 28*, 335–347.

Folk, C. L., Remington, R. W., & Wright, J. H. (1994). The structure of attentional control: Contingent attentional capture by apparent motion, brightness and color. *Journal of Experimental Psychology: Human Perception and Performance, 20*, 317–329.

Gainotti, G., Messerli, P., & Tissot, T. (1972). Qualitative analysis of unilateral spatial neglect in relation to laterality of cerebral lesion. *Journal of Neurolology, Neurosurgery and Psychiatry, 35*, 545–550.

Gibson, B., & Egeth, H. (1994). Inhibition of return to object-based and environment-based location. *Perception & Psychophysics, 55*, 323–339.

Grabowecky, M., Robertson, L. R., & Treisman, A. M. (1993). Preattentive processes guide visual search: Evidence from patients with unilateral visual neglect. *Journal of Cognitive Neuroscience, 5*, 288–302.

Harms, L., & Bundesen, C. (1983). Color segregation and selective attention in a onsearch task. *Perception & Psychophysics, 33*, 11–19.

Hoffman, D. D., & Richards, W. A. (1984). Parts of recognition. *Cognition, 18*, 65–96.

Holmes, G. (1918). Disturbances of visual orientation. *British Journal of Ophthalmology, 2*, 449–506.

Holmes, G., & Horax, G. (1919). Disturbances of spatial orientation and visual attention with loss of stereoscopic vision. *Archives of Neurology and Psychiatry, 1*, 385–407.

Jonides, J. (1981). Voluntary versus automatic control over the mind's eye's movement. In J. Long & A. Baddeley (Eds.), *Attention and performance, IX* (pp. 187–203). Hillsdale, NJ: Lawrence Erlbaum Associates.

Kahneman, D., Treisman, A., & Gibbs, B. (1992). The reviewing of object files. *Cognitive Psychology, 24*, 175–219.

Kanizsa, G., & Gerbino, W. (1976). Convexity and symmetry in figure-ground organization. In M. Henle (Ed.), *Art and artifacts*. New York: Springer.

Kartsounis, L. D., & Warrington, E. K. (1991). Failure of object recognition due to a breakdown of figure-ground discrimination in a patient with normal acuity. *Neuropsychologia, 29*, 969–980.

Klein, R. (1988). Inhibitory tagging system facilitates visual search. *Nature, 334*, 430–431.

Klymenko, V., & Weisstein, N. (1986). Spatial frequency difference can determine figure-ground organization. *Journal of Experimental Psychology: Human Perception and Performance, 12*, 324–330.

Koffka, K. (1935). *Principles of Gestalt psychology*. London: Routledge and Kegan Paul.

Kramer, A. F., & Jacobson, A. (1991). Perceptual organization and focused attention. *Perception & Psychophysics, 50*, 267–284.

Kramer, A. F., Tham, M. P., & Yeh, Y. Y. (1991). Movement and focused attention. *Perception and Psychophysics, 50*, 537–546.

Mach, E. (1885/1959). *The analysis of sensation* (translated 1959). New York: Dover.

Marshall, J. C., & Halligan, P. W. (1994). The yin and yang of visuo-spatial neglect: A case study. *Neuropsychologia, 32*, 1037–1057.

Peterson, M. A. (1994). Object recognition processes can and do operate before figure-ground organization. *Current Directions in Psychological Science, 3*, 105–111.

Peterson, M. A., & Gibson, B. S. (1993). Shape recognition inputs to figure-ground organization in three-dimensional displays. *Cognitive Psychology, 25*, 383–429.

Peterson, M. A., & Gibson, B. S. (1994). Must figure-ground organization precede object recognition? An assumption in peril. *Psychological Science, 5*, 253–259.

Peterson, M. A., Harvey, E. M., & Weidenbacher, H. (1991). Shape recognition contributions to figure-ground organization: Which routes count? *Journal of Experimental Psychology: Human Perception and Performance, 17*, 1075–1089.

Posner, M. I. (1980). Orienting of attention. *Quarterly Journal of Experimental Psychology, 32*, 3–26.

Posner, M. I., & Cohen, Y. (1984). Components of visual orienting. In H. Bouma & D. Bouwhuis (Eds.), *Attention and performance, X.* Hillsdale, NJ: Lawrence Erlbaum Associates.

Pylyshyn, Z., & Storm, R. W. (1988). Tracking multiple independent targets. *Spatial Vision, 3*, 179–197.

Rock, I., & Gutman, D. (1981). The effect of inattention on form perception. *Journal of Experimental Psychology: Human Perception and Performance, 7*, 275–285.

Rubin, E. (1915). *Visuell wahrgenommene figuren* [The determination of visual figures]. Copenhagen: Glydendalske.

Tipper, S. P., Driver, J., & Weaver, B. (1991). Object-centred inhibition of return of visual attention. *Quarterly Journal of Experimental Psychology, 43A*, 289–298.

Waltz, D. L. (1975). Generating semantic descriptions from scenes with shadows. In P. H. Winston (Ed.), *The psychology of computer vision.* New York: McGraw-Hill.

Watt, R. J. (1988). *Visual processing.* Hillsdale, NJ: Lawrence Erlbaum Associates.

Wertheimer, M. (1915). Untersuchen zu lehre von der Gestalt I [Studies on the determination of form I]. *Psychologische Forschung, 3*, 47–58.

Wertheimer, M. (1923). Untersuchen zu lehre von der Gestalt II [Studies on the determination of form II]. *Psychologische Forschung, 3*, 47–58.

Weisstein, N., & Wong, E. (1987). Figure-ground organization affects the early visual processing of information. In M. A. Arbib & A. R. Hanson (Eds.), *Vision, brain and cooperative computation.* Cambridge, MA: MIT Press.

Wong, E., & Weisstein, N. (1982). A new perceptual context-superiority effect: Line segments are more visible against a figure than against a ground. *Science, 218*, 587–589.

Yantis, S. (1992). Multielement visual tracking: Attention and perceptual organization. *Cognitive Psychology, 24*, 295–340.

Yantis, S. (1993). Stimulus-driven attentional capture. *Current Directions in Psychological Science, 2*, 156–161.

Yantis, S., & Jonides, J. (1984). Abrupt visual onsets and visual attention. *Journal of Experimental Psychology: Human Perception and Performance, 10*, 601–621.

Chapter 9

Frontal Lobe Function During Infancy: Implications for the Development of Cognition and Attention

Martha Ann Bell
Virginia Polytechnic Institute and State University

While there is strong evidence for frontal cortex involvement in studies of adult attentional abilities, memory processes, and emotional mood, only recently have we begun to consider this cortical area as an intricate component of infant development. This chapter examines the recent evidence implicating frontal cortex in a variety of infant behaviors. The first section is a brief overview of evidence for development of the frontal cortex during the first 12 months of life. The second section is an examination of the evidence for frontal involvement in a specific behavior, the A-not-B task. Behavioral neuroscience work on this Piagetian task, as well as our own electrophysiological work is highlighted, along with the proposition that left frontal cortex may play a specific role in A-not-B performance.

The third section is a presentation of evidence of frontal involvement in higher order attentional processes during infancy. Implications that the right frontal area may be involved not only in sustained attention but also in the level of vigilance necessary for A-not-B performance will be noted. Special note is made of our work on a looking version of the A-not-B task that enabled us to utilize the ongoing EEG during task performance. The next section is a discussion of some of the developmental literature presenting electrophysiological evidence for individual differences in left and right frontal EEG activation patterns and temperamental style. Finally, the last section is an attempt to interrelate research implicating frontal involvement in A-not-B performance, attentional processes, and temperamental style.

DEVELOPMENT OF FRONTAL CORTEX DURING INFANCY

Recently we have reported on brain development during infancy by examining the ontogeny of the EEG (Bell, in press; Bell & Fox, 1994). The classic infant EEG development studies that grew out of Berger's (1932) report of EEG differences between children and adults ignored maturation of the EEG at anterior scalp locations. Many of these early researchers affixed electrodes over frontal sites (e.g., Hagne, 1968; Henry, 1944; Smith, 1938), but never reported on frontal recordings. In fact, Hagne (1968) specifically noted that the frontal EEG recordings were unusable because of artifact from eye movements. It may have been more likely, however, that the complex functions associated with frontal functioning were thought beyond the realm of infant behavior (Bell, in press).

Neuroimaging (e.g., Chugani, 1994; Chugani & Phelps, 1986), morphological (e.g. Huttenlocher, 1979, 1990), and neuropsychological (e.g., Davidson & Fox, 1982; Fox & Davidson, 1987, 1988) studies, however, have shown that the frontal cortex is not undeveloped and static during infancy. Our own brain-behavior work has been directed at frontal development during infancy. In both monthly EEG recordings (Bell & Fox, 1992, 1994) and a weekly EEG case study (Bell & Schmauder, 1995) we have shown that frontal EEG recordings follow a pattern of increases and decreases in power during the 6- to 12-month age range, with a positive slope indicating an overall pattern of increasing EEG power values. In the infant EEG developmental literature, increases in power, magnitude, and/or peak frequency are considered indices of maturation of the EEG signal and, hence, indices of brain development. Spectral analyses of our infant data demonstrate that the 6–9 Hz frequency band displays this developmental function during the first year of life (Bell, in press).

Behavioral neuroscience studies have indicated that the frontal cortex undergoes a major synaptogenesis around 8 months of age (Goldman-Rakic, 1987) and that both frontal and occipital cortex areas are divided into regions involved with object vision and spatial vision (Wilson, O-Scalaidhe, & Goldman-Rakic, 1993). Electrophysiological work with human infants has shown that the connectivity of frontal cortex with occipital cortex, measured via EEG coherence, increases dramatically at 8 months before declining with specific environmental experiences (Bell & Fox, 1996). Thus, both behavioral neurosicence and electrophysiological work confirm frontal cortex development during infancy.

EVIDENCE FOR FRONTAL INVOLVEMENT IN THE A-NOT-B TASK

Description of the A-not-B Task

Classic research on cognitive functioning during infancy has relied heavily on the phenomena described by Piaget (1954). In particular, Piaget's notions of Stage 4 object permanence, the search for a hidden object in two different locations, have been subjected to rigorous scrutiny. Three lines of research have developed. Some studies have been designed to test theoretical implications drawn from Piaget's writings of object permanence (e.g., Baillargeon, 1987, 1995; Butterworth, 1977; Butterworth, Jarrett, & Hicks, 1982; Gratch, Appel, Evans, LeCompte, & Wright, 1974; Munakata, McClelland, Johnson, & Siegler, 1994). Other researchers have examined individual difference variables affecting infant performance on object permanence tasks (e.g., Bell & Fox, 1992, in press; Diamond, 1990b; Diamond & Goldman-Rakic, 1983, 1989; Horobin & Acredolo, 1986; Kermoian & Campos, 1988).

During the A-not-B task, a desirable object is hidden in one of two possible adjacent locations in full view of the infant. When allowed to manually search for the hidden object, the 8- or 9-month-old infant will typically retrieve the object from multiple hidings at one location (side A). When the object is switched to the other location (side B) in full view of the infant, however, the typical infant will automatically reach back to the side of the original hidings (A). Thus, the infant reaches to side A, not side B. The phenomenon received its name from infants' behavior. This counterintuitive mistake made by younger infants has generated a wealth of research (see Bremner, 1985; Harris, 1983, 1987, for reviews; see Wellman, Cross, & Bartsch, 1986, for a meta-analysis of the A-not-B error literature) and much speculation about the skills and abilities associated with proficiency on the task.

Abilities Associated With Successful Performance on the A-not-B Task

Harris (1987) has noted two aspects of the A-not-B phenomenon from a Piagetian perspective. First, the infant making the A-not-B error does not understand that objects continue to exist when no longer in sight. The objects are made and unmade by the infant's action of searching at location A. When the object disappears at location B, the infant acts again on location A to re-create it. Therefore, second, the infant's own actions are actually re-creating the object rather than finding it. This Piagetian explanation for the infant's search errors appears to attribute faulty searches to the infant's lack of knowledge about how objects exist in the physical world.

Baillargeon (1995) contended that infants actually do have a great deal of knowledge about the physical world. For example, using a violation-of-expectation paradigm, she has demonstrated 8-month-old infants look longer at an "impossible event," where an object is retrieved from location B after having been hidden at location A, than they do a "possible event," with an object retrieved from location A after being hidden at location A (Baillargeon & Graber, 1988). Baillargeon has also shown that infants as young as

3.5 months of age look reliably longer during testing at an impossible event where an object failed to come into view at a window, yet appeared to have traveled past the window in its movement from one end of a screen to another (Baillargeon & DeVos, 1991). Baillargeon proposed that infants perform poorly on Piagetian search tasks because they have difficulty planning manual means–end search sequences (Baillargeon, Graber, De-Vos, & Black, 1990). Although Baillargeon's paradigms do not assess the classic Piagetian A-not-B concept, they do demonstrate that young infants have some level of understanding about the dynamics of the physical world.

Diamond (1991) suggested that infants actually do understand the object concept and spatial relations that Piaget was examining, even though they are unable to demonstrate this ability until 8 or 9 months of age (Diamond, 1985). She proposed that the behaviors Piaget required of the infants involve more than just relating two actions together in a sequence, however. In order to successfully perform the classic A-not-B task, infants must be able to relate information over a separation in time and inhibit predominant response tendencies (Diamond, 1988, 1990a, 1990b). The integration of these two skills is a primary competency of dorsolateral prefrontal cortex (Diamond, 1991). Others (Fuster, 1989; Goldman-Rakic, 1987; Knight & Grabowecky, 1995; Pribram, 1973) have suggested that the prefrontal cortex has interactive functions: a temporal retrospective function of working memory, a temporal prospective function of anticipatory set, and an interference-control mechanism that suppresses behavior incompatible with the goal. Recently, West (1996) proposed a model that views the primary process of the prefrontal cortex as the temporal organization of behavior. Secondary processes associated with the dorsolateral portion of the prefrontal cortex are retrospective memory, prospective memory, and prepotent inhibition, whereas the secondary process associated with orbital prefrontal cortex is interference control.

The behavioral neuroscience work accomplished by Diamond and colleagues has provided enticing evidence that the dorsolateral prefrontal cortex is involved at some level in successful performance of Piaget's A-not-B task. As a foundation for the neuroscience work implicating this brain area, Diamond's comparative research has demonstrated that as human infants and infant monkeys grow older, they are able to tolerate longer delays on the A-not-B task (Diamond, 1990b). Diamond (1985) tested 25 human infants biweekly from 6 to 12 months of age and reported that the A-not-B error was demonstrated by all infants throughout the study, not just by the 8- to 9-month-old infants, as long as a delay procedure was used. The delay was initiated between the hiding of the object and the time when the infant was allowed to search. Diamond used a delay of 2 seconds between hiding and retrieval and increased the delay in 2-second increments across the course of this longitudinal study. As part of the same study, Diamond (1985) also tested a cross-sectional sample of 84 infants (12 infants at each age from 6 to 12 months) and reported a similar developmental progression in delay tolerated at each age. It should be noted that attempts to replicate Diamond's claim of 12-month-old infants tolerating a 10-second delay have failed (e.g., Bell & Fox, 1992; Matthews, Ellis, & Nelson, 1996). Replication of increasing delay across the last half of the first year of life have been successful, however (e.g., Bell & Fox, 1992; Matthews et al., 1996).

In comparative work, Diamond and Goldman-Rakic (1986) tested four infant rhesus monkeys on the A-not-B task every day from the age when they first could uncover a hidden object until they passed the A-not-B task with a 12-second delay. Like human infants, these infant monkeys showed a developmental progression in the length of delay tolerated. Infant monkeys showed a progression between 1.5 to 4 months on the A-not-B task that was comparable to that shown by human infants between 7.5 to 12 months of age. Graphs of the human infant data and the infant monkey data appear identical (Diamond, 1990b).

Neuroscience Work on A-not-B and Frontal Plasticity

Behavioral neuroscience work validates Diamond's claim of dorsolateral prefrontal involvement in A-not-B performance. Diamond and Goldman-Rakic (1989) tested 10 adult rhesus monkeys that either received lesions of the dorsolateral prefrontal cortex (Broadmann's Areas 8, 9, and 10; n = 4), received lesions of the parietal cortex (Broadmann's Area 7; $n = 3$), or were unoperated ($n = 3$). Diamond, Zola-Morgan, and Squire (1989) studied 6 adult cynomolgus monkeys that either received lesions of the entire hippocampal formation ($n = 3$) or were unoperated ($n = 3$). These adult monkeys were tested on the A-not-B task at delays of 2, 5, and 10 seconds. Diamond reported that the unoperated rhesus and cynomolgus monkeys, the rhesus monkeys with parietal lesions, and the cynomolgus monkeys with hippocampal lesions all succeeded on the A-not-B task at each tested delay (Diamond & Goldman-Rakic, 1989; Diamond et al., 1989). However, adult rhesus monkeys with prefrontal lesions made the A-not-B error at each delay tested (Diamond & Goldman-Rakic, 1989).

Diamond (1990b) noted that lesions performed on the infant monkey do not necessarily yield the same results as lesions in the adult monkey. She asserted that lower areas of the brain mediate the infant monkey's performance, although performance by the adult monkey is likely mediated by the later maturing prefrontal area (Diamond, 1990b). To determine if lesions of the dorsolateral prefrontal cortex would have the same effect on the infant monkey as on the adult monkey, Diamond and Goldman-Rakic (1986) tested two infant rhesus monkeys who received lesions at 4.5 months after being tested on the A-not-B task from 1.5 to 2.5 months of age. Testing resumed at 5.5 months and continued until 8 months of age, with the two infant monkeys who received the prefrontal lesions exhibiting the A-not-B error at delays of 2 and 5 seconds. The infant monkeys displayed random reaching, or what Diamond calls deteriorated performance, at the 10-second delay (Diamond & Goldman-Rakic, 1986).

It should be noted, however, that the neuroscience evidence associating prefrontal cortex and A-not-B performance is questionable. Previous work by Goldman-Rakic (e.g., Goldman, 1971, 1976; Goldman & Mendelson, 1977) has highlighted the plasticity of the prefrontal cortex in nonhuman primates. For example, rhesus monkeys receiving either dorsolateral or orbital prefrontal cortex lesions as infants, age 48–52 days, were compared on a set of prefrontal tasks to monkeys receiving the lesions as juveniles, age 18–24 months (Goldman, 1971). Initial testing occurred 10 months after the lesions were received. Infant monkeys with orbital lesions performed as poorly as the juveniles with orbital lesions. Infant monkeys with dorsolateral lesions performed very well, whereas juveniles with the same lesions did poorly. At the second testing session 9 months later, the results were reversed. Infant monkeys who had received orbital lesions performed very well, whereas those who had received dorsolateral lesions were impaired. Goldman-Rakic proposed that the dorsolateral prefrontal cortex may have been functionally immature and may not have been contributing to skills necessary for testing at the initial session (Goldman, 1971).

Recently, Diamond (1994) developed an animal model of early-treated phenylketonuria (PKU) where the rat pups are injected with an inhibitor of the enzyme that metabolizes phenylalanine (Phe) to tyrosine. Impairment on delayed alternation, a task related to prefrontal functioning, was evident in the rat pups. Diamond noted that dopamine metabolism was reduced in the prefrontal area of these rats and speculated that lower levels of tyrosine in the prefrontal cortex affected neuronal firing in that area. In a longitudinal study comparing human infants with early-treated PKU deficiency to their siblings and to matched controls, Diamond (1994) reported lower levels of performance on the A-not-B task (i.e., infants could tolerate briefer delays) among the early-treated PKU infants. Diamond suggested that even small reductions in tyrosine affect dopamine levels in the prefrontal cortex and the cognitive performance associated with prefrontal cortex function.

Nelson (1995) suggested that the dorsolateral prefrontal cortex is probably involved with the memory requirement of the A-not-B task. Citing evidence from behavioral neuroscience, neuroimaging, and morphological studies, he noted that this cortical area is likely mature enough by the last half of the first year of life to support memory functions, but that the other skills required for successful performance probably rely on the coordination of dorsolateral and orbital prefrontal areas, the mediodorsal nucleus, and the anterodorsal caudate nucleus. Developmentally, Nelson (1995) proposed that the caudate nucleus has major responsibility for the types of skills, other than memory ones, needed for A-not-B performance during infancy and that the dorsolateral prefrontal cortex takes over these skills later in life. Based on available evidence, however, there can be no speculation as to the age at which this assumption of skills occurs (Nelson, 1995).

Frontal EEG Maturation and Developing Skills on the A-not-B Task

In a longitudinal study examining relations between EEG and cognitive development from 7 to 12 months of age, we (Bell & Fox, 1992) observed 13 infants monthly for EEG recordings and A-not-B task testing. Using Diamond's data as a foundation, we hypothesized that differences in the development of A-not-B task performance would be related to differences in frontal EEG development. We further hypothesized that these EEG differences would not be apparent in other brain regions.

Utilizing cluster analysis techniques, we found two patterns of development in performance of the A-not-B task. By 12 months of age one group of infants was able to tolerate a 13-second delay and successfully retrieve the hidden object from the *B* hiding site. The other group of infants could tolerate a 3-second delay by 12 months of age. Age-related EEG differences at 6–9 Hz between these two groups of infants were found for the frontal region. Specifically, the group of infants tolerating increasing delay from 7 to 12 months of age displayed gradual increases in EEG power from 7 to 12 months of age. In infant EEG research, changing power values in the more "mature" frequency bands (in this case, 6 to 9 Hz) are associated with maturation of the EEG (e.g., Hagne, 1968, 1972). In the occipital EEG data, the long-delay group exhibited greater left hemisphere power values than right hemisphere power values at each age. There was no group by age interaction.

We confirmed our results of group differences in A-not-B task performance and 6–9 Hz EEG development with a cross-sectional sample of infants (Bell & Fox, 1992). Infants at each age in the cross-sectional sample were divided into those tolerating "long" delays at the A-not-B task and those tolerating "short" delays at the A-not-B task. EEG differences between the two groups were evident in the frontal leads. Specifically the group tolerating long delay at each age had greater power values in both of the frontal EEG leads.

Individual Differences in A-not-B and Frontal EEG

The search for hidden objects is considered a benchmark of cognitive development during infancy (Wellman & Somerville, 1982) and the research literature contains suppositions that differences exist among individual infants in the performance of these types of tasks. Diamond reported a wide range of individual differences in A-not-B performance among same-age infants (Diamond, 1990b). Among some other infant cognitive behaviors, individual differences have been shown to persist into early childhood (Colombo, 1993; Colombo & Janowsky, chap. 12, this volume). However, it is not yet known whether the individual differences in A-not-B performance represent differences in rate of development, differences in strategies, or long-term differences (Acredolo, 1990).

We found that differences in A-not-B performance across age were associated with differences in frontal EEG maturation across age (Bell & Fox, 1992). The next level of inquiry was whether individual differences in A-not-B performance among same-age infants would be associated with different levels of frontal EEG maturation. In a study of 8-month-old infants, we investigated the notion of individual differences in A-not-B performance by examining not only the contributions of frontal EEG but also locomotor experience (Bell & Fox, in press). Developmentalists have long noted a relation between onset of hands-and-knees crawling and development of cognitive behaviors (e.g., Acredolo, 1990; Bai & Bertenthal, 1992; Kermoian & Campos, 1988) and have speculated that locomotor experience may aid in the processing of spatial information (e.g., Bertenthal, Campos, & Kermoian, 1994).

We (Bell & Fox, in press) recruited 80 infants for this study of individual differences and placed them into groups according to their amount of hands-and-knees crawling experience (none, 1–4 weeks, 5–8 weeks, 9+ weeks). We found that crawling infants performed at a higher level on the A-not-B task, confirming previous developmental work. We also found that infants who performed at a higher level on the A-not-B task (i.e., achieved success on A-not-B, as opposed to making the A-not-B error) displayed greater frontal and occipital EEG power values at 6–9 Hz than infants performing at a lower level on the task, confirming our previous longitudinal study. Interestingly, there was no 3-way interaction among A-not-B performance, crawling experience, and frontal EEG. So it appears that frontal EEG and crawling experience may independently contribute to A-not-B performance.

The Programming of Reaching Behaviors Associated With A-not-B Performance and the Left Frontal Cortex

The posterior parietal lobe is involved in the processing of sensory stimuli essential for purposeful movement (Ghez, 1985; Ghez, Gordon, Ghilardi, & Sainburg, 1995). The initiation of movement is also controlled by this cortical region (Mountcastle, Lynch, Georgopoulos, Sakata, & Acuna, 1975). Specifically, there are "arm projection neurons" that fire only when a monkey reaches for food and "hand manipulation neurons" that fire when a monkey manually explores objects. Individual neurons in the posterior parietal cortex are active when a monkey produces an arm reaching movement in different directions (Georgopoulos, 1987) and the posterior parietal cortex is linked with the motor cortex in the generation of reaching in space (Georgopoulos, 1995).

However, although the motor cortex and posterior parietal cortex are essential in the production of reaching movements, the frontal cortex is essential in the programming of those complex movement sequences (Ghez, 1985). Different areas of the cortex are active when adults are asked to perform motor tasks that vary in complexity (Roland, Larsen, Larsen & Skinjoh, 1980). For example, motor and parietal cortices are active in thumb and finger compression. However, a complex sequence of movements utilizing all of the fingers involves not only the motor and parietal cortices but also the supplementary motor area (SMA) of the frontal cortex. More importantly, when adults are instructed to mentally rehearse the complex sequence without actually performing the movements, cerebral blood flow increases only in the SMA (Roland et al., 1980). There is evidence from the nonhuman primate literature that the SMA is involved in memorized sequential motor movements, as opposed to visually guided motor movements (Mushiake & Inase, 1993), whereas the prefrontal cortex is functional in the initiation and controlling of visually initiated hand movements (Sasaki & Gemba, 1993).

In other work, adults who had undergone unilateral frontal lobe excision or temporal lobectomy were given a stack of cards with the same pictures on each card arranged in rows and columns (Milner, 1982; Milner, Petrides, & Smith, 1985). The relative positions of the pictures were different for each card. The patients performed a subject-ordered pointing task where they were instructed to go through a stack of cards and touch only one item on each card, taking care not to touch the same picture again on subsequent cards. Thus, the individual determined the order of the responding. The supposition was that this sequential task was directly related to the concept of planning of motor movements. In contrast to the temporal lobe patients, frontal lobe patients were unable to keep track of their own responses, with those patients with left frontal excision displaying the greatest deficit in performance (Milner, 1982; Milner et al., 1985). These findings were consistent with the notion of left frontal lobe dominance in the programming of voluntary actions (Milner, 1982).

Although there are no data indicating that frontal involvement in A-not-B performance is hemisphere specific, these neuroscience studies and adult clinical studies allow us to speculate that perhaps the programming of the arm movement to reach toward the hiding site and uncover the hidden object is governed by the left frontal lobe. In a later section of this chapter, we show that the left frontal lobe is associated with specific temperamental styles or mood states during infancy.

EVIDENCE FOR FRONTAL INVOLVEMENT IN HIGHER ORDER ATTENTIONAL PROCESSES

Posner (Posner, 1992, 1995; Posner & Peterson, 1990; Posner & Raichle, 1994) proposed that there are three attention networks in the brain. The orienting (or posterior) attention network is associated with posterior parietal lobe, superior colliculus, and pulvinar and is the center for covert shifts in attention (Posner, 1988; Posner, Inhoff, Friedrich, & Cohen, 1987; Posner & Raichle, 1994; Posner, Walker, Friedrich, & Rafal, 1984; Posner, Walker, Friedrich, & Rafal, 1987). This attention network allows shifting attention from one place in the visual field to another without muscular or eye-position changes. Associated brain structures allow the individual to disengage attention from a cued location, move attention to an anticipated target location, and enhance attention to the new target (Posner & Raichle, 1994). Developmental research has demonstrated that this orienting attention network is fully functioning by 6 to 8 months of age (e.g., Hood, 1993, 1995; Hood, Atkinson, & Braddick, chap. 7, this volume; Johnson, Posner, & Rothbart, 1991; Rothbart, Posner, & Boylan, 1990).

Ruff and Rothbart (1996) proposed that an orienting–investigative system, akin to Posner's orienting attention network, is strongly governed by novelty. This system involves both a spatial orienting network in the parietal cortex and an object recognition pathway in the temporal cortex. Ruff and Rothbart (1996) noted that these lower level processes are later controlled to some extent by a higher level attention system involving the frontal cortex.

According to Posner (Posner, 1992, 1995; Posner & Peterson, 1990; Posner & Raichle, 1994), the executive (or anterior) attention network functions to bring an object into conscious awareness (Posner & Raichle, 1994), with attention jointly decided by events in the environment and the individual's predominant goals at a particular point in time (Posner, 1995). The site of control of the executive network is the anterior cingulate gyrus, which has alternating bands of cells that connect to the dorsolateral prefrontal cortex and the posterior parietal lobe (Posner, 1995). Thus, this executive attention network is highly involved in both working memory and visual orienting (Posner & Raichle, 1994). Posner has noted that the more this executive network is involved in a task requiring a motor response, the more cortical involvement there is in the supplementary motor area of the frontal cortex (Posner & Raichle, 1994).

In the developmental literature Ruff and Rothbart (1996) described a higher-order attention system that is involved in the inhibition of responses and the planning of goal-directed behavior. This attention system involves the frontal cortex and emerges in the last half of the first year of life. Ruff and Rothbart (1996) have also proposed that this higher-order attention system relies on social input for its development. Parents help the young infant acquire the underlying skills instrumental for maintaining an attentive state. With development, children become able to regulate their own attentional processes.

The Vigilance Network and Right Frontal Cortex

The frontal cortex has also been implicated in studies of sustained attention or vigilance with adult subjects. Adult patients with lesions of the right frontal lobe have been found to be impaired on a sustained attention task (Salmaso & Denes, 1982; Wilkins, Shallice, & McCarthy, 1987). Lesion, split brain, and blood flow studies done while adult subjects were in an alert and attentive state implicated right frontal cortex as essential for maintaining sustained attention (Posner & Peterson, 1990; Posner, Peterson, Fox, & Raichle, 1988).

In a task designed to detect momentary lapses in attention, patients were required to respond to stimuli at two different presentation rates: 1 per second and 7 per second (Wilkins et al., 1987). Frontal patients with right hemisphere excisions, compared to left frontal and temporal patients, made a greater number of errors at the 1 Hz presentation rate. However, at the 7 Hz presentation rate, these right frontal patients displayed no impairment. The researchers concluded that the slower rate was monotonous to the right frontal patients and they were unable to voluntarily sustain attention to it.

Posner has labeled the brain areas involved in maintaining a sustained state of alertness as the vigilance (Posner & Raichle, 1994) or alerting network (Posner, 1995, Posner & Peterson, 1990). Data from PET studies have shown that as vigilance and right frontal activation increase, activation in the anterior cingulate decreases, demonstrating that this attention network is behaviorally and anatomically different from the executive attention network (Posner, 1995; Posner & Raichle, 1994). Vigilant activity also involves the right parietal lobe, as alertness also involves orienting (Posner & Raichle, 1994). Although Posner's work has utilized PET data, it may be that heart-rate defined attention phases index this sustained state of alertness in infants (Richards & Hunter, chap. 4, this volume).

Although there are no data indicating that frontal involvement in A-not-B performance is hemisphere specific, the adult studies allow us to speculate that perhaps the sustained level of alertness, or vigilance, essential for performance of the looking version of the A-not-B task is influenced by the right frontal lobe. In a later section of this chapter, I show that the right frontal lobe is associated with specific temperamental styles or mood states during infancy.

Frontal EEG, Attention, and a Looking Version of the A-not-B Task

The ongoing EEG recorded in our previous studies (Bell & Fox, 1992, in press) was accomplished during a baseline condition, rather than during task performance. This is necessary because of the nature of the standard object permanence task requiring that the infant reach and uncover a hidden object. In the adult neurophysiological literature, however, ongoing EEG is digitized while participants are cognitively engaged in formulating answers to cognitive problems (e.g., Davidson, Chapman, Chapman, & Henriques, 1990; Ray & Cole, 1985, West & Bell, 1997). These types of studies are the foundation of our scientific knowledge of adult brain function and cognitive processing. There is no comparable body of work for infancy utilizing ongoing EEG during cognitive processing. There is, however, a body of infant work using ERP measures to examine the development of attention and memory (Nelson & Dukette, chap. 11, this volume). Based on our previous findings on relations between baseline measures of frontal EEG power and A-not-B performance, we designed a looking version of the classic reaching A-not-B task so that EEG could be recorded during cognitive performance (Bell, 1996). We proposed that this looking version of the A-not-B task would require activation of the anterior attention network (Posner & Peterson, 1990; Posner & Raichle, 1994).

Sixty-three 8-month-old infants were assessed on both the classic reaching version and the new looking version of the A-not-B task. From the developmental literature, we knew that by 4 months of age infants have the neural structures in place to allow saccadic movements to peripheral locations (Johnson, Gilmore, & Csibra, chap. 3, this volume; Maurer & Lewis, chap. 2, this volume). The use of 8-month-old infants in this study would allow for comparison with our previous reaching studies. At the laboratory testing session, EEG was recorded during baseline and during looking task performance from 6 frontal and 4 posterior scalp locations. Complete behavioral and electrophysiological data were available for 58 of the infants. Preliminary analyses of these data have shown that infants are more successful on the looking version of the task than on the reaching version. This finding is consistent with recent between-subjects research using a Delayed Response reaching versus looking paradigm (Hofstadter & Reznick, 1996) and may reflect the simpler response required by looking compared with reaching (Diamond, 1991; Munakata et al., 1994).

Preliminary analyses of the EEG data have shown higher power values at 6–9 Hz during the looking task than during the baseline recording (see Fig.

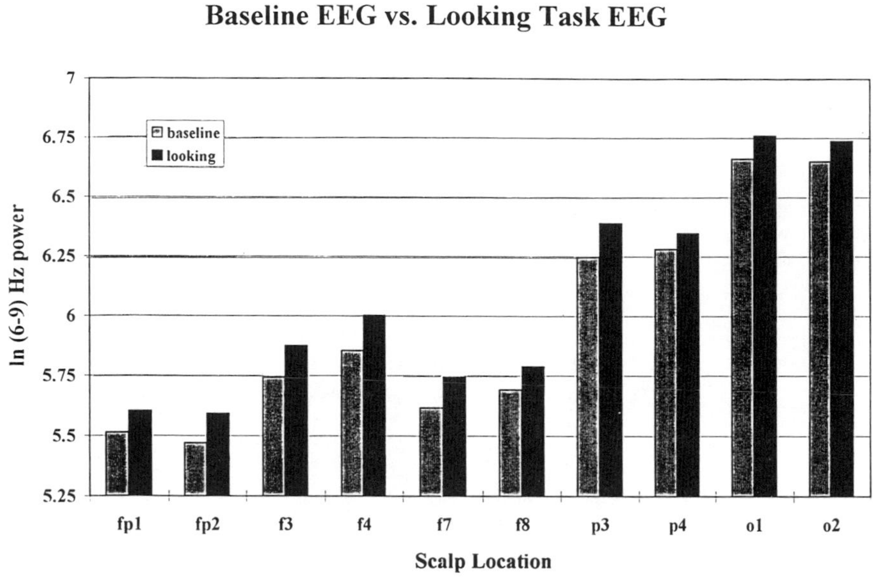

Baseline EEG vs. Looking Task EEG

FIG. 9.1. EEG power in 8-month-old infants at anterior and posterior scalp locations during baseline EEG and during a looking version of the A-not-B task.

9.1). This finding was surprising in light of the adult EEG literature. Adults tend to show less EEG power in the 8–13 Hz band with sensory stimulation and mental activity, so this band has been the standard frequency used in many adult EEG studies of cognitive processing (Ray, 1990). We had hypothesized that the infant 6–9 Hz band would exhibit this same "suppression" tendency during cognitive processing. These data, however, demonstrated that there is increased power at 6–9 Hz with infant cognitive processing.

The task-related EEG was event-marked to delineate the three looking task conditions: (1) display and hide object, (2) brief delay while gaze is broken from hiding site and the "search" (i.e., eye movement toward a hiding site), and (3) retrieval of object by experimenter and verbal reward to infant. EEG power data were analyzed separately for the anterior and poster EEG leads. Analysis of the frontal EEG 6–9 Hz power values revealed main effects for condition and for area, as seen in Fig. 9.2. Specifically, there were greater power values during condition 2 (delay and search) and greater power values at the medial frontal leads (F3, F4). There was also a condition by area interaction, where the EEG power values at F3 and F4 remained elevated during condition 3 (retrieval by experimenter and verbal praise). At Fp1, Fp2, F7, and F8 power values decreased during condition 3.

Anterior EEG during Looking Task Conditions

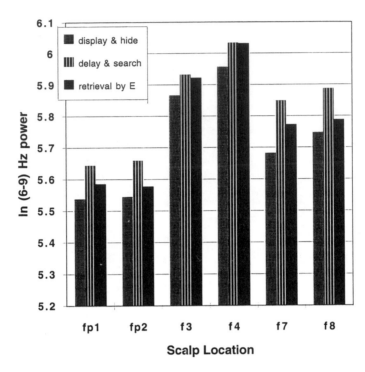

FIG. 9.2. EEG power at frontal scalp locations during 3 conditions of the looking version of the A-not-B task. Condition 1 is the display and hiding of the object. Condition 2 is the delay (while visual gaze to the correct hiding site is broken) and the infant's subsequent search by moving the eyes to the correct hiding location. Condition 3 is the retrieval of the hidden object by the Experimenter after the infant's eye movement.

For the posterior EEG power values, there were main effects for condition (higher power at condition 2, delay and search), area (greater power at occipital O1 and O2 than parietal), and hemisphere (greater power at left than right hemispheres). These main effects can be seen in Fig. 9.3. There were no interactions in the posterior EEG data.

These data are valuable not only because they were recorded during performance of a looking version of the classic A-not-B task, but also because of the information they give us concerning the nature of the 6–9 Hz frequency band. We have shown previously that this 6–9 Hz band may be a marker of frontal development (Bell & Fox, 1992), as well as a marker of individual differences in object permanence performance during infancy

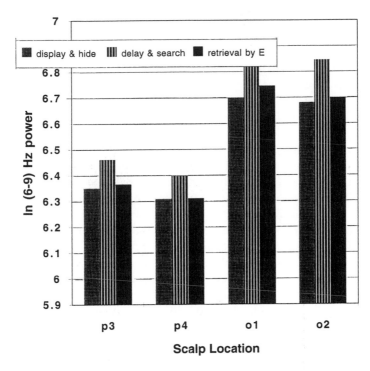

Posterior EEG during Looking
Task Conditions

FIG. 9.3. EEG power at parietal and occipital scalp locations during 3 conditions of the looking version of the A-not-B task.

(Bell & Fox, in press). This band, however, does not behave as adult alpha 8–13 Hz. These infants did not display "alpha suppression" during cognitive processing. Instead, EEG power at 6–9 Hz appears to increase during the most cognitively challenging portion of the task, the time when memory for the hiding location and inhibition of looking back to previous hiding locations may predominant cognition. Power at 6–9 Hz also does not decrease at F3 and F4 after cognitive processing is completed, as it did in all other leads. This may be related to two different processes (Bell, 1996). It may be related to the emotional content of verbal praise the Experimenter gave upon successful search (Dawson, 1994a). On the other hand, as noted by Nelson and Dukette (chap. 11, this volume), memory and attention functions share neural substrates. Therefore, it is more likely that the elevation of power at medial frontal may be related to the anterior attention network (Posner, 1992; Posner & Peterson, 1990; Poser & Raichle,

1994) that continued to be activated upon retrieval of the hidden object by the Experimenter.

EVIDENCE FOR FRONTAL LOBE INVOLVEMENT
IN TEMPERAMENTAL STYLE DURING INFANCY

In the adult EEG literature, Davidson reported that asymmetries in frontal cortical functioning are associated with variations in emotional behavior (e.g., Davidson, 1992, 1994, 1995; Davidson, Ekman, Saron, Senulis, & Friesen, 1990; Tomarken, Davidson, & Henriques, 1990; Wheeler, Davidson, & Tomarken, 1993). Specifically, greater levels of left frontal activation relative to right frontal activation are associated with positive affect or approach behaviors. Greater levels of right frontal activation, relative to left frontal, are associated with negative affect or withdrawal behaviors. These hemispheric differences can be seen in situations designed to elicit different emotional responses.

Likewise in the developmental literature, Dawson (1994a, 1994b; Dawson, Panagiotides, Grofer Klinger, & Hill, 1992) reported that type and intensity of emotional expression is related to specific patterns of left and right hemisphere frontal EEG activation in infants. Infants exhibited frontal activation relative to baseline during a brief maternal separation. Furthermore, during emotion eliciting situations, infants exhibited right frontal activation during sad, or withdrawal, situations and left frontal activation during angry, or approach, situations. Dawson (1994b) proposed that these frontal activation asymmetries reflect regulatory, coping, and experiential factors more than innate approach or withdrawal tendencies.

Over the last several years, the developmental work of Fox has examined individual differences in frontal EEG asymmetry (1991, 1994; Bell & Fox, 1994; Calkins, Fox, & Marshall, 1996; Davidson & Fox, 1989; Fox, Bell, & Jones, 1992; Fox & Calkins, 1993; Fox, Calkins, & Bell, 1994; Fox & Davidson, 1987). For example, 10-month-old infants who exhibited greater relative right frontal EEG activation during a baseline EEG recording were more likely to cry at maternal separation than infants exhibiting greater relative left frontal activation (Davidson & Fox, 1989). Facial expressions did not differ during baseline between the infants who subsequently cried at separation and those who did not.

Longitudinal work by Fox has revealed that frontal EEG asymmetry may reflect a stable temperamental disposition rather than a developmental pattern of behavior (Bell & Fox, 1994; Calkins et al., 1996; Fox et al., 1992; Fox et al., 1994). Utilizing the infants from our longitudinal A-not-B study (Bell & Fox, 1992), we sought to replicate the Davidson and Fox (1989) study on the relation between baseline frontal EEG asymmetries and subsequent crying to maternal separation. After cognitive testing, mothers stood up, waved and said "bye-bye," and left the testing room, closing the door behind them. We timed the latency for the infants to cry, up to 30 seconds. We used K-means cluster analysis and found that from 7 to 12 months of age, there were two groups of infants defined by their behavior at maternal separation (see Fig. 9.4). One group of infants ($n = 8$) consistently showed a long latency to cry at maternal separation at each testing session, averaging about 25 seconds. The other group of infants ($n = 5$) declined from a latency to cry of about 25–30 seconds at the 7- and 8-month testing sessions, to a latency of 0–5 seconds at the 11- and 12-month testing sessions (Bell & Fox, 1994; Fox et al., 1992).

We computed frontal and parietal EEG asymmetry scores for each infant at each age by subtracting the EEG power value of the left hemisphere from

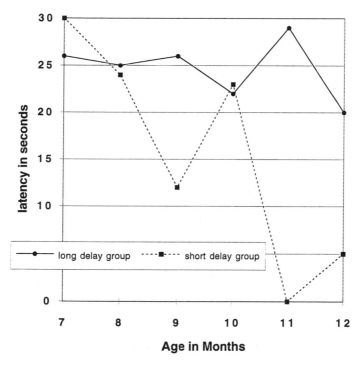

FIG. 9.4. Latency to cry at maternal separation for the 2 K-means cluster analysis groups. Adapted from Fox, Bell, and Jones (1992). Copyright 1992 by Lawrence Erlbaum Associates, Inc. (Reprinted with permission from the publisher.)

the EEG power value of the right hemisphere (lnRIGHT − lnLEFT). Thus, negative values reflected right hemisphere activation and positive values reflected left hemisphere activation. We found that infants who consistently exhibited a shorter latency to cry at maternal separation displayed right frontal activation during baseline EEG (see Fig. 9.5, left), whereas infants with a longer latency to cry at separation consistently exhibited left frontal activation during baseline EEG (Bell & Fox, 1994; Fox et al., 1992). In contrast, there was no difference in parietal EEG asymmetry scores between the long and short latency to cry groups (see Fig. 9.5, right).

Fox (1994) proposed that these differences in left and right frontal activation reflect varying regulatory styles among same-age infants. He has extended the model beyond the dichotomy of left frontal activation associated with approach behaviors–positive affect and right frontal activation associated with withdrawal behaviors–negative affect. Rather than simply manifesting positive and negative emotions, these approach and withdrawal responses may be involved in the regulation of an infant's response to emotionally arousing situations (Fox, 1994). Thus, the infants who exhibited right frontal activation during the baseline EEG recordings and cried during maternal separation did so because of their temperamental tendency to withdraw from arousing stimuli as a way to regulate their stress to anxiety-producing events.

Both cortical and subcortical networks appear to be associated with emotional responses, discrimination, and interpretation. Although evidence for frontal involvement in regulatory styles is apparent from the work reviewed earlier, subcortical involvement in emotions is thought to involve such structures as the amygdala and the thalamus working in concert with the cortex to form the limbic system. Posner, Rothbart, and Harman (1994) suggested that this emotional brain network interacts with the executive attention network. Specifically, the anterior cingulate gyrus is the site of control for the executive attention network and this same brain structure receives input from emotion networks associated with distress. In the next section, we attempt to interrelate the research on frontal lobe involvement in cognition and temperamental style.

INTERRELATIONS AMONG COGNITIVE PROCESSING, TEMPERAMENTAL STYLE, AND FRONTAL CORTEX

Adult Literature on Personality, Cognition, and EEG

There is evidence from normal adults (e.g., Davidson, 1995), clinical populations (e.g., Davidson, Schaffer, & Saron, 1985), and developmental studies (Calkins et al., 1996) of a relation between individual differences in EEG

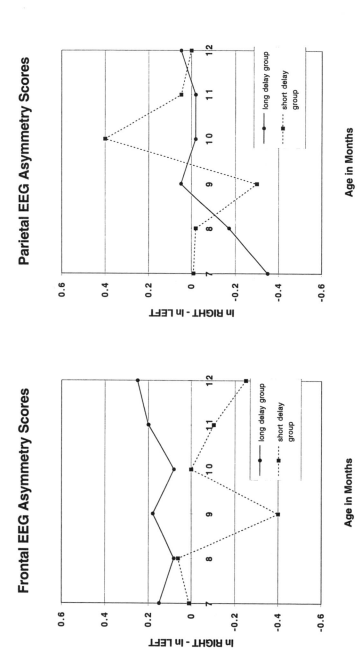

FIG. 9.5. Frontal EEG asymmetry values (left) and parietal EEG asymmetry values (right) for the 2 latency to cry at maternal separation groups. Adapted from Fox, Bell, and Jones (1992). Copyright 1992 by Lawrence Erlbaum Associates, Inc. (Reprinted with permission from the publisher.)

activity and certain aspects of personality. Other studies have examined the relations between adult cognitive performance and personality characteristics (e.g., Ackerman, Kanfer, & Goff, 1995). Levy (1983) proposed a model in which tonic hemispheric arousal is related to performance on cognitive tasks involving hemispheric specialization. She found that performance on paper and pencil tasks requiring left hemisphere involvement was enhanced in individuals with tonic left hemispheric arousal. Performance was diminished on these same tasks for individuals with tonic right hemisphere arousal (Levy, Heller, Banich, & Burton, 1983). Few studies, however, have examined variations in adult personality, cognitive performance, and hemispheric activation in a normal population.

The relation between mood state or personality and brain activity in a normal population may be related to the work done with clinical populations. Researchers working with depressed patients have reported tonic levels of right hemisphere brain activation among these patients (e.g., Henriques & Davidson, 1990; Matousek, Capone, & Okawa, 1981; Schaffer, Davidson, & Saron, 1983). Other researchers have reported that depressed patients display greater right hemisphere activation during cognitive tasks thought to involve the right hemisphere (Flor-Henry & Koles, 1984; Flor-Henry, Koles, & Tucker, 1982). In addition, these researchers have reported that depressed patients show deficiencies on certain right hemisphere tasks.

This work with clinical populations may have implications for work with normal adults. Recently, Howard and colleagues (Howard, Fenwick, Brown, & Norton, 1992) reported social extraversion was associated with left hemisphere activity during verbal and spatial tasks. Likewise, we (Bell & Fox, 1997) have noted that adults selected to be high on positive or negative affectivity displayed differences in spatial task performance, with high-negative adults performing poorly on a spatial task and exhibiting high levels of EEG activation in the right hemisphere. Thus, it appears that in a normal adult population differences in personality may interact with cognitive performance and the hemispheric activation associated with that performance. The potential for parallel findings in infant populations is great, given the infancy literature linking frontal EEG maturation with cognitive development and frontal EEG activation with temperamental reactivity.

Speculation Concerning Interrelations Among A-not-B Performance, Temperamental Style, and Frontal EEG During Infancy

Within a normal infant population, there is the potential for individual differences in mood state or temperament and the brain activation associated with a particular temperamental style to interact with cognitive performance (Rothbart et al., 1990; Rothbart, Posner, & Rosicky, 1994; Ruff

& Rothbart, 1996). Our previous work has shown that there is a relation between 7- to 12-month-old infants' temperamental reactivity during a brief maternal separation and frontal brain electrical activity recorded during baseline EEG prior to the separation (Bell & Fox, 1994; Fox et al., 1992). Specifically, it was possible to predict which infants would cry at maternal separation based on frontal EEG recordings. Infants who cried exhibited right frontal EEG activation. There were no associations between reactivity at maternal separation and EEG recorded from other scalp locations.

In other work, we have reported a relation between frontal brain electrical activity and cognitive development during infancy. Using frontal EEG as a marker of brain development in a longitudinal study, we noted that changes in frontal EEG from 7 to 12 months of age are associated with changes in object permanence performance during that same age period (Bell & Fox, 1992). Object permanence, the knowledge that an object continues to exist even when out of sight, is a classic marker of infant cognitive development. We also reported that individual differences in frontal EEG among same-age infants are related to differences in frontal EEG activity (Bell & Fox, in press). Specifically, higher levels of performance on an object permanence scale were associated with greater EEG power values at the frontal scalp locations.

While both temperamental reactivity to maternal separation and object permanence performance have been shown to be related to specific patterns of frontal EEG activity during infancy, there is no direct evidence in the infancy literature that cognitive processing interacts with individual differences in temperament and EEG activation. In a study of visual orienting from 2 to 4 months of age, however, Johnson et al. (1991) speculated that attention development would be related to the development of individual differences in infant temperament. They reported that at 4 months of age the ability to disengage attention is positively related to temperamental soothability, as rated by maternal report on the Infant Behavior Questionnaire (IBQ; Rothbart, 1981). The ability to disengage was inversely related to maternal-rated temperamental aspects of fear and frustration. Thus, not only was orienting related to development of the neural circuits associated with visual attention (Johnson, 1990, 1995), it was also related to individual differences in emotional reactivity and regulation.

Rothbart, Derryberry, and Posner (1994) proposed a developmental model examining the interrelations of temperamental style and attentional capacities. These authors have specifically related individual differences in negative emotionality at the newborn period, frustration–anger tendencies beginning at 2 months of age, and fearful behaviors from 6 months of age to the beginnings of effortful control (via the anterior attention system) prior to the first birthday. Through intricate interrelations among temperament style, environmental rewards and punishments, and socialization, attentional processes are developed. What is missing from this model are other cognitive behaviors related to frontal functioning during infancy.

Although there is much speculation that a relation exists between temperamental reactivity and cognitive processing (e.g., Fox, 1994; Rothbart et al., 1990; Rothbart et al., 1994; Ruff & Rothbart, 1996), no studies have been designed to examine the associations among temperament, EEG activation, and cognitive development during infancy. In our research lab, we presently are examining in a nonselected infant population the premise that differences in infant temperamental reactivity, and the frontal lobe EEG activation associated with temperamental style, interact with cognitive processing. These data will further our knowledge of brain–behavior relations during infancy and provide the impetus for study of the effects of extreme temperament style influences on cognitive development and for longitudinal study of the interrelations between temperament and cognitive development during the first few months of life.

SUMMARY AND CONCLUSIONS

There is growing evidence of frontal involvement in cognitive behaviors during the first year of life. There also is increasing confirmation that the ongoing EEG provides evidence of the development of the frontal cortex, as well as individual differences in frontal development and functioning, during infancy. This is an especially pertinent point because not all cognitive behaviors assessed during infancy are amenable to the same methods of electrophysiological testing. For example, while ERP methodology has proven invaluable in assessing the development of recognition memory and attention during infancy (see Nelson & Dukette, chap. 11, this volume), this methodology is not usable with A-not-B testing. Considering the way we assess A-not-B performance at the present time, it is not possible to have enough trials during A-not-B assessment to make use of ERP techniques.

An intriguing notion for future A-not-B research is the use of heart rate (HR) defined measures of sustained attention (see Richards & Hunter, chap. 4, this volume). Our looking version of the A-not-B task was invaluable because it allowed us to record the ongoing EEG during A-not-B performance. During the task, however, we were making suppositions that the directional gaze of the infants meant that they were "paying attention" to the task. Richards (e.g., 1995; Richards & Casey, 1992) has shown that gaze fixation and sustained attention are not necessarily coincident. That is, infants are not distractible from a stimulus during the time when HR has decreased after stimulus orienting. Conversely, infants are distractible from a stimulus during the time the HR returns to prestimulus levels. Future A-not-B work would benefit from autonomic measures of sustained attention. It would be intriguing if infants who made the A-not-B error did so during the HR-defined attention termination phase, while those who succeeded on the task did so during the HR-defined sustained attention phase. Even more fascinating would be evidence that within the same infants, successful trials occurred during HR-defined sustained attention, while error trials occurred during HR-defined attention termination.

In this chapter evidence has been presented for frontal involvement in infant cognitive and socioemotional behaviors. By focusing on the A-not-B task, we have proposed that EEG measures implicate frontal development in increasing performance on this classic infant task. We have also suggested that among same-age infants individual differences in A-not-B performance are related to individual differences in frontal development. With a looking version of the classic reaching task, we measured EEG online and reported differences in frontal EEG during different task conditions and suggested involvement of the executive attention network in this version of the task. We also reviewed data on frontal EEG activation and temperamental style during infancy and then proposed that there are interrelations among frontal activation, higher order attentional processes, and temperamental style in A-not-B performance.

Studies reported here and elsewhere in 1997 are adding greatly to our body of knowledge concerning brain–behavior relations during infancy. As we continue to examine infant development with both behavioral and electrophysiological measures, we are able gather more precise information about the dynamics of cognitive development.

ACKNOWLEDGMENTS

Portions of the research reported in this chapter were conducted while the author was a Visiting Assistant Professor at the University of South Carolina and were supported by a Research and Productive Service award from the University. Work done in collaboration with Nathan A. Fox was supported by grants HD17889 and HD26728 from the National Institutes of Health to NAF. The assistance of Anne Luebering, Nancy Aaron-Jones, Anne Schubert, Glenda Insabella, and Kathleen Wallner-Allen at the University of Maryland, and Stephanie Adams, Sabrina Pope, Jonathan Roberts, and numerous undergraduate research assistants at the University of South Carolina is gratefully acknowledged. Appreciation is expressed to Robin Panneton Cooper, Nathan A. Fox, and John E. Richards for comments on an earlier version of this manuscript.

REFERENCES

Ackerman, P. L., Kanfer, R., & Goff, M. (1995). Cognitive and noncognitive determinants and consequences of complex skill acquisition. *Journal of Experimental Psychology: Applied, 1,* 270–304.

Acredolo, L. (1990). Individual differences in infant spatial cognition. In J. Colombo & J. Fagen (Eds.), *Individual differences in infancy: Reliability, stability, prediction* (pp. 321–340). Hillsdale, NJ: Lawrence Erlbaum Associates.

Bai, D. L., & Bertenthal, B. I. (1992). Locomotor experience and the development of spatial search skills. *Child Development, 63*, 215–226.

Baillargeon, R. (1987). Object permanence in 3.5- and 4.5-month-old infants. *Developmental Psychology, 23*, 655–664.

Baillargeon, R. (1995). Physical reasoning in infancy. In M. Gazzaniga (Ed.), *The cognitive neurosciences* (pp. 181–204). Cambridge, MA: MIT Press.

Baillargeon, R., & DeVos, J. (1991). Object permanence in young infants: Further evidence. *Child Development, 62*, 1227–1246.

Baillargeon, R., & Graber, M. (1988). Evidence of location memory in 8-month-old infants in a nonsearch AB task. *Developmental Psychology, 24*, 502–511.

Baillargeon, R., Graber, M., DeVos, J., & Black, J. (1990). Why do young infants fail to search for hidden objects? *Cognition, 36*, 255–284.

Bell, M. A. (1996, October). *Frontal EEG activation in 8-month-old infants during a looking version of the classic A-not-B object permanence task.* Paper presented at the annual meeting of the Society for Psychophysiological Research, Vancouver, BC.

Bell, M. A. (in press). The ontogeny of the EEG during infancy and childhood: Implications for cognitive development. In B. Garreau (Ed.), *Neuro imaging in childhood psychiatric disorders.* Paris: Springer-Verlag.

Bell, M. A., & Fox, N. A. (1992). The relations between frontal brain electrical activity and cognitive development during infancy. *Child Development, 63*, 1142–1163.

Bell, M. A., & Fox, N. A. (1994). Brain development over the first year of life: Relations between electroencephalographic frequency & coherence and cognitive & affective behaviors. In G. Dawson & K. W. Fischer (Eds.), *Human behavior and the developing brain* (pp. 314–345). New York: Guilford.

Bell, M. A., & Fox, N. A. (1996). Crawling experience is related to changes in cortical organization during infancy: Evidence from EEG coherence. *Developmental Psychobiology, 29*, 551–561.

Bell, M. A., & Fox, N. A. (1997). *Personality correlates of EEG activity during verbal and spatial tasks.* Manuscript submitted for publication.

Bell, M. A., & Fox, N. A. (in press). Individual differences in object permanence performance at 8 months: Locomotor experience and brain electrical activity. *Developmental Psychobiology.*

Bell, M. A., & Schmauder, A. R. (1995, April). *Frontal lobe development from 6 to 10 months of age: An EEG case study.* Paper presented at the Society for Research in Child Development, Indianapolis.

Berger, H. (1932). Uber das elektrenkephalogramm des menschen. V [On the electroencephalogram of man. V]. *Archiv fur Psychiatrie und Nervenkrankheiten, 98*, 231–254.

Bertenthal, B. I., Campos, J. J., & Kermoian, R. (1994). An epigenetic perspective on the development of self-produced locomotion and its consequences. *Current Directions in Psychological Science, 5*, 140–145.

Bremner, J. G. (1985). Object tracking and search in infancy: A review of data and a theoretical evaluation. *Developmental Review, 5*, 371–396.

Butterworth, G. (1977). Object disappearance and error in Piaget's stage IV task. *Journal of Experimental Child Psychology, 23*, 391–401.

Butterworth, G., Jarrett, N., & Hicks, L. (1982). Spatiotemporal identity in infancy: Perceptual competence or conceptual deficit? *Developmental Psychology, 18*, 435–449.

Calkins, S. D., Fox, N. A., & Marshall, T. R. (1996). Behavioral and physiological antecedents of inhibited and uninhibited behavior. *Child Development, 67*, 523–540.

Chugani, H. T. (1994). Development of regional brain glucose metabolism in relation to behavior and plasticity. In G. Dawson & K. W. Fischer (Eds.), *Human behavior and the developing brain* (pp. 153–175). New York: Guilford.

Chugani, H. T., & Phelps, M. E. (1986). Developmental changes in cerebral function in infants determined by FDG Positron Emission Tomography. *Science, 231*, 840–843.

Colombo, J. (1993). *Infant cognition: Predicting later intellectual functioning.* Newbury Park, CA: Sage.

Davidson, R. J. (1992). Anterior cerebral asymmetry and the nature of emotion. *Brain and Cognition, 20*, 125–151.

Davidson, R. J. (1994). Temperament, affective style, and frontal lobe asymmetry. In G. Dawson & K. W. Fischer (Eds.), *Human behavior and the developing brain* (pp. 518–536). New York: Guilford.

Davidson, R. J. (1995). Cerebral asymmetry, emotion, and affective style. In R. J. Davidson & K. Hugdahl (Eds.), *Brain asymmetry* (pp. 361–387). Cambridge, MA: MIT Press.

Davidson, R. J., Chapman, J. P., Chapman, L. J., & Henriques, J. B. (1990). Asymmetrical brain electrical activity discriminates between psychometrically matched verbal and spatial cognitive tasks. *Psychophysiology, 27*, 528–543.

Davidson, R. J., Ekman, P., Saron, C. D., Senulis, J. A., & Friesen, W. V. (1990). Approach/withdrawal and cerebral asymmetry: Emotional expression and brain physiology I. *Journal of Personality and Social Psychology, 58*, 330–341.

Davidson, R. J., & Fox, N. A. (1982). Asymmetrical brain activity discriminates between positive versus negative affective stimuli in human infants. *Science, 218*, 1235–1237.

Davidson, R. J., & Fox, N. A. (1989). Frontal brain asymmetry predicts infants' response to maternal separation. *Journal of Abnormal Psychology, 98*, 127–131.

Davidson, R. J., Schaffer, C. E., & Saron, C. (1985). Effects of lateralized stimulus presentations on the self-report of emotion and EEG asymmetry in depressed and non-depressed subjects. *Psychophysiology, 22*, 353–364.

Dawson, G. (1994a). Development of emotional expression and emotion regulation in infancy: Contributions of the frontal lobe. In G. Dawson & K. W. Fischer (Eds.), *Human behavior and the developing brain* (pp. 346–379). New York: Guilford.

Dawson, G. (1994b). Frontal electroencephalographic correlates of individual differences in emotion expression in infants: A brain systems perspective on emotion. In N. A. Fox (Ed.), The development of emotion regulation: Biological and behavioral considerations (pp. 135–151). *Monographs of the Society for Research in Child Development, 59* (2-3, Serial No. 240).

Dawson, G., Panagiotides, H., Grofer Klinger, L., & Hill, D. (1992). The role of frontal lobe functioning in the development of self-regulatory behavior in infancy. *Brain and Cognition, 20*, 152–175.

Diamond, A. (1985). Development of the ability to use recall to guide action, as indicated by infants' performance on AB. *Child Development, 56*, 868–883.

Diamond, A. (1988). Abilities and neural mechanisms underlying AB performance. *Child Development, 59*, 523–527.

Diamond, A. (Ed.). (1990a). Developmental time course in human infants and infant monkeys, and the neural bases, of inhibitory control in reaching. In *The development and neural bases of higher cognitive functions* (pp. 637–676). New York: New York Academy of Sciences Press.

Diamond, A. (Ed.). (1990b). The development and neural bases of memory functions as indexed by the AB and delayed response tasks in human infants and infant monkeys. In *The development and neural bases of higher cognitive functions* (pp. 267–317). New York: New York Academy of Sciences Press.

Diamond, A. (1991). Neuropsychological insights into the meaning of object concept development. In S. Carey & R. Gelman (Eds.), *The epigenesis of mind: Essays on biology and knowledge* (pp. 67–110). Hillsdale, NJ: Lawrence Erlbaum Associates.

Diamond, A. (1994). Phenylalanine levels of 6–10 mg/dl may not be as benign as once thought. *Acta Paediatrica Supplement, 407*, 89–91.

Diamond, A., & Goldman-Rakic, P. S. (1983). Comparison of performance on a Piagetian object permanence task in human infants and rhesus monkeys: Evidence for involvement of prefrontal cortex. *Society for Neuroscience Abstracts, 9*, 641.

Diamond, A., & Goldman-Rakic, P. S. (1986). Comparative development in human infants and infant rhesus monkeys of cognitive functions that depend on prefrontal cortex. *Society for Neuroscience Abstracts, 12*, 742.

Diamond, A., & Goldman-Rakic, P. S. (1989). Comparison of human infants and rhesus monkeys on Piaget's AB task: Evidence for dependence on dorsolateral prefrontal cortex. *Experimental Brain Research, 74*, 24–40.

Diamond, A., Zola-Morgan, S., & Squire, L. R. (1989). Successful performance by monkeys with lesions of the hippocampal formation on AB and object retrieval. *Behavioral Neuroscience, 103*, 526–537.

Flor-Henry, P., & Koles, Z. J. (1984). Statistical quantitative EEG studies of depression, mania, schizophrenia, and normals. *Biological Psychology, 19*, 257–279.

Flor-Henry, P., Koles, Z. J., & Tucker, D. M. (1982). Studies in EEG power and coherence (8–13 Hz) in depression, mania, and schizophrenia compared to controls. *Advances in Biological Psychiatry, 9*, 1–7.

Fox, N. A. (1991). If it's not left, it's right: Electroencephalogram asymmetry and the development of emotion. *American Psychologist, 46*, 863–872.

Fox, N. A. (Ed.). (1994). Dynamic cerebral processes underlying emotion regulation. In The development of emotion regulation: Biological and behavioral considerations (pp. 152–166). *Monographs of the Society for Research in Child Development, 59* (2-3, Serial No. 240).

Fox, N. A., Bell, M. A., & Jones, N. A. (1992). Individual differences in response to stress and cerebral asymmetry. *Developmental Neuropsychology, 7*, 161–184.

Fox, N. A., & Calkins, S. D. (1993). Pathways to aggression and social withdrawal: Interactions among temperament, attachment, and regulation. In K. Rubin & J. Asendorpf (Eds.), *Social withdrawal, inhibition, and shyness in children* (pp. 81–100). Hillsdale, NJ: Lawrence Erlbaum Associates.

Fox, N. A., Calkins, S. D., & Bell, M. A. (1994). Neural plasticity and development in the first two years of life: Evidence from cognitive and socio-emotional domains of research. *Development and Psychopathology, 6*, 677–698.

Fox, N. A., & Davidson, R. J. (1987). EEG asymmetry in ten month old infants in response to approach of a stranger and maternal separation. *Developmental Psychology, 23*, 233–240.

Fox, N. A., & Davidson, R. J. (1988). Patterns of brain electrical activity during the expression of discrete emotions in ten month old infants. *Developmental Psychology, 24*, 230–236.

Fuster, J. M. (1989). *The prefrontal cortex*. New York: Raven.

Georgopoulos, A. (1987). Cortical mechanisms subserving reaching. *Motor areas of the cerebral cortex* (pp. 125–132). New York: Wiley.

Georgopoulos, A. (1995). Motor cortex and cognitive processing. In M. Gazzaniga (Ed.), *The cognitive neurosciences* (pp. 507–517). Cambridge, MA: MIT Press.

Ghez, C. (1985). Voluntary movement. In E. R. Kandel & J. H. Schwartz (Eds.), *Principles of neural science* (2nd ed., pp. 487–501). New York: Elsevier.

Ghez, C., Gordon, J., Ghilardi, M. F., & Sainburg, R. (1995). Contributions of vision and proprioception to accuracy in limb movements. In M. Gazzaniga (Ed.), *The cognitive neurosciences* (pp. 549–564). Cambridge, MA: MIT Press.

Goldman, P. S. (1971). Functional development of the prefrontal cortex in early life and the problem of neuronal plasticity. *Experimental Neurology, 32*, 366–387.

Goldman, P. S. (1976). The role of experience in recovery of function following orbital prefrontal lesions in infant monkeys. *Neuropsychologia, 14*, 401–412.

Goldman, P. S., & Mendelson, M. J. (1977). Salutary effects of early experience on deficits caused by lesions of frontal association cortex in developing rhesus monkeys. *Experimental Neurology, 57,* 588–602.

Goldman-Rakic, P. S. (1987). Development of cortical circuitry and cognitive function. *Child Development, 58,* 601–622.

Gratch, G., Appel, K. J., Evans, W. F., LeCompte, G. K., & Wright, N. A. (1974). Piaget's stage IV object concept error: Evidence of forgetting or object conception? *Child Development, 45,* 71–77.

Hagne, I. (1968). Development of the waking EEG in normal infants during the first year of life. In P. Kellaway & I. Petersen (Eds.), *Clinical electroencephalography of children* (pp. 97–118). New York: Grune & Stratton.

Hagne, I. (1972). Development of the EEG in normal infants during the first year of life. *Acta Pediatrica Scandinavia,* Supplement 232, 25–53.

Harris, P. L. (1983). Infant cognition. In M. M. Haith & J. J. Campos (Eds.), P. H. Mussen (Series Ed.), *Handbook of child psychology: Vol. 2. Infancy and developmental psychobiology* (pp. 689–782). New York: Wiley.

Harris, P. L. (1987). The development of search. In P. Salapatek & L. B. Cohen (Eds.), *Handbook of infant perception: Vol. 2.* New York: Academic Press.

Henriques, J. B., & Davidson, R. J. (1990). Regional brain electrical asymmetries discriminate between previously depressed and healthy control subjects. *Journal of Abnormal Psychology, 99,* 22–31.

Henry, J. R. (1944). Electroencephalograms of normal children. *Monographs of the Society for Research in Child Development, 9*(3, Serial No. 39).

Hofstadter, M., & Reznick, J. S. (1996). Response modality affects human infant delayed-response performance. *Child Development, 67,* 646–658.

Hood, B. M. (1993). Inhibition of return produced by covert shifts of visual attention in 6-month-old infants. *Infant Behavior and Development, 16,* 245–254.

Hood, B. M. (1995). Shifts of visual attention in the human infant: A neuroscientific approach. In C. Rovee-Collier & L. P. Lipsitt (Eds.), *Advances in infancy research. Vol. 9* (pp. 163–216). Norwood, NJ: Ablex.

Horobin, K., & Acredolo, L. (1986). The role of attentiveness, mobility history, and separation of hiding sites on stage IV search behavior. *Journal of Experimental Child Psychology, 41,* 114–127.

Howard, R. C., Fenwick, P., Brown, D., & Norton, R. (1992). Relationship between CNV asymmetries and individual differences in cognitive performance, personality, and gender. *International Journal of Psychophysiology, 13,* 191–197.

Huttenlocher, P. R. (1979). Synaptic density of human frontal cortex: Developmental changes and effects of aging. *Brain Research, 163,* 195–205.

Huttenlocher, P. R. (1990). Morphometric study of human cerebral cortex development. *Neuropsychologia, 28,* 517–527.

Johnson, M. H. (1990). Cortical maturation and the development of visual attention in early infancy. *Journal of Cognitive Neuroscience, 2,* 81–95.

Johnson, M. H. (1995). The development of visual attention: A cognitive neuroscience perspective. In M. S. Gazzaniga (Ed.), *The cognitive neurosciences* (pp. 735–747). Cambridge, MA: MIT Press.

Johnson, M. H., Posner, M. I., & Rothbart, M. K. (1991). Components of visual orienting in early infancy: Contingency learning, anticipatory looking, and disengaging. *Journal of Cognitive Neuroscience, 3,* 335–344.

Kermoian, R., & Campos, J. J. (1988). Locomotor experience: A facilitator of spatial cognitive development. *Child Development, 59,* 908–917.

Knight, R. T., & Grabowecky, M. (1995). Escape from linear time: Prefrontal cortex and conscious experience. In M. Gazzaniga (Ed.), *The cognitive neurosciences* (pp. 1357–1371). Cambridge, MA: MIT Press.

Levy, J. (1983). Individual differences in cerebral hemisphere asymmetry: Theoretical issues and experimental considerations. In J. B. Hellige (Ed.), *Cerebral hemisphere asymmetry: Method, theory, and aplication* (pp. 465–497). New York: Praeger.

Levy. J., Heller, W., Banich, M. T., & Burton, L. (1983). Are variations among right-handers in perceptual asymmetries caused by characteristic arousal differences in the hemispheres? *Journal of Experimental Psychology: Human Perception and Performance, 9,* 329–359.

Matousek, M., Capone, C., & Okawa, M. (1981). Measurement of the interhemispheral differences as a diagnostic tool in psychiatry. *Advances in Biological Psychiatry, 6,* 76–80.

Matthews, A., Ellis, A., & Nelson, C. A. (1996). Development of AB, recall memory, transparent barrier detour, and means-end task performance in pre-term and full-term infants. *Child Development, 67,* 2658–2676.

Milner, B. (1982). Some cognitive effects of frontal-lobe lesions in man. *Philosophical Transactions of the Royal Society of London, 298,* 211–226.

Milner, B., Petrides, M., & Smith, M. L. (1985). Frontal lobes and the temporal organization of memory. *Human Neurobiology, 4,* 137–142.

Mountcastle, V. B., Lynch, J. C., Georgopoulos, A., Sakata, H., & Acuna, C. (1975). Posterior parietal association cortex of the monkey: Command functions for operations within extrapersonal space. *Journal of Neurophysiology, 38,* 871–908.

Munakata, Y., McClelland, J. L., Johnson, M. H., & Siegler, R. S. (1994). *Now you see it, now you don't: A gradualistic framework for understanding infants' successes and failures in object permanence tasks* (Tech. Rep. No. PDP.CNS.94.2). Pittsburgh, PA: Carnegie Mellon University.

Mushiake, J. T. H., & Inase, M. (1993). Premotor and supplementary motor cortex in sequential motor tasks. In T. Ono, L. R. Squire, M. E. Raichle, D. I. Perrett, & M. Fukuda (Eds.), *Brain mechanisms of perception and memory* (pp. 464–472). New York: Oxford University Press.

Nelson, C. A. (1995). The ontogeny of human memory: A cognitive neuroscience perspective. *Developmental Psychology, 31,* 723–738.

Piaget, J. (1954). *The construction of reality in the child.* New York: Basic.

Posner, M. I. (1988). Structures and functions of selective attention. In T. Boll & B. Bryant (Eds.), *Master lectures in clinical neuropsychology* (pp. 173–202). Washington, DC: American Psychological Association.

Posner, M. I. (1992). Attention as a cognitive and neural system. *Current Directions in Psychological Science, 1,* 11–14.

Posner, M. I. (1995). Attention in cognitive neuroscience: An overview. In M. Gazzaniga (Ed.), *The cognitive neurosciences* (pp. 615–624). Cambridge, MA: MIT Press.

Posner, M. I., Inhoff, A. W., Friedrich, F. J., & Cohen, A. (1987). Isolating attentional systems: A cognitive-anatomical analysis. *Psychobiology, 15,* 107–121.

Posner, M. I., & Peterson, S. E. (1990). The attention system of the human brain. *Annual Review of Neuroscience, 13,* 25–42.

Posner, M. I., Peterson, S. E., Fox, P. T., & Raichle, M. E. (1988). Localization of cognitive operations in the human brain. *Science, 240,* 1627–1631.

Posner, M. I., & Raichle, M. E. (1994). *Images of mind.* New York: Scientific American Library.

Posner, M. I., Rothbart, M. K., & Harman, C. (1994). Cognitive science's contributions to culture and emotion (pp. 197–216). Washington, DC: American Psychological Association.

Posner, M. I., Walker, J. A., Friedrich, F. J., & Rafal, R. D. (1984). Effects of parietal injury on covert orienting of attention. *The Journal of Neuroscience, 4,* 1863–1874.

Posner, M. I., Walker, J. A., Friedrich, F. A., & Rafal, R. D. (1987). How do the parietal lobes direct covert attention? *Neuropsychologia, 25,* 135–145.

Pribram, K. H. (1973). The primate frontal cortex: Executive of the brain. In K. H. Pribram & A. R. Luria (Eds.), *Psychophysiology of the frontal lobes* (pp. 293–314). New York: Academic Press.

Ray, W. J. (1990). Electrical activity of the brain. In J. T. Cacioppo & L. G. Tassinary (Eds.), *Principles of psychophysiology: Physical, social, and inferential elements* (pp. 385–412). Cambridge, England: Cambridge University Press.

Ray, W. J., & Cole, H. W. (1985). EEG alpha activity reflects attentional demands, and beta activity reflects emotional and cognitive processes. *Science, 228,* 750–752.

Richards, J. E. (1995). Infant cognitive psychophysiology. Normal development and implications for abnormal developmental outcomes. In T. H. Ollendick & R. J. Prinz (Eds.), *Advances in clinical child psychology* (Vol. 17 , pp. 77–107). New York: Plenum Press.

Richards, J. E., & Casey, B. J. (1992). Development of sustained visual attention in the human infant. In B. A. Campbell, H. Hayne, & R. Richardson (Eds.), *Attention and information processing in infants and adults: Perspectives from human and animal research* (pp. 30–60). Hillsdale, NJ: Lawrence Erlbaum Associates.

Roland, P. E., Larsen, B., Larsen, N. A., & Skinhoj, E. (1980). Supplementary motor area and other cortical areas in organization of voluntary movements in man. *Journal of Neurophysiology, 43,* 118–136.

Rothbart, M. K. (1981). Measurement of temperament in infancy. *Child Development, 52,* 569–578.

Rothbart, M. K., Derryberry, D., & Posner, M. I. (1994). A psychobiological approach to the development of temperament. In J. E. Bates & T. D. Wachs (Eds.), *Temperament: Individual differences at the interface of biology and behavior* (pp. 83–116). Washington, DC: American Psychological Association.

Rothbart, M. K., Posner, M. I., & Boylan, A. (1990). Regulatory mechanisms in infant development. In J. T. Enns (Ed.), *The development of attention: Research and theory* (pp. 47–66). Amsterdam: Elsevier.

Rothbart, M. K., Posner, M. I., & Rosicky, J. (1994). Orienting in normal and pathological development. *Development and Psychopathology, 6,* 635–652.

Ruff, H. A., & Rothbart, M. K. (1996). *Attention in early development.* New York: Oxford University Press.

Salmaso, D., & Denes, G. (1982). Role of the frontal lobes on an attentional task: A signal detection analysis. *Perceptual and Motor Skills, 55,* 127–130.

Sasaki, K., & Gemba, H. (1993). Prefrontal cortex in the organization and control of voluntary movement. In T. Ono, L. R. Squire, M. E. Raichle, D. I. Perrett, & M. Fukuda (Eds.), *Brain mechanisms of perception and memory* (pp. 473–496). New York: Oxford University Press.

Schaffer, C. E., Davidson, R. J., & Saron, C. (1983). Frontal and parietal EEG asymmetries in depressed and non-depressed subjects. *Biological Psychiatry, 18,* 753–762.

Smith, J. R. (1938). The electroencephalogram during normal infancy and childhood: II. The nature and growth of the alpha waves. *Journal of Genetic Psychology, 53,* 455–469.

Tomarken, A. J., Davidson, R. J., & Henriques, J. B. (1990). Resting frontal brain asymmetry predicts affective responses to films. *Journal of Personality and Social Psychology, 59,* 791–801.

Wellman, H. M., Cross, D., & Bartsch, K. (1986). Infant search and object permanence: A meta-analysis of the A-not-B error. *Monographs of the Society for Research in Child Development, 51*(3, Serial No. 214).

Wellman, H. M., & Somerville, S. C. (1982). The development of human search ability. In M. E. Lamb & A. E. Brown (Eds.), *Advances in developmental psychology* (Vol. 2, pp. 44–84). Hillsdale, NJ: Lawrence Erlbaum Associates.

West, R. L. (1996). An application of prefrontal cortex function theory to cognitive aging. *Psychological Bulletin, 120*, 272–292.

West, R. L., & Bell, M. A. (1997). Stroop color-word interference and EEG activation: Evidence for age-related decline in the anterior attention system. *Neuropsychology, 11*, 421–427.

Wheeler, R. W., Davaidson, R. J., & Tomarken, A. J. (1993). Frontal brain asymmetry and emotional reactivity: A biological substrate of affective style. *Psychophysiology, 30*, 82–89.

Wilkins, A. J., Shallice, T., & McCarthy, R. (1987). Frontal lesions and sustained attention. *Neuropsychologia, 25*, 359–365.

Wilson, F. A. W., O-Scalaidhe, S. P., & Goldman-Rakic, P. S. (1993). Dissociation of object and spatial processing domains in primate prefrontal cortex. *Science, 260*, 1955–1958.

Chapter 10

Summary and Commentary: Developing Attentional Skills

Michael I. Posner
Mary K. Rothbart
University of Oregon

DEVELOPING ATTENTIONAL SKILLS

The four chapters on which we comment all address the skill of visual orienting, that is, the ability to shift the eyes or attention toward a source of visual input. A great deal is known about the neural control of eye movements. Systems controlling eye movements are both complex and distributed, involving a number of anterior and posterior cortical centers as well as many subcortical areas. In this commentary we tie together some of the interesting ideas that have emerged from studies described in these chapters and suggest some relationships to other aspects of attention.

Visual Orienting of Attention

The relatively close connection between eye movements and visual orienting of attention makes it tempting to conclude that all there is to attention is eye movements. In fact, in their selection-for-action chapter, Hood et al. come very close to making this identification when they say, "likewise it is not possible to maintain fixation on an object of interest at the same time as one has to orient to a peripheral target" (p. 220). If by "orient" they mean a shift of attention, this is just not so. Many studies have demonstrated shifts of covert attention as fixation is maintained. However, at times eye movements can be taken as a fairly direct indicant of attention—

as in studies where eye-movement protocols supplement speaking aloud. A major reason for examining covert orienting as a separate category is the hope that its mechanisms might help us understand more general cases of attention, such as when information is stored in memory and not currently present in the environment.

If the eyes are kept fixed, attention can be given to another location in the field. Attending away from the fovea does little to improve acuity—this depends on hard wiring of the fovea which cannot be shifted—but it does provide greater priority to the attended area. Even in the earliest papers in this area (e.g., Posner, 1980), it was pointed out that eye movements and covert attention shifts were not completely independent, but rather that they had a strong functional relationship. Hood et al. support a prefrontal theory, holding that attention movements, like eye movements, involve frontal motor systems. Although this may be true, it is not very helpful to label either process as prefrontal only because a part of the circuitry of each might involve frontal areas. The prefrontal theory holds that each attention shift is an act of readying an eye movement. However, both lesion (Posner, 1988) and PET studies (Corbetta, Miezen, Shulman, & Petersen, 1993) have been quite clear in implicating an area of the parietal lobe involved in covert shifts of attention that seems to be very different than the frontal area mediating saccades.

Although covert and overt attention are not identical, one may still hope that what we know about eye movements can help guide our understanding of the orienting of attention. Rafal successfully illustrates this possibility by showing how lesions can influence covert and overt shifts of orienting. He finds specific parts of the network to overlap between the two systems, and this seems a more adequate approach than emphasizing that a part of each network is frontal.

Rafal presents several good examples of how model tasks related to particular anatomical areas by brain injury can help us understand development. To illustrate what we can learn from this approach, consider the difficult question of when one can attend to more than a single item. When the task is searching a complex field, studies indicate only a single focus of attention. However, patients with the corpus callosum split can search items presented in two visual fields much faster than when presented with items only in a single field (Luck, Hillyard, Mangun, & Gazzaniga, 1994). We now know that communication between separate controllers imposes a unified focus of attention for visual orienting in adults. We need to find out if this conclusion can be generalized to other attentional functions. Because the corpus callosum continues to develop in children past the period of infancy, this may make possible a developmental method for examining the integration of orienting mechanisms.

Visual Search

What is covert attention for? Visual search is surely one of its main functions. Visual search forms a very strong link between the Rafal and Hood et al. chapters dealing with the neurology of orienting, and the chapter by Baylis dealing directly with visual search. One should not be misled by the apparent controversy between the space-based and object-based models of visual orienting that concern Baylis in the early parts of his chapter. In fact, the common characteristic that almost defines the set of things we call objects is that they occupy space, even though this location may move from moment to moment. Hood et al. also raise the controversy between space- and object-based attention in discussing inhibition of return. Inhibition of return is, of course, a form of novelty preference or a one-trial habituation. It should be no surprise to students of infancy that habituation can be obtained by repeated presentation of an object. Indeed, this has been a standard method in studying infant cognition for many years.

There never could be any doubt, based on subjective experience, that we often attend to objects and move attention overtly or covertly as the object moves. Baylis illustrates this quite well in his Fig. 8.1. There is also excellent PET data arguing that the same anatomical areas involved in visual cuing experiments are also involved in searching the visual field (Corbetta, Shulman, Miezin, & Petersen, 1995).

Baylis cites the advantage of shifts of attention within objects rather than between objects (Egly, Driver, & Rafal, 1994). It appears that the brain performs a surprising trick by integrating a left hemisphere orienting system that is very greatly dependent upon the segmentation of the field into objects, and a right hemisphere mechanism that is less influenced by articulation of the visual field. As discussed earlier, in normal subjects the corpus callosum integrates the two mechanisms, but when the brain is split they reveal their independent character.

There are now very good methods for tracing the development of orienting in early infancy (Ruff & Rothbart, 1966). Indeed, Rovee Collier and her associates (Rovee Collier, Bhatt, & Chazin, 1996) have shown that even 6-month-old infants perform visual search with similar mechanisms as adults. We (Posner, Rothbart, Thomas-Thrapp, & Gerardi, in press) have been able to show that selection of locations and selection of objects both develop in the period of 3–6 months, but as two independent mechanisms. The studies of Baylis and associates of 6-month-olds show how advanced these mechanisms become, even at an age before the emergence of language.

Visual search can be quite sophisticated in adults, involving many frontal structures. For example, when subjects are instructed to attend to color there is increased neuronal activity in the occipital areas that process color (Corbetta, Miezin, Dobmeyer, Shulman, & Petersen, 1991). When trials involving selective attention were compared with trials in which the subjects passively observed the same stimuli, frontal areas were active. In visual search there appear to be three major ways of detecting a target. If the target differs in a single feature from the surround, it pops out and only the final report depends on attention. In these conditions there is activation of the ventral occipital pathway involved in object recognition and nowhere else. If the target is similar to the surround, it is necessary to orient to each object in turn, in much the same way as Baylis describes. Under these conditions there is activation of the same parietal brain areas involved in other forms of covert orienting. In some difficult visual search tasks, search can be guided by confining orienting to those objects with some feature in common, for example, color, form, or motion. In this case, one finds input from frontal areas involved. Thus small changes in the way the task is understood and executed by the subject can recruit different brain areas.

Working Memory

Although there can be involvement of frontal areas even in tasks that involve orienting to visual objects as in visual search, the performance of many tasks rests very substantially upon attentional control from frontal areas. In her chapter, Bell discusses the role of frontal structures in infant memory (e.g., the A-not-B task) and in higher-order attention skills (the anterior or executive network).

Recent PET data on working memory in adults largely supports her suggestion of dorsolateral prefrontal activity in these tasks (Smith & Jonides, 1994). Working memory for objects, locations, and verbal information all have strong lateral frontal activation in addition to posterior activations. These systems are also likely to have common attentional control, and all show activation of the frontal midline. These results support the general idea that lateral frontal areas are involved in representing different domains of information (e.g., location or object) in the absence of a stimulus, with midline frontal structures supporting attentional control of these representations.

Resolution of Conflict

As Bell stresses in her chapter, the development of these frontal structures represent an important achievement of infancy and early childhood. It is not enough, however, merely to identify areas of the frontal cortex as important in development. The work of Diamond (1990) is important, because it illustrates a model of how the development of one part of the frontal lobes (dorsolateral prefrontal cortex) influences very specific aspects of the infant's behavior. From 9 to 12 months the infant achieves the ability to control reaching independent of the line of sight. This represents initial freeing of the infant's behavior from control by the visual orienting system, the major subject of the first three chapters of this section.

The development of the ability to use stored information rather than current stimulus events to control behavior is marked by the ability of the infant to resist basing responses on a previously rewarded location, instead basing it on a cue provided on this trial by the experimenter. The A-not-B task represents a resolution of conflict between two forms of stored information. The conflict is manifest when the infant moves the eyes toward the visually marked location where the target is located, while the hand moves to the previously rewarded location where there is no target. This dissociation between the information that controls hand and eye can be found even in adults under speeded conditions (Posner & Cohen, 1980), but the months of early childhood mark the development of common control systems that serve to resolve the conflict and produce integrated behavior that can be controlled by absent events.

In our recent work we have employed a nonverbal conflict task modeled after the familiar Stroop task (Gerardi, 1997). In this task infants press a key corresponding to a picture shown on a computer monitor. The picture may occur on the side of the correct key (compatible) or on the opposite side (incompatible). In adults, conflict trials of the Stroop task produce activation within the anterior cingulate gyrus of the frontal midline, a brain area we believe is related to executive control. Our data suggest very substantial development in this function between 24 and 36 months of age. During the early period a few infants were so dominated by location that they responded correctly 100% of the time on compatible trials, but were rarely or never correct on incompatible trials. Over a very short period of time, infants became capable of resolving this form of conflict. We believe this represents a much more general skill of conflict resolution than shown by the ability to dissociate reaching from the line of sight.

Gerstadt, Hong, and Diamond (1994) used a more complex Stroop-like task requiring a verbal response and showed its development between 3.5 and 7 years. For children of this age we introduced an additional complexity to our conflict task. Children were asked to obey the instruction from one source while inhibiting instructions from another (Simon says task). At 42 months children did poorly in the task, but just 4 months later they performed it without apparent difficulty. We believe that the sudden mastery of various forms of conflict resolution marks the development of frontal systems capable of providing priority to the instructed attributes. This admittedly speculative hypothesis about frontal development rests on the developmental results already obtained for visual orienting and the data of Diamond, both of which have established close connections between rapid and systematic behavioral changes and underlying brain maturation. Adult PET and lesion data also suggest that many of these changes involve frontal attentional systems.

Temperament and Self-Regulation

Bell's chapter discusses asymmetries between the right and left hemisphere in relation to infant temperament and affect. The study of affect has benefited greatly from the current emphasis on brain activity, because even more than cognition, the study of affect has had its roots in physiology. PET studies of depression (Drevets et al., 1992) have suggested special importance of dysregulation of amygdala—midfrontal interactions. Apparently, in depression, there is a lack of ability to disengage attention from negative affect. This abnormality is strongest in the left cerebral hemisphere and may relate to the differences in emotional tone between the two hemispheres that Bell discusses.

In our work we have studied self-regulation in infants 4 months of age as visual orienting ability develops, allowing the infant to be distracted from distress (Harman, Rothbart, & Posner, in press). As suggested before, we think of later childhood as an important period in which more general attentional regulation of negative ideation develops. Normal adults who report themselves as low in negative affect also report more highly developed skills of orienting attention (Derryberry & Rothbart, 1988). We believe this is a function of frontal attentional systems that show very substantial development during early childhood. Of course these relationships differ greatly among individuals, as Bell points out. Nonetheless, here once again the study of visual orienting provides us with a way of thinking about complex attentional interactions that may serve to regulate adult emotions.

These four chapters illustrate progress in understanding purely internal mechanisms that control attentional functions. Although we know the most about visual orienting, we need to continue to examine clues that visual orienting mechanisms may provide us about more complex forms of attentional control that develop in childhood, and provide the basis for self-regulation in adults.

REFERENCES

Corbetta, M., Miezin, F. M., Dobmeyer, S., Shulman, G. L., & Petersen, S. E. (1991). Selective and divided attention during visual discrimination of shape, color, and speed: Functional anatomy by positron emission tomography. *Journal of Neuroscience, 11,* 2383–2402.
Corbetta, M., Miezin, F. M., Shulman, G. L., & Petersen, S. E. (1993). A PET study of visuospatial attention. *Journal of Neuroscience, 13,* 1202–1226.

Corbetta, M., Shulman, G. L., Miezin, F. M., & Petersen, S. E. (1995). Superior parietal cortex activation during spatial attention and visual feature conjunction. *Science, 270,* 803–805.

Derryberry, D., & Rothbart, M. K. (1988). Affect, arousal and attention as components of temperament. *Journal of Personality and Social Psychology, 55,* 958–966.

Diamond, A. (Ed.). (1990). Developmental time course in infants and infant monkeys and the neural bases of inhibitory control in reaching. In *The development and neural bases of higher cognitive functions* (pp. 637–676). New York: New York Academy of Sciences Press.

Drevets, W. C., Videen, T. O., Price, J. L., Preskorn, S. H., Carmichael, S. T., & Raichle, M. E. (1992). A functional anatomy of unipolar depression. *Journal of Neuroscience, 12,* 3628–3642.

Egly, R., Driver, J., & Rafal, R. (1994). Shifting visual attention between objects and locations: Normality and pathology. *Journal of Experimental Psychology: General, 123,* 161–177.

Gerardi, G. (1997). *Development of executive attention and self-regulation in the third year of life.* Unpublished doctoral dissertation, University of Oregon.

Gerstadt, C. L., Hong, Y. J., & Diamond, A. (1994). The relationship between cognition and action: Performance of children 3.5 to 7 years old on a stroop-like day-night test. *Cognition, 53,* 129–153.

Harman, C., Rothbart, M. K., & Posner, M. I. (1997). Distress and attention interactions in early infancy. *Motivation and Emotion.*

Luck, S., Hillyard, S. A. Mangun, G. R., & Gazzaniga, M. S. (1994). Independent attentional scanning in the separated hemispheres of split-brain patients. *Journal of Cognitive Neuroscience, 6,* 84–91.

Posner, M. I. (1980). Orienting of attention. The 7th Sir F. C. Bartlett Lecture. *Quarterly Journal of Experimental Psychology, 32,* 3–25.

Posner, M. I. (1988). Structures and functions of selective attention. In T. Boll & B. Bryant (Eds.), *Master lectures in clinical neuropsychology and brain function: Research, measurement, and practice* (pp. 171–202). Washington, DC: American Psychological Association.

Posner, M. I., & Cohen, Y. (1980). Attention and the control of movements. In G. E. Stelmach & J. Requin (Eds.), *Tutorials in motor behavior* (pp. 243–258). Amsterdam: North Holland.

Posner, M. I., Rothbart, M. K., Thomas-Thrapp, L., & Gerardi, G. (in press). Development of orienting to locations and objects. In R. Wright (Ed.), *Visual attention* (pp.). New York: Oxford University Press.

Rovee Collier, C., Bhatt, R. S., & Chazin, S. (1996). Set size, novelty and visual pop-out in infancy. *Journal of Experimental Psychology: Human Perception and Performance, 22,* 1178–1187.

Ruff, H. A., & Rothbart, M. K. (1996). *Attention in early development.* New York: Oxford University Press.

Smith, E. E., & Jonides, J. J. (1994). Working memory in humans: Neuropsychological evidence. In M. S. Gazzaniga (Ed.), *The cognitive neurosciences* (pp. 1009–1020). Cambridge, MA: MIT Press.

Part III

ATTENTION, MEMORY, AND LIFE-SPAN CHANGES

A Cognitive Neuroscience Perspective on the Relation Between Attention and Memory Development

Charles A. Nelson
Dianne Dukette
University of Minnesota

Although both attentional and memorial abilities undergo dramatic development during the first year of postnatal life (see Nelson, 1995, 1997; Ruff & Rothbart, 1996), significant improvements in both domains continue through childhood. With regard to attention, for example, the more volitional aspects of attention, such as spontaneous alternation, vigilance, selective attention, and sustained attention, begin to appear during the second half of the first year of life and continue to mature well into the school age period (Enns, 1990; Enns & Cameron, 1987; Johnson, 1990; Johnson, Posner, & Rothbart, 1991; Lane & Pearson, 1982; Ruff & Rothbart, 1996). These systems appear to rely primarily on frontal, prefrontal, and limbic circuitry. Coincidentally, these same brain areas (particularly prefrontal and limbic) have also been implicated in memory development. It is not surprising, therefore, that although memory improves significantly during the first 1–2 postnatal years, continued improvement is observed through the middle childhood years.

In the developmental literature, attention and memory have most often been studied as independent functions, and we do not depart from this precedent in the work we discuss in this chapter. This is unfortunate, as not only do these functions mutually service one another, but they also share neural substrate. As work in this volume demonstrates, however, although attention can be studied in the absence of memory, it is far more difficult to study memory in the absence of attention. This is certainly reflected in our work, which has historically focused on memory. We offer these observations, as they bear directly on the content of our chapter.

We begin with a review of the neural bases of memory development. Included in this review is discussion of the event-related potential studies we have conducted on memory with infants and children; highlighted are those studies from which some conclusions can be drawn about attention. We then turn to the literature on attentional development. This is not our main area of expertise, and because this work is so competently reviewed elsewhere in the volume, we focus our review narrowly. We begin with an exposition of the neural bases of attention (focusing most on the network that subserves visual selective attention), and then turn to a discussion of our own recent efforts on studying attention in infants and young children using event-related potentials. We conclude with an integrative summary and some recommendations for future work.

WHAT DO WE MEAN BY "MEMORY"?

A prominent doctrine of many contemporary memory theorists is that memory is not a unitary trait. Rather, two "types" of memory have been proposed: explicit (or declarative) memory, and implicit memory. Explicit memory is typically thought of as memory that can be declared, about which one is consciously aware, and that can be brought to mind as an image or proposition. It is also a type of memory that can occur quickly, perhaps in as little as one trial in an experimental paradigm (e.g., a single exposure to a visual stimulus is sufficient for the subject to recall or recognize this stimulus at a later point in time). Examples include what has traditionally been called recall memory, as well as recognition memory (for discussion, see Squire, 1986, 1987; Tulving, 1985). Implicit memory, in contrast, reflects a constellation of abilities that have in common the *lack* of conscious awareness, which may require multiple trials in order for memory to occur. Thus, skilled motor learning (e.g., mirror tracing) is an example of implicit memory, as is procedural learning, perceptual priming, and conditioning (for discussion, see Schacter, 1987).

Needless to say, what differentiates explicit from implicit memory is not always well defined, and some have argued that what masks for different types of memory are really different underlying processes (see Roediger, 1990; Roediger, Rajaram, & Srinivas, 1990). For example, in a serial reaction time (SRT) task, a subject must push a button that corresponds to the position of a particular light. A pattern is eventually formed by each successive light, and the extent to which the subject has learned the pattern is inferred from increasingly shorter reaction times to push each button. Although this task is assumed to be learned "unconsciously," some subjects are, in fact, aware of the emerging pattern, and may perhaps be using strategies to acquire this knowledge. Our point is that the boundary between implicit and explicit memory is not always clear cut.

Neuroscientists have also examined the division between types of memory using a variety of approaches, such as inducing lesions in experimental animals or conducting neuroimaging studies (e.g., Positron Emission Tomography, or PET; functional Magnetic Resonance Imaging, or fMRI) with healthy human adults, and adults with circumscribed brain damage. It is now believed, for example, that all forms of explicit memory depend on structures that lie in the medial temporal lobe and surrounding cortex, such as the hippocampus and entorhinal cortex. It is also known that implicit memory does not rely on these structures, although which structures subserve implicit memory depend on the type of implicit memory being evaluated. For example, visual priming likely depends on areas of the visual cortex, auditory priming depends on the auditory cortex, some forms of conditioning rely on the cerebellum, and so forth.

Collectively, the proposition that there are different types of memory that are subserved by different neural systems has received support from both cognitive psychologists and neuroscientists. Unfortunately, knowledge of the *development* of these memory systems remains an enigma: We know much about behavioral development, but little about the neural bases of development. In the next section we review current thinking on this subject.

NEURAL BASES OF MEMORY DEVELOPMENT

Although many of the procedures used to evaluate memory in the adult can easily be adopted with verbal children, surprisingly little is known about implicit memory development (for review, see Thomas, 1996). Far more is known about explicit memory, although much of this work has been confined to the nonhuman primate (e.g., Bachevalier, 1990, 1992; Webster, Bachevalier, & Ungerleider, 1995), and only recently, to the human infant and child (for reviews, see Janowski, 1993; Johnson, 1997; Nelson, 1995, 1996, 1997). Focusing specifically on the infancy period, one of us (Nelson, 1995, 1997) has presented a model of the neural bases of memory. This model is summarized next.

Citing work with both nonhuman primates and adult humans with focal brain damage, Nelson proposed that a number of tasks used with infants can be interpreted as reflecting the adult equivalent of explicit memory. Such tasks include cross-modal recognition memory; visual recognition memory, when delays are imposed between familiarization and test; delayed nonmatch to sample; and possibly deferred imitation. The basis for this claim is indirect, as with the exception of work with event-related potentials (ERPs), there have been few direct studies of brain function in the infant. Rather, a number of "infant" paradigms (those listed earlier) have been adopted for use with either the monkey or the adult with focal lesions.

Thus, monkeys with bilateral lesions of the hippocampus and surrounding cortex (see Webster et al., 1995, for discussion) or human adults with comparable lesions (see McKee & Squire, 1993) fail to show novelty preferences in the visual paired comparison task of recognition memory with even very short delays. Adults with these same lesions also do poorly on deferred imitation tasks (McDonough, Mandler, McKee, & Squire, 1995). Similarly, monkeys with bilateral lesions of medial temporal lobe structures perform poorly on the delayed nonmatch to sample task (e.g., Bachevalier & Mishkin, 1984). Finally, it is not until 8–12 months that human infants begin to perform well on tasks of cross-modal recognition memory (see Rose & Ruff, 1989) and deferred imitation (see Bauer, Hertsgaard, & Dow, 1994; Meltzoff, 1995). Assuming that both the monkey and human adult approach these "infant" tasks the same way as do human infants, it appears, then, that human infants are capable of what would be called "explicit" memory. This claim is bolstered by the fact that many of the structures that lie in the medial temporal lobe that are thought to subserve explicit memory do, in fact, develop over the first year of life (see Nelson, 1997, for review).

However, the observations that adult-like tasks of explicit memory are successfully negotiated by young infants and that the medial temporal lobe structures that support explicit memory develop over the first year does not necessarily mean that infants are capable of explicit qua explicit memory. Nelson argues that there may be a form of *pre*-explicit memory that depends critically on the hippocampus, but not surrounding cortex and/or adjacent (e.g., area TE), that is in place shortly after birth. This form permits simple novelty detection and provides for the ability to tolerate short delays, and still allow discrimination of a novel from familiar stimulus. However, it will require further maturation of the hippocampus (particularly the dentate region) and more importantly, the surrounding cortex, in order for more adult-like forms of explicit memory to develop. Thus, it is not until later in the first year that infants are able to distinguish novel information from familiar information that is presented infrequently (Nelson & Collins, 1991, 1992); that they can negotiate a cross-modal recognition memory task (Nelson, Henschel, & Collins, 1993); and that they can show evidence of deferred imitation (see Bauer, Hertsgaard, & Dow, 1994; Meltzoff, 1995). Nelson proposed that these more adult-like forms of explicit memory make their appearance closer to 1 year of age, although tremendous development follows. What is responsible for the changes after 1 year likely include further development of the dentate and perhaps most critically, of the surrounding temporal cortex (e.g., area TE). In addition, consistent with current views of memory development in children (see Kail, 1990, for review), it may not be memory capacity that changes during the preschool and elementary school years as much as the strategies one employs in order to remember increasingly complex material. Although no support was provided, Nelson (1995, 1997) speculated that the use of strategies may depend on the emergence of executive functions subserved by the prefrontal cortex, a cognitive landmark that does not begin until the preschool years (for recent findings on the functional emergence of this area of the brain, see Luciana & Nelson, in press).

Collectively, a form of explicit memory (referred to as "preexplicit") makes its appearance during the first 6–9 months of life, which is gradually supplanted by a more adult-like form of explicit memory as infants approach their first birthday. However, there is continued refinement through the preschool years, due in part to development in regions of the hippocampal formation and the inferior temporal cortex, and in part to the development of the prefrontal structures that support the use of strategies.

EVENT-RELATED POTENTIAL STUDIES OF MEMORY WITH IMPLICATIONS FOR ATTENTION

The model just described has not been exhaustively evaluated, due in part to the paucity of measures currently available for examining structure–function relations in young children. A few approximations have been made, however, using event-related potentials (ERPs). These studies are reviewed next.

Most ERP studies with infants use a variant of the oddball paradigm traditionally used with adults. In the case of the infant, a series of high- and low-probability events is presented, with the former assumed to be more familiar (due to their more frequent occurrence) than the latter. In our lab, we have modified this procedure further by first familiarizing infants to one stimulus, and then presenting an interlace of flashed presentations of the familiar stimulus and a novel stimulus (for review, see Nelson, 1994).

In either paradigm (that is, with and without a familiarization period), a concern with presenting high- and low-probability events is that the subject could respond to the low-probability event because of some proclivity to respond to a stimulus that is presented infrequently, not necessarily because it is novel. Of course, the same could be said for the most commonly used behavioral methods of evaluating visual recognition memory in infants, the habituation and paired-comparison procedures. Here infants are preexposed to one event (for a relatively lengthy period of time), and then later tested on their recognition of that event and a novel event. Infants might respond to the latter because it is novel *or* because it is seen so infrequently (relative to the familiar stimulus). There is, then, a potential confound between probability of occurrence and novelty: by default, novel stimuli are also infrequent stimuli.

To disentangle the frequency with which events are presented from whether such events are familiar or novel, we conducted a series of studies, first with children, then with infants. In the child study (Nelson & Nugent, 1990), 4- to 6-year-old subjects were presented with an interlace of two different facial expressions (happy and fear) posed by the same model. In Condition 1 subjects were told to attend to the rare event (presented 20% of the time); in Condition 2 they were told to attend to the frequent event (presented 80% of the time). Which expression served as rare or frequent was counterbalanced across subjects. As predicted, subjects in Condition 1 evinced a prominent P300 response to the rare, target event. As for Condition 2, it was predicted that subjects would also show a P300 to the target event, but of smaller amplitude due to its more frequent occurrence. What was actually observed, however, was a prominent P300 to the rare, *nontarget* event, despite having overtly attended to the frequent, target event. These results suggested that children as "old" as 4–6 years are sensitive to event probability.

In our infant studies we could not, of course, issue verbal instructions. In addition, we were interested in teasing apart probability information from both novelty and familiarity information. This was accomplished using the following design: Infants were first presented with two, alternating faces (50% probability each), for a total of 20 trials. We assumed that this would result in equal familiarization, a prediction that was confirmed when the familiarization data were examined (i.e., the ERP response to both events was the same). Immediately following the test period, infants were presented with three types of events. On 60% of the trials, one of the familiar faces was presented ("frequent-familiar"). On a random 20% of the trials, the other familiar face was presented ("infrequent-familiar"). Finally, on *each* of the remaining 20% of the trials a different face was presented ("infrequent-novel"). In one study we tested 6-month-old infants (Nelson & Collins, 1991) and in another 4- and 8-month-old infants (Nelson & Collins, 1992). If infants were able to dissociate probability information from whether a stimulus was novel or familiar, then during the test trials they should respond identically to both familiar stimuli (and in theory, the response to these events should be equivalent to their response to the same event presented as a familiarization stimulus). This response, in turn, should differ from that of the novel event. Although this pattern was, in fact, obtained for the 8-month-olds tested, it was not for the two younger groups. At 4 months the response to all three events was sufficiently ambiguous that no clear conclusions could be drawn. At 6 months infants responded to the frequent-familiar event as predicted: a negative peak we associate with obligatory attention (see Fig. 11.1; this is discussed in more detail in a subsequent section of this chapter). Their response to the infrequent-familiar event, however, took the form of a positive slow wave

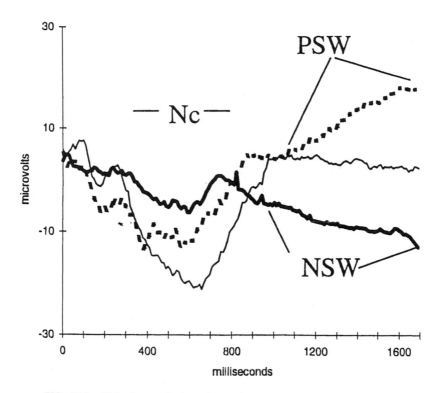

FIG. 11.1. This figure depicts the major components that have been observed in the infant ERP waveform. The negative component (labeled "Nc"), thought to reflect an obligatory aspect of attention, can be seen most clearly in the thin, solid line, peaking between 400 and 800 ms after stimulus onset. As depicted by this same curve (thin, solid line), this negative peak resolves to baseline. This baseline response is thought to reflect a fully encoded stimulus. In contrast, if the stimulus is partially encoded into memory, but must be updated, the negative peak shifts positive, and becomes a positive slow wave (labeled "PSW"). This is illustrated by the dashed line. Finally, if the infant attends to the stimulus, but merely detects its presence against a background of recurring other events, the negative peak shifts further negative, manifesting itself in a negative slow wave (labeled "NSW"). This is reflected by the thick, solid line. From Nelson (1996). Electrophysiological correlates of memory development in the first year of life. In H. W. Reese & M. D. Franzen (Eds.), *Thirteenth West Virginia University Conference on Life-Span Developmental Psychology: Biological and Neuropsychological Mechanisms.* Mahwah, NJ: Lawrence Erlbaum Associates. Reprinted by permission.

that we associate with the updating of working memory (see Fig. 11.1). It was as though infants had some recognition of having seen this event before, but were not completely certain. Finally, the response to the infrequent-novel events took the form of a negative slow wave, a response we interpret as novelty detection (see Fig. 11.1). It was as though infants responded both to how often events were presented *and* to whether they were novel or familiar. As stated earlier, it was only at 8 months that infants responded equivalently to the two classes of familiar events, discriminating those from the novel class.

These results, then, suggest that novelty reactions may to some extent be obligatory or reflexive; to infants below approximately 8 months, an infrequently presented stimulus can, under some conditions, be mistaken for a novel stimulus. It may only be after this age that responses to novelty come under voluntary control.

A second way we have approached the question of ERP correlates of explicit memory is to examine the scalp topography and morphology of the ERP waveform, and to conduct experiments that permit one to infer what neural systems should be required to perform the task (see Bell, chap. 9, this volume, for an example of this approach in the context of the EEG and attention). With regard to the former, we have consistently observed that a positive slow wave with a latency of 800 to 1,500 ms, and a central-frontal scalp maximum, appears to reflect the updating of memory for a partially encoded stimulus (see Fig. 11.1). If we assume further that this type of memory (visual recognition memory) is mediated by structures that lie in the medial temporal lobe, then it seems reasonable to suggest that the source of this positive slow wave is the medial temporal lobe.[1]

With regard to inferring neural systems from well-designed experiments, we attempt to design studies that are logically tight; that is, that permit us to be specific about the type of process or ability that is evaluated. If comparable studies have been done with animals or adult humans with known lesions, we can also attempt to link the processes or ability in question with underlying neural sources.

An illustration of this approach is reflected in work we have done on cross-modal recognition memory. Here a subject is presented with a stimulus in one sense modality (e.g., he or she is allowed to feel or manually manipulate the object without benefit of seeing it). Following some famili-

---

[1]It must be noted that inferring the source or sources of scalp-recorded ERPs is challenging at best, and at worst may be untenable without extensive scalp coverage. Essentially one must solve the "inverse problem" of attempting to work backwards from the actual scalp according to its underlying neural generator. Given that ERPs conduct through extracellular space, and must pass through layers of high impedance material (neuropil, pia, dura, skull, skin, hair), solving this problem can be problematic. Although as we, and other groups (e.g., M. Johnson, personal communication) move toward electrode montages that provide for greater scalp coverage and thus improved ability to triangulate sources, we must be content with performing well-designed studies that tap known sources; thus, a form of memory that depends on the rhinal cortex, or a form of attention that depends on the right posterior parietal lobe. By manipulating waveforms using such experimental conditions, we may be able to draw inferences about underlying sources, although additional information will ultimately be required to validate such inferences (e.g., such as cross-registration of ERPs with MRI).

arization period, the subject is presented with the same and a different object in a different sense modality (e.g., pictures of the object they felt, and a novel object). We know from work with monkeys that lesions of the amygdala impair cross-modal recognition memory (Murray & Mishkin, 1985), although more recently the suggestion has been made that the amygdala may facilitate stimulus–stimulus associations generally, not just cross-modal associations (see Murray & Gaffan, 1994). We also know that recognition memory in general is mediated by structures that lie in the medial temporal lobe, including the hippocampus. From an ERP perspective, if the subject has been able to transfer from one sense modality (touch) to another (vision) the representation of the familiar object, the ERP response to that object should take the form of the baseline response we have come to associate with well-encoded events (see Fig. 11.1). In contrast, the novel stimulus can be responded to one of two ways: If it has been presented often enough (e.g., 50% of the trials) so that infants begin to remember it, the ERP should take the form of a positive slow wave indicative of memory updating for a partially encoded stimulus (see Fig. 11.1). Alternatively, if it was presented rarely, such that no memory consolidation occurred, the novel stimulus should invoke a negative slow wave, indicative of novelty detection.

We (Nelson et al., 1993) conducted a study similar to this with 8-month-old infants. Infants were allowed to manipulate a small block fashioned into a certain shape. They felt the object for 60 seconds but were never allowed to see it. Shortly thereafter (a delay of 1–2 minutes) they were presented with alternating pictures of the object they felt, and a novel object (with equal probabilities). Consistent with our predictions, the ERP response to the familiar object took the form of a baseline response. In contrast, the picture of the novel object invoked a positive slow wave, indicative of memory updating for a partially encoded stimulus. This positive slow wave had the same morphology, latency, and scalp topography we have observed in our visual recognition memory work. In addition, pilot work with 6-month-old healthy infants and 8-month-old premature infants (uncorrected for prematurity; Richards, Thomas, Georgieff, & Nelson, 1994) have failed to observe differences between the novel and familiar objects. Collectively, these results suggest that (a) it is not until 8 months that infants show ERP evidence of cross-modal recognition memory (which is consistent with the behavioral literature on this subject; see Rose & Ruff, 1989), and (b) the positive slow wave invoked by the novel stimulus reflects a form of memory mediated by the medial temporal lobe, and as such, (c) the positive slow wave may have been generated by those structures.

Overall, although indirect, our ERP studies are in line with the proposal that adult-like forms of explicit memory do not come on line until the second half of the first year of life.

INTERSECTION OF ATTENTION AND MEMORY

Studies With Infants

As stated at the outset of this chapter, much of the work on infant memory has confounded memory with attention. Our work is certainly no exception to that. Recently, however, we have begun to perform experiments that at least increase the demands on attention, and minimize the demands on memory. It is this work we discuss next.

Before describing our studies, it is important to define a component of the ERP that has been observed primarily in children, and has been interpreted by a number of authors as reflecting some aspect of attention. Under a variety of task conditions a negative component (central-frontal scalp maximum) peaking at around 400 ms has consistently been observed to both target and nontarget events (labeled "Nc" by Courchesne, 1978; also see Friedman, Sutton, Putnam, Brown, & Erlenmeyer-Kimling, 1988; Kestenbaum & Nelson, 1992; Kok & Rooijakkers, 1985; Nelson & Nugent, 1990). Although a consensus has not been reached on the functional significance of this component, most investigators agree that it reflects the commitment of attentional resources.

Courchesne, Ganz, and Norcia have also observed an Nc component in 6-month-old infants. Unlike the latency of the child Nc, the infant Nc had a latency of approximately 700 to 800 ms, although like the child component the infant Nc did have a central-frontal scalp maximum. Other investigators have also observed this component in infants (e.g., Karrer & Ackles, 1987, 1988).

In our studies we have also observed this component very reliably. We have found that this component has a central-frontal scalp distribution and a latency of approximately 700 ms at 6 months, gradually shortening to 400–500 ms at 1 year (see Fig. 11.2).

In our standard memory studies (e.g., Nelson & Collins, 1991, 1992; Nelson & Salapatek, 1986; see Nelson, 1994, for review), this component appears not to distinguish between novel and familiar stimuli; that is, the Nc is not larger to the infrequent or novel stimulus as Karrer and Ackles (1987, 1988) have observed. Recently, however, we have found that this component *does* reliably distinguish stimuli that are highly familiar to the infant: the mother's face or certain facial expressions.

Attention to Facial Expressions

Building on a series of behavioral studies examining infants' discrimination and categorization of facial expressions, in which it has been observed that infants "prefer" to look at fearful faces relative to happy faces (as inferred by longer looking times), Nelson and de Haan (1996) conducted two

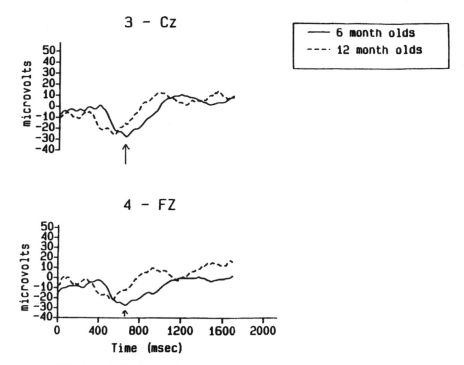

FIG. 11.2. This figure displays the prominent negative peak described in the text (and labeled "Nc" in Fig. 11.1), thought to reflect an obligatory attentional response. The ERP pattern displayed in this figure was invoked by presenting infants with the same face for a total of 20 times. This peak (seen as a downwards deflection) occurs at approximately 750 ms at 6 months (solid line) and 500 ms at 12 months (dashed line). From Nelson (1996). Electrophysiological correlates of memory development in the first year of life. In H. W. Reese & M. D. Franzen (Eds.), *Thirteenth West Virginia University Conference on Life-Span Developmental Psychology: Biological and Neuropsychological Mechanisms.* Mahwah, NJ: Lawrence Erlbaum Associates. Reprinted by permission.

experiments with 7-month-olds. To parallel behavioral preference studies (e.g., Nelson & Dolgin, 1985), infants in Experiment 1 were presented with alternating pictures of one model posing happy, and a second model posing fear. To control for the possibility that responses to happy and fear could be influenced less by these discrete emotions per se than by choosing emotions that come from very different categories of affect (positive vs. negative), infants in Experiment 2 were presented with alternating pictures of fear and anger (both negative emotions). Based on previous observations that infants evince looking preferences for fear over happy, and that the midlatency negative component ("Nc") is sensitive to the allocation of attentional resources, it was predicted that fear would invoke a greater amplitude negative component as contrasted to happy (Experiment 1). It was additionally expected that no such differences would obtain to fear and anger (Experiment 2) because infants would distribute their attention equally between these two expressions.

The results of this study were largely in line with the predictions. In Experiment 1, infants evinced a larger negative component to fear than to happy (see Fig. 11.3, lead T4 in particular). However, an unexpected finding was that following this negative component, infants also showed a more pronounced positive component (positive slow wave, or PSW; see Fig. 11.1) to happy relative to fear (see Fig. 11.3). In previous research

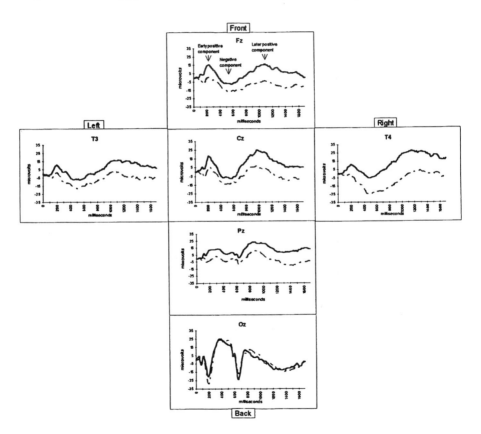

FIG. 11.3. Here infants were presented with alternating pictures (500 ms each) of a happy face and a fearful face, posed by the same model. The data displayed are grand averages ($n = 19$) for happy (solid line) and fearful (dashed line) faces. The center plots represent the midline leads moving in an anterior (Fz) to posterior (Oz) direction. The left (T3) and right (T4) temporal leads are displayed on the outside. From Nelson and de Haan (1996). Neural correlates of infants' visual responsiveness to facial expressions of emotion. *Developmental Psychobiology, 29*, 577–595. Reproduced with permission of John Wiley & Sons.

this PSW has been interpreted as a reflection of memory updating for a partially familiar stimulus. Thus, these results suggested that infants showed partial recognition of happy and none for fear. Finally, there were no ERP differences observed to fear and anger, suggesting that attentional resources were distributed equally between these expressions, and that neither was recognized as familiar.

These results revealed that the midlatency negative component can, under some circumstances, be manipulated by attentional load, but perhaps only when infants are presented with stimuli with which they are at least partially familiar (due to exposure to such events in the natural environment). To examine this hypothesis further, we next consider another study in which the familiarity of the stimuli was controlled.

Attention to Facial Features Other Than Expressions

de Haan and Nelson (1997) conducted a series of studies with 6-month-old infants designed to examine recognition of the mother's face. In two experiments, the mother's face was contrasted with that of a stranger who looked either dissimilar to the mother (Experiment 1) or similar to the mother (Experiment 3). In two additional experiments, infants were presented with two different strangers' faces. In one case these strangers were judged to be dissimilar looking (Experiment 2) or similar looking (Experiment 4). Across all four experiments, infants were presented with alternating digitized images of the two faces presented on a computer monitor while ERPs were recorded from a total of 10 electrodes. Similar to what was predicted in the Nelson and de Haan (1996) study on facial expressions, it was predicted that the midlatency negative component would be sensitive to attentional load. Thus, this component should be larger to mother vs. stranger, and not differ to stranger vs. stranger.

What was observed was slightly more complicated than the predictions. When infants were presented with the mother and a dissimilar looking stranger (Experiment 1), the negative component was, in fact, larger to mother vs. stranger (see Fig. 11.4, in particular, lead Cz and T4). The pattern was reversed when the stranger was similar looking to the mother (Experiment 3; see Fig. 11.5, in particular, lead Pz at 700–800 ms). Note, however, that a critical difference between these experiments was the scalp topography of these differences. In Experiment 1 the negative component was maximal at midline scalp lead Cz (consistent with previous studies) and at right anterior temporal scalp lead T4. In Experiment 3, this component was maximal at posterior midline scalp lead Pz. Thus, it was not only the amplitude of this component that distinguished between mother and stranger but also the scalp topography. As predicted, there were no ERP differences to the two strangers, be they dissimilar looking (Experiment 2) or similar looking (Experiment 4).

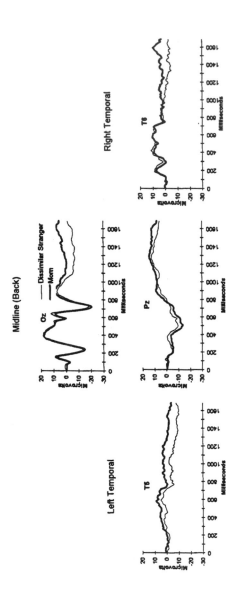

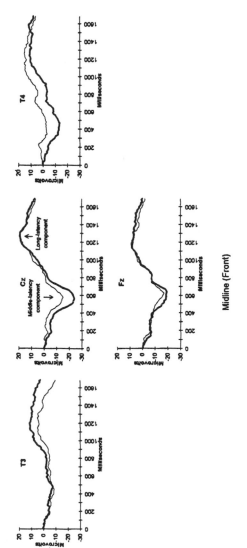

FIG. 11.4. Infants ($n = 22$) were presented with alternating pictures (500 ms presentations) of the mother's face (thick solid line) and a dissimilar-looking stranger's face (thin solid line). The center plots represent the midline electrodes from anterior (Fz) to posterior (Oz) and the outside plots represent the left (T3, T5) and right (T4, T6) temporal electrodes. From de Haan, M., & Nelson, C. A. (in press). Recognition of the mother's face by 6-month-old infants: A neurobehavioral study. *Child Development*. Reproduced by permission of University of Chicago Press.

341

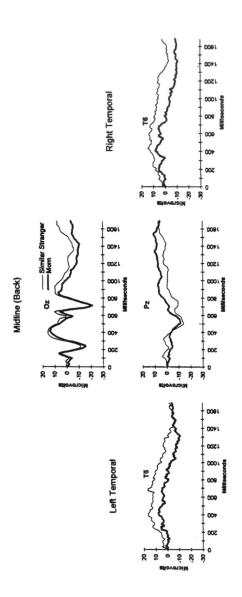

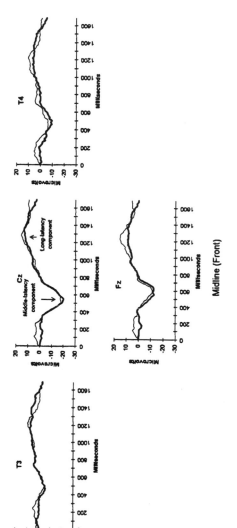

FIG. 11.5. Infants ($n = 22$) were presented with alternating pictures (500 ms presentations) of the mother's face (thick solid line) and a similar-looking stranger's face (thin solid line). The center plots represent the midline electrodes from anterior (Fz) to posterior (Oz) and the outside plots represent the left (T3, T5) and right (T4, T6) temporal electrodes. From de Haan, M., & Nelson, C. A. (in press). Recognition of the mother's face by 6-month-old infants: A neurobehavioral study. *Child Development.* Reproduced by permission of University of Chicago Press.

343

These results are partially consistent with those observed in our facial expression study. Specifically, the amplitude of the negative component was found to vary with how attention was distributed among different stimuli. When infants were presented with pictures of their mother and a stranger who looked very different than the mother, the characteristic negative component thought to reflect the allocation of attention was larger to the mother than to the stranger. However, when the task was made more difficult, as when the mother was contrasted to a stranger judged to be similar looking to mother, then the negative component was larger to the stranger. The scalp distribution in this case differed than in the former case, suggesting that a different neural network was activated. These topographic differences notwithstanding, the finding from Experiment 3 suggests that as task difficulty increases, infants attend to the more novel event. (In Experiment 1, infants showed greater amplitudes to the mother not because she was novel, but because the task was relatively easy, thus permitting infants to focus their attention on the appetitively motivating stimulus.) This interpretation is consistent with the results of the two stranger–stranger experiments (Experiments 2 and 4), in which both stimuli were equally novel. Finally, they are also consistent with what we observed in our facial expression study, in which the negative component was larger to fear than to happy.

Collectively, the results of our work with facial expressions and highly familiar faces (i.e., mother's face) depart from our previous work using unfamiliar faces. Here we have observed that the negative component thought to reflect attention allocation covaries with degree of familiarity, with infants showing larger negative components to nonfamiliar (novel) faces. This general pattern of results is also consistent with what we have observed in children presented with facial expressions of emotion, a topic to which we next turn our attention.

STUDIES WITH CHILDREN

Attention to Facial Expressions

As discussed in an earlier section, Nelson and Nugent (1990) presented 4- to 6-year-old children with happy and fearful expressions posed by strangers in order to study the P300 response. Recall that in Experiment 1 one of these expressions served as target and was presented on a random 20% of the trials, whereas the other expression served as nontarget and was presented on 80% of the trials (the design was counterbalanced). In Experiment 2 these same expressions were also presented, except children were now instructed to attend to the high-probability event instead of the low-probability event. Consistent with the extant ERP literature on the development of the P300, in Experiment 1 children evinced a P300 (latency

= approximately 800 ms, Pz/Cz maximum) to the target (low probability) event, independent of expression (i.e., there was only a main effect of condition). A negative component with a latency of approximately 400 ms (labeled N400) was also observed. Interestingly, this component was larger to angry when angry was the target event, and was also larger to angry when angry was the *nontarget event*. Thus, although the P300 data suggested that children were following the instructions to attend to the low-probability event, they were also devoting more attention to the negative emotion.

The results of this study are intriguing, for two reasons. First, consistent with our infant studies, it appears that the negative component is sensitive to certain facial expressions; specifically, in the case of infants, fear results in a larger amplitude negative component (when contrasted with happy), and in the case of children, anger results in a larger amplitude negative component (when contrasted with happy). Second, when task demands are greatly increased by asking children to attend to a high-probability event, the task becomes virtually impossible, with children—perhaps involuntarily—drawn to the low-probability event. Under these conditions, attention is drawn most to the rare event, with few resources left to be allocated to emotion.

Summary

Overall, these results complement those from our studies with infants, revealing that across the first 6 years of life, children are drawn to infrequently presented events, and to novel events. Although the PSW in infants, and the P300 in children seems to be manipulated by memory load, the midlatency negative component (latency = 500–700 ms in 6–12-month-old infants and 400 ms in children) appears to be manipulated by attentional demands. This conclusion opens the door to asking why it is in our studies of memory (using unfamiliar events) the negative component rarely discriminated among different classes of stimuli (although the component itself was always present). Infants may allocate their cognitive resources according to the demands of the task. If the task is one of memory, particularly when the stimuli are unfamiliar, then the negative component is invoked involuntarily, freeing up resources to be devoted to the memory demands of the task. In contrast, if the task makes fewer demands on memory, such as when familiar stimuli are presented (e.g., mother's face, certain facial expressions) or the task reflects simple preferences (choice of two stimuli presented equally often), then resources are allocated towards attentional load. Needless to say, these conclusions should be considered speculative, given how little research has been conducted to address this question directly.

Thus far we have discussed our own research that pertains to attention, even though most of the work reviewed often confounded attention and memory. In the next section, we turn to studies of attentional development that have attempted to disentangle attention and memory. We begin with a brief exposition on the neural basis of attention, and then turn to work by ourselves and others in which ERPs have been used to study attention in children.

NEURAL BASES OF ATTENTION

Depending on the context, attention can mean many things: moving one's eyes toward a new sound or object in the environment, searching for a particular object in space, concentrating on a single task over time, or staying alert to detect a specific event or change.

We describe three distinct networks in the attentional system—orienting, vigilance, and selection—and we concentrate on visual selective attention. Although each network consists of a unique group of brain subsystems, they are not entirely independent and may interact in the deployment of attention.

Much work has been done in the area of covert orienting to visual locations. As discussed by others in this volume (see Rafal, chap. 6; Hood et al., chap. 7), this attentional process is analogous to training a "spotlight" on a particular location in space so that objects or events in the spotlight are highlighted (Posner, 1980; Triesman & Gelade, 1980). This type of orienting occurs in the absence of eye movements, hence the designation "covert." In an extensive series of behavioral, PET, and lesion studies of normal adults and neurological patients, Posner and colleagues (Peterson, Fox, Posner, Mintun, & Raichle, 1988; Posner, 1988; Posner et al., 1984; Posner & Peterson, 1990) have provided a description of the neural network responsible for orienting to spatial location (see chap. 9 by Bell, this volume, for additional detail on Posner's model). This covert orienting network is also referred to as the posterior attentional system. Posner describes three primary functional components of this network: disengaging attention from the present focus, moving attention to the target, and selectively attending to the target. Three areas, the posterior parietal cortex, the superior colliculus and surrounding midbrain, and the pulvinar nucleus of the thalamus, each seems to carry out one of these distinct operations. The posterior parietal lobe plays a critical role in the ability to disengage from the present attentional focus. Damage to the superior colliculus interferes with shifting attention to the target, and the pulvinar nucleus of the thalamus restricts sensory input to the attended target area. This network is active under conditions of both involuntary and voluntary attentional orienting.

ERP studies of adults have demonstrated that the early sensory-evoked potentials, P100 and N100, are larger in response to valid versus invalid target cues in Posner's behavioral paradigm (Harter, Miller, Price, LaLonde, & Keyes, 1989; Mangun & Hillyard, 1991). These findings suggest that the attentional orienting network has an effect early in the processing stream, at the point of extrastriate cortex (upstream from area V1).

Less is known about the two other networks of brain areas thought to carry out the attentional functions of vigilance and of selection. The vigilance network acts on attention to enhance the speed of target detection. For example, when carrying out a long and tedious task such as monitoring radar screens for enemy planes, there is evidence that target detection is faster if one remains "alert." Right frontal and parietal brain areas appear to be part of this vigilance network (Posner, 1995).

VISUAL SELECTIVE ATTENTION

Our ability to attend to a specific object or spatial location in our environment while ignoring others is a basic skill that underlies and makes possible most other cognitive functions such as learning, memory, and language. This attentional selection is usually jointly determined by the external environment and the organism's goals (Maunsell, 1995; Posner, 1995) and is thought to act on visual input as early in the processing stream as the extrastriate cortex (Heinze, et al., 1994; Moran & Desimone, 1985). It is at the extrastriate cortex that sensory processing divides into two streams, temporal (ventral) and parietal (dorsal). Although these streams are not completely independent, areas in the temporal pathway are specialized for object recognition and identification, whereas those in the parietal pathway are primarily involved in the analysis of motion and spatial relations (Ungerleider & Mishkin, 1982). Single cell recordings of neurons in the cortex of behaving nonhuman primates have shown that the animal's attentional focus impacts on neuronal firing patterns in both temporal and parietal processing streams (Maunsell, 1995). These so-called state-dependent modulations serve to enhance the visual information that is important to the animal at the time. In the temporal pathway neuronal responses in inferotemporal cortex (IT) are stronger to stimuli or stimulus features that are the target of the animal's attention (Richmond & Sato, 1987; Spitzer & Richmond, 1991). Similarly, in the parietal processing stream, the responses of many neurons increase when a stimulus is the target of an eye movement or a hand movement (Barash, Bracewell, Fogassi, Gnadt, & Anderson, 1991; Bushnell, Goldberg, & Robinson, 1981).

The primary brain areas participating in the selective attention network are dorsolateral prefrontal cortex (DLPC), anterior cingulate cortex, the pulvinar nucleus of the thalamus, and the posterior parietal cortex (PPC). The anterior cingulate, located in the medial ventral area of the frontal lobe, is part of the limbic association cortex. It consists of alternating bands of neurons with reciprocal connections to DLPC and PPC and has been found to be active in tasks involving language and visual target detection (Goldman-Rakic, 1988). It is therefore thought to serve an integrative function between spatial information in the PPC and semantic processing in the lateral frontal cortex. There are numerous direct connections between DLPC and PPC as well (see Fig. 11.6). It has also been suggested that DLPC may serve an executive function in activating and controlling the posterior orienting network (via the PPC) (Peterson et al., 1988). The pulvinar, DLPC, and PPC also appear to form a triangulated circuit within this network. There are reciprocal connections between the pulvinar and DLPC and between the pulvinar and PPC. It is likely that PPC provides input, via the pulvinar, to DLPC concerning target location within the selective attention network.

Development of the Visual Selective Attention Network

Efforts have been made to describe patterns of synaptogenesis, synapse elimination, axonal myelination, and glucose metabolism within different subcortical and cortical brain regions during development. It is thought that comparison in the timing of these processes across areas may provide insight into the maturational sequence of regions and networks in the human brain. Although these measures have provided provocative data, relatively little is known about the developmental time courses within and between specific cortical regions. We briefly discuss the available information on the maturation of the brain areas that subserve visual selective attention.

Generally the phylogenetically older brain structures mature earlier in development than does the newer neocortex. For example, the pulvinar nucleus of the thalamus is the first structure in the visual selective attention network to mature. Within the neocortex the frontal lobe, in general, is late in maturation, relative to other cortical areas. Evidence for this comes from several converging lines of investigation with humans. First, synaptic elimination begins late, at about 7 years of age and continues to adolescence. This is in contrast to the visual cortical area in which synapse reduction begins at about 10 months and continues to approximately age 6 (Huttenlocher, 1979, 1990, 1994). Second, myelination in frontal cortex is also late, possibly continuing into the second decade of life (Jernigan, Trauner, Hesselink, & Tallal, 1991; Yakovlev & LeCours, 1967). Third, in terms of glucose utilization (from which some inference can be drawn about synapse formation), Chugani and colleagues (Chugani, 1994;

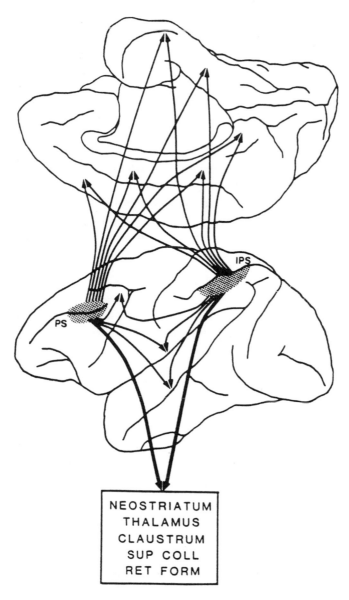

NEOSTRIATUM
THALAMUS
CLAUSTRUM
SUP COLL
RET FORM

FIG. 11.6. Some of the connections between the posterior parietal cortex and the prefrontal cortex (principal sulcal region of the dorsolateral prefrontal cortex). The major targets of the prefrontal and parietal projections are limbic areas on the medial surface of the brain, and the opercular and superior temporal cortices on the lateral surface. In this figure, the stippled areas represent the intraparietal sulcus (IPS) and the principal sulcus (PS). From Goldman-Rakic, P. S. (1987). Circuitry of the prefrontal cortex and the regulation of behavior by representational knowledge. In F. Plum & V. Mountcastle (Eds.), *Handbook of Physiology: Section I: The nervous system.* Vol. 5. *Higher functions of the brain* (pp. 373–417). Bethesda, MD: American Physiological Society. Reproduced with permission of the author and the publisher.

Chugani & Phelps, 1986) have reported that prefrontal cortex is the last brain area to show adult patterns, at about 12 months. Consistent with this time course for anatomical development are data from behavioral studies, indicating that children's selective attention abilities continue to undergo developmental change through the middle school age period (e.g., Enns, 1990; Enns & Cameron, 1987; Lane & Pearson, 1982).

Developmental Studies of Visual Selective Attention

There is very little work on the neural networks that underlie visual selective attention in young children and on how those brain areas and connections develop. The main reason for this is that most of the brain imaging techniques used to study adult humans and nonhuman primates of all ages are not appropriate to use with normal children. The radioactive contrast agent (e.g., ^{15}O) required for PET studies presents too much of a risk to be used with children who have no clinical reasons for such scans. And, although great strides have recently been made in studying cognitive abilities in healthy children using functional Magnetic Resonance Imaging (fMRI), it is difficult to test children below the age of 6 years (although for children older than this, see Casey et al., 1995; Truwit et al., 1996). In addition, this procedure is very expensive and sufficiently technically sophisticated to preclude its use on a wide scale. Thus, the use of ERP techniques is particularly attractive, as such techniques are non-invasive, inexpensive, and can be used across the entire life span.

In research with human adults the ERP methodology has proven useful in investigating the neurophysiological basis of selective attention (for reviews, see Hillyard & Hansen, 1986; Näätänen, 1982, 1990). Adult selective attention has been studied in several modalities (auditory, visual, and somatosensory), but the greatest amount of work has been done on the auditory modality. In a typical ERP study, subjects alternately attend to tones of a particular pitch in one ear while ignoring tones of a different pitch in the other ear. A major finding has been that stimuli processed in the attended ear elicited a larger N100 (a component of negative polarity occurring 100 ms post stimulus onset) than identical tones presented to the unattended ear (Hillyard, Hink, Schwent, & Picton, 1973). It has since been determined that this N100 enhancement was due to an endogenous processing negativity superimposed on the exogenous N100 component (Näätänen, 1990; Näätänen & Michie, 1979). This processing negativity has been operationalized as the Nd wave, the difference between the processing negativity elicited by stimuli in the attended ear and that elicited by stimuli in the unattended ear (Hansen & Hillyard, 1980). Both an early and late Nd have been identified (Näätänen, 1990). The early sensory component is thought to reflect the discrimination of stimuli in the attended channel and is localized to the auditory cortex (Näätänen, 1990). The later (and longer duration) Nd component is thought to reflect selective rehearsal to maintain the attentional trace (Näätänen, 1990).

Berman and Friedman (1995) conducted a developmental study of auditory selective attention with children (average age of 8), adolescents (average age of 14), and young adults. They found that the early component of the Nd waveform increased in amplitude and its latency decreased with age (see Fig. 11.7). According to the authors this finding suggests that

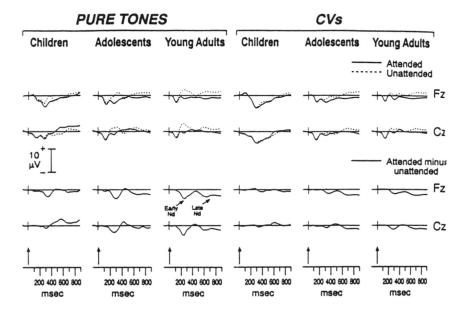

FIG. 11.7. In this study subjects were presented with two sequences of pure tones (low- and high-pitched) or consonant–vowel combinations (e.g., ba vs. da). Subjects were instructed to attend to one of the two stimuli in order to detect a deviant target stimulus (which was embedded in the train of "attended" stimuli), while simultaneously ignoring the sequence comprised of the other stimulus. The infrequent target stimuli were always slightly longer in duration than the frequent nontargets. The data presented in the top half of this figure represent grand averages for the different conditions (e.g., attend, ignore) for the midline frontal (Fz) and central (Cz) scalp leads. The stimuli to which subjects attended are represented by the solid line, whereas the ones that were ignored are represented by the dashed line. The data displayed in the bottom half of the figure are also grand means for the Fz and Cz leads, except these are difference waves; that is, the response to the "unattend" stimulus subtracted from the "attend" stimulus. The arrows indicate stimulus onset. From Berman and Friedman (1995). The development of selective attention as reflected by event-related brain potentials. *Journal of Experimental Child Psychology, 59,* 1–31. Reproduced with permission of Academic Press.

with development, fewer processing resources are allocated to the unattended channel. In other words, as has been demonstrated by behavioral data, children become better able to ignore irrelevant information with development. Berman and Friedman also found topographical differences in the early Nd component among the age groups. The topography was relatively more posterior for the young adults than it was for the children and adolescents, also suggesting qualitative differences in the strategies used by the younger subjects when selectively attending to competing input. The authors also found that the later component of the Nd waveform showed age-related changes. The amplitude of the late Nd was larger for adolescents and adults. In addition, for the older subjects the component has a widespread scalp distribution, but for the children it is centered at Fz and laterally at the temporal sites. The smaller Nd amplitude found in the children was described by the authors as suggesting that they were having difficulty in maintaining the attentional trace necessary for further processing of the to-be-attended stimuli. Finally, Berman and Friedman speculated that the age-related shift in the scalp distribution of the late Nd component is consistent with developmental changes in frontal lobe activity, which are known to continue well into adolescence. It is interesting to note that late Nd amplitude is significantly reduced in adult patients with lesions to the dorsolateral prefrontal cortex (Knight, Hillyard, Woods, & Neville, 1981), providing further evidence that this component is an index of frontal lobe activity. Taken together, these data are consistent with behavioral findings of children's increasing ability to focus attention on relevant information while ignoring irrelevant information as they grow older, and with the protracted development of frontal cortex, known to be a critical component of the selective attention network.

In the visual modality, the ERP patterns associated with selective attention are different from those seen for auditory processing. In a study of adults, Mangun, Hillyard, and Luck (1993) found enhancement of the early sensory-evoked P100 (80–120 ms) and N100 (140–190 ms) components when subjects were asked to focus attention on a particular point in space. The P100 component was focused over ventrolateral extrastriate cortex, whereas the N100 effect was localized over occipito-parietal cortex. The authors concluded that early spatial attention acts as a "sensory gain control" modulating the flow of information in multiple extrastriate areas. When subjects are asked to select stimuli based on color, size, shape, and so forth, rather than spatial location, the attentional effects are seen in later (150–350 ms) endogenous ERP components such as N200 and P300. As with the auditory Nd component, the amplitude and latency of the exogenous N200 and P300 components provide information about the timing and order of the selection of different features of the visual stimuli (Hillyard, Mangun, Woldorff, & Luck, 1995).

We have recently begun to examine a different facet of selective attention in children, using ERPs. There exists an extensive literature documenting adults' processing of complex spatial patterns. Typical stimuli used in these studies are hierarchical letter patterns. These patterns have two interrelated levels, consisting of the parts, (the *local* level) which are arranged to form the larger whole (the *global* level). An example is a large H shape (global level) made of small S's (local level). Behavioral measures (reaction time and accuracy) have shown normal adults are faster at identifying the letter at the global level than at the local level. Also, there is evidence that global level information interferes with the processing of the local level of the stimulus, but not vice versa (Kinchla & Wolfe, 1979; Miller, 1981; Navon, 1977). In numerous studies of adults with unilateral posterior (tempo-parietal junction) lesions it has been shown that the right hemisphere is relatively more critical in attending to the global level of a stimulus, whereas the left hemisphere appears to be specialized for processing local level information (Delis, Robertson, & Effron, 1986; Robertson & Lamb, 1991). Behavioral studies of children who experienced congenital neonatal focal lesions to these posterior brain areas have also demonstrated a pattern of deficit similar to that seen in adult patients (Stiles, Dukette & Nass, 1992; Stiles & Thal, 1993).

Data derived from studies of adult and child patients concerning the differential contribution of right and left hemisphere networks to visual selective attention served as the impetuous for an ERP study conducted in our laboratory (Dukette & Nelson, 1996). In this study, hierarchical letter patterns similar to those described earlier served as stimuli. The subject was seated in front of a computer monitor and button box. For each block of trials, hierarchical letter stimuli were presented one at a time in the center of the computer screen. Each stimulus remained visible for 200 ms. Prior to one block of trials, the subject was instructed to "pay attention" only to the large letter shape (global level) and to press one button if the letter at that level was an "H" and the other button if it was an "S." For the other block of trials the same subject was told to switch and attend only to the small letters (local level) and to press the H or the S button depending on the identity of those letters. Order of presentation of "global attention" and "local attention" blocks was counterbalanced. In addition, the identity of the letter at the nonattended level of the stimulus was systematically varied in one of three ways: (a) The letter at the nonattended level was the other possible target letter (H or S, depending on the identity of the letter at the target level) and thus provided a potential "conflict" response with the information at the to-be-attended level, (b) the identity of the letter at the nonattended level was other than that of the two target letters, and was therefore "neutral," and (c) the letter at the nonattended level was identical to the one at the attended level, so the two levels provided "redundant" information. These stimulus variations were used in order to evaluate the functioning of the selective attention network when the relevance of the competing information varied.

Third graders (average age = 8.5 years) served as subjects. All were right-handed and had normal or corrected to normal vision. Both RT and ERP data were recorded. As expected, the RT data revealed that the children were faster in their letter identifications when they were told to attend selectively to the global level than when they attended to the local level. In global attention condition, the identity (conflict, neutral, or redundant) of the letter on the nonattended local level had no apparent effect on performance (see Fig. 11.8). However, in the local attention condition, the identity of the non-attended global level did seem to influence RT. These data suggest that in the conflict stimulus condition, global information interfered with children's ability to attend selectively to the local level, but not vice versa.

Based on the ERP data, however, we cannot necessarily conclude that the RT differences reflect variation in the children's ability to attend selectively to certain stimulus features. We examined the N200 component of the ERP waveform because it is considered to reflect endogenous or volitional attentional processing. There were no statistically significant dif-

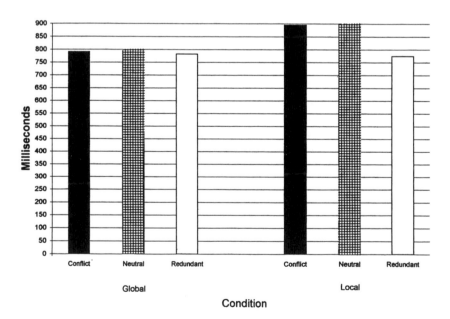

FIG. 11.8. Reaction time data from Dukette and Nelson (1996) study. The data displayed are for the three test contrasts (conflict, neutral, and redundant) for subjects tested under the two conditions (attend global, attend local).

ferences between the global and local attentional conditions in the amplitude or latency of this component. For both conditions, N200 amplitude was larger at posterior sites (O1, O2, T5, T6, P3, and P4) and larger over the right hemisphere than the left (see Fig. 11.9). Latency data also suggest that the generator for this component is located in the area of the occipital-temporal-parietal junction. These data were compared to the N200 patterns of a group of adults in a similar task (Dukette, 1995). Although the overall latency was approximately 50 ms earlier in the adults, the morphology of the N200 component was virtually identical in these two groups.

There were also no significant differences in the P300 component between the global and local attentional conditions, providing further evidence that the global advantage and local interference seen in the children's behavioral data do not reflect differences in their ability to selectively attend to these aspects of the stimuli. The average peak amplitude of the

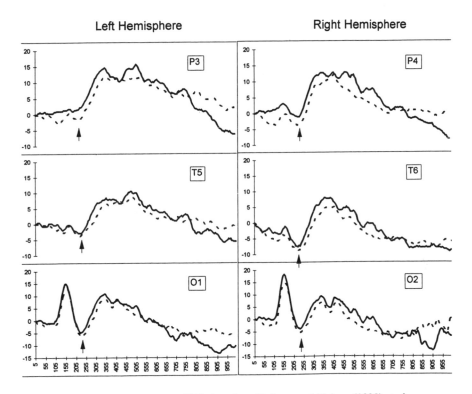

FIG. 11.9. Grand average ERP data from Dukette and Nelson (1996) study. Shown on the left are the data from the left hemisphere leads (P3 = left parietal; T5 = left temporal; O1 = left occipital) and on the right those from the right hemisphere leads (P4 = right parietal; T6 = right temporal; O2 = right occipital). The arrow indicates the N200 response discussed in the text.

N200 occurred between 230–350 ms, whereas the RT latencies were in the range of 780–900 ms. It is possible that the observed RT differences between attention conditions might reflect cognitive processing which occurs later in the stream, beyond visual selection but prior to response initiation.

Summary

Overall, these results provide support for behavioral data from other laboratories, confirming that at least by the early school age period children are readily able to selectively attend to aspects of a visual array, and to shift their attentional focus as directed. The ERP data reveal, however, that the neural networks that subserve this ability may continue to develop beyond the first 8 years of life. Although the patterns of the N200 component were very similar in the children and adults, there were peak latency differences which may reflect changes in the efficiency of this attentional network, possibly continuing to adolescence. This would be consistent with the maturational timecourse of dorsolateral prefrontal cortex, a critical brain region in the visual selective attention network.

In their studies of auditory selective attention, Berman and Friedman (1995) also found evidence for some continuing maturation of this network through the school age period. Although the behavioral and ERP data suggested that the children were quite competent in their selective attentional processing, they also revealed subtle differences between them and the adults.

Taken together, these findings point to the critical role of the frontal cortex for fully developed, adult-like selective attention function. At least by the age of 8, children are very good at selective attention tasks in both the auditory and visual modalities. But, they do not exhibit full competence until the completion of the maturation of frontal cortex.

SUMMARY AND CONCLUSIONS

Attention and memory are intricately related, although in the context of studying infants and children, these abilities are often difficult to disentangle experimentally. As should be evident, there is some similarity between the time course for the development of attentional abilities, and for memorial abilities. It is not clear whether this similarity is due to development of those neural systems that support attention and memory coming on-line at the same (or similar) times, or is an artifact of our methods for studying both behavioral and neurological development. Regarding the former, it is entirely possible that the neural systems involved in, for example, vigilance, happen to develop on the same time scale as those that are involved in the development of explicit memory. Accordingly, it would appear that both vigilance and explicit memory come online together. On the other hand, our methods for studying attention and memory development, particularly in the earliest portions of the life span, are severely limited. As a result, it is also possible that the crudeness of our methods contributes most to our observations about similarities in developmental course. Clearly, then, developmental science would profit from expanding the methodological armamentarium for studying both attention and memory, and in particular, the relation between attention and memory.

It is in this context that we offer the following recommendations. First, it would seem beneficial for the developmental psychologist interested in attention and memory to begin to explore the methods used by the cognitive neuroscientist who studies mature functioning. Although invasive methods such as PET are likely not feasible except for clinical populations, methods such as fMRI may be. Indeed we (Truwit et al., 1996) have enjoyed tremendous success in evaluating working memory in children older than 6 years of age using this procedure. Children are remarkably tolerant of undergoing fMRI studies, in part because they are more comfortable than many adults in being confined to small spaces, and, in part, because it is possible to take repeated breaks while scanning a subject. Of course, motion artifacts remain a big problem (e.g., even the smallest movement, even the movement of the heart in the chest cavity, can cause distortion in the image), but it is hoped that motion correction algorithms currently being developed will go a long way toward solving this problem.

As we tried to make clear in this chapter, the use of ERPs holds great promise in studying attentional development. ERPs can be recorded in a matter of minutes, do not require a verbal or motor response, and can be used across the entire life span. Further, relative to fMRI, ERP research is relatively inexpensive to conduct. Although there will always be the dilemma of inferring neural sources from scalp recorded brain activity, new methods of recording from 128 scalp sites are currently being developed. In addition, outside of the purview of neural sources, ERPs are also useful for studying problems that do not lend themselves to behavioral analysis, such as fast-occurring events.

A final approach we would like to encourage concerns the use of clinical populations. Although the study of individuals with brain damage, even when discrete and highly localized, can be problematic (e.g., will the results generalize to normative samples?), their use nonetheless can complement the study of normal, healthy individuals. Infants and children do suffer from localized neural insults, often leaving them *relatively* unimpaired, with perhaps only selective deficits. Studying such children using a combination of behavioral, electrophysiological (e.g., ERP), and perhaps even magnetic (e.g., fMRI) methods would greatly complement the study of normal children, essentially providing converging information on normative processes.

Overall, it is our hope that developmental psychologists will increasingly embrace the methods used by those studying adult functioning from a cognitive neuroscience perspective and apply them to the study of infants and children. In so doing we would gain not only important information about development, but as well, our insight into mature functioning will also have profited.

ACKNOWLEDGMENTS

The writing of this chapter was made possible, in part, by training grants from the NIH to the Center for Research in Learning, Perception, and Cognition, University of Minnesota (HD07151; Al Yonas, P.I.) and the Institute of Child Development, University of Minnesota (HD07279; Megan Gunnar and Charles A. Nelson, P.I.s); and by grants from the NINDS to the first author (NS32976 and NS32755).

REFERENCES

Bachevalier, J. (1990). Ontogenetic development of habit and memory formation in primates. In A. Diamond (Ed.), *Development and neural bases of higher cognitive functions* (pp. 457–484). New York: New York Academy of Sciences Press.

Bachevalier, J. (1992). Cortical versus limbic immaturity: Relationship to infantile amnesia. In M. R. Gunnar & C. A. Nelson (Eds.), *Minnesota Symposia on Child Psychology: Developmental Neuroscience* (Vol. 24, pp. 129–153). Hillsdale, NJ: Lawrence Erlbaum Associates.

Bachevalier, J., & Mishkin, M. (1984). An early and a late developing system for learning and retention in infant monkeys. *Behavioral Neuroscience, 98,* 770–778.

Barash, S., Bracewell, R. M., Fogassi, L., Gnadt, J. W., & Andersen, R. A. (1991). Saccade-related activity in the lateral intraparietal area: II. Spatial properties. *Journal of Neurophysiology, 66,* 1109–1124.

Bauer, P. J., Hertsgaard, L. A., & Dow, G. A. (1994). After 8 months have passed: Long-term recall of events by 1- and 2-year-old children. *Memory, 2,* 353–383.

Berman, S., & Friedman, D. (1995). The development of selective attention as reflected by event-related brain potentials. *Journal of Experimental Child Psychology, 59,* 1–31.

Bushnell, M. C., Goldberg, M. E., & Robinson, D. L. (1981). Behavioral enhancement of visual responses in monkey cerebral cortex: I. Modulation in posterior parietal cortex related to selective visual attention. *Journal of Neurophysiology, 46,* 755–771.

Casey, B. J., Cohen, J. D., Jezzard, P., Turner, R., Noll, D. C., Trainor, R. J., Giedd, J., Kaysen, D., Hertz-Pannier, L., & Rappaport, J. L. (1995). Activation of prefrontal cortex in children during a non-spatial working memory task with functional MRI. *Neuroimage, 2,* 221–229.

Chugani, H. T. (1994). Development of regional brain glucose metabolism in relation to behavior and plasticity. In G. Dawson & K. Fischer (Eds.), *Human behavior and the developing brain* (pp. 153–175). New York: Guilford Press.

Chugani, H. T., & Phelps, M. E. (1986). Maturational changes in cerebral function in infants determined by [18]FDG positron emission Tomography. *Science, 231,* 840–843.

Courchesne, E. (1978). Neurophysiological correlates of cognitive development: Changes in long-latency event-related potentials from childhood to adulthood. *Electroencephalography and Clinical Neurophysiology, 45,* 468–482.

de Haan, M., & Nelson, C. A. (1997). Recognition of mother's face by 6-month-old infants: A neurobehavioral study. *Child Development, 68,* 187–210.

Delis, D. C., Robertson, L. C., & Efron, R. (1986). Hemispheric specialization of memory for visual hierarchical stimuli. *Neuropsychologia, 24,* 205–214.

Dukette, D. (1995, March). Neural activity during global and local processing: An ERP study. Paper presented at the *Cognitive Neuroscience Society Meeting, San Francisco.*

Dukette, D., & Nelson, C. A. (1996). *Children's selective attention to global and local information.* Manuscript in preparation.

Enns, J. T. (1990). Components of attention. In J. T. Enns (Ed.), *The development of attention: Research and theory.* New York: North-Holland.

Enns, J. T., & Cameron, S. (1987). Selective attention in young children: The relations between visual search, filtering, and priming. *Journal of Experimental Child Psychology, 44,* 38–63.

Fox, P. T., Peterson, S., Posner, M., & Raichle, M. E. (1988). Is Broca's area language-specific? *Neurology, 38*(Suppl.), 172.

Friedman, D., Sutton, S., Putnam, L., Brown, C., & Erlenmeyer-Kimling, L. (1988). ERP components in picture matching in children and adults. *Psychophysiology, 25,* 570–590.

Goldman-Rakic, P. S. (1988). Topography of cognition: Parallel distributed networks in primate association cortex. *Annual Review of Neuroscience, 11,* 137–156.

Hansen, J. C., & Hillyard, S. A. (1980). Endogenous brain potentials associated with selective auditory attention. *Electroencephalography and Clinical Neurophysiology, 49,* 277–290.

Harter, M. R., Miller, S. L., Price, N. J., LaLonde, M. E., & Keyes, A. L. (1989). Neural processes involved in directing attention. *Journal of Cognitive Neuroscience, 1,* 223–237.

Heinze, H. J., Mangun, G. R., Burchert, W., Hinrichs, S. M., Munte, T. F., Gos, A., Scherg, M., Johannes, S., Hundeshagen, H., Gazzaniga, M. S., & Hillyard, S. A. (1994). Combined spatial and temporal imaging of brain activity during visual selective attention in humans. *Nature, 372,* 543–546.

Hillyard, S. A., & Hansen, J. C. (1986). Attention: Electrophysiological approaches. In M. G. H. Coles, E. Donchin, & S. W. Porges (Eds.), *Psychophysiology* (pp. 227–243). New York: Guilford Press.

Hillyard, S. A., Hink, S., Schwent, V., & Picton, T. (1973). Electrical signs of selective attention in the human brain. *Science, 162,* 177–180.

Hillyard, S. A., Mangun, G. R., Woldorff, M. G., & Luck, S. J. (1995). Neural systems mediating selective attention. In M. Gazzaniga (Ed.), *The cognitive neurosciences.* Cambridge, MA: MIT Press.

Huttenlocher, P. R. (1979). Synaptic density in human frontal cortex—Developmental changes and effects of aging. *Brain Research, 163,* 195–205.

Huttenlocher, P. R. (1990). Morphometric study of human cerebral cortex development. *Neuropsychologia, 28,* 517–527.

Huttenlocher, P. R. (1994). Synaptogenesis, synapse elimination, and neural plasticity in human cerebral cortex. In C. A. Nelson (Ed.), *Threats to optimal development: Integrating biological, psychological, and social risk factors.* Minnesota Symposium on Child Psychology, Vol. 27 (pp. 35–54). Hillsdale, NJ: Lawrence Erlbaum Associates.

Janowsky, J. (1993). The development of memory systems. In M. H. Johnson (Ed.), *Brain development and cognition: A reader.* Cambridge, MA: Blackwell.

Jernigan, T. L., Trauner, D. A., Hesselink, J. R., & Tallal, P. A. (1991). Maturation of human cerebrum observed in vivo during adolescence. *Brain, 114,* 2037–2049.

Johnson, M. H. (1990). Cortical maturation and the development of visual attention in early infancy. *Journal of Cognitive Neuroscience, 2,* 81–95

Johnson, M. H. (1997). *Developmental cognitive neuroscience.* London: Blackwell Publishers.

Johnson, M. H., Posner, M. I., & Rothbart, M. K. (1991). Components of visual orienting in early infancy: Contingency learning, anticipatory looking, and disengagement. *Journal of Cognitive Neuroscience, 3,* 335–344.

Kail, R. (1990). *The development of memory in children* (3rd ed.). New York: Freeman.

Karrer, R., & Ackles, P. K. (1987). Visual event-related potentials of infants during a modified oddball procedure. In R. Johnson, Jr., J. W. Rohrbaugh, & R. Parasuraman (Eds.), *Current trends in event-related potential research* (EEG Suppl. 40), 603–608.

Karrer, R., & Ackles, P. K. (1988). Brain organization and perceptual/cognitive development in normal and Down syndrome infants: A research program. In P. Vietze & H. G. Vaughan, Jr. (Eds.), *The early identification of infants at risk for mental retardation* (pp. 210–234). Orlando, FL: Grune & Stratton.

Kestenbaum, R., & Nelson, C. A. (1992). Neural and behavioral correlates of emotion recognition in children and adults. *Journal of Experimental Child Psychology, 54,* 1–18.

Kinchla, R. A., & Wolfe, J. M. (1979). The order of visual processing: "Top-down," "bottom-up," or "middle-out". *Perception & Psychophysics, 25*(3), 225–231.

Knight, R. T., Hillyard, S. A., Woods, D. L., & Neville, H. J. (1981). The effects of frontal cortex lesions on event-related potentials during auditory selective attention. *Electroencephalography and Clinical Neurophysiology, 52,* 571–582.

Kok, A., & Rooijakkers, J. A. J. (1985). Comparison of event-related potentials of young children and adults in a visual recognition and word reading task. *Psychophysiology, 22,* 11–23.

Lane, D. M., & Pearson, D. A. (1982). The development of selective attention. *Merrill-Palmer Quarterly, 28,* 317–337.

Luciana, M. L., & Nelson, C. A. (in press).

Mangun, G. R., & Hillyard, S. A. (1991). Modulations of sensory-evoked brain potentials provide evidence for changes in perceptual processing during visual-spatial priming. *Journal of Experimental Psychology (Human Perception), 17,* 1057–1074.

Mangun, G. R., Hillyard, S. A., & Luck, S. J. (1993). Electrocortical substrates of visual selective attention. In D. Meyer & S. Kornblum (Eds.), *Attention and performance, Vol. 14* (pp. 219–243). Cambridge, MA: MIT Press.

Maunsell, J. H. R. (1995). The brain's visual world: Representation of visual targets in cerebral cortex. *Science, 270,* 764–769.

McDonough, L., Mandler, J. M., McKee, R. D., & Squire, L. R. (1995). The deferred imitation task as a nonverbal measure of declarative memory. *Proceedings of the National Academy of Sciences, 8,* 7580–7584.

McKee, R. D., & Squire, L. R. (1993). On the development of declarative memory. *Journal of Experimental Psychology: Learning, Memory, and Cognition, 19,* 397–404.

Meltzoff, A. N. (1995). What infant memory tells us about amnesia—long-term recall and deferred imitation. *Journal of Experimental Child Psychology, 59,* 497–515.

Miller, E. K., & Desimone, R. (1994). Parallel neuronal mechanisms for short-term memory. *Science, 263,* 520–522.

Miller, J. (1981). Global precedence in attention and decision. *Journal of Experimental Psychology: Human Perception and Performance, 7*(6), 1161–1174.

Moran, J., & Desimone. R. (1985). Selective attention gates visual processing in extrastriate cortex. *Science, 229,* 782–784.

Murray, E. A., & Gaffan, D. (1994). Removal of the amygdala plus subjacent cortex disrupts the retention of both intramodal and crossmodal associative memories in monkeys. *Behavioral Neuroscience, 108,* 494–500.

Murray, E. A., & Mishkin, M. (1985). Amygdalectomy impairs cross-modal association in monkeys. *Science, 228,* 604–606.

Näätänen, R. (1982). Processing negativity: An evoked-potential reflection of selective attention. *Psychology Bulletin, 92,* 605–640.

Näätänen, R. (1990). The role of attention in auditory information processing as revealed by event-related potentials and other measures of cognitive function. *Behavioral and Brain Sciences, 13,* 201–288.

Näätänen, R., & Michie, P. T. (1979). Early selective attention effects on the evoked potential: A critical review and reinterpretation. *Biological Psychology, 8,* 81–136.

Navon, D. (1977). Forest before trees: The precedence of global features in visual perception. *Cognitive Psychology, 9,* 353–383.

Nelson, C. A. (1994). Neural correlates of recognition memory in the first postnatal year of life. In G. Dawson & K. Fischer (Eds.), *Human development and the developing brain* (pp. 269–313). New York: Guilford Press.

Nelson, C. A. (1995). The ontogeny of human memory: A cognitive neuroscience perspective. *Developmental Psychology, 31,* 723–735.

Nelson, C. A. (1996). Electrophysiological correlates of Early Memory Development. In H. W. Reese & M. D. Franzen (Eds.), *Thirteenth West Virginia University Conference on Life Span Developmental Psychology: Biological and Neuropsychological Mechanisms* (pp. 95–131). Mahwah, NJ: Lawrence Erlbaum Associates.

Nelson, C. A. (1997). The neurobiological basis of early memory development. In N. Cowan (Ed.), *The development of memory in childhood.* London: University College London Press.

Nelson, C. A., & Collins, P. F. (1991). Event-related potential and looking time analysis of infants' responses to familiar and novel events: Implications for visual recognition memory. *Developmental Psychology, 27,* 50–58.

Nelson, C. A., & Collins, P. F. (1992). Neural and behavioral correlates of recognition memory in 4- and 8-month-old infants. *Brain and Cognition, 19,* 105–121.

Nelson, C. A., & de Haan, M. (1996). Neural correlates of infants' visual responsiveness to facial expressions of emotion. *Developmental Psychobiology, 29,* 577–595.

Nelson, C. A., & Dolgin, K. (1985). The generalized discrimination of facial expressions by 7-month-old infants. *Child Development, 56,* 58–61.

Nelson, C. A., Henschel, M., & Collins, P. F. (1993). Neural correlates of cross-modal recognition memory in 8-month-old infants. *Developmental Psychology, 29,* 411–420.

Nelson, C. A., & Nugent, K. (1990). Recognition memory and resource allocation as revealed by children's event-related potential responses to happy and angry faces. *Developmental Psychology, 26,* 171–179.

Nelson, C. A., & Salapatek, P. (1986). Electrophysiological correlates of infant recognition memory. *Child Development, 57,* 1483–1497.

O'Neil, J. B., Friedman, D. P., Bachevalier, J., & Ungerleider, L. G. (1986). Distribution of muscarinic receptors in the brain of a newborn rhesus monkey. *Society for Neuroscience Abstracts, 12,* 809.

Peterson, S. E., Fox, P. T., Posner, M. I., Mintun, M., & Raichle, M. E. (1988). Positron emission Tomographic studies of the cortical anatomy of single-word processing. *Nature, 331,* 585–589.

Peterson, S. E., Fox, P. T., Posner, M. I., Mintun, M., & Raichle, M. E. (1990). Positron emission tomographic studies of the processing of single words. *Journal of Cognitive Neuroscience, 1,* 153–170.

Posner, M. I. (1980). Orienting of attention. *Quarterly Journal of Experimental Psychology, 32,* 3–25.

Posner, M. I. (1988). Structures and functions of selective attention. In T. Boll & D. K. Bryant (Eds.), *Clinical neuropsychology and brain function: Research, assessment and practice.* Washington, DC: American Psychological Association.

Posner, M. I. (1995). Attention in cognitive neuroscience: An overview. In M. S. Gazzaniga (Ed.), *The cognitive neurosciences.* Cambridge, MA: MIT Press.

Posner, M. I., & Peterson, S. E. (1990). The attention system of the human brain. *Annual Review of Neuroscience, 13,* 25–42.

Richards, M. L. M., Thomas, K., Georgieff, M. K., & Nelson, C. A. (1994, February). *Evoked potential responses of recognition memory in premature infants.* Paper presented at the Western Society for Pediatric Research, Carmel, CA.

Richmond, B. J., & Sato, T. (1987). Enhancement of inferior temporal neurons during visual discrimination. *Journal of Neurophysiology, 58,* 1292–1306.

Robertson, L. C., & Lamb, M. R. (1991). Neuropsychological contributions to theories of part/whole organization. *Cognitive Psychology, 23,* 299–230.

Roediger, H. L., III (1990). Implicit memory: Retention without remembering. *American Psychologist, 45,* 1043–1056.

Roediger, H., III, Rajaram, S., & Srinivas, K. (1990). Specifying criteria for postulating memory systems. In A. Diamond (Ed.), *The development and neural bases of higher cognitive functions.* New York: New York Academy of Sciences.

Rose, S. A., & Ruff, H. A. (1989). Cross-modal abilities in human infants. In J. D. Osofsky (Ed.), *Handbook of infant development* (pp. 318–362). New York: Wiley.

Ruff, H. A., & Rothbart, M. K. (1996). *Attention in early development.* New York: Oxford University Press.

Schacter, D. L. (1987). Implicit memory: History and current status. *Journal of Experimental Psychology: Learning, Memory, and Cognition, 13,* 501–518.

Spitzer, H., & Richmond, B. J. (1991). *Experimental Brain Research, 83,* 340.

Squire, L. R. (1986). Mechanisms of memory. *Science, 232,* 1612–1619.

Squire, L. R. (1987). *Memory and brain.* New York: Oxford University Press.

Stiles, J., & Dukette, D. (1985). *The effects of early focal brain injury on children's reproductions of hierarchical patterns.* Manuscript in preparation.

Stiles, J., Dukette, D., & Nass, R. (1992). *Selective deficits of visuospatial processing in children with early right or left posterior focal brain injury.* Paper presented at the Child Neurology Society Conference, New Orleans.

Stiles, J., & Thal, D. (1993). Linguistic and spatial cognitive development following early focal brain injury: Patterns of deficit and recovery. In M. Johnson (Ed.), *Brain development and cognition: A reader* (pp. 643–664). Oxford: Blackwell.

Thomas, K. M. (1996). *The development of implicit processing: Brain and behavior.* Special area written examination, University of Minnesota.

Thomas, K. M., & Nelson, C. A. (1996). Age-related changes in the electrophysiological response to visual stimulus novelty: A topographic approach. *Electroencephalography and Clinical Neurophysiology, 98,* 294–308.

Triesman, A. M., & Gelade, G. (1980). A feature-integrative theory of attention. *Cognitive Psychology, 12,* 97–136.

Truwit, C. L., Le, T. H., Lim, J. C., Hu, X., Carver, L., Thomas, K. M., Monk, C., & Nelson, C. A. (1996, June). *Functional MR imaging of working memory task activation in children: Preliminary findings.* Paper presented to the American Society of Neuroradiology meeting, Seattle, WA.

Tulving, E. (1985). How many memory systems are there? *American Psychologist, 40,* 385–398.

Ungerleider, L. G., & Mishkin, M. (1982). Two cortical visual systems. In D. J. Ingle, M. A. Goodale, & R. J. W. Mansfield (Eds.), *Analysis of visual behavior* (pp. 549–586). Cambridge, MA: MIT Press.

Webster, M. J., Bachevalier, J., & Ungerleider, L. G. (1995). Development and plasticity of visual memory circuits. In B. Julesz & I. Kovacs (Eds.), *Maturational windows and adult cortical plasticity.* New York: Addison-Wesley.

Yakovlev, P. I., & Lecours, A. R. (1967). The myelogenetic cycles of regional maturation of the brain. In A. Minkowski (Ed.), *Regional development of the brain in early life.* Philadelphia: F. A. Davis.

Chapter 12

A Cognitive Neuroscience Approach to Individual Differences in Infant Cognition

John Colombo
University of Kansas

Jeri S. Janowsky
Oregon Health Sciences University

Although the study of individual differences in infant cognition dates back to the 1970s, the amount of attention devoted to research on this topic has increased dramatically over the past decade. Such interest has been fueled largely by the finding that measures of early cognition show modest but significant prediction of intellectual function in childhood and adolescence (Bornstein & Sigman, 1986; Colombo, 1993; Fagan, 1981; McCall & Carriger, 1993; McCall & Mash, 1995). That is, individual differences in performance on some cognitive tasks show some continuity from infancy to early childhood.

Among the puzzling features of this phenomenon concerns what cognitive processes and neural substrates mediate this continuity. Indeed, a current and fundamental focus of research in this area concerns the determination of what cognitive process(es) underlie those individual differences that persevere from infancy to maturity (Colombo & Frick, in press). From the basic-science frame of reference, a clear resolution of this issue would contribute greatly to the understanding of the structural development of cognition. From an applied viewpoint, such an understanding would ultimately contribute to the development of early interventions that might effectively ameliorate cognitive deficits in childhood.

The inquiry into the processes that underlie individual differences in infant cognition and the continuity of such individual differences into childhood may well be enhanced by the cognitive neuroscience approach. Cognitive neuroscience seeks to understand the component processes of these distinct cognitive functions and their associated neural bases. Among the core tenets of this interdisciplinary meld of cognitive psychology and neuroscience is the notion that particular cognitive processes can be reliably identified with specific loci, pathways, or systems in the normally developed and intact CNS. The study of cognitive processes in the context of what is known about their underlying neural substrates has many merits, along with the simple fact that such an approach constrains cognitive theorizing to what is biologically plausible.

In keeping with the theme of this volume, the present chapter examines the various possible neural underpinnings of individual differences in performance on those tasks or paradigms that tap cognitive functions that are continuous from infancy to childhood and adolescence. From the cognitive neuroscience perspective, the ultimate task is to define the paradigms and techniques for assessing infant cognition by their primary components, understand how continuity in individual differences on these components is preserved during development, and determine how the neural substrate maintains this continuity. Although the reader should not expect any definitive statements in this regard, we begin here the process through which such questions may eventually be answered.

INDIVIDUAL DIFFERENCES IN INFANT COGNITION

To this point, several specific measures of infant cognition have been shown to yield meaningful individual differences. As noted earlier, such meaning has typically been equated with the predictive validity of these measures with respect to intellectual function later in childhood. Although much of this literature has been reviewed elsewhere, a brief recapitulation may be useful. In this section, we describe the measures, indicate the nature of the measures' relationship to later cognitive function, and provide some updating on the earlier summarizations of this area.

The Measures

The first of these measures is long-term retention in the conjugate reinforcement paradigm. This paradigm is a variant of operant conditioning that is applicable with infants beyond 2 months of age, and yields several measures of learning and retention. Fagen and Ohr (1990) reported that infants with better long-term retention during the first and second years of life scored higher on standardized measures of intelligence and achievement administered at age 3.

A second set of predictive measures come from the visual expectation paradigm. In this paradigm (Haith, Hazan, & Goodman, 1988) an infant is exposed to visual stimuli that are presented in a regular and predictable spatiotemporal pattern. Individual differences on two specific measures gleaned from this paradigm appear to be predictive of cognitive outcome at maturity. The first of these is a simple ocular–oculocephalic reaction time; DiLalla et al. (1990) reported that infants who fixate more quickly to the locus in which a visual stimulus has appeared scored higher on standardized tests of intelligence in early childhood. Additionally, after repeated experience with predictable sequences of visual stimuli, some infants will begin to "anticipate" the appearance of a stimulus in a particular spatial location. Although the DiLalla et al. (1990) analyses did not show these anticipations to be significantly related to later childhood measures (see Colombo, 1993), more recent reports suggest that individual differences in the ability to anticipate such occurrences were related to subsequent performance childhood cognitive tests. That is, infants who anticipated more frequently showed higher scores on childhood tests of intelligence than those who showed fewer anticipations (Dougherty & Haith, 1993).

Further, the visual habituation paradigm (Horowitz, Paden, Bhana, & Self, 1972) has yielded a number of measures for which modest predictive validity has been reported from infancy. In this paradigm, infants' attention is monitored across repetitive presentations of a stimulus. The decline in responding that is typically observed has been interpreted as a crude form of learning (Sokolov, 1963). Various measures gleaned from this "learning curve" during infancy were correlated with later performance on tests of intelligence, achievement, cognition, and language in later childhood (Bornstein & Sigman, 1986). Colombo and Mitchell (1990) argued that these various indicants are driven by the length of looking observed during the initial portions of the habituation. The duration of such looks was reported to be negatively correlated with later measures of cognition (see Jacobson, Chiodo, & Jacobson, 1996; Mitchell, McCollam, O'Brien, Horowitz, & Embretson, 1991; Rose, Slater, & Perry, 1986; Sigman, Cohen, Beckwith, & Parmelee, 1986; Sigman, Cohen, Beckwith, Asarnow, & Parmelee, 1991; Tamis-LeMonda & Bornstein, 1989); that is, across much of the first year of life, briefer fixations are associated with more optimal cognitive outcomes.

Finally, individual differences in infants' performance in the paired-comparison or familiarization-novelty procedure were shown to be meaningful across the long term. In this paradigm, the infant is exposed to a two- or three-dimensional stimulus for some time period and is then presented with the choice of fixating that same stimulus or a novel one. Typically, under conditions where the length of the initial exposure has been sufficient, infants over 2 months of age show a preference for the novel stimulus, although systematic familiarity preferences are sometimes observed with three-dimensional stimuli or when familiarization is marginally sufficient.

Higher novelty preferences during infancy were linked with higher performance on measures of intelligence and language in childhood in several samples (Fagan & McGrath, 1981; Fagan & Shepard, 1986/1987; Fagan & Singer, 1983; Fagan, Singer, Montie, & Shepard, 1986; Rose & Feldman, 1995a, 1995b; Rose, Feldman, & Wallace, 1992; Rose, Feldman, Wallace, & Cohen, 1991).

Some Caveats

The preservation of individual differences in cognitive performance from infancy to maturity indicates that early individual differences are in fact meaningful indicants of later cognitive function. The existence of such prediction, however, should by no means be interpreted to mean that individual parameters in such cognitive function are fixed from early in life. Indeed, although the predictive validity of these measures attains statistical significance, the absolute level of prediction is relatively modest (see Colombo, 1993; McCall & Carriger, 1993). Correlations range in magnitude from about .20 to about .60, with typical magnitudes in the range of .35 to .45. The factors that may work to constrain the predictive power of these measures include their relatively low test–retest reliability and internal consistency (Benasich & Bejar, 1992; Colombo, 1993). Additionally, measurement of these cognitive parameters in isolation ignore the obvious and important contribution of variables in the child's environment to his or her ultimate cognitive outcome. The inclusion of such variables during infancy appreciably raises the level of prediction (see Mitchell et al., 1991; Tamis-LeMonda & Bornstein, 1989; see also related studies by Bornstein & Tamis-LeMonda, 1994; Saxon, Frick, & Colombo, 1997).

Summary

The consistent finding of modest continuity of cognitive function from infancy constitutes a remarkable phenomenon in and of itself. For the cognitive developmentalist, however, the basic and fundamental questions raised by these findings concern the underlying cognitive processes that give rise to continuity in early individual differences. For the developmental cognitive neuroscientist, the question reduces even further, asking which brain loci, functions, or systems might mediate such processes.

These are not easy questions to address, and they will not be definitively answered in this chapter. What we do attempt, however, is to delineate some of the possible candidate processes that might be involved in these individual differences, and identify what CNS systems have been identified to mediate those processes (at least in the adult). We start by examining two broad classes of cognitive theories in which these individual differences have been previously considered.

GENERAL–UNITARY MODELS

The first of these two classes of theories holds that individual differences in infant cognitive performance across all of these tasks is in fact reducible to a single underlying process. The continuity of individual differences from infancy, then, is attributable to continuity in that process (see Fig. 12.1). These unitary- or general-factor theories (Colombo & Frick, in press) are subject to several criticisms (Mitchell & Colombo, in press), but are appealing because of their apparent simplicity and parsimony (Fagen, 1995; McCall, 1994; McCall & Carriger, 1993).

This position includes the hypothesis that such performance is attributable to a general factor of intelligence (g). Although many of the allusions to a unitary mechanism underlying continuity in cognitive function from infancy have in fact been based on g (see Colombo, 1993; Fagan, 1984a; Mitchell & Colombo, in press), the single-construct model for explaining continuity has taken other forms as well. For example, a general-factor model has been recently proposed by McCall (1994; McCall & Carriger, 1993). McCall (1994) argued that the continuity in performance from habituation and familiarization–novelty paradigms in infancy to intelligence in childhood is mediated by a general inhibitory process. Such a process would work to both accelerate habituation and increase novelty preferences, in that each may be interpreted as involving the inhibition of looking to a familiar stimulus.

Evidence for a General Process

Indeed, there is some empirical evidence for such a general factor in infant cognition. One of the earlier reviews of the prediction literatures (Colombo, 1993) suggested that all of the predictive measures showed modest correlations with one another. Additionally, individual differences on some

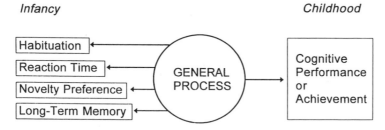

FIG. 12.1. Depiction of a general-process model of infant cognition, and the continuity of infant cognitive performance to later cognitive measures in childhood. Here, all infant measures are driven by this general factor (and are thus correlated), as is children's performance on later outcome measures of cognitive performance.

measures of visual habituation and recognition memory have been reported to covary with other global developmental indices, such as motor development (Colombo, Mitchell, O'Brien, & Horowitz, 1987b), reaction time (Jacobson, Jacobson, O'Neill, Padgett, Frankowski, & Bihun, 1992; Lamarre & Pomerleau, 1985), general psychophysiological indices (Linnemeyer & Porges, 1986; Richards, 1985), and behavioral manifestations of arousal (Frick, Colombo, & Gorman, 1997).

Additional evidence comes from the pattern of longitudinal associations; for example, individual differences in infant novelty preferences correlate better with childhood IQ than with childhood measures of recognition memory (Fagan, 1984b). This might suggest that such continuity is not due to a preservation of recognition memory abilities per se, but rather to some other construct that underlies both the cognitive measure assessed in infancy and standardized test performance assessed later in childhood.

The Substrate of General–Unitary Processes

The cognitive neuroscience of general-factor models has only rarely been considered (Detterman, 1994), but it can be argued that a cognitive neuroscience approach to a general-factor model of early individual differences might be limited to two general classes of mechanisms (see Fig. 12.2).

First, such differences might be explained in terms of overall quality of the individual's CNS. For example, if one hypothesizes (as some have) that g is reducible to individual differences in processing speed, then individual differences in cognitive performance across the lifespan might be explained in terms of the preservation of some widespread characteristic that affects overall speed of neural transmission (Colombo, 1995b; Sigman, Cohen, & Beckwith, 1996). Such a characteristic might be manifest at any level of the CNS (anatomical, physiological, biochemical, or mechanical). Indeed, researchers investigating the physical basis of g have attempted to isolate a measure of central processing speed or efficiency that is dissociable from the speed of peripheral nerve conduction (e.g., Jensen, 1993; Reed & Jensen, 1992; Vernon & Mori, 1992).

Alternatively, it is possible that such general, widespread differences might be attributed to individual differences in a critical CNS structure that is far enough "upstream" in the organizational hierarchy of the brain to contribute to the organization or function of other numerous "downstream" structures that mediate a broad spectrum of behavioral–cognitive manifestations. No such hypothesis has to our knowledge been posited for individual differences in infant cognition, but just such a hypothesis has been posited recently to account for the organic basis of autism. Based on both neuroimaging data and a knowledge of the interconnections of the CNS systems that mediate this wide variety of behavioral systems, Courchesne (1989,

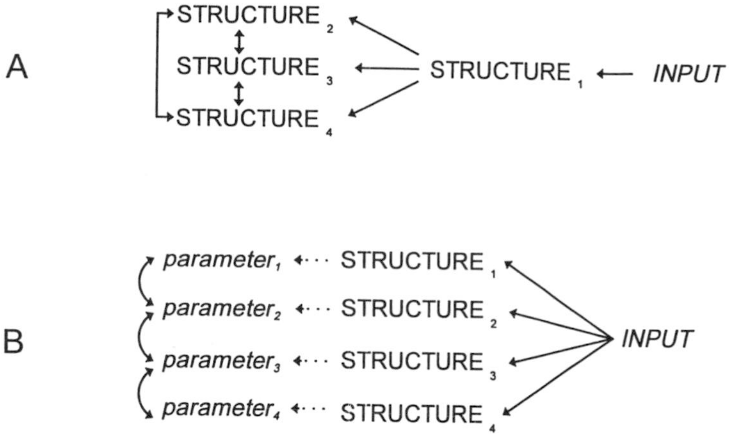

FIG. 12.2. Two schematics for the potential substrate of a general, or single-factor model of cognitive function. Model A is the simplest of a number of structural models. Here, the function of many substrates or structures (Structures 2 through 4) is dependent upon the functional integrity or parameters of one "upstream" structure (Structure 1). Deficits in the function of Structure 1 will cause correlated deficits in each of the functions mediated by Structures 2 through 4. Model B is the simplest of a number of parametric models. Here, various structures are structurally independent of one another, but all share a common quantitative parameter (as indicated by the bidirectional arcs). For example, each structure might have slow transmission speed or efficiency.

1995) has suggested that cerebellar abnormalities (Berntson & Torello, 1982; Schmahmann, 1991) may represent a common neurocognitive denominator for the pervasive deficits in attention (Casey, Gordon, Mannheim, & Rumsey, 1993), higher-order cognition (McEvoy, Rogers, & Pennington, 1993), and social cognition (Rutter, 1978) that characterize the disorder.

MODULAR MODELS

Recent evidence suggests that a second class of theories provide an alternative that is at least as plausible as a general model of individual differences in infant cognition. From the view of this position, measures of attention and recognition memory reflect dissociable and independent cognitive functions (see Fig. 12.3). Indeed, if neuroscientists are correct in their assertions that any one neuron (or neuronal circuit) makes contact with a relatively small proportion of other neurons in the CNS (Damasio, 1994), then modular explanations of both behavior and cognition may correspond more closely with the actual organization of the CNS (see Fig. 12.4). In the following sections, we consider the evidence and theoretical implications of such modular processes in individual differences in early cognition.

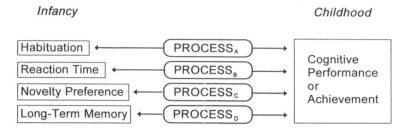

FIG. 12.3. Depiction of a multiple and modular-process model of infant cognition, and the continuity of infant cognitive performance to later cognitive measures in childhood. Here, different infant measures are driven by different factors (and thus may be uncorrelated). All of the independent processes tapped by the infant measures are represented on the childhood outcome measure, and thus each shows some prediction to that childhood assessment of cognitive performance.

Evidence for the Modular Position

Modular models have recently been proposed to account for the constructs and structures underlying individual differences in infant cognition. Colombo (1993) proposed an initial form of such a model, although this was essentially a minor extension of the more general models in vogue at

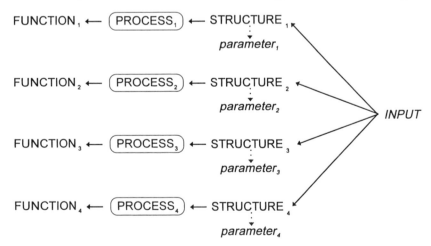

FIG. 12.4. A schematics for one potential substrate of a modular, multiple-process model of cognitive function. The structures, their parameters, the processes they represent, and functions that they mediate are all theoretically independent from one another, and deficits in any one is not necessarily correlated with deficits in any other. Given certain conditions and tasks, they may be shown to be correlated with one another, or to correlate in particular combinations, but such correlation is not inevitable, and is not attributable to any inherent commonality of the substrate.

the end of the last decade. This two-factor model involved separable and independent contributions of both processing speed and memory to individual differences in, and the continuity of cognitive function in infancy (Colombo, 1993; see also Anderson, 1992).

The two-factor model was initially supported by both a pattern of longitudinal findings and a factor analysis reported by Jacobson (1995; Jacobson et al., 1992). Jacobson et al. (1992) initially collected data on novelty preference, reaction time, and fixation duration on over 100 infants. A factor analysis of these data yielded one factor on which fixation duration and reaction time loaded positively, and a second factor on which novelty preference loaded significantly. Jacobson (1995) has since reported additional data suggesting that looking time and novelty preferences tap dissociable underlying constructs. Jacobson, Fein, Jacobson, Schwartz, and Dowler (1985) had earlier reported that infants prenatally exposed to polychlorinated biphenyls (PCB) showed significantly lower novelty preferences than nonexposed controls. Subsequently, Jacobson, Jacobson, Sokol, Martier, and Ager (1993) found that infants prenatally exposed to high levels of alcohol showed longer looking and slower reaction times than infants not so exposed. However, Jacobson (1995) has presented extended analyses that show novelty preferences *not* to be sensitive to prenatal alcohol exposure, and fixation duration *not* to be sensitive to differential status of PCB exposure.

Further evidence for modular function may be derived from data reported by Rose and Feldman (1995a, 1995b). Rose and Feldman (1995b) found significant multivariate relationships between infant visual recognition memory performance at 7 and 11 months of age and four specific abilities (language, memory, perceptual speed, and nonverbal spatial abilities) at 11 years of age. They extracted a factor from the four specific abilities that they characterized as "speed of processing," but also found that not all of the correlations between the infancy measures and the specific abilities were reduced by partialling 11-year IQ. This suggests the influence of multiple processes from infancy, beyond that represented simply by speed of processing.

Summary. In essence, then, these data suggested that the relationships between infant attention, recognition memory and later cognitive function are probably complex, and may be more amenable to explanation in terms of multiple, modular underlying processes. Although the notion of multiple processes in early individual differences is currently gaining momentum, the potential complexity of this proposal should not be underestimated. Indeed, the prospect of multiple cognitive processes in individual differences in infant visual attention and cognition opens a veritable floodgate of possibilities. For example, the same measure (e.g., look duration from habituation sessions) may reflect different processes (e.g., rapidity of stimulus processing, attention span) at different ages. It is also possible that the same measure (e.g., novelty preference) assessed under different task parameters (e.g., at brief vs. long familiarization lengths) may also reflect different processes (e.g., visual discrimination, recognition memory, or simply a positive response to novelty). Finally, it is possible, if not likely, that a single measure may well reflect the contribution of multiple processes (Vecera, Rothbart, & Posner, 1991). In any case, this position at the very least suggests that the meaningful cognitive processes represented by, for example, habituation–look duration and novelty preference may be best considered as reflections of independent processes, and as being mediated by different CNS substrates.

In the sections that follow, we take look duration and novelty preferences as examples of measures to which the modular model and the cognitive neuroscience approach might be applied. In each of these measures, the underlying process is still a matter of debate. We first examine the evidence on the various processes that might contribute to individual differences in these measures; we then discuss the possible CNS substrates that might contribute to these processes in infancy.

INDIVIDUAL DIFFERENCES IN INFANT LOOK DURATION

Individual differences in looking time (i.e., in the length of fixation duration to stimuli) were initially drawn from infant controlled habituation sequences (Horowitz et al., 1972) but data suggest that, at least during much of the first year (see Saxon et al., 1997), it is correlated with measurements of looking time taken through other procedures as well (Colombo, Frick, Ryther, & Gifford, 1996; Colombo, Mitchell, Coldren, & Freeseman, 1991; Frick & Colombo, 1996; Frick et al., 1997).

Colombo and Mitchell (1990) argued that look duration may most closely reflect individual differences in the visual learning or acquisition that occurs during visual habituation (see also Bornstein & Tamis-LeMonda, 1994; Tamis-LeMonda & Bornstein, 1989). Longitudinal research indicates that fixation duration is negatively correlated with cognitive and intellectual outcome in childhood (Jacobson et al., 1996; Mitchell et al., 1991; Rose et al., 1986; Sigman et al., 1986, 1991; Tamis-LeMonda & Bornstein, 1989).

Originally, individual differences in look duration were conceptualized in terms of a logical extension of the comparator model of habituation (Sokolov, 1963). As such, longer looking should reflect slower or less-efficient information processing (Cohen, 1988; Morrongiello, 1988). This interpretation has been supported by the observation of prolonged looking in younger infants (Cohen, 1988; Colombo & Mitchell, 1990; Mayes & Kessen, 1989), in some reports on premature infants (e.g., Sigman & Beckwith, 1980) and infants with Down Syndrome (e.g., Cicchetti & Ganiban, 1990; Cohen, 1981), and in infants exposed prenatally to alcohol (Jacobson et al., 1993). Longer looking has also been observed in primate infants who have been nutritionally deprived (Reisbick, Neuringer, Gohl, Wald, & Anderson, 1997). Within-age variation in look duration has been associated with variation in the rapidity or efficiency of stimulus encoding in low-risk populations as well (e.g., Colombo et al., 1991, 1996; Colombo, Freeseman, Coldren, & Frick, 1995; Freeseman, Colombo, & Coldren, 1993; Frick & Colombo, 1996; Gifford, Colombo, Ryther, Gorman, & Stowe, 1995).

Look Duration and Visual Encoding

We have reviewed data suggesting that individual differences in look duration covary with differences in the rapidity of stimulus processing. However, it has also been suggested that such individual differences in the rapidity of visual information processing may be due to differences with which long- and short-looking infants attend to, and perhaps encode, different properties of visual information.

Most of this work has focused on the processing of the overall ("global") configuration of visual stimuli versus the featural ("local") details that also comprise such stimuli (see Fig. 12.5). The global–local distinction has a long history in the behavioral literature in the form of debates between the holistic–Gestalt–differentiation and reductionist–feature analysis–integration theories of perception and perceptual development. Indeed, attention to these two properties of the visual environment appears to be orthogonal (see Corbetta, Miezin, Dobmeyer, Shulman, & Petersen, 1990; Kinchla, Solis-Macias, & Hoffman, 1983; Marshall & Halligan, 1995). The global–local distinction is most evident in the current literatures with reference to the global precedence phenomenon (Hughes, Layton, Baird, & Lester, 1984; Lamb & Yund, 1993; Navon, 1977, 1983; see also Nelson & Dukette, chap. 11, this volume). Recently, the distinction has also been the focus of arguments over the nature of local and global properties; it has been hypothesized that these properties may be isomorphic with high- and low-spatial frequency components in visual displays (Badcock, Whitworth, Badcock, & Lovegrove, 1990; Breitmeyer, 1975; Breitmeyer & Ganz, 1976; Hughes, Fendrich, & Reuter-Lorenz, 1990; Hughes, Nozawa, & Kitterle, 1996; Hughes & Sprague, 1986).

Research on the possibility that long- and short-lookers vary in the quality of their visual encoding started at the end of the last decade. A series of initial studies (Colombo et al., 1991; Freeseman et al., 1993) suggested that individual differences in look duration covaried only with the rapidity with which infants processed both of the two visual properties. However,

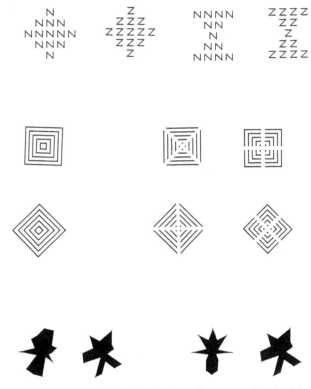

FIG. 12.5. Examples of stimuli used in studies summarized in this section. The top panel shows hierarchically organized stimulus sets used in Colombo et al. (1995). Infants were familiarized with a particular target (e.g., a diamond made of Ns) and then novel properties were put in competition with one another on paired-comparison trials (e.g., an hourglass made of Ns versus a diamond made of Zs). The middle panel shows the stimuli from Frick and Colombo (1996). Infants were familiarized with a complete stimulus (square or diamond, far left column), and then tested with targets with either the vertex deleted (middle column) or the midsegment deleted (far right column). The bottom panel shows the discriminations tested in Gifford et al. (1995). The right-hand pair show the stimuli used for the symmetrical–asymmetrical discrimination, and the left-hand pair show the stimuli used for the asymmetrical–asymmetrical discrimination.

Colombo et al. (1995) subsequently reported tests of the perceptual dominance of the two visual properties in short- and long-looking infants. This was accomplished by taking advantage of infants' predilection to attend to novel stimuli after sufficient familiarization. Novel global and novel local properties were put in competition with one another after such familiarization, and the direction of infants' attention was noted. The results suggested that, for short-looking infants, novel global properties were dominant at brief familiarization, and local properties became dominant when familiarization was extended (Paquet & Merikle, 1984, report such a pattern for adults). For long-looking infants, however, a dominant property did not emerge until after extended familiarization, at which point the local properties were selectively attended-to.

Gifford et al. (1995) approached the processing of global versus local visual processing in long- and short-looking infants by testing for differences in the processing of symmetrical versus asymmetrical stimuli (see Fig. 12.5). Given that both adults (Palmer & Hemenway, 1987) and infants (Bornstein, Ferdinandsen, & Gross, 1981) process vertically symmetrical visual forms faster than asymmetrical ones, and that visual symmetry is recognized through globally directed attention (Locher & Nodine, 1973, 1987), subjects suspected of being biased toward local visual analysis should not show an advantage of processing symmetrical over asymmetrical forms. Thus, long- and short-lookers were tested for processing of vertically symmetrical versus asymmetrical visual stimuli within standard paired-comparison discrimination paradigms and across varying levels of familiarization. The results of these studies were in direct accord with the predictions made: Short-looking infants encoded symmetrical forms at briefer familiarization than that necessary for encoding of asymmetrical forms. Long-looking infants, on the other hand, needed more extensive familiarization to encode either type of stimulus and, in fact, actually showed evidence for encoding asymmetrical stimuli *before* encoding symmetrical stimuli.

Frick and Colombo (1996) addressed the issue via another avenue. They assessed 4-month-old long- and short-looking infants' recognition of visual targets that were degraded in different ways (see Fig. 12.5). If long-looking infants were in fact reliant on local elements or particular visual contours for visual encoding, then this should be reflected in difficulty in recognizing forms in which contours have been deleted, or "degraded." Targets were degraded by removing the contour at either stimulus vertices (i.e., contour intersections) or at contour midsegments; length of familiarization was varied systematically. Short-looking infants recognized midsegment-deleted stimuli under conditions of brief familiarization, and recognized vertex-deleted stimuli after familiarization was increased. Long-looking infants recognized midsegment-deleted stimuli only at extended levels of familiarization, and never showed recognition of vertex-deleted stimuli, even after maximizing familiarization with a habituation procedure. Long-looking infants, then, appeared to be dependent on particular local contour for recognition of visual stimuli. This possibility has been examined in a convergent manner in Colombo et al. (1996), with similar results.

The Cognitive Neuroscience of Global–Local Processing. If individual differences in look duration covary with the processing of local and global visual properties, then three distinct alternatives can be plausibly considered from a cognitive neuroscience approach.

First, if indeed global and local visual properties are simply reducible to low and high spatial frequencies in the visual display, then individual differences in processing these frequencies may be mediated by particular subdivisions of the geniculostriate system whose responses are thought to more optimally responsive to either low- or high-spatial frequency information (Hickey, 1977; Hickey & Peduzzi, 1987; Livingstone & Hubel, 1987, 1988; Merigan & Maunsell, 1993; Regan, 1982; see also Colombo, 1995a).

Second, if differences in the perceptual precedence of, or reliance on, one or other of these properties is interpreted as individual differences in the ability to direct and focus attention to either of these properties, then a number of studies point to either prestriate visual cortex (Fink et al., 1996) or the superior temporal gyrus (Lamb, Robertson, & Knight, 1990; Polster & Rapscak, 1994; Robertson & Lamb, 1991; Robertson, Lamb, & Knight, 1988) as the potential substrates involved.

Finally, if these differences are interpreted in terms of infants' ability to *switch* or *allocate* attention to and from global and local properties, then parietal areas may be the locus of interest, based on studies suggesting that parietal damage affects the distribution of attentional resources (i.e., covert shifting) to the temporal lobe subsystems (Lamb et al., 1990; Polster & Rapscak, 1994; Robertson & Lamb, 1991; see also Rafal & Robertson, 1995) and that temporal-parietal activation is observed when subjects are asked to switch attention between such properties in a visual display (Fink et al., 1996).

Look Duration and Disengagement of Attention

Although individual differences in look duration have long been considered to be reflective of information processing, some theorists (Cohen, 1976; Colombo, 1995a) have speculated that such individual differences might simply reflect the ability of infants to disengage their attention from loci in the visual field or from visual stimuli (see also Hood, Atkinson, & Braddick, chap. 7, this volume; Richards & Hunter, chap. 4, this volume).

Several studies have been conducted indicating a relationship between look duration and disengagement of attention. In Frick, Colombo, and Saxon (1996), 3- and 4-month-old infants were first assessed on their characteristic look duration. Following this pretest, infants were engaged in a peripheral-stimulus detection task under conditions where either (a) a central stimulus remained illuminated when the peripheral stimulus was presented, or (b) where the central stimulus was withdrawn before the peripheral stimulus appeared. In (a), the infant was required to disengage attention before shifting to the peripheral stimulus, whereas in (b) such disengagement was not required. Three-month-olds' RTs to move toward the peripheral target were slower than 4-month-olds' RTs, and these younger infants were especially impaired on trials that required disengagement. Furthermore, at both ages, individual differences in look duration were significantly correlated with the latency of eye movements during tasks requiring disengagement of attention, but not on trials that did not require such disengagement. These results strongly suggest that longer fixations may be associated with difficulties in attentional disengagement. Just as importantly, however, the findings suggest that individual differences in look duration may be independent of overall differences in RT.

More evidence for the role of disengagement has come from a recent study of 4-month-old infants' heart rate (HR) patterns during infant-controlled habituation sessions to facial stimuli (Colombo, Frick, Gorman, & Casebolt, 1997). In this study, HR was continuously monitored simultaneous with infants' looking, so that it was possible to know, for example, the infants' HR just prior to the onset of a look, during a look, just before the termination of a look, and just after the termination of a look. Both long- and short-looking infants showed significant HR decelerations during fixations, relative to their HR prior to the initiation of a look. However, on average, short-looking infants terminated their looks *before* their HR levels returned to prelook levels. Long-looking infants terminated their fixations only when their HRs had returned to, or exceeded, prelook levels. Richards (1988; Richards & Casey, 1991) suggested that infants' visual fixations may be segregated into three HR-defined phases of attention: "orienting" (the initial decelerative decline), "sustained attention" (the decelerative asymptote, the period during which the greatest amount of information processing presumably occurs), and "attention termination" (the period during which HR returns to baseline levels). These findings suggest that short-looking infants do not continue looking during the entire attention termination phase, and that long-looking infants typically do not "let go" of their looking until attention termination ends. Again, this is entirely consistent with the hypothesis that the ability to disengage attention contributes to individual differences in look duration.

The Cognitive Neuroscience of Attentional Disengagement. Thanks to research over the last two decades, the cognitive neuroscience of attentional disengagement is relatively clear. In the adult, a CNS substrate composed of the superior colliculus, thalamus, and parietal cortex, is believed to mediate the disengagement, shifting, and engagement of attention to various features of the visual environment (e.g., Posner, 1980; Posner, Walker, Friedrich, & Rafal, 1984, 1987). Specific difficulties in disengagement of attention have been most closely linked to parietal cortex (Harvey & Milner, 1995; Pierrot-Deseilligny, Gray, & Brunet, 1986; Posner et al., 1984, 1987; Rafal & Robertson, 1995), the most extreme condition of which is the "gaze apraxia" seen in Bàlint's syndrome (Hausser, Robert, & Girard, 1980;

Husain & Stein, 1988; see also Baylis, chap. 8, this volume; Rafal, chap. 6, this volume).

Of further interest to the developmental audience is the observation that the behaviors associated with the collicular–thalamic–parietal system that mediates attentional disengagement in the adult appear to emerge somewhere between 2 and 6 months of age (Clohessy, Posner, Rothbart, & Vecera, 1991; Hood, 1993; Johnson, Posner, & Rothbart, 1991; Johnson & Tucker, 1993; Vecera et al., 1991). This is exactly the period during which (a) look durations may best reflect differences between individuals (Colombo, Mitchell, O'Brien, & Horowitz, 1987a, 1987b), (b) the course of look durations exhibits the greatest developmental change (Colombo & Mitchell, 1990), and (c) the correlations of look duration with later measures of cognitive status are robust (McCall & Carriger, 1993; Rose et al., 1986).

Summary and Synthesis

At this point, the various processes reflected by look duration imply the involvement of various CNS substrates (see Fig. 12.6). The candidate substrates include the geniculostriate subpathways, prestriate cortex, the tem-

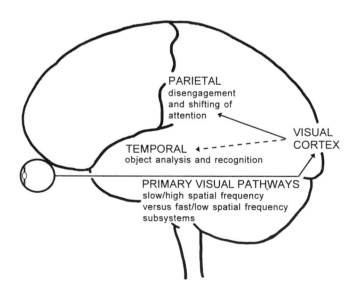

FIG. 12.6. A highly simplified depiction of the dissociable substrates that may mediate individual differences in habituation/look duration performance (solid lines) and individual differences in novelty preference (dashed lines). The presence of different substrates mediating the two tasks would be in accord with the observation that correlations between infants' performance are possible, but not necessarily inevitable.

poral lobe, and the parietal cortex. It is of interest that the adult function of the parietal cortex overlaps to some degree with respect to individual differences in both the response to global and local visual properties and in the disengagement of attention from stimuli. The parietal lobe appears to have a role in the biasing of attention between the local and global aspects of the visual field, and there are anecdotal references to local interference with global processing in patients afflicted with Bàlint's syndrome (Rafal & Robertson, 1995). Furthermore, in the adult, the role of the parietal lobe in the disengagement of attention seems clear. Thus, a parsimonious model for the substrate mediating individual differences in look durations during infancy could involve the development of the parietal area. However, further work is obviously necessary to examine each of these areas in more detail, and to determine which substrate(s) contribute to the preservation of cognitive function from infancy to later childhood.

INDIVIDUAL DIFFERENCES IN NOVELTY PREFERENCES

This section addresses the possible neural substrates mediating individual differences in infant performance in the familiarization–novelty paired-comparison paradigm. Again, the discriminative response most typically observed in this paradigm is the novelty preference.

The catalogue of candidate processes that may be brought to bear on individual differences in novelty preferences is actually much larger than that for look duration (e.g., Fagan, 1990). This is because the occurrence of the novelty preference is dependent upon at least three different and conceivably independent cognitive functions: The infant must be able to (a) encode some representation of the visual stimulus with which she or he has been familiarized, (b) remember which one of those stimuli was previously shown, and (c) exhibit the discriminative response (i.e., prefer to fixate) to the novel stimulus. Thus, the requisite components for showing a novelty preference may be derived from at least three different domains: the facility of perceptual encoding, the function of recognition memory processes, and the infant's disposition to actually fixate the novel stimulus.

As such, the neural substrate that one proposes to mediate infant performance on this measure will vary with the process that one assumes it reflects. As an example, one may contend that the primary contributor to infants' novelty preference performance is individual differences in visual acuity or resolution. From this position, it is obvious that any lower-order component of the visual system may be brought to bear as underlying substrates in a cognitive neuroscience analysis. However, given that most considerations of the long-term implications for individual differences in novelty-preference performance assume intact and normal visual function in the infant, we are left with the consideration of higher-order cognitive processes that follow.

Novelty Preferences as Facility of Encoding

Facility of encoding clearly contributes to the manifestation of the novelty preference. Perhaps the best evidence of this is the fact that success with the paired-comparison technique is virtually dependent on the length of the familiarization that precedes the choice-trial preference tests (Colombo, 1993). Familiarization that is too brief will yield either random responding on the part of the infant, or even a preference for the familiarized stimulus. Familiarization that is too long will result in attrition or variable performance on the part of the infant. From this point of view, then, infants who do not show novelty preferences may in fact be characterized to have failed to sufficiently process the familiarized stimulus in the study time allotted prior to choice-trial tests.

As such, then, novelty preference performance may be interpreted in terms of a parameter of encoding speed. This construct has been long considered to underlie individual differences in this measure, although it is worth noting that no clear and prospective evidence has been collected to implicate rapidity of encoding as the primary source of predictive validity in the novelty preference. If this rapidity of encoding does in fact underlie the predictive validity of this measure, then the underlying model would resemble the parametric form of the general-process schematic depicted in Fig. 12.2B.

Novelty Preferences as Recognition Memory

Although rapidity of encoding is a logical consideration in interpreting individual differences in novelty preferences, such individual differences in novelty preferences may be more commonly interpreted as a reflection of early recognition memory processes (Nelson, 1995; Overman, Bachevalier, Sewell, & Drew, 1993; see also Colombo, Mitchell, Dodd, Coldren, & Horowitz, 1989).

If recognition memory is given such consideration, however, then Bachevalier's (1990) program of research on animal models of recognition memory deficits may be brought to bear on the issue. Much of this research program focuses on structures that have been commonly implicated in memory function, such as the limbic system (e.g., hippocampus) and cortical structures adjacent to the limbic system. To some degree, an understanding of the function of these structures is problematic, because it is still uncertain whether performance deficits incurred by lesions to these

areas are attributable to deficits in recognition memory *per se*, or to difficulties in the encoding process (Grady, McIntosh, Horwitz, & Maisog,
1995). On the other hand, however, a strength of this research is the fact
that it has employed animal testing paradigms that are very similar to those
used with preverbal infants (Bachevalier, Brickson, & Hagger, 1993). Thus,
it is likely that the results of such studies are directly relevant to a consideration of individual differences in infant performance.

Bachevalier and Mishkin (1984) initially reported a functional, anatomical, and developmental dissociation of cortico-limbic and nonlimbic memory systems in the monkey; visual recognition memory was linked to the
former (Malkova, Mishkin, & Bachevalier, 1995), while habit memory was
linked to the latter (Bachevalier & Mishkin, 1986). Subsequent work established the validity of these dissociations in the human infant as well
(Overman, Bachevalier, Turner, & Peuster, 1992). Recent evidence strongly
suggests that performance on the paired-comparison task is impaired by
lesions to limbic structures, such as the amygdaloid complex and hippocampus (Bachevalier et al., 1993; Bachevalier & Mishkin, 1994), and perhaps also
by perirhinal cortex (Meunier, Bachevalier, Mishkin, & Murray, 1993).
Similar findings have also been reported for human subjects with limbic
system damage (McKee & Squire, 1993). Nelson (1995) has further posited
that memory systems that derive input from temporal cortex (see Bachevalier, Brickson, Hagger, & Mishkin, 1990; Phillips, Malamut, Bachevalier, &
Mishkin, 1988) also probably contribute to novelty preference performance
in the paired-comparison paradigm during infancy.

Novelty Preference as a Preference for Novelty

First, novelty preferences may be interpreted in a very literal sense, as Berg
and Sternberg (1985) have done. That is, novelty preferences may be
considered to reflect a predilection for attending to novel stimuli or events
in the environment. If this is the case, the response-to-novelty construct
(variously measured) has been attributed to the function of frontal cortex
(e.g., Paradowski, Zaretsky, Brucker, & Alba, 1980), to fronto-limbic pathways (Levine & Prueitt, 1989; Metcalfe, 1993; Roberts & Tarassenko, 1994),
or to more holistic CNS systems whose presumed purpose is novelty detection (Tulving, Markowitsch, Kapur, Habib, & Houle, 1994). Indeed, in
chapter 11 of this volume, Nelson and Dukette have suggested that increased fixation to a novel stimulus (at least in the oddball paradigms that
dominate EEG work with subjects of all ages) may in some way be "obligatory" in nature. If a mechanism in fact mediated such detection and steer-
ing of attention to novel elements in the environment, then it would fit
within this realm.

There is one serious drawback to the consideration of novelty preferences as reflecting simply a positive response for novelty, however. This is

the fact that under conditions where processing demands are increased on infants (e.g., when three-dimensional stimuli are used, or when familiarization is marginal), the discriminative response in the paired-comparison paradigm is often expressed in the form of a familiarity preference, which has also been found to be predictive of childhood cognitive status (see Colombo, 1993, for a detailed exposition). This suggests that the critical components involved in novelty preference are probably more cognitive than motivational in nature.

Summary

Clearly, we favor a matrix of visual encoding and recognition memory as the primary determinants mediating individual differences in novelty preference. If this is the case, then it would appear that cortical and subcortical temporal structures, such as the limbic system and temporal cortex (Nelson, 1995) would presumably constitute the best candidates for substrates contributing to individual differences in early performance on this measure. Again, as we have noted, recognition memory tasks are resistant to componential analyses, and more work is necessary to delineate the influence of other cognitive and neural contributors to such individual differences. However, if temporal-limbic structures constitute the primary influence on novelty preference performance, then it is possible that novelty preference and look duration is mediated by different substrates (see Fig. 12.6). Such would account for the dissociation of these measures in previous behavioral work (Jacobson, 1995; Jacobson et al., 1992).

DIRECTIONS AND QUESTIONS FOR FUTURE RESEARCH

The Cognitive Neuroscience of Early Individual Differences

Since the discovery that individual differences in infants' performance on information-processing tasks might in fact represent meaningful differences in cognitive ability, investigators have attempted to enumerate, dissociate, and isolate particular cognitive constructs or underlying substrates that contribute to such performance. As should be evident from the preceding text of this chapter, this is not a trivial undertaking. In examining only a few measures of early visual cognition, we have summoned a plethora of cognitive processes and neural substrates that might account for, or contribute to, individual differences in performance on these measures.

This is probably attributable to the fact that the current methods for assessing infant cognition were designed neither to yield cleanly defined cognitive constructs nor to be amenable to a cognitive neuroscience analysis (Janowsky, 1996). The existing tasks and paradigms (e.g., visual habituation, paired-comparison, visual expectation) were constructed to tap the *functional* cognitive abilities of infants. Thus, at least for the present time and with current methods of infant assessment, the dissection or divination of specific cognitive structures or substrates may always be a difficult, speculative, and frustrating endeavor. How, then, might the cognitive neuroscience of individual differences in infancy best proceed? Two possibilities come to mind.

First, cognitive developmental studies might simply consider the component processes of the tasks used and evaluate which of those processes predict continuity in individual differences and which do not. This strategy does not, however, address the neural basis for the continuity in individual differences in cognition; this would require an additional survey of the neural bases of these processes from studies from the adult cognitive neuroscience literature. Second, it might be possible to use tasks that have been examined in cognitive neuroscience studies of adults in which both the component processes have been delineated as well as their associated neural bases.

Both of these approaches are problematic, however, for the following reasons. First, we cannot assume that the neural basis of a particular component process is the same throughout development. Two examples suggest that this may not be the case. First, consider the fact that newborn infants show a developmental stepping reflex that looks similar to actual walking later in development, but which is probably not mediated at all by the motor cortex (Thelen & Ulrich, 1991). A second more cognitive example is provided by Goldman-Rakic and colleagues (Goldman & Rosvold, 1972; Goldman, Rosvold, & Mishkin, 1970a, 1970b), who have shown that regions such as the frontal lobe that appear to play only a small role in delayed response performance early in development actually play a critical role later, whereas the caudate nucleus is critical for delayed response performance early in development and may be unimportant for performance later in development. Thus the neural basis of cognitive functions, and possibly even component processes, may shift across the lifespan.

The Cognitive Neuroscience of Continuity from Infancy

Although we have dealt with the cognitive neuroscience of individual differences in infant cognition in this chapter, we have not dealt with the cognitive neuroscience of continuity per se. That is, we have held at arm's length the question of which CNS substrates mediate the continuity of processes reflected by tasks that measure infant cognition.

A cognitive neuroscience of continuity must satisfactorily address the fact that the neural systems of interest change dramatically over the first months and years of life. The numbers of synapses, efficiency of neural transmission, myelination, and so forth, are all modified during early development. So possibly the biggest quandary for the future of developmental cognitive neuroscience is not *what* cognitive processes show continuity in individual differences or what neural system subserves the cognitive process, but *how* continuity is maintained when the neural hardware mediating the processes is continuously modified. From the cognitive neuroscience point of view, it may be very difficult to attribute such continuity to the simple survival of individual differences on a single component or parameter of information processing from infancy. Instead, it may be necessary to invoke a much more complex developmental course of events, similar to that which is routinely considered within the framework of developmental systems theory (Turkewitz & Devenny, 1993).

ACKNOWLEDGMENTS

Preparation of this chapter was supported in part by NIH Grants HD29960 to J.C., and AG12611 to J.S.J. We are grateful to Shelley Francis, Dr. Janet Frick, and W. Allen Richman for editorial help with an earlier draft of this chapter.

REFERENCES

Anderson, M. (1992). *Intelligence and development: A cognitive theory.* Oxford: Blackwell.

Bachevalier, J. (1990). Ontogenetic development of habit and memory formation in primates. *Annals of the New York Academy of Sciences, 608,* 457–484.

Bachevalier, J., Brickson, M., & Hagger, C. (1993). Limbic-dependent recognition memory in monkeys develops early in infancy. *Neuroreport, 4,* 77–80.

Bachevalier, J., Brickson, M., Hagger, C., & Mishkin, M. (1990). Age and sex differences in the effects of selective temporal lobe lesion on the formation of visual discrimination habits in rhesus monkeys (Macaca mulatta). *Behavioral Neuroscience, 104,* 885–899.

Bachevalier, J., & Mishkin, M. (1984). An early and late developing system for learning and retention in infant monkeys. *Behavioural Neuroscience, 98,* 770–778.

Bachevalier, J., & Mishkin, M. (1986). Visual recognition impairment follows ventromedial but not dorsolateral prefrontal lesions in monkeys. *Behavioural Brain Research, 20,* 249–261.

Bachevalier, J., & Mishkin, M. (1994). Effects of selective neonatal temporal lobe lesions on visual recognition memory in rhesus monkeys. *Journal of Neuroscience, 14,* 2128–2139.

Badcock, J. C., Whitworth, F. A., Badcock, D. R., & Lovegrove, W. J. (1990). Low-frequency filtering and the processing of local-global stimuli. *Perception, 19,* 617–629.

Benasich, A. A., & Bejar, I. I. (1992). The Fagan Test of Infant Intelligence: A critical review. *Journal of Applied Developmental Psychology, 13,* 153–171.

Berntson, G. G., & Torello, M. W. (1982). The paleocerebellum and the integration of behavioral function. *Physiological Psychology, 10,* 2–12.

Berg, C., & Sternberg, R. J. (1985). Response to novelty: Continuity versus discontinuity in the developmental course of intelligence. In H. W. Reese (Ed.), *Advances in child development and behavior* (Vol. 15, pp. 1–47). New York: Academic Press.

Bornstein, M. H., Ferdinandsen, K., & Gross, C. G. (1981). Perception of symmetry in infancy. *Developmental Psychology, 17*, 82–86.

Bornstein, M. H., & Sigman, M. D. (1986). Continuity in mental development from infancy. *Child Development, 57*, 251–274.

Bornstein, M. H., & Tamis-Lemonda, C. S. (1994). Antecedents of information-processing skills in infants: Habituation, novelty responsiveness, and cross-modal transfer. *Infant Behavior and Development, 17*, 371–380.

Breitmeyer, B. G. (1975). Simple reaction time as a measure of the temporal response properties of transient and sustained channels. *Vision Research, 15*, 1411–1412.

Breitmeyer, B. G., & Ganz, L. (1976). Implications of sustained and transient channels for theories of visual pattern masking, saccadic suppression, and information processing. *Psychological Review, 83*, 1–36.

Casey, B. J., Gordon, C. T., Mannheim, G. B., & Rumsey, J. M. (1993). Dysfunctional attention in savants. *Journal of Clinical and Experimental Neuropsychology, 15*, 933–946.

Cicchetti, D., & Ganiban, J. M. (1990). The organization and coherence of developmental processes in infants and children with Down syndrome. In R. M. Hodapp, J. A. Burack, & E. Zigler (Eds.), *Issues in the developmental approach to mental retardation* (pp. 169–225). New York: Cambridge University Press.

Clohessy, A. B., Posner, M. I., Rothbart, M. K., & Vecera, S. P. (1991). The development of inhibition of return in early infancy. *Journal of Cognitive Neuroscience, 3*, 345–350.

Cohen, L. B. (1976). Habituation of infant visual attention. In T. Tighe & R. Leaton (Eds.), *Habituation* (pp. 241–253). Hillsdale, NJ: Lawrence Erlbaum Associates.

Cohen, L. B. (1981). Examination of habituation as a measure of aberrant infant development. In S. L. Friedman & M. D. Sigman (Eds.), *Preterm birth and psychological development* (pp. 241–253). New York: Academic Press.

Cohen, L. B. (1988). An information processing approach to infant cognitive development. In L. Weiskrantz (Ed.), *Thought without language* (pp. 211–228). Oxford, England: Clarendon Press.

Colombo, J. (1993). *Infant cognition: Predicting childhood intelligence.* Newbury Park, CA: Sage.

Colombo, J. (1995a). On the neural mechanisms underlying developmental and individual differences in infant fixation duration: Two hypotheses. *Developmental Review, 15*, 97–135.

Colombo, J. (1995b). *Some hypotheses about speed of processing in infancy.* Society for Research in Child Development, Indianapolis, Indiana.

Colombo, J., Freeseman, L. J., Coldren, J. T., & Frick, J. E. (1995). Individual differences in infant visual fixation: Dominance of global and local stimulus properties. *Cognitive Development, 10*, 271–285.

Colombo, J., & Frick, J. E. (in press). Recent advances and issues in the study of preverbal intelligence. In M. Anderson (Ed.), *Development of intelligence.* London: University College of London Press.

Colombo, J., Frick, J. E., Gorman, S. A., & Casebolt, K. (1997). *Infant heart rate patterns during infant-controlled habituation sessions.* Society for Research in Child Development, Washington, DC.

Colombo, J., Frick, J. E., Ryther, J. S., & Gifford, J. J. (1996). Individual differences in infant visual attention: Four-month-olds' recognition of forms connoted by complementary contour. *Infant Behavior and Development, 19*, 113–119.

Colombo, J., & Mitchell, D. W. (1990). Individual and developmental differences in infant visual attention. In J. Colombo & J. W. Fagen (Eds.), *Individual differences in infancy* (pp. 193–227). Hillsdale, NJ: Lawrence Erlbaum Associates.

Colombo, J., Mitchell, D. W., Coldren, J. T., & Freeseman, L. J. (1991). Individual differences in infant visual attention: Are short lookers feature processors or faster processors? *Child Development, 62,* 1247–1257.

Colombo, J., Mitchell, D. W., Dodd, J. D., Coldren, J. T., & Horowitz, F. D. (1989). Longitudinal correlates of infant attention in the paired comparison paradigm. *Intelligence, 13,* 33–42.

Colombo, J., Mitchell, D. W., O'Brien, M., & Horowitz, F. D. (1987a). Stability of infant visual habituation during the first year. *Child Development, 58,* 474–489.

Colombo, J., Mitchell, D. W., O'Brien, M., & Horowitz, F. D. (1987b). Stimulus and motoric influences on visual habituation at three months. *Infant Behavior and Development, 10,* 173–181.

Corbetta, M., Miezin, F. M., Dobmeyer, S., Shulman, G. L., & Petersen, S. E. (1990). Attentional modulation of neural processing of shape, color, and velocity in humans. *Science, 248,* 1556–1559.

Courchesne, E. (1989). Neuroanatomical systems involved in infantile autism: Implication of cerebellar abnormalities. In G. Dawson (Ed.), *Autism: Nature, diagnosis, and treatment* (pp. 119–143). New York: Guilford Press.

Courchesne, E. (1995). Infantile autism. Part II: A new neurodevelopmental model. *International Pediatrics, 10,* 155–165.

Damasio, A. R. (1994). *Descartes' error.* New York: Avon.

Detterman, D. K. (1994). Intelligence and the brain. In P. A. Vernon (Ed.), *The neuropsychology of individual differences* (pp. 35–58). New York: Academic Press.

DiLalla, L. F., Thompson, L. A., Plomin, R., Phillips, K., Fagan, J. F., Haith, M. M., Cyphers, L. H., & Fulker, D. W. (1990). Infant predictors of preschool and adult IQ: A study of infant twins and their parents. *Developmental Psychology, 26,* 759–769.

Dougherty, T. M., & Haith, M. M. (1993, March). *Relations between manual RT, visual RT, and IQ.* Society for Research in Child Development, Indianapolis, IN.

Fagan, J. F. (1981). Infant intelligence. *Intelligence, 5,* 239–243.

Fagan, J. F. (1984a). The intelligent infant: Implications. *Intelligence, 8,* 1–9.

Fagan, J. F. (1984b). The relationship of novelty preferences during infancy to later intelligence and recognition memory. *Intelligence, 8,* 339–346.

Fagan, J. F. (1990). The paired-comparison paradigm and infant intelligence. *Annals of the New York Academy of Sciences, 608,* 337–364.

Fagan, J. F., & McGrath, S. K. (1981). Infant recognition memory and later intelligence. *Intelligence, 5,* 121–130.

Fagan, J. F., & Shepard, P. A. (1986/1987). *The Fagan test of infant intelligence.* Cleveland, OH: Infantest Corporation.

Fagan, J. F., & Singer, L. T. (1983). Infant recognition memory as a measure of intelligence. In L. P. Lipsitt & C. K. Rovee-Collier (Eds.), *Advances in infancy research* (Vol. 2, pp. 31–79). Norwood, NJ: Ablex.

Fagan, J. F., Singer, J., Montie, J., & Shepard, P. A. (1986). Selective screening device for the early detection of normal or delayed cognitive development in infants at risk for later mental retardation. *Pediatrics, 78,* 1021–1026.

Fagen, J. W. (1995). Predicting IQ from infancy: We're getting closer. *Contemporary Psychology, 40,* 19–20.

Fagen, J. W., & Ohr, P. S. (1990). Individual differences in infant conditioning and memory. In J. Colombo & J. W. Fagen (Eds.), *Individual differences in infancy* (pp. 155–192). Hillsdale, NJ: Lawrence Erlbaum Associates.

Fink, G. R., Halligan, P. W., Marshall, J. C., Frith, C. D., Frackowiak, R. S. J., & Dolan, R. J. (1996). Where in the brain does visual attention select the forest from the trees? *Nature, 382,* 626–628.

Freeseman, L. J., Colombo, J., & Coldren, J. T. (1993). Individual differences in infant visual attention: Four-month-olds' discrimination and generalization of global and local stimulus properties. *Child Development, 64,* 1191–1203.

Frick, J. E., & Colombo, J. (1996). Individual differences in infant visual attention:Recognition of degraded visual forms by 4-month-olds. *Child Development, 67*, 188–204.

Frick, J. E., Colombo, J., & Gorman, S. A. (1997). *Sensitization during visual habituation sequences: Procedural effects and individual differences.* Society for Research in Child Development, Washington, DC.

Frick, J. E., Colombo, J., & Saxon, T. F. (1996, April). *Long looking infants are slower to disengage fixation.* International Conference on Infant Studies, Providence, RI.

Gifford, J. J., Colombo, J., Ryther, J. S., Gorman, S. A., & Stowe, K. (1995, April). *Long and short looking infants' recognition of symmetrical and asymmetrical forms.* Society for Research in Child Development, Indianapolis, IN.

Goldman, P. S., & Rosvold, H. E. (1972). The effects of selective caudate lesions in infant and juvenile rhesus monkeys. *Brain Research, 43*, 53–66.

Goldman, P. S., Rosvold, H. E., & Mishkin, M. (1970a). Evidence for behavioral impairment following prefrontal lobectomy in the infant monkey. *Journal of Comparative Physiological and Psychology, 70*, 454–463.

Goldman, P. S., Rosvold, H. E., & Mishkin, M. (1970b). Selective sparing of function following prefrontal lobectomy in infant monkeys. *Experimental Neurology, 29*, 221–226.

Grady, C. L., McIntosh, A. R., Horwitz, B., & Maisog, J. M. (1995). Age-related reductions in human recognition memory due to impaired encoding. *Neuroscience, 269*, 218–221.

Haith, M. M., Hazan, C., & Goodman, G. (1988). Expectation and anticipation of dynamic visual events by 3.5-month-old babies. *Child Development, 59*, 467–479.

Harvey, M., & Milner, A. D. (1995). Bálint's patient. *Cognitive Neuropsychology, 12*, 261–281.

Hausser, C. O., Robert, F., & Girard, N. (1980). Bálint's syndrome. *Canadian Journal of Neurological Science, 1*, 405–422.

Hickey, T. L. (1977). Postnatal development of the human lateral geniculate nucleus: Relationship to a critical period for the visual system. *Science, 198*, 836–838.

Hickey, T. L., & Peduzzi, J. D. (1987). Structure and development of the visual system. In L. Cohen & P. Salapatek (Eds.), *Handbook of infant perception* (pp. 1–42). New York: Academic Press.

Hood, B. M. (1993). Inhibition of return produced by covert shifts of visual attention in 6-month-old infants. *Infant Behavior and Development, 16*, 245–254.

Horowitz, F. D., Paden, L. Y., Bhana, K., & Self, P. A. (1972). An infant control procedure for studying infant visual fixations. *Developmental Psychology, 7*, 90.

Hughes, H. C., Fendrich, R., & Reuter-Lorenz, P. A. (1990). Global versus local processing in the absence of low spatial frequencies. *Journal of Cognitive Neuroscience, 2*, 272–282.

Hughes, H. C., Layton, W. M., Baird, J. C., & Lester, L. S. (1984). Global precedence in visual pattern recognition. *Perception and Psychophysics, 35*, 361–371.

Hughes, H. C., Nozawa, G., & Kitterle, F. (1996). Global precedence, spatial frequency, and the statistics of natural images. *Journal of Cognitive Neuroscience, 8*, 197–230.

Hughes, H. C., & Sprague, J. M. (1986). Cortical mechanisms for local and global analysis of visual space in the cat. *Experimental Brain Research, 6*, 332–354.

Husain, M., & Stein, J. (1988). Rezsö Bálint and his most celebrated case. *History of Neurology, 45*, 89–93.

Jacobson, S. W. (1995, March). *Evidence for speed of processing and recognition memory components of infant information processing.* Society for Research in Child Development, Indianapolis, IN.

Jacobson, S. W., Chiodo, L. M., & Jacobson, J. L. (1996). *Predictive validity of infant recognition memory and processing speed to 7-year IQ in an inner-city sample.* International Conference on Infant Studies, Providence, RI.

Jacobson S. W., Fein, G. G., Jacobson, J. L., Schwartz, P. M., & Dowler, J. K. (1985). The effects of intrauterine PCB exposure on visual recognition memory. *Child Development, 56*, 853–860.

Jacobson, S. W., Jacobson, J. J., O'Neill, J. M., Padgett, R. J., Frankowski, J. J., & Bihun, J. T. (1992). Visual expectation and dimensions of infant information processing. *Child Development, 63,* 711–724.

Jacobson, S. W., Jacobson, J. L., Sokol, R. J., Martier, S. S., & Ager, J. W. (1993). Prenatal alcohol exposure and infant information processing ability. *Child Development, 64,* 1706–1721.

Janowsky, J. S. (1996). *The effects of fatty acid supplementation on the brain and language development.* Paper presented at the International Conference on Infant Studies, Providence, RI.

Jensen, A. R. (1993). Why is reaction time correlated with psychometric *g? Current Directions in Psychological Science, 2,* 53–55.

Johnson, M. H., Posner, M. I., & Rothbart, M. K. (1991). Components of visual orienting in early infancy: Contingency learning, anticipatory looking, and disengaging. *Journal of Cognitive Neuroscience, 3,* 335–344.

Johnson, M. H., & Tucker, L. A. (1993, April). *The ontogeny of covert visual attention: Facilitatory and inhibitory effects.* Society for Research in Child Development, New Orleans, LA.

Kinchla, R. A., Solis-Macias, V., & Hoffman, J. (1983). Attending to different levels of structure in a visual image. *Perception and Psychophysics, 33,* 1–10.

Lamarre, G., & Pomerleau, A. (1985, July). *The meaning of individual differences in early habituation.* International Society for the Study of Behavioral Development, Tours, France.

Lamb, M. R., Robertson, L. C., & Knight, R. T. (1990). Component mechanisms underlying the processing of hierarchically organized patterns: Inferences from patients with unilateral cortical lesions. *Journal of Experimental Psychology: Learning, Memory, and Cognition, 16,* 471–483.

Lamb, M. R., & Yund, E. W. (1993). The role of spatial frequency in the processing of hierarchically organized stimuli. *Perception and Psychophysics, 54,* 773–784.

Levine, D. S., & Prueitt, P. S. (1989). Modeling some effects of frontal lobe damage—Novelty and perseveration. *Neural Networks, 2,* 103–116.

Linnemeyer, S. A., & Porges, S. W. (1986). Recognition memory and vagal tone in 6-month-old infants. *Infant Behavior and Development, 9,* 43–56.

Livingstone, M., & Hubel, D. H. (1987). Psychophysical evidence for separate channels for the perception of form, color, movement, and stereopsis. *Journal of Neuroscience, 7,* 3416–3468.

Livingstone, M., & Hubel, D. (1988). Segregation of form, color, movement, and depth: Anatomy, physiology, and perception. *Science, 240,* 740–749.

Locher, P. J., & Nodine, C. G. (1973). Influence of stimulus symmetry on visual scanning patterns. *Perception and Psychophysics, 13,* 408–413.

Locher, P. J., & Nodine, C. G. (1987). Symmetry catches the eye. In J. K. O'Regan & A. Levy-Schoen (Eds.), *Eye movements: From physiology to cognition* (pp. 353–361). North-Holland: Elsevier.

Malkova, L., Mishkin, M., & Bachevalier, J. (1995). Long-term effects of selective neonatal temporal lobe lesions on learning and memory in monkeys. *Behavioral Neuroscience, 109,* 212–226.

Marshall, J. C., & Halligan, P. W. (1995). Seeing the forest but only half the trees? *Nature, 373,* 521–523.

Mayes, L., & Kessen, W. (1989). Maturational changes in measures of habituation. *Infant Behavior and Development, 12,* 437–450.

McCall, R. B. (1994). What process mediates prediction of childhood IQ from infant habituation and recognition memory? Speculations on the roles of inhibition and rate of information processing. *Intelligence, 18,* 107–124.

McCall, R. B., & Carriger, M. (1993). A meta-analysis of infant habituation and recognition memory performance as predictors of later IQ. *Child Development, 64,* 57–79.

McCall, R. B., & Mash, C. (1995). Infant cognition and its relation to mature intelligence. In G. Whitehurst (Ed.), *Annals of child development* (Vol. 11, pp. 27–56). Greenwich, CT: JAI.

McEvoy, R. E., Rogers, S. J., & Pennington, B. F. (1993). Executive function and social communication deficits in young autistic children. *Journal of Child Psychology and Psychiatry and Allied Disciplines, 34*, 563–578.

McKee, R. D., & Squire, L. R. (1993). On the development of declarative memory. *Journal of Experimental Psychology: Learning, Memory, and Cognition, 19*, 397–404.

Merigan, W. H., & Maunsell, J. H. R. (1993). How parallel are the primate visual pathways? *Annual Review of Neurosciences, 16*, 369–402.

Metcalfe, J. (1993). Novelty monitoring, metacognition, and control in a composite holographic associative recall model: Implications for Korsakoff Amnesia. *Psychological Review, 100*, 3–22.

Meunier, M., Bachevalier, J., Mishkin, M., & Murray, E. A. (1993). Effects on visual recognition of combined and separate ablations of the entorhinal and perirhinal cortex in rhesus monkeys. *Journal of Neuroscience, 13*, 5418–5432.

Mitchell, D. W., & Colombo, J. (in press). Infant cognition and general intelligence. In W. Tomic & J. Kingma (Eds.), *Advances in cognition and education: Reflections on the concept of intelligence*. Greenwich, CT: JAI.

Mitchell, D. W., McCollam, K., Horowitz, F. D., Embretson, S. E., & O'Brien, M. (1991, April). *The interacting contribution of constitutional, environmental, and information processing factors to early developmental outcome.* Society for Research in Child Development, Seattle, WA.

Morrongiello, B. A. (1988). Habituation, visual fixation, and cognitive activity: Another "look" at the evidence. *European Bulletin of Cognitive Psychology/Cahiers de Psychologie Cognitive, 8*, 482–488.

Navon, D. (1977). Forest before trees: The precedence of global features in visual perception. *Cognitive Psychology, 9*, 353–383.

Navon, D. (1983). How many trees does it take to make a forest? *Perception, 12*, 239–254.

Nelson, C. A. (1995). The ontogeny of human memory: A cognitive neuroscience perspective. *Developmental Psychology, 31*, 723–738.

Overman, W. H., Bachevalier, J., Sewell, F., & Drew, J. (1993). A comparison of children's performance on two recognition memory tasks: Delayed nonmatch-to-sample versus visual paired-comparison. *Developmental Psychobiology, 26*, 345–357.

Overman, W. H., Bachevalier, J., Turner, M., & Peuster, A. (1992). Object recognition versus object discrimination: Comparison between human infants and infant monkeys. *Behavioral Neuroscience, 106*, 15–29.

Palmer, S., & Hemenway, K. (1987). Orientation and symmetry: Effects of multiple, rotational, and near symmetries. *Journal of Experimental Psychology: Human Perception and Performance, 4*, 691–702.

Paquet, L., & Merikle, P. M. (1984). Global precedence: Effect of exposure duration. *Canadian Journal of Psychology, 38*, 45–53.

Paradowski, W., Zaretsky, H., Brucker, B., & Alba, A. (1980). Recognition of matching tasks and stimulus novelty as a function of unilateral brain damage. *Perceptual and Motor Skills, 51*, 407–418.

Phillips, R. R., Malamut, B. L., Bachevalier, J., & Mishkin, M. (1988). Dissociation of the effects of inferior temporal and limbic lesions in object discrimination learning with 24-hour intertrial intervals. *Behavioural Brain Research, 27*, 99–107.

Pierrot-Deseilligny, Ch., Gray, F., & Brunet, P. (1986). Infarcts of both inferior parietal lobules with impairment of visually guided eye movements, peripheral visual inattention and optic ataxia. *Brain, 109*, 81–97.

Polster, M. R., & Rapcsak, S. Z. (1994). Hierarchical stimuli and hemispheric specialization: Two case studies. *Cortex, 30*, 487–497.

Posner, M. I. (1980). Orienting of attention. *Quarterly Journal of Experimental Psychology, 32,* 3–25.

Posner, M. I., Walker, J. A., Friedrich, F. A., & Rafal, R. D. (1984). Effects of parietal lobe injury on covert orienting of visual attention. *Journal of Neuroscience, 4,* 1863–1874.

Posner, M. I., Walker, J. A., Friedrich, F. A., & Rafal, R. D. (1987). How do the parietal lobes direct covert attention? *Neuropsychologia, 25,* 135–145.

Rafal, R. D., & Robertson, L. (1995). The neurology of visual attention. In M. S. Gazzaniga (Ed.), *The cognitive neurosciences* (pp. 625–648). Cambridge, MA: MIT Press.

Regan, D. (1982). Visual information channelling in normal and disordered vision. *Psychological Review, 89,* 407–444.

Reisbick, S., Neuringer, M., Gohl, E., Wald, R., & Anderson, G. J. (1997). Visual attention in infant monkeys: Effects of dietary fatty acids and age. *Developmental Psychology, 33,* 387–395.

Reed, T. E., & Jensen, A. R. (1992). Conduction velocity in a brain nerve pathway of normal adults correlates with intelligence. *Intelligence, 16,* 259–272.

Richards, J. E. (1985). Respiratory sinus arrhythmia predicts heart rate and visual responses during visual attention in 14 and 20 week old infants. *Psychophysiology, 22,* 101–109.

Richards, J. E. (1988). Heart rate changes and heart rate rhythms, and infant visual sustained attention. In P. K. Ackles, J. R. Jennings, & M. G. H. Coles (Eds.), *Advances in psychophysiology* (Vol. 3, pp. 189–221). Greenwich, CT: JAI.

Richards, J. E., & Casey, B. J. (1991). Heart-rate variability during attention phases in young infants. *Psychophysiology, 28,* 43–53.

Roberts, S., & Tarassenko, L. (1994). A probabilistic resource allocating network for novelty detection. *Neural Computation, 6,* 270–284.

Robertson, L. C., & Lamb, M. R. (1991). Neuropsychological contributions to theories of part/whole organization. *Cognitive Neuropsychology, 23,* 299–330.

Robertson, L. C., Lamb, M. R., & Knight, R. T. (1988). Effects of lesions on temporal-parietal junction on perceptual and attentional processing in humans. *Journal of Neuroscience, 8,* 3757–3769.

Rose, S. A., & Feldman, J. F. (1995a). Prediction of IQ and specific cognitive abilities at 11 years from infancy measures. *Developmental Psychology, 31,* 685–696.

Rose, S. A., & Feldman, J. F. (1995b, March). *Cognitive continuity from infancy: A single thread or a twisted skein?* Presented at the meeting of the Society for Research in Child Development, Indianapolis, IN.

Rose, S. A., Feldman, J. F., & Wallace, I. F. (1992). Infant information processing in relation to six-year outcomes. *Child Development, 63,* 1126–1141.

Rose, S. A., Feldman, J. F., Wallace, I. F., & Cohen, P. (1991). Language: A partial link between infant attention and later intelligence. *Developmental Psychology, 27,* 798–805.

Rose, D., Slater, A., & Perry, H. (1986). Prediction of childhood intelligence from habituation in early infancy. *Intelligence, 10,* 251–263.

Rutter, M. (1978). Diagnosis and definition. In M. Rutter & E. Schopler (Eds.), *Autism: A reappraisal of concepts and treatments* (pp. 1–25). New York: Plenum.

Saxon, T. F., Frick, J. E., & Colombo, J. (1997). Individual differences in infant visual fixation and maternal interactional styles. *Merrill-Palmer Quarterly, 43,* 48–66.

Schmahmann, J. D. (1991). An emerging concept: The cerebellar contribution to higher function. *Archives of Neurology, 49,* 1178–1187.

Sigman, M. D., & Beckwith, L. (1980). Infant visual attentiveness in relation to caregiver-infant interaction and developmental outcome. *Infant Behavior and Development, 3,* 141–154.

Sigman, M., Cohen, S. E., & Beckwith, L. (1996). *Why does infant attention predict adolescent intelligence?* International Conference on Infant Studies, Providence, RI.

Sigman, M. D., Cohen, S. E., Beckwith, L., & Parmelee, A. H. (1986). Infant attention in relation to intellectual abilities in childhood. *Developmental Psychology, 22,* 788–792.

Sigman, M. D., Cohen, S. E., Beckwith, L., Asarnow, R., & Parmelee, A. H. (1991). Continuity in cognitive abilities from infancy to 12 years of age. *Cognitive Development, 6,* 47–57.

Sokolov, E. (1963). *Perception and the conditioned reflex.* Oxford: Pergamon.

Tamis-LeMonda, C. S., & Bornstein, M. H. (1989). Habituation and maternal encouragement of attention in infancy as predictors of toddler language, play, and representational competence. *Child Development, 60,* 738–751.

Thelen, E., & Ulrich, B. D. (1991). Hidden skills: A dynamic systems analysis of treadmill stepping during the first year. *Monographs of the Society for Research in Child Development, 56*(1), Serial No. 223.

Tulving, E., Markowitsch, H. J., Kapur, S., Habib, R., & Houle, S. (1994). Novelty encoding networks in the human brain: Positron emission tomography data. *Neuroreport, 5,* 2525–2528.

Turkewitz, G., & Devenny, D. A. (Eds.). (1993). *Developmental time and timing.* Hillsdale, NJ: Lawrence Erlbaum Associates.

Vecera, S. P., Rothbart, M. K., & Posner, M. I. (1991). Development of spontaneous alternation in infancy. *Journal of Cognitive Neuroscience, 3,* 351–354.

Vernon, P. A., & Mori, M. (1992). Intelligence, reaction times, and peripheral nerve conduction velocity. *Intelligence, 16,* 273–288.

Chapter 13

Selective Attention Over the
Life Span: Behavioral Measures

James T. Enns
University of British Columbia

Darlene A. Brodeur
Acadia University

Lana M. Trick
Kwantlen University College

In this chapter we highlight some of the emerging patterns we have seen in our research on the development of visual attention over the life span. We began our studies of visual attention in children over 10 years ago (e.g., Enns & Brodeur, 1989; Enns & Girgus, 1985), but it is only within the past few years that we have begun to compare the trends observed at the beginning of life with those at the other end of life (Brodeur & Enns, 1997; Plude, Enns, & Brodeur, 1994; Trick & Enns, in press; Trick, Enns, & Brodeur, 1996). We hope the following story will explain why we have been at times very optimistic, and at other times more cautious, about the possibility of linking behavioral changes over the life span to theories of development, theories of attention, and to the growing understanding of the underlying neural basis of both attention and development.

Our motivation in this work has been threefold. First, data from life-span studies are relevant to theories of perceptual and cognitive development. Some theories propose that development primarily reflects the changing effects of experience and knowledge on task performance (Chi, 1977; Roth, 1983). In childhood, performance improves with age because of the associated changes occurring in various skill domains. The young child as "novice" eventually becomes the older child and young adult as "expert." Other theories account for life-span change with general biological mechanisms that are believed to wax and wane in a large inverted U-shape (Kail & Salthouse, 1994; Salthouse, 1985, 1991). They begin with the premise that the speed of any performance is limited by the maximum rate at which elementary cognitive operations can be executed. This limit is set by factors that would have very general consequences, such as the number of transient cortical connections and the degree of neural myelinization; candidates in adulthood include increased neural noise through weakened inhibitory connections and decreased levels of key neurotransmitters. These two classes of theory thus propose very different views on the issue of task-specific life-span changes.

A second motivation, and one sometimes overlooked, is that developmental studies provide a unique opportunity to test the validity of general theories of attention (Enns, 1993). Developmental studies do this in the same way they do neuropsychological, cross-cultural, and species-comparative studies. First, important differences among participant groups are noted. Second, a mapping is established between theoretical constructs and these group differences. Finally, data are collected to determine whether performance on theory-relevant tasks is systematically related to the group differences. One of the unique strengths of developmental studies in this regard is the inherent continuity that can be studied, as the observer moves from childhood, to adulthood, and eventually to old age.

Finally, there is a need for normative and comparable data on measures of attention over the life span. It is fair to say that far more is known about life-span changes in many basic visual and auditory functions than is known about changes in attention (see Coren, Ward, & Enns, 1994, for typical textbook coverage). Yet, one observation that keeps driving us to collect more data is that the apparently limiting factor on performance in many developmental studies (even those putatively studying low-level sensory function) is something that can go by no other name than attention.

In this chapter we first summarize our views on what constitutes attention by focusing on three separable aspects of attention that are known to vary in childhood as well as in old age. We then summarize several different views on "What develops?" in these aspects of attention. Finally, we present life-span data from our labs on these components of attention, considering these data in light of the several different theoretical viewpoints.

WHAT IS ATTENTION?

In order to investigate life-span changes in attention, it is first necessary to agree on the concept of attention. At this point, we believe there is considerable consensus on the central concepts. That is, attention is seen by everyone to involve issues of *processing selectivity*, whether that selectivity concerns locations of the visual field for closer inspection (see Schiller, chap. 1, this volume), shapes and objects that constitute "figure" amidst other shapes and objects that constitute "ground" (see Baylis, chap. 8, this volume), attributes of objects that are relevant to the performance of some task (see Hood, Atkinson, & Braddick, chap. 7, this volume), or even actions that must be inhibited while other actions are performed (see Rafal, chap. 6, this volume). However, we acknowledge at the same time that there is considerably less consensus about the boundaries of the concept. Does attention always involve conscious awareness? How do biologically determined biases in selection (e.g., the orienting reflex to abrupt visual and auditory stimuli) interact with knowledge-based biases (e.g., the voluntary effort to maintain fixation in the face of moving stimuli elsewhere in the visual field)? Our strategy has been to steer clear of the contentious border issues, while trying to stay firmly rooted on the islands of agreement. In the sections that follow we describe the tasks we have studied and the dominant theoretical perspectives associated with each.

Covert Orienting

One aspect of attention is the ability to detect change in the environment, whether that change results from the sudden appearance of a new object or an attribute change in an existing object. The ability to shift visual attention toward the location of such a change, without accompanying physical movements of the eye, head, and body, has been called *covert orienting* by Posner (1980). In a typical covert orienting task, participants make a speeded response to the onset of a target, or they are asked to discriminate rapidly to one of two possible targets. Response time (RT) and accuracy are measured. Cues are presented prior to the onset of the target, indicating possible target locations. Comparisons are made between trials in which the cue correctly indicates the subsequent target location (*valid* trials), trials in which the cue incorrectly indicates one of the possible locations (*invalid* trials), and trials in which no specific location is indicated by the cue stimulus (*neutral* trials).

   In studies of this kind, responses are typically fastest and most accurate when cues are valid, even if eye movements are prevented. According to Posner's (1980) theory of visual orienting, this is because attention resembles a spotlight that can be moved independently of eye movements. This spotlight is responsible for detailed analysis; objects falling within its focus receive enhanced perceptual processing. However, the spotlight cannot process every object in the image at once because the cognitive resources it demands are limited. Disengaging the focus from one location, moving the position of the focus in the visual field, and engaging the focus on a new location each require time and effort. Consequently, performance is expected to be best on valid cue trials, because the spotlight has been given a head start to move to the target location before the target actually appears. When there is no information about where to put the attentional focus (neutral trials), or worse, incorrect information (invalid trials), performance suffers because the attentional focus has to be disengaged from its location of current activity, moved to the location of the source of change, and re-engaged on the new object.

Studies using single-cell recording techniques in monkeys (Wurtz, 1996), studies of human patients with various forms of brain injury (Rafal, chap. 6, this volume), and studies of brain imaging in humans engaged in cognitive tasks (Posner & Raichle, 1994) have converged in pointing to the superior colliculus (a midbrain structure) as being central in the normal functioning of covert orienting. In the most primitive form of orienting, this structure is the home of a subcortical reflex, which abruptly orients both attention and the direction of gaze to the location of a new stimulus in the visual field. This reflex is modulated by another complimentary reflex, controlled by other neurons in the same structure, to fix attention and gaze on the current object of interest. It is also modulated by cortical input from the parietal lobes, signaling the strategic goal of the organism to voluntarily orient toward a location in space. This complex array of relations, between the opposing reflexes to orient and fixate, and between the reflex to orient in one direction versus the higher-order goal to orient toward another, are thus a very promising place to begin examining developmental changes in attention.

Visual Search

Another aspect of attention is the ability to search for certain objects or attributes that are presented among other task-irrelevant objects or attributes. Visual search involves discriminating the presence versus absence of a particular target item among a varying number of distractor items. This task requires the ability to distinguish between targets and distractors, as well as the ability to deal with spatial uncertainty, multiple items, and displays that occupy large areas of visual space. Participants make a speeded response to indicate the presence or absence of the target on each trail. Again, response time and accuracy can be measured. The most important measure, however is RT slope, which is a summary measure of the increase in task difficulty as a function of the total number of items in the display.

Previous research has revealed two broad patterns of performance on visual search tasks (e.g., Treisman & Gelade, 1980). When targets and distractors differ by an easily discriminable feature such as brightness, color, size, or orientation, RT slopes are small or even zero. When targets and distractors are not easily discriminable, or differ by a conjunction of features (e.g., a particular combination of brightness and orientation), RT slope is relatively large.

A popular interpretation of these results comes from Feature Integration Theory (Treisman & Gelade, 1980). This theory proposes that visual features such as brightness and orientation are initially registered in separate topographically organized regions of the brain. Consequently, information from remote brain regions must be brought together (integrated) to determine that a particular conjunction of features share the same location or belong to the same object. The theory also proposes the existence of a master map of spatial locations to which all feature maps have access. However, the binding together of different features at one location is a serial operation that can only be performed in relatively small regions at a time (perhaps as small as that occupied by one object).

Thus, according to feature integration theory, RT slopes in conjunction search are high because the effortful feature integration operation must be performed for each item in the display until the target is found. RT slopes in feature search, on the other hand, are low because targets can be identified on the basis of unique activity in a single feature map. No linkage between different feature maps is required and so display size is unimportant. Although the theory has undergone several modifications since its origin (Treisman, 1988; Treisman & Gormican, 1988; Treisman & Sato, 1990), it is widely accepted that targets defined by conjunctions demand more attentional processing than those defined by features (see Bundesun, 1990; Duncan & Humphreys, 1989; Wolfe, 1994).

Single-cell recording studies in awake monkeys (Moran & Desimone, 1985; Motter, 1993), studies of human patients with various forms of brain injury (Cohen & Rafal, 1991) and studies of brain imaging in humans engaged in cognitive tasks (Posner & Raichle, 1994) indicate that visual search involves coordinated activity between several cortical regions in addition to activity in the superior colliculus. In particular, the temporal lobes are engaged in processing aspects of object identity (e.g, form and color), the parietal lobes are involved in the voluntary guidance of spatial attention to visual field locations, and the superior colliculus is critical in the actual movements of the eye and attention to locations in space. As with covert orienting then, the task of visual search shows a great deal of promise in being able to provide behavioral indices of developmental changes in the brain interactions involved in visual attention.

Visual Enumeration

A third component of attention is the ability to register the presence of two or more distinct items in a display. Visual enumeration is the term given to the ability to specify the number of target items in a spatial array. Like visual search, enumeration involves the ability to deal with multiple-item displays that cover extended areas. However, unlike visual search, participants must register the presence of every single target, not just the first they see. In order to avoid missing targets or enumerating them more than once, targets must be kept distinct from one another. This process is referred to as *individuation.*

Typically, there are two patterns of response in tasks of this kind. When there are only a small number of targets (up to 3–5 for most adults), the error rate is minimal, and the increase in RT with each additional item (the slope) is relatively shallow (40–100 ms per item). When there are larger numbers (5 or more) the error rate grows rapidly and the RT slope is much larger (250–300 ms per item). *Subitizing* is the term given to the cognitive processes involved when the slope is shallow, and thus the *subitizing range* is the range over which this shallow slope remains linear. *Counting* is the term applied to the cognitive processes involved when the slopes are steeper, and the *counting range* refers to the numbers of items that are beyond the elbow in the RT function.

Interestingly, subitizing only occurs in some situations. Participants can subitize complex objects (i.e., with multiple contours) of varying sizes; they can subitize O targets in X distractors, and items of one color or orientation amidst a variety of distractor items of other colors or orientations. However, when spatial attention is required to differentiate the target item as a whole from its background (e.g., the enumeration of nested concentric items), or to distinguish the target from distractors (e.g., the enumeration of O's in Q's, items connected by a line, or items with a particular conjunction of orientation and color), then subitizing does not occur (Trick & Pylyshyn, 1993). In these cases, the discontinuity in the RT function is absent; RT slopes are uniformly high throughout the number range, as if the more effortful counting process were used for both large and small numbers of items.

From data such as these, Trick and Pylyshyn (1994a) have surmised that subitizing is performed by a limited-capacity mechanism that individuates and selects a small number of distinctive items for further processing (Pylyshyn, 1989). This mechanism can be used for enumeration when the items to be enumerated are preattentively discriminable from distractors (Trick & Pylyshyn, 1994b), provided that the number of items does not exceed a limited number of internal reference tokens. When attention is required to discern individual items, either because they are spatially overlapping, or not sufficiently distinct from distractors, or when the number of items exceeds the number of available reference tokens, enumeration requires attention. The counting process therefore involves moving an attentional focus from location to location, using and reusing the same limited number of reference tokens at successive locations.

This behavioral analysis of visual enumeration indicates that it has much in common with both covert orienting and visual search. Like voluntary orienting and search, enumeration requires the planning and execution of movements of the attentional spotlight to specific locations in space.

As such, the superior colliculus and parietal lobes must be involved. Also like search, enumeration requires the repeated inspection of visual items to determine whether they match the criteria of the target item. This would suggest that temporal lobe function is also involved. However, what makes the enumeration task unique from both orienting and search is that it demands that some record be kept of target items that have already been determined to belong to the target set. The behavioral data indicating that this record keeping can be accomplished with little effort for small numbers of items, but is cognitively demanding for larger numbers, strongly suggests that different brain regions are probably involved for subitizing and counting. For instance, whereas the individuation of a small number of items may be accomplished by subcortical mechanisms that are shared between nonhuman mammals, human infants, and adults, the individuation of larger numbers may require complex cognitive strategies and the involvement of distributed cortical regions. Unfortunately, there is as yet no relevant neurophysiological evidence on this issue. Perhaps the developmental dissociations reported below for subitizing and counting may help to initiate such studies.

WHAT DEVELOPS?

Armed with this range of attentional measures, constructs, and theories, it makes sense to ask the question "What is developing?" when performance changes over the life span.

Developmental Theories

According to almost all developmental theories, RT in each of these tasks should vary in a U-shaped fashion over the life span. However, the reason for the U-shape is very different for an expertise view than it is for the speed of processing view. The expertise view holds that increasing amounts of practice in childhood, together with the "use it or lose it" principle in old age, account for the U-shaped trend. Speed of processing makes the same prediction because each task taps into a common set of cognitive operations that are subject to the neural factors contributing to cognitive slowing. For the present tasks, these might include sensory registration, perceptual identification of shapes, response selection, and response execution.

These two views differ considerably, however, in their predictions for the life-span patterns of measures that are specifically attentional. Consider, for example, the RT difference between valid and invalid cues in covert orienting, the RT slope in visual search, or the subitizing and counting slopes in visual enumeration. The speed of processing view would contend that each of these measures should show a U-shape function over the life span, since each involves neural processing of the sort that is speeded and slowed by developmental processes. The expertise view, on the other hand, permits more diversity. Some of the measures may not change at all over the life span (e.g., if they are tapping into operations that are not changed with practice and use), others may show improvement even into old age (e.g., if they reflect operations that are in consistent use throughout life) and others may show the familiar U-shape (e.g., if the operations are exercised most vigorously in young adulthood). The difficulty lies, of course, in the mapping of practice and exercise onto the cognitive components of laboratory tasks.

Attention Theories

The three theories of attention we have summarized provide for a large number of theoretical constructs. These theories, however, are for the most part silent on the issue of development. This has given us opportunities to consider the possible life-span course for each of them. In some cases, it is not too difficult to make a plausible conjecture, based on other (nondevelopmental) characteristics that are claimed for the construct by the theory. For example, if a theory proposes that some operation is "low-level" and therefore impervious to strategy and intention on the part of the observer, then it is tempting to hypothesize that this operation will show little developmental change. For the majority of the proposed attentional constructs, however, the question of developmental change is still open. Consequently, life-span data can be used to evaluate the plausibility of the theories.

Neurodevelopmental Data

A number of constructs in the neurodevelopmental literature may eventually prove to hold the key to understanding the relation between development and visual attention. We give examples of several, but hasten to add that none of these is at present developed fully enough to make specific predictions, especially with regard to early development versus aging. They can and should, however, guide research at the level of informing the choices made concerning the ages of observers that are tested and the types of tasks that are chosen.

One very natural place to begin looking for developmental change is in the relative rates at which various regions of the brain become fully myelinated in childhood. Neuroanatomical studies indicate that youthful development is fastest for the brainstem and midbrain, slower for the primary cortical areas and parietal lobes, and slowest for the prefrontal cortex. One of the more striking findings of these studies is that the brainstem is fully mylenized in early infancy whereas the cortex continues to mature through the teen years (Lecours, 1975). Thus one might expect attentional functions supported by lower brain centers to develop faster (or appear earlier) in childhood than those supported by higher cortical centers.

Another promising avenue can be seen in anatomical research on neuron number, density, and interconnectedness (Huttenlocher, 1990). One lesson of this research is that neural development is not about number of neurons, but rather about the density of synaptic connections. In childhood, one measure of synaptic density (the number of synapses per neuron) has an inverted U-shaped function over age. There is rapid growth in this measure following birth, which peaks at 2 years of age. The measure then declines, reaching a stable adult level at approximately 11 years of age. In senior adults there is yet another decline toward the end of life. It is, of course, tempting to relate such a trend in neuroanatomy to various behaviors that can be correlated with these age markers. To do this properly, however, behaviors must be carefully linked to the brain centers that are undergoing the change. Sadly, at this point we know little more on this score than that brain development follows a pattern of inside-out development, meaning that the cortical centers are the last to develop.

Finally, there is very promising research elsewhere in this volume (see chapters by Shiller, Maurer & Lewis, Johnson & Gilmore, Richards & Hunter, Rafal, and Hood et al.) on developmental changes in the way various brain centers coordinate their activity. Clearly, behavior guided by attention is the final output of a complex interaction among competing forces in various brain regions. A successful cognitive neuroscience of attentional development will therefore rely equally on (a) behavioral tasks that isolate separable functions of attention, (b) behavioral tasks that are appropriately linked to brain activity in specialized centers, (c) an understanding of the computations performed by given brain regions, and (d) studies of the developmental course of brain region activity. The studies that follow contribute most to the first objective.

RESULTS OF LIFE-SPAN STUDIES

In three studies we compared healthy volunteer participants with normal, or corrected-to-normal vision, from five groups with mean ages of 6, 8, 10, 22 and 72 years. The senior adults were screened for both glaucoma and cataracts. For each task, participants responded by pressing one of two keys. Their instructions were always to respond as quickly as they could, without sacrificing accuracy. These instructions were understood uniformly across the age groups, as shown by the high levels of response accuracy. As a result, we focus our discussion on the RT data, although it should be born in mind that the patterns discussed were also always evident in the accuracy data.

Covert Orienting

Both theory and research point to an important distinction between orienting that is elicited by a *stimulus* cue (usually abrupt luminance transients at the location to be attended) and an *information* cue (typically arrows or digits at the center of gaze that to refer to predesignated locations). Stimulus-induced shifts are often said to be reflexive because they are not easily influenced by higher-level goals such as voluntary shifts in attention (Jonides, 1981; Jonides & Yantis, 1988; Muller & Rabbitt, 1989; Nakayama & Mackeben, 1989; Yantis & Jonides, 1984, 1990). Moreover, stimulus-driven shifts generally result in rapid effects of a short duration, whereas information cues produce effects that are slower to emerge and longer lasting (Jonides, 1981; Muller & Rabbitt, 1989; Nakayama & Mackeben, 1989; Posner & Cohen, 1984). These theoretical and empirical distinctions suggest that there might be different life-span courses for these two forms of cuing.

Brodeur and Enns (1997) compared orienting to the two cues over a range of cue–target intervals from 133 to 800 ms. Participants were instructed to press one key if the target was an O and another if the target was an X, and targets were centered in one of four locations: 2.0° left, 2.0° right, 6.0° left, or 6.0° right of fixation. Targets were preceded by 50 ms cues: stimulus cues in one condition and information cues in another. The stimulus cue was a small black disk that could appear at fixation (neutral cue), or at one of four target locations. The information cue was either an equal sign (neutral cue), or arrows pointing left or right. The cues were valid in 20% of the trials for stimulus cues (i.e., entirely non-predictive), as compared to 80% of the trials for information cues (i.e., highly predictive).

Participants in both conditions were instructed to keep their eyes at fixation throughout the trial sequence and to blink, when necessary, between trials. Eye movements were monitored with a video camera. Participants in the stimulus cue task were warned that there would be a flash in one of the target locations before the target (the cue), but they were told to ignore it. In contrast, participants in the information cue condition were told to use the arrow cues as a very helpful indicator of the target's likely location.

The results indicated that stimulus-driven covert orienting undergoes relatively minor developmental change over the life span, as shown in Fig. 13.1. The three groups of children are combined in this graph because there were no significant differences among them. All age groups showed

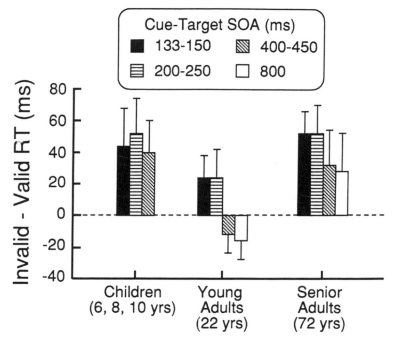

FIG. 13.1. Orienting effects (Invalid RT minus Valid RT) in a stimulus cuing task, where the cue is a noninformative flash at a potential target location. Children were tested at the three cue-target intervals of 133, 250, 450 ms; young and senior adults were tested at the four cue-target intervals of 133, 200, 400, and 800 ms. Adapted and redrawn from Brodeur and Enns (1997).

an orienting effect, which diminished at longer intervals. This is consistent with previous reports made separately for children (Akhtar & Enns, 1989; Enns & Brodeur, 1989) and senior adults (Hartley, Kieley, & Slabach, 1990; Hoyer & Familant, 1987; Madden, 1990). The young adults showed slightly less orienting than the other groups, perhaps because they were best able to follow the explicit instructions to ignore the stimulus cues. They were also the only group to show any signs of the inhibition of return effect at the longer intervals.

There were larger age-related changes for information cues. The young adult group demonstrated the most consistent orienting effects across the temporal intervals, as shown in Fig. 13.2. By comparison, all three groups of children showed strong effects at short intervals with marked decreases in the effects after 200 ms. Senior adults were different again, showing an information cue orienting effect only at the longest interval.

These results concur with those from previous studies on information cues. Children have often been reported to have difficulty sustaining stra-

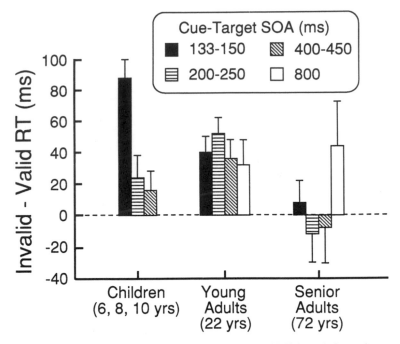

FIG. 13.2. Orienting effects (Invalid RT minus Valid RT) in an information cuing task where the cue is a predictive arrow at the center of the screen. Children were tested at the three cue-target intervals of 133, 250, 450 ms; the adults were tested at the four cue-target intervals of 133, 200, 400, and 800 ms. Adapted and redrawn from Brodeur and Enns (1997).

tegic aspects of attention over time (e.g., Kupietz & Richardson, 1978), and senior adults have previously been shown to be slower in the use of information cues for spatial orienting (e.g., Hartley et al., 1990; Hoyer & Familant, 1987). However, contrary to theories appealing to similar mechanisms for the reduced levels of performance at the beginning and end of life (e.g., cognitive slowing, see Kail, 1990, and Salthouse, 1985), these results suggest different underlying mechanisms. Children were able to make use of the information cue very rapidly (i.e., at least by 150 ms), but they clearly had difficulty sustaining their attention voluntarily in the cued location. In contrast, older adults were simply unable to respond very quickly to the cue. A theory premised on a common mechanism for U-shaped age changes in information-based orienting would have difficulty accounting for the differences observed here.

A second experiment in the same study (Brodeur & Enns, 1997) looked more closely at the interaction between the two types of orienting. Stimulus and information cues were presented together in the same trial in the following sequence. An information cue was presented for 50 ms upon the offset of the fixation marker. After a variable interval (140, 400, or 800 ms), a stimulus cue was presented. The stimulus cue-to-target interval was a constant 133 ms. Participants were instructed to use the information cue, as in first experiment, and told that there would also be a flash (the stimulus cue) on each trial, which they should try to ignore.

Although the design and associated data were complex, there was one finding of particular importance to the question of the separability of the two forms of cuing. Only the young adults were capable of partially discounting the information cue when the stimulus cue was valid. This is shown in Fig. 13.3, where the interval between the informative arrow cue and the target was 800 ms, and the interval between the noninformative stimulus cue and the target was 133 ms. Whereas the children and the senior adults showed additive contributions of the two forms of cuing (the validity effects of one cue type were constant over the validity effects of the other cue type), the young adults showed a clear cue interaction. The invalid stimulus cue was clearly less effective in the face of a valid informational cue. This indicates that only the young adults were able to override the orienting reflex in this case with the intention to orient to the location indicated by the arrow. This kind of cognitive flexibility is in general con-

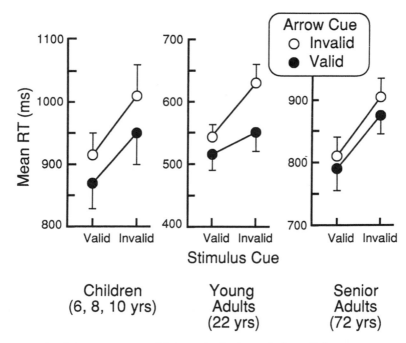

FIG. 13.3. Mean correct RT in a mixed cuing task. A predictive arrow cue preceded the target by 800 ms and a nonpredictive flash preceded the target by 133 ms. Adapted and redrawn from Brodeur and Enns (1997).

sistent with other research showing young adults to be most adaptive in their approach to a task (e.g., Enns & Girgus, 1985; Guttentag, 1989; McDowd & Craik, 1988). However, in the present case it points to a very specific form of adaptability in regard to visual orienting. In everyday terms, it can probably be related to the ability to "stay on task" with overt and covert gaze mechanisms in the face of abrupt and unexpected visual events.

Visual Search

Two findings are well established in regard to this aspect of attention. One is that there is a U-shaped pattern of performance over the life span: Visual search speed improves in childhood and declines again in old age. The second finding is that in conjunction search tasks this pattern is true of both baseline RT (intercepts of the search function over display size) and the increase in RT with display size (RT slope). When feature search has been tested it seems only to be true of baseline RT (Plude et al., 1994). RT slopes in feature search tasks are almost flat for children as young as 5–6 years of age and in seniors as old as 80 years. This suggests at a minimum that not all aspects of the search task are subject to the same developmental limitations.

We considered the possibility that the age-related changes in RT slope in conjunction search might originate from a number of sources, including changes in peripheral acuity, eye movement speed, feature integration ability, attentional filtering of distractors, movement of the attentional focus, or responses to spatial uncertainty. In order to determine which, if any, of these factors were important, observers were tested on three variations of a search task (Trick & Enns, in press). In the first condition, which we called Fixed Location–No Distractors, all uncertainty about the location of the target was eliminated. A single item always appeared at the center of the display and observers indicated as rapidly as possible whether or not it was the target. If feature conjunction was relatively more difficult than feature discrimination for some age groups, it would suggest a fundamental difficulty in feature integration for that age group.

We then added location uncertainty in a condition we called Random Location–No Distractors. The single item now appeared in random locations anywhere in the display area and observers judged whether it was the target or not. Two questions were of interest. First, did the addition of spatial uncertainty and increased foveal eccentricity influence any age groups disproportionately? Such a result would point to a fundamental difficulty in either peripheral acuity and/or moving attention to a new location in the visual field. Second, was the relationship between conjunction and feature discrimination any different across ages in this task than the previous one? If so, it would suggest that the difficulty of feature integration for that age group was only observed when spatial attention was not already focused on the target location.

Finally, we added varying numbers of distractor items to the displays and called the condition Random Location–Distractors. The task was identical to the previous one except there were now an additional 1, 9, or 17 distractor items randomly positioned in the display on target present trials. If the mere presence of distractors hindered search selectively for some age groups, it would indicate difficulty in ignoring items that were competing for attention. Furthermore, as the number of distractors increased, if Conjunction search became disproportionately more difficult than Feature search for some age groups, it would suggest a problem specific to voluntary movements of attention from one search item to another.

For all search tasks, participants were given the task of indicating the presence or absence of the same target—a dark outline circle. In feature detection the distractors were randomly divided between light gray outline circles and squares, making the target distinctive on the basis of brightness alone. In conjunction detection the distractors were randomly divided between light gray outline circles and dark gray outline squares, making the target distinctive on the basis of a particular combination of brightness and shape.

The results from the three tasks are presented in Figs. 13.4 and 13.5. We found no evidence that the efficiency of feature integration changed with age. There were, of course, baseline differences in the mean correct RT across age. As expected, RT decreased with age from childhood to young adulthood, and then increased again in old age. The important findings, however, concerned the RT differences between conditions. When a single item was presented at a fixed location in the display (Fig. 13.4), conjunction detection was indeed more difficult than feature detection. Remarkably, however, the age of the observer had no effect on this degree of difficulty. Similarly, when a single item was presented at a random location, conjunction detection was slower than feature detection by approximately the same amount, and there was no age-related change in this difference.

Moreover, there was no evidence that age affected the efficiency of moving the attentional focus to a single display item. Responding to a single item in a random location was slower than responding to an item at a fixed location for all observers, but age played no role in this difference. These stable RT differences across age are an important finding, because they rule out age differences in peripheral visual acuity (Akhtar, 1990), simple eye-movement speed (Miller, 1973), and the speed of reflexive orienting to new stimuli (Enns & Brodeur, 1989) as sources for the age effects in search. At least we can say that such age differences were not evident when the search task involved responding to a single item in an otherwise empty display field.

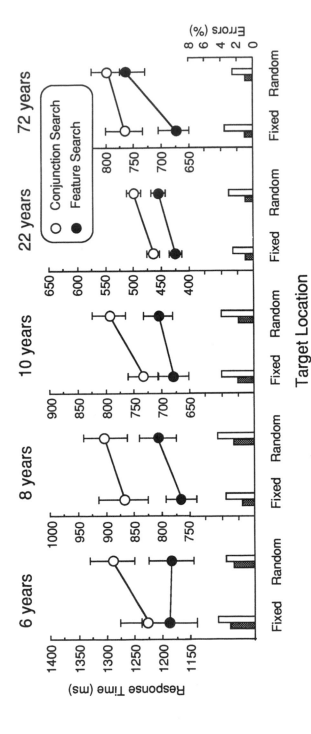

FIG. 13.4. Mean correct RT and percentage errors in the two No Distractor search tasks. Items were presented either at a fixed or random screen location, and targets differed from distractors by either a simple feature or a conjunction of features. Bars represent standard errors of the mean. Adapted and redrawn from Trick and Enns (in press).

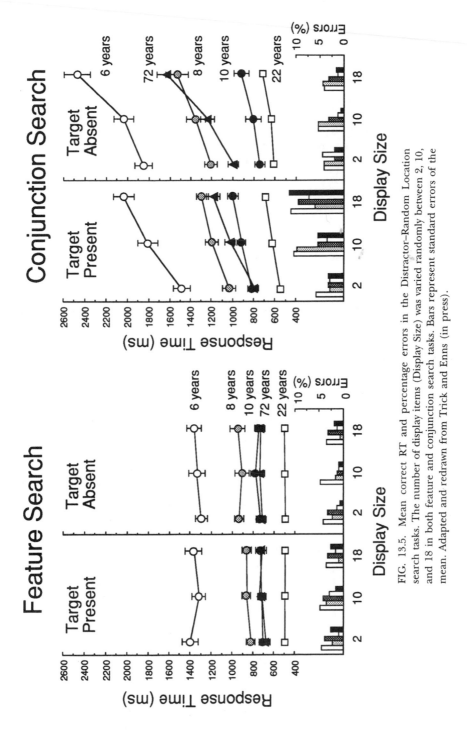

FIG. 13.5. Mean correct RT and percentage errors in the Distractor–Random Location search tasks. The number of display items (Display Size) was varied randomly between 2, 10, and 18 in both feature and conjunction search tasks. Bars represent standard errors of the mean. Adapted and redrawn from Trick and Enns (in press).

In fact, the age differences in performance only emerged when there was more than one item in the display. Although there were no age differences in the RT slope in the feature search task as a function of the number of distractors, there was a large U-shaped life-span trend in the conjunction search task. These data are shown in Fig. 13.5. We attribute this slope effect to a difficulty in voluntary movements of attention from item to item. This conclusion is warranted because we were able to rule out differences in the processes of feature integration, as well as in the processes involved in moving attention to a single item in a visual display. Both of these are ordinarily valid candidate mechanisms for explaining slope differences in conjunction search.

Visual Enumeration

How might subitizing and counting RT slopes be expected to change with age? Subitizing involves registering target items as discrete items, individuating them, and selecting the appropriate number name response (Trick & Pylyshyn, 1994b). With the exception of response selection, most of the current literature suggests that these processes change little with age. For example, visual search for simple features is comparable in children, senior adults, and young adults (see the previous study and Plude et al., 1994) and even very young infants can distinguish between 2 and 3 items (e.g., Starkey & Cooper, 1980; van Loosbroek & Smitsman, 1990). Therefore, the reported decline in the subitizing slope during childhood (Chi & Klahr, 1975; Svenson & Sjoberg, 1978) probably reflects improving efficiency in retrieving number names from memory and matching them to individuated items in order to select a response. Once the process of retrieving number names from memory is overlearned, however, there is no reason to expect it to deteriorate with normal aging, and consequently, no reason to expect the subitizing slope to increase again for senior adults. Thus, the subitizing slope should decline with age to adulthood, and then stabilize.

In contrast, the counting process involves a number of operations in addition to those required for subitizing, including moving the attentional focus from item to item. The findings of the previous two studies would thus predict that counting slopes should be higher for both elderly subjects and children than they would be for young adults.

We investigated enumeration with a number discrimination task (Trick et al., 1996). In each condition, random arrangements of one of two alternative numbers had to be discriminated by the observers: 1 vs. 2; 3 vs. 4; 6 vs. 7; and 8 vs. 9.

RTs are shown in Fig. 13.6. The data revealed a different pattern over the life span for numbers in the subitizing range (1–4 items) versus those in the counting range (6–9 items). The RT slope in the small number

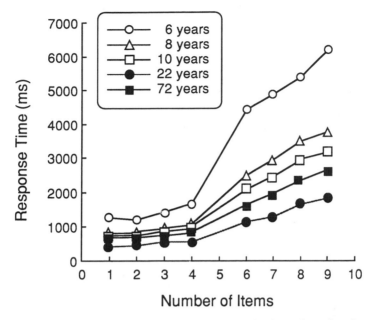

FIG. 13.6. Mean correct RT in the number discrimination task as a function of the number of items and age of the subjects. From Trick, Enns, and Brodeur (1996).

range decreased monotonically with age between 6 and 22 years (from 159 ms per item to 62 ms per item) and then did not decline significantly thereafter. In fact, the 72-year age group had the smallest slope estimates of all (51 ms per item). This might be expected if the process that was changing with age involved matching individuated display items with number names retrieved from memory. Once this process becomes automatic, there would be no reason to expect it to deteriorate with age.

In contrast, RT slopes in the large number range declined into young adulthood (547 ms, 438 ms, 399 ms 260 msm for 6-, 8-, 10-, and 22-year-olds, respectively), but then increased again in old age (354 ms per item). Given that the position of the attentional focus has been shown to be important in the counting range (Trick & Pylyshyn, 1994a), and that other studies have shown children and elderly subjects to be less efficient at shifting attention (see previous two studies and Plude et al., 1994), it seems likely that attentional factors are responsible for this change. Though the counting process involves many other operations, such as storing and retrieving information from short-term memory, and performing addition, attentional factors logically precede these operations. Therefore, it is parsimonious to conclude that voluntary control over spatial attention is a primary candidate for the U-shaped life-span trend in counting slopes.

SUMMARY AND CONCLUSIONS

These results indicate that some measures of attention are relatively stable between 6 and 72 years of age, whereas others follow a U-shaped trend. Among the stable components are reflexive covert orienting to the location of an abrupt visual event, search for a target that stands out from distractors because it differs in a simple visual feature, the ability to discriminate a visual item based on a conjunction of two features, and the ability to rapidly enumerate small numbers of items. The attentional components following a U-shaped trend include voluntary covert orienting to nonfoveal locations, visual search for a target amidst distractors when the target is defined by a conjunction of two features, and the ability to enumerate items for numbers larger than 5. An obvious common element to these measures of attention is voluntary control over, and guidance of, the location of attention.

Implications for Theories of Development

It appears that the highly touted U-shaped pattern of performance over the life span accurately describes mean response time and accuracy in our tasks, but it does not account for all measures of performance that are specifically attentional. Some of these measures show no hint of a U-shaped pattern.

Why is there a discrepancy between measures of overall task perform-ance and finer grained measures of attention? We think the answer lies in the observation that a measure of overall task performance, in even the simplest of tasks, involves influential cognitive components that do indeed follow the U-shaped pattern predicted by both expertise-based and speed of processing theories. However, these components serve to obscure most of the theoretically interesting attentional effects.

For example, most of the response time measures reflect cognitive op-erations that are of little interest to the visual attention theorist. This would include the target identification stage, the response decision stage, and the response execution stage. In the case of visual search, these components are reflected in the baseline RT (intercept). The slope of the RT function over display size reflects the unique contribution of the increasing number of display items. If there is a measurable difference in RT between condi-tions, and this difference does not change with age despite large changes in baseline RT, then one is compelled to conclude that it reflects a cognitive operation that does not wax or wane over the life span. Exclusive reliance on overall response time would make it impossible to investigate the changes unique to attention. Instead, finer grained analysis is required.

The studies reported in this chapter employ measures useful for investigating age-related changes in the components of attention. We found that of our two measures of covert orienting, one of them changes very little with age (stimulus-cued orienting), while the other changes a great deal (information-based orienting). Furthermore, even the age changes in this latter case were not unidimensional over the life span. Children had more difficulty than young adults sustaining their attention voluntarily to a cued location, whereas senior adults needed more time than young adults to take advantage of the cue.

In visual search we found that targets defined by simple features showed no age-related change, whereas search for conjunction-defined targets showed a U-shaped pattern. Closer examination of several possible reasons underlying this pattern pointed to a factor that appears to have much in common with information-based orienting. In visual search this manifested itself as a U-shaped trend in the ability to voluntarily shift attention among multiple items.

For visual enumeration we again found a dissociation for separate cognitive components. The enumeration of small numbers of items showed a monotonically improving trend even into old age, whereas the enumeration of larger numbers showed a U-shaped pattern. Once again, it appears that this pattern can be traced to difficulties directing the spatial focus of attention among multiple objects.

This diversity of life-span patterns among components of visual attention can be understood from either an expertise or a speed of processing perspective, but it certainly complicates research in both areas. For example, for the expertise theory, it now becomes important to understand how factors of practice and knowledge preserve some aspects of attention while other aspects deteriorate. For the speed of processing view, it becomes important to understand why some cognitive operations are impervious to factors influencing neural conduction rates and conduction fidelity. Are different brain regions responsible for different attentional components? Do development and aging influence the neural speed and fidelity of these brain regions differentially? Although no direct data is available, it is tantalizing to hypothesize these kinds of connections, especially given the rapid growth in the understanding of the neural bases of attention (e.g., Posner & Raichle, 1994; Zeki, 1993).

Implications for Theories of Attention

How do these life-span data constrain theories of attention? Consider first feature integration theory (Treisman & Gelade, 1980), which proposes that RT slopes in conjunction search tasks reflect the incremental time associated with integrating visual features one item at a time. Furthermore, the initial location of the focus of attention should be critical for predicting performance, because features can only be integrated once attention is focused on the location of visual features in question. If this were true, then the difference between feature and conjunction search should have been larger in our Random Location task than in our Fixed Location task. The data did not support this prediction. This result, taken together with the failure to find age differences in feature integration itself, suggests that the mechanisms emphasized by feature integration theory do not play a large role in age-related trends in visual search. This should also lead researchers to question the degree to which feature integration is a "high-level" cognitive operation.

The implications for Posner's visual orienting theory (Posner, 1980) are less specific. According to this theory, conjunction search is less efficient than feature search because the target item does not trigger reflexive orienting mechanisms. As a consequence, observers must intentionally guide the spotlight of attention from item to item. This involves repeated uses of the *disengage, move,* and *engage* operations (Posner & Petersen, 1990; Posner & Raichle, 1994). The present studies suggest that the youngest and oldest participants had difficulty moving their attentional focus systematically through other items, though they are capable of moving the focus in response to stimulus and information cues.

This difficulty could stem from any or all of Posner's three operations, which in itself suggests promising avenues for future research. For example, the *disengage* operation could be studied directly by using search tasks in which there are variable temporal gaps between the offset of a currently attended stimulus and the onset of a stimulus to be attended (Fisher & Breitmeyer, 1987; Kingstone & Klein, 1993). Similarly, the *move* operation could be studied by manipulating the spacing and configuration of items in the display. Finally, the *engage* operation could be tested by comparing psychometric functions of visual acuity in regions of the display that were either attended or not attended. Some researchers have already begun to speculate on which subset of the three attention orienting components are at issue when age differences are found, but at this point the directly relevant research has yet to be done.

Implications for Understanding the Normative Development of Attention

These behavioral data represent only the beginning of what must be studied if a foundation is to be laid for the normative development of attention. Progress will only be made if behavioral researchers of attention and development work hand-in-hand with neurophysiological researchers of these topics. Because so few attempts to build bridges among these four disciplines have been made to date, there is still plenty of room for widely diverse approaches to the problem. In our view, among the most important of these is the collection of more data of all kinds. The paucity of current theory on these links, we think, is a direct reflection of the paucity of data relevant to the links. For example, in the behavioral literature, there are at present only a handful of studies that have attempted to use comparable measures across the life span. The portions of the age range that have been sampled are sparse. The measures of attention tested represent only a tiny fraction of what is possible. We suspect a similar story is true in the neurophysiological literature. Although this may appear discouraging to the reader who yearns for immediate application and a guiding theory, it should also be taken as an invitation to those researchers who are looking for an area in which to make their mark. Present technological advances in the form of precise brain imaging techniques, the present maturity in methods for the objective behavioral testing of a wide range of populations, the present climate of research funding, which places a high premium on collaborative and interdisciplinary ventures, and the present cultural interest in improving the quality of life and education for all, have conveniently conspired to make the cognitive neuroscience of attentional development a research area of rapid projected growth.

ACKNOWLEDGMENTS

The research reported in this chapter was supported by grants from the BC Health Research Foundation and the Natural Science and Engineering Research Council of Canada.

REFERENCES

Akhtar, N. (1990). Peripheral vision in young children: Implications for the study of visual attention. In J. T. Enns (Ed.), *The development of attention: Research and theory* (pp. 139–158). Amsterdam: Elsevier.

Akhtar, N., & Enns, J. T. (1989). Relations between covert orienting and filtering in the development of visual attention. *Journal of Experimental Child Psychology, 48*, 315–334.

Brodeur, D., & Enns, J. T. (1997). Covert visual orienting across the lifespan. *Canadian Journal of Experimental Psychology, 51*, 20–35.

Bundesun, C. (1990). A theory of visual attention. *Psychological Review, 97*, 523–547.

Chi, M. T. H. (1977). Age differences in the speed of processing: A critique. *Developmental Psychology, 13*, 543–544.

Chi, M., & Klahr, D. (1975). Span and rate of apprehension in children and adults. *Journal of Experimental Child Psychology, 19*, 434–439.

Cohen, A., & Rafal, R. D. (1991). Attention and feature integration: Illusory conjunctions in a patient with a parietal lobe lesion. *Psychological Science, 2*, 106–110.

Coren, S., Ward, L., & Enns, J. (1994). *Sensation and perception* (4th ed.). New York: Harcourt Brace.

Duncan, J., & Humphreys, G. (1989). Visual search and stimulus similarity. *Psychological Review, 96,* 433–458.

Enns, J. T. (1993). What can be learned about attention from studying its development?. *Canadian Psychology, 34,* 271–281.

Enns, J. T., & Brodeur, D. A. (1989). A developmental study of covert orienting to peripheral visual cues. *Journal of Experimental Child Psychology, 48,* 171–189.

Enns, J., & Girgus, J. (1985). Developmental changes in selective and integrative visual attention. *Journal of Experimental Child Psychology, 40,* 319–337.

Fischer, B., & Breitmeyer, B. (1987). Mechanisms of visual attention revealed by saccadic eye movements. *Neuropsychologia, 25,* 73–83.

Guttentag, R. (1989). Age differences in dual task performance: Procedures, assumptions, and results. *Developmental Review, 9,* 146–170.

Hartley, A., Kieley, J., & Slabach, E. (1990). Age differences and similarities in the effects of cues and prompts. *Journal of Experimental Psychology: Human Perception and Performance, 16,* 523–537.

Hoyer, W., & Familant, M. (1987). Adult age differences in the rate of processing expectancy information. *Cognitive Development, 2,* 59–70.

Huttenlocher, P. R. (1990). Morphometric study of human cerebral cortex development. *Neuropsychologia, 28,* 517–527.

Jonides, J. (1981). Voluntary versus automatic control over the mind's eye's movement. In J. Long & A. Baddeley (Eds.), *Attention and performance* (pp. 187–204). Hillsdale, NJ: Lawrence Erlbaum Associates.

Jonides, J., & Yantis, S. (1988). Uniqueness of abrupt visual onset in capturing attention. *Perception and Psychophysics, 43,* 346–354.

Kail, R. (1990). More evidence for a common, central constraint on speed of processing. In J. T. Enns (Ed.), *The development of attention: Research and theory* (pp. 159–173). Amsterdam: North-Holland.

Kail, R., & Salthouse, T. A. (1994). Processing speed as a mental capacity. *Acta Psychologica, 86,* 199–225.

Kingstone, A., & Klein, R. (1993). Visual offsets facilitate saccadic latency: Does predisengagement of visuospatial attention mediate this gap effect? *Journal of Experimental Psychology: Human Perception and Performance, 19,* 1251–1265.

Kupietz, S., & Richardson, E. (1978). Children's vigilance performance and inattentiveness in the classroom. *Journal of Child Psychology and Psychiatry, 19,* 145–154.

Lecours, A. R. (1975). Myelogenetic correlates of development of speech and language. In E. H. Lenneberg & E. Lenneberg (Eds.), *Foundations of language and development: A multidisiplinary approach* (pp. 121–135). New York: Academic Press.

Madden, D. (1990). Adult age differences in the time course of visual attention. *Gerontology, 45,* 9–16.

McDowd, J., & Craik, F. (1988). Effects of aging and task difficulty on divided attention performance. *Journal of Experimental Psychology: Human Perception and Performance, 14,* 267–280.

Miller, L. K. (1973). Developmental differences in the field of view during covert and overt search. *Child Development, 44,* 247–252.

Moran, J., & Desimone, R. (1985, August). Selective attention gates visual processing in the extrastriate cortex. *Science, 229,* 782–784.

Motter, B. C. (1993). Focal attention produces spatially selective processing in visual cortical areas V1, V2, and V4 in the presence of competing stimuli. *Journal of Neurophysiology, 70,* 909–919.

Muller, H., & Rabbitt, P. (1989). Reflexive and voluntary orienting of visual attention: Time course of activism and resistance to interruption. *Journal of Experimental Psychology: Human Perception and Performance, 15,* 315–330.

Nakayama, K., & Mackeben, M. (1989). Sustained and transient components of focal visual attention. *Vision Research, 29,* 1631–1647.

Plude, D., Enns, J. T., & Brodeur, D. A. (1994). The development of selective attention: A lifespan overview. *Acta Psychologia, 86,* 227–272.

Posner, M. I. (1980). Orienting of attention. *Quarterly Journal of Psychology, 32,* 3–25.

Posner, M., & Cohen, Y. (1984). Components of visual orienting. In H. Bouma & D. Bowhuis (Eds.), *Attention and performance* (pp. 531–556). Hillsdale, NJ: Lawrence Erlbaum Associates.

Posner, M. I., & Peterson, S. E. (1990). The attention system of the human brain. *Annual Review of Neuroscience, 13,* 25–42.

Posner, M. I., & Raichle, M. E. (1994). *Images of mind.* New York: Freeman.

Pylyshyn, Z. (1989). The role of location indexes in spatial perception: A sketch of the FINST spatial-index model. *Cognition, 32,* 65–97.

Roth, C. (1983). Factors affecting developmental changes in the speed of processing. *Journal of Experimental Child Psychology, 35,* 509–528.

Salthouse, T. (1985). Speed of behavior and its implications for cognition. In J. E. Birren & K. W. Schaie (Eds.), *Handbook of the psychology of aging* (2nd ed., pp. 400–426). New York: Van Nostrand Reinhold.

Salthouse, T. (1991). *Theoretical perspectives on cognitive aging.* Hillsdale, NJ: Lawrence Erlbaum Associates.

Starkey, P., & Cooper, R. (1980). Perception of number by human infants. *Science, 210,* 1033–1035.

Svenson, O., & Sjoberg, K. (1978). Subitizing and counting processes in young children. *Scandinavian Journal of Psychology, 19,* 247–250.

Treisman, A. (1988). Features and objects: The 14th Bartlett memorial lecture. *Quarterly Journal of Experimental Psychology, 40A,* 201–327.

Treisman, A., & Gelade, G. (1980). A feature integration theory of attention. *Cognitive Psychology, 12,* 97–136.

Treisman, A., & Gormican, S. (1988). Feature analysis in early vision: Evidence from search asymmetries. *Psychological Review, 95,* 15–48.

Treisman, A., & Sato, S. (1990). Conjunction search revisited. *Journal of Experimental Psychology: Human Perception and Performance, 16,* 459–478.

Trick, L., & Enns, J. T. (in press). Lifespan changes in attention: The visual search task. *Cognitive Development.*

Trick, L. T., Enns J. T., & Brodeur, D. (1996). Lifespan changes in visual enumeration: The number discrimination task. *Developmental Psychology, 32,* 925–932.

Trick, L., & Pylyshyn, Z. (1993). What enumeration studies can show us about spatial attention: Evidence for a limited capacity *preattentive* processing. *Journal of Experimental Psychology: Human Perception and Performance, 19,* 331–351.

Trick, L., & Pylyshyn, Z. (1994a). Cueing and counting: Does the position of the attentional focus affect enumeration? *Visual Cognition, 1,* 67–100.

Trick, L., & Pylyshyn, Z. (1994b). Why are small and large numbers enumerated differently? A limited capacity preattentive stage in vision. *Psychological Review, 101,* 80–102.

Yantis, S., & Jonides, J. (1984). Abrupt visual onsets and selective attention: Evidence from visual search. *Journal of Experimental Psychology: Human Perception and Performance, 10,* 601–620.

Yantis, S., & Jonides, J. (1990). Abrupt visual onsets and selective attention: Voluntary versus automatic allocation. *Journal of Experimental Psychology: Human Perception and Performance, 16,* 121–134.

Van Loosbroek, E., & Smitsman, A. (1990). Visual perception of numerosity in infancy. *Developmental Psychology, 26,* 911–922.

Wolfe, J. M. (1994). Guided search 2.0: A revised model of visual search. *Psychonomic Bulletin & Review, 1,* 202–238.

Wurtz, R. H. (1996). Vision for the control of movement. *Investigative Ophthalmology & Visual Science, 37,* 2131–2145.

Zeki, S. (1993). *A vision of the brain.* Boston, MA: Blackwell Scientific Publications.

Chapter 14

Summary and Commentary. Selective Attention: Its Measurement in a Developmental Framework

Holly A. Ruff
Albert Einstein College of Medicine

The preceding three chapters are rich in the amount of data presented and in the discussion of methods for studying attention. They also offer the reader some intriguing ideas about the cognitive and neural processes that underlie attention. The challenge for me has been to integrate three very different approaches to the issue of visual selective attention. The approaches differ in both the techniques used and the age range being investigated, and yet they all contribute to our understanding of a number of key issues. These issues are: the conceptualization of selective attention; the role of attention in performance, learning, and memory; and the course of development of attention, or to borrow a phrase from Enns, Brodeur, and Trick, "What develops?"

THE CONSTRUCT OF ATTENTION

As Enns and his colleagues point out, selectivity is central to the construct of attention. Selection is an ongoing, dynamic process; not only is it essential that we orient to only some events and objects out of the multitude of possibilities that are available, we must be able to sustain selection whenever it is appropriate and adaptive to do so. This "maintenance of a stimulus selective state" (Näätänen, 1992, p. 396) requires an active resistance to distracting events. Dynamic, active selectivity involves both facilitation and inhibition; selection effectively enhances the perception of the target object or event by increasing the receptivity and responsivity of the relevant neurons and pathways *and* by reducing the receptivity and responsivity of neurons and pathways not currently relevant (Näätänen & Michie, 1979). On the other hand, it is important for us to be able to shift attention from one target to another when appropriate. The only way to define whether sustained attention or shifting is appropriate is in terms of the individual's goals and adaptation to current demands for action. Because selective attention is important for adaptation, it is closely allied to the facilitation of appropriate actions and to the reduction of response competition (Allport, 1987; Tipper, 1992; see also Hood et al., chap. 7, this volume). Selective processes that affect sensory pathways are complemented by selective processes affecting motor pathways (Näätänen, 1992).

The authors creatively use a variety of tasks to tease apart different aspects of selective attention. For Colombo and Janowsky, the primary approach is to assess individual differences in infants' duration of looking in the context of familiarization or habituation. By systematically manipulating stimulus displays and the duration of exposure, Colombo and his colleagues (see Colombo, 1995, for a review) have tested a number of interesting hypotheses about the role of attention in determining what types of displays individual infants learn and later recognize. Here, Colombo and Janowsky offer some highly detailed speculation motivating further behavioral investigation. Nelson and Dukette, also studying recognition memory, combine behavior and ERP data in studies with somewhat older infants. They separate ERP components related to memory from those related more directly to visual attention by varying the stimulus displays and the context and by referring to studies—their own and others'—with older children and adults where more experimental control is possible. Enns, Brodeur, and Trick focus on development of attention across the life span, specifically from 6 to 72 years. Their research involves three paradigms—a version of Posner's covert orienting task, search tasks involving single features and conjunctions of features, and a counting task. By examining reaction time and errors, these investigators draw conclusions about a U-shaped development of attention.

Although only Nelson and Dukette are studying neural activity directly, the behavioral work in all the chapters raises questions, confirms some hypotheses, and suggests others that should help to guide future integration of behavioral and neurological levels into our understanding of attention. I agree with the assessment of Enns and his colleagues, however, that the field needs a great deal more descriptive behavioral work to both test and guide thinking about underlying processes.

The diversity of procedures and measures used by these authors is important because it helps us to avoid defining attention in terms of a single measure or task, a limitation that interferes with our understanding of the underlying neural structures and processes. For this reason, I take issue with Enns and colleagues when they equate their *tasks* with different *aspects* of attention. The results from their three tasks converge and provide information about the general processes of shifting and sustaining attention. Valuable as these paradigms are, they present subjects with highly atypical situations and are therefore limited in what they can tell us about attention. Likewise, measurement of ERPs require many, atypically brief exposures. Although a degree of artificiality is necessary for gaining the control necessary to ask some questions, it is useful to supplement such data with data from less constrained situations. The work described by Colombo and Janowsky is a case in point. They use looking as a reflection of visual attention. Although we know that the target of visual attention is not necessarily the current fixation point (Posner, 1980) and that attention during looking can vary in intensity (Richards & Casey, 1992), the direction and duration of looking under normal circumstances is likely to follow shifts and pauses in visual attention. No measure and no method, however, is a perfect index of the underlying constructs, and thus, it helps to integrate as many different ones as possible into our thinking about attention.

In studying the development of attention, we also need to be mindful that attention is determined in part by the goals and needs of the individual; the goals of infants and children are not as likely to coincide with the needs of the experimenter as those of adults. For this reason, I am more skeptical than Nelson and Dukette about the ready application to infants and children of "methods used by those studying adult functioning." When subjects at different ages are presented with the same tasks, as in the studies by Enns et al., we cannot attribute all age differences to changes in basic functions because motivational factors certainly contribute. There may be paradigms that are particularly suited for children and will engage their motivation and skills, and thus their attention, in ways that paradigms used with adults do not. Although assessing attention across age with the same tasks provides valuable information, such an approach tells us about children relative to adults in only those circumstances. Children's deployment of attention may be more efficient and better controlled in other circumstances.

In sum, each chapter illustrates the limitations inherent in only one approach; more important, however, together they illustrate the variety and richness of approaches available to us.

ATTENTION IN PERFORMANCE, LEARNING, AND MEMORY

What we select and how well we maintain selectivity makes a difference in how well we perform tasks and how well we learn and remember. Nelson and Dukette argue that cross-modal transfer and recognition memory can be seen as reflecting explicit memory. Colombo and Janowsky base many of their conclusions and speculations on results from recognition memory tasks. If these are explicit memory tasks, then attention to the original events is necessary. We could also argue with Logan (1988) that "encoding into memory is an obligatory, unavoidable consequence of attention" (p. 493). Attention in this context implies awareness. Implicit learning of actions and sequences can occur without awareness, but learning may be better and faster with it (Curran & Keele, 1993). In this view, the ERP components reflecting attention, according to Nelson and Dukette, are a necessary part of the flow of neural signals that contain other components reflecting memory of events.

Colombo and Janowsky elaborate the attention–memory link in infancy by inferring different patterns of selective attention from differential performance on recognition memory tests. For example, long-looking infants seem to attend more to the local details of stimulus displays during familiarization because, on the recognition tests, they respond to changes at that level as novel; short-looking infants show the opposite pattern. The authors offer evidence from neuroscience investigations to suggest that different neural systems dominate the selective attention of these two groups. Based on data from older children and adults who were instructed to attend to either the global or local level of the stimulus displays, Nelson and Dukette report that the attention components of the ERPs did not differ with the level presumably attended to, but manual reaction times did. This finding cautions us to separate selective attention to the displays from possible response competition. That is, we may reasonably infer earlier direction of attention from later performance, but performance is also influenced by selective processes operating at the time of responding.

Enns, Brodeur, and Trick minimize the memory requirements in their tasks, although an element of search tasks is certainly maintaining selectivity for the relevant feature or conjunction of features. In this way, ongoing attention is an influence on performance in that task. As Enns et al. argue, however, aspects of attention are involved in all of their tasks, which require systematic shifting of attention from one location to another. When sustained attention is interrupted by irrelevant events or when shifts are not governed by strategy, performance suffers.

In summary, performance is affected by the ability to sustain and shift attention as well as by the particular elements of the situation that are selected, whether the tasks probe memory and have implications for earlier attention or the tasks assess attention and performance simultaneously. Electrophysiological measures, such as ERPs, may help us to distinguish interruptions or disruptions in performance caused by failure to detect and attend to target events and disruption caused by failure to inhibit responses to detected nontarget events.

WHAT DEVELOPS?

In global terms, a critical trend in the development of attention is a shift from external control of attention to more voluntary control. All of the authors of these three chapters address this distinction at some level. Enns and colleagues address it most directly in the covert orienting paradigm by manipulating both stimulus cues and information cues. Stimulus cues, such as abrupt brightening in the peripheral visual field, tend to elicit attention automatically; information cues, such as arrows instructing the subject to shift attention in a particular direction, govern voluntary attention. The results suggest that 6- to 10-year-old children have more difficulty than adults ignoring the stimulus cues even when explicitly instructed to do so. Also, although the children responded quickly to information cues, their voluntary attention to the peripheral locations was not sustained as long as the attention of adults. The first seems to be a failure of inhibition in the face of biologically potent stimuli, and the latter, a failure to maintain cognitively directed attention. The data, therefore, suggest that strategic voluntary attention is less readily maintained in childhood than in early adulthood, and responding on the basis of potent external cues is less inhibited. When automatic responding to stimulus cues is appropriate, however, children perform more like adults.

Nelson and Dukette report results with an ERP component in response to auditory stimulation. The results are consistent with the thesis that school-aged children have more difficulty ignoring competing nontargets and maintaining the attentional trace (Näätänen, 1992). A relative weakness in children's voluntary attention under these circumstances may be related to immaturity of pathways in the frontal cortex.

Although there are important developments in voluntary attention over the course of childhood (Ruff & Rothbart, 1996), some functions related to it to emerge in infancy. An important element of voluntary attention is the ability to disengage from highly salient stimulation. Colombo and Janowsky suggest that individual differences in infants' looking times may be related to the facility for disengaging attention. In one study, infants who characteristically looked longer at standard visual displays were slower than "short lookers" to respond to peripheral targets if they were already looking at a central target; their latencies were no different, however, if the central target disappeared before the peripheral target appeared. These results suggest that infants with long looks disengaged less readily from the central target. Furthermore, long-looking infants were slower to look away even when their heart rate patterns suggested that attention to the target was beginning to terminate (Richards, 1988). Interestingly, if long-looking infants were *not* slower than short-looking infants to begin the attention termination phase, then perhaps the results could be interpreted as differences in the speed with which a shift in looking follows a shift in attention.

Individual differences in duration of looking parallel age trends, with younger infants looking longer than older infants. The data suggest that age differences in infants' tendency to prolong looking are also related to the development of underlying attentional processes such as disengaging and shifting. The ability to disengage attention can thus be seen as an essential step in the development of voluntary attention.

Nelson and Dukette refer to selective attention as "volitional"; they describe the underlying network as involving the dorsolateral prefrontal cortex, an area of the brain that begins to become functional toward the end of the first year of life. It is worth emphasizing, however, that there are many different bases for selection (Ruff & Rothbart, 1996). Attention is by its nature selective, and even newborn infants are biased to attend to some aspects of their environment rather than others. Selectivity, however, may be determined relatively automatically by variations in physical salience or reinforcement history, or it may be more deliberate and based on cognitive goals or instruction. The difference between stimulus cues and information cues as used by Enns et al. is an example. The development of the frontal cortex seems to be related to the voluntary aspects of selective attention in that it helps to inhibit or facilitate lower level processes, such as those controlled by the posterior parietal cortex (Posner, 1982; Näätänen, 1992).

Before concluding this section on development, a word about the life-span approach of Enns, Brodeur, and Trick is in order. These authors take a broad development perspective and offer some fascinating data on the performance of 72-year-olds. The results suggest that attentional processes do change with aging, with older adults showing lower levels of inhibition and slower responses. The results also suggest that the changes in aging are not simply the reverse of developmental changes in childhood. A relative weakness in higher-level controls may be seen at both ends of the age spectrum and reflect changes in frontal cortex. The picture provided by Enns and colleagues, however, suggests that practice and knowledge may partly compensate for diminished attentional control in older adults.

CONCLUSION

This brief summary and integration cannot do justice to these chapters, where much interesting information is contained in the details. Each chapter reveals an impressive attempt to probe different attentional processes. The authors all offer speculation about accompanying activity in neural networks and report data that will help to constrain and direct future investigations combining behavioral and neuroscience approaches. And perhaps most important, given the purpose of this volume, all of the authors offer insights into the development of the skills that constitute attention.

REFERENCES

Allport, A. (1987). Selection for action: Some behavioral and neurophysiological considerations of attention and action. In H. Heuer & A. F. Sanders (Eds.), *Perspectives on perception and action* (pp. 395–419). Hillsdale, NJ: Lawrence Erlbaum Associates.

Colombo, J. (1995). On the neural mechanisms underlying developmental and individual differences in visual fixation in infancy: Two hypotheses. *Developmental Review, 15*, 97–135.

Curran, T., & Keele, S. W. (1993). Attentional and nonattentional forms of sequence learning. *Journal of Experimental Psychology: Learning, Memory, and Cognition, 19*, 189–202.

Logan, G. D. (1988). Toward an instance theory of automatization. *Psychological Review, 95*, 492–527.

Näätänen, R. (1992). *Attention and brain function.* Hillsdale, NJ: Lawrence Erlbaum Associates.

Näätänen, R., & Michie, P. T. (1979). Early selective-attention effects on the evoked potential: A critical review and reinterpretation. *Biological Psychology, 8*, 81–136.

Posner, M. I. (1980). Orienting of attention. *Quarterly Journal of Experimental Psychology, 32*, 3–25.

Posner, M. I. (1982). Cumulative development of attentional theory. *American Psychologist, 37*, 168–179.

Richards, J. E. (1988). Heart rate responses and heart rate rhythms, and infant visual sustained attention. *Advances in Psychophysiology, 3*, 189–221.

Richards, J. E., & Casey, B. J. (1992). Development of sustained visual attention in the human infant. In B. Campbell, H. Hayne, & R. Richardson (Eds.), *Attention and information processing in infants and adults* (pp. 30–60). Hillsdale, NJ: Lawrence Erlbaum Associates.

Ruff, H. A., & Rothbart, M. K. (1996). *Attention in early development: Themes and variations.* New York: Oxford University Press.

Tipper, S. P. (1992). Selection for action: The role of inhibitory mechanisms. *Current Directions in Psychological Science, 1*(3), 105–109.

Author Index

Subject Index

A

accessory optic system, 38-42
acuity, 318
affect, 322
amygdala, 335
A-not-B task, 320, 321
   EEG, 298-309,
   frontal lobe, 295-309
   HR, 297, 308, 309
   looking version, 298-302
   reaching version, 294-296
anterior cingulate cortex, 321, 347, 348
antisaccades, 121, 212-214
asymmetry, 322
assigned edges, 274
attention, 144-158, 317, 318, 365, 369,
   371, 375-378, 421
   allocation, 344
   arousal systems, 146, 147, 152
   attention-directed saccade, 132,
     133, 151, 153, 157
   attention termination, 145, 146,
     150, 151, 152, 153, 376-379, 423
   cognitive limits, 394
   components, 422
   development of, 423, 165-168
   disengaging, 229, 231, 234, 244,
     423, 424
   disorders, 268-273
   endogenous, 121, 220-222, 226, 227,
     228, 234, 235, 240-244, 263, 265,
     354
   environment-based, 236-239
   eye movements, 131-158
   exogenous, 221, 222, 226-228, 234,
     235, 243, 244, 263, 265, 423
   figure-ground assignment, 263-265
   head and eye movements, 148-153
   heart rate, 66, 377, 423
   inattention, 146, 148, 149, 155, 157
   infant memory, 336-339
   infant measures, 165-168
   internal control of, 423
   load, 339, 345
   life span development of, 393-415
   memory, 327-358, 422
   object-based, 236-239, 252, 253, 255,
     257-259, 273
   object-limited, 255-257
   obligatory, 106, 332, 333, 334, 337
   posterior attention system, 14-16,
     22, 23 34, 134, 151, 152, 346
   premotor theory, 237, 243, 244
   selection-for-action, 219, 220, 225,
     226, 231, 234, 237, 243, 244, 317
   selective attention, 254, 320, 327,
     394, 420, 422, 424
   shift, 318
   space based, 252
   span, 371, 372, 377
   spatial, 352, 398
   spotlight, 227, 235, 236, 252
   trace, 351, 423
   vigilance, 327, 357
   voluntary, 424
auditory cortex, 329
auditory priming, 329
auditory selective attention, 351
autism, 368
automatic interrupt, 145

B

Babinski sign, 182
Balint's syndrome, 232, 233, 272, 273,
   377, 379
basal ganglia, 136

DATE DUE